Zo-

Cover & flap / Umschlag & Klappe: FRANZ ACKERMANN, BOARDING, 2002, oil on canvas, 110 1/4 x 212 5/8" / 280 x 540 cm.

Inside cover & page 1 / Innere Umschlagseite & Seite 1: DAN GRAHAM, TWO-WAY MIRROR PAVILION WITH ONE CURVED SIDE, 1996, "Artscape Nordland," Norway / Norwegen.

Back cover / Rückseite: EIJA-LIISA AHTILA, CONSOLATION SERVICE, 1999, stills from 35-mm film / Bilder aus dem 35-mm-Film.

All images slightly cropped / Alle Bilder leicht beschnitten.

PARKETT Zürich New York

Bice Curiger Chefredaktorin/Editor-in-Chief; **Jacqueline Burckhardt** Redaktorin/Senior Editor; **Cay Sophie Rabinowitz** Redaktorin USA / Senior Editor US; **Suzanne Schmidt** Textredaktion und Produktion / Editing and Production; **Hanna Koller · Simone Eggstein** Graphik / Design, **Trix Wetter** (beurlaubt / on temporary leave); **Catherine Schelbert** Englisches Lektorat / Editorial Assistant for English; **Claudia Meneghini Nevzadi** Korrektorat/Proof Reading

Beatrice Fässler Vorzugsausgaben, Inserate / Special Editions, Advertising; **Nicole Stotzer** Buchvertrieb, Administration / Distribution, Administration; **Mathias Arnold** Abonnemente / Subscriptions; **Ali Subotnick** Redaktion, Vorzugsausgaben und Marketing USA / Associate Editor, Editions and Marketing US; **Monika Condrea** Abonnemente USA / Subscriptions US; **Cliff Borress** Praktikant USA/Intern US; **Adrian Koerfer** Deutsche Verlagsvertretung/German Representative

Jacqueline Burckhardt – Bice Curiger – Dieter von Graffenried Herausgeber/Parkett Board;
Jacqueline Burckhardt – Bice Curiger – Dieter von Graffenried – Walter Keller – Peter Blum Gründer/Founders

Dieter von Graffenried Verleger/Publisher

www.parkettart.com

PARKETT-VERLAG AG, QUELLENSTRASSE 27, CH-8031 ZÜRICH, TEL. 41-1-271 81 40, FAX 41-1-272 43 01
PARKETT, NEW YORK, 155 AV. OF THE AMERICAS, N.Y. 10013, PHONE (212) 673-2660, FAX (212) 271-0704

EDITORIAL

Ein Erforschen von Gleichzeitigkeiten, von multiperspektivischen Betrachtungspunkten steht im Zentrum dieser Ausgabe von Parkett mit Franz Ackermann, Eija-Liisa Ahtila und Dan Graham. Das Flugzeug auf dem Titelblatt kündet von diesen Reisen, auf welchen die Zeit- und Raumbegriffe tüchtig durcheinander geraten.

Dan Graham, der älteste unter den hier vorgestellten Künstlern, dessen Werk heute von einer Zeitreise durch die Rezeptionsgeschichte der vergangenen Jahrzehnte geprägt ist, habe die «Atomisierung des einheitlichen modernen Subjekts, eine Kritik des aristotelischen Raum-Zeit-Kontinuums und die Demontage der Renaissance-Perspektive samt ihrer gesellschaftsordnenden Wirkung» zum Kern seiner gesamten Arbeit gemacht, heisst es im Text von Karin Schneider und Nicolás Guagnini (S. 103). Sowohl Ackermann wie Ahtila knüpfen bei diesen Erfahrungen an. Während jedoch bei Graham die Menschen sowohl als Bewohner, Besucher und Benutzer von öffentlichen, privaten und halbprivaten Räumen betont ins Zentrum der Arbeit selber gerückt werden, bleibt der Mensch in Franz Ackermanns Malerei und in seinen riesigen farbigen Installationen ausgeblendet. Strukturen, Arteriensysteme und zerschnittene Schichtungen sind die halluzinationsähnlichen Schmelzformen, die gleichzeitig das Naturgegebene wie das von Menschen Gemachte darstellen. Das sichtbare Leben erscheint nur in abstrahierter Form, aber umso eindringlicher beschworen als schematisierte Abwesenheitsgrösse.

In Eija-Liisa Ahtilas Werk hingegen stehen die Menschen im Brennpunkt, doch öffnet sich der mentale Raum zwischen ihnen in kaleidoskopartiger Vielgestalt. Wenn der Ausdruck «Borderline» fällt (etwa im Text von Taru Elfving), so steht er auch für das formale Prinzip in den Videofilmen und Photographien, wo Stillstand und Bewegung, Fiktion und Dokumentation, Schönheit von Farbe, Licht und Raum und die Härte einer sozialen Wirklichkeit fliessend ineinander übergehen.

Eine ganz andere Bezugnahme, eine Art «Test» mit den Errungenschaften einer früheren künstlerischen Generation findet sich im Insert. Jonathan Monk greift einen Satz aus der Blütezeit der Konzeptkunst auf, um ihn auf eine Reise durch die Sprachen rund um den Erdball zu schicken – bis der Satz schliesslich wieder in die Ausgangssprache Englisch zurückübersetzt ist. Die dabei entstandenen Sinnverschiebungen sind mehr als nur ein Witz. Sie künden von den Aromen anderer Kulturen und Vorstellungswelten und kratzen sanft an einer vergangenen künstlerischen Geisteshaltung, die auf puristische Bedingungen setzte. Die Übersetzungsreise kommt so einer Kontamination gleich: Robert Barrys ursprünglicher Satz, die Beschreibung der Idee, allein durch Telepathie ein Kunstwerk entstehen zu lassen, liest sich nach der Einverleibung durch eine auf Animismus, Geister- und Seelenbeschwörung spezialisierten Welt vollkommen anders und ist nicht minder ernsthaft als vorher.

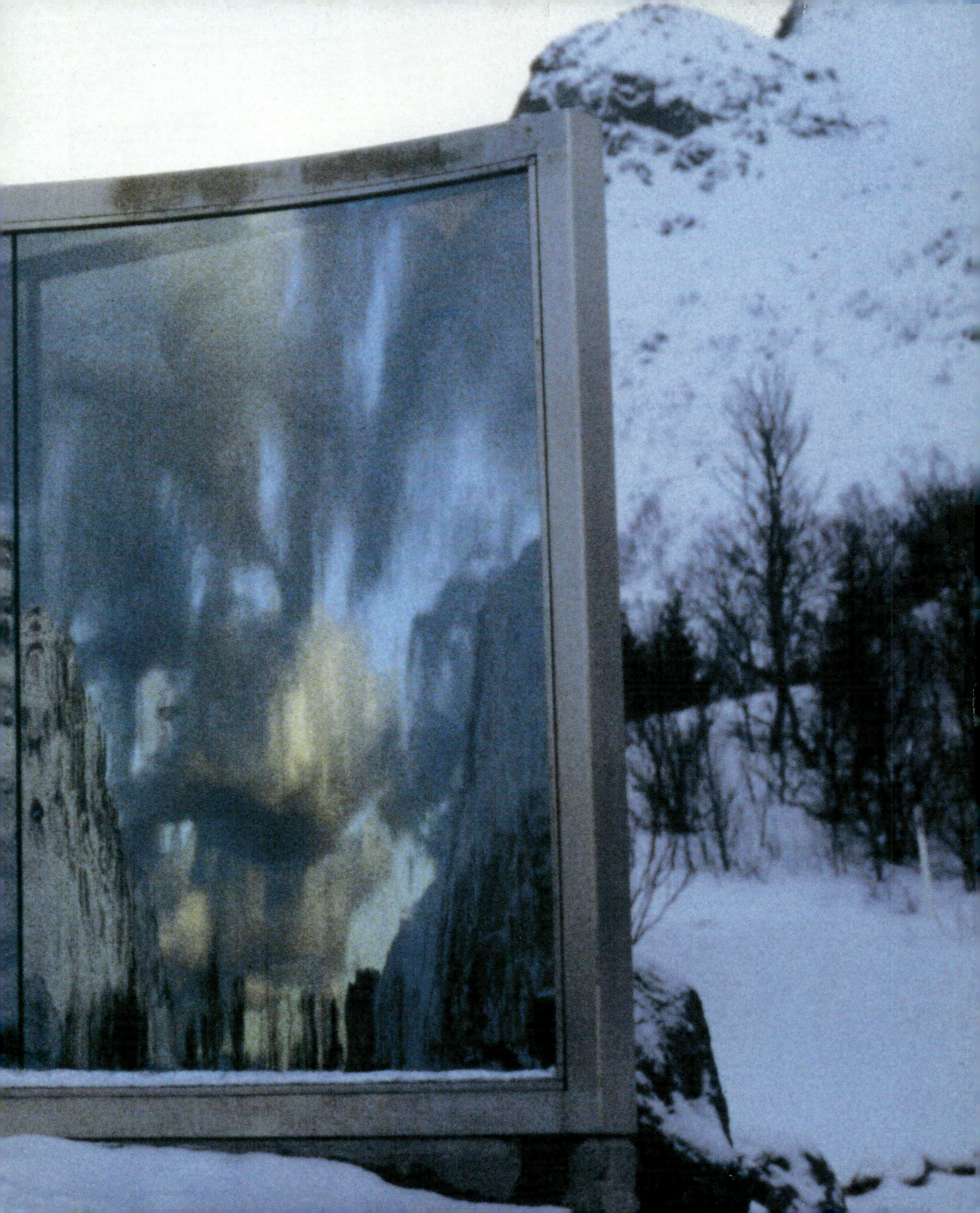

DIE PARKETT-REIHE MIT GEGENWARTSKÜNSTLERN / THE PARKETT SERIES WITH CONTEMPORARY ARTISTS

Book Series with contemporary artists in English and German, published three times a year. Each volume is created in collaboration with artists, who contribute an original work specially made for the readers of Parkett. The works are reproduced in the regular edition and available in a limited and signed Special Edition.

Buchreihe mit Gegenwartskünstlern in deutscher und englischer Sprache, erscheint dreimal im Jahr. Jeder Band entsteht mit Künstlern oder Künstlerinnen, die eigens für die Leser von Parkett einen Originalbeitrag gestalten. Diese Werke sind in der gesamten Auflage abgebildet und zusätzlich in einer limitierten und signierten Vorzugsausgabe erhältlich.

PARKETT NR. 69 ENTSTEHT IN COLLABORATION MIT • **FRANCIS ALŸS, ISA GENZKEN, ANISH KAPOOR** • WILL BE COLLABORATING ON PARKETT NO. 69

JAHRESABONNEMENT (DREI NUMMERN) / ANNUAL SUBSCRIPTION (THREE ISSUES) SFR. 116.– (SCHWEIZ), € 78 (BRD), € 82 (ÜBRIGES EUROPA), US$ 80 (USA AND CANADA ONLY)

ZWEI- UND DREIJAHRESABONNEMENTPREISE SIEHE GELBE BESTELLKARTE IM HEFT / FOR TWO & THREE YEAR RATES, PLEASE CONSULT YELLOW ORDER FORM.

Zürichsee Druckereien AG (Stäfa) Satz, Litho, Druck/Copy, Printing, Color Separations

PARKETT-VERLAG AG ZÜRICH SEPTEMBER 2003 PRINTED IN SWITZERLAND ISBN 3-907582-18-7 ISSN 0256-0917

EDITORIAL

Studies in the multiple perspectives of several simultaneous vantage points mark the pages of this volume of Parkett with Franz Ackermann, Eija-Liisa Ahtila, and Dan Graham. The aircraft on the cover presages artistic journeys that thoroughly ruffle our ingrained notions of time and space.

The work of Dan Graham, the oldest of the artists presented here, represents a journey in time through the history of artistic reception over the past decades. In the words of Karin Schneider and Nicolás Guagnini, "An atomization of the unified modern subject, a critique of Aristotelian time-space continuity, and a dismantling of Renaissance perspective and its organizing social presence are at the core of Graham's overall project." (p. 99) Both Ackermann and Ahtila address similar experiences. However, while Graham's agenda explicitly involves residents, visitors and users of public, private and semiprivate spaces, human beings do not figure at all in Franz Ackermann's painting or his vast, colorful installations. Structures, arterial systems, and intercut layers produce a melting pot of hallucinatory forms that at once represent the givens of nature and the products of human culture. Although visible life appears only in abstract form, its presence is evoked all the more intensely as schematized absence.

In contrast, people lie at the heart of Eija-Liisa Ahtila's oeuvre, which posits between them a mental space of kaleidoscopic, protean proportions. When the term "borderline" appears, as in Taru Elfving's essay, it stands for the formal principle of video films and photographs that enables boundaries to flow into each other and subvert such distinctions as stasis vs. movement, fiction vs. documentation, and the beauty of color, light, and space vs. the harshness of social reality.

In the Insert, readers encounter an entirely different referential standpoint, one that seems to be 'testing' the achievements of an earlier artistic generation. Jonathan Monk has appropriated a sentence from the heyday of conceptual art and sent it on a journey through the languages of the world until it comes full circle, having been translated back into the language of its origin: English. The semantic shifts that result do not simply amuse; they are redolent with the fragrance of other cultures and mindsets as they gently scratch the surface of an artistic mentality that once put all its stakes on purist parameters. The journey of translation is tantamount to contamination: Robert Barry's original statement, in which he speaks of attempting to "communicate telepathically a work of art," reads entirely differently and certainly no less seriously after being incorporated into a world specialized in animism and the invocation of spirits and souls.

BICE CURIGER

Das war es, was er Tag für Tag vergeblich zu erfassen versuchte, das war es, was ihn seit dem Einfall des unwahrnehmbaren, blendenden Lichthofs ohne Unterlass verfolgt hatte. Die äusserste Grenze, die das Denken erreichen kann, ist nichts Seiendes, kein Ort oder Ding, selbst ohne alle Eigenschaft, sondern sein eigenes absolutes Vermögen, das reine Vermögen der Darstellung selbst...

– Giorgio Agamben[1)]

DANIEL KURJAKOVIC

NAHE bei ETWAS und NICHTS und ETWAS

Die Arbeit des 1974 geborenen, in Paris lebenden Bojan Šarčević ist von einem Humor zweiter Ordnung geprägt. Dieser bezieht sich nicht auf diese oder jene Erfahrung, sondern auf das Spiel mit den Bedingungen von Erfahrung. Die kulissenhafte Welt der Stummfilme, voll hintergründiger Spässe und Effekte, kann dies gut verdeutlichen. Wenn der Protagonist – meist zu spät – merkt, dass er, nachdem er aus dem Haus getreten ist, nicht in der umgebenden Landschaft steht, sondern fast im Nichts, nämlich auf gefährlichste Weise nah am Abgrund, in den er trotz der charakteristischen Wiederholung der Szene natürlich nicht stürzen wird, dann amüsiert mich dies als Zuschauer vor allem deshalb, weil ich vom Zwiespalt zwischen Annahme und Wirklichkeit weiss, während der Protagonist darin handelt und dabei das Gesetz des Alltags von der notwendigen Deckungsgleichheit zwischen Annahme und Tatsache suspendiert. Wir bekommen sozusagen den paradoxen «Beweis» geliefert (eine Kategorie, mit der der Film natürlich halsbrecherisch jongliert), dass das Gesetz, dem wir uns im Rahmen einer täglichen Rationalität ohne weiteres unterzuordnen bereit sind, nicht greift – und damit eben gar kein Gesetz ist.

Etwas Ähnliches ging mir jedenfalls bei Šarčević's Arbeit POINT D'APPUI (2001) durch den Kopf, einer mehrteiligen Skulptur mit architektonischen Ver-

DANIEL KURJAKOVIC, Kunsthistoriker und Kurator, lehrt zurzeit an der Hochschule für Gestaltung und Kunst in Zürich.

satzstücken.[2] Sie liess mich an die Aussenfassade eines im Bau befindlichen Hauses denken, wie man sie zum Beispiel in Südosteuropa antreffen kann. POINT D'APPUI besteht aus einer Art Zwischenboden aus Beton, der über einem Portal in den Raum greift; daran fügen sich seitlich zwei «kaskadenartige» Strukturen – alles nicht begehbar –, kurz: ein Ensemble, das etwas ortlos und doch viel Raum schaffend dastand. Interessanterweise verführt diese Struktur dazu, den Innenraum (hier des Bonner Kunstvereins) mit dem Charakter eines Aussenraums zu überblenden. Der Titel, POINT D'APPUI, im übertragenen Sinn als Anhaltspunkt und wörtlich als Stützpunkt zu übersetzen, schien diese Unbestimmtheit zwischen Innen und Aussen auf der Ebene der Bedeutung selbst zu reproduzieren, nämlich als Dilemma zwischen Metapher und Metonymie.

Wo immer Bedeutung erzeugt wird, stellt sich früher oder später die Frage, ob Gedanken subjektive Assoziationen sind oder vom betrachteten Objekt herrühren. Viele von Šarčević's Arbeiten steuern auf diese Schwelle zu. Auf wunderbare, leicht verschrobene Weise hat Šarčević dieses Subjekt-Objekt-Problem anhand einiger architektonischer Entwürfe thematisiert, und zwar in einer mehrteiligen Zeichnungsserie ohne Titel aus dem Jahr 2001. Šarčević hat den Lauf der Sonne und des Mondes in Form transparenter Kurven, die sich teilweise kreuzen, in die Fassade eines Hauses «eingepasst». Was ich im Haus sehen würde, wäre theoretisch die sehr langsame Laufbahn einer Kugel aus Licht – Sonne/Mond –, das durch die gekurvten offenen Bänder von aussen eindringt. Die Kugel würde, so stelle ich mir das wenigstens vor, derart in der Passform der Kurvenbänder «sitzen», dass ich sie zugleich als klein und als gross erleben würde, als Element eines Bildes wie auch eines Raumes.[3]

In erkenntnispraktischer Hinsicht verunreinigt Šarčević's Arbeit Unterscheidungen wie jene zwischen Innen und Aussen, subjektiv und objektiv, ohne sie je zu verleugnen. So liess Šarčević für die Videoarbeit COVER VERSIONS (2001) das Istanbuler Maquam-Ensemble Barbaros Erköse einige Pop-, Reggae- und Soul-Songs, wie «Come as you are» von Nirvana, «Could you be loved» von Bob Marley, «I heard it through the grapevine» von Marvin Gaye

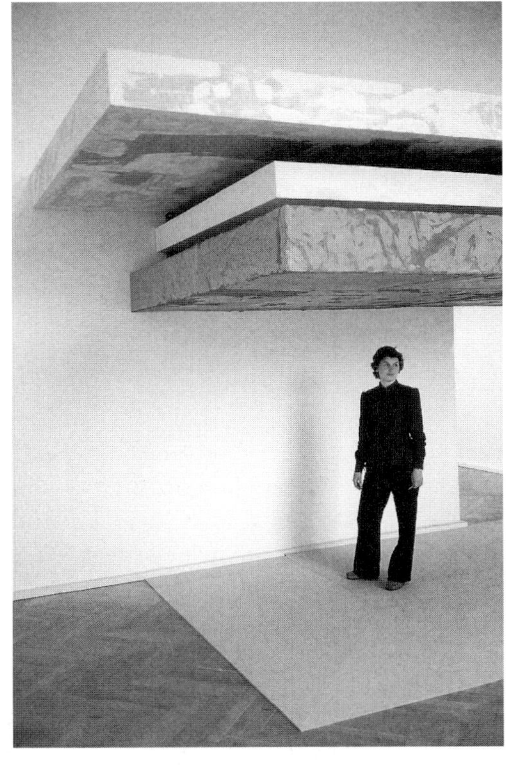

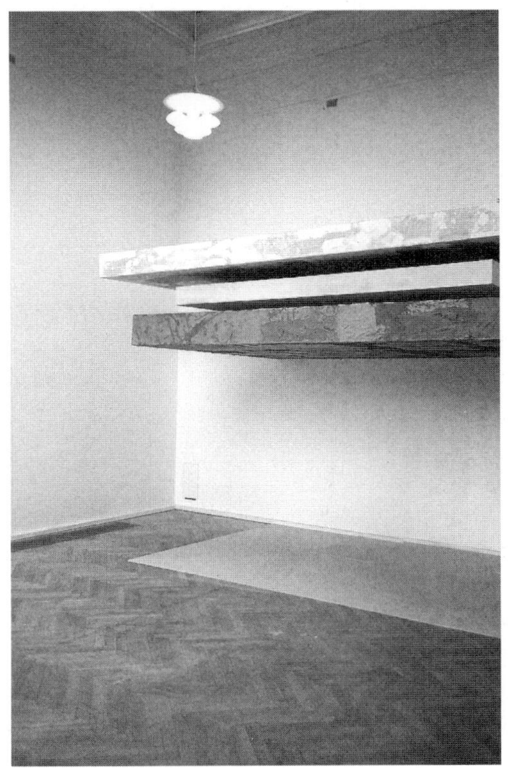

BOJAN SARCEVIC, POINT D'APPUI, 2002, concrete, plaster, wood, installation view, "My head is on fire but my heart is full of Love", Charlottenborg exhibition space, Copenhagen / Beton, Gips, Holz, Museum Charlottenburg, Kopenhagen.

sowie eine Technoversion von «Block Rockin' Beats» der Chemical Brothers einspielen.[4] Die Installation führt auf drei Projektionen verteilt die musikalische Umsetzung vor, wobei in der Bildmitte das Ensemble in der Totalen auftaucht und die seitlichen Projektionen Details wie Blicke und Gesten der kommunizierenden Musiker präsentieren.

Gezeigt wird nicht nur die tastende Annäherung und die graduelle Appropriation, sondern auch die «Erfindung» einer bislang nur potenziellen musikalischen Schicht – die sozusagen aus einem imaginären musikalischen Untergrund «gehievt» wird. Dabei stellt sich durch die arabische Instrumentierung der diversen Songs nicht nur ein Verfremdungseffekt ein – die Arbeit geht über diesen mimetischen Impuls hinaus. Vielmehr erscheinen die Songs so, als würde man hinter einem milchigen Glas die Konturen einer vorübergehenden Person wahrnehmen: Man erkennt diese Person zwar, aber nicht weil man die bekannten Züge identifiziert, sondern weil einem annäherungsweise einige individuelle Eckdaten, etwa die Gesichtsproportionen vertraut sind. Nochmals: Es geht nicht eigentlich um die Verfremdung *per se*, um die Versetzung von einem Kontext in den anderen (dies hielte ich für eine etwas «mechanistische» Deutung); Thema scheint eher die Verunklärung, das Eindringen in einen perzeptiven und kognitiven Graubereich zu sein. COVER VERSIONS wirft – als Verunklärung eines phänomenologischen Verhältnisses von Innen und Aussen – die Frage auf, welche Musik sozusagen in welcher Musik «steckt» beziehungsweise wie sich das eine im anderen ausbreitet (um eine räumliche Metapher zu gebrauchen).

Allen Anzeichen einer «dokumentarischen» Filmsprache zum Trotz bin ich sogar – vielleicht etwas übereifrig – versucht zu verneinen, dass es um das Thema der kulturellen Differenz geht, das in COVER VERSIONS und vielen anderen Arbeiten von Šarčević so offensichtlich zu sein scheint. Was Šarčević macht, ist einfacher und komplexer zugleich – einfacher in der Intention, komplexer auf der Ebene möglicher Lektüren. In OHNE TITEL (BAMAKO) (2001), einem 16-mm-Film, ruht sich eine schwarze Frau, umringt von ihren Töchtern und anderen Halbwüchsigen, auf einer Liege in dörflicher Atmosphäre vor einem Haus aus. Ist es ein Innenhof, ein auf die Strasse hin offener Vorplatz? Eine der Töchter legt eine Kassette mit Gesang von Nina Simone in den Recorder ein. Erneut könnte man die Arbeit metaphorisieren, sich beispielsweise auf kulturelle Identität beziehen, auf lokales Wissen o.ä. Das hiesse allerdings, den metonymischen Aspekt zu unterdrücken. Šarčević operiert denn auch eher mit einer zirkulären Struktur,

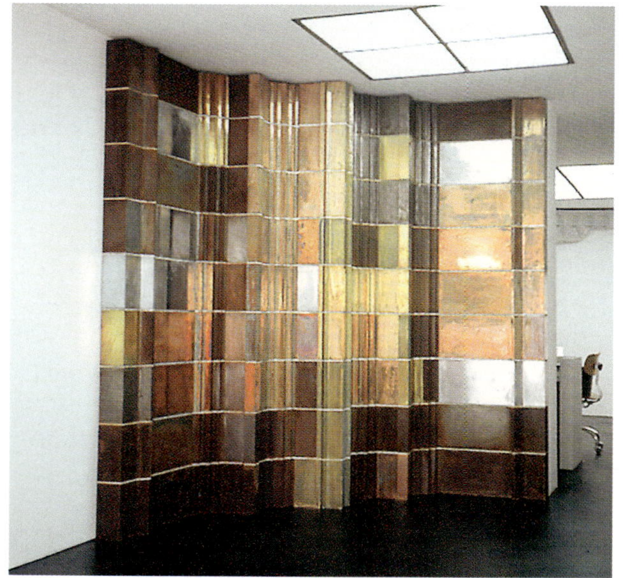

BOJAN SARCEVIC, SPIRIT OF INCLUSIVENESS, 2002, copper, brass, zinc, BQ Gallery, Cologne, 110¼ x 110¼" / GEIST DER EINSCHLIESSLICHKEIT, Kupfer, Messing, Zink, Galerie BQ, Köln, 280 x 280 cm.

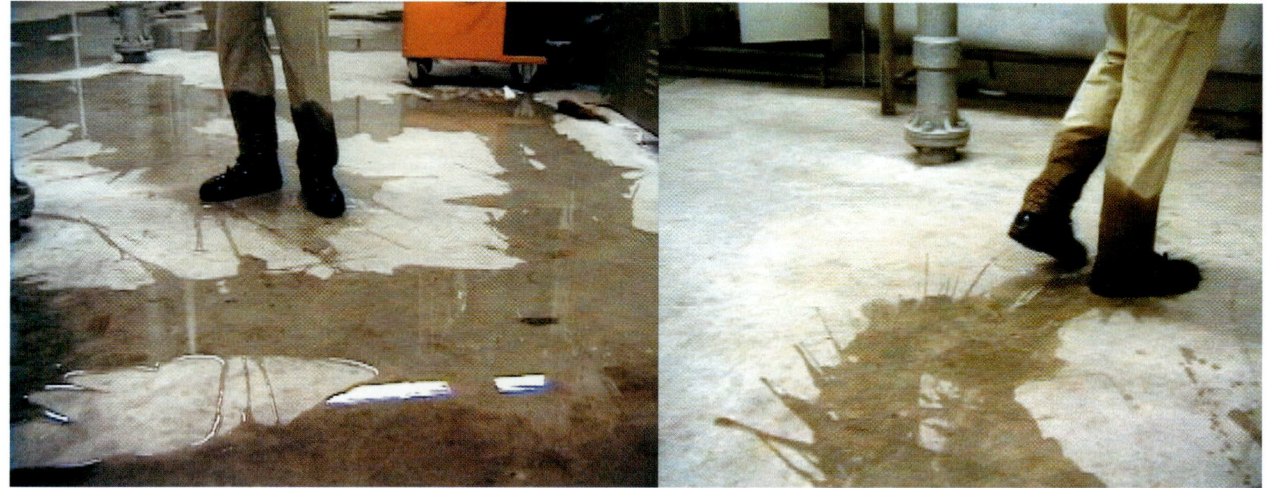

BOJAN SARCEVIC, IRRIGATION-FERTILISATION, 1999, 9-min. video & 12 offset prints; 2 video stills (above), 1 offset print (right) / 9-Minuten-Video & 12 Offsetprints; 2 Videostills (oben), 1 Offsetprint (rechts).

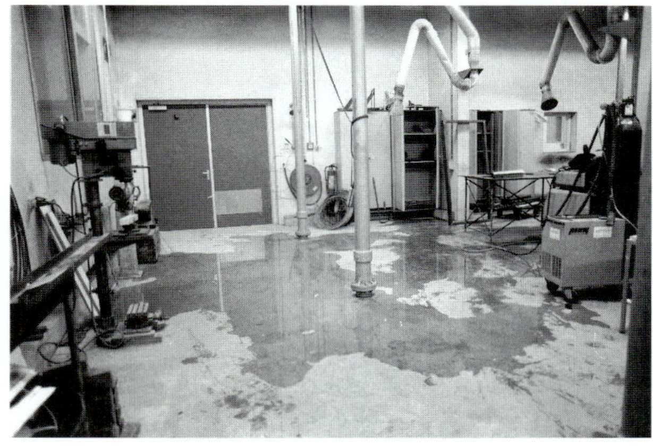

das heisst mit der Tatsache, dass das Lied von Simone zwar als buchstäblich Fremdes eingeführt, doch nach kürzester Zeit als «natürliches» Zeichen aufgefasst wird. Das Lied erweist sich weder als dem Kontext fremd noch als blosse Überlagerung im Sinne eines Soundteppichs.

Wie kommt es zu dieser zirkulären Bewegung? Ist sie zirkulär oder beinahe zirkulär? Ich meine, einer inneren Logik folgend und sie abschliessend oder diese letztlich doch aushebelnd? Ist sie in ein Netz von Verweisen eingetaucht, das an einen Ausgangspunkt (welchen?) zurückführen wird? Und wo ist dieser Ausgangspunkt, bei mir oder in der Welt? Ist er subjektiv oder objektiv? Hier mögen drei Beispiele interessant sein.

Das erste ist IRRIGATION-FERTILISATION (1999), ein Werk, das aus einem neun Minuten langen Video und zwölf Schwarzweisspostern besteht. Das Video zeigt einen Werkraum und fokussiert dabei auf einen Mann, der mäandrierend im Raum umhergeht und Maschinen ein- und ausschaltet, wobei aus seinen Schuhen ununterbrochen Wasser sickert und dabei die hellen Hosenbeine dunkel verfärbt. Allmählich wird der Boden überschwemmt. Teile des Raumes, allerdings kaum mehr als die Neonröhren an der Decke, spiegeln sich in der Lache. Durch den Bildausschnitt, der immer unter Augenhöhe bleibt, wird die Abgeschlossenheit des Raums, eines Innenraums, betont. Er ist allerdings bar jeder intimen Atmosphäre. Der Maschinenpark macht ihn unpersönlich. Der gleichsam absichtslose – und zugleich «masslose» – Akt des Bewässerns nähert ihn noch stärker einem Aussenraum an. Aber was genau bewässert und befruchtet wird, bleibt offen. Auch hier

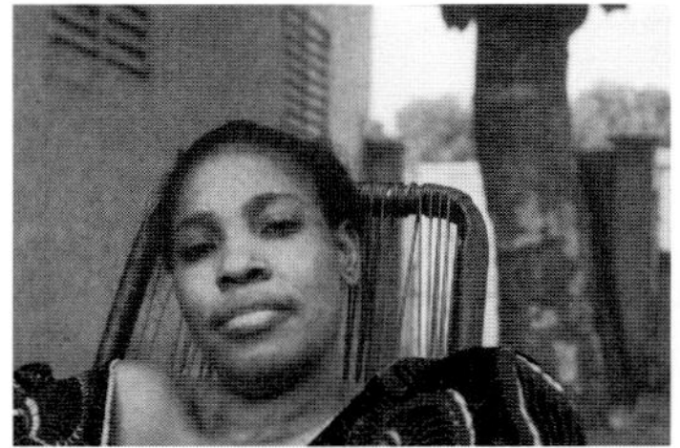

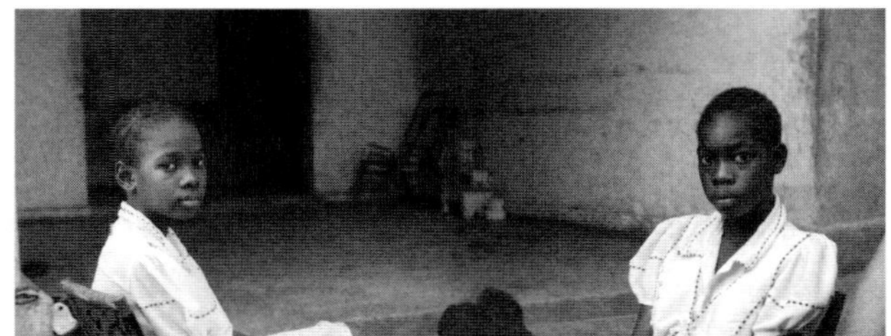

BOJAN SARCEVIC, UNTITLED (BAMAKO), 2001, stills from 16-mm film, duration: 6 min. / Bilder aus dem 16-mm-Film, Dauer: 6 Min.

dienen Begriffe des Titels, wie «Irrigation» und «Fertilisation», als Hinweise für eine sowohl buchstäbliche als auch übertragene Lektüre, die unbestimmt zwischen mechanoiden und organischen Konnotationen hin und her schwingt.

Zweites Beispiel: der achtminütige DVD-Film OHNE TITEL (BANGKOK) (2002). Hier ist die zirkuläre oder beinahe zirkuläre Struktur auf die Stadt projiziert: Diese wird zum Ort, an dem der Protagonist – Šarčević selbst – mit der Zeitung in der Hand durch Strassen und Gassen geht. In Form einer Schnitt-Gegenschnitt-Montage sehen wir ihn nahen und immer wieder hinter einer Hausecke verschwinden. Dies wiederholt sich unablässig. Die Szenen variieren leicht: Mal sind die Strassen bevölkert, mal leer, mal kommt Verkehr auf, mal ist kein Fahrzeug zu sehen. Die Zeitung in der Hand täuscht eine alltägliche Handlung vor, doch mit zunehmender Dauer greift diese Erklärung nicht mehr, die Handlung findet nicht statt. Der Betrachter fängt an, sich wahlweise dem halluzinativen Sog hinzugeben oder umgekehrt nach einem «tiefen» Sinn zu suchen, der durch den filmischen Kode suggeriert, aber nicht eingelöst wird.

Das dritte Beispiel ist MINIATURES (2002), ein weiterer DVD-Film, während dessen gesamter Dauer von elf Minuten wir im Inneren eines Autos sitzen, das durch eine Stadt fährt. Die minimale Handlung, die folgt, verdankt sich gewissermassen dem einfachen, für Šarčević's phänomenologische Sensibilität prägenden Umstand, dass es im Autoinneren warm ist und draussen kalt. Denn dadurch beschlägt sich die Frontscheibe mehr und mehr, wobei der Fahrer mit der linken Hand eine zunehmend labyrinthische Struktur aus mal grösseren, mal kleineren, sich überlagernden Rechtecken darauf zeichnet. Handelt es sich um gedankenlos hingekritzelte, vielleicht bedeutungslose Notate? Oder sind es bereits Manifestationen einer, wenn auch kaum verständlichen, psychischen Tätigkeit, Aufzeichnungen feinster geistiger Regungen? Man wäre versucht dem zuzustimmen, wenn Šarčević nicht in allen Arbeiten so sorgfältig – und irgendwo auch unausweichlich – Handlungsräume ausgewählt hätte, die einer subjektivierenden Deutung entgegenlaufen. Sie sind oft wenig vertraut, nicht spezifisch, opak. Oder beinah auratisch, was vielleicht am verstörendsten zum Ausdruck kommt in Werken wie der Serie der *Points d'appui,* in SPIRIT OF INCLUSIVENESS, einer Art fragmentarischer Rekonstitution des Sockelteils des Kölner Doms aus Holz-, Kupfer-, Stahl-, Messing- und Zinkelementen, oder SPIRIT OF VERSATILITY, einer orientalischen Muqarnas nachgebildeten, hellgrauen Decken-Eckskulptur, bis zu OÙ LA MAIN N'ENTRE PAS LA CHALEUR S'INSINUE, einer Art transparenter Kuppelsektion, eine nicht begehbare, den Betrachter aussperrende Struktur, die zugleich den Eckraum schützt und gewissermassen erst wahrnehmbar macht.

Wenn sich Šarčević so mit den Bedingungen von Erfahrung auseinander setzt und in einen erkenntnistheoretisch unreinen Bereich vorstösst, wenn er beinah-zirkuläre, beinah-auratische Ereignisse schafft, dann scheint er an einer bestimmten, sagen wir, innerweltlichen Transzendenz interessiert. Es ist, als ob Šarčević's Arbeit dem Betrachter jene schützende ungläubige Verwunderung verliehe, die ihn, ähnlich dem sorglosen und von seiner Aufgabe erfüllten Protagonisten aus dem Stummfilm, nahe am Abgrund balancieren lässt.

1) Giorgio Agamben, *Idee der Prosa,* Suhrkamp, Frankfurt am Main 2003, S. 12–13.
2) Unter diesem Titel sind mehrere Arbeiten entstanden, die ich allerdings nicht Versionen nennen möchte. Es scheint eher so, als hätte Šarčević das Vokabular weiterentwickelt unter Berücksichtigung der jeweiligen geographisch-architektonischen Kontexte.
3) Vgl. in diesem Zusammenhang das sehr schöne Künstlerbuch *Spirit of Versatility and Inclusiveness,* das anlässlich von Šarčević's Einzelausstellung im Jahr 2002 bei BQ, Köln, entstanden ist.
4) Vgl. hierzu auch Anja Dorn, «Appropriations», Text zur Ausstellung «Cover Versions», 24.3.–6.5.2001, in der Ausstellungsbroschüre Nr. 59, Stedelijk Museum Bureau Amsterdam, 2001, unpaginiert.

BOJAN SARCEVIC, OÙ LA MAIN N'ENTRE PAS LA CHALEUR S'INSINUE / WHERE THE HAND DOESN'T ENTER, HEAT INFUSES, 2003, Plexiglas and steel, Institut d'Art Contemporain, Villeurbanne/Lyon, 157 1/2 x 157 1/2" / WO DIE HAND NICHT HINREICHT, MACHT SICH HITZE BREIT, Plexiglas und Stahl, 400 x 400 cm.

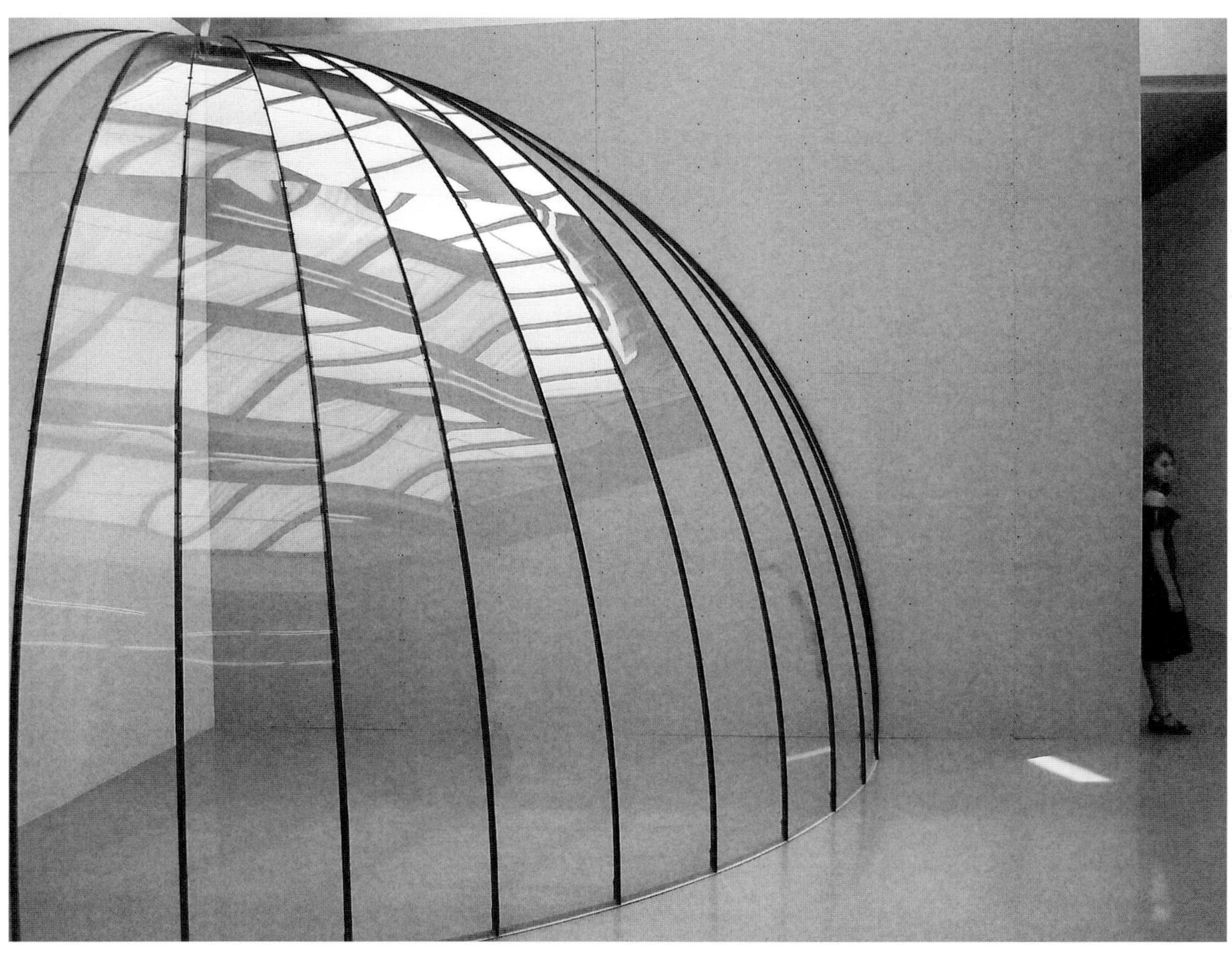

It was this that he had been so futilely trying to grasp day after day, it was this that he had unceasingly pursued by the light of the brief flash of the unglimpsable, blinding halo. The uttermost limit thought can reach is not a being, not a place or thing, no matter how free of any quality, but rather, its own absolute potentiality, the pure potentiality of representation itself…

– Giorgio Agamben, *Idea of Prose,* 1987

DANIEL KURJAKOVIC

NEAR to SOMETHING and NOTHING and SOMETHING

The work of Bojan Šarčević, born in 1974 and now living in Paris, is permeated by a humor of the second order, which derives not from this or that experience, but from a game with the conditions of experience, as in the coulisse-filled world of silent films, with its in fact serious jokes and effects. When the protagonist steps out of his house and notices—usually too late—that he is not in the surrounding landscape but almost in a form of nothingness, that is to say, dangerously close to the abyss—which he will not plunge into despite the characteristic repetition of the scene—then this amuses me, as the viewer, above all because I know of the discrepancy between supposition and reality, whereas the protagonist acts within that context, thereby suspending the usual law of the necessary congruence between supposition and fact. It is as though we are being provided with the paradoxical "proof" (a category that the film tosses around rather hazardously) that the law which we are glibly willing to accept within the framework of ordinary rationality, does not apply here—and hence cannot be a law.

Something of that sort certainly crossed my mind when I saw Šarčević's POINT D'APPUI (2001), a multi-

DANIEL KURJAKOVIC, art historian and curator, is currently lecturing at the Hochschule für Gestaltung und Kunst in Zurich.

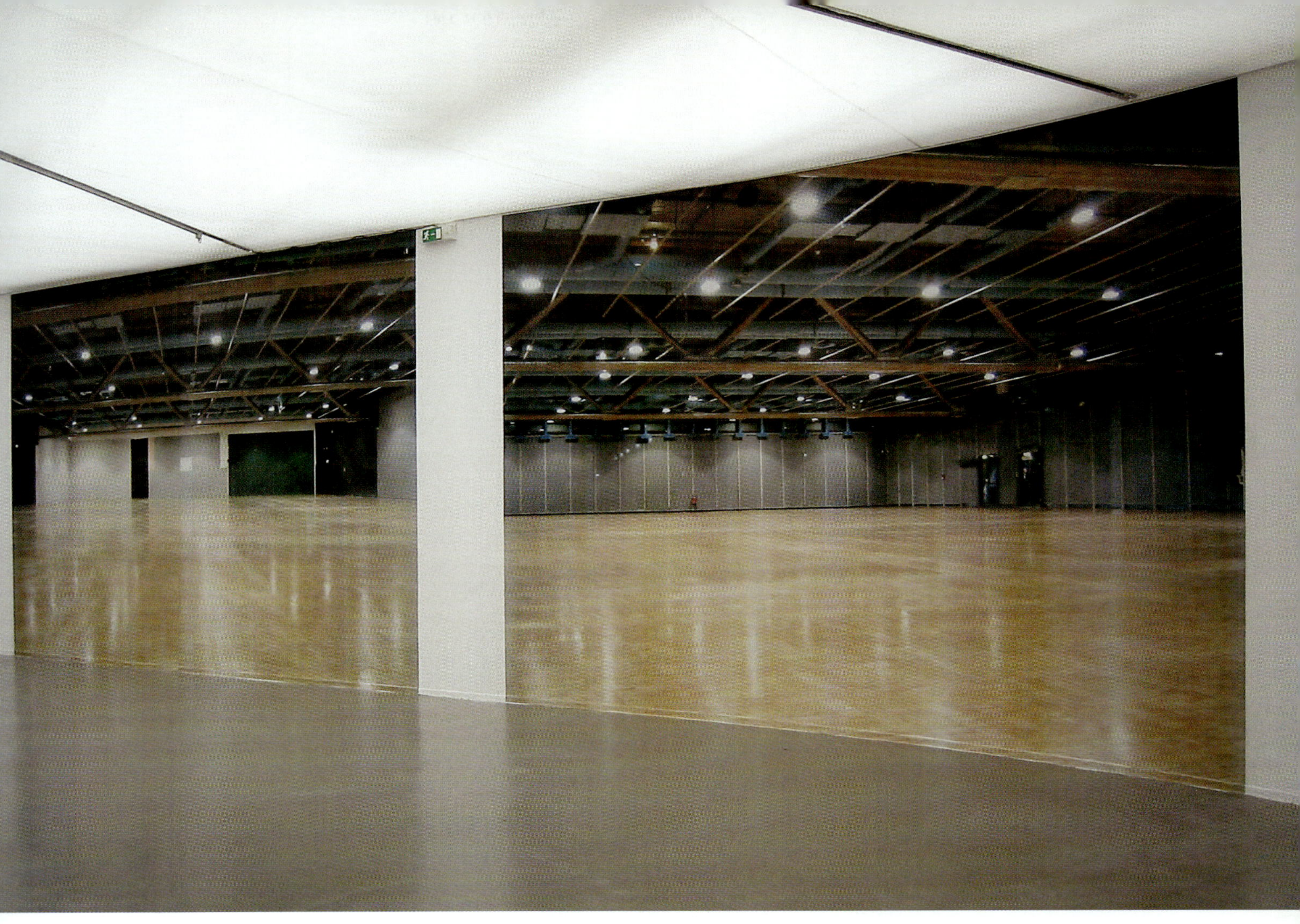

BOJAN SARCEVIC, TROMPE L'OEIL, 2003, 2 ink-jet prints, 13 1/8 x 19 11/16', Musée d'Art Moderne de la Ville de Paris / 2 Ink-Jet-Prints, je 400 x 600 cm.

part sculpture with architectural props.[1] It reminded me of the façade of a building still under construction, of the kind found in south-eastern Europe, for instance. POINT D'APPUI consists of a form of concrete mezzanine floor that extends forwards above a doorway; on either side of this are fixed two "cascade-like" structures—none of which is for walking on; in short, as an ensemble it stood there, rather placeless, yet creating a great deal of space. Intriguingly, this structure encourages one to superimpose the character of an exterior space on the interior in which it stands (in this case the Bonn Kunstverein). The title, POINT D'APPUI, may be taken metaphorically as grounds or literally as ground (in the sense of a base) and seemed, in its meaning, to reproduce this indeterminacy between inner and outer, as a dilemma between metaphor and metonymy.

Wherever there is meaning, sooner or later the question arises as to whether thoughts are subjective associations or derive from the object under consideration. Many of Šarčević's works steer towards this threshold. In a miraculous, faintly quirky way Šarčević has turned the spotlight on this subject-object problem in a number of architectural pieces, specifically in a multi-part series of untitled drawings, made in 2001. Šarčević has "fitted" the course of the sun and the moon—in the form of transparent arcs, intersecting here and there—into the façade of a house. Theoretically, inside the house I would see the very slow trajectory of a ball of light—sun/

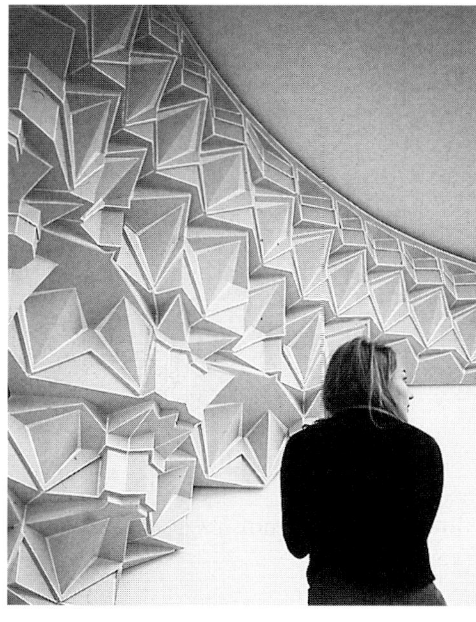

BOJAN SARCEVIC, SPIRIT OF VERSATILITY, 2002, BQ Gallery, Cologne, 70⅞ x 70⅞" / GEIST DER WANDELBARKEIT, Galerie BQ.

moon—penetrating the interior by passing along the open arcs. The ball, or at least this is how I imagine it, would "sit" in the carefully fitting arcs in such a way that I would see it simultaneously as small and as big, as an element in a picture and in a space.[2]

From the point of view of practical epistemology, Šarčević's work clouds distinctions such as those between inside and outside, subjective and objective, without ever denying their existence. In this spirit, for his video work COVER VERSIONS (2001), Šarčević engaged a Maquam ensemble from Istanbul, Barbaros Erköse, to cover a number of pop, reggae and soul tracks—including "Come as you are" by Nirvana, "Could you be loved" by Bob Marley, "I heard it through the grapevine" by Marvin Gaye—and a techno version of "Block Rockin' Beats" by the Chemical Brothers.[3] The video installation of these new musical versions is split between three walls, with the ensemble as a whole in the central projection, and the two sides given over to details, such as the glances and gestures of the musicians communicating with each other.

The projections show not only the tentative approach and gradual appropriation of the original tracks by the ensemble, but also the "invention" of a hitherto purely potential musical layer—which is as it were "hauled" up out of an imaginary musical underground. The Arabian instrumentation of the various tracks produces more than just an alienation effect, for the work goes beyond this mimetic impulse. The effect of the songs is much more akin to the sight of the silhouette of someone passing behind a pane of frosted glass: we recognize the person not because we identify known characteristics but because certain salient points, such as the proportions of that person's face, are familiar to us. Once again: this is not alienation *per se,* where one situation is displaced and transposed into another (in my view that would be a rather "mechanistic" interpretation); it seems rather that this is about disclarifying, about entering into a gray area of perception and cognition. COVER VERSIONS—as a disclarification of the phenomenological relationship of inside and outside—raises the question as to which music already "inhabits" which music or, alternatively, how one spreads itself within the other (to take a spatial metaphor).

Despite the apparent use of a "documentary" film language in COVER VERSIONS, I am even tempted—perhaps a little rashly—to suggest that it is not about cultural difference, which seems to be so obvious in this video and in many of Šarčević's other works. What Šarčević does is simpler and more complex in one—simpler in its intentions, more complex on the level of possible interpretations. In the 16mm film UNTITLED (BAMAKO) (2001) a black woman—surrounded by her daughters and other children—lies on a folding chair outside a house in a rural atmosphere. Is this an interior courtyard, or a front yard open to the street? One of her daughters puts on a cassette by the singer Nina Simone. Again, it would be possible to derive a metaphorical meaning from the work, referring to cultural identity, to local knowledge and the like. But that would mean suppressing the metonymic aspect of the work. In any case Šarčević is, if anything, working with a circular structure, that is, with the fact that the song by Nina Simone is introduced as a literally alien element but very quickly becomes a "natural" feature of the scene. The song neither seems alien in this context nor is it simply an extra layer in the sense of musical wallpaper.

How does this circular movement come about? Is it circular or only almost circular? I mean, does it conform to some inner logic which it takes full circle or does it in fact unhinge that original logic? Is it cloaked in a web of references which will lead back to the starting point (whatever that was)? And where is that starting point, within me or out in the world? Is it subjective or objective? Let us turn to three different examples of Šarčević's work, which are possibly of interest here.

The first is IRRIGATION-FERTILISATION (1999), a work that consists of a nine-minute video and twelve black-and-white posters. The video shows a workshop and focuses on a man wandering around in it, switching machines on and off; all the while water is continuously seeping out of his shoes and darkening his pale trouser legs. Gradually the floor is flooded. Parts of the room, albeit not much more than the fluorescent lights under the ceiling, are reflected in the pool of water. The camera view, always shot from below eye-level, emphasizes the hermetic nature of the workshop, an internal room. Yet there is no sense of intimacy. The presence of the machines gives it an impersonal feel. The seemingly unintentional—yet also "immeasurable"—act of watering makes it seem more like an exterior. But exactly what is being watered and fertilized remains unclear. Once again the terms used in the title—"irrigation" and "fertilization"—point to both a literal and a metaphorical meaning, which wavers indeterminately between mechanical and organic connotations.

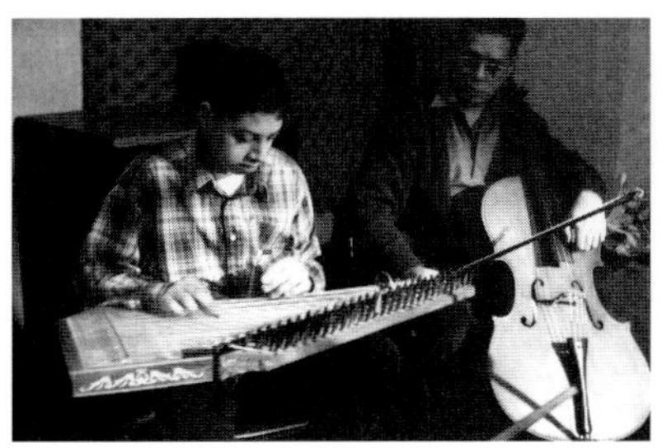

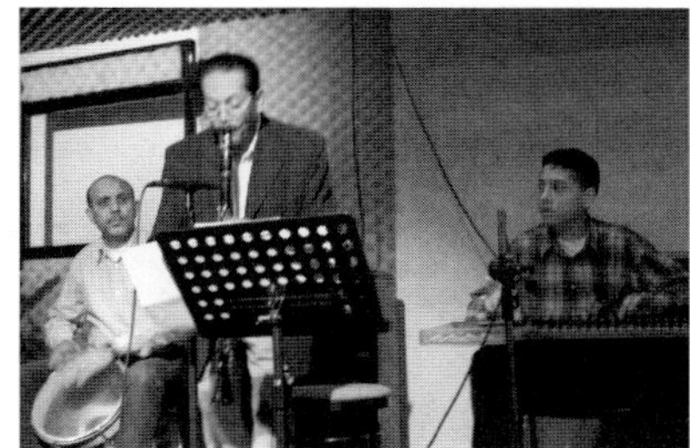

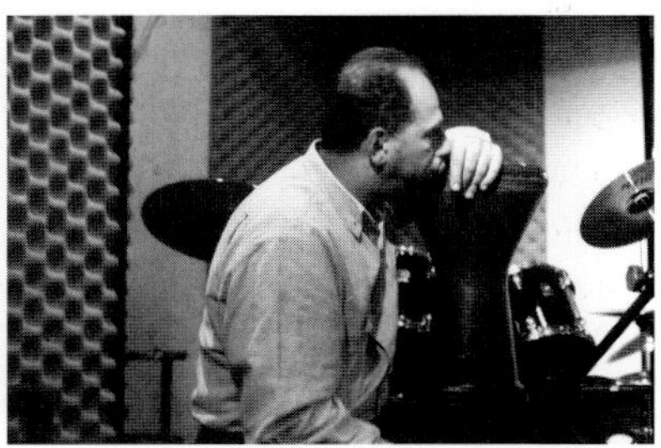

BOJAN SARCEVIC, COVER VERSIONS, 2001,
video projection on 3 screens, duration 30 min. /
Videoprojektion auf 3 Bildschirmen, Dauer: 30 Min.

Second example: the eight-minute film UNTITLED (BANGKOK) (2002). In this case, the circular or almost circular structure is projected onto the city: this becomes a place where the protagonist—Šarčević himself—walks up and down streets and lanes, a newspaper in his hand. In a cut/cross-cut montage we see him approaching and constantly disappearing around the side of a building. This is repeated again and again. The scenes vary just a little: sometimes the streets are bustling, sometimes empty, sometimes there is traffic, sometimes not a single vehicle. The newspaper in the protagonist's hand makes the situation look like an everyday action, but as it continues this explanation no longer suffices, there is no real action. The viewer starts either to sink into the hallucinative vortex or, alternatively, to search for a "deeper" meaning, which is suggested by the cinematic code but never resolved.

The third example is MINIATURES (2002), another DVD, which has us sitting, for its entire duration (eleven minutes), inside a car driving through a town. The ensuing minimal action in a sense springs from the simple fact—which is crucial to Šarčević's phenomenological sensibility—that it is warm inside the car and cold outside. This causes the windscreen to mist over more and more; and as it does so, the driver, using his left hand, draws an increasingly labyrinthine structure made up of now larger, now smaller rectangles, one on top of the other. Are these just thoughtless doodles, possibly meaningless scribbles? Or are these manifestations of a—perhaps barely comprehensible—psychic activity, signs of elevated mind impulses? It might be tempting to go along with the latter but for the fact that in all his works Šarčević has taken great care—almost with a sense of inevitability—to choose settings that parry subjective interpretations. The settings are often hardly familiar, not specific, opaque. Or almost auratic, which is perhaps seen at its most disturbing in works like the series of *Points d'appui*, in SPIRIT OF INCLUSIVENESS, a kind of fragmented reconstruction of the base of Cologne Cathedral using wood, copper, steel, brass, and zinc, or in SPIRIT OF VERSATILITY, a pale-gray ceiling sculpture after an oriental muqarna, right through to OÙ LA MAIN N'ENTRE PAS LA CHALEUR S'INSINUE (Where the Hand Doesn't Enter, Heat Infuses), a kind of transparent section of a dome, not to be entered, indeed keeping the viewer at a distance, both protecting the corner space and in a sense rendering it perceptible at all.

Given that Šarčević engages with the conditions of experience in this way, and enters into an unclear epistemological zone, given that he creates almost circular, almost auratic events, it seems that he may be interested in a certain, shall we say, inner-worldly transcendence. It is as though Šarčević's work lends the viewer that protective, disbelieving wondering, which allows him/her—like the carefree protagonist in the silent film, entirely wrapped up in his task—to balance on the brink of the abyss.

(Translation: Fiona Elliott)

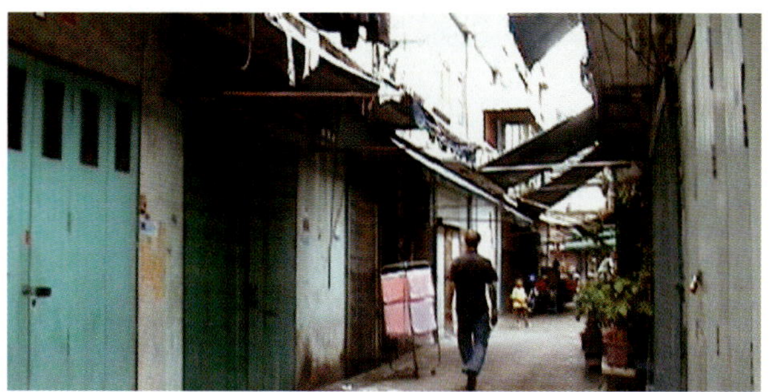

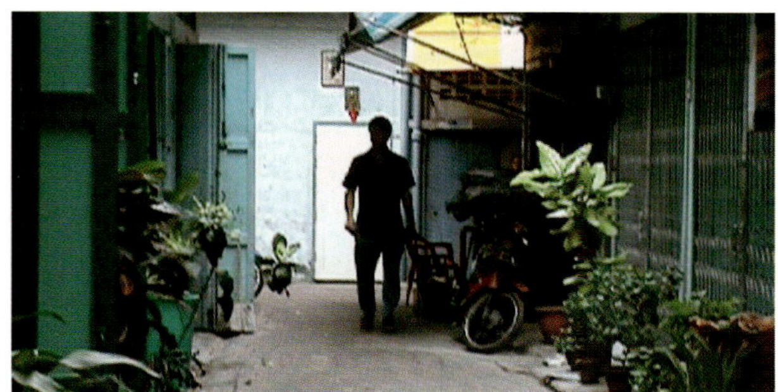

1) Šarčević has produced a number of works with this title, although I would not like to call them versions. It seems rather that Šarčević has continued to develop his vocabulary, in response to new geographical and architectural contexts.
2) In this connection, see the very beautiful artist's book *Spirit of Versatility and Inclusiveness,* which was published to coincide with Šarčević's solo exhibition in 2002 at BQ in Cologne.
3) For more on this see also Anja Dorn's "Appropriations," on the exhibition "Cover Versions" (24 March–6 May 2001), in the exhibition brochure No. 59, Stedelijk Museum Bureau Amsterdam, 2001, unpaginated.

BOJAN SARCEVIC, UNTITLED (BANGKOK), 2002, stills from 7 min. video / Bilder aus dem 7-Min.-Video.

Franz Ackermann

GEBOREN 1963 IN NEUMARKT ST. VEIT, DEUTSCHLAND,

LEBT UND ARBEITET IN BERLIN UND KARLSRUHE /

BORN 1963 IN NEUMARKT ST. VEIT, GERMANY,

LIVES AND WORKS IN BERLIN AND KARLSRUHE.

Eija-Liisa Ahtila

GEBOREN 1959 IN HÄMEENLINN

LEBT UND ARBEITET IN HELSINK

BORN 1959 IN HÄMEENLINNA, F

LIVES AND WORKS IN HELSINKI.

Dan Graham

BORN 1942 IN URBANA, ILLINOIS, USA,

LIVES AND WORKS IN NEW YORK /

GEBOREN 1942 IN URBANA, ILLINOIS, USA,

LEBT UND ARBEITET IN NEW YORK.

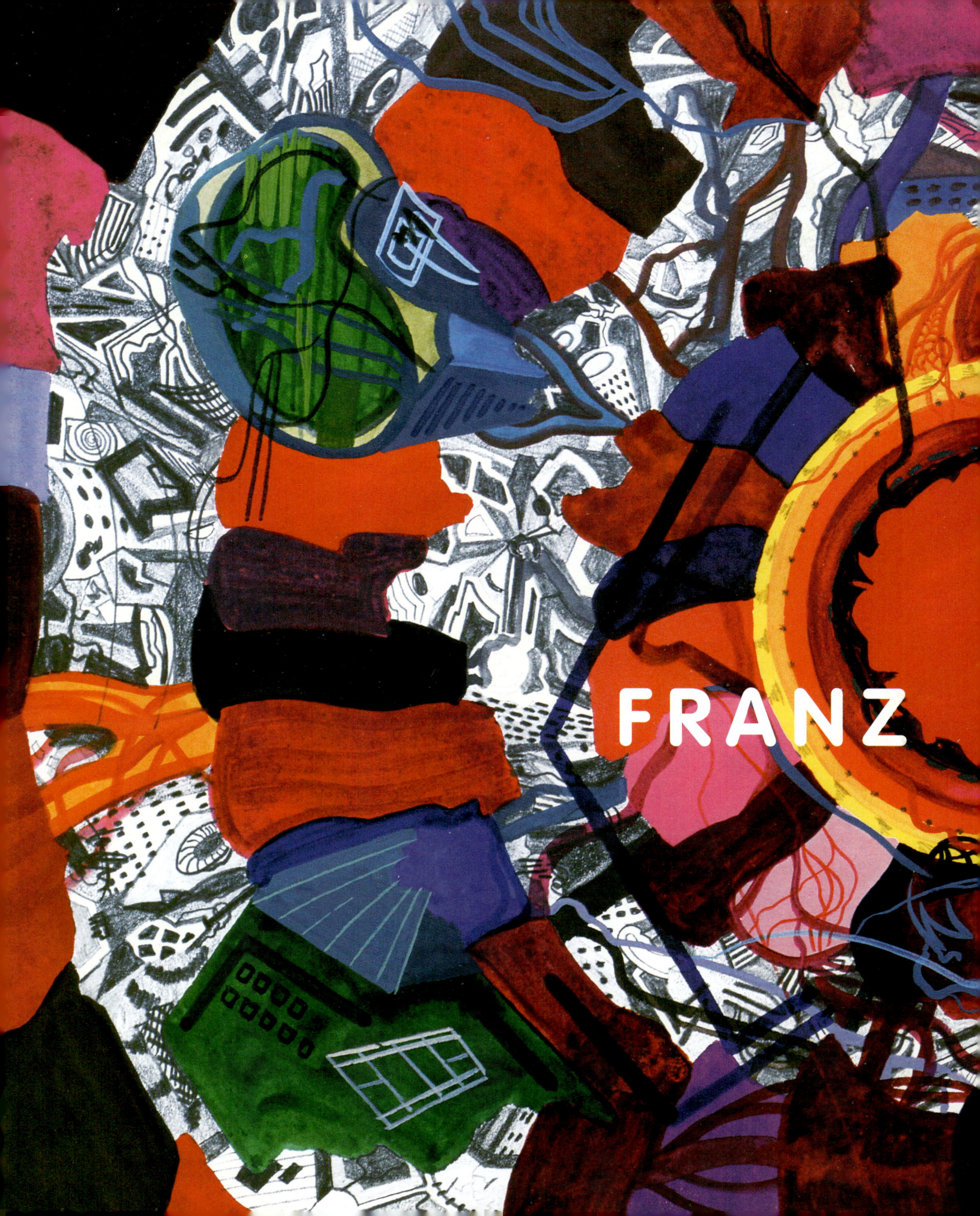
FRANZ

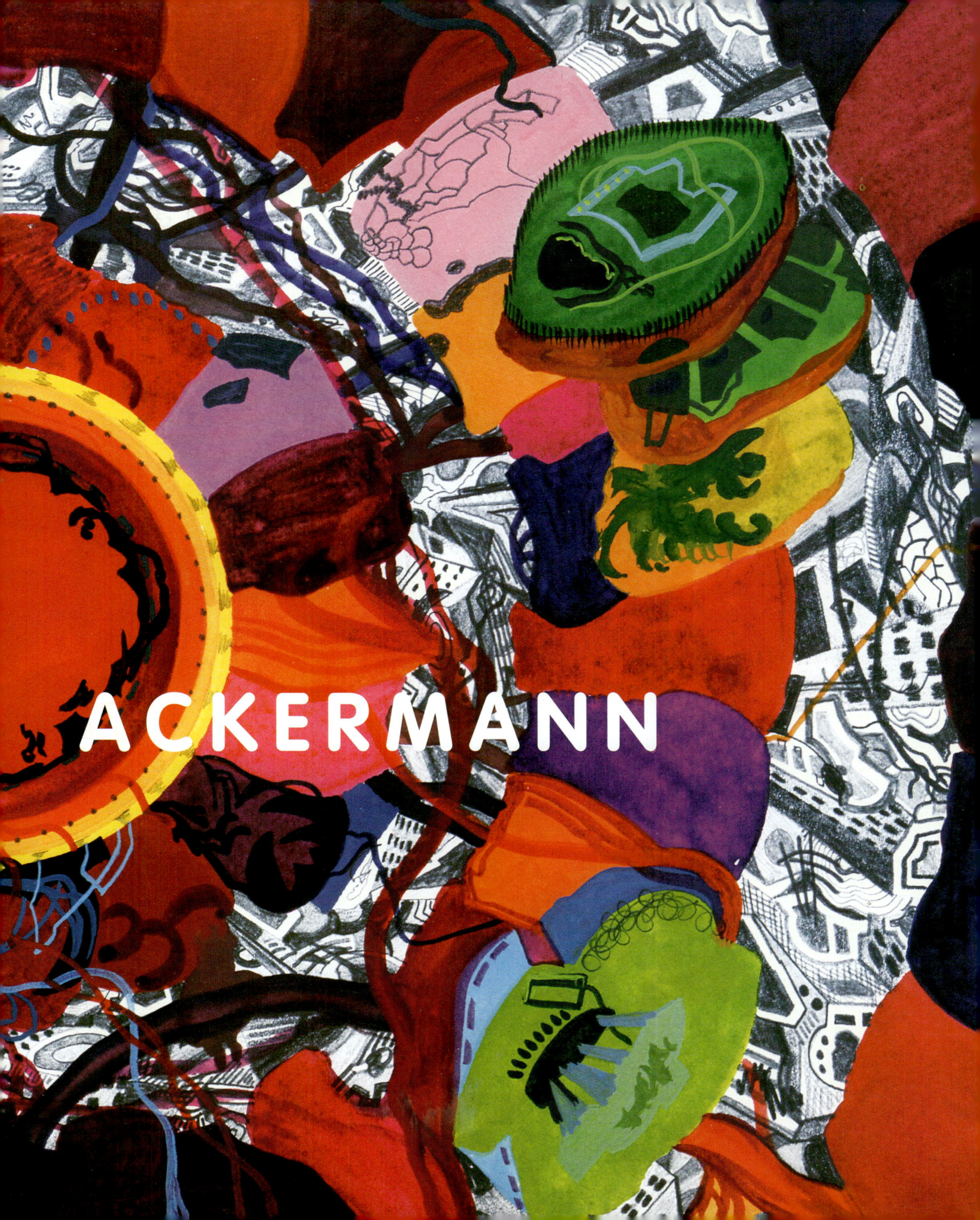
ACKERMANN

The Occidental Tourist

DOUGLAS FOGLE

Club Med—a cheap holiday in other people's misery.

During the upheavals of May 1968 in Paris, this Situationist-inspired indictment of the Western tourist industry could be found scrawled on the walls of buildings and on the barricades that had been erected in the streets. In the years leading to the uprisings, tourism in general and the vacation in particular would come to stand in for all of the ills of a materialist consumer culture that Guy Debord would anoint "the society of the spectacle." One only needs to think of the apocalyptic "holiday" scenario played out in Jean Luc Godard's film *Weekend* (1967) to see the full extent of the slippage of this critique from the counter culture to the culture industry. Nearly a decade later, this critique would be reborn as the avatars of punk rock, the Sex Pistols, would appropriate this phrase as the opening line of their fourth and final single "Holidays in the Sun" (1977). Wailing in a machine gun staccato and accompanied by the feedback-laced chords of his partners, Johnny Rotten's lyrics for this song would present an even more damning critique of the middle-class values of the "package tours" offered by local travel agencies, suggesting a trip not to Club Med but to Bergen-Belsen, the infamous site of one of the Third Reich's concentration camps. These critiques are just as relevant in the situation we find ourselves in today. Although world travel is hardly an invention of the twentieth let alone the twenty-first century, tourism is a particularly contemporary mode of being in the modern world. We are now confronted with a myriad of possibilities for travel from the newly minted more exotic forms of adventure and eco-tourism to the familiar and well-worn package tours to Europe, North America, or Asia. If one has the right amount of money, even the International Space Station isn't outside the limits of a determined tourist courtesy fueled by the entrepreneurial desperation of the Russian space program. But despite the more enlightened, less imperialistic forms of travel at our disposal today, and a full knowledge of their economic importance to developing countries, what precisely does it mean to participate in the global tourist economy?

This is the question that Franz Ackermann confronts in his work both directly and obliquely. Ackermann is a painter for whom travel is a categorical necessity. However, when looking at his work, it is clear that the road he travels is not that which we might associate with the classical grand tour. For Ackermann tourism is both a topic and a methodology. Since making his first international trip to Asia in 1991 on a DAAD grant, during which he spent a year living in Hong Kong, Ackermann has evolved a set of Situationist-inspired visual practices that have actively investigated the "psychogeographical" aspects of travel as embodied in the figure of the tourist.[1] A major part of Ackermann's work can be found in the form of what he has termed his "mental maps"—small drawings rendered in pencil, ink, and gouache.

DOUGLAS FOGLE is Associate Curator of Visual Arts at the Walker Art Center in Minneapolis.

Preceding double page / Vorangehende Doppelseite: FRANZ ACKERMANN, MENTAL MAP: PANIC BUTTON, 2003, Mischtechnik auf Papier, 21 x 36 cm / mixed media on paper, $8^1/_4$ x $14^3/_{16}$".

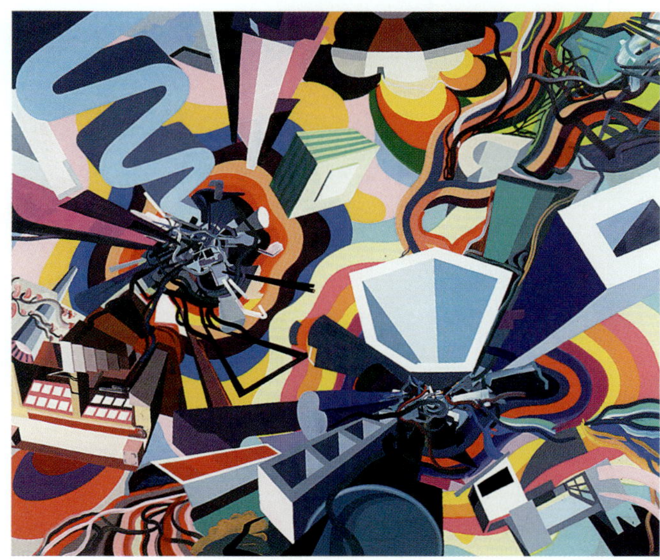

FRANZ ACKERMANN, EVASION XVII (TWO PIPELINES DELIVERING A CITY—BUILD ME UP TO KNOCK ME DOWN), 1998, Öl auf Leinwand, 250 x 300 cm / oil on canvas, 98 1/2 x 118 1/8".

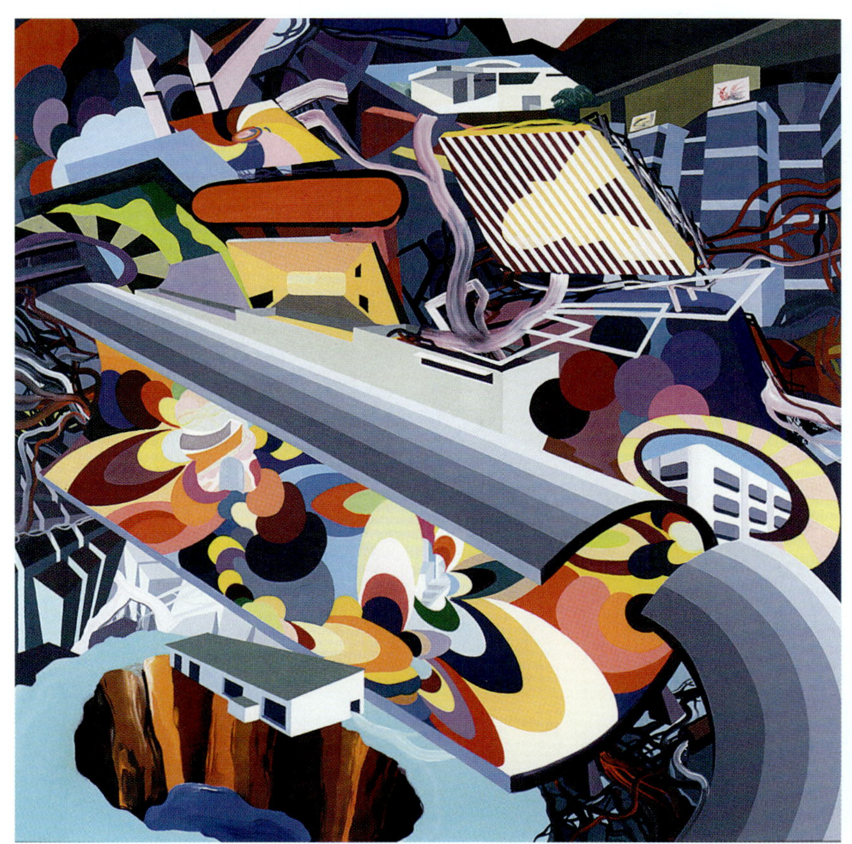

FRANZ ACKERMANN, EVASION XVI (THE DISASTER), 1998, Öl auf Leinwand, 280 x 290 cm / oil on canvas, 110 1/4 x 114 3/16".

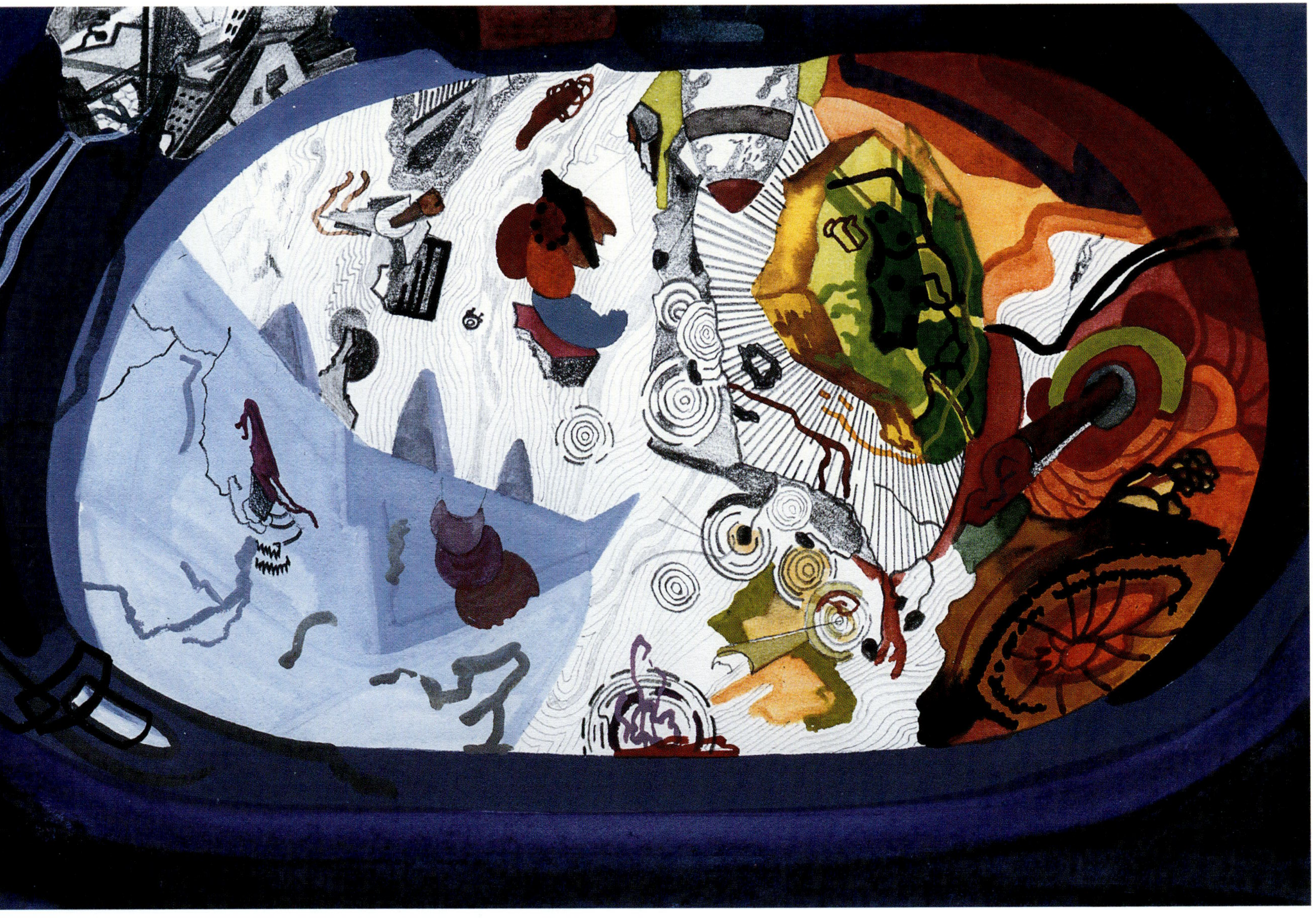

FRANZ ACKERMANN, OHNE TITEL (MENTAL MAP: DIE ÜBERRASCHUNG), 2003, Mischtechnik auf Papier, 19 x 13 cm / mixed media on paper, $7^1/_2$ x $5^1/_8$".

These mental maps are executed on the fly, in hotel rooms during the artist's travels, and they constitute what we might think of as a type of highly subjective GPS technology rendered at the level of the hand. Graphically abstracting characteristic architectural elements of the specific urban landscapes in which he finds himself, the artist creates colorful graphic networks that act as highly subjective records of the built environment of his various global destinations. Fast, expressionistic, and infused with a critical cartographic impulse, Ackermann's mental maps are more akin to Guy Debord's psychogeographical drawings of Paris or the architect/painter Constant's sketches of his New Babylon, than to any rationally ordered traveler's city guide.

The explosive character of urban space within the burgeoning confines of our contemporary global hyper-cities finds itself realized in the contorted geometries of Ackermann's larger canvas-based work he calls "evasions." Often developed out of his more delicate and contemplative mental maps, these vertiginous agglomerations of vibrant color confront the viewer with a collapsed sense of perspective in which pictorial, geographical and architectural space are forced through a vortex. Moving from work to work, a soccer stadium in São Paulo morphs into an office building in Hong Kong or later into an advertising billboard in Minneapolis. Nothing is recognizable yet everything is vaguely familiar. We are confronted with a traveler's sense of déjà vu. It is as if in these works Ackermann has injected the *Michelin Guide* or *London A to Z* with a pyschedelia-infused mixture of pigments leaving the viewer with an experience reminiscent of looking at a painting by Hieronymus Bosch on acid or a Cimabue dropped through the looking glass. But instead of looking on a tortured landscape of hell or on the compressed architectonics of medieval architecture, we gaze out on the very modern and highly subjective traces of an artist's movement through space and time via the travel machine known as tourism.

Ackermann's "evasions" are commonly mounted by the artist on top of even larger site-specific wall paintings. In January of 2001, Ackermann arrived in Minneapolis in order to complete just such a project for an exhibition that I was curating at the Walker Art Center. It was strange to think about Ackermann becoming a tourist in Minneapolis, a moderately scaled city situated squarely in the Upper Midwest of the American continent. Spending time here, however, one soon realizes that the recent demographic history of the city itself reflects the ebbs and flows of the tumultuous upheavals of the global political and economic situation. Over the past twenty years, Minneapolis has seen an incredible influx of immigrants first from Southeast Asia and now East Africa. It was in this context that Ackermann set out to make a work entitled HELICOPTER NO. 15 (WATCH ME FALLING) (2001). Working in the touristically inhospitable dead of winter, Ackermann rendered a phantasmatic portrait of the city. Abstracted portions of an office tower by Philip Johnson melted into other vernacular visual elements culled by the artist from his walks through the city, creating a lurching, graphic tower of Babel. Mounted at the base of this massive psychedelic monolith next to a mental map of Minneapolis rendered in graphite were two photographs. One image was an archetypal view of a decades old beer sign by the Mississippi River that has taken on a kind of monumental iconic significance within the city. The other was the view from the window of the artist's hotel room where much of this work was mapped out. What became clear to me after seeing this completed project was that Ackermann not only travels physically, garnering more frequent flier miles with every project. He also travels psychically, producing hallucinatory visions of cities that are every bit as accurate as any tourist map. Looking at HELICOPTER NO. 15 (WATCH ME FALLING) one enters one's very own daydream nation.

If this contemporary mode of travel is a constant presence in Ackermann's practice and if his paintings are themselves dependent on his own movements across the globe, the artist does not leave his own complicity with this mode of being untouched by his critical stance. In his work HAUS AM STRAND (House on the Beach) (1997), for example, we see a photographic self-portrait of the artist standing with his back to the camera. The artist looks off into the distance, resembling, as the critic Jörg Heiser has suggested, "one of Caspar David Friedrich's Romantic protagonists."[2] But unlike Friedrich's WANDERER

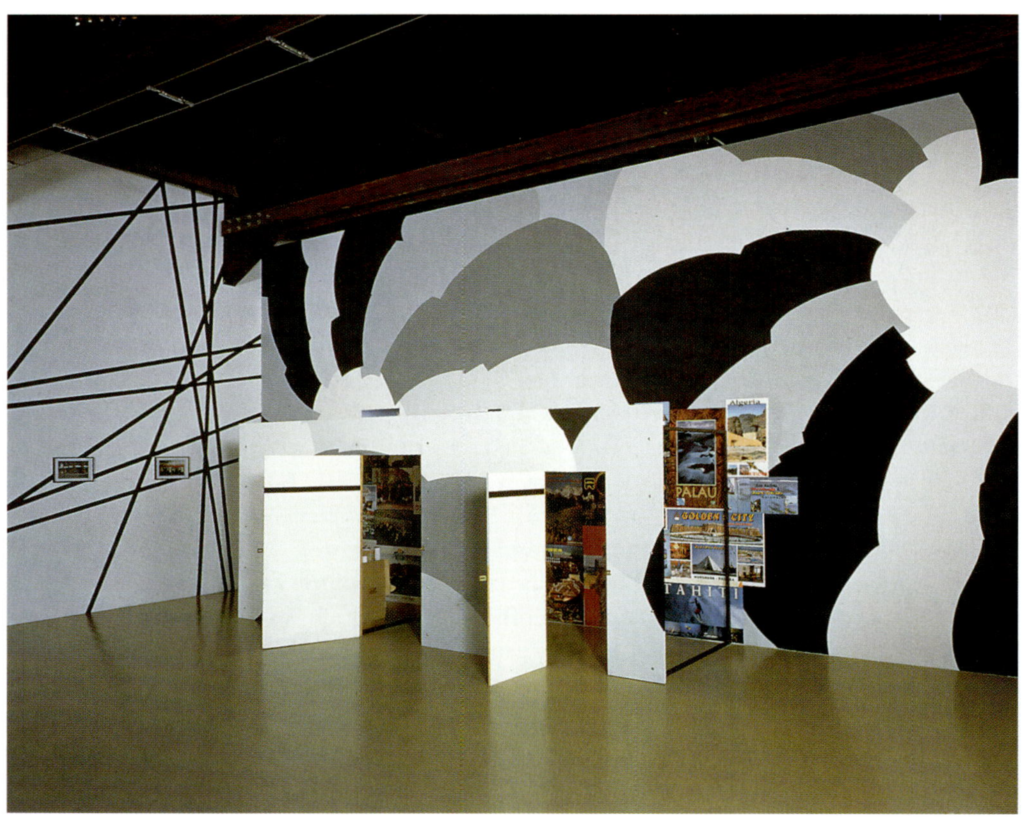

FRANZ ACKERMANN, BOLOGNA, 2000, Acryl auf Holz, 205 x 518 cm, Wandmalerei, 446 x 1202 cm / acrylic on wood, 80 7/8 x 204", wall painting, 175 5/8 x 473 1/4", installation view, Castello di Rivoli, Torino.
(PHOTO: PAOLO PELLION, TORINO)

IN THE MIST (1818), this wanderer is wearing a military grade flak jacket emblazoned with the graphic invocation "tourist." Of course, courtesy of satellite television and the likes of CNN, the world has spent the better part of the last decade looking at journalists in bulletproof vests reporting from war zones such as Bosnia. In the last year, however, we have seen a quantum leap in the touristic aspects of the news media with the insertion of so-called "embedded" journalists into the United States and British military in the war in Iraq. Has tourism, once a subtly implied form of neo-colonial subjugation, now come clean and owned up to its imperialistic roots? Is this signage on the artist's flak jacket a target or a warning? Ackermann lets us think about this question within the context of the travel industry as he surrounds this self-portrait with an architectural framework of posters advertising slide presentations of travels to exotic locales such as China, Nepal, and Burma, which are commonly put on in Berlin and other German cities. In light of recent events, Ackermann's work begins to make me think about the implications of the Sex Pistols' "Holiday in the Sun" for the Christianne Amanpours of the world.

Some of the first American tourists to Asia in the post-war period were the "advisors" sent by the U.S. military to Vietnam. We all know the results of that holiday in the sun. Today, the embedded reporters in Iraq have undertaken their own more virulent kind of tourism. In his work, Franz Ackermann has taken note of this and seemingly replaced the idyllic slogan of May '68 "beneath the paving stones, the beach" with a more recent incantation brought to us by Francis Ford Coppola in his 1979 film *Apocalypse Now:* "Charlie don't surf." Perhaps he would if he had seen the slide shows.

1) In 1955 Guy Debord suggested that a new field of inquiry of "psychogeography could set for itself the study of the precise laws and specific effects of the geographical environment, consciously organized or not, on the emotions and behavior of individuals." See Guy Debord, "Introduction to a Critique of Urban Geography" in: *Situationist International Anthology,* ed. by Ken Knabb (Berkeley: Bureau of Public Secrets, 1981), p. 5.

2) Jörg Heiser, "Travelling Light," *Frieze,* no. 66, April 2002, p. 57.

Die Reisen des Franz Ackermann & der abendländische Tourismus

DOUGLAS FOGLE

Club Med – eine billige Reise ins Elend anderer Leute.

Diese von den Situationisten inspirierte Verurteilung der westlichen Tourismusindustrie war während der Maiunruhen 1968 in Paris als Parole auf Hauswänden und Strassenbarrikaden allgegenwärtig. In den Jahren unmittelbar davor galt der Tourismus allgemein und insbesondere der Ferientourismus als Inbegriff aller Übel der materialistischen Konsumgesellschaft, die Guy Debord feierlich zur «Gesellschaft des Spektakels» erklärte. Man braucht nur an die apokalyptischen «Ausflugs»-Szenen in Jean-Luc Godards Film *Le week-end* (1967) zu denken, um zu realisieren, wie sehr diese Kritik auf ihrem Weg von der Subkultur in die Kulturindustrie an Schärfe verloren hat. Fast genau ein Jahrzehnt später sollte sie erneut auferstehen, als die Galionsfiguren des Punk Rock, The Sex Pistols, diesen Ausspruch in der ersten Zeile ihrer vierten und letzten Single, «Holidays in the Sun» (1977), wieder aufgriffen. Geschrien im Stakkato eines Maschinengewehrs und von den rückgekoppelten Saitenklängen seiner Partner begleitet stellt Johnny Rottens Songtext sogar eine noch schärfere Kritik jener Werte der Mittelklasse dar, welche Pauschalreisen lokaler Anbieter zulassen, die nicht nur den Club Med im Angebot haben, sondern auch Bergen-Belsen, Standort eines Konzentrationslagers im Dritten Reich. Bis heute hat diese Kritik nichts von ihrer Brisanz eingebüsst. Auch wenn Weltreisen keine Erfindung des zwanzigsten, geschweige denn des einundzwanzigsten Jahrhunderts sind, so ist der Tourismus doch eine typische Erscheinung unserer modernen Welt. Wir sind mit einer ungeheuren Vielfalt von Reisemöglichkeiten konfrontiert: von den neueren, eher exotischen Formen des Abenteuer- und Ökotourismus bis zu den bekannten und bewährten Pauschalreisen nach Europa, Nordamerika oder Asien. Ja, dank dem verzweifelten unternehmerischen Wagemut der Betreiber des russischen Raumfahrtprogramms ist nicht einmal

DOUGLAS FOGLE ist Associate Curator of Visual Arts am Walker Art Center in Minneapolis.

die internationale Raumstation ausser Reichweite eines zielstrebigen Touristen, sofern er nur über genügend Geld verfügt. Aber selbst wenn uns aufgeklärtere, weniger ausgeprägt imperialistische Formen des Reisens offen stehen, und im vollen Bewusstsein um die wirtschaftliche Bedeutung des Tourismus für die Entwicklungsländer: Was genau bedeutet es eigentlich, an der globalen Tourismusindustrie teilzuhaben?

Das ist die Frage, die Franz Ackermann in seiner Arbeit auf direkte und versteckte Weise stellt. Ackermann ist ein Maler, für den das Reisen ein kategorischer Imperativ ist. Sieht man jedoch auf sein bisheriges Werk zurück, wird klar, dass seine Reiseroute nicht dem entspricht, was wir uns unter einer klassischen Weltreise vorstellen. Für Ackermann ist das Reisen Thema und Methode zugleich. Seit seiner ersten Asienreise 1991 mit einem DAAD-Stipendium in der Tasche, in deren Verlauf er ein Jahr in Hongkong verbrachte, hat Ackermann eine Reihe von den Situationisten inspirierte, visuelle Praktiken entwickelt, um die «psychogeographischen» Aspekte des Reisens, verkörpert in der Gestalt des Touristen, genauer zu untersuchen.[1] Einen grossen Teil von Ackermanns Arbeiten machen die von ihm so genannten *Mental Maps* aus – kleine Zeichnungen mit Bleistift, Tusche und Gouache. Diese geistigen Landkarten entstehen jeweils flugs, im Vorbeigehen, in Hotelzimmern, wenn der Künstler auf Reisen ist, und stellen eine Art hyper-subjektiver GPS-Technologie in manueller Form dar. Indem er architektonische Elemente der urbanen Landschaft, in der er sich gerade befindet, zeichnerisch abstrahiert, schafft der Künstler farbintensive graphische Netzwerke, die eine ganz und gar subjektive Aufzeichnung der gebauten Umgebung an all seinen wechselnden, über die ganze Welt verstreuten Aufenthaltsorten darstellen. Schnell hingeworfen, expressiv und mit einem kritisch-kartographischen Impetus versehen stehen Ackermanns geistige Landkarten Guy Debords psychogeographischen Zeichnungen von Paris oder den Neu-Babylon-Skizzen des Architekten und Malers Constant näher als irgendeinem rational aufgebauten Stadtreiseführer.

Den explosiven Charakter des urbanen Raumes innerhalb der aus allen Nähten platzenden Grenzen der heutigen globalen Hyper-Städte finden wir in der «verrenkten» Geometrie von Ackermanns grösseren Arbeiten auf Leinwand wieder, die er *Evasionen* nennt. Diese oft aus seinen delikateren und kontemplativen geistigen Landkarten heraus entwickelten, Schwindel erregenden Ansammlungen vibrierender Farbe vermitteln dem Betrachter das Gefühl eines perspektivischen Kollapses, bei dem malerischer, geographischer und architektonischer Raum von einem gewaltigen Strudel erfasst werden. Bewegen wir uns von einem Bild zum nächsten, verwandelt sich ein Fussballstadion in São Paulo zu einem Bürogebäude in Hongkong und später zu einer Plakatwand in Minneapolis. Nichts ist mit Sicherheit wiederzuerkennen, aber alles ist vage vertraut. Wir haben das *Déjà-vu*-Erlebnis eines Reisenden. Es ist, als ob Ackermann diesen Arbeiten den *Guide Michelin* oder *London von A bis Z* zusammen mit einer psychedelischen Pigmentmischung injiziert hätte und dem Besucher dadurch das Gefühl vermittelte, er betrachte ein Bild, das Hieronymus Bosch auf einem LSD-Trip gemalt habe, oder einen durch den Spiegel gefallenen Cimabue. Doch statt eine qualvolle Höllenlandschaft oder die gedrungene Architektur des Mittelalters zu erblicken schauen wir hinaus auf die sehr neuzeitlichen und höchst subjektiven Spuren der Bewegungen eines Künstlers durch Zeit und Raum mittels jener Reisemaschine, die uns unter dem Namen Tourismus vertraut ist.

Ackermanns *Evasionen* werden vom Künstler gewöhnlich in noch grössere, ortsbezogene Wandbilder gehängt. Im Januar 2001 kam Ackermann nach Minneapolis um ein solches Projekt für eine von mir kuratierte Ausstellung im Walker Art Center fertigzustellen. Es war seltsam, sich vorzustellen, dass Ackermann zu einem Touristen in Minneapolis würde, einer mittelgrossen Stadt, die zentral im oberen Mittleren Westen des nordamerikanischen Kontinents liegt. Verbringt man einige Zeit hier, erkennt man, dass die jüngere demographische Entwicklung dieser Stadt das Auf und Ab der gewaltigen Veränderungen der globalen politischen und wirtschaftlichen Situation widerspiegelt. Während der letzten zwanzig Jahre hat Minneapolis einen unglaublichen Zustrom von Immigranten erlebt, zuerst aus Südostasien, danach aus Ostafrika. Vor diesem Hinter-

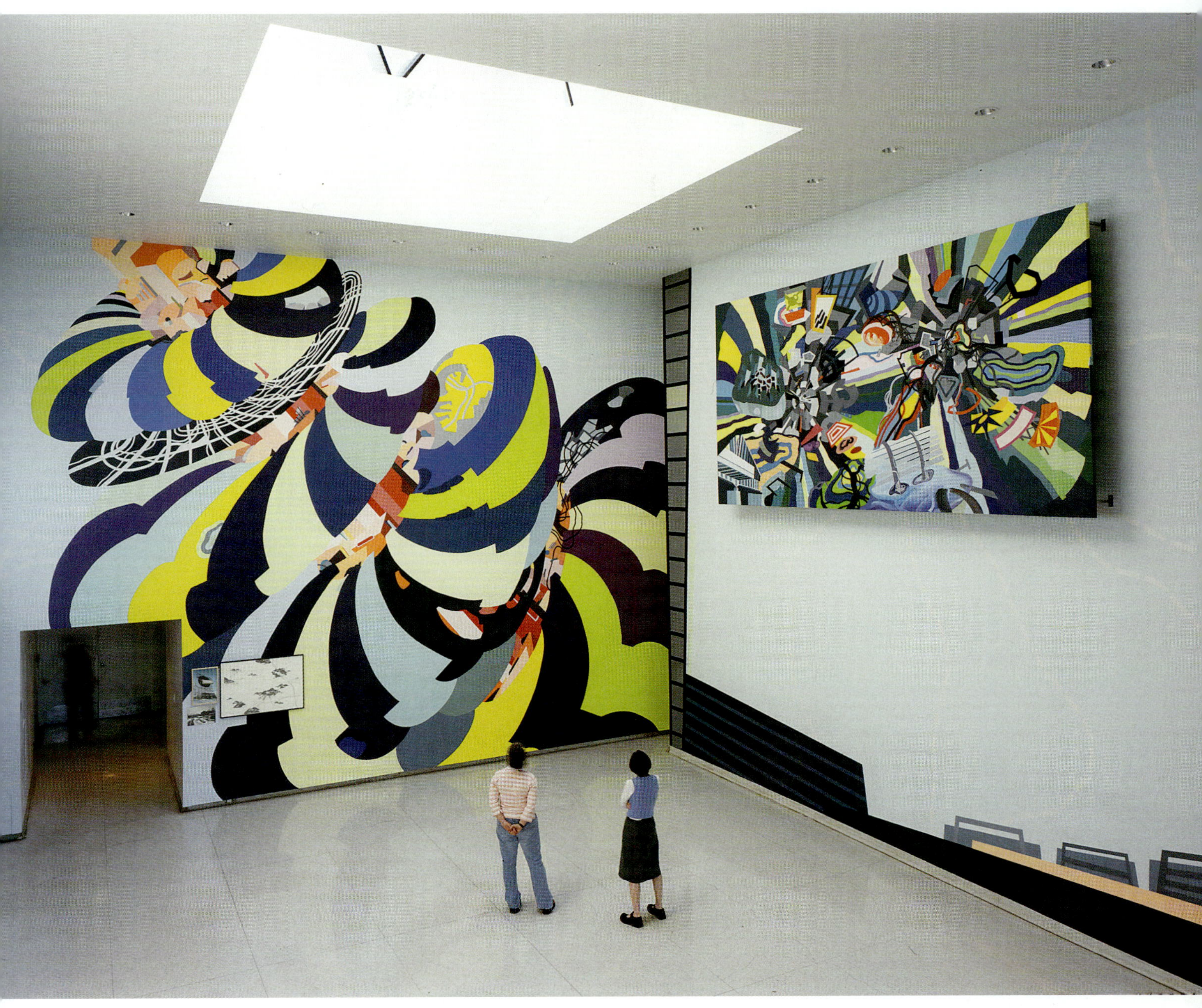

FRANZ ACKERMANN, HELICOPTER GIVE ME YOUR BED, 2001, Wandmalerei, 1100 x 1000 cm / wall painting, installation view, Walker Art Center, Minneapolis, 433 x 393 11/16".

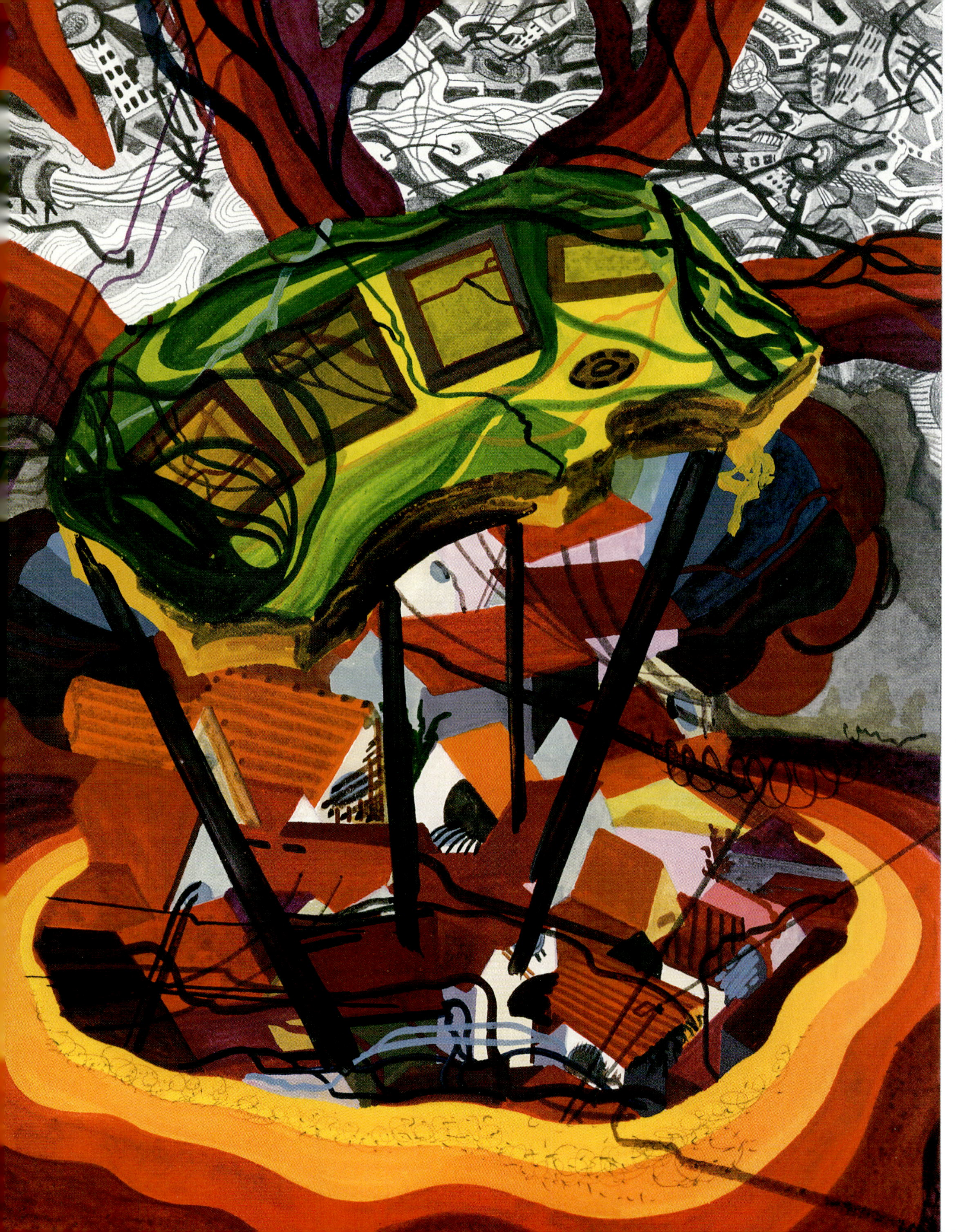

grund entschloss sich Ackermann zu seiner Arbeit HELICOPTER NO.15 (WATCH ME FALLING) (2001) – Helikopter Nr.15 (Schau mir beim Fallen zu). Bei seiner Arbeit mitten im touristisch nicht sehr attraktiven Winter zeichnete Ackermann ein Phantasieporträt der Stadt. Abstrahierte Teile eines Büroturms von Philip Johnson verbanden sich mit anderen lokalen Bildelementen, die der Künstler auf seinen Spaziergängen durch die Stadt aufgeschnappt hatte, um schliesslich zu einem taumelnden Turm von Babel zu verschmelzen. An der Basis dieses massiven psychedelischen Monolithen waren, neben einer geistigen Karte von Minneapolis in Graphit, zwei Photographien angebracht. Eine zeigte eine archetypische Ansicht einer Jahrzehnte alten Bierreklame am Mississippi, die für die Stadt mittlerweile die Bedeutung einer monumentalen Ikone gewonnen hat. Die andere zeigte die Aussicht aus dem Hotelzimmer des Künstlers, wo ein grosser Teil dieser Arbeit ausgeheckt worden war. Nachdem ich das vollständige Werk gesehen hatte, wurde mir klar, dass Ackermann nicht nur physisch reist und mit jedem Projekt mehr Flugmeilen auf sein Konto bucht. Nein, er reist auch psychisch und schafft halluzinationsartige Visionen von Städten, die ebenso präzis sind wie ein touristischer Stadtplan. Beim Betrachten von HELICOPTER NO.15 (WATCH ME FALLING) betritt jeder sein ureigenes Tagtraumland.

Auch wenn diese zeitgemässe Art des Reisens in Ackermanns Arbeit immer gegenwärtig ist und seine Bilder mit seinen eigenen Reisen rund um die Welt zusammenhängen, so steht der Künstler seiner eigenen Komplizenschaft mit diesem Seinsmodus nicht unkritisch gegenüber. In seiner Arbeit HAUS AM STRAND (1997), zum Beispiel, sehen wir ein photographisches Selbstporträt des Künstlers mit dem Rücken zur Kamera. Er schaut in die Ferne und ähnelt, wie der Kritiker Jörg Heiser meinte, «einem von Caspar David Friedrichs romantischen Helden».[2] Aber anders als Friedrichs REISENDER ÜBER DEM NEBELMEER (1818) trägt dieser Wanderer eine militärische Flakjacke, die mit der Aufschrift «Tourist» versehen ist. Natürlich sind Journalisten, die in kugelsicheren Westen aus Kriegsgebieten wie Bosnien berichten, dank Satellitenfernsehen und CNN in den letzten zehn Jahren zu einem vertrauten Anblick geworden. In diesem Jahr jedoch erlebten wir einen Quantensprung hinsichtlich des touristischen Aspekts der neuen Medien, nämlich mit dem Einsatz so genannter *embedded journalists*, der «Einbettung» von Journalisten in der amerikanischen und britischen Armee während des Irakkrieges. Bekennt der Tourismus, einst eine subtil implizite neokolonialistische Herrschaftsform, hier definitiv Farbe und steht zu seinen imperialistischen Wurzeln? Ist dieser Schriftzug auf der Flakjacke des Künstlers eine Art Zielmarke oder eine Warnung? Ackermann bringt uns im Kontext der Tourismusindustrie zum Nachdenken über solche Fragen, indem er diesem Selbstporträt einen architektonischen Rahmen aus Plakaten verpasst, die Diareportagen von so exotischen Reisezielen wie China, Nepal oder Burma anpreisen, Plakate, wie sie in Berlin und anderen deutschen Städten gang und gäbe sind. Im Licht der jüngsten Ereignisse bringt mich Ackermanns Arbeit dazu, mir die Frage zu stellen, was der Sex-Pistols-Song «Holidays in the Sun» für die Christianne Amanpours[3] dieser Welt implizieren mag.

Zu den ersten amerikanischen Asienreisenden der Nachkriegszeit gehörten auch die «Berater», die von der US-Army nach Vietnam entsandt wurden. Wir alle kennen das Resultat dieser *Holidays in the Sun*. Jetzt haben die «eingebetteten» Reporter im Irak ihre eigene, rabenschwarze Spielart von Tourismus durchgezogen. Franz Ackermann nimmt das in seiner Arbeit zur Kenntnis und hat anscheinend den idyllischen Slogan der 68er, «Unter dem Pflaster liegt der Strand», durch eine aktuellere Zeile – aus Francis Ford Coppolas *Apocalypse Now* (1979) – ersetzt: «Charlie don't surf.» Vielleicht täte er es doch, wenn er die Diareportagen gesehen hätte.

(Übersetzung: Suzanne Schmidt)

FRANZ ACKERMANN, OHNE TITEL (MENTAL MAP: DAS NEST), 2003, Mischtechnik auf Papier, 24,5 x 18 cm / mixed media on paper, $9^5/_8$ x $7^1/_8$".

1) 1955 plädierte Guy Debord für eine neue wissenschaftliche Disziplin, die Psychogeographie, welche sich dem Studium der genauen Gesetze und spezifischen Einflüsse des geographischen Umfeldes – ob bewusst gewählt oder nicht – auf die Gefühle und das Verhalten von Individuen widmen sollte. Guy-Ernest Debord, «Introduction à une critique de la géographie urbaine», in: *Les Lèvres Nues,* Nr. 6/1955, S. 11. (Reprint in: Collection complète, 1954–1958, Editions Plasma, Paris 1978.)

2) Jörg Heiser, «Travelling Light», *Frieze,* No. 66, April 2002, S. 57.

3) Christianne Amanpour: Kriegsberichterstatterin bei CNN.

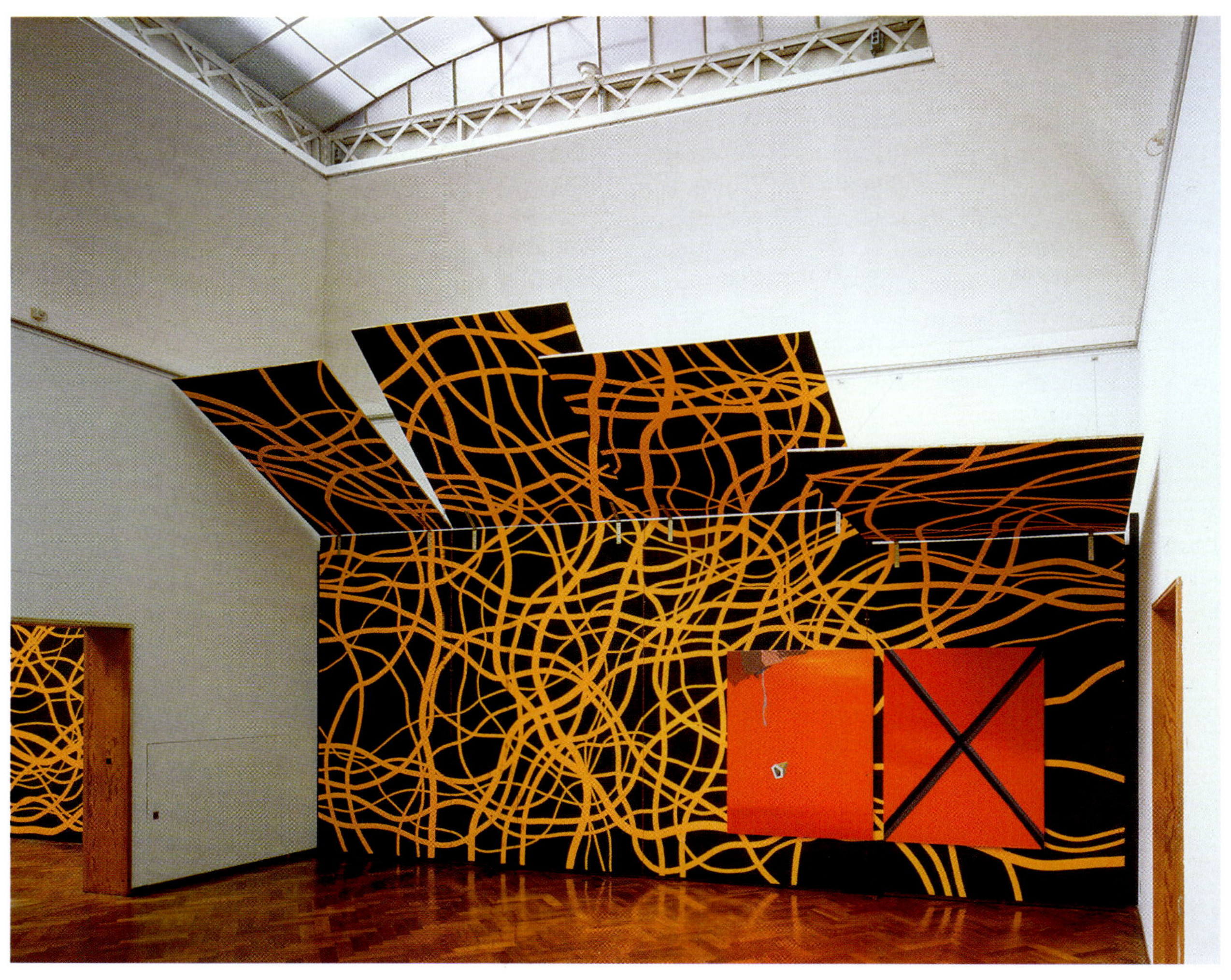

FRANZ ACKERMANN, SEASONS IN THE SUN, 2002,
Acryl auf Holz und Öl auf Leinwand, Installation im Stedelijk Museum, Amsterdam, ca. 5,2 x 15,7 m / acrylic on wood and oil on canvas, ca. 17 x 51 1/2'.
(PHOTO: NEUGERRIEMSCHNEIDER, BERLIN)

FRANZ ACKERMANN, CAN'T BE A MANGO TREE HERE OR SOMETHING, 2002, Öl auf Leinwand (MENTAL MAP: BEACH PARTY), Holz, Wandmalerei, Einbau, Zeichnung, Video, Schwarzweissphotographie, Hängematte, Photokopie, Farbphotographien, Grösse variabel / oil on canvas (MENTAL MAP: BEACH PARTY), wood, wall painting, built-in elements, drawing, video, b/w photograph, hammock, xerox, color photographs, dimensions variable.

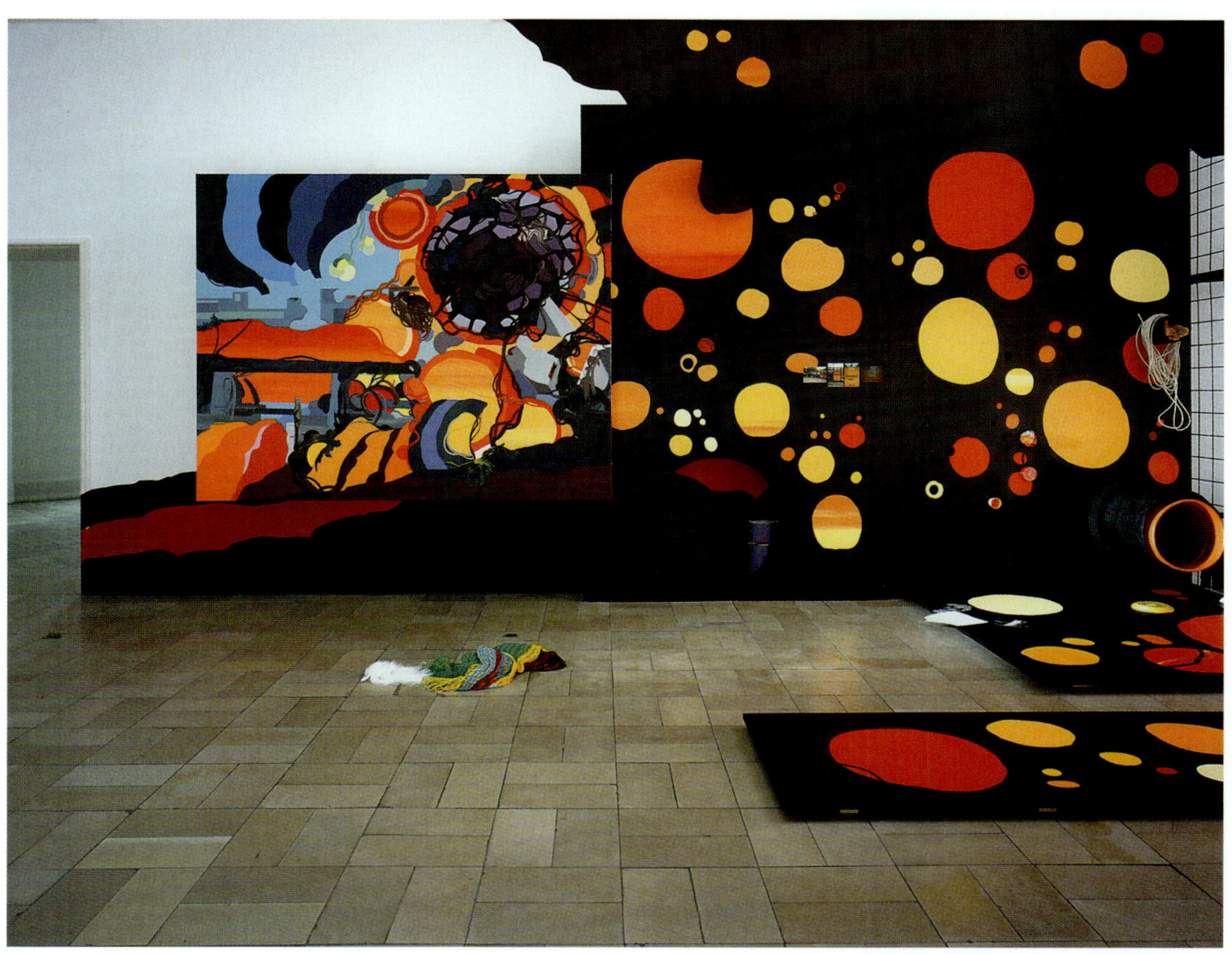

ACKERMANN HALLUCINATING MAPS

JOSHUA DECTER

...A memory wanders, becomes dispersed, then partially reassembled: conceivably, we first met at the home of...

...It would seem that I initially encountered Franz Ackermann somewhere in...

...or near my friend's house, proximate to...

...Yes, it was somewhere within the environs of Los Angeles...

...Is this an imaginary memory... or the recovering of an imagined event?...

...It was around 1994 or 1995, on one of my occasional trips to the West Coast...

...Ackermann had been moving about, inhabiting different places... re-locating himself... iterating these re-locations through drawings...

...If I can recall accurately, memory often being a slippery substance, on at least one evening, Ackermann and I shared a taxicab to navigate through various neighborhoods scattered across LA's de-centered territories...

...traversing the multi-centered city space in a vehicle, navigating by an endless interconnectivity of imagination and objective topographical scanning...

...networked, interlaced, urban, and post-urban nodes...

...taking advantage of mobility, really there was no other choice, to negotiate relatively unknown social spaces...

...through territories that seemed mobile themselves, interpenetrating conduits of activity and inertia...

...echoing in his phantasmagoric drawings...

...Now I recall that Ackermann had used LA's public transportation system, the buses, to move through the city's arteries...

...It became evident that there was a certain synergy between his method of working and Los Angeles...

...In Ackermann's works, it was possible to discern his way of navigating through places known and unknown, consuming the unfamiliar into a language of ...

...a continuous re-generation of cartographic lo-

JOSHUA DECTER is a New York-based writer, curator, and art historian. He is currently writing a book on video art, commissioned by Taschen. Decter has organized exhibitions for the Kunsthalle Vienna, The Museum of Contemporary Art in Chicago, and P.S.1, New York, among other institutions.

FRANZ ACKERMANN, OHNE TITEL (MENTAL MAP: CROSSING CITIES), 1999, Mischtechnik auf Papier, 70 x 50 cm / mixed media on paper, 27 9/16 x 19 11/16".

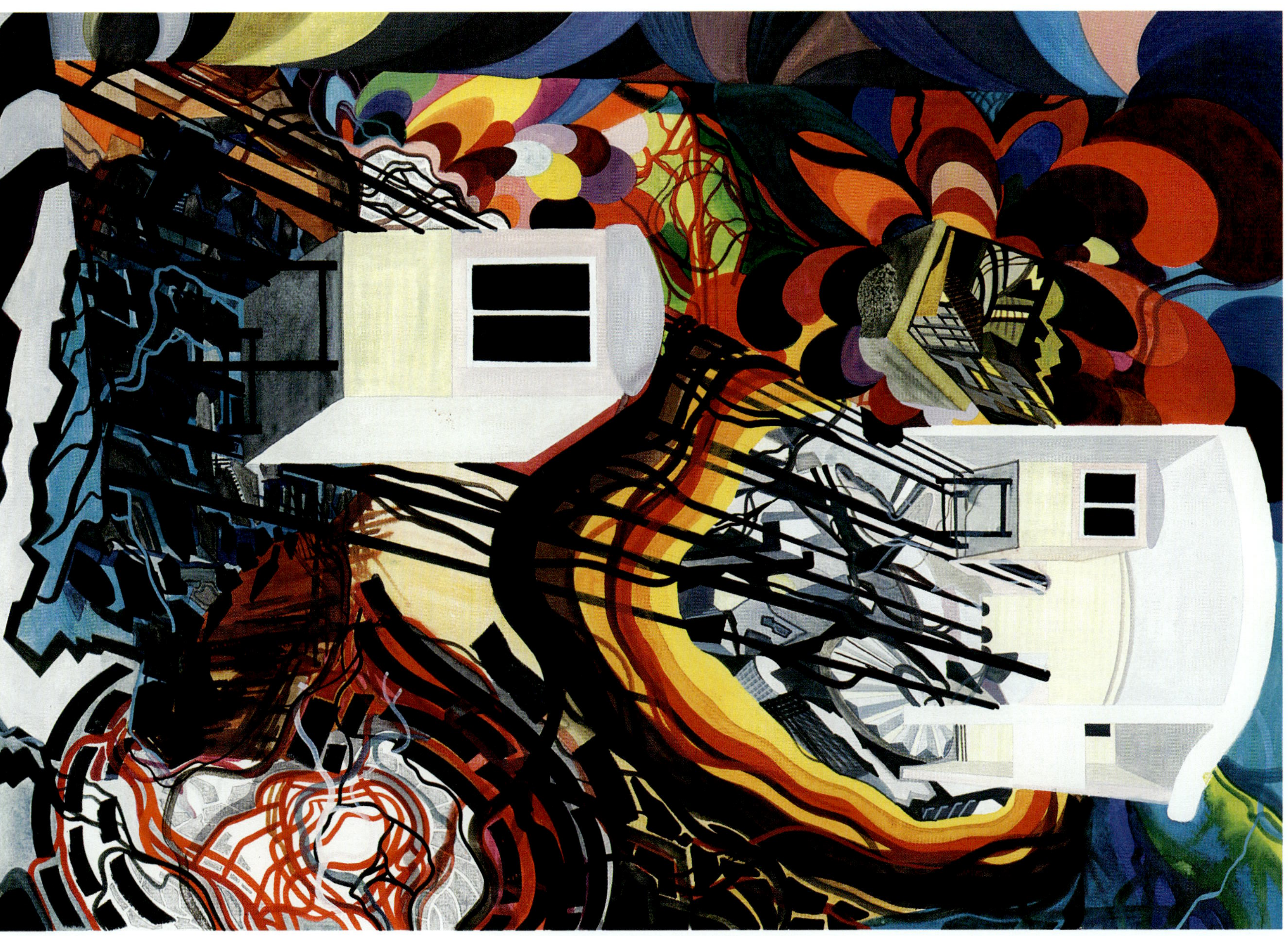

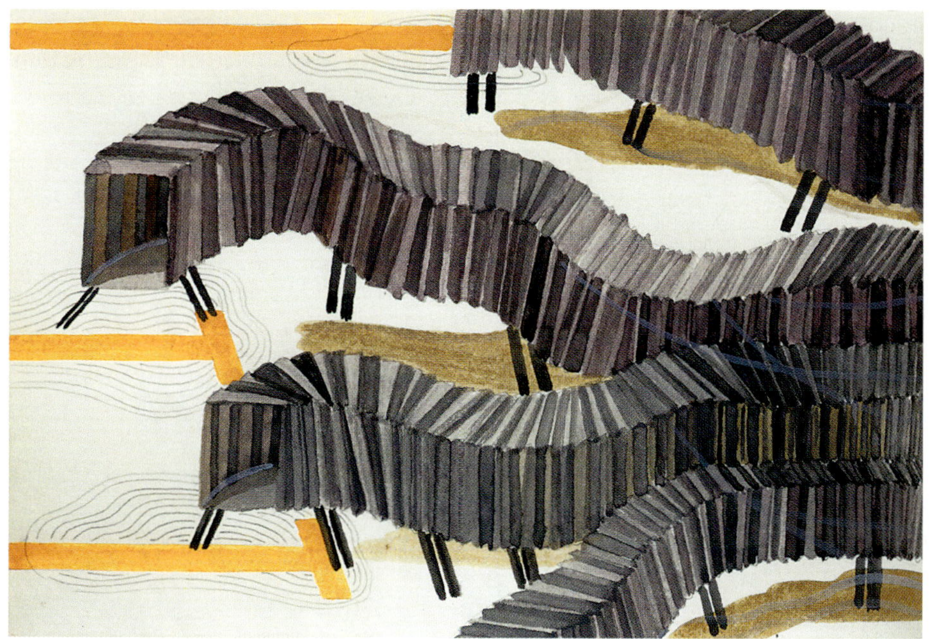

FRANZ ACKERMANN, OHNE TITEL (MENTAL MAP: SEAT 52A), 1998, Mischtechnik auf Papier, 13 x 19 cm / mixed media on paper, 5 1/8 x 7 1/2".

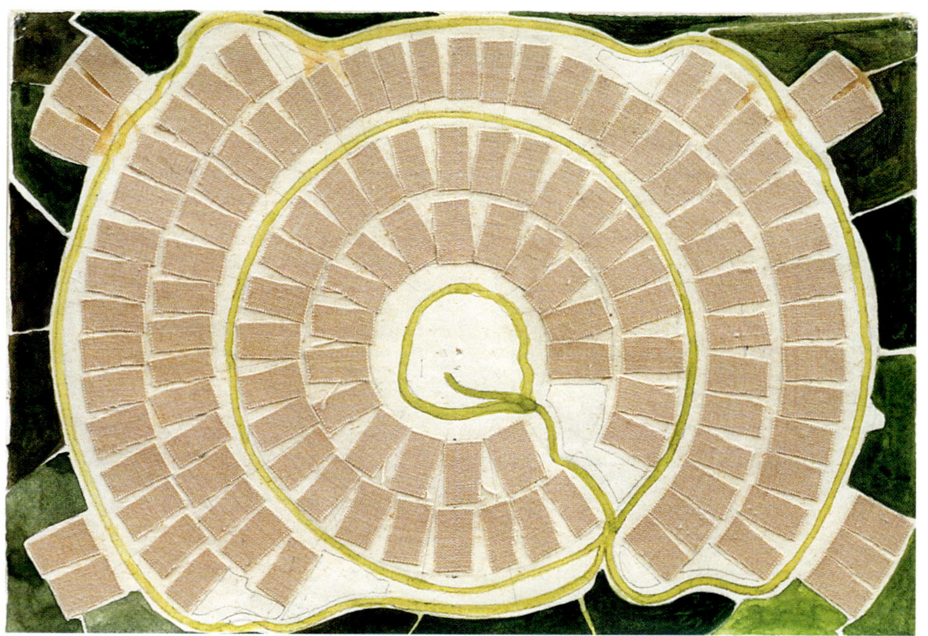

FRANZ ACKERMANN, OHNE TITEL (MENTAL MAP), 1992–1994, Mischtechnik auf Papier, 13 x 19 cm / mixed media on paper, 5 1/8 x 7 1/2".

cation and un-location... an intoxication brought on by immersion into the flux of a place....

...and how to render the interpenetration of location, time, space, and subjectivity into image...

...a palimpsest... a topography of simultaneously erupting, and then systematized, places and non-places...

...if memory is more than a re-imaging, or re-imagining, of some events that unfolded at a different time and location, a place that can only be revisited through conjecture.

Recently, just some days ago, I scanned through Paul Virilio's small book, *A Landscape of Events,* and was struck by a number of observations that seem quite illuminating in relation to my current thinking on Franz's work. In the foreword to the book, the architect Bernard Tschumi offers a condensation of Virilio's ideas: "Indeed, rarely has a contemporary writer so engaged in an exacerbated analysis of the acceleration of time, to the point where space itself becomes engulfed in time. Space becomes temporal."[1)]

For Tschumi, Virilio is engaged with the notion that "...duration is really a conjunction of simultaneities"; and "...in Virilio's global temporal space, landscapes become a random network of pure trajectories whose occasional collisions suggest a possible topography..."[2)]

In evoking Virilio (initially via Tschumi), I would like to propose a relationship, albeit oblique, between Ackermann's approach to art making and elements of Situationist thinking. Virilio, in the first chapter of his book, refers to Debord: "... the Situationist Guy Debord was to remark, 'We didn't try to find the formula for overthrowing the world in books but by roaming around.'"[3)]

In relation to contemporary society, and the notion of traversing—or wandering—through space conceived of as a temporal condition, Virilio posits: "...specialists in time differences, revolutionary jetsetters amidst a general roaming in which the dislocation of the real world derives spontaneously from the delocalization and accelerated displacement of bodies (dislocate is from the Latin, *dislocare:* to move about, displace)."[4)]

I can recall thinking of Ackermann's mental map drawings as both visionary and modest, meticulous and provisional, a kind of spontaneously (post-utopian?) impulse to offer reflection upon the notion of the artist as the inhabitant of an intangible space in which local experience and global self-awareness become sensuously interpenetrated.

"At this point, cognitive mapping in the broader sense comes to require the coordination of existential data (the empirical position of the subject) with unlived, abstract conceptions of the geographic totality."[5)]

Ackermann articulates a language, at once cartographic and anti-cartographic, that moves far beyond the parochial distinctions between (pictorial) representation and (organic-cultural) abstraction. One spatial condition displaces and then reinvents the other, continuously, rhythmically.

If only it were possible to generate this text, my text, so that it would function as an analogue to one of Ackermann's works, as a way of mapping an aesthetic language. An implausible notion, to be sure, but there is an occasional desire in the writer to produce textual counterparts to what is observed in the body of artworks, to recreate, by alternative means, the phenomenal reality, or irreality, of the artwork.

To attempt such a thing would take the writer, and needless to say the reader, along multiple meandering, even colliding pathways of logic and illogic, sense and nonsense, stable and unstable meanings. A kind of drive through intertextual architectures and spaces, to find a way back in Ackermann's world through a network of textual fragments, strands of ideas... perhaps this is already unfolding here...

Ackermann's quirky, subtly hallucinatory works might reveal how a mobility of existence can engender a fecund elasticity of imagination, wherein empirical observation of place undergoes poetic erosion as a result of the vagaries of subjective experience.

Mental mapping, as literal method and figurative relationship to the objective world, is the creation of a territory that may have its basis in the real. Here, things inevitably break down into multiple tendrils of imagined geography, and a thousand streams of possible bearings... and are then reorganized... and then begin to fall apart, all of which again leads me to Debord and Situationist thinking:

"The production of psychogeographic maps, or even the introduction of alterations such as more or less arbitrarily transposing maps of two different regions, can contribute to clarifying certain wanderings that express not subordination to randomness but complete insubordination to habitual influences (influences generally categorized as tourism, that popular drug as repugnant as sports or buying on credit). A friend recently told me that he had just wandered through the Harz region of Germany while blindly following the directions of a map of London."[6)]

Ackermann's works suggest a hybridity of source materials and references: souvenirs of the memory's engagement with place. I would imagine that Ackermann considers himself something of a wanderer who collects sensations in unfamiliar social and cultural territories, sensations that mutate through his act of recollection and re-/de-construction. Cities, non-cities, the spaces (in) between urban zones, and other interstitial spaces are reprocessed as events akin to psychic hallucinations.

Philosopher Henri Lefebvre's early theoretical writings on "everyday life" influenced the Situationists, as he considered the city to be an arena for the encounter between differences, a space which both produces social relations and is produced by social relations. Lefebvre suggests that we tend to think about the contemporary urban environment in contradictory terms: as both an abstract space modeled upon hierarchical orderings (e.g. center, periphery) that may reinforce dominant economic relations, and as a space of ruptures, disjunctions, flux, and pulverizations.

How to trace the contours of the meeting ground between imagination and place? What is a map if not a demarcation of the self in relation to a location, or a network of locations? Mapping is a procedure at once instinctual and rational, intellectual and intuitive. In order to inhabit the known, we map it. In order to inhabit a world yet to be known, we invent new maps, which may indeed be post-rational, beyond empirical notions of "order," indeed, mischievously psychological geographies.

If Ackermann does practice an eccentric kind of cultural geography, he also manifests a desire for an aggressive decomposition of the territorial order usually associated with structured social spaces. Ackermann is able to access the character of an architectural location by accentuating the subjective interplay between the perception of place, and the place itself, creating a lyrical reconfiguration of that which we recognize as tangent to our lived social spaces, and that which exceeds the real.

We often reflect upon the status of certain artists as migratory or nomadic creatures, continuously shifting from one context to the other, moving across boundaries, slipping in and out of identifiable political and cultural affiliations, reinventing identity positions within an increasingly liquid field of trans-global relations.

Ackermann has moved through various places, known and unknown, throughout the world, perhaps even suggesting a kind of late modern version of *vagabondage,* a notion that Walter Benjamin introduces in his *Arcades Project,* in relation to the notion of the flaneur's phantasmagoric engagement with place and space.

For Ackermann, it seems there is a continuous intercourse of movement, a dance or interplay, between literal location/place and imagination, and the increasing difficulty of distinguishing between these ways of inhabiting the world.

"The figure of the flaneur. He resembles the hash eater, takes space up into himself like the latter. In hashish intoxication, the space starts winking at us: 'What do you think may have gone on here?' And with the very same question, space accosts the flaneur."[7)]

Collapsing together inscrutability and legibility, Ackermann unravels reference and denotation, triggering a continuous oscillation between inscription and erasure, memory and invention. His lyrical meta-travelogues explode linear narrative, delivering us into the controlled rapture of an artist's intercourse with the unknown...

...mental mapping, the marking of a territory that may have its basis in the real, yet inevitably breaks down into multiple tendrils of imagined geography, and a thousand streams of possible bearings...

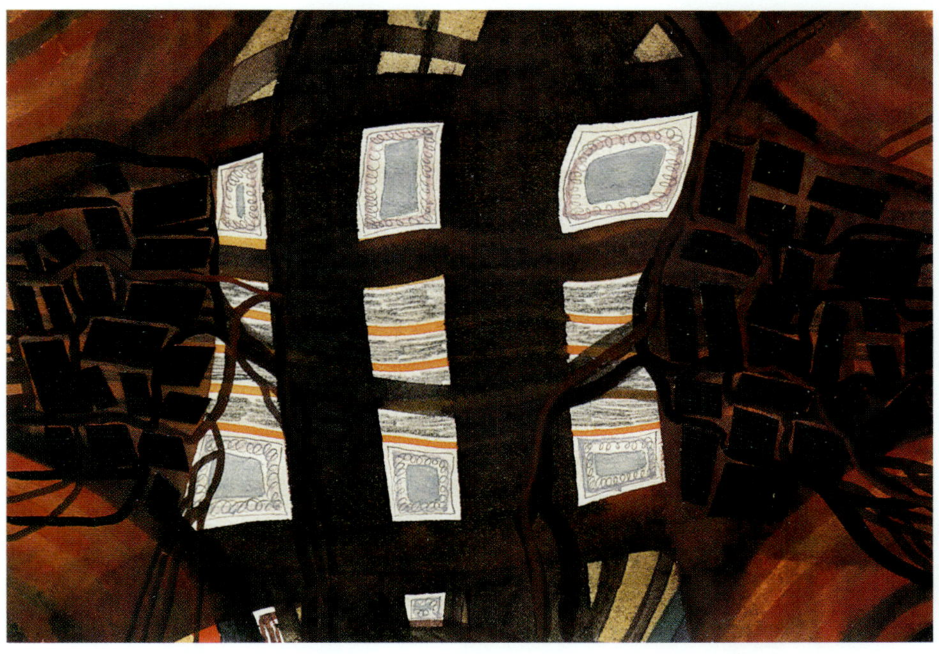

FRANZ ACKERMANN, OHNE TITEL (MENTAL MAP: JUST ANOTHER PLACE FOR RIOTS III), 1995,
Mischtechnik auf Papier, 13 x 19 cm / mixed media on paper, $5^{1}/_{8}$ x $7^{1}/_{2}$".

...If Ackermann practices a quirky kind of cultural geography in his works, we might say that his rationalist tendencies are filtered through the unpredictable mess of intuition and imagination, and vice versa...

...His subjective anti-maps decompose the territorial order usually associated with various kinds of urban and suburban spaces, willfully corroding the representational protocol of topographical systems, while suggesting that there is always an interconnection between organization and chaos...

...Each of Ackermann's works might be understood as an event of reconstructed and deconstructed memory, the synthesizing of memory-fragments, at once indexical and solipsistic...

...the need to throw away maps, or to hallucinate new cartographic representations and counter-representations...

...A map is its own territory, a territory inside of a representation of a place, becoming a meta-world...

...a beautiful jumble of impossibly linked geographies... a geography of imagined geographies... the apparition of the known interfaces with the phantasmagoria of the unknown...

...Now, where did I initially meet Franz Ackermann... perhaps, nowhere?

1) Bernard Tschumi, forward to Paul Virilio, *A Landscape of Events,* transl. by Julie Rose (Cambridge: The MIT Press, 2000), p. viii.
2) Ibid., pp. viii-ix.
3) Ibid., p. 6.
4) Ibid.
5) Fredric Jameson, "Postmodernism, or the Cultural Logic of Late Capitalism," *New Left Review,* no. 146, July/August 1984, p. 90.
6) Guy-Ernest Debord, "Introduction à une critique de la géographie urbaine," *Les Lèvres Nues,* no. 6, 1955, p. 14. (English translation in *Situationist International Anthology,* ed. by Ken Knabb (Berkeley: Bureau of Public Secrets, 1981).
7) Walter Benjamin, *The Arcades Project,* transl. by Howard Eiland and Kevin McLaughlin (Cambridge, MA: The Belknap Press of Harvard University Press, 1999), p. 841.

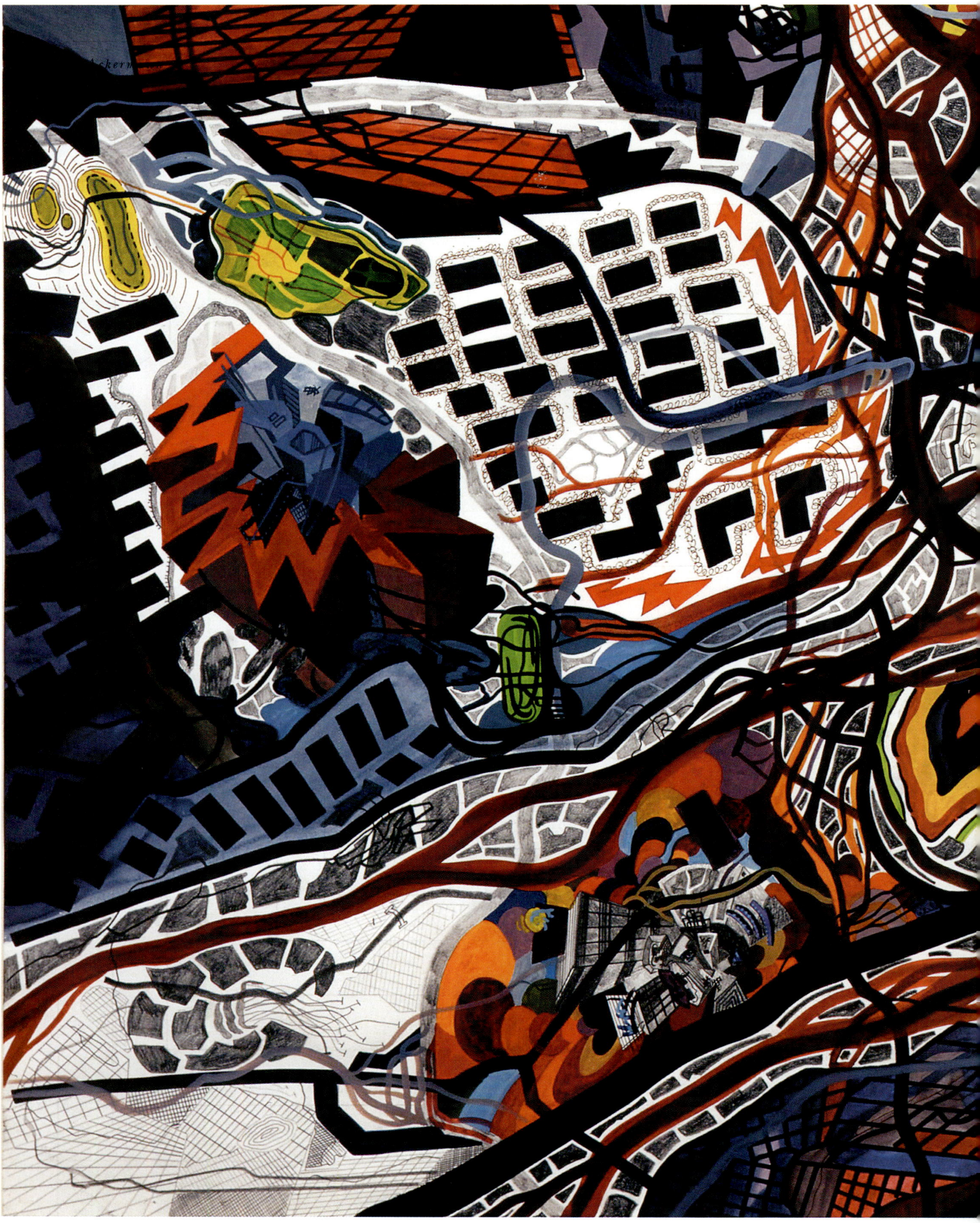

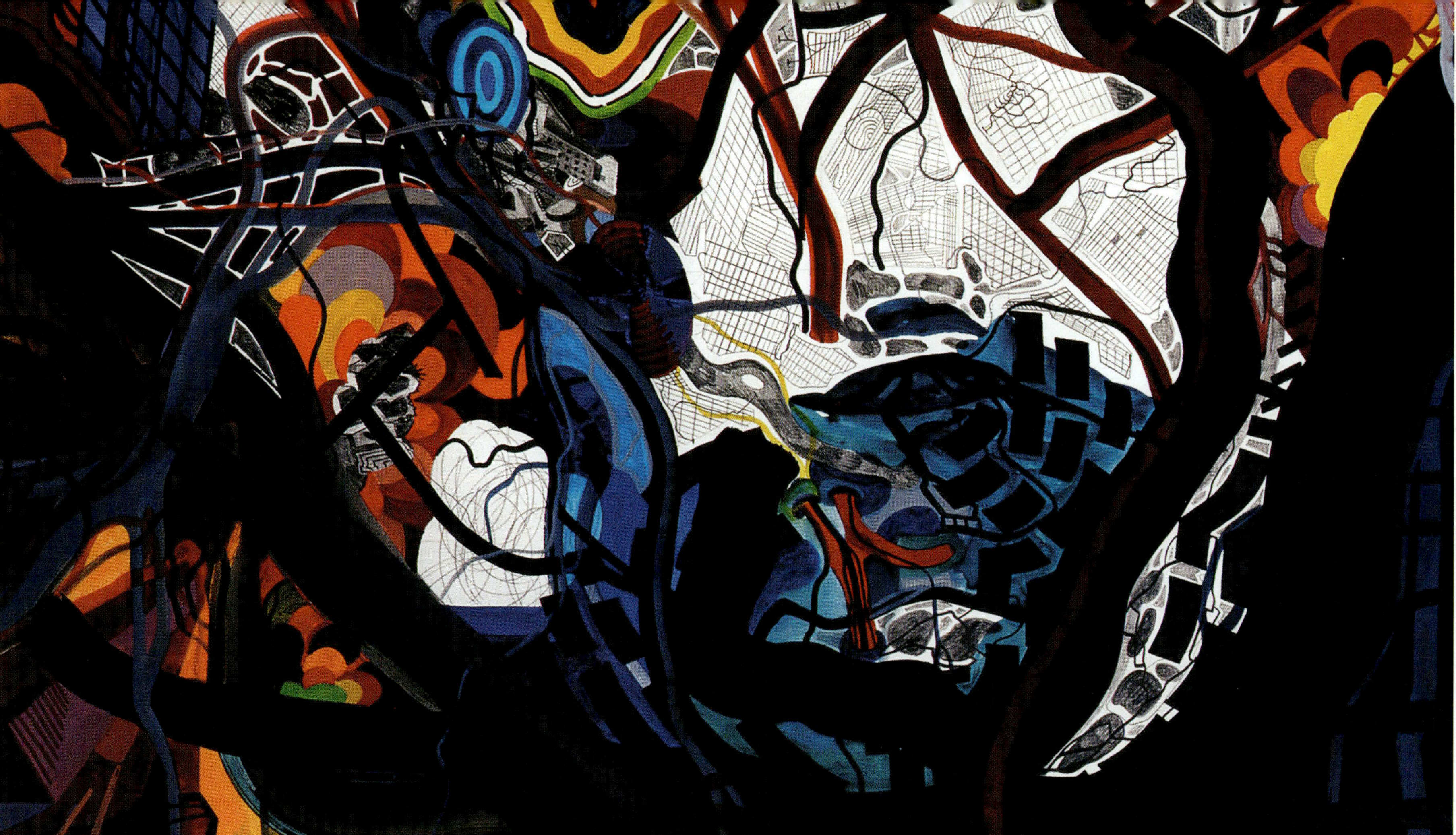

FRANZ ACKERMANN, GSP (GREATER SÃO PAULO), 2001, Mischtechnik auf Papier, 70 x 100 cm / mixed media on paper, $27\frac{9}{16}$ x $39\frac{3}{8}$".

LANDKARTEN WIE HALLUZINATIONEN

JOSHUA DECTER

Eine Erinnerung verliert sich, löst sich auf und setzt sich dann stückweise wieder zusammen: möglich, dass wir uns zum ersten Mal gesehen haben bei...

...vermutlich begegnete ich Franz Ackermann ursprünglich irgendwo in...

...oder aber in der Nähe des Hauses, wo mein Freund wohnt, in der Gegend von...

...ja, es war irgendwo in der Umgebung von Los Angeles...

...Ist das eine imaginäre Erinnerung... oder erinnere ich mich an ein imaginäres Ereignis?...

...Es war um 1994 oder 1995 herum, auf einer meiner diversen Reisen an die Westküste...

...Ackermann war damals unterwegs, wohnte an verschiedenen Orten..., sich selbst immer wieder aufspürend und dieses fortwährende Aufspüren in Zeichnungen wiederholend...

...Wenn ich mich richtig erinnere, auch wenn sich mir die Erinnerung oft aalglatt wieder entzieht, teilten Ackermann und ich uns zumindest an einem Abend ein Taxi, um durch verschiedene, querbeet in Los Angeles und seinen Vororten verstreute Gegenden zu fahren...

...den Stadtraum mit seinen vielen Zentren in einem Fahrzeug durchquerend und uns dabei an einer endlosen Vernetzung von Imagination und objektiver topographischer Beobachtung orientierend...

...vernetzte, verknüpfte, urbane und posturbane Knoten...

...von der Mobilität profitierend, eigentlich hatten wir keine andere Wahl, um zu den relativ unbekannten Treffpunkten zu gelangen...

...durch Gebiete, die selbst mobil zu sein schienen, sich gegenseitig durchdringende Kanäle von Aktivität und Reglosigkeit...

...die sich in seinen phantasmagorischen Zeichnungen widerspiegelten...

...Jetzt fällt mir wieder ein, dass Ackermann L.A.'s öffentliche Verkehrsmittel, die Busse, benützte, um sich in die Verkehrsadern der Stadt einzuspeisen.

...Es war klar zu erkennen, dass es eine gewisse Synergie gab zwischen seiner Arbeitsweise und Los Angeles...

...Ackermanns Arbeiten konnte man entnehmen, wie er bekannte und unbekannte Orte bereiste und das Unvertraute auflöste in eine Sprache des...

JOSHUA DECTER ist Kritiker, Kurator und Kunsthistoriker. Gegenwärtig schreibt er im Auftrag des Taschen-Verlags ein Buch über Videokunst. Unter anderem hat er Ausstellungen für die Kunsthalle Wien, das Museum of Contemporary Art in Chicago und P.S.1 in New York organisiert.

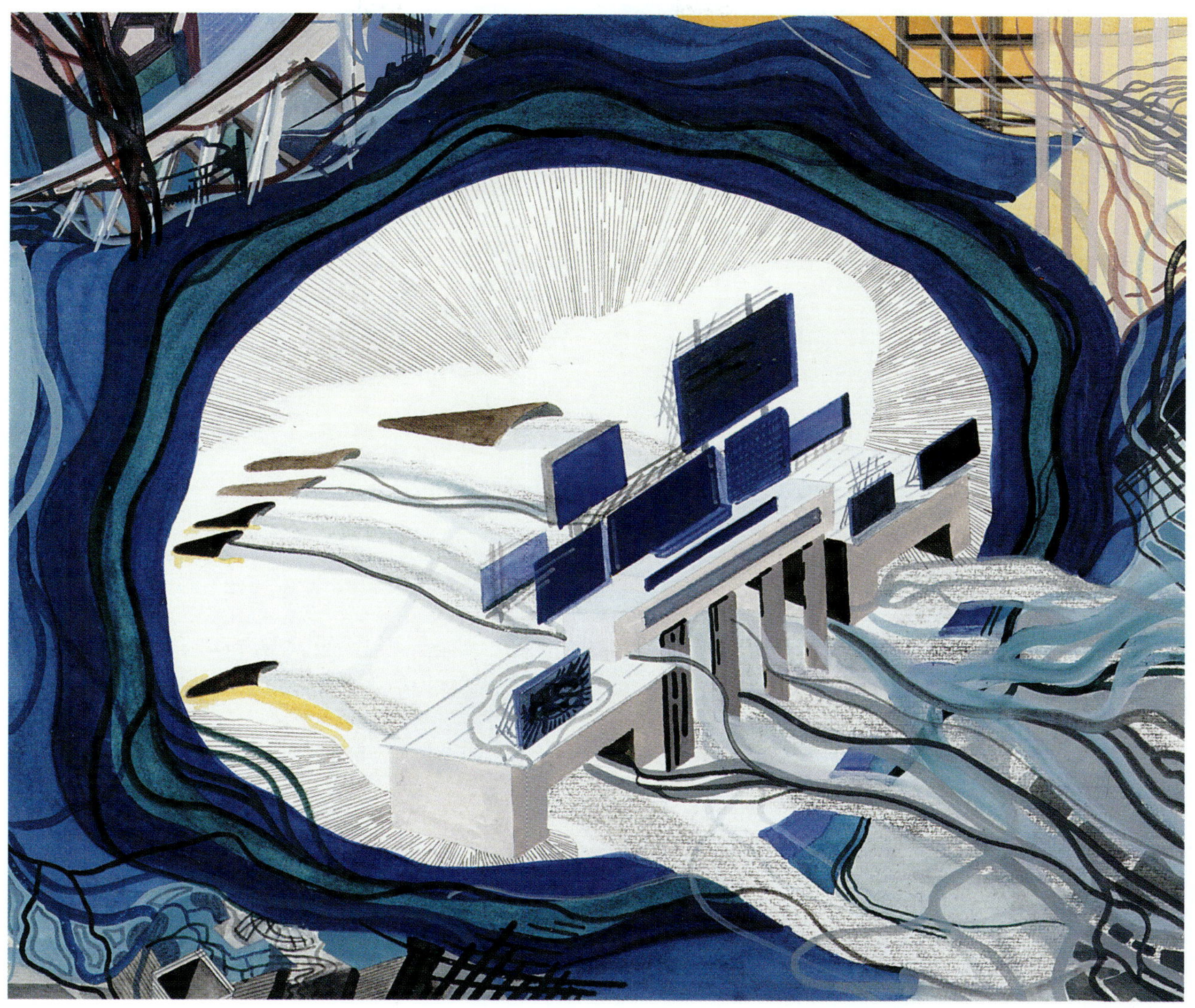

FRANZ ACKERMANN, OHNE TITEL (MENTAL MAP: YOU WON'T GIVE UP WITHOUT A FIGHT), 1999, Mischtechnik auf Papier, 29 x 34,5 cm / mixed media on paper, $11^{7}/_{16}$ x $13^{9}/_{16}$".

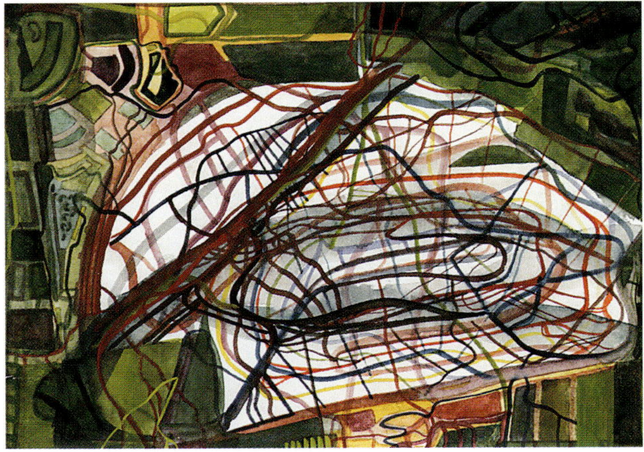

FRANZ ACKERMANN, OHNE TITEL (MENTAL MAP: CROSSING COUNTRIES), 1993, *Mischtechnik auf Papier, 13 x 19 cm / mixed media on paper, 5 1/8 x 7 1/2".*

FRANZ ACKERMANN, OHNE TITEL (MENTAL MAP: SOON FINISHED), 1997, *Mischtechnik auf Papier, 13 x 19 cm / mixed media on paper, 5 1/8 x 7 1/2".*

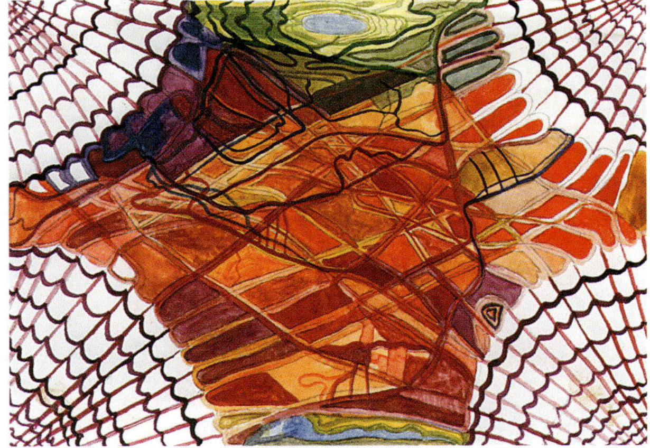

...eine fortwährende Re-Generation kartographischer Orte und Unorte... ein Rausch, der durch das Eintauchen in den Fluss einer bestimmten Lokalität ausgelöst wurde...

...und wie sich die gegenseitige Durchdringung von Ort, Zeit, Raum und Subjektivität zu einem Bild verarbeiten lässt...

...ein Palimpsest... eine Topographie gleichzeitig aufbrechender und danach systematisierter Orte und Unorte...

...falls die Erinnerung mehr ist als ein Nachbilden oder nachträgliches Einbilden von Ereignissen, die zu einer anderen Zeit an einem anderen Ort stattgefunden haben, einem Ort, der nur mutmasslich wieder aufgesucht werden kann.

Kürzlich, es ist erst wenige Tage her, blätterte ich in Paul Virilios kleinem Buch *Ereignislandschaft* und machte dabei einige Beobachtungen, die mir im Hinblick auf meine jetzigen Gedanken zu Ackermanns Arbeiten durchaus erhellend scheinen. Im Vorwort zur englischen Ausgabe fasst der Architekt Bernard Tschumi Virilios Gedanken wie folgt zusammen: Tatsächlich habe sich kaum ein zeitgenössischer Denker auf eine derart scharfe Analyse der Beschleunigung der Zeit eingelassen, bis zu dem Punkt, wo der Raum von der Zeit verschlungen beziehungsweise selbst zu etwas Zeitlichem werde.[1)]

Laut Tschumi vertritt Virilio die Idee, dass die Dauer eigentlich eine Verbindung von Gleichzeitigkeiten sei, und Landschaften werden in Virilios globalem zeitlichem Raum zu einem zufälligen Netzwerk blosser Bewegungsbahnen, deren gelegentliche Kollisionen eine mögliche Topographie andeuten...[2)]

Wenn ich (zunächst indirekt via Tschumi) an Virilio erinnere, so deshalb, weil ich eine, wenn auch unterschwellige Beziehung zwischen Ackermanns Weise des Kunst Machens und gewissen Gedankenelementen der Situationisten zu erkennen glaube. Im ersten Kapitel des genannten Buches nimmt Virilio Bezug auf Debord und zitiert dessen Satz: «Die Formel für den *Umsturz der Welt* haben wir nicht in den Büchern gesucht, sondern beim *Herumirren.*»[3)]

Entsprechend redet Virilio im Zusammenhang mit der zeitgenössischen Gesellschaft und ihrer Vorstellung von der Durchquerung oder Durchwanderung des Raums als etwas zeitlich Bedingtem von: «...Fachleuten der Zeitverschiebung, dem revolutionären Jet-set eines allgemeinen Umherirrens, bei dem die Auflösung der realen Welt unversehens aus der Delokalisierung und der beschleunigten Fortbewegung der Körper hervorgeht.»[4]

Ich weiss noch, dass ich Ackermanns Zeichnungen geistiger Landkarten zugleich als visionär und bescheiden, als sehr genau und provisorisch empfand, als eine Art spontanen (postutopischen?) Impuls, der dazu anregte, sich den Künstler als Bewohner eines unberührbaren Raums vorzustellen, in welchem sich lokale Erfahrung und globales Selbstverständnis auf sinnliche Weise verknüpfen.

«An diesem Punkt wird für das kognitive Karten Zeichnen im weiteren Sinn die Koordination von existenziellen Daten (der empirischen Position des Subjekts) und ungelebten, abstrakten Ideen einer geographischen Totalität notwendig.»[5]

Ackermann spricht eine Sprache, die zugleich kartographisch und antikartographisch ist und weit über die zu kurz greifende Unterscheidung zwischen (bildlicher) Repräsentation und (organisch-kultureller) Abstraktion hinausgeht. Ein Raumzustand verdrängt den anderen und erfindet ihn in einem unaufhörlichen Rhythmus neu.

Wäre es nur möglich, diesen Text, meinen Text, auf eine Weise zu schreiben, dass er als Analogon zu einer von Ackermanns Arbeiten funktionierte, als mögliche kartographische Aufzeichnung einer ästhetischen Sprache. Zweifellos eine wenig plausible Idee, aber gelegentlich taucht beim Schreiben dieser Wunsch auf, ein Gegenstück zu dem, was in Kunstwerken, im Werkkorpus eines Künstlers zu beobachten ist, in Textform hervorzubringen beziehungsweise mit anderen Mitteln die Erscheinungswirklichkeit oder -unwirklichkeit des Kunstwerks nachzubilden.

Allein der Versuch würde für den Schreibenden – vom Leser gar nicht zu reden – bedeuten, zahllosen verschlungenen Mäandern zu folgen, ja selbst miteinander im Widerstreit liegenden Wegen des Logischen und Unlogischen, des Sinnvollen und Unsinnigen, der fixen und schwankenden Bedeutungen. Eine Art Umweg durch intertextuelle Architekturen und Räume, um schliesslich in Ackermanns Welt zurückzufinden durch ein Netzwerk von Textfragmenten, Gedankensträngen... vielleicht geschieht das hier bereits...

Ackermanns eigenwilligen, das Halluzinative streifenden Arbeiten gelingt es vielleicht, aufzuzeigen, wie die Mobilität der Existenz zu einer fruchtbaren Elastizität der Vorstellungskraft führen kann, in welcher die empirische Beobachtung von Orten dank der Unwägbarkeiten der subjektiven Erfahrung eine poetische Erosion erfährt.

Das geistige Kartographieren – als nüchterne Methode wie als figurative Bezugnahme auf die objektive Welt – bedeutet die Schaffung eines Territoriums, das durchaus auf der Realität basieren kann. Hier gehen die Dinge unweigerlich in den vielfachen Verästelungen einer imaginären Geographie auf und in tausend möglichen Querverbindungen und Konsequenzen... und werden neu geordnet... und beginnen auseinander zu fallen, was mich noch einmal zu Debord und dem Denken der Situationisten führt:

Die Erstellung psychogeographischer Karten oder auch nur das Herbeiführen von Änderungen, wie etwa das mehr oder weniger freiwillige Vertauschen von Karten zweier verschiedener Gebiete, kann zur Klärung bestimmter Bewegungen beitragen, die nicht eine Unterwerfung unter das Zufällige zum Ausdruck bringen, sondern den totalen Widerstand gegen die üblichen Einflüsse – Einflüsse, die man gewöhnlich als Tourismus bezeichnet, jene beliebte Droge, die genauso widerwärtig ist wie Sport oder das Kaufen auf Kredit.

Ein Freund hat mir kürzlich erzählt, er habe eben eine Harzwanderung hinter sich, auf der er sich blindlings den Angaben eines Stadtplans von London anvertraut habe.[6]

Ackermanns Arbeiten scheinen eine Mischform aus Quellenmaterialien und Verweisen zu sein: ein Andenken an ortsbezogene Erinnerungen. Ich vermute, dass Ackermann sich selbst als eine Art Wanderer versteht, der Sinneserfahrungen in ihm nicht vertrauten sozialen und kulturellen Gebieten sammelt, Erfahrungen, die sich im Akt der Erinnerung und der Re- oder Dekonstruktion verwandeln. Stadtzentren, Nichtstädtisches, die Spannen zwischen urbanen Zonen und andere Zwischen-Räume werden als halluzinationsähnliche Ereignisse wieder aufbereitet.

Die Situationisten standen unter dem Einfluss der frühen theoretischen Schriften des Philosophen Henri Lefebvre über das «Alltagsleben»: Er verstand

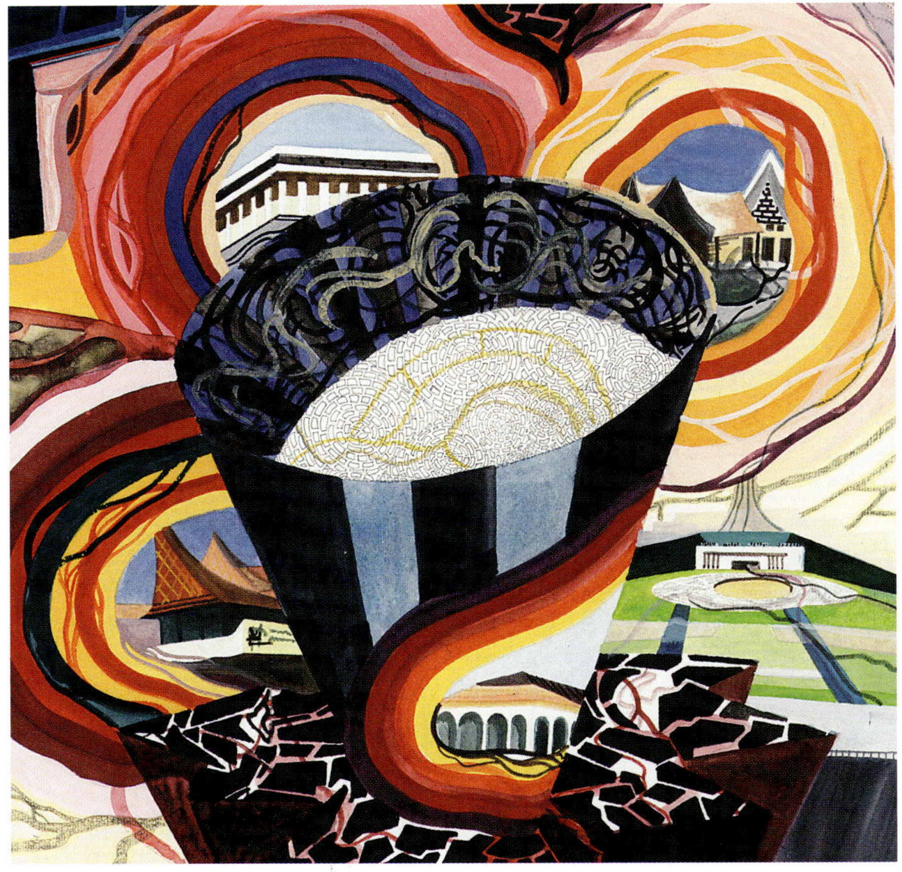

FRANZ ACKERMANN, UNTITLED (PACIFIC: MONUMENT OF CORRUPTION), 1999,
Mischtechnik auf Papier, 29 x 34,5 cm / mixed media on paper, 11 7/16 x 13 9/16".

die Stadt als Schauplatz der Begegnung zwischen Differenzen, als Raum, der sowohl soziale Beziehungen schafft, als auch selbst durch soziale Beziehungen entsteht. Lefebvre meint, dass unsere Auffassung des zeitgenössischen urbanen Lebensraums widersprüchlich sei: Einerseits verstehen wir ihn als abstrakten Raum, der hierarchischen Ordnungsbegriffen unterliegt (Zentrum, Peripherie u.a.), welche die herrschenden Wirtschaftsverhältnisse zementieren, andrerseits aber auch als Raum der Brüche, der Trennungen, des Flusses und der Zertrümmerung.

Wie lassen sich die Umrisse des Aufeinandertreffens zwischen Phantasie und Ort nachzeichnen? Was ist eine Karte, wenn nicht eine Demarkationslinie zwischen dem Selbst und einem bestimmten Ort oder einem Netz von Orten? Das Kartographieren ist ein gleichzeitig instinktiver und rationaler, intellektueller und intuitiver Prozess. Um das Bekannte zu besetzen zeichnen wir es auf. Um eine Welt zu besetzen, die wir erst noch kennen lernen müssen, erfinden wir neue Karten, die in der Tat postrational sein können, ja sogar jenseits aller empirischen Vorstellungen von «Ordnung», übermütige psychologische Geographien.

Wenn Ackermann eine exzentrische Form von Kulturgeographie praktiziert, so bringt er gleichzeitig den Wunsch nach einer aggressiven Zerstörung jener territorialen Ordung zum Ausdruck, die man gewöhnlich mit strukturierten sozialen Räumen in Verbindung bringt. Ackermann versteht es, den Charakter einer baulichen Lokalität zu erfassen, indem er das subjektive Wechselspiel zwischen der Ortswahrnehmung und dem Ort selbst unterstreicht und dadurch eine lyrische Nachbildung schafft, in der wir unsere erlebten sozialen Räume wieder erkennen, die aber gleichzeitig über diese Realität hinausgeht.

Oft denken wir über den Status gewisser Künstler als Migranten oder Nomaden nach und wechseln dabei laufend den Kontext, überschreiten Grenzen, machen identifizierbare politische und kulturelle Verwandtschaften aus, lassen sie wieder fallen und erfinden auf dem sich zunehmend verflüssigenden Boden transglobaler Beziehungen neue Identitätspositionen.

Ackermann hat sich an verschiedenen, bekannten und unbekannten Orten auf der ganzen Welt herumgetrieben, vielleicht spielt er sogar auf eine spätmoderne Spielart von Müssiggang an, ein Begriff, den Walter Benjamin in seinem *Passagen-Werk* einführt, und zwar im Zusammenhang mit der phantasmagorischen Beziehung, die der Flaneur zu Ort und Raum unterhält.

Bei Ackermann scheint ein ständiges Hin und Her von Bewegung, Tanz und wechselseitigen Einflüssen im Gange zu sein, zwischen dem Ort selbst und der Phantasie sowie auch der wachsenden Schwierigkeit, zwischen diesen verschiedenen Arten des in der Welt Seins zu unterscheiden.

Die Figur des Flaneurs. Er gleicht dem Haschischesser, nimmt den Raum in sich auf wie dieser. Im Haschischrausch beginnt der Raum uns anzublinzeln: «Nun, was mag denn in mir sich alles zugetragen haben?» Und mit der gleichen Frage macht der Raum an den Flanierenden sich heran.[7)]

Indem Ackermann das Unergründliche und das Lesbare zusammenfallen lässt, dröselt er Referenz und Denotation auseinander und löst ein fortwährendes Oszillieren aus zwischen Einschreiben und Auslöschen, Erinnerung und freier Erfindung. Seine lyrischen Meta-Reiseberichte sprengen jeden linearen Erzählstrang und überlassen uns dem kontrollierten Rausch eines Zwiegesprächs des Künstlers mit dem Unbekannten...

...geistiges Kartographieren, Markieren eines Territoriums, das im Realen gründen mag und sich dennoch unweigerlich in den vielfachen Verästelungen einer imaginären Geographie auflöst und in tausend möglichen Verbindungen und Konsequenzen...

...Wenn Ackermann eine exzentrische Form von Kulturgeographie praktiziert, so könnte man sagen, dass seine rationalistischen Tendenzen durch das unberechenbare Durcheinander von Intuition und Phantasie gefiltert werden und umgekehrt...

...Seine subjektiven Anti-Landkarten zersetzen die territoriale Ordnung, die man gewöhnlich mit urbanen und suburbanen Räumen assoziiert, und zerstören bewusst die für topographische Systeme vorgeschriebene Darstellungsform, wobei sie nahe legen, dass es immer eine Verknüpfung zwischen Ordnung und Chaos gibt...

Jede von Ackermanns Arbeiten kann als rekonstruierender und dekonstruierender Erinnerungsprozess verstanden werden, als ein Zusammensetzen von Erinnerungsfetzen, zugleich systematisch und ohne jede Rücksicht auf Zusammenhänge...

...das Bedürfnis Karten wegzuwerfen oder neue kartographische Darstellungen und Gegendarstellungen zu halluzinieren...

...Eine Karte ist ihr eigenes Territorium, ein Territorium innerhalb der Darstellung eines Ortes, und wird zu einer Metawelt...

...ein schönes Durcheinander von Geographien in unmöglicher Verknüpfung – eine Geographie der imaginären Georgraphien – die Erscheinung des Bekannten kurzgeschlossen mit der Phantasmagorie des Unbekannten...

...Wo nur, bin ich Franz Ackermann zum ersten Mal begegnet..., vielleicht nirgendwo?

(Übersetzung: Suzanne Schmidt)

1) Bernard Tschumi in seinem Vorwort zu Paul Virilio, *A Landscape of Events*, übers. v. Julie Rose, The MIT Press, Cambridge, Mass., 2000), S. viii.
2) Ebenda, S. viii–ix.
3) Paul Virilio, *Ereignislandschaft*, Hanser, München 1998, S. 18.
4) Ebenda.
5) Fredric Jameson, «Postmodernism, or the Cultural Logic of Late Capitalism», *New Left Review*, Nr. 146, Juli/August 1984, S. 90.
6) Guy-Ernest Debord, «Introduction à une critique de la géographie urbaine», *Les Lèvres Nues*, Nr. 6/1955, S. 14. (Reprint in: Collection complète, 1954–1958, Editions Plasma, Paris 1978.)
7) Walter Benjamin, *Das Passagen-Werk*, hrsg. v. Rolf Tiedemann, Suhrkamp, Frankfurt am Main 1982, S. 1009.

RAIMAR STANGE

Ein utopischer Bürger?

Die Zeichnungen und Gemälde von Franz Ackermann sind in aller Regel menschenleer, das Subjekt ereignet sich hier, wenn man so will, in absoluter Abwesenheit. Selbst auf dem kleinformatigen MENTAL MAP: SAILORS (1994) findet sich, trotz des viel versprechenden Titels, keine Darstellung der dort angesprochenen reisenden, genauer: seefahrenden Personen. Tattooähnliche Muster, karthographische Einschreibungen und abstrakt-expressive Farbflächen protokollieren statt dessen die (anonymen) Er-fahr-ungen nomadischer Existenz. So verwundert es nicht, dass auch die frühen Arbeiten von Franz Ackermann, die als Selbstporträt gelesen werden können, auf die visuelle Repräsentation des Künstlers bewusst verzichten. Vielmehr ist da auf Umwegen ein Bild des Künstlers von ihm selbst entworfen. Etwa in der Dia-Installation HERE: PROMISING ABSENCE (1996): Gut 160 farbenfrohe Cover gängiger Tourismusprospekte werden hier in Überblendprojektionen vorgestellt. Ein dunkelhäutiger «Eingeborener» und sein Kanu preisen die «experience to all the senses» in Papua Neu Guinea an, eine weite und karge Landschaft inklusive Gebirge und endlos blauem Himmel wirbt für Tibet, und ein grüner Dschungel steht ein für den vermeintlich naturnahen «Ekotourismus» in Panama. Wir kennen diese kitschigen Motive alle, diese Klischees, die seit Jahrhunderten auf unterschiedliche Weise programmiert werden von – *pars pro toto* – Alexander von Humboldt und Paul Gauguin bis zu Cook's Reisebüro und Hollywood. Trotz ihrer redundanten Abgedroschenheit und offensichtlichen Realitätsferne künden diese Klischees gefühlsecht von unseren Seh(n)süchten nach abenteuerlicher Exotik und einer längst fälligen Flucht aus dem vergleichsweise grauen Alltag. Entscheidend aber ist der gemeinsame Nenner all der gezeigten Tourismusprospekte: Es handelt sich bei den darin präsentierten Ländern allesamt um solche, die der Künstler damals noch nicht selbst besucht hatte. *Ex negativo* also erzählt uns Franz Ackermann von seiner eigenen Reisetätigkeit, die, wie wir inzwischen wissen, bis heute zentral ist für seine Kunst.

Ein weiteres Beispiel für diese frühen Selbstporträts stellt das Projekt SOFT ROOM (1997) dar. Wieder stehen Momente des Unterwegs- beziehungsweise Zuhauseseins im Mittelpunkt:

RAIMAR STANGE ist freier Kurator und Kritiker; er schreibt u. a. für *Kunst-Bulletin* (Zürich), *Texte zur Kunst* (Berlin) und *Frieze* (London). Jüngste Buchpublikationen: *Sur.Faces* (Frankfurt 2002) und *Zurück in die Zukunft* (Hamburg 2003). Ausserdem ist er Mitherausgeber des Berliner Artfanzines *Neue Review.*

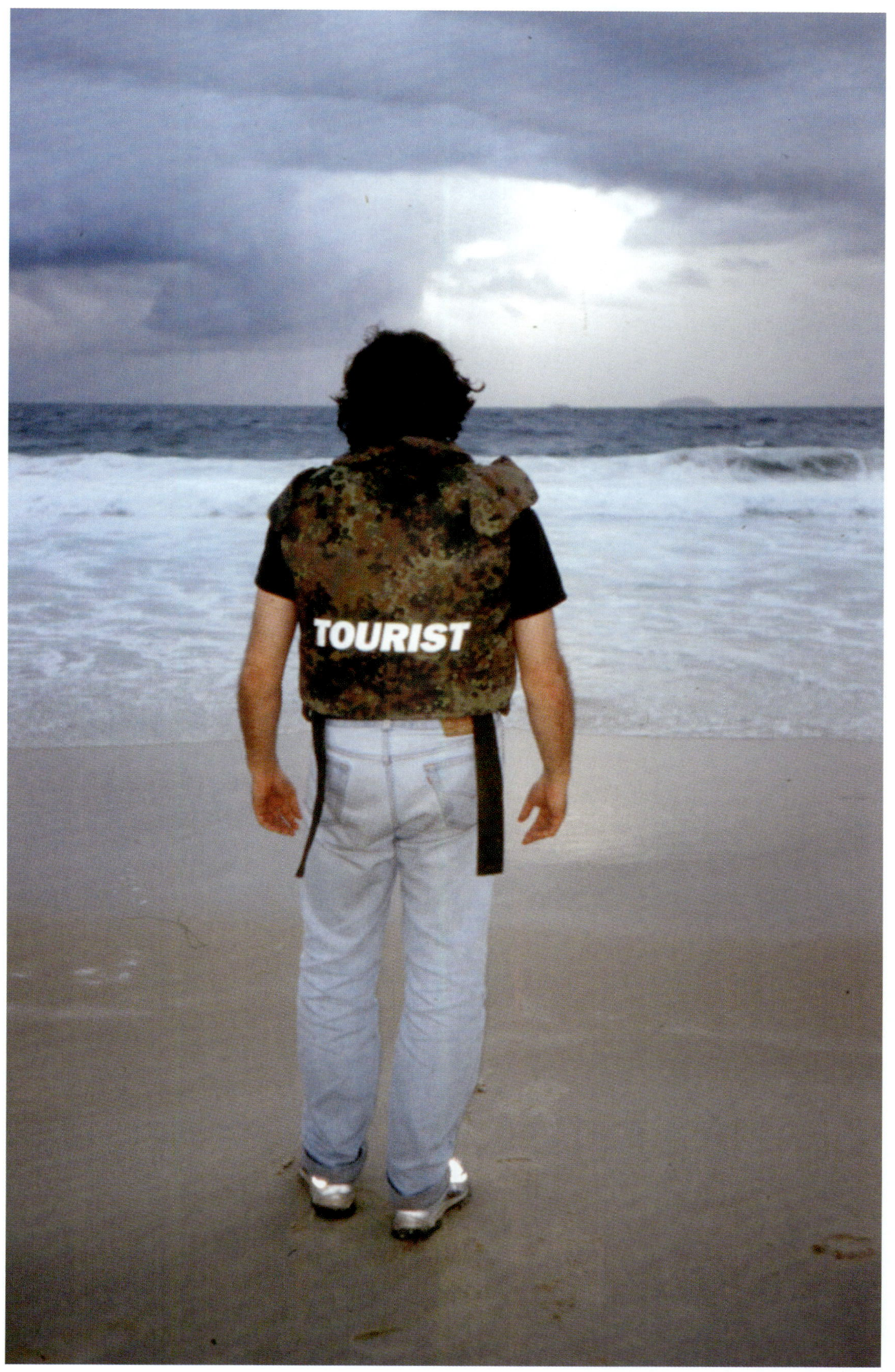

FRANZ ACKERMANN, RIO DE JANEIRO, COPACABANA, 1999, *Farbphotographie / color photograph.*

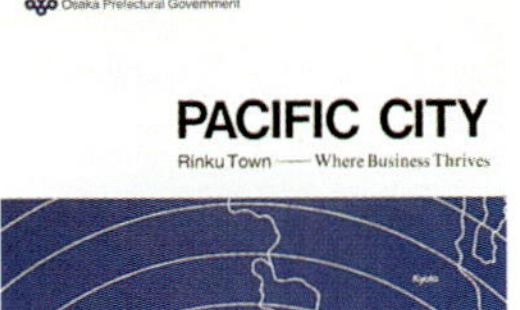

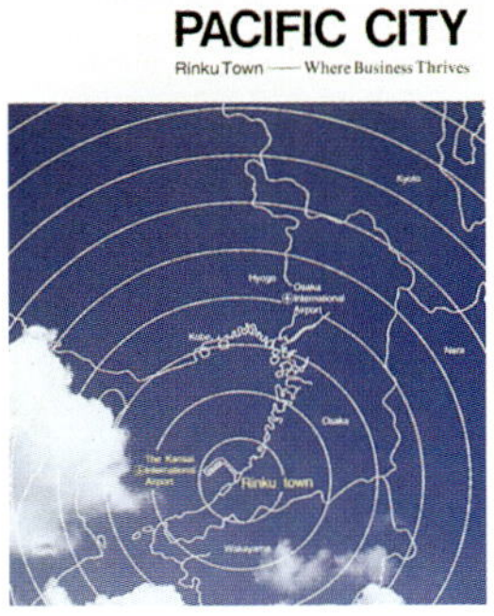

FRANZ ACKERMANN, HERE: PROMISING ABSENCE (ALL THE PLACES I'VE NEVER BEEN TO), 1995, 3 von 160 Dias in 2 Karussells (ohne Projektoren) / 3 of 160 slides in 2 Carousels (without projectors).

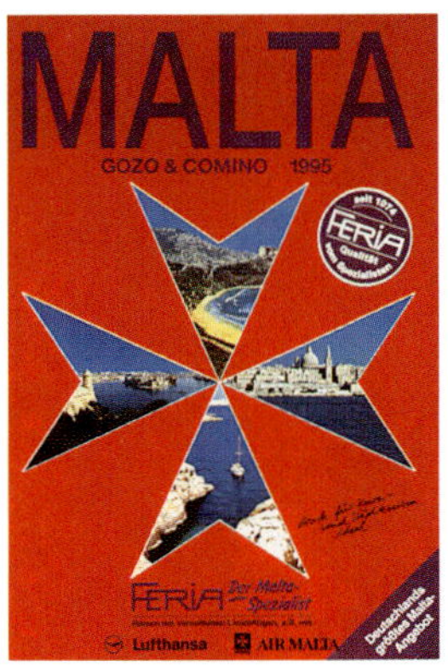

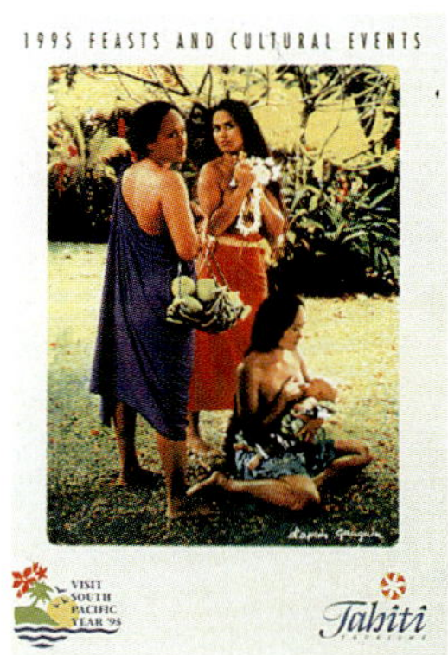

Der Künstler hat die Masse aller rund 150 Zimmer samt der darin befindlichen Möbel vermessen und notiert, in denen er in den Jahren zuvor einmal, wie lange auch immer, «gewohnt» hatte. Aus diesen Massen hat er dann die Durchschnittswerte errechnet und anschliessend aus einfachen MDF-Platten einen gleichsam exemplarischen Lebensraum in Form von «platonischen» Möbelmodellen nachgestellt. Schrank, Tisch, Stuhl und Bett konstruieren einen auf die Grundelemente reduzierten (flüchtigen) Ort, der überall und nirgends stehen könnte und so eine überaus säkularisierte Form von Utopie inszeniert. Diese Flüchtigkeit betonend wählte der Künstler einen scheinbar beliebigen Ort und Raum, ein Fachwerkhaus in Hannoversch Münden unweit der «documenta»-Stadt Kassel aus. Mit dem SOFT ROOM porträtiert sich Franz Ackermann wiederum in gänzlicher Abwesenheit; nicht die Präsenz seines abgebildeten Körpers gibt Auskunft über ihn und seine Haltung zur Welt, sondern die Art und Weise seines «kurzweiligen» Wohnens. Eine Variante dieser Arbeit stellt in mancherlei Hinsicht die Textarbeit OHNE TITEL (1997) dar: Ohne Punkt und Komma sind hier in asyndetischer, im wahrsten Sinne des Wortes «subjektloser» Reihung die Namen all der Strassen aufgelistet, in denen sich der Künstler in den letzten Jahren länger aufgehalten hat: «...Street Santa Monica Boulevard North Fairfax Avenue Potsdamer Strasse Adalbert Strasse...». Die (Photo-)Tapete ALLE ORTE AN DENEN ICH JEMALS WAR (2002) schliesslich zeigt mit vergleichbarer Logik in Bild und Karthographie alle Orte auf...

Ein wirklich kurzer theoretischer Exkurs: «...man entweicht an den Nicht-Ort der Geschwindigkeit. Der Weltbürger wird zum utopischen Bürger, der nur noch die Transportmittel und die Transitstätten bewohnt», schreibt Paul Virilio 1975 in seinem Essay «Fahrzeug».[1] Vor allem die Errungenschaften der modernen Technik haben, so Paul Virilios Argumentation, die Kategorien von Zeit und Raum, die doch nach dem Königsberger Philosophen Immanuel Kant die Bildung von Subjektivität erst ermöglichen, ausser Kraft gesetzt und so das Individuum entfremdet von jedweder (transzendentalen) Verortung. Genau ein Vierteljahrhundert später greifen Michael Hardt/Antonio Negri in ihrer (Anti-)Globalisierungsfibel *Empire* diese Argumentation auf, betonen jetzt aber die emanzipatorischen Seiten der von Paul Virilio beschriebenen Deterritorialisierungen. Die beiden Theoretiker sprechen von einer «globalen Staatsbürgerschaft» und von der «Tugend» des Nomadismus als «erste moralische Praktik». Gerade der Wegfall von nationalen Grenzen und die «Virtualität des Welt-Raums» eröffne eben auch die Möglichkeit einer grenzenlosen «Liebe und Gemeinschaft».[2] Genau dieser Spannung von leidvoller Entfremdung und lustvoller Entgrenzung stellt sich immer wieder auch die Kunst von Franz Ackermann. Der Themenkreis Tourismus etwa, ich habe es oben ausgeführt, erlaubt ihm sowohl die Macht des besagten Dienstleistungszweiges wie auch das individuelle Begehren der Reisenden zu untersuchen.

Die Macht, ja die Gewalt des Tourismus steht auch in der wohl ersten Arbeit Franz Ackermanns im Blickpunkt, in der er selbst als Person zu sehen ist. Noch zaghaft und vorsichtig betritt sein repräsentierter Körper die Areale der Kunst, denn seinen Rücken hat er den Betrachtern eines Photos zugedreht, das in die Installation DAS HAUS AM STRAND (1998–2003) integriert ist. Auf diesem Selbstporträt trägt der Künstler nicht nur ein Paar Nike-Sneakers, einen der Fetische der neuen globalisierten Welt, sondern auch eine schusssichere Weste, auf deren Rücken, in der von der UNO benützten Typographie, das Wort «Tourist» zu lesen ist. Verschiedene Fluchtlinien werden hier also kurzgeschlossen, in erster Linie aber die des weltweiten, oftmals wenig rücksichtsvollen Einflusses von *global players* wie dem Nike-Konzern, der – inzwischen allerdings zunehmend entmachteten – UNO oder dem Dienstleistungssektor Tourismus. Spätestens mit diesem Photo beginnt zudem eine ästhetische Strategie, in der Franz Ackermann sich nicht bloss als kritischer Inspekteur, sondern auch als aktiv involvierter Teilnehmer der von ihm beobachteten Prozesse positioniert.

Das Selbstporträt FACELAND (2001) bestimmt diese teilnehmende Rolle als eine mit Warencharakter,[3] die den Künstler auch zum Klischee seiner selbst werden lässt. Das Porträt zeigt im «passbildtauglichen» Ausschnitt das Konterfei Franz Ackermanns, das sich im Stil Arcimboldos aus unzähligen Versatzstücken seines eigenen bisherigen Formenvokabulars zusammensetzt. Architektonische Ansichten und karthographische Notate, dynamische Farbkreise und perspektivisch sich widersprechende geometrische Ornamente bilden hier ein ruhig nach vorne schauendes Antlitz. So ist dieser Arbeit einerseits die Aussage «Ich bin, wie ich reise und wohne» ins Gesicht geschrieben, andererseits zeugt das aus Selbstzitaten gesampelte Porträt von dem Bild, das sich das Betriebssystem Kunst und sein längst weltweit mehr oder weniger florierender Markt heute von der Ware Franz Ackermann macht: der Artist als «Spurensucher, Kartenleser», als «reisender Beobachter»[4] und ästhetisch reflektierender Urbanist. Als solcher, auch dies führt das Blatt FACELAND bewusst vor, setzt er während des artistischen Prozesses eigentlich fragmentarisch bleibende Erfahrungen und Erkenntnisse in künstlerische Werte um; zwangsläufig stellt sich dabei eine werkhafte Ganzheit her, die hier dennoch in sich zersplittert und unzusammenhängend erscheint.

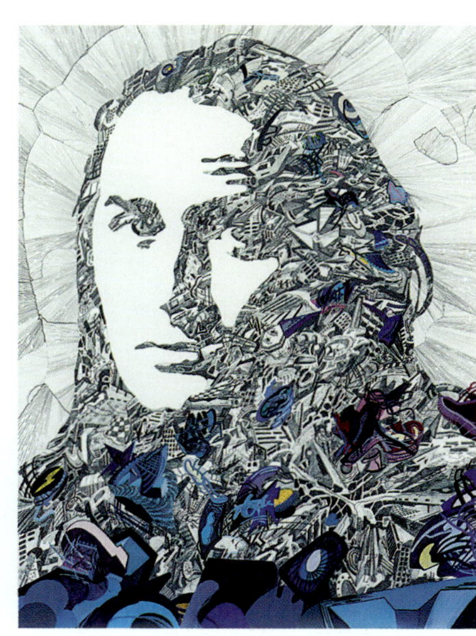

FRANZ ACKERMANN, FACELAND, 2001, Mischtechnik auf Papier, 84,5 x 64,5 cm / mixed media on paper, 33 1/4 x 25 3/8".

Schliesslich sei noch die Arbeit FACELAND II (2002) angeführt, die das Problem von der Stellung des Menschen in nicht mehr hinterfragten, nicht mehr von einem «real-existierenden» Sozialismus bekämpften Marktverhältnissen endgültig politisch zuspitzt. Ein sich aus unzähligen Glühbirnen zusammensetzender kugelförmiger Leuchtkörper hängt da erhellend schön von der Decke herab. Auf ihm ist genau das flächige Konterfei des Künstlers in prägnantem Schwarz montiert, das schon in FACELAND als auszufüllende Fläche seine Verwendung fand. Die Glühbirnen der globusartigen Lampe blinken verführerisch in unterschiedlichen Farbkonstellationen auf, lassen uns aber auch an Weltkarten denken, mit denen global agierende Unternehmen ihre im internationalen «Wettbewerb» zu erobernden Territorien abstecken. Vor diesem zwiespältigen Hintergrund erinnert das markant stilisierte Antlitz des Künstlers einerseits an eingängige Logos für marktfähige Produkte – etwa an *Uncle Ben's* (Reis) –, andererseits an piktoriale Heroisierungen von diktatorischen Herrschern. So promotet Franz Ackermann sich hier selbst als einleuchtende Ikone, in der die visuellen Grammatiken von ökonomischem Diktat und politischer Diktatur parallel gesetzt werden. Das Selbstporträt Marke Franz Ackermann behauptet sich – und nicht nur hier! – also weder als ach so psychologisierendes Protokoll individueller Persönlichkeit noch als mehr oder weniger eitle Bühne für postmoderne Rollenspiele. Stattdessen bietet es sich an als suggestives Modell für die spannungsvollen Beziehungen von Kapital und Macht in unserer längst globalisierten Welt. Und diese Beziehungen sind, wie es im Titel einer Zeichnung des Künstlers heisst, «incredible, terrible, beautiful» zugleich.

1) Paul Virilio, «Fahrzeug», in: *Fahren, fahren, fahren...*, Merve Verlag, Berlin 1978, S. 32.
2) Alle Zitate aus: Michael Hardt, Antonio Negri, *Empire*, Campus Verlag, Frankfurt am Main u.a. 2003, S. 369.
3) Das Subjekt als Ware: «Tourists are money». Diese Textzeile aus dem Song «God save the Queen» der legendären Punkband The Sex Pistols hat Franz Ackermann 1997 in seiner Installation URBAN LIVING grossflächig an die Wand geschrieben.
4) Beide Zitate: Gregor Jansen, in: *Art Now*, Taschen, Köln 2002, S. 12.

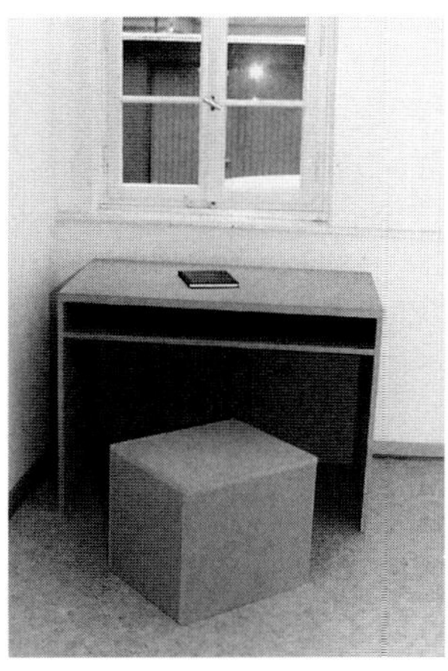

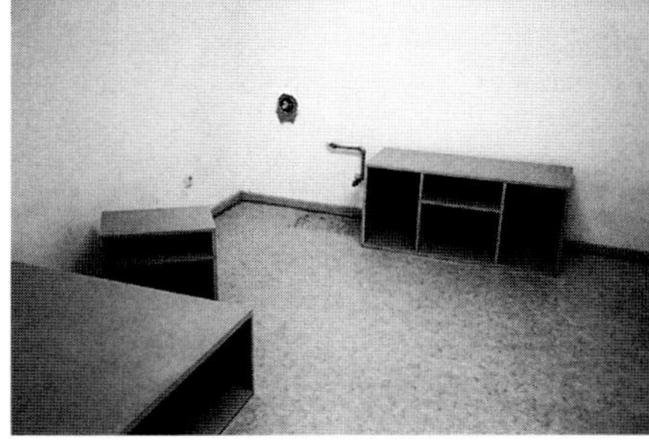

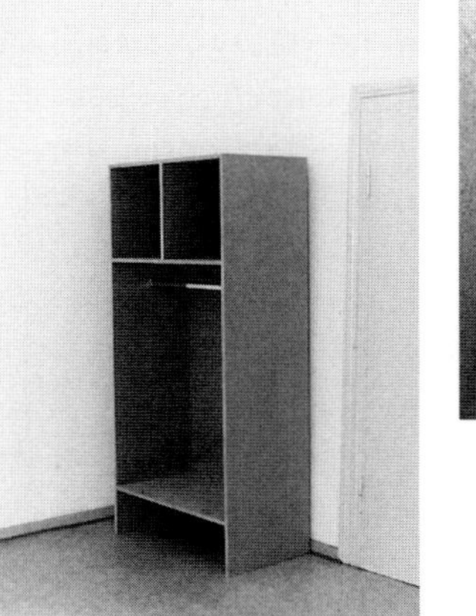

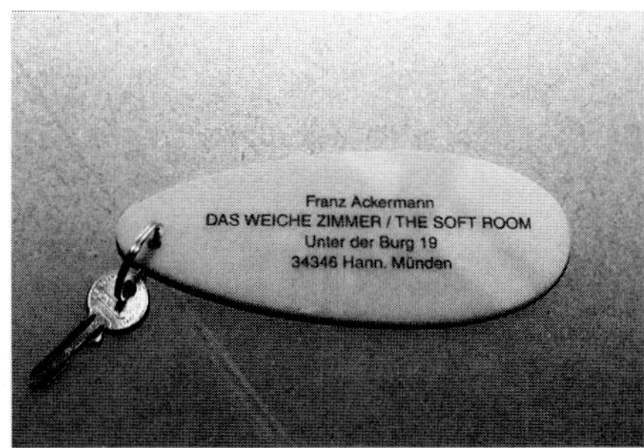

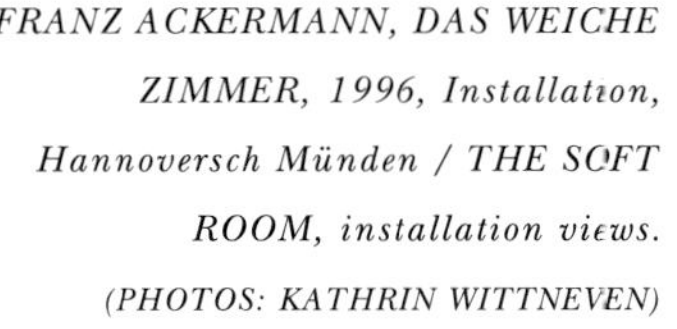

FRANZ ACKERMANN, DAS WEICHE ZIMMER, 1996, Installation, Hannoversch Münden / THE SOFT ROOM, installation views.
(PHOTOS: KATHRIN WITTNEVEN)

RAIMAR STANGE

A Utopian Citizen?

As a rule, Franz Ackermann's drawings and paintings do not show any people; the subject emerges in them as absolute absence, so to speak. Despite the promising title, even the small-format MENTAL MAP: SAILORS (1994) does not contain a depiction of the traveling, more precisely, sea-faring people mentioned. Instead, tattoo-like patterns, cartographic inscriptions and abstract-expressive color planes record the (anonymous) experiences of a nomadic existence. It is no surprise, therefore, that Franz Ackermann's early works, which can be read as self-portraits, also deliberately forego any visual representation of the artist. Instead, the artist has indirectly drafted an image of himself in those works, for example, in the slide installation HERE: PROMISING ABSENCE (1996), in which a good 160 colorful covers from typical travel brochures are presented as superimposed projections. A dark-skinned "native" and his canoe extol the "experience to all the senses" available in Papua New Guinea; a wide empty landscape, mountains, and an eternal blue sky promote Tibet; and a green jungle symbolizes the supposedly nature-friendly "eco-tourism" in Panama. We are all familiar with those kitsch motifs, those clichés promulgated for centuries—*pars pro toto*—from Alexander von Humboldt and Paul Gauguin to Cook's travel agency and Hollywood. Despite their redundant triteness and obvious disregard for reality, these clichés lend expression to genuine longings for adventurous exoticism and for long overdue escape from the dull routines of everyday life. The important thing, however, is the lowest common denominator in Ackermann's choice of travel brochures on display: all the countries presented are ones the artist had not yet visited at the time. So, *ex negativo,* Franz Ackermann tells us about his own travels, which, as we have learned by now, are pivotal to his art.

The SOFT ROOM project (1997) is another example of these early self-portraits. Again, the focus is on being abroad or being at home. The artist measured and recorded the size of all the approximately 150 rooms, plus furniture, in which he had "lived" in the previous years, for whatever period of time. He then calculated the average size and built an exemplary living space, as it were, in the form of "Platonic" furniture models, using simple MDF boards. A

RAIMAR STANGE is a free-lance curator and critic; he regularly contributes to art magazines like *Kunst-Bulletin* (Zurich), *Texte zur Kunst* (Berlin), and *Frieze* (London). His more recent book publications include *Sur.Faces* (Frankfurt 2002) and *Zurück in die Zukunft* (Hamburg 2003). He is also co-editor of the Berlin art fanzine *Neue Review.*

cupboard, table, chair, and bed define a (fleeting) space reduced to its basic elements, a space that could be located everywhere and nowhere and thus constitutes an altogether secularized form of utopia. To underscore the fleetingness, the artist chose an apparently arbitrary site, a half-timber house in Hannoversch Münden, not far from the city of Kassel, venue of the "documenta." In SOFT ROOM, Franz Ackermann once again portrays himself through complete absence; information about him and his attitude to the world is not provided by the presence of his depicted body, but by the way in which he "temporarily" lives. In many ways, the text work O.T. (Untitled, 1997) represents a variation on this: in a truly "subject-less," asyndetic sequence with neither periods nor commas, he lists the names of all the streets that he lived on over the past few years: "... Street Santa Monica Boulevard North Fairfax Avenue Potsdamer Strasse Adalbert Strasse..." The same logic underlies the images and cartography in his wallpaper of photographs titled ALLE ORTE, AN DENEN ICH JEMALS WAR (All the Places I Have Ever Been, 2002).

A really brief theoretical excursus: "...one escapes to the non-place of speed. The global citizen becomes the utopian citizen, who dwells merely in the means of transportation and the places of transit," wrote Paul Virilio in his 1975 essay "Véhicule."[1] Paul Virilio argues that the achievements of modern technology have invalidated the categories of time and space, the very categories that, according to the Königsberg philosopher Immanuel Kant, enable the formation of subjectivity. The individual has therefore been alienated from any kind of (transcendental) locality. Exactly a quarter of a century later, in their (anti-)globalization reader *Empire,* Michael Hardt and Antonio Negri took up Virilio's argument. However, the two theorists emphasize the emancipatory aspects of the deterritorializations described by Paul Virilio. They speak of a "global citizenship" and the "virtue" of nomadism as one of the "first ethical practices." The very disappearance of national borders and "the virtuality of world space" also present the possibility of an unbounded "love and community."[2] Franz Ackermann's art repeatedly confronts this tension between painful alienation and pleasurable openness. The above-mentioned theme of tourism, for example, allows him to examine both the power of that service sector and the individual longing of the travelers.

The power, indeed the force of tourism, is also the focal point of the first work by Franz Ackermann in which his person is to be seen. The representation of his body enters the arena of art timidly and cautiously, for he has turned his back to the viewers of the photograph that is integrated into the installation DAS HAUS AM STRAND (The House on the Beach, 1998–2003). In this self-portrait, the artist is wearing not only a pair of Nike sneakers, a fetish of the new globalized world, but also a bullet-proof jacket on the back of which the word "tourist" is written in the typography used by the UN. Various vanishing lines come together here, first and foremost those of the often not very respectful influence of global players like the Nike concern, the – increasingly powerless – UN, and the service sector of tourism. In addition, the photograph launches an aesthetic strategy in which Franz Ackermann positions himself not just as a critical inspector, but also as an actively involved participant in the processes under observation.

The self-portrait FACELAND (2001) defines this participation as a commodity-like role,[3] which also turns the artist into a cliché of himself. In a frame that could qualify as a passport photo, we see a likeness of Franz Ackermann consisting of countless set pieces from his own formal vocabulary assembled in the style of Archimboldo. Architectonic views and cartographic notations, dynamic color circles and perspectivally contradictory geometric ornaments make up a face that is looking calmly ahead. Written all over it, so to speak, is the statement: "I am as I travel and live." On the other hand, this sampling of self-citations bears witness to the image that the art business and its long since global and more or less flourishing market has created of the commodity Franz Ackermann: the artist as "tracker, map-reader," as "roving observer"[4] and aesthetically reflecting urbanist. Moreover, as FACELAND deliberately demonstrates, the artistic process transforms essentially fragmentary experiences and insights into artistic values; unavoidably, this gives rise to a holistic work which here nevertheless seems splintered and disjointed.

Finally, mention should be made of the work FACELAND II (2002) which takes to political extremes the issue of man's position in power relations that are no longer questioned and no longer combated by any "real existing" Eastern bloc socialism. Hanging from the ceiling is a beautifully luminous, spherical lamp made up of countless bulbs. Mounted on this, in a striking black, is the same planar likeness of the artist that filled the picture surface of FACELAND. The bulbs of the globe-like lamp flash seductively in various color combinations, but we are also reminded of the maps on which global concerns stake out the territories they aim to conquer worldwide by eliminating the competition. Seen against this ambiguous background, the artist's strikingly stylized face is reminiscent both of eye-catching logos for marketable products—for example, *Uncle Ben's* (rice)—and of heroicizing portraits of dictatorial rulers. So Franz Ackermann is promoting himself as a shining icon in which the visual grammars of economic dictates and political dictatorship are equated. The Franz Ackermann self-portrait brand asserts itself—and not just here—as neither a psychologizing record of an individual personality, nor as a more or less vainglorious stage for postmodern role-play. Instead it functions as a suggestive model for the tense relationship between capital and power in our long since globalized world. And, as the title of one of the artist's drawings says, this relationship is at once "incredible, terrible (and) beautiful."

(Translation: Pauline Cumbers)

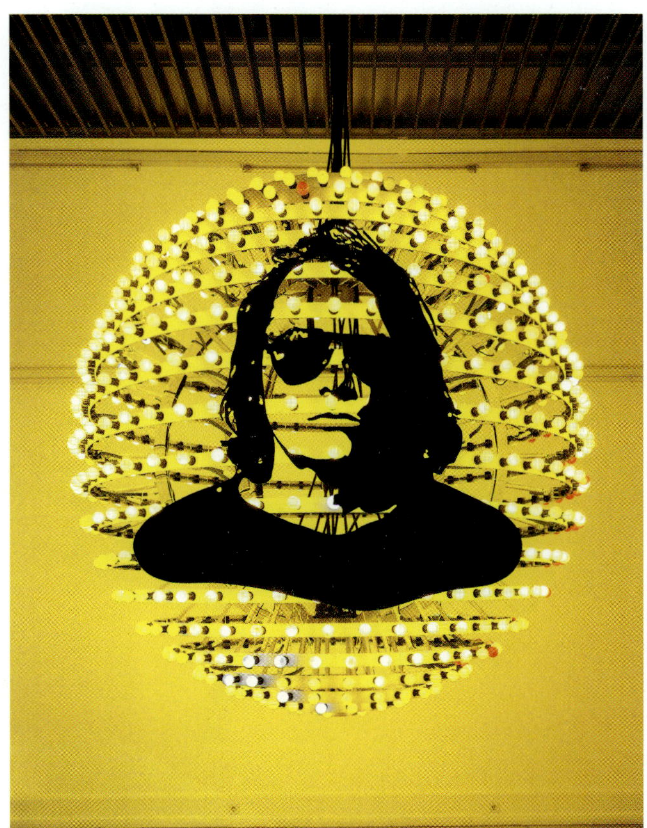

FRANZ ACKERMANN, FACELAND II (YOU BETTER KEEP THE LIGHT ON), 2002, Aluminium, Licht, Metall, Installation, Kunsthalle Nürnberg, Durchmesser ca. 280 cm / aluminum, light, metal, installation view, diameter ca. 110¼".

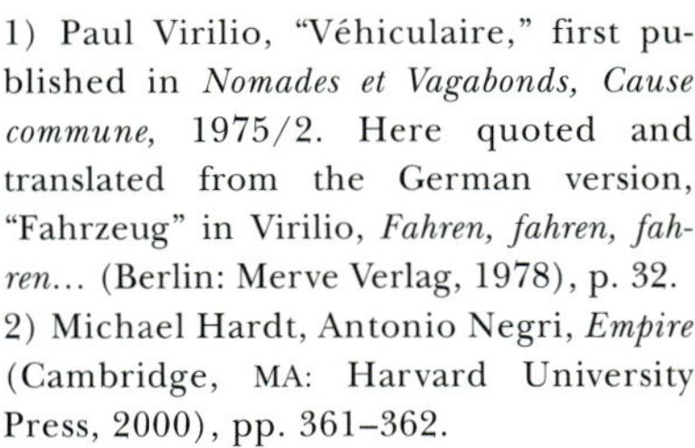

1) Paul Virilio, "Véhiculaire," first published in *Nomades et Vagabonds, Cause commune,* 1975/2. Here quoted and translated from the German version, "Fahrzeug" in Virilio, *Fahren, fahren, fahren…* (Berlin: Merve Verlag, 1978), p. 32.
2) Michael Hardt, Antonio Negri, *Empire* (Cambridge, MA: Harvard University Press, 2000), pp. 361–362.
3) The subject as commodity: "Tourists are money." Franz Ackermann wrote this line from the song "God save the Queen" by the legendary punk band, the Sex Pistols, in large lettering on the wall of his 1997 installation URBAN LIVING.
4) Gregor Jansen, "Franz Ackermann" in *Art Now,* Taschen, Cologne 2002, p. 12.

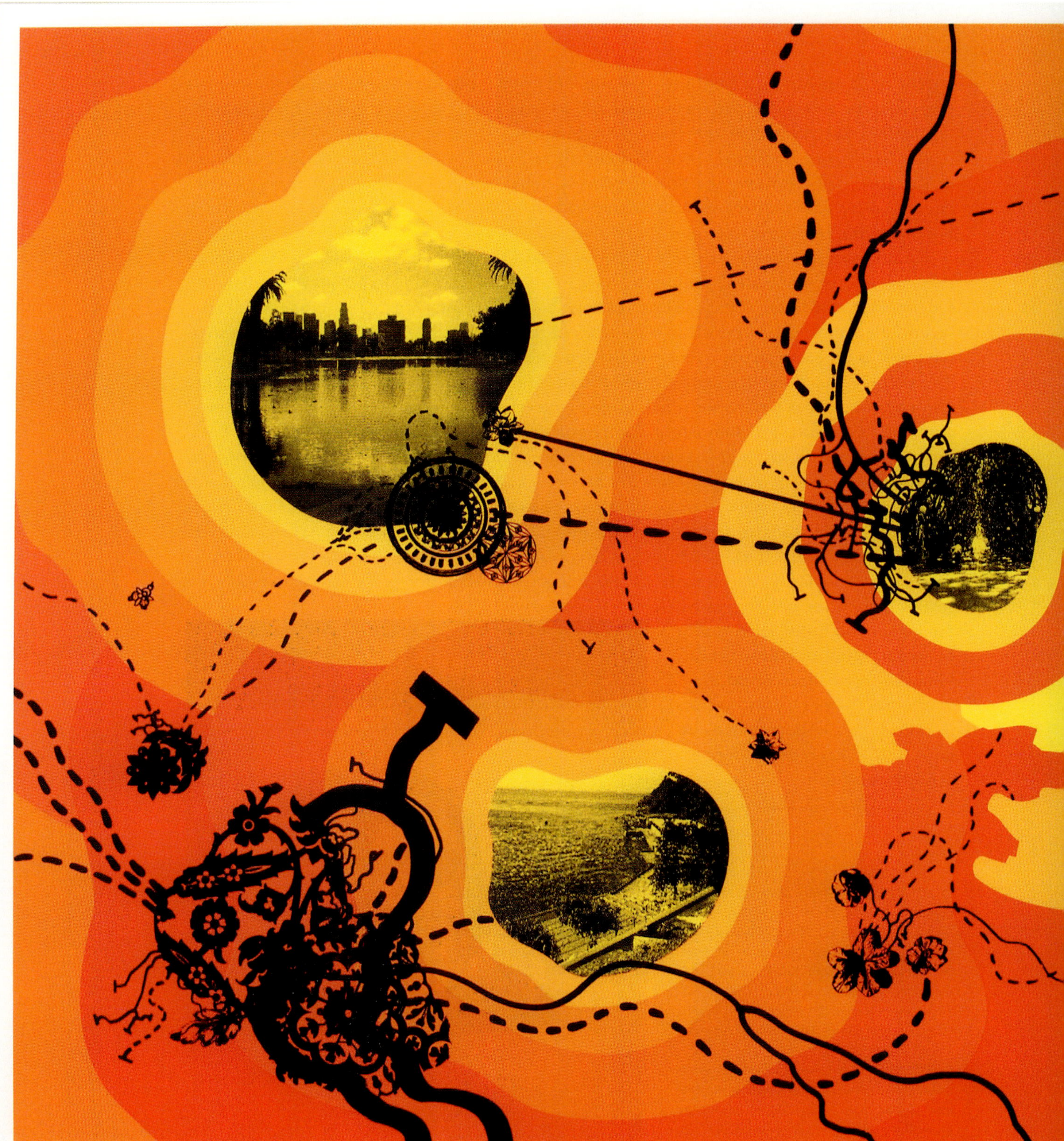

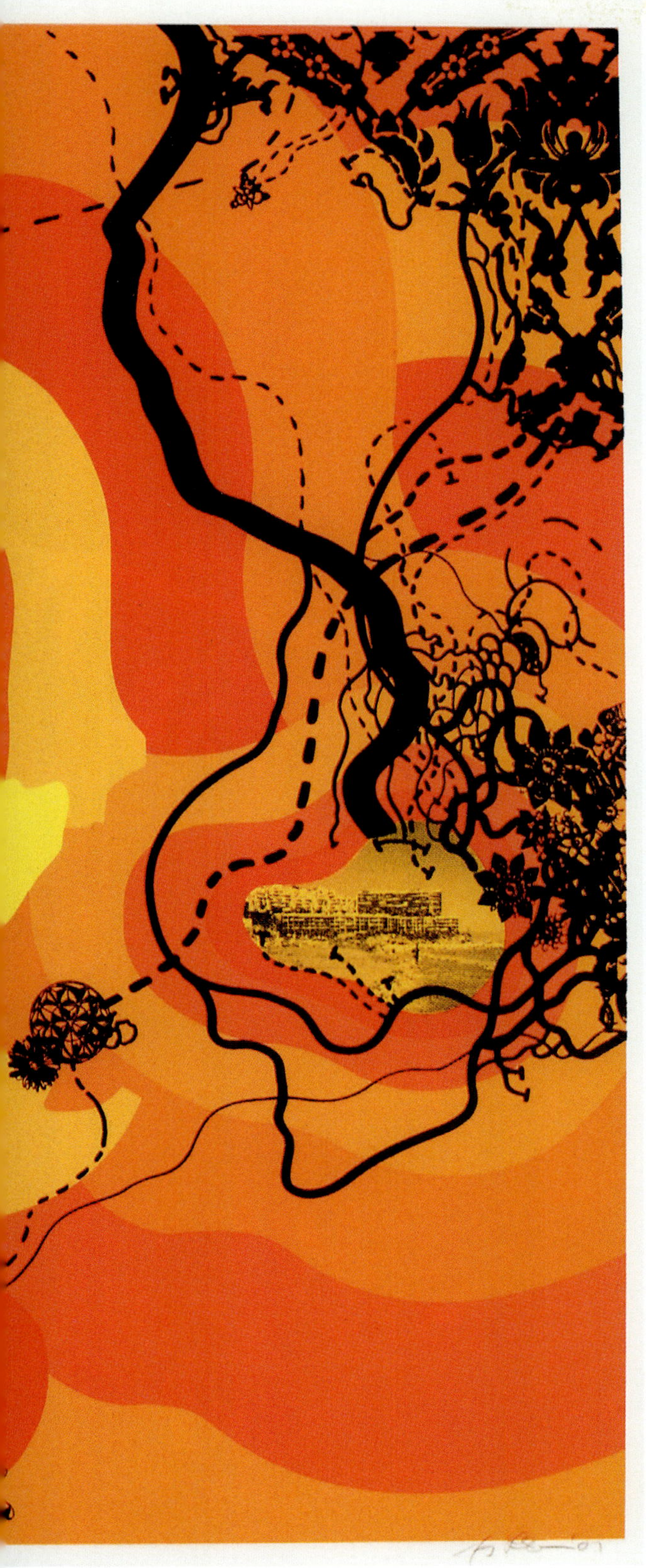

EDITION FOR PARKETT
FRANZ ACKERMANN

PEAK SEASON, 2003

Siebdruck (10 Farben) auf Somerset 300g/m^2;

Blattformat 50 x 70 cm, Bildformat 48 x 68 cm.

Druck: Werkstatt für Kunstsiebdruck München.

Auflage: 70, signiert und nummeriert.

10-color silkscreen print on Somerset 300 g/m^2;

paper size 19 11/16 x 27 9/16", image size 18 7/8 x 26 3/4".

Printed by Werkstatt für Kunstsiebdruck Munich.

Edition of 70, signed and numbered.

(PHOTO: MANCIA/BODMER, FBM STUDIO, ZÜRICH)

EIJA-LIISA AHTILA

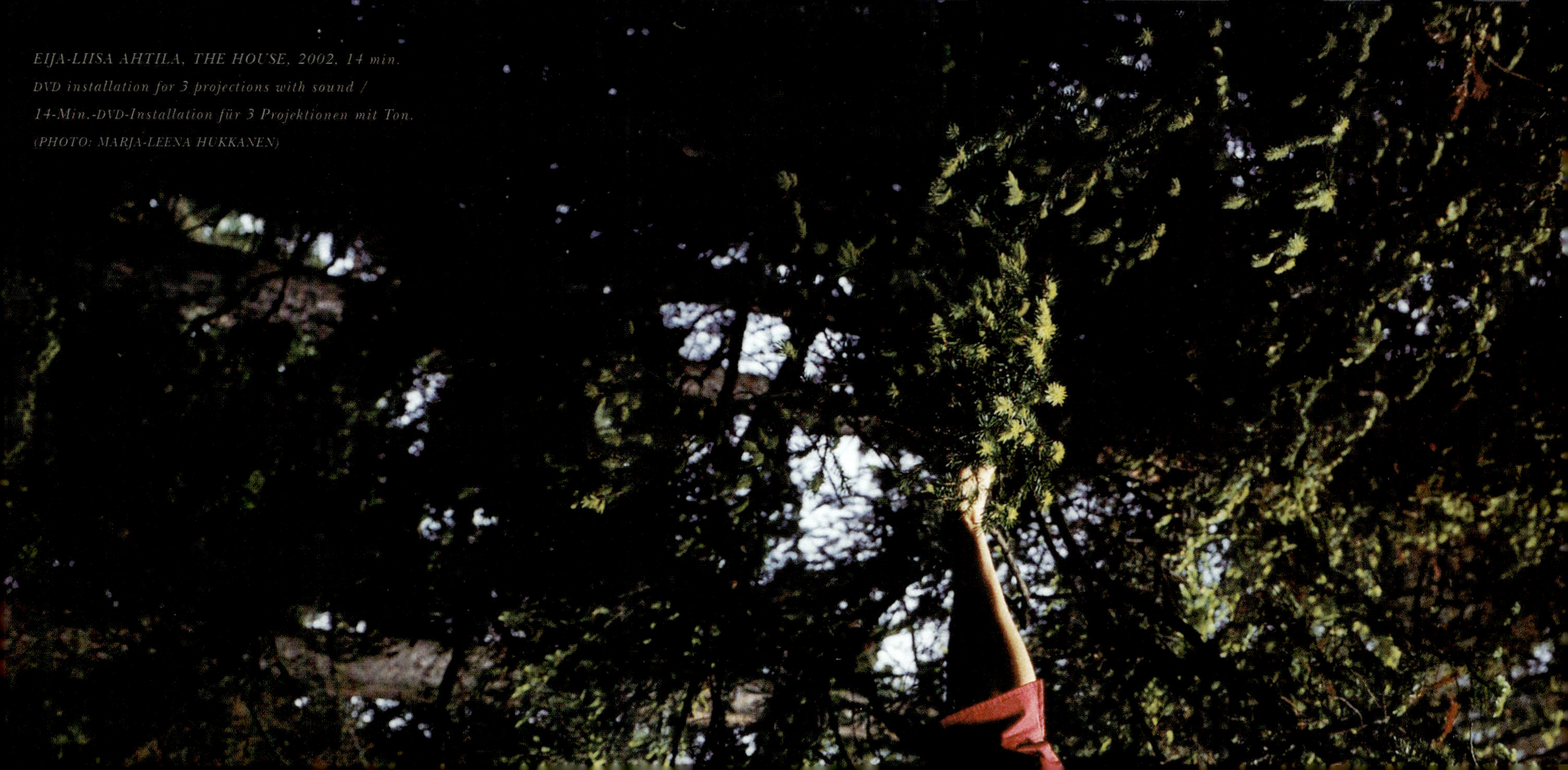

EIJA-LIISA AHTILA, THE HOUSE, 2002, 14 min.
DVD installation for 3 projections with sound /
14-Min.-DVD-Installation für 3 Projektionen mit Ton.
(PHOTO: MARJA-LEENA HUKKANEN)

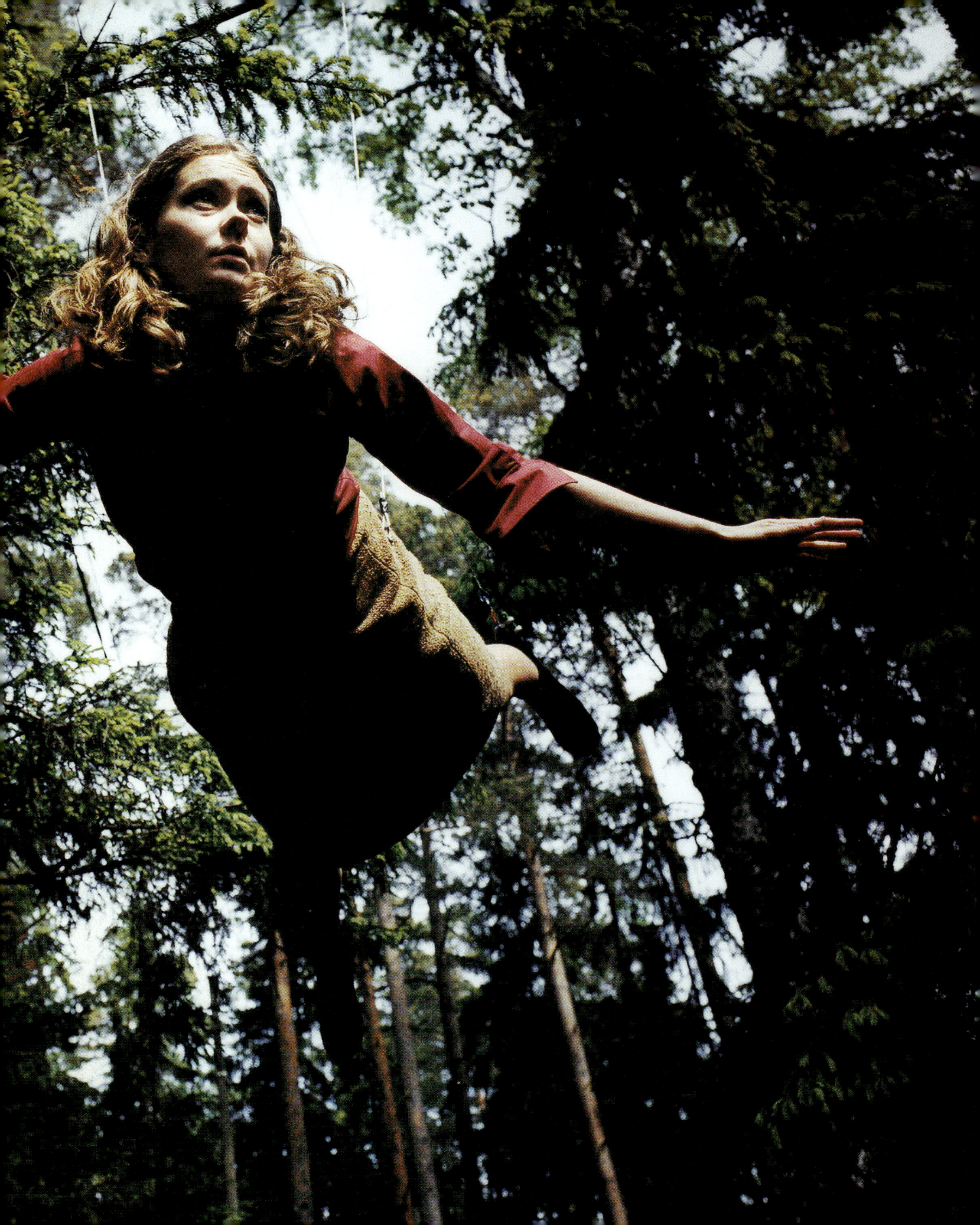

THINKING IN FILM

EIJA-LIISA AHTILA in Conversation with CHRISSIE ILES

Chrissie Iles: Perhaps we should start by talking about a phrase in the subtitle of Daniel Birnbaum's essay about your work, "extended cinema." When I went through the different pieces chronologically, it became clear that the boundaries between fiction and documentary, ego and the loss of self, and between the still and the moving image, all very cinematic issues, were present from the beginning. Yet the "extended cinema" that you have created is very different from the approach to cinema that most artists took after 1989 in Europe and Scandinavia. You are one of the few artists who trained in film, in both America and England, and you incorporated the black box of cinema into the white cube of the gallery from the beginning. So what does extended cinema mean in your work? And how is it different from others who have incorporated the cinematic?

Eija-Liisa Ahtila: My approach to cinema and the moving image has to do with my background. I graduated as a painter and painted for a couple of years, and then I became interested in photography and started making photo and text installations. During that period I also read art theory and followed what was going on internationally. In 1987 I took part in a video course with some of my friends and found the medium fascinating. I did some little things with video and at the beginning of the nineties went to study film. The plan was to give up visual arts, but that didn't happen—I got stuck somewhere between the two traditions.

I feel that because of my background as a painter, my approach to film is more about how to express something through the medium of the moving image. The question "what is a moving image?" became more important to me than whether the context was cinema, visual art or new media. When making the works, "what" frequently turns into "how." How to express sadness in images? Can a feeling be expressed without its opposite? How is understanding related to time, and what is the role of causality in installations? Making films and installations became a matter of identifying the links between images, sounds, rhythms, light, characters, and words, and using them

CHRISSIE ILES is Curator of Film and Video at the Whitney Museum of American Art, New York.

to approach and construct the story. So, I think my approach is still an artist's.

CI: During your training, you must have been exposed to film history and film theory, and you also come out of the strong context of Finnish cinema.

EA: Because I was quite old already when I thought about the transition from art to film, I didn't want to spend time taking technical courses such as how to use a camera. Instead, I felt I needed to concentrate on the different ways of expressing things with the medium, so I chose courses on editing and cinematography and learned about the different choices that cinematographers had made in order to suggest the emotions they wanted to express. And I also took some courses on film history and theory.

You asked about my use of still images. I try to think about these issues in relation to telling a story or creating a narrative. Usually in films the image is subordinate to the story, which means that when you cut from one image to another—let's say from a long shot to a close up—you've got to give more information about a character or events. That's the motivation for cutting—images are always ...

CI: ... vehicles for the narrative.

EA: Exactly. The meaning of the image comes from the story. I'd like to do it differently and still maintain the coherence of the story. There are many possibilities that the moving image offers.

CI: Was film an early influence on you in Finland?

EA: There was a cinema club in this small town where I lived as a child that I remember going to. They showed a Louis Malle film about a young woman and her first sexual experiences. I thought it had a weird symbolism, but I enjoyed it. I think it's called *Black Moon*. I was thirteen or fourteen; another one I saw was Robert Altman's *Three Women*. And Ingmar Bergman's films.

CI: Was Ingmar Bergman a strong presence in Finland?

EA: Yes. His films were also shown on TV.

CI: In your installations, you shift between foregrounding image and narrative. Do the multiple screens help abstract or forefront the image, both compositionally, within the frame, and in the physical construction of the pieces? What is the difference between watching your films linearly in a cinema, and

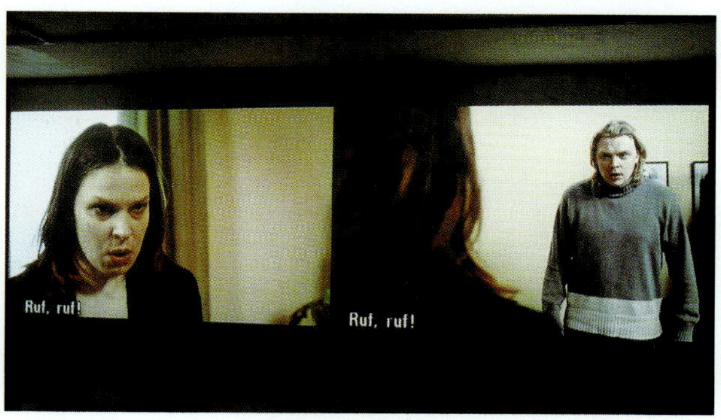

EIJA-LIISA AHTILA, CONSOLATION SERVICE, 1999, still from 24 min. 35-mm film / Bild aus dem 24-minütigen 35-mm-Film.

seeing them as installations, watching the narrative unfold spatially, within multiple screens, in a gallery?

EA: An installation with three screens definitely gives much more emphasis to the image, and it also allows lots more experimentation. But we are still talking about the moving image and storytelling—a moving image narrative seems to have this great potential to glue everything together. Sound is always about space and distances, and two images close to each other always connect. This is of course a question about perception and I'm also thinking about the set of rules we use to create a narrative. Take CONSOLATION SERVICE, which was made for Venice ("End of Story," La Biennale di Venezia, 49th International Art Exhibition, Nordic Pavilion, 1999) as an example. I wanted to explore the difference between a story told either with one or two images: in the cinema, the aim is to find the best possible vantage point for viewers in regard to the linear events taking place on screen within a single projective frame. Everything has been constructed in relation to this, from the microphone positioning at the locations to the editing of the images from one shot to the other. In a multi-screen installation, you can't experience the narrative singularly, as several things are happening in the space. Also, several screens make it possible, for example, to show the reaction shot and the action shot at the same time. This means that the viewer has to choose. At Kiasma, when there was a screening of the film CONSOLATION SERVICE, the installation version was on view as well. People I spoke with mentioned that the experience in the installa-

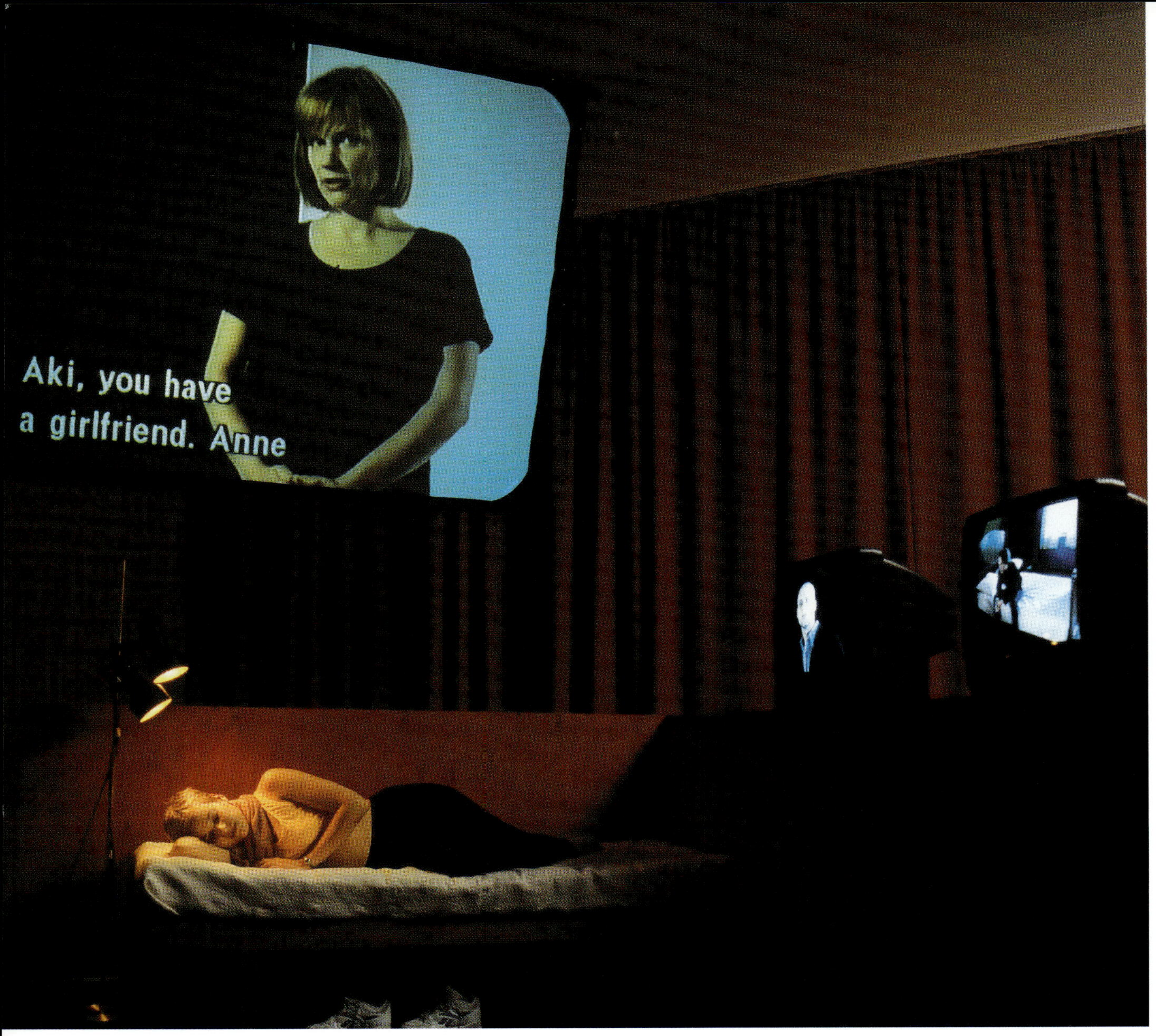

EIJA-LIISA AHTILA, ANNE, AKI AND GOD, 1998, 30 min. DVD installation for 2 projections and 5 monitors with sound; wooden structure, furniture, text / DVD-Installation für 2 Projektionen und 5 Monitore mit Ton, Dauer: 30 Min.; Holzgerüst, Möbel, Text.

tion felt more realistic, you couldn't choose sides: the woman's point of view in the story didn't appear to be emphasized. In the film, it became more obvious that the main character's presence directed the story.

CI: Was that what you had intended or did this surprise you?

EA: No, I didn't intend that. So I was happy to hear the comments. My aim was to explore different ways of telling a story—it is actually part of my thesis work for the Academy of Fine Arts in Helsinki. With two screens, you can't really guide the experience as precisely as with one screen.

CI: In CONSOLATION SERVICE, the viewer could only enter at the beginning of the film. Why did you insist on this for that particular piece and not for the others?

EA: When I was writing the story, I wanted to explore how to move from one emotion to another—how this kind of building of a work functions in an installation. After seeing the finished work, I felt that you have to learn to know the events and the characters in order to understand them. You need to stay with them to be able to react emotionally when, for example, they fall through the ice or the man materializes and disappears. These things depend on the chosen structure of the story.

CI: Fragmentation occurs in your work as a metaphor of psychological disturbance, touching on the boundaries of psychosis, particularly in your relation to women. In a single screen format, these boundaries are represented in a very different way from an installation like ANNE, AKI AND GOD (1998) where the breaking down of the understanding of where reality ends and fantasy begins is literalized. Aki's bed, with a screen above it, becomes, like Barthes' description of cinema, like slipping into bed and dreaming.

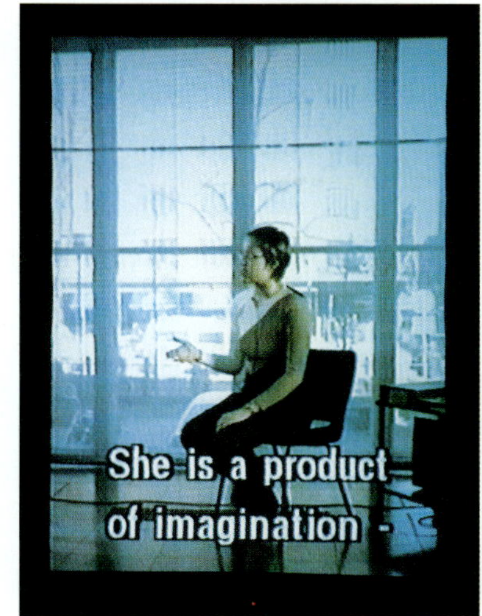

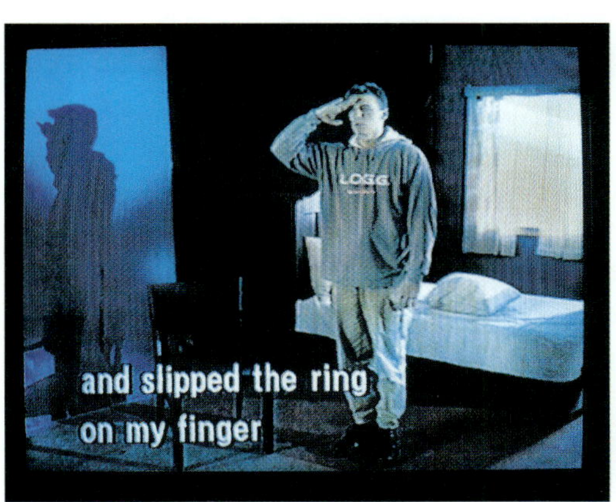

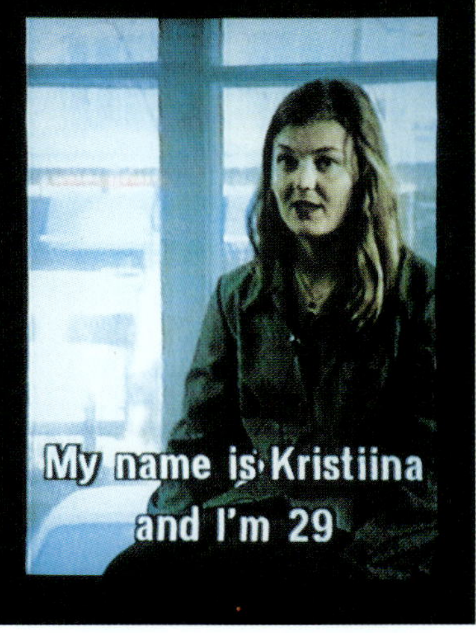

EIJA-LIISA AHTILA, ANNE, AKI AND GOD, 1998, stills from the 30 min. DVD / Stills aus der 30-minütigen DVD.

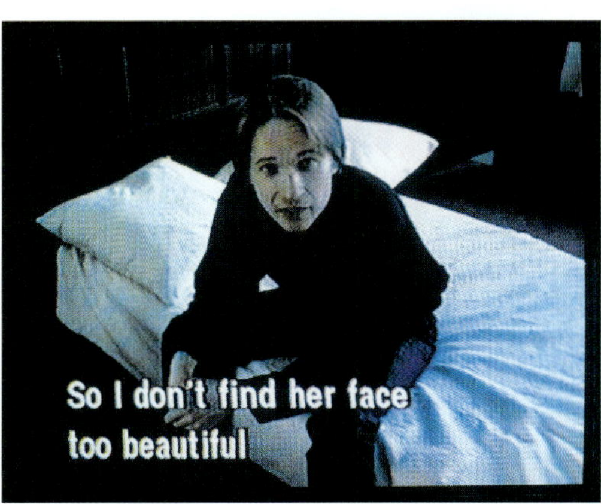

EA: ANNE, AKI AND GOD is based on a true story that happened to a young guy in Helsinki. A friend of mine told me about this man's extraordinary psychotic experience, and we agreed that he would interview Aki. So he did, and the tapes were transcribed. The installation is based on that material. Because the experience existed only in his imagination, I thought it would be nice to concretize it. In the story, God appeared on the screen above his bed and told him, "Aki, you have a girlfriend, Anne. Look around, it's so dirty, you have to clean it here. Anne can't come here." This is how the psychosis started. Since Anne lived only in Aki's dreams, I wanted Anne to be present—to be there for everyone to see. So I put out a casting call, took the job description to the employment office, and fourteen women responded. Seven of the short interviews with them appear on another screen, making the process of making the film more visible.

CI: Is this the piece in which the process of the making of the film is most clearly evident? The contrast between fiction and reality is very precise there, because the realism of the actresses being interviewed contrasts so strongly with Aki's fantasies. It reminds me of Brechtian theater, where the mechanics of how the drama is created are made evident.

EA: When the actor suddenly directs the words to the audience ...

CI: ... and the illusion is broken.

EA: Since Brecht and Godard, and long nights with TV, I feel that illusion has become material to work with. Sometimes it's interesting to think about, rather than to create illusion.

CI: Your process of disrupting illusion could be argued to relate to the conceptual practices of the sixties, which you've developed within a narrative cinematic framework. You also use the performative as part of this questioning.

EA: I haven't thought of this in relation to my work but it's funny that many of my friends are from theater. I remember enjoying Meyerhold's ideas as a young student.

CI: Also related to the Brechtian element is your resonance with Finnish cinema, which is often semi-documentary, and socially based. In your work, we encounter young men and women, teenagers, older women, all with complex problems. We can identify with them, because they're not romanticized.

EA: I want the characters to be straightforward, but on the other hand also poetic.

CI: They also have a surreal quality.

EA: Maybe that's because of the combination I mentioned. All the stories and characters are fictional, but based on research. When I start thinking about a work, I like to be certain about the facts—I need to know that it could have happened, and that it's believable. Then again, the knowledge that you gain through research gives you the freedom to invent things.

CI: An aspect of your work reminds me of Hollywood melodrama, and its heightened psychological fear.

EA: I like Robert Altman, Rainer Werner Fassbinder and John Cassavetes, among others—but during the working process, books I've read are more important.

CI: You're more influenced by literature than by film?

EA: It depends. When I'm planning the work, making notes and writing the script, text is material with which I have a kind of communication. For example, in a book I bought yesterday, there's a paragraph with a simple description of a phone ringing on the wall. This gave me an idea about a transition from one scene to another. In the book, it wasn't an important thing, but it gave me an idea that was suitable for the atmosphere of the scene. I enjoy reading Paul Bowles, Ian McEwan, Patrick McGrath, Don DeLillo. Now I'm reading Virginia Woolf's short stories. I usually read material about the subject matter I'm working on as well.

CI: In your recent works, the intimacy of a domestic environment heightens the claustrophobia of the darkened space, creating a kind of container for the emotional intensity that is expressed. In THE WIND (2002), the construction of space within the film is conveyed both materially and psychologically, through physical space: the walls and curtains close in, then the bookshelves fall over.

EA: I like to keep the different elements of moving images equal, to use sounds, colors and light instead of giving information only through dialogue. But I like words ...

CI: This kind of equality was already present in your earliest wall pieces, in which you combined text and images within a single metal frame. Those structures seem to anticipate the screen structures in your projective installations. In THE WIND or THE HOUSE (2002), we look up towards the screens, which suggest both cinematic viewing and large-scale painting. This seems to be a key to the relationship between your still images and your installations. And there was a moment where this relationship shifted, from external subjects to a more personal subject matter. In GRAY (1997), one persona recounts the effects of nuclear accident on the environment, through different voices.

EA: I made that work in 1993, when I was invited to take part in two different exhibitions, one in Stockholm and one in Moscow. I got the idea for the work one evening when I was at home. I don't remember what I was doing. The TV was on, but I wasn't really watching it. I noticed an advertisement, then I went on doing what I was doing, then after a while, I saw it again. I wasn't quite sure if it was exactly the same as before or another version of it. This made me think about the way adverts work, the special needs of a short slot, and the relationship between fiction and the advertisements. I became interested in doing a work in the space reserved for adverts on TV. The themes of both exhibitions happened to be "identity." I made three short spots of which the last one deals with national identity and culture in relation to the pervasiveness of nuclear disaster.

CI: You often use different personae to tell a story. One voice starts and another voice picks up where the other left off, until the origin of the voice becomes confused. It becomes especially ambiguous because we move back and forth between documentary and fiction. We don't know what you've written and what you've read. That fragmentation of the single voice through language seems to be an expression of the fragmented self.

EA: Using different voices, male and female, with one actor on screen, was a means of questioning the boundaries between self and other. With the work IF 6 WAS 9 (1995), I tried to use the split screen as a metaphor of the teenage girl's identity. It was the first work in which I used several projections. I planned the work when I was still living in L.A. I saw a series of billboard advertisements made of huge black-and-white photos showing models standing in a composite of several images, and you could see the cut between them. I thought the split screen suggested the idea of girls growing up.

CI: Within this approach, what does "personal" mean? You have adopted a non-personal—non-autobiographical—approach in constructing your work, but you also want us to think about the personal as a structure, as a way of creating what is around you.

EA: When an artist makes a film, people often assume that everything rises from their personal life—that the topic is autobiographical, and the events in the film have happened to the artist and are presented more or less in the way that they occurred in real life. This kind of approach eliminates the process of making the work, the distance between an idea and the finished film, everything that actually makes the work what it really is. It completely overlooks the creative process—the ways of creating meaning within the medium itself. For example, in film, emotions are created from a knowledge of the characters, the use of sounds, juxtapositions of material, rhythms of editing, etc. Also, this attitude forgets the important input of the members of the crew—the cinematographer, the sound designer, the set designer, the editor, just to mention a few.

On the other hand, I don't wish to deny the importance of the personal when making the work, in terms of my own point of view and my relationship to society. This leads me to think of how the "personal" functions in making works with moving images. Sometimes I'm asked questions like "Have you been mentally ill?" But I'd rather talk about the ways the personal can be seen in the rhythm of the work, the editing, and maybe in the way light functions as part of the story.

CI: In relation to your photographic works, in particular the constructed domestic interiors, you have talked of the doll's house, and the construction of an interior space in which the raw edges of the walls are visible—the artifice of the room, as almost a stage set, is revealed.

EA: I usually make one photographic series per year. I like to make a series, not just single pieces. In one frame, there are usually two to four images. Since I started working with moving images, it's been difficult for me to work with just one image. It feels too fixed, without time and a possibility to make an error. An error is a chance, a crack, a break of an order. I don't use film stills or the same material as in the films, but the different works can be linked thematically. After finishing the installation THE HOUSE and the film LOVE IS A TREASURE (2002), I still wanted to work with the themes of perception and giving

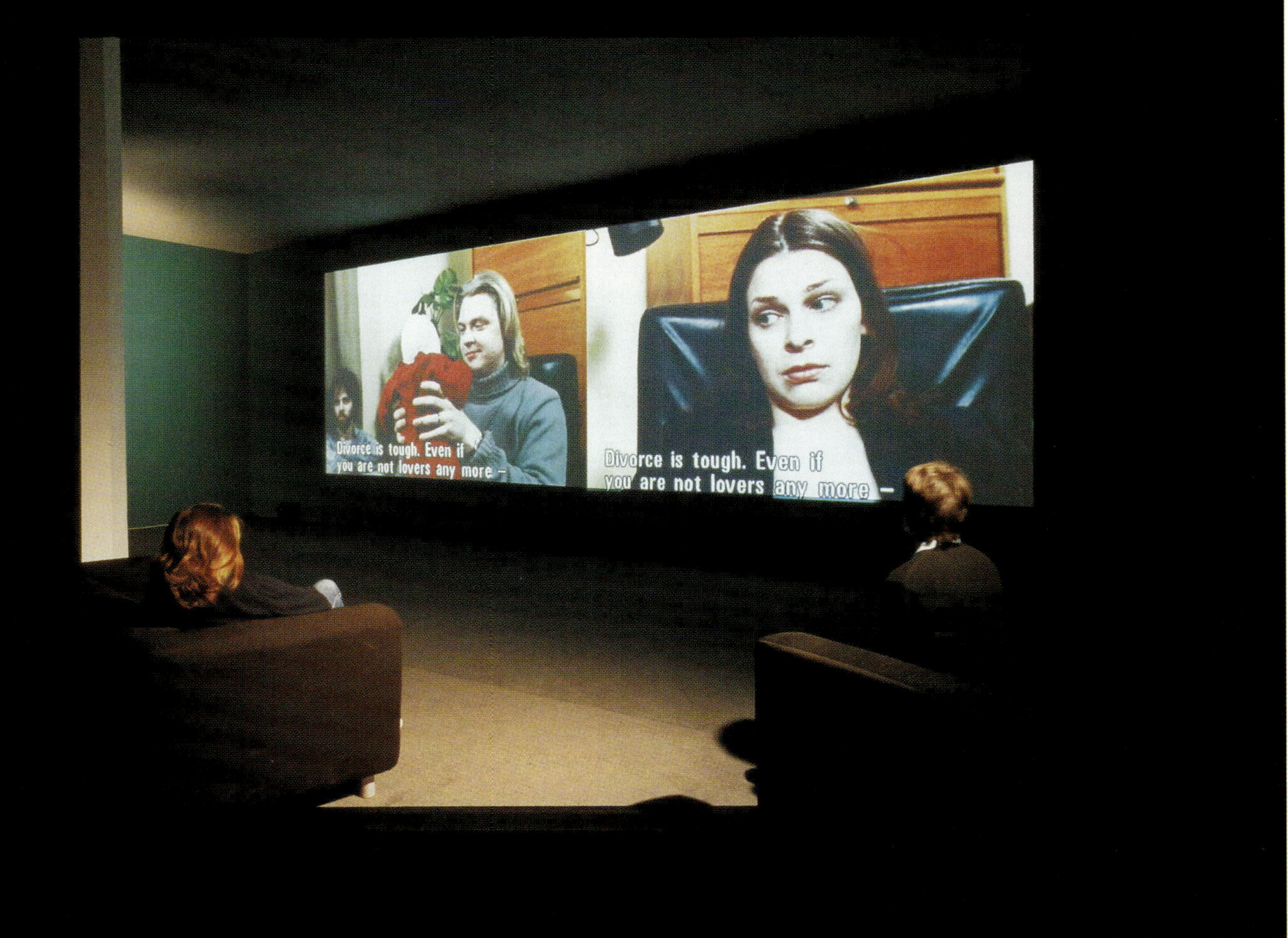

EIJA-LIISA AHTILA, CONSOLATION SERVICE, 1999, 24 min. 35-mm film, installation view / 24-minütiger 35-mm-Film, Installationsansicht.

meaning to things around you—creating a coherent world that makes sense. This is similar to what a scenographer does in her/his work; finding different places and constructing them in such a way that a believable world comes together. This is how the series SCENOGRAPHER'S MIND (2002) was named. One of the photographs includes kind of a doll's house for adults. This is something I still would like to work on, not with photographs, but in a more sculptural context.

CI: Does your fragmentation of fictional narrative into real-life action relate to Godard's techniques and philosophical thinking about cinema?

EA: I don't know how to answer that question—on one hand, he is an extremely important figure in film history, and on the other, he's one of the filmmakers, along with Bergman and Buñuel, whose films I saw a lot when I was young and without a filmmaker's point of view. One thing I remember fascinating me was the way in which the female characters turned and talked to us in the middle of the story, and I had a feeling of meeting new people, or characters, inside the film.

As I mentioned earlier, I don't usually consciously think about other films, filmmakers or different approaches when I'm working on a new film or installation; but certainly Godard is the director you need to know about if you are interested in experimenting with film and narrative. I try to see as many new films as possible that experiment with narrative; unfortunately Helsinki is nowadays not such a good place for that.

DENKEN IN FORM VON FILM

EIJA-LIISA AHTILA im Gespräch mit CHRISSIE ILES

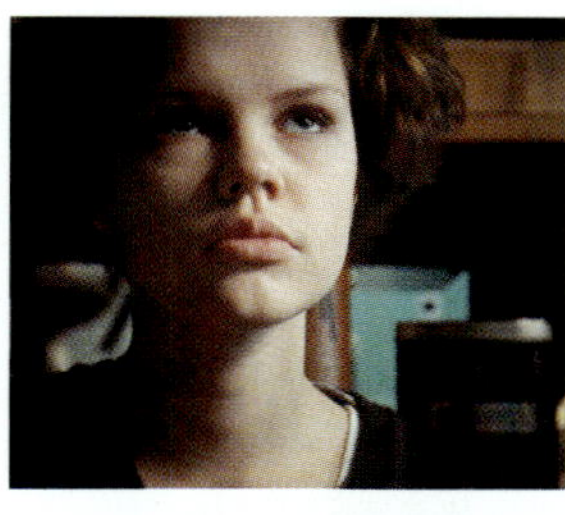

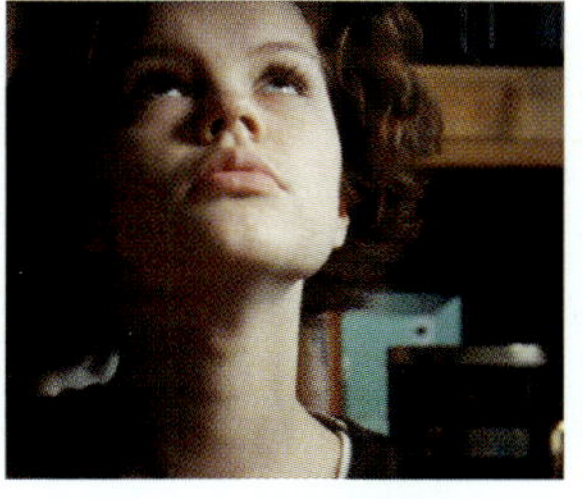

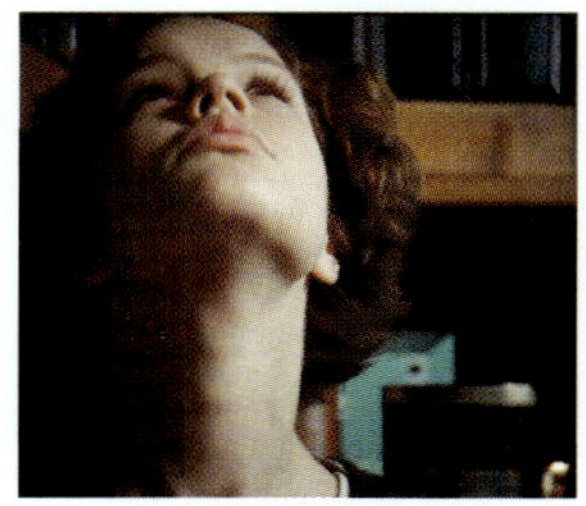

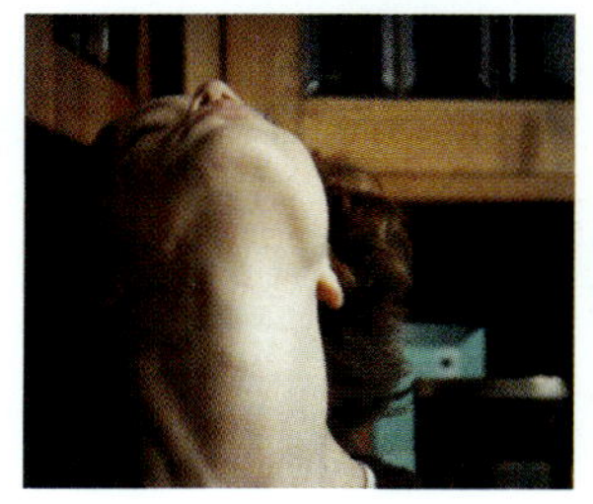

EIJA-LIISA AHTILA, IF 6 WAS 9, 1995, 35-mm film, details.

CHRISSIE ILES: Vielleicht sollten wir zunächst über einen Begriff reden, den Daniel Birnbaum im Untertitel eines Essays zu deinem Werk verwendet: *extended cinema,* erweiterter Film. Als ich mir die verschiedenen Arbeiten in der Reihenfolge ihres Entstehens anschaute, zeigte sich, dass die Grenzen zwischen Fiktion und Dokumentation, Ich und Selbstverlust sowie zwischen Standaufnahme und bewegtem Bild – alles klassische Filmthemen – von Anfang an präsent waren. Dennoch sind die «erweiterten Filme», die du gemacht hast, etwas ganz anderes als die Filme der meisten Künstlerinnen und Künstler in Europa und Skandinavien nach 1989. Du bist eine der wenigen, die das Filmemachen in Amerika und England gelernt haben, und du hast die Black Box des Kinos von Anfang an in den White Cube der Galerie integriert. Was also bedeutet «erweiterter Film» im Rahmen deiner Arbeit? Und wo liegt der Unterschied gegenüber anderen, die den Film in ihre Arbeit einbeziehen?

EIJA-LIISA AHTILA: Mein Umgang mit Film und bewegten Bildern hängt mit meinem Background zusammen. Ich habe eine Ausbildung in Malerei abgeschlossen und malte einige Jahre lang, dann begann ich mich für Photographie zu interessieren und machte Installationen mit Photos und Texten. In dieser Zeit habe ich auch kunsttheoretische Schriften gelesen und verfolgte die interna-

---

CHRISSIE ILES ist Kuratorin für Film und Video am Whitney Museum of American Art, New York.

tionalen Entwicklungen in der Kunst. 1987 nahm ich mit einigen Freunden an einem Videokurs teil und war von diesem Medium fasziniert. Ich machte einige kleine Videoarbeiten und begann Anfang der 90er Jahre Film zu studieren. Eigentlich wollte ich die bildende Kunst aufgeben, aber es kam anders: Ich blieb irgendwo zwischen den beiden Traditionen hängen.

Ich habe das Gefühl, dass ich mich, weil ich von der Malerei herkomme, vor allem dafür interessiere, wie sich etwas durch das Medium des bewegten Bildes ausdrücken lässt. Die Frage «Was ist ein bewegtes Bild?» war mir wichtiger als jene, ob Kino, bildende Kunst oder neue Medien den Kontext bildeten. Während der konkreten Arbeit wird das «was» häufig zum «wie». Wie lässt sich Traurigkeit in Bildern ausdrücken? Kann man ein Gefühl ohne sein Gegenteil zum Ausdruck bringen? Wie hängt Verstehen mit Zeit zusammen, und welche Rolle spielt die Kausalität bei Installationen? Das Schaffen von Filmen und Installationen wurde zu einer Frage des Erkennens der Verbindungen zwischen Bildern, Tönen, Rhythmen, Licht, Charakteren und Worten sowie deren Einsatz bei der Gestaltung und Konstruktion der Geschichte. Ich glaube, mein Vorgehen ist immer noch das einer Künstlerin.

CI: Während deiner Ausbildung musst du mit der Geschichte und Theorie des Films in Berührung gekommen sein, und dann kommst du ja auch aus dem starken Kontext des finnischen Kinos.

EA: Weil ich schon relativ alt war, als ich von der Kunst auf Film umzusteigen gedachte, wollte ich meine Zeit nicht mit technischen Kursen verschwenden, etwa, «Wie arbeitet man mit einer Kamera?» Stattdessen hatte ich das Gefühl, mich auf die verschiedenen Ausdrucksmöglichkeiten in diesem Medium konzentrieren zu müssen, also belegte ich Kurse in Filmschnitt und Kinematographie und lernte einiges über die verschiedenen Entscheidungen, die Filmemacher getroffen hatten, um die jeweils gewünschten Gefühle auszudrücken. Und ich belegte auch einige Vorlesungen in Filmgeschichte und Filmtheorie.

Du hast nach meiner Verwendung von Standaufnahmen gefragt: Ich versuche solche Fragen im Zusammenhang mit dem Erzählen einer Geschichte oder der Schaffung eines Handlungsstranges zu sehen. Im Film ist das Bild normalerweise der Geschichte untergeordnet, also muss man, wenn man schneidet und von einem Bild auf ein anderes überblendet – etwa von einem Bild aus der Ferne auf eine Nahaufnahme –, mehr Informationen über Figuren oder Ereignisse gewinnen: Das ist der eigentliche Grund fürs Schneiden – Bilder sind immer...

CI: ... Handlungsträger.

EA: Genau. Die Bedeutung des Bildes ergibt sich aus der Geschichte. Ich möchte das gern anders machen und dennoch den Handlungszusammenhang aufrechterhalten. Das bewegte Bild birgt viele Möglichkeiten.

CI: Hat der Film in Finnland früh Einfluss auf dich ausgeübt?

EA: In dem Städtchen, in dem ich aufwuchs, gab es einen Filmclub, den ich besucht habe. Sie zeigten dort einen Film von Louis Malle über eine junge Frau und ihre ersten sexuellen Erfahrungen. Ich fand, er hätte eine etwas verkorkste Symbolik, aber er gefiel mir. Ich glaube, er heisst *Black Moon* (1975). Ich war dreizehn oder vierzehn; ein anderer Film, den ich dort sah, war Robert Altmans *3 Women* (1977). Und die Filme von Ingmar Bergman...

CI: War Ingmar Bergman in Finnland sehr präsent?

EA: Ja. Seine Filme liefen auch im Fernsehen.

CI: In deinen Installationen wechselst du jeweils zwischen dem dominierenden Bild und der Erzählung dahinter hin und her. Helfen die mehrteiligen Projektionsflächen dabei, vom Bild zu abstrahieren beziehungsweise es in den Vordergrund zu rücken, sowohl kompositorisch, innerhalb des vorgegebenen Rahmens, als auch beim konkreten Aufbauen der Arbeiten? Was ist der Unterschied zwischen der linearen Betrachtung deiner Filme in einem Kino und ihrer Betrachtung im Rahmen einer Installation in einer Galerie, wo sich die Geschichte auf mehreren Leinwänden auch räumlich entwickelt?

EA: Eine Installation mit drei Projektionsflächen verleiht dem Bild viel mehr Nachdruck und ermöglicht weit mehr Experimente. Aber wir reden noch immer über das bewegte Bild und das Geschichten Erzählen – eine Geschichte in bewegten Bildern scheint dieses unerhörte Potenzial zu haben, alles zusammenzuschweissen. Beim Ton geht es immer um Räume und Distanzen, aber zwei Bilder, die nah beieinander sind, verbinden sich immer miteinander. Das ist natürlich eine Frage der Wahrnehmung und ich denke auch über die Regeln nach, die wir anwenden, um eine Geschichte zu erzeugen. Nehmen wir zum Beispiel CONSOLATION SERVICE (Trostservice), eine Arbeit, die für Venedig entstanden ist («End of Story», 49. Biennale Venedig, 1999, Skandinavischer Pavillon). Darin wollte ich den Unterschied des Erzählens einer Geschichte in einem beziehungsweise in zwei Bildern untersuchen: Im Kino soll der Betrachter möglichst gut platziert sein, damit er sieht, was sich linear auf der einzigen Leinwand abspielt. Alles ist darauf ausgerichtet, von der Position des Mikrophons am Drehort bis zum Zusammenschnitt der verschiedenen Szenen. Bei einer Installation mit mehreren Projektionsflächen kann man die Geschichte nicht auf einmal aufnehmen, da sich verschiedene Dinge gleichzeitig im Raum ereignen. Mehrere Leinwände erlauben zum Beispiel auch, die Aufnahme der Aktion und jene der Reaktion gleichzeitig zu zeigen. Also muss der Betrachter eine Wahl treffen. In Kiasma war gleichzeitig mit dem Film CONSOLATION SERVICE auch die Installationsversion zu sehen. Einige Leute, mit denen ich gesprochen habe, erlebten die Installation als realistischer, man konnte keine Partei ergreifen: Der Standpunkt der Frau in der Geschichte hatte nicht mehr Gewicht, als jener der anderen Figuren. Im Film kam deutlich zum Ausdruck, dass die Hauptfigur die Geschichte bestimmte.

CI: Hattest du dies beabsichtigt oder war das eine Überraschung?

EA: Nein, ich war nicht darauf aus. Deshalb freute ich mich über diese Kommentare. Mein Ziel war es, verschiedene Arten des Erzählens einer Geschichte zu untersuchen – tatsächlich ist das Teil meiner Dissertation an der Kunstakademie in Helsinki. Mit zwei Projektionsflächen kann man das Erleben des Betrachters weniger genau kanalisieren als mit einer.

CI: In CONSOLATION SERVICE durften die Besucher nur zu Beginn des Films eintreten. Warum hast du bei dieser Arbeit darauf bestanden, bei anderen dagegen nicht?

EA: Als ich diese Geschichte schrieb, ging es mir darum, zu untersuchen, wie man von einem Gefühl zu einem anderen gelangt – wie diese Art des Werkaufbaus in einer Installation funktioniert. Und nachdem ich die fertige Arbeit gesehen hatte, fand ich, man müsse die Ereignisse und die Charaktere zuerst kennen lernen, um sie zu verstehen. Man muss zuerst mit ihnen zusammen sein, damit man emotional reagieren kann, wenn sie, zum Beispiel, durchs Eis fallen oder wenn der Mann auftaucht und verschwindet. Diese Dinge hängen mit der besonderen Struktur dieser Geschichte zusammen.

CI: Fragmentierung ist in deinen Arbeiten eine Metapher für psychische Störungen, für das Streifen der Grenze zur Psychose, insbesondere wo es Frauen betrifft. Auf einer einzigen Leinwand sind diese Grenzen ganz anders dargestellt als in einer Installation wie ANNE, AKI AND GOD (1998), wo der Zusammenbruch des Wissens darum, wo die Realität endet und die Phantasie beginnt, ausformuliert wird. Akis Bett und die Projektionsfläche darüber verkörpern – entsprechend Roland Barthes' Beschreibung des Kinos – quasi das Ins-Bett-Schlüpfen-und-Träumen.

EA: ANNE, AKI AND GOD beruht auf einer wahren Geschichte, die einem jungen Burschen in Helsinki widerfuhr. Ein Freund erzählte mir von der aussergewöhnlichen psychotischen Erfahrung dieses Menschen und wir beschlossen, dass er ein Interview mit Aki machen würde. Das tat er und die Tonaufzeichnungen wurden transkribiert. Die Installation beruht auf diesem Material. Weil diese Erfahrung nur in seiner Phantasie existierte, dachte ich, es wäre schön, sie konkret werden zu lassen. In der Geschichte erschien Gott auf der Leinwand über seinem Bett und sagte: «Aki, du hast eine Freundin, Anne. Schau dich um, hier ist es so schmutzig, du musst sauber machen. Anne kann nicht hierher kommen.» So begann die Psychose. Und weil es Anne nur in Akis Träumen gab, wollte ich, dass sie gegenwärtig wäre – für jedermann sichtbar. Also schrieb ich die Rolle aus, brachte die Beschreibung des Jobs zur Arbeitsvermittlung, worauf sich vierzehn Frauen meldeten. Sieben der Kurzinterviews mit ihnen sieht man auf einer anderen Leinwand, um den Entstehungsprozess des Filmes sichtbarer zu machen.

CI: Ist das die Arbeit, in der dieser Entstehungsprozess am deutlichsten sichtbar wird? Der Kontrast zwischen Fiktion und Realität ist hier sehr scharf, weil die Realität der Interviews mit den Schauspielerinnen so stark mit Akis Phantasien kontrastieren. Es erinnert mich ans Brechtsche Theater, in dem die Techniken des Theatermachens offen demonstriert werden.

EA: Wenn der Schauspieler sich plötzlich direkt ans Publikum wendet...

CI: ... und die Illusion zerstört wird.

EA: Seit Brecht und Godard und einigen endlosen Fernsehabenden habe ich das Gefühl, dass Illusion zu einem Material geworden ist, mit dem man arbeiten muss. Oft ist es interessanter, über Illusionen nachzudenken als sie zu erzeugen.

CI: Deine Art des Durchbrechens der Illusion könnte man in Beziehung zu konzeptuellen Taktiken der 60er Jahre setzen und sagen, dass du sie in einem narrativen filmischen Rahmen weiterentwickelt hast. Auch die Schauspielerei setzt du in diesem Sinn ein.

EA: Ich habe das nie mit meiner Arbeit in Zusammenhang gebracht, aber es ist schon komisch, dass viele meiner Freunde Theater machen. Ich erinnere mich, dass mir Meyerholds Ideen als Studentin gefallen haben.

CI: Auch in deiner Prägung durch den finnischen Film, der oft halb dokumentarisch und sozial ausgerichtet ist, steckt ein Brechtsches Element. In deinen Arbeiten begegnen wir jungen Männern und Frauen, Teenagern und älteren Frauen, alle mit vielfältigen Problemen. Wir können uns mit ihnen identifizieren, weil sie nicht romantisiert dargestellt sind.

EA: Ich will, dass meine Figuren aufrichtig, aber dennoch poetisch sind.

CI: Sie haben auch etwas Surreales.

EA: Vielleicht ist das wegen dieser Kombination, von der ich sprach. Alle Geschichten und Figuren sind fiktiv, beruhen aber auf Recherchen. Wenn ich über eine Arbeit nachzudenken beginne, weiss ich gern Bescheid über die Fakten – ich muss wissen, dass es hätte passieren können und dass es glaubhaft ist. Und natürlich verleiht einem erst das durch Recherchen gewonnene Wissen die Freiheit, Dinge zu erfinden.

CI: Ein Aspekt deiner Arbeiten erinnert mich an den melodramatischen Hollywoodfilm mit seinen überspitzten psychischen Angstzuständen.

EA: Ich mag Robert Altman, Rainer Werner Fassbinder und John Cassavetes, um nur einige zu nennen, aber für meinen Arbeitsprozess sind die Bücher, die ich gelesen habe, jeweils wichtiger.

CI: Du bist mehr von der Literatur beeinflusst als vom Film?

EA: Das kommt darauf an. Wenn ich eine Arbeit vorbereite, mir Notizen mache und das Drehbuch schreibe, ist Text das Material, mit dem ich kommunikativ in Verbindung stehe. Zum Beispiel steht in einem Buch, das ich gestern gekauft habe, ein Absatz mit einer einfachen Beschreibung eines klingelnden Telefons an der Wand. Das brachte mich auf eine Idee für einen Szenenwechsel. Im Buch war das nicht wichtig, aber es brachte mich auf eine Idee, die in die Atmosphäre dieser Szene passt. Ich lese gern Paul Bowles, Ian McEwan, Patrick McGrath, Don DeLillo. Momentan lese ich die Kurzgeschichten von Virginia Woolf. Meistens lese ich auch Dinge zum Thema, an dem ich gerade arbeite.

CI: In deinen neueren Arbeiten verstärkt jeweils das Intime einer häuslichen Umgebung das Klaustrophobische des verdunkelten Raums und bereitet das Feld für die emotionale Intensität, die zum Ausdruck gebracht werden soll. In THE WIND (2002) wird die Konstruktion des Raumes im Film sowohl materiell wie psychisch durch den physischen Raum vermittelt: Die Wände und Vorhänge rücken zusammen, die Bücherwände kippen um.

EA: Ich behandle die verschiedenen Elemente bewegter Bilder gern gleichwertig und arbeite mit Ton, Farben und Licht, statt die Informationen nur über den Dialog zu vermitteln. Aber ich mag Worte...

CI: Diese Gleichwertigkeit gab es schon in deinen ersten Wandarbeiten, in denen du Text und Bilder in ein und demselben Metallrahmen kombiniert hast. Jene Strukturen scheinen die Organisation der Projektionsflächen in deinen Installationen vorwegzunehmen. In THE WIND oder THE HOUSE (2002) schauen wir zu Leinwänden hinauf, was uns sowohl ans Kino erinnert wie an grossflächige Malerei. Das scheint ein Hinweis auf das Verhältnis zwischen deinen Standaufnahmen und Installationen zu sein. Und es gab einen Moment, in dem sich diese Beziehung von äusseren Gegenständen auf eine persönlicher gefärbte Thematik verlagerte, nämlich

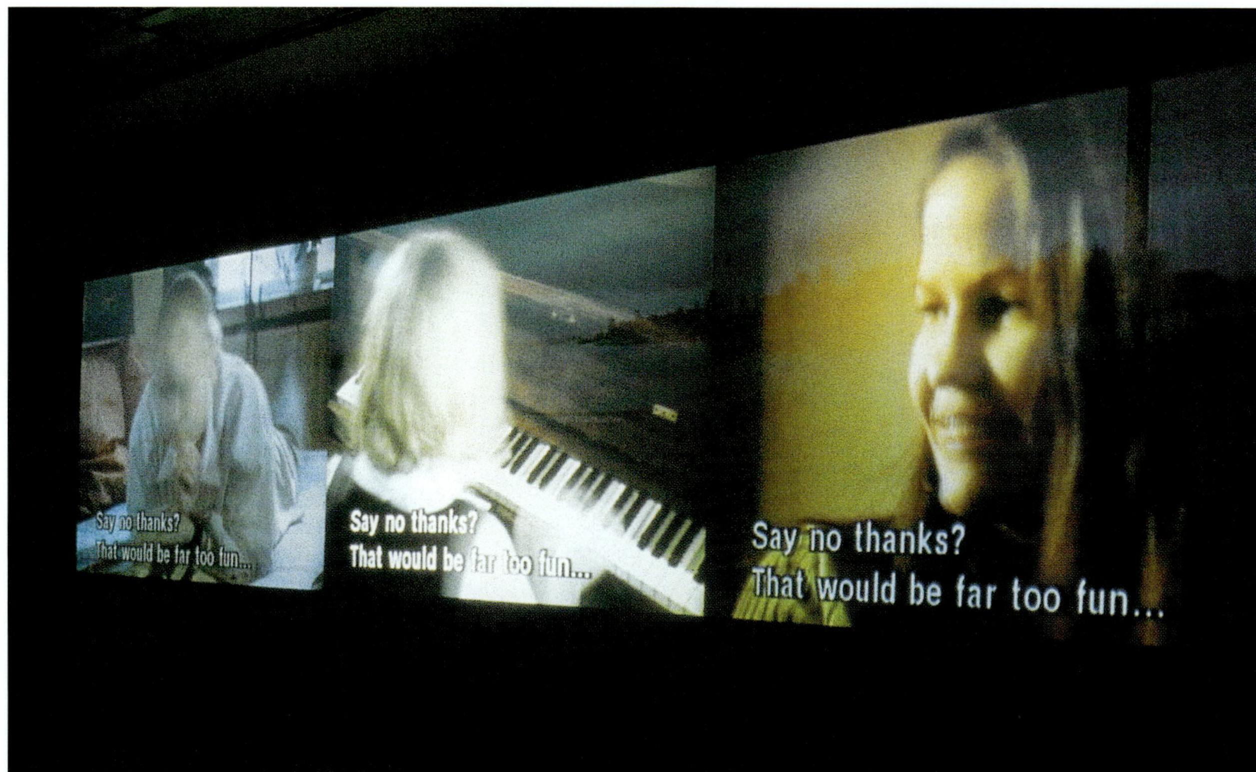

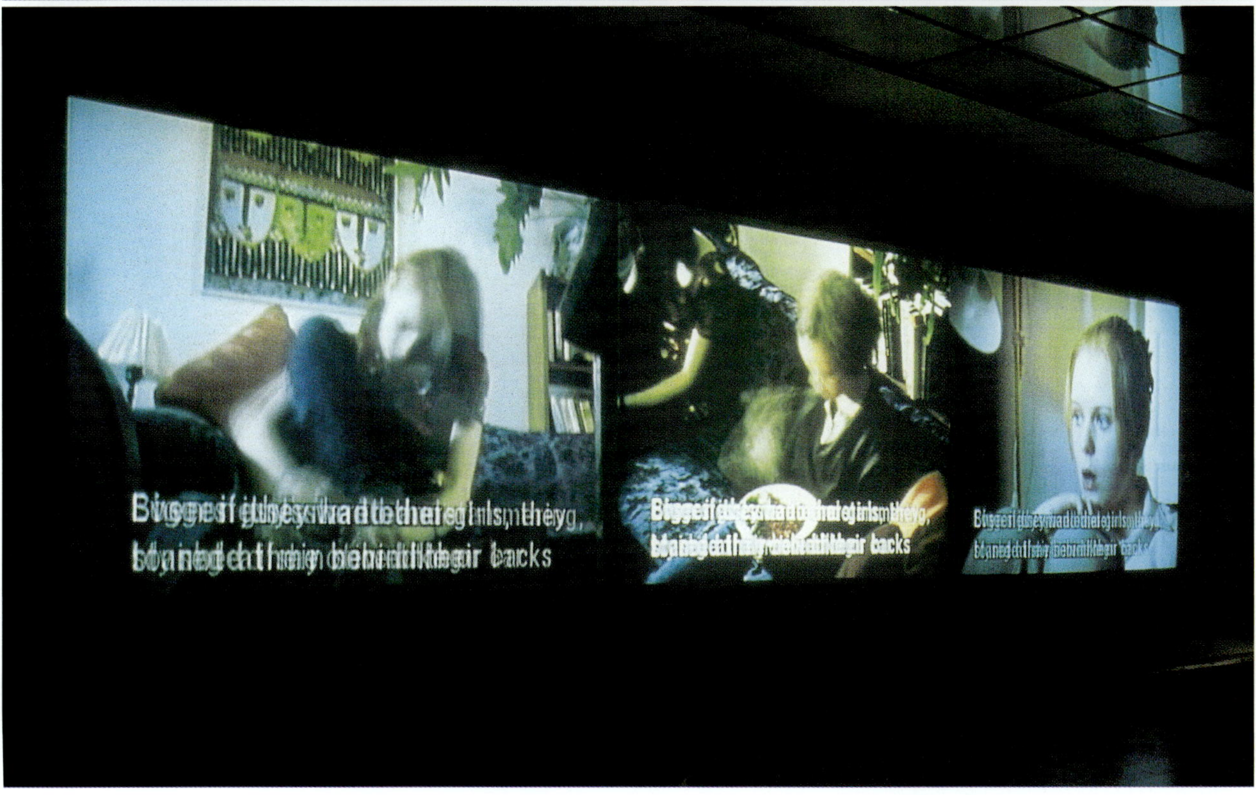

EIJA-LIISA AHTILA, IF 6 WAS 9, 1995, 10 min. 35-mm film and DVD installation for 3 projections with sound / 35-mm-Film- und DVD-Installation für 3 Projektionen mit Ton, Dauer: 10 Min.

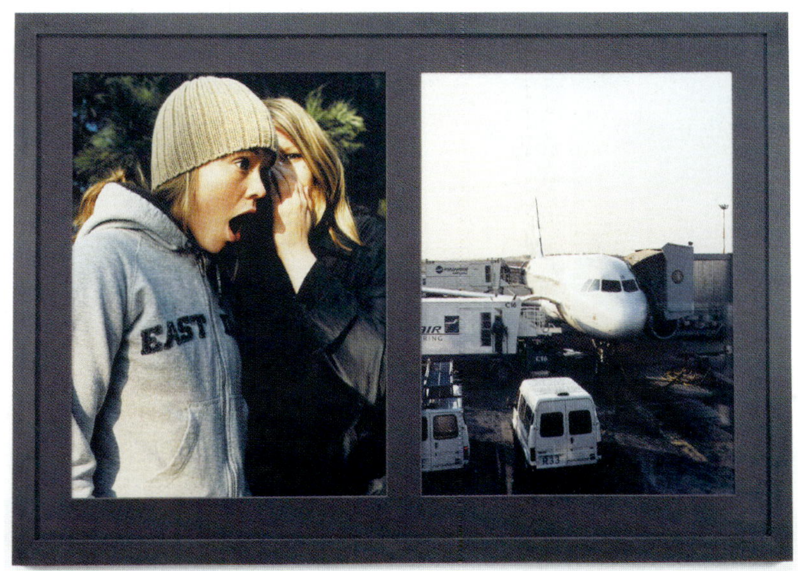

EIJA-LIISA AHTILA, SCENOGRAPHER'S MIND V, 2002, 2 color prints, set with hand-colored mat and frame, 42 1/8 x 66 15/16" / 2 Farbprints, Set mit handkoloriertem Passepartout und Rahmen, 107 x 170 cm.

in GRAY (1993), wo eine Person mit verschiedenen Stimmen die Wirkungen eines nuklearen Unfalls auf die Umwelt beschreibt.

EA: Ich habe diese Arbeit 1993 gemacht, als ich zu zwei verschiedenen Ausstellungen eingeladen war, eine in Stockholm, die andere in Moskau. Die Idee dazu kam mir eines Abends, als ich zu Hause mit irgendwas beschäftigt war, ich weiss nicht mehr was. Der Fernseher lief, aber ich schaute nicht wirklich fern. Ein Werbespot fiel mir auf, dann fuhr ich fort zu tun, was ich gerade tat, und etwas später sah ich dieselbe Werbung wieder. Ich war mir nicht ganz sicher, ob es wirklich derselbe Spot war oder eine leicht veränderte Version. Das brachte mich dazu, darüber nachzudenken, wie Werbung funktioniert, über die besonderen Bedürfnisse der kurzen Sendezeit und die Beziehung zwischen Fernsehfilmen und Werbesendungen. Ich interessierte mich dafür, eine Arbeit für dieses, der Werbung vorbehaltene Zeitfenster im Fernsehen zu machen. Das Thema beider Ausstellungen war zufällig «Identität». Ich machte drei kurze Spots, von denen der letzte sich mit nationaler Identität und Kultur im Hinblick auf das Grenzüberschreitende der nuklearen Katastrophe auseinander setzt.

CI: Du lässt eine Geschichte oft von verschiedenen Personen erzählen. Eine Stimme beginnt, eine andere fährt dort weiter, wo die erste aufhört, bis schliesslich unklar wird, woher die Stimme überhaupt kommt. Besonders undeutlich wird es, weil wir uns zwischen Dokumentation und Fiktion hin und her bewegen. Wir wissen nicht, was du geschrieben und was du gelesen hast. Diese Fragmentierung der einzelnen Stimme beim Sprechen scheint Ausdruck des zersplitterten Selbst zu sein.

EA: Die Verwendung verschiedener männlicher und weiblicher Stimmen mit nur einem Schauspieler auf der Leinwand war ein Weg, die Grenzen zwischen dem Selbst und dem Anderen auszuloten. In IF 6 WAS 9 (1995) versuchte ich die geteilte Leinwand als Metapher für die Identität des weiblichen Teenagers zu benützen. Das war das erste Mal, dass ich mit mehrfachen Projektionen arbeitete. Die Vorbereitungen dazu hatte ich noch in Los Angeles begonnen. Ich hatte dort eine Reihe von Werbeplakatwänden gesehen, die aus riesigen Schwarzweissphotos von Models bestanden, die in einem aus mehreren Bildern zusammenmontierten Bild standen, wobei der Schnitt zwischen den verschiedenen Bildteilen deutlich zu sehen war. Ich dachte mir, die gespaltene Leinwand deute auf das Erwachsenwerden von Mädchen.

CI: Was heisst «persönlich» in diesem Zusammenhang? Du pflegst nicht persönlich – nicht autobiographisch – an deine Arbeiten heranzugehen, aber

gleichzeitig willst du, dass wir über das Persönliche als Struktur, als Methode, das zu erschaffen, was um uns herum ist, nachdenken.
EA: Wenn ein Künstler einen Film macht, nehmen die Leute oft an, dass alles aus seinem Privatleben heraus entstehe, das heisst, dass das Thema autobiographisch sei und dass die Ereignisse im Film dem Künstler selbst widerfahren sind und mehr oder weniger so präsentiert werden, wie sie im wirklichen Leben stattgefunden haben. Diese Annahme übersieht den Entstehungsprozess des Werkes, die Distanz zwischen der ersten Idee und dem fertigen Film, also alles, was das Werk schliesslich zu dem macht, was es wirklich ist. Sie vernachlässigt den ganzen kreativen Prozess – die verschiedenen Arten in diesem spezifischen Medium Bedeutung zu erzeugen. Im Film, zum Beispiel, werden Gefühle erzeugt durch die Vertrautheit mit den Charakteren, die Verwendung von Tönen, die Gegenüberstellung von Materialien, den Rhythmus des Schnitts usw. Diese Auffassung vergisst auch völlig den wichtigen Beitrag anderer Mitarbeiter – des Kameramannes, des Tontechnikers, des Bühnenbildners, des Cutters, um nur einige zu nennen.

Andrerseits will ich die Bedeutung des Persönlichen bei der Entstehung eines Werks nicht leugnen, insofern es um meinen eigenen Standpunkt und mein Verhältnis zur Gesellschaft geht. Das wiederum lässt mich darüber nachdenken, wie das «Persönliche» bei der Arbeit mit bewegten Bildern funktioniert. Wenn man mir Fragen stellt wie: «Waren Sie selbst geisteskrank?», möchte ich in der Regel lieber darüber diskutieren, wie das Persönliche im Rhythmus des Werks, in der Montage zum Ausdruck kommt, und vielleicht darin, wie das Licht als Teil der Geschichte funktioniert.
CI: Im Zusammenhang mit deinem photographischen Werk, insbesondere den konstruierten privaten Innenräumen, hast du vom Puppenhaus gesprochen und von der Konstruktion eines Innenraumes, in dem die rohen Enden der Wände sichtbar sind und das Künstliche des Raums fast wie eine Bühnenkulisse freigelegt wird.
EA: Gewöhnlich mache ich jährlich eine Photoserie. Ich mache lieber Serien als Einzelbilder. In einem Rahmen sind meist zwei bis vier Bilder. Seit ich mit bewegten Bildern zu arbeiten begonnen habe, fällt es mir schwer, mit nur einem Bild zu arbeiten. Es ist mir zu starr, so ganz ohne Zeitfaktor und ohne die Möglichkeit Fehler zu machen. Ein Fehler ist eine Chance, ein Riss, ein Bruch in der Ordnung. Ich verwende keine Filmstills und auch nicht dasselbe Material wie in den Filmen, aber die verschiedenen Arbeiten sind manchmal thematisch miteinander verbunden. Nach Beendigung der Installation THE HOUSE und des Films LOVE IS A TREASURE (2002) wollte ich weiterarbeiten an den Themen «Wahrnehmung» und «den Dingen um sich herum eine Bedeutung geben, um eine zusammenhängende sinnvolle Welt zu erzeugen». Das gleicht der Arbeit eines Bühnenbildners: verschiedene Orte finden und sie so miteinander verbinden, dass eine glaubwürdige Welt entsteht. So kam die Serie SCENOGRAPHER'S MIND (Bühnenbildnerdenken, 2002) zu ihrem Titel. In einer der Photographien findet sich eine Art Puppenhaus für Erwachsene. Daran möchte ich noch weiterarbeiten, nicht mit Photos, sondern in einem eher skulpturalen Kontext.
CI: Nimmst du in deiner Fragmentierung fiktiver Erzählstränge durch reale Handlungen Bezug auf Godards Techniken und seine Filmphilosophie?
EA: Ich weiss nicht, was ich darauf antworten soll. Einerseits ist er eine extrem wichtige Figur der Filmgeschichte und andrerseits gehört er – mit Bergman und Buñuel – zu jenen Filmemachern, deren Filme ich sehr jung, sehr oft und ohne jedes Wissen ums Filmemachen gesehen habe. Etwas, woran ich mich erinnere, ist, dass ich fasziniert war von der Art, wie die weiblichen Figuren sich mitten im Film umdrehten und sich direkt an uns wandten, und ich hatte das Gefühl im Film neue Leute oder Charaktere kennen zu lernen.

Wie ich schon sagte, mache ich mir gewöhnlich keine Gedanken über andere Filme, Filmemacher oder Vorgehensweisen, wenn ich selbst an einem neuen Film oder an einer Installation arbeite; aber natürlich ist Godard der Regisseur, den man in erster Linie kennen muss, wenn man sich für filmische und narrative Experimente interessiert. Ich versuche mir so viele neue Filme wie möglich anzusehen, die mit den narrativen Strukturen experimentieren; leider ist Helsinki dafür momentan nicht der ideale Ort.

(Übersetzung: Suzanne Schmidt)

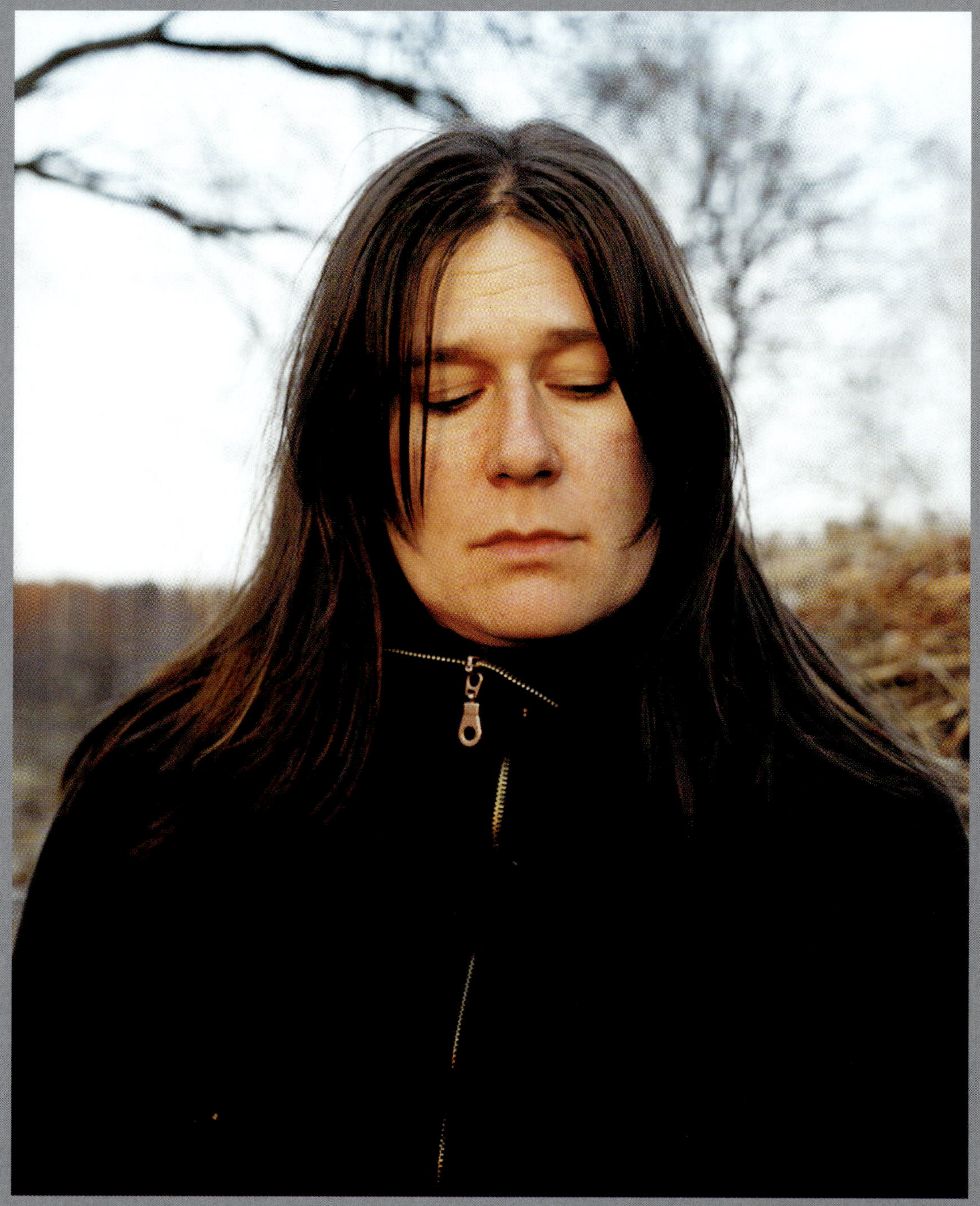

EIJA-LIISA AHTILA, SCENOGPAPHER'S MIND III, 2002, 2 color prints, set with hand-colored mat and frame 42 1/8 x 66 15/16" / 2 Farbprints, Set mit handkoloriertem Passepartout und Rahmen, 107 x 170 cm.

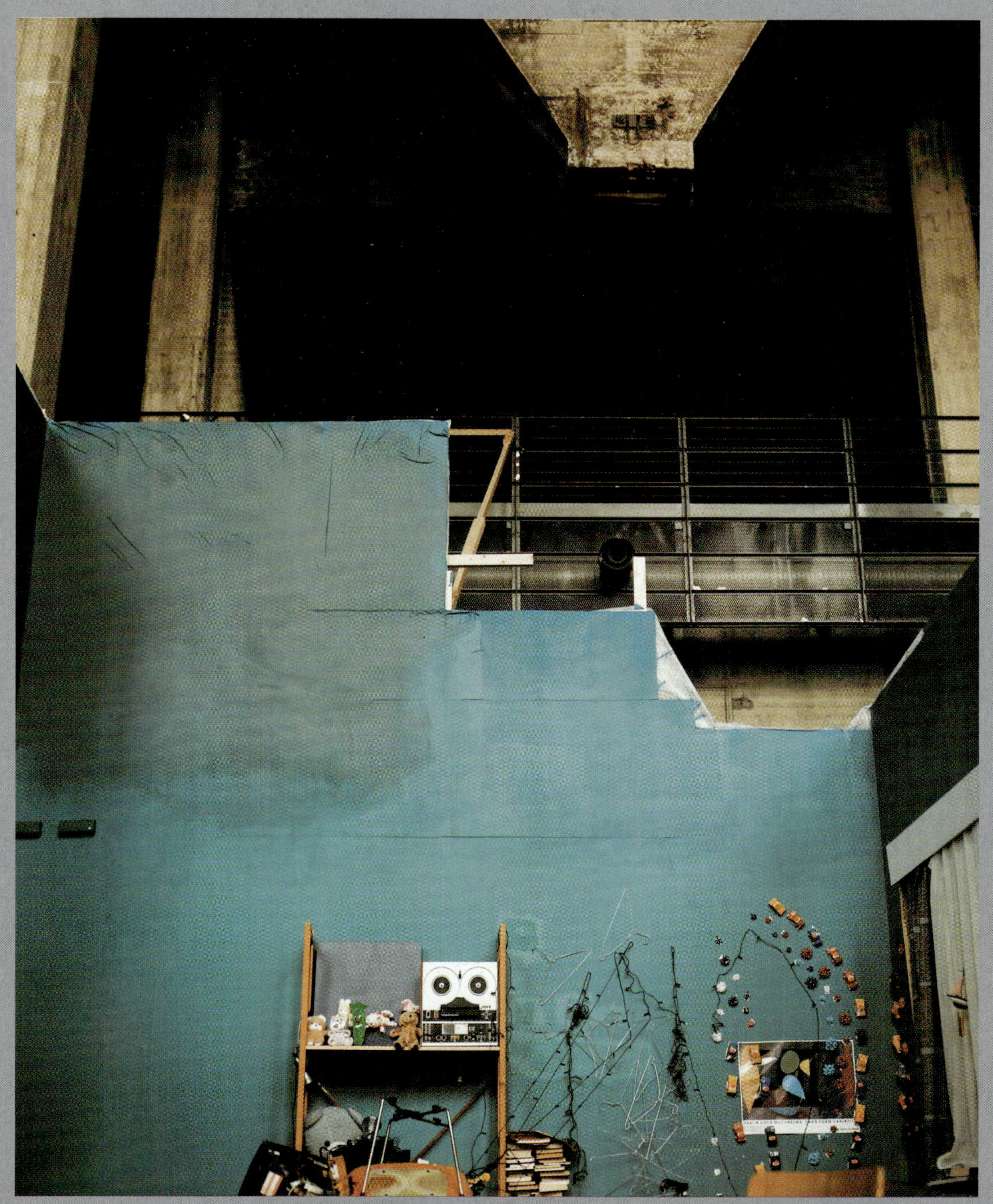

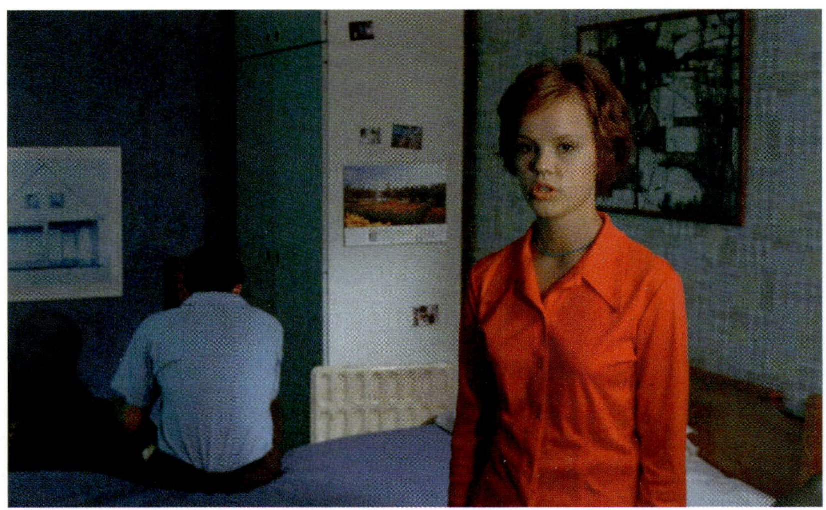

Seeing Red

... a little detail that starts to swell and carries you off ...
– Gilles Deleuze & Félix Guattari [1)]

TARU ELFVING

The baby girl in red.

Lucia embodies a border between her parents, simultaneously separating and binding them inseparably together. She is a silent witness of her parents' divorce in Eija-Liisa Ahtila's CONSOLATION SERVICE (1999). Irreducible to, yet indistinguishable from them, she is a site where all clear distinctions collapse. Baby girl, whose name refers to purity, in a bright red jumpsuit. What does the redness matter?

Red garments seem to be haunting my attempts to write about Ahtila's video installation works. It may be too late for exorcism. So I give up and write about, with, and in red. Instead of asking what is veiled by red, I wonder what this veiling does. Maybe it actually unveils knots of relations and connections, where linear coordinates collapse.

The girl in a red shirt.

In TODAY (1996–1997) a girl hovers awkwardly on the thresholds of inhabited spaces, and on the surface of the image. When she steps into her father's bedroom for a moment their two realities seem to be enfolded together, but with a tangible spatio-temporal distance between the girl and her convulsively crying father. She speaks to me, the viewer, reaching out of her father's reality, as a narrator in his tragedy.

TARU ELFVING is a Finnish writer, curator, and researcher in Visual Culture, Goldsmiths College, University of London, London, UK.

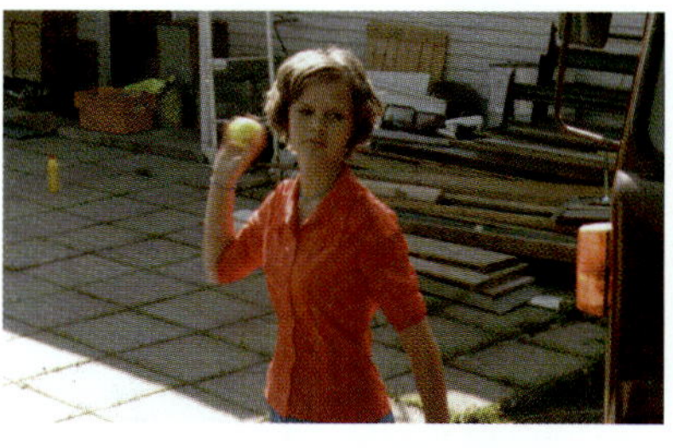

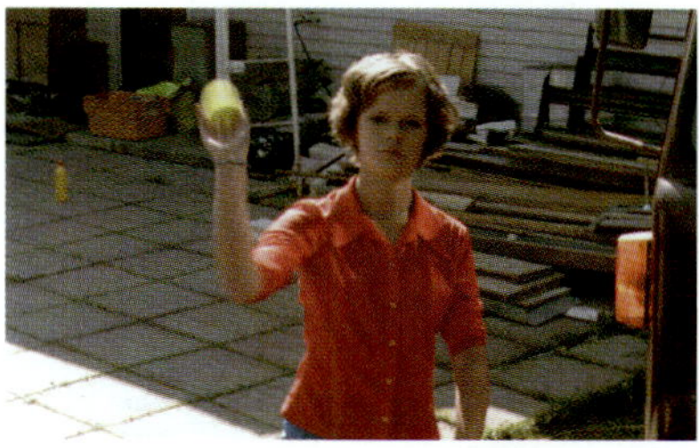

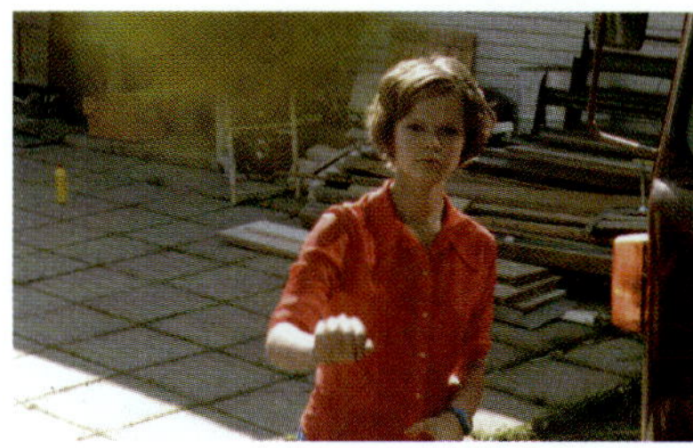

EIJA-LIISA AHTILA, TODAY, 1996–97, stills from 10 min. 35-mm film / Stills aus dem 10-minütigen 35-mm-Film.

Vera's faded redness.

From the girl's closing screen, my gaze glides to Vera's, who in my view is the girl in mature age. Her room is flooded with a sensuous red glow, but her shirt does not stand out anymore. The redness of the girl's shirt has spread to her surroundings. The boundary between Vera and her space has blurred, whereas before she inhabited the borders of the space(s). Is Vera's case just another example of the impossibility of a unified, stable subjectivity? Coherent identity demands a position with a sovereign perspective to the surrounding space, where one then appears as an object for others.[2] This can, however, never be fully secured. The subject is always entwined with the occupied space in a constant process of negotiation.

Elisa's red shirt.

THE HOUSE (2002) explores women's experiences of psychosis; the relation between subject and space is investigated with an intense attention to collapsing boundaries. Elisa inhabits her house surrounded by various red details, as another red spot in the interior. Her body does not seem to offer a rooted point from which to map one's position in relation to the surroundings. First just sounds from other places, such as her car and an unknown boat, but towards the end other people also take over her embodied being: "I meet people. One at a time they step inside me and live inside me."

All coordinates have become muddled. She is not just part of space, but a layered site, where all places collapse into one. The establishment of one's location in space is disrupted when the self and body fail to interlock.[3] Is this Elisa's fate? The prioritization of mind over matter presents a model of identity as a self-contained unity, where the body is a passive container for interior depth. But as Luce Irigaray amongst others claims, a female subject cannot take her own place, because her being is marked as a place, matter, for others.[4] Maybe Elisa is revealing the absurdity of this position, and resisting it?

Iines in a red polo neck.

Iines in THE PRESENT (2002) crawls with determination over a bridge, dragging her red bag along. When safely above solid ground again, she stands up, straightens her clothes and walks on. Defying expectations she proclaims: "I realized that I looked mad. That that's where the madness is. Or is it just me? I don't know. Still, they let me do what I have to do."

Their symptoms refer to possession. Elisa is possessed by the world around her, Iines by some inexplicable inner necessity. Are they comparable to the female figures in horror films, who often appear as battlegrounds where boundaries are challenged and reinforced again with renewed vigor? Are their bodies possessed, open vessels or tools for someone else's self-expression? On the contrary, they seem to challenge the whole notion of possession, refusing to accept the role of passive receptacle and victim.

The possession story tends to be driven by a desire to make the female body speak and leak evidence of its difference that escapes from vision. The similarities between occult horror stories and psychological dramas, exorcism and talking cure, are notable here.[5] Both possession and madness seem to thus depend on visibility and bodily signs. But if the border between sanity and insanity is crossed in the visible, what remains in the invisible? When Iines consciously chooses to act in a manner that appears mad, what do we actually see? What can I then do with my evidence, the red signs that do not seep from a hidden interior?

Another girl in a red top.

IF 6 WAS 9 (1995) plays with a charged symbol of femininity, the hole, a break in the wholeness of normative subjectivity. The repetition of passages and gaps underlines their ambiguity within structures based on strictly separate public and private, inside and outside. The girls actively look and speak this imagery of in-betweens. In the end, a girl in a red top recalls an article listing places around the city where people have sex. She had cut out and shared the images of these sites with the other girls, occupying symbolically the sexualized public sphere. The signification of female embodied subjectivity as open and penetrable is spatialized in the imag(in)ed topography of the city. The three holes of the female body, which the girl factually refers to, are multiplied into an endless flow of thresholds, creating further openings for me to bridge.

Seeing red.

Elisa leaps further over the borders of the visible. She occupies her house according to learned patterns. In a similar manner, she describes her surroundings and the events unfolding both around her and in her mind. In vain, she tries to interpret the world and her place in it by mapping the visual. Therefore, she decides to ward off the confusion by eliminating the field of vision, as this is where the blurring boundaries cause most trouble. Elisa darkens her house and retreats into the alternative space(s) where the voices are, where border crossing and simultaneity may be allowed.

As a viewer, I am denied a coherent point of view in Ahtila's installations. In THE HOUSE, I look through Elisa's eyes in one image, at her in another, and from her side in a third. She escapes my gaze, and then suddenly becomes two. At times, her voice breaks free from her image. I join Elisa in a frustrated struggle to grasp a singular, solid perspective on the surrounding space. Or am I the only anxious one here? Am I projecting my frustration on to Elisa, unable to adapt to the changes as serenely as she does?

Thinking red.

Normative subjectivity is disrupted in various ways in Ahtila's works, but unlike the possessed female characters in horror films, her figures are not forced through exorcism. There are no demands to re-stabilize them, or to make their bodies speak truths. Their speech is not talking cure, neither compulsive confession nor hysterical vomiting.

Many of Ahtila's characters seem to inhabit the borders of language. They speak to me, like narrators reading a memorized script, occupying a threshold between our space-time and theirs. The lack of expression makes their words strange, as if they were speaking a foreign language, although completely fluently. Maybe they are thinking aloud, inhabiting the hazy area between the structures of language and the free flow of thought. Ambiguities merge harmoniously within the factual statements. Speech keeps detaching itself from the speakers. When the girls in IF 6 WAS 9 interact with each other, I cannot hear their voices at all. Who is talking to whom, and what about? Instead of clear messages, the words deliver further layers and fragments for me to get lost amongst. Like the narrator in CONSOLATION SERVICE, "I am standing in the middle of characters' lines."

Do ghosts wear red?

Are these women haunted? Or are they the ones who haunt? Like ghosts, they do not respect set divisions and structures, but fly effortlessly over all borders. They appear in formless form, invisible visibility, immaterial materiality. Like Jacques Derrida's specter, they are always more than one, and no more one.[6] They share their unbounded and ungrounded perspective with me to some extent, but slip from my grasp time after time. My vision begins to stumble. They seem to be asking whether we have to fight against the loss of clear boundaries. Instead of embodying borderline states, the characters mobilize points of ambiguity and the border zone itself, unsettling the distinctions it is supposed to guarantee. They question how normality can be distinguished from the pathological, self from its other. Are we not all borderline cases of some kind?

My red shirts.

To possess a specter means to be possessed by it, claims Derrida.[7] Am I haunted, or becoming a ghost myself? I am repeatedly caught wearing red shirts when speaking about Ahtila's work. In my attempts to get to grips with the characters, I have been absorbed into this parade of red shirts. In all their loose ends and fractures, the works are daring me to leap into new unfolding stories, as a participant.

The red shirts have disrupted both the flow of linear narrative in the works and my position as a viewer. My supposedly objective distance has transformed into a kind of suspended in-between that is not simply proximity, nor its opposite. I am denied both the familiar pleasures of immersion and critical detachment. Ahtila's works invite me to a borderline that no longer distinguishes but unites. It is no more clear, or even relevant, whether I am on the screen or in the audience. Like the girl in TODAY, I can only wonder whose father is crying—Lucia's, Vera's, Elisa's, Iines's, or Taru's.

1) Gilles Deleuze and Félix Guattari, *A Thousand Plateaus* (Minneapolis: University of Minnesota Press, 1987), p. 292.
2) On the threat presented by space to the subject, see e.g. Roger Caillois, "Mimicry and Legendary Psychastenia" in *October*, 31 (Winter), 1984, pp. 12–32; Elizabeth Grosz, *Space, Time, and Perversion* (New York and London: Routledge, 1995), pp. 83–101.
3) Grosz, op. cit., p. 89.
4) Luce Irigaray, *Ethics of Sexual Difference* (London: The Athlone Press, 1993), pp. 10–12; see also pp. 34–55.
5) See e.g. Carol C. Clover, *Men, Women, and Chainsaws* (Princeton, NJ: Princeton University Press, 1992).
6) Jacques Derrida, *Specters of Marx* (New York/London: Routledge, 1994), p. xx.
7) Ibid., p. 132.

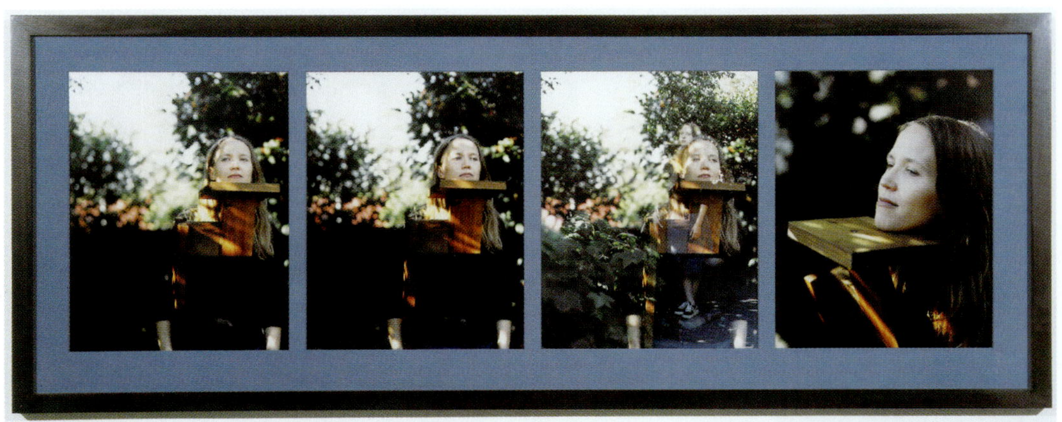

EIJA-LIISA AHTILA, ASSISTANT SERIES: SUPPORT, 2000, series of 4 color prints, framed set with hand-colored mat, each print 15 3/4 x 19 1/2", frame 27 1/8 x 73 7/16" / Serie aus 4 Farbprints, gerahmt, mit handkoloriertem Passepartout, je 40 x 49,5 cm, Rahmen 69 x 186,5 cm.

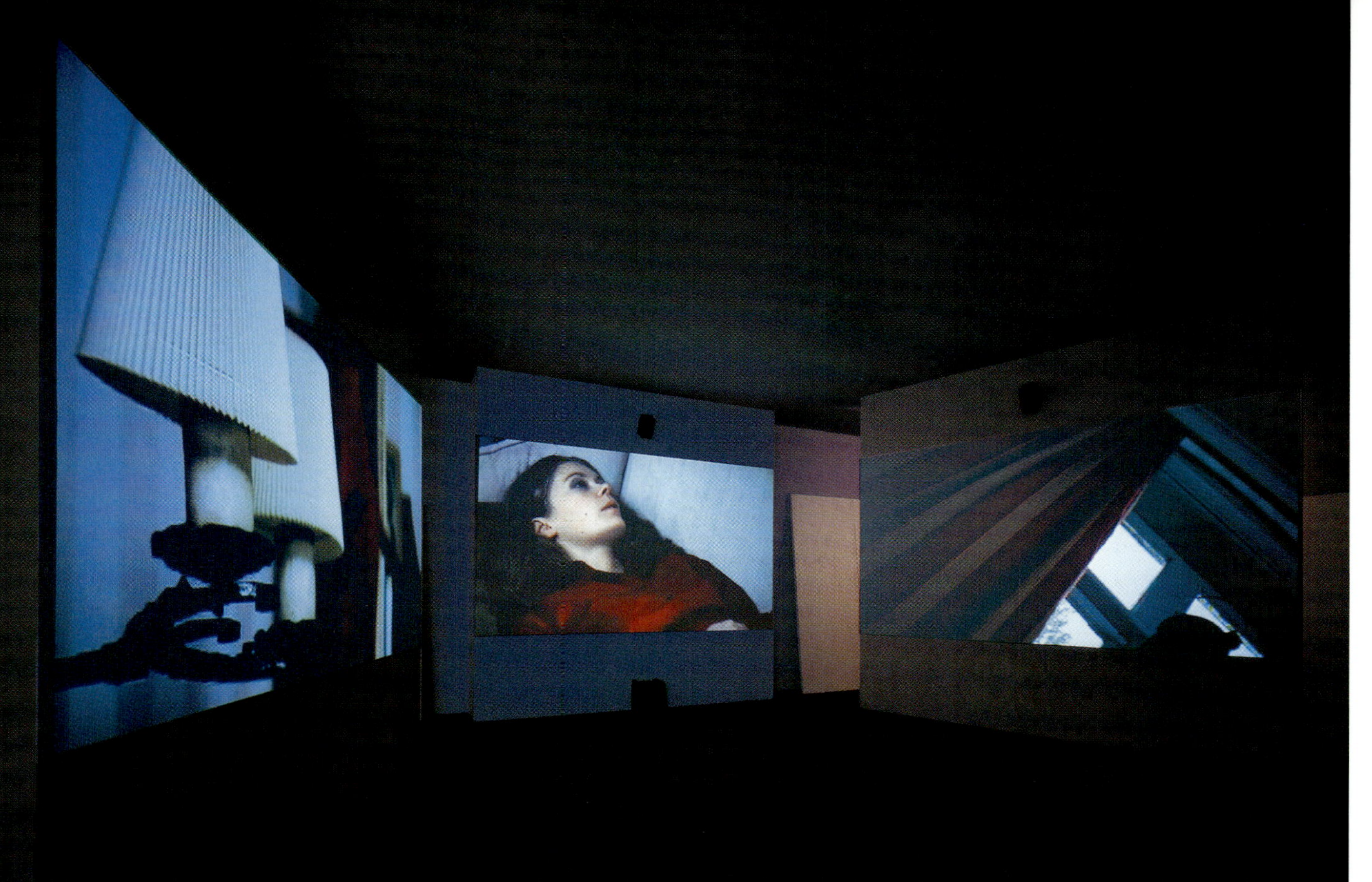

EIJA-LIISA AHTILA, THE HOUSE, 2002, 14 min. DVD installation for 3 projections with sound, installation view, "Trasparente," Rome, 2003 / DVD-Installation für 3 Projektionen mit Ton, Dauer: 14 Min., Ausstellung «Trasparente», Rom.

TARU ELFVING

Rot sehen

... ein kleines Detail (...), das immer wichtiger wird und von dem man mitgerissen wird.
– Gilles Deleuze & Félix Guattari [1)]

Das kleine Mädchen in Rot.
Lucia verkörpert eine Grenze zwischen ihren Eltern, sie trennt und verbindet sie gleichzeitig unauflöslich miteinander. In Eija-Liisa Ahtilas CONSOLATION SERVICE (Trostservice, 1999) ist sie stumme Zeugin der Scheidung ihrer Eltern. Zwar nicht mit ihnen identisch, aber dennoch untrennbar mit ihnen verbunden, wird Lucia zum Ort, an dem alle klaren Unterscheidungen zu Bruch gehen. Welche Rolle spielt das Rot?

In all meinen Versuchen, über Ahtilas Video-Installationen zu schreiben, scheinen rote Kleidungsstücke herumzuspuken. Für einen Exorzismus dürfte es wohl zu spät sein. Ich strecke also die Waffen und schreibe über, mit und in Rot. Statt zu fragen, was das Rot verhüllt, frage ich mich, was dieses Ver-

TARU ELFVING ist Kuratorin und Publizistin. Die gebürtige Finnin ist wissenschaftliche Mitarbeiterin für Visual Culture am Goldsmiths College der University of London.

hüllen bewirkt. Vielleicht enthüllt es ja auch Beziehungs- und Verbindungsknoten, wo lineare Koordinaten zusammenbrechen.

Das Mädchen im roten Oberteil.

In TODAY (Heute, 1996–1997) lungert ein Mädchen verlegen auf der Bildfläche und auf den Türschwellen bewohnter Räume herum. Als sie das Zimmer ihres Vater betritt, scheinen ihre beiden Realitäten für einen Augenblick ineinander zu greifen, jedoch mit einer spürbaren räumlich-zeitlichen Distanz zwischen dem Mädchen und ihrem von Weinkrämpfen geschüttelten Vater. Dann wendet sie sich aus der Realität ihres Vaters heraus an mich, die Betrachterin, und wird zur Erzählerin seiner Tragödie.

Veras verblichenes Rot.

Von der letzten Einstellung mit dem Mädchen wandert mein Blick zu Vera, die für mich das Mädchen als erwachsene Frau verkörpert. Ihr Zimmer glüht in einem roten, sinnlichen Licht, doch ihre Bluse hebt sich nicht mehr ab. Das Rot der Kleidung hat auf die Umgebung abgefärbt. Während Vera sich zuvor noch an den Grenzen der Räume aufhielt, sind jetzt die Grenzen zwischen Vera und dem Raum verschwommen. Zeigt Veras Beispiel einfach einmal mehr die Unmöglichkeit eines identischen, stabilen Subjekts? Eine gefestigte Identität setzt einen Standpunkt voraus, der einen souveränen Blick auf den umgebenden Raum erlaubt, in dem man von anderen als Objekt wahrgenommen wird.[2] Das ist jedoch nie wirklich gewährleistet. Denn das Subjekt ist in eine fortwährende Auseinandersetzung mit dem Ort verstrickt, an dem es sich befindet.

Elisas rote Bluse.

THE HOUSE (Das Haus, 2002) erforscht psychotische Erfahrungen von Frauen; die Beziehung zwischen

EIJA-LIISA AHTILA, THE HOUSE, 2002, DVD still.

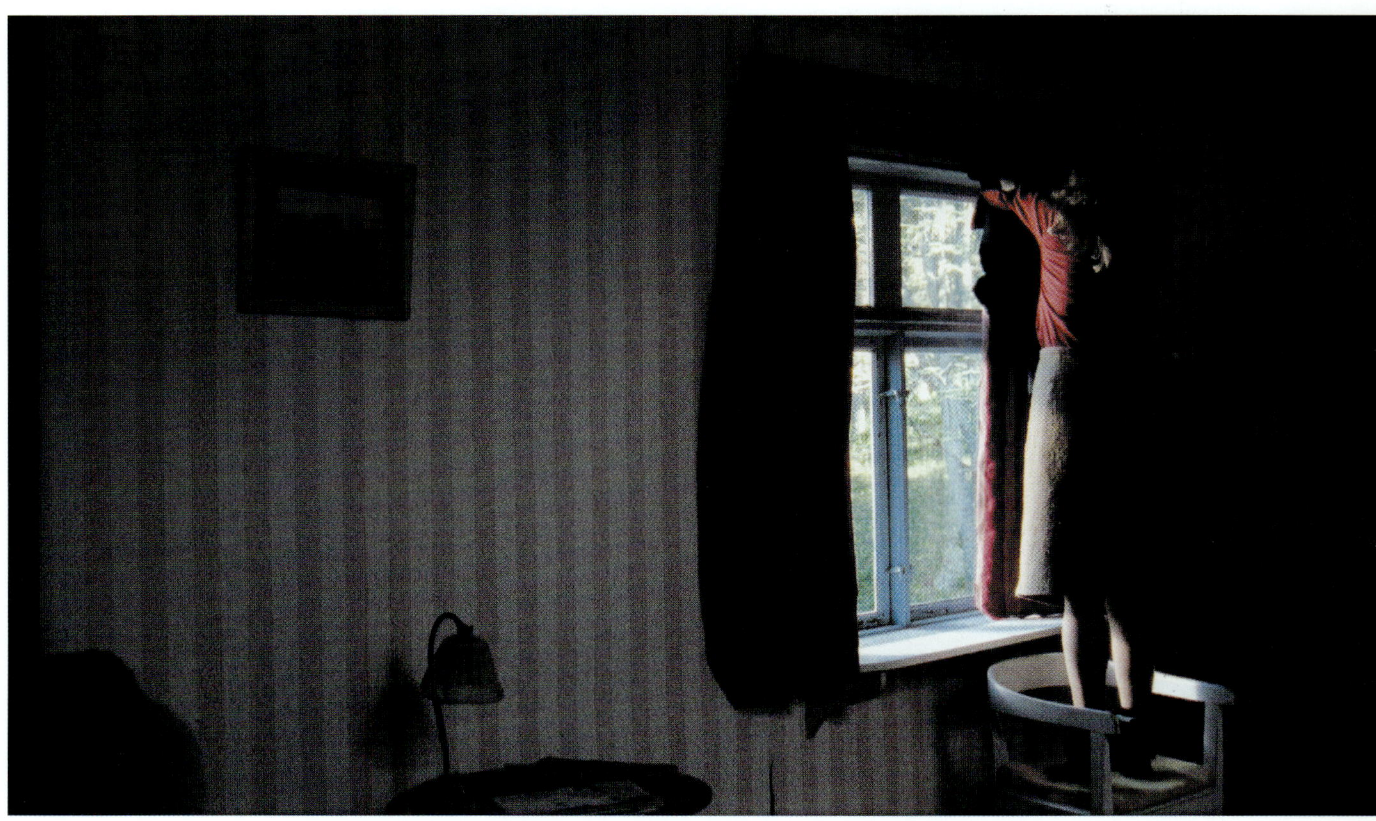

Subjekt und Raum wird mit einem besonderen Augenmerk auf bröckelnde Grenzen untersucht. Umgeben von diversen roten Dingen ist Elisa in ihrem Haus lediglich ein roter Fleck unter vielen. Ihr Körper scheint keinen festen Bezugspunkt zu bieten, der eine klare Orientierung im Verhältnis zu ihrer Umgebung erlauben würde. Zunächst sind es nur entfernte Geräusche, etwa die ihres Autos oder irgendeines Bootes, die sich ihres körperlichen Ichs bemächtigen, aber am Ende sind es auch Menschen: «Ich begegne Leuten. Einer nach dem anderen dringen sie in mich ein und leben in mir.»

Alle Koordinaten sind durcheinander geraten. Elisa ist nicht mehr nur Teil des Raums, sondern ein vielschichtiger Ort, an dem alle anderen Orte zu einem einzigen zusammenfallen. Wenn das Ich nicht fest im Körper verankert ist, wird die Positionierung im Raum unmöglich.[3)] Ist das Elisas Schicksal? Stellt man den Geist über die Materie, so erscheint Identität als in sich ruhende Einheit, wobei der Körper lediglich passives Gefäss innerer Tiefen ist. Doch wie Luce Irigaray und andere meinen, kann ein weibliches Subjekt gar keinen eigenen Platz einnehmen, da das weibliche Wesen selbst als Ort, Materie für andere definiert ist.[4)] Vielleicht enthüllt Elisa die Absurdität dieser Position und rebelliert dagegen?

Iines im roten Poloshirt.

In THE PRESENT (Die Gegenwart, 2002) kriecht Iines zielstrebig über eine Brücke, ihre rote Handtasche hinter sich herschleifend. Als sie wieder festen Boden unter den Füssen hat, steht sie auf, streicht ihre Kleider glatt und geht weiter. Überraschenderweise erklärt sie: «Mir war klar, dass ich total wahnsinnig wirkte. Das ist ja der Wahnsinn. Oder ist das nur mein Problem? Ich weiss nicht, jedenfalls lässt man mich tun, was ich tun muss.»

All diese Symptome haben mit Besessenheit zu tun. Elisa ist besessen von ihrer Umwelt. Iines ist getrieben von einem unerklärlichen inneren Zwang. Sind sie mit den Protagonistinnen von Horrorfilmen vergleichbar, die häufig als das Schlachtfeld fungieren, auf dem Grenzen in Frage gestellt werden, um schliesslich noch fester zementiert fortzubestehen? Sind ihre Körper besessene, offene Gefässe oder Werkzeuge der Selbstdarstellung anderer? Das Gegenteil scheint der Fall, eher scheinen sie den Begriff der Besessenheit überhaupt in Frage zu stellen, indem sie die Rolle des passiv empfangenden Opfers verweigern.

Die Geschichte mit der Besessenheit entspringt häufig dem Wunsch, den weiblichen Körper zum Sprechen zu bringen und einen Beweis für seine nicht sichtbare Andersartigkeit zu liefern. Die Gemeinsamkeiten zwischen okkulten Horrorgeschichten und psychologischen Dramen, Exorzismus und Gesprächstherapie, sind augenfällig.[5)] Besessenheit wie Wahnsinn scheinen deshalb beide von sichtbaren Körpersignalen abhängig zu sein. Wenn aber die Grenze zwischen Normalität und Wahnsinn im Bereich des Sichtbaren überschritten wird, was bleibt dann im Unsichtbaren übrig? Wenn Iines bewusst in einer Weise agiert, die wahnsinnig wirkt, was sehen wir dann? Und was fange ich mit meinen Beweisen, den roten Signalen, an, wenn sie nicht aus einer verborgenen Innenwelt stammen?

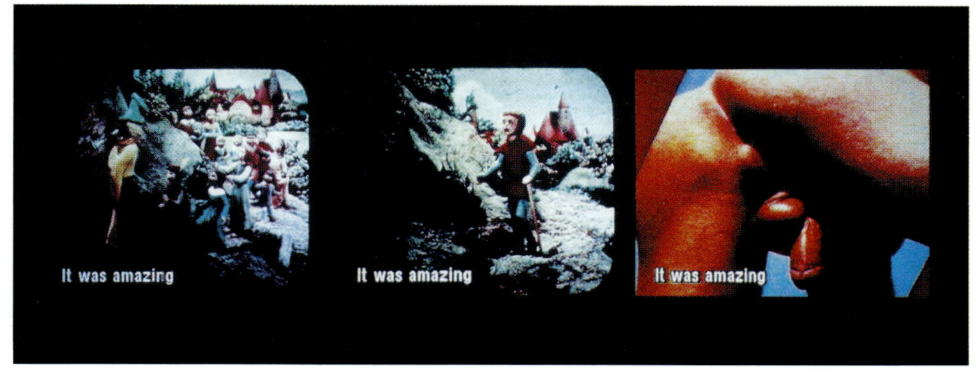

EIJA-LIISA AHTILA, IF 6 WAS 9, 1995, 10 min. 35-mm film and DVD installation for 3 projections with sound, / 35-mm-Film- und DVD-Installation für 3 Projektionen mit Ton, Dauer: 10 Min.

Ein weiteres Mädchen in rotem Oberteil.

IF 6 WAS 9 (Wenn 6 9 wäre, 1995) spielt mit einem strapazierten Symbol der Weiblichkeit, dem Loch, dem Riss im heilen Gewebe der geltenden Norm. Die wiederholten Bilder von Durchgängen und Ritzen unterstreichen den Zwiespalt dieser Frauen innerhalb von Strukturen, die auf der strikten Trennung von Öffentlichem und Privatem, Innen und Aussen, beruhen. Die Mädchen bringen diese Bildsprache der Zwischenräume lebhaft zum Ausdruck. Am Ende erinnert sich ein Mädchen in rotem Oberteil an einen Zeitungsartikel, der alle Orte in der Stadt auflistet, wo Sex angeboten wird. Sie hatte sich die Bilder dieser Orte ausgeschnitten und schaut sie sich mit den anderen Mädchen zusammen an, womit sie sich symbolisch diese öffentlichen Zonen der Sexualität aneignen. Das Weibliche als Verkörperung einer jederzeit offenen und zugänglichen Subjektivität bekommt durch diese illustrierte (und phantasierte) Topographie der Stadt eine räumliche Dimension. Die drei Öffnungen des weiblichen Körpers, auf die das Mädchen konkret Bezug nimmt, vervielfachen sich und werden zu einem steten Fluss immer neuer Schwellen, immer neuer Klüfte, die ich überbrücken muss.

Rot sehen.

Elisa geht noch weiter über die Grenzen des Sichtbaren hinaus. Sie lebt in ihrem Haus nach vorgegebenen Mustern. Entsprechend beschreibt sie auch ihre Umgebung und was sich um sie herum und in ihrer Vorstellung abspielt. Erfolglos versucht sie, die Welt und ihren Platz darin anhand des Sichtbaren zu verstehen. Sie beschliesst deshalb, der Verwirrung ein Ende zu bereiten und den Bereich des Sichtbaren zu liquidieren, da dessen unscharfe Grenzen ihr die grössten Probleme bereiten. Elisa verdunkelt ihr Haus und zieht sich in andere Räume zurück, dorthin, wo die Stimmen herkommen und wo vielleicht auch Grenzüberschreitungen und Simultaneität möglich sind.

Als Betrachter wird mir in Ahtilas Installationen eine klare und eindeutige Sicht der Dinge verweigert. In THE HOUSE sehe ich in einem Bild mit Elisas Augen, in einem anderen schaue ich sie an und im dritten befinde ich mich an ihrer Seite. Sie entzieht sich meinem Blick und verdoppelt sich dann plötzlich. Manchmal löst sich ihre Stimme auch von ihrem Bild. Ich nehme teil an Elisas verzweifeltem Kampf, einen einzigen, zuverlässigen Blick auf den sie umgebenden Raum zu erhaschen. Oder bin nur ich es, die verunsichert ist? Projiziere ich meine Frustration auf Elisa, unfähig, die ständigen Veränderungen so gelassen hinzunehmen, wie sie es tut?

Rot denken.

Die normale Erfahrung subjektiven Bewusstseins wird in Ahtilas Arbeiten auf verschiedenste Art aufgebrochen, aber im Gegensatz zu den besessenen Heldinnen der Horrorfilme werden die Frauen nicht zum Exorzismus gezwungen. Es besteht kein Anspruch, sie wieder zu stabilisieren oder ihre Körper zum Sprechen zu bringen. Wenn sie dennoch sprechen, hat es nie therapeutischen Charakter und ist weder zwanghaftes Bekenntnis noch hysterischer Erguss.

Viele von Ahtilas Figuren scheinen in den Grenzgebieten der Sprache zu Hause zu sein. Sie sprechen mit mir wie Erzählerinnen, die eine einstudierte Rolle abrufen, und befinden sich auf einer Schwelle zwischen unserer Raumzeit und ihrer eigenen. Ihre Ausdruckslosigkeit lässt ihre Worte seltsam klingen, als würden sie – wenn auch fliessend – in einer fremden Sprache sprechen. Vielleicht denken sie auch nur laut in einer diffusen Zone zwischen sprachlichen Strukturen und freiem Gedankenfluss. Doppeldeutiges verbindet sich harmonisch mit klaren Aussagen. Und immer wieder löst sich die Sprache von den Sprechenden. Wenn die Mädchen in IF 6 WAS 9 miteinander kommunizieren, sind ihre Stimmen nicht zu hören. Wer spricht mit wem und worüber? Anstelle klarer Botschaften vermitteln die Worte nur weitere Schichten und Bruchstücke, die mir die Orientierung rauben. Wie die Erzählerin in CONSOLATION SERVICE stehe ich inmitten der sprechenden Protagonisten.

Tragen Gespenster Rot?

Werden diese Frauen von Gespenstern heimgesucht? Oder gehen sie selbst um? Wie Gespenster respektieren sie keine Wände und Widerstände, sondern setzen sich mühelos über alle Grenzen hinweg. Sie erscheinen als formlose Form, als unsichtbar Sicht-

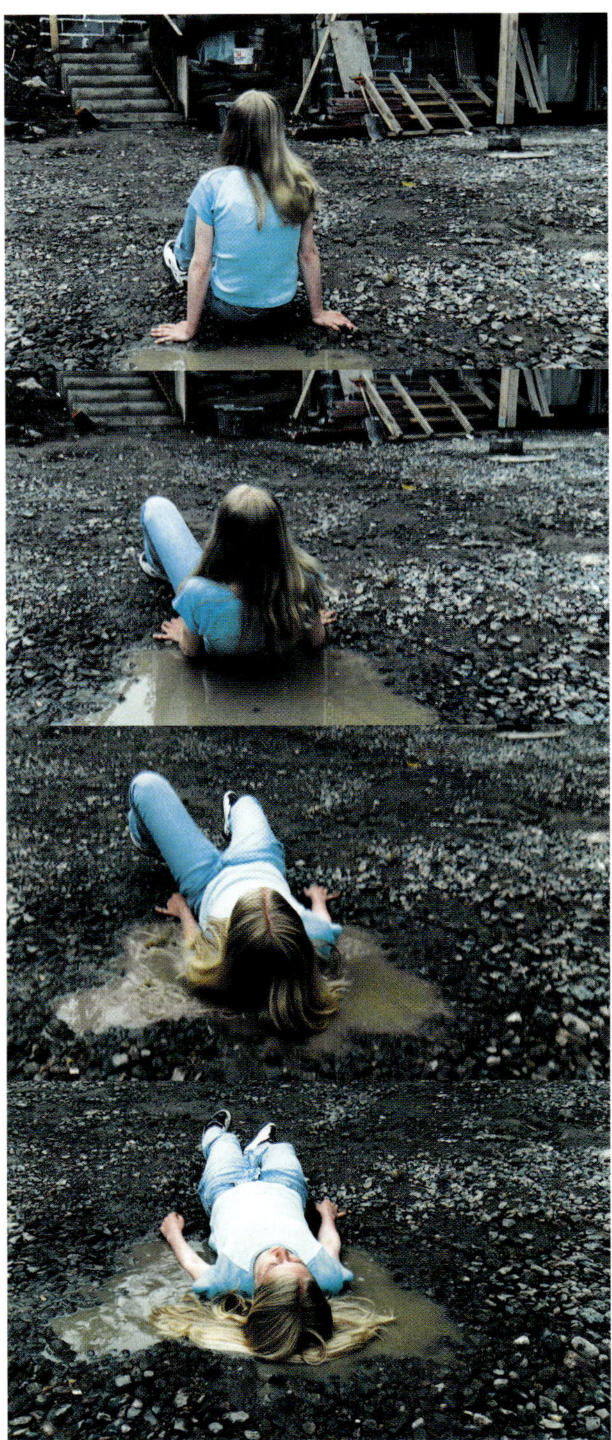

EIJA-LIISA AHTILA, THE PRESENT, 2001, DVD stills.

bares und entstofflichte Stofflichkeit. Wie das Gespenst bei Jacques Derrida sind sie immer mehr als eins, gleichzeitig aber auch weniger als eins.[6] Bis zu einem gewissen Grad teilen sie ihre grenzen- und bodenlose Perspektive mit mir, entschlüpfen meinem Zugriff aber auch immer wieder. Meine Wahrnehmung beginnt zu straucheln. Sie scheinen zu fragen, ob man sich gegen den Verlust klarer Grenzen wehren müsse. Statt Borderline-Zustände zu verkörpern benützen diese Figuren die Doppeldeutigkeiten und den Grenzbereich selbst, um auch noch jene Unterscheidungen aufzulösen, die er eigentlich garantieren soll. Sie hinterfragen die Unterscheidung zwischen Normalität und Krankheit, zwischen dem Selbst und seinem Anderen. Leiden wir nicht alle unter einer Art Borderline-Syndrom?

Meine roten Shirts.

Ein Gespenst besitzen heisst, laut Derrida, von ihm besessen zu werden.[7] Werde ich von einem Geist heimgesucht oder werde ich selbst zum Gespenst? Ich ertappe mich immer wieder in einem roten Shirt, wenn ich über Ahtilas Arbeiten rede. Beim Versuch, mir über ihre Figuren Klarheit zu verschaffen, bin ich in diese Parade roter Blusen hineingezogen worden. All die offenen Enden und Brüche in diesen Arbeiten sind ein einziger Appell, mich als aktiv Beteiligte in sich neu entfaltende Geschichten hineinzustürzen.

Die roten Blusen haben sowohl den linearen Erzählfluss der Arbeiten unterbrochen als auch meine Position als Betrachterin aus den Angeln gehoben. Meine angeblich objektive Haltung hat sich in einen schwebenden Zwischenzustand verwandelt, der weder einfach nur Nähe, noch das Gegenteil davon ist. Beides wird mir verweigert: das vertraute, lustvolle Eintauchen und die kritische Distanz. Ahtilas Arbeiten führen mich an eine Grenze, die nicht mehr unterscheidet, sondern verbindet. Es ist nicht mehr klar oder auch nur von Bedeutung, ob ich mich auf dem Bildschirm befinde oder im Publikum. Wie dem Mädchen in TODAY bleibt mir nichts anderes übrig als mich zu fragen, wessen Vater wohl weint: Lucias, Veras, Elisas, Iines' oder Tarus?

(Übersetzung: Goridis/Parker)

1) Gilles Deleuze und Félix Guattari, *Tausend Plateaus,* Merve Verlag, Berlin 1992, S. 397.
2) Über die Bedrohung, die der Raum für das Subjekt darstellt, siehe u.a.: Roger Caillois, «Mimicry and Legendary Psychastenia», *October* Nr. 31 (Winter), 1984, S. 12–32; Elizabeth Grosz, *Space, Time, and Perversion,* Routledge, New York/London 1995, S. 83–101.
3) Grosz, op. cit., S. 89.
4) Luce Irigaray, *Ethik der sexuellen Differenz,* Suhrkamp, Frankfurt am Main 1991, S. 15ff.; vgl. auch S. 46–70.
5) Vgl. auch Carol C. Clover, *Men, Women, and Chainsaws,* Princeton University Press, Princeton 1992.
6) Jacques Derrida, *Marx' Gespenster,* Fischer Taschenbuch Verlag, Frankfurt am Main 1996, S. 17.
7) Ebenda, S. 208.

EIJA-LIISA AHTILA, THE PRESENT, 2001, DVD installation for 5 monitors and 5 TV spots with sound, duration: 5 x 70–120 sec. and 5 x 30 sec., installation view, Marian Goodman Gallery, Paris / DVD-Installation für 5 Monitore und 5 TV-Spots mit Ton, Dauer 5 x 70–120 Sek. bzw. 5 x 30 Sek. (PHOTO: MARC DOMMAGE)

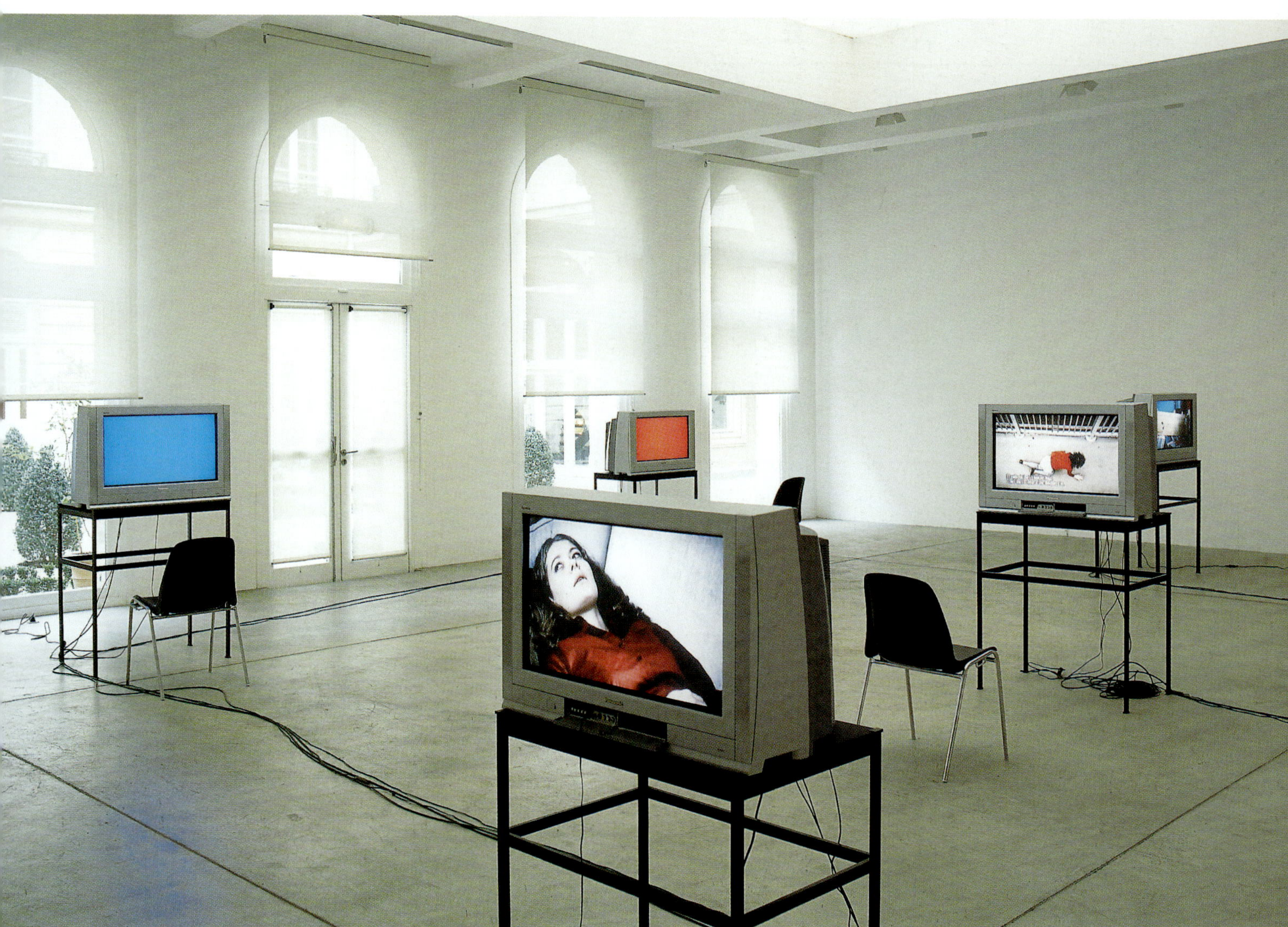

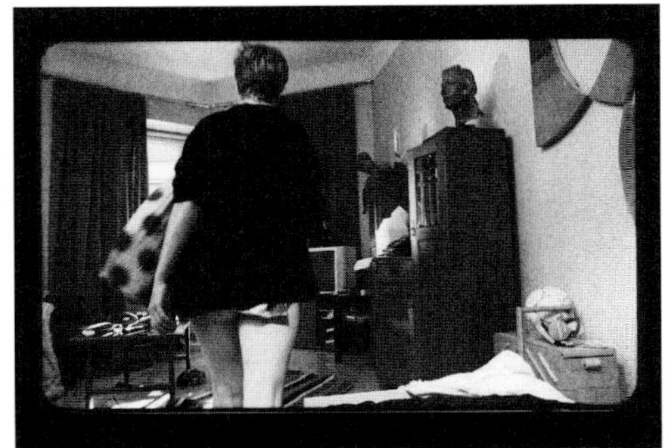

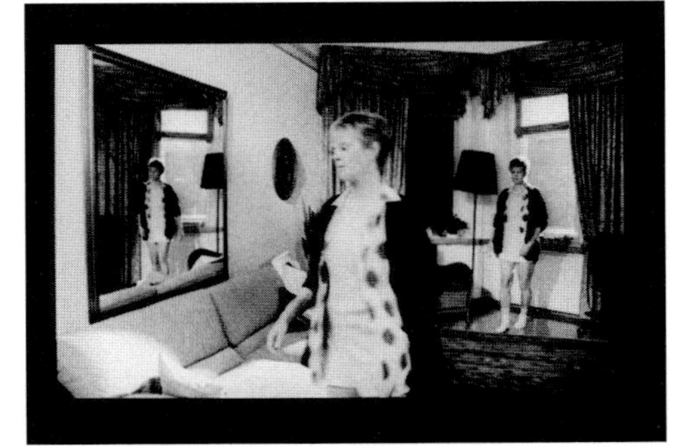

EIJA-LIISA AHTILA, ME/WE; OKAY; GRAY, 1993, 35-mm film stills.

HOME MOVIES oder die Schwierigkeit vom Leben in Häusern

EIJA LIISA-AHTILAS BEWEGTE BILDER VON LEBEN UND TOD

GERTRUD KOCH

Wie wohnt man in einem Haus, wie verlässt man es und wie findet man eine Unterkunft?

Die bewegten Bilder Ahtilas drehen sich oft um das Haus und um die Gegenstände und Personen, die es nach innen öffnen und nach aussen isolieren. Zufahrten, Parkplätze, Brücken auf dem Weg, Türen, die von aussen nach innen von merkwürdigen Besuchern aufgestossen werden, Gardinen, die den Lichteinfall der Fenster verschliessen, Autos, die auf den Wänden im Zimmer fahren, Betten, unter denen man sich verbergen kann, Windstösse, die alles zunichte machen. Das Bild des Hauses, das Ahtila entwirft, ist eine fragile Angelegenheit. Etwas zwischen Puppenstube und Kartenhaus, Modellbau und Baustelle. In einem Film gibt es ein Haus, das aufgeschnitten im Hof steht wie ein riesiges Puppenhaus oder wie Jacques Tatis gläserne Funktionalbauten in *Playtime*. In einem anderen Film klebt eine Frau an einer Stelle der Wand, die sonst nur elegante Musicaltänzer in Überwindung der Schwerkraft zu «betreten» vermögen. Es gibt aber auch Häuser, die sich nicht betreten lassen: Die Betontreppen scheinen nur an sie angelehnt zu sein und bevor man dort reingeht, legt man sich lieber in eine schmutzige Pfütze vor dem Haus, das von der

---

GERTRUD KOCH ist Professorin für Filmwissenschaft an der Freien Universität in Berlin. Ihre jüngste Publikation ist der Essayband *Kunst als Strafe: zur Ästhetik der Disziplinierung* (Fink, München 2003).

Mutter versperrt scheint, die am oberen Ende der Treppe steht.

Anders als das HAUS UR, das Gregor Schneider 2001 an der Biennale in Venedig in den Deutschen Pavillon einbaute, sind Ahtilas Häuser weniger architektonische oder skulpturale Gebilde als vielmehr Bildräume, die selbst jene akrobatische Beweglichkeit aufweisen, die Schneider den Besuchern des HAUSES UR abverlangt. Die Häuser Ahtilas werden digital – oder auch mithilfe der Kamera vor Ort – geschrumpft und verdoppelt: Am Boden vor dem riesigen, dreidimensionalen Spitalgebäude steht eine Miniaturausgabe desselben – das Kameraobjektiv und die Bewegung des Schwenkarmes lassen beide Versionen real erscheinen. Die filmische, photographische Welt aus dreidimensionalen Objekten wird durch *special effects* zum *haunted house:* jenem Haus des Horrorfilms, das in der Terminologie Sigmund Freuds das «Heimelige» des Heims mit dem Unheimlichen tabuisierter Zonen verbindet. Freuds Analyse bemüht bekanntlich die Figur des Sandmanns aus E. T. A. Hoffmanns phantastischer Erzählung, um die Nähe von Familienheim und Horrorhaus zu belegen. In Hoffmanns Erzählung wird die wunderliche Verwandlung des väterlichen Hauses zuerst durch allerlei optische Gerätschaften orchestriert, welche die natürliche Sicht der Welt in Unordnung bringen. Der «Opticus» Spalanzani verkauft dem jungen Nathanael ein «Perspektiv» (ein kleines Taschenfernrohr), durch das der Anblick der Puppe Olimpia zum Affektbild (im Sinne der Filmtheorie von Gilles Deleuze) transformiert wird. Im Close-Up des ausgezogenen Perspektivs animiert sich die Puppe zum idealen Frauenbild: «Noch im Leben war ihm kein Glas vorgekommen, das die Gegenstände so rein, scharf und deutlich dicht vor die Augen rückte.»[1)] In der optischen Transformation entsteht das obsessive Bild: «Nun erschaute Nathanael erst Olimpias wunderschön geformtes Gesicht. Nur die Augen schienen ihm gar seltsam starr und tot. Doch wie er immer schärfer und schärfer durch das Glas hinschaute, war es, als gingen in Olimpias Augen feuchte Mondesstrahlen auf. Es schien, als wenn nun erst die Sehkraft entzündet würde; immer lebendiger und lebendiger flammten die Blicke.»[2)] Hoffmanns Erzählung ist nicht nur von Freud aufgegriffen worden, gerade in der Filmtheorie sind die optischen Prämissen einer neuen Sicht auf die Welt nicht unbemerkt geblieben. Im Zusammenhang mit den unheimlichen Häusern Ahtilas bekommt Spalanzanis verrückende Optik aber noch eine zusätzliche Dimension. Bei Hoffmann bildet sie eine Prämisse, die in Ahtilas phantastischen Grotesken wirksam geblieben ist: Entgleist dort die Wahrnehmung der Welt in ihrer genauen Beobachtung, so sind es bei Ahtila Beschreibungen psychotischer Wahrnehmungen, welche die Welt erst konstituieren. Auf dem Umschlag des Videobandes LOVE IS A TREASURE (2002) steht, dass dieser Film aus fünf Episoden bestehe, die verschiedene Geschichten von Frauen erzählen, welche Psychosen entwickelt hätten, und dass spezielle Filmtechniken verwendet worden seien, um im Kopf entstandene unmögliche Situationen nahtlos in die realistische Kulisse einzufügen.[3)] Dem Film liegen Recherchen und Gespräche mit Personen zugrunde, die von ihren psychotischen Störungen berichten. Bilder, Töne, Charaktere und Texte dieser Interviews sind frei montiert und erhalten dadurch einen fiktionalen Status. Es geht also keinesfalls um die Prosa dokumentarischer Verfahren in Bezug zu den Verzerrungen der Wahrnehmungswelt. Es geht vielmehr um die transformatorische Kraft der Verrückung selber als einem Prozess, die optische Welt umzukonstruieren. Trotz des dramatischen Ausgangsgeschehens bleiben die Filme und Videos kühl, so als wollten sie selbst das «Perspektiv» sein, das sehen lässt, und nicht der enthusiasmierte Seher.

ZWANGSVORSTELLUNG

In «Ground Control», einer Episode von LOVE IS A TREASURE, wird ein weiblicher Teenager zur Assistentin der UFOs, die alle Töne auf der Erde kontrollieren.[4)] Die Transformationen finden akustisch über

Geräusch und optisch über Objekte statt: Ein Streitgespräch mit der Mutter endet in einer Fahrt vom Gesicht der lamentierenden Mutter auf einen Knopf an ihrer Bluse, der als Detailaufnahme festgehalten wird; ein Schnitt von einem merkwürdig aussehenden Beton-Wasserturm, der oben eine Art Schale trägt, führt auf ein Detail einer ovalen Verkleidung, die dem ovalen Ornament dieses Knopfes ähnelt. Später werden wie Knöpfe aussehende, digitalisierte metallische Kugeln, die sich aus dem Nachthimmel lösen und durch die Strasse rasen, zu wirklichen Knöpfen, die als Mobile an Fäden im Zimmer hängen. Die UFO-Phantasien sind zwar technisch perfekt, aber mit Alltagsgegenständen gebastelt, statt mit Hightech-Allusionen versehen. So wird das digitale Bild selbst fast ironisch unterlaufen. Die Verschmelzung von mentalem Bild und photographischem beziehungsweise elektronischem Bild favorisiert den lakonischen Zug. Es geht weder darum, den Illusionismus der Wahrnehmung zu denunzieren, noch den der Phantasie.

Die Zwangshandlung, das kommt in der Logik dieser Bilder zum Ausdruck, setzt die Anerkennung ihrer Selbstverständlichkeit voraus: Wenn UFOs es befehlen, lege ich mich selbstverständlich wieder in die Pfütze, auf die nächtliche Strasse und so weiter. Die Natürlichkeit meiner Handlungen ergibt sich aus den Vorstellungen, die ich habe und die mir keine andere Wahl lassen. Wenn ich an UFOs glaube, ist es selbstverständlich, dass ich tue, was sie sagen.

In der Episode «Underworld» krallt sich eine Frau unter das Bett im Zimmer einer psychiatrischen Abteilung. Wenn die Ärztin elektronisch zur Miniatur geschrumpft unter das Bett marschiert, wird die Faust der Patientin gross und schlägt sie zurück. Im Prinzip sind das keine spektakulären *special effects,* wie wir sie aus Sciencefiction- oder Phantasyfilmen kennen. Ihre Schlagkraft im metaphorischen Sinn erhalten sie durch eine Struktur der Wiederholung, welche die Bilderfolge auf eine Zeitachse legt, in der sich die vorgenommenen Verrückungen in ihrer Zwanghaftigkeit als selbstverständlich etablieren und Teil einer Alltagswelt werden. Das verleiht den skurrilen Bildern ihren grotesken, aber eben auch lakonischen Zug. Denn nicht immer werden Zwangsordnungen ins Bild gerückt. Es gibt auch grossartige visuelle Metaphern, die Verdichtungen von Affekten bündeln, wie zum Beispiel in der Episode «Der Wind», in der die Selbstverständlichkeit vollends zur Natürlichkeit wird, wenn der Zorn einer Frau als Wind durchs Zimmer fegt und alles umstürzt.

Im Spiel mit den Dingen und Verrückungen werden Ordnungen aufgebaut und vernichtet, die sich meist als topographische Ordnungen etablieren. Es ist die Ordnung von Häusern, Strassen und Brücken, die umgebaut werden.

Raumprojektionen

Auch wenn die Bildkonstruktionen Ahtilas eher auf dem Flächigen des Bildes aufbauen als am Skulpturalen der Architektur interessiert sind, fällt es doch auf, wie wichtig Gebäude, Häuser, Zimmer, Strassen und Brücken in ihren Arbeiten sind. Auf der Fläche wird das Haus zum Bild, in der Rauminstallation aber das Bild zur Wand, drei Bilder zu einem Raum, und der Betrachter sieht sich in einen Raum versetzt, der zwar eine Ordnung hat, einen zeitlichen Ablauf, der auf der Wiederholungsschleife, dem Loop basiert; schliesslich muss er sich doch räumlich orientieren, da er die meist drei Bildflächen nicht auf einen Blick erfassen kann. Anders als bei der Film- oder Videoprojektion auf e i n e Leinwand, sieht sich nun der Betrachter von der Flächigkeit der Projektionsleinwand zurückgeworfen in einen Bildraum ohne festen Standpunkt. Ihre ganze Stärke entfalten die Projektionsbilder Ahtilas eigentlich erst im Raum. Das hängt zuallererst an den Proportionen. Die teilweise direkt in die Kamera sprechenden und blickenden Protagonistinnen stehen dem Betrachter auf Augenhöhe gegenüber, er sieht sich einen Raum betreten, der einen Raum zeigt, in dem ihn jemand anzusprechen scheint. Hier entfalten auch die vielen Stimmen und Geräusche erst ihre volle Wirkung.

In den Rauminstallationen werden die Proportionen so sistiert, dass der Raum des Bildes mich auf merkwürdige Art mit einschliesst. Gegenüber dem kleinen Format selbst des grössten Fernsehapparats und gegenüber der optimalen Distanz, die man zur Kinoleinwand einzunehmen pflegt, um das ganze Bild auf einen Blick erfassen zu können, hält einen diese Rauminstallation auf Armlänge und Augenhöhe. Der Raum der Bilder hat die abstrakte Form eines Zimmers mit Wänden und wenn in diesen Installationsräumen die Zimmertheater Ahtilas zur Aufführung kommen, so stellt sich leicht das Gefühl ein, Besucher zu sein in einem bewohnten Zimmer, in dem uns Stimmen ansprechen oder klagend Episoden, Geschichten erzählen, wie man sie zu erahnen meint, wenn man beim Überqueren der Strasse in eine Parterrewohnung guckt und dort unverhofft Leuten beim Fernsehen zuschauen kann.

Diese Mischung aus *special effects* der Verrückung, die an Valie Exports frühe Arbeiten erinnern, und der Evozierung einer Welt auf Augenhöhe ist höchst disparat und macht den ästhetischen Reiz der Werke Ahtilas aus, denn oft kommt zu diesen beiden Aspekten ein dritter hinzu: ein Standort, der ein bisschen *point-of-nowhere* ist, weder narrativ an die Figuren gebunden, noch spezifisch für mentale Projektionen, sondern eine Art dritter Blick, der jene Unheimlichkeit und visuelle Neugier erzeugt, den das ehrwürdige «Perspektiv» des Opticus Spalanzani schon einmal in die Welt getragen hat. Die Unheimlichkeit freilich ist eine, die vor jeder Erkennbarkeit liegt, in Erwartung von Müttern, UFOs oder Unfällen.

1) E.T.A. Hoffmann, *Der Sandmann,* (1816), Reclam, Stuttgart 1969, S. 28.
2) Ebenda, S. 28–29.
3) "... consists of five episodes containing five different stories about women who have developed psychoses. Special cinematic techniques have been used to seamlessly situate impossibilities thrown up by the mind into realistic settings." LOVE IS A TREASURE (2002), (55 min.:1:1.85, DD5.1), Copyright: Crystal Eye, 2002.
4) Ebenda. ("... a teenage girl becomes an assistant to the UFOs who control sounds on earth.")

EIJA-LIISA AHTILA, DOG BITES (1992–97), 4 of a series of 8 color photographs, 24 3/8 x 36 1/4" each / 4 aus einer Serie von 8 Farbphotographien, je 62 x 92 cm.

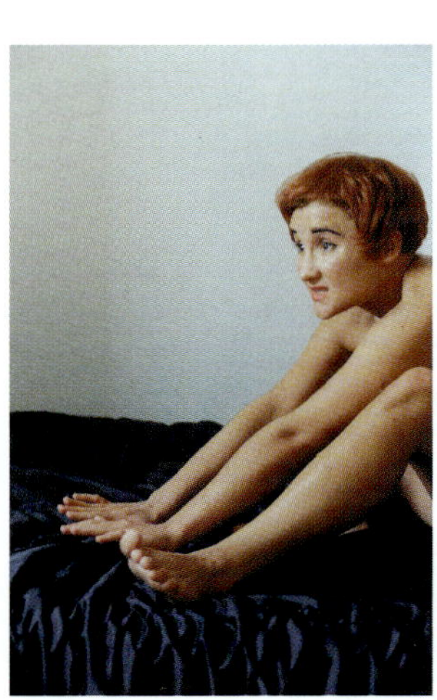

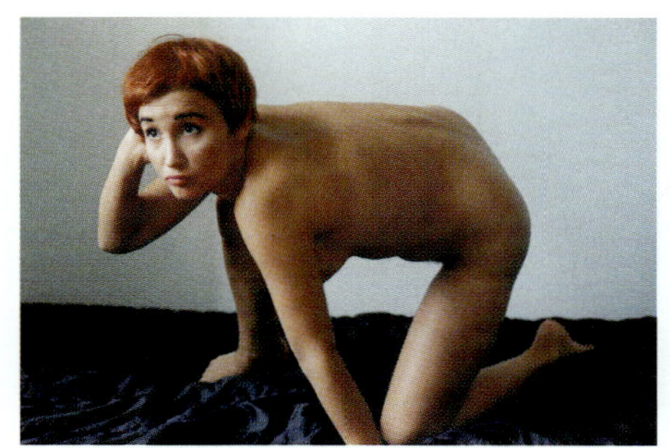

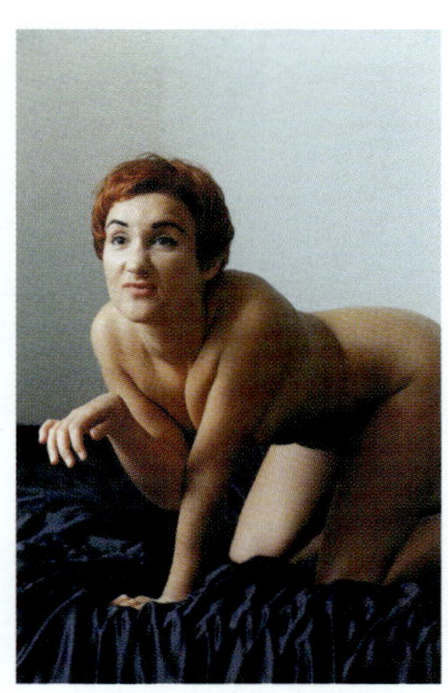

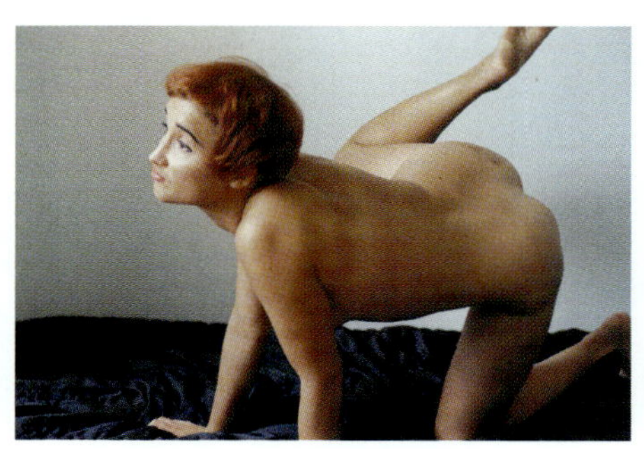

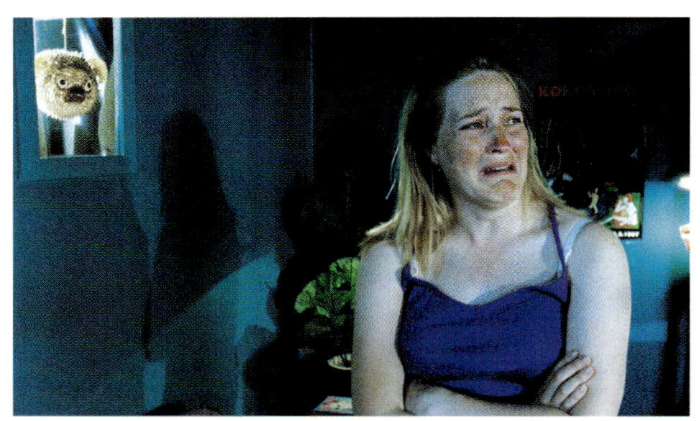

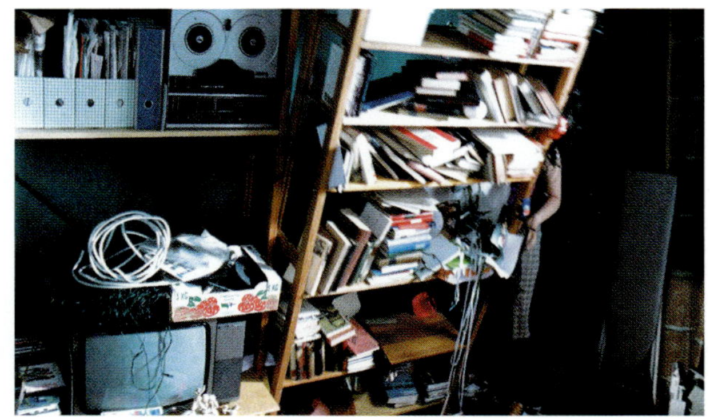

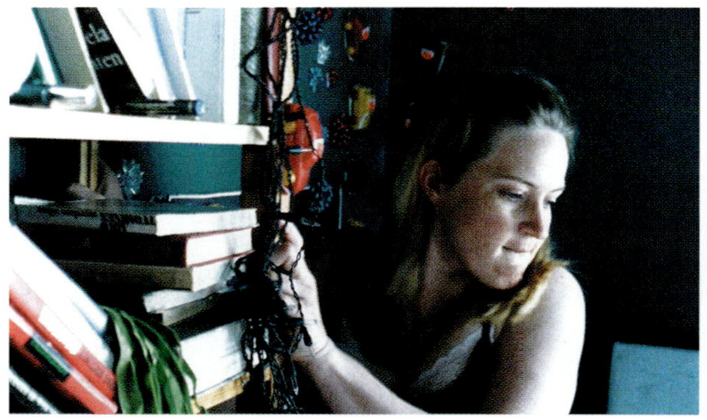

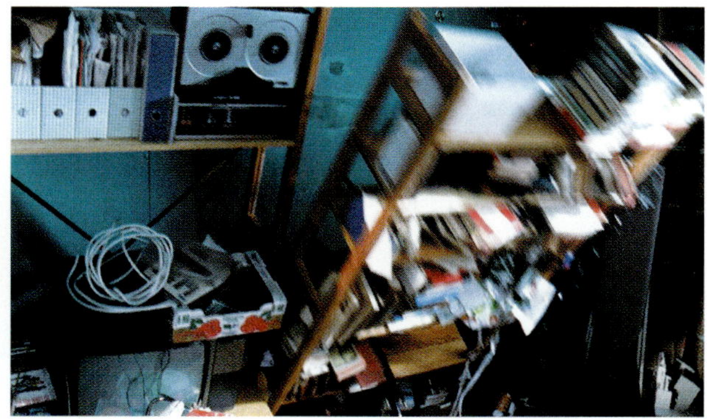

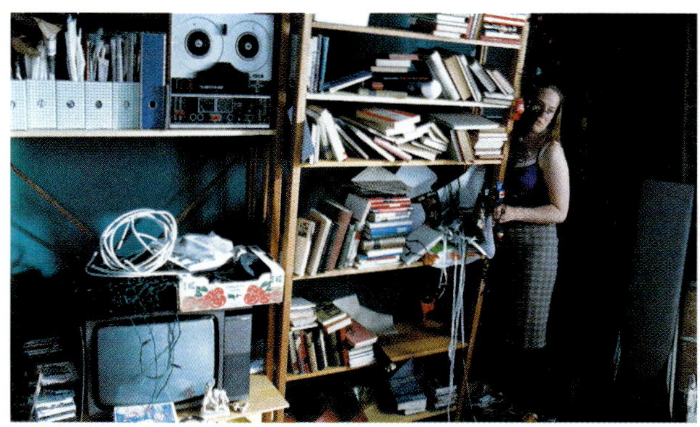

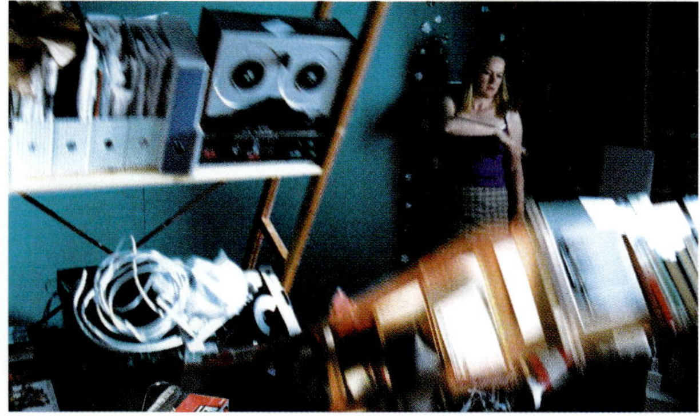

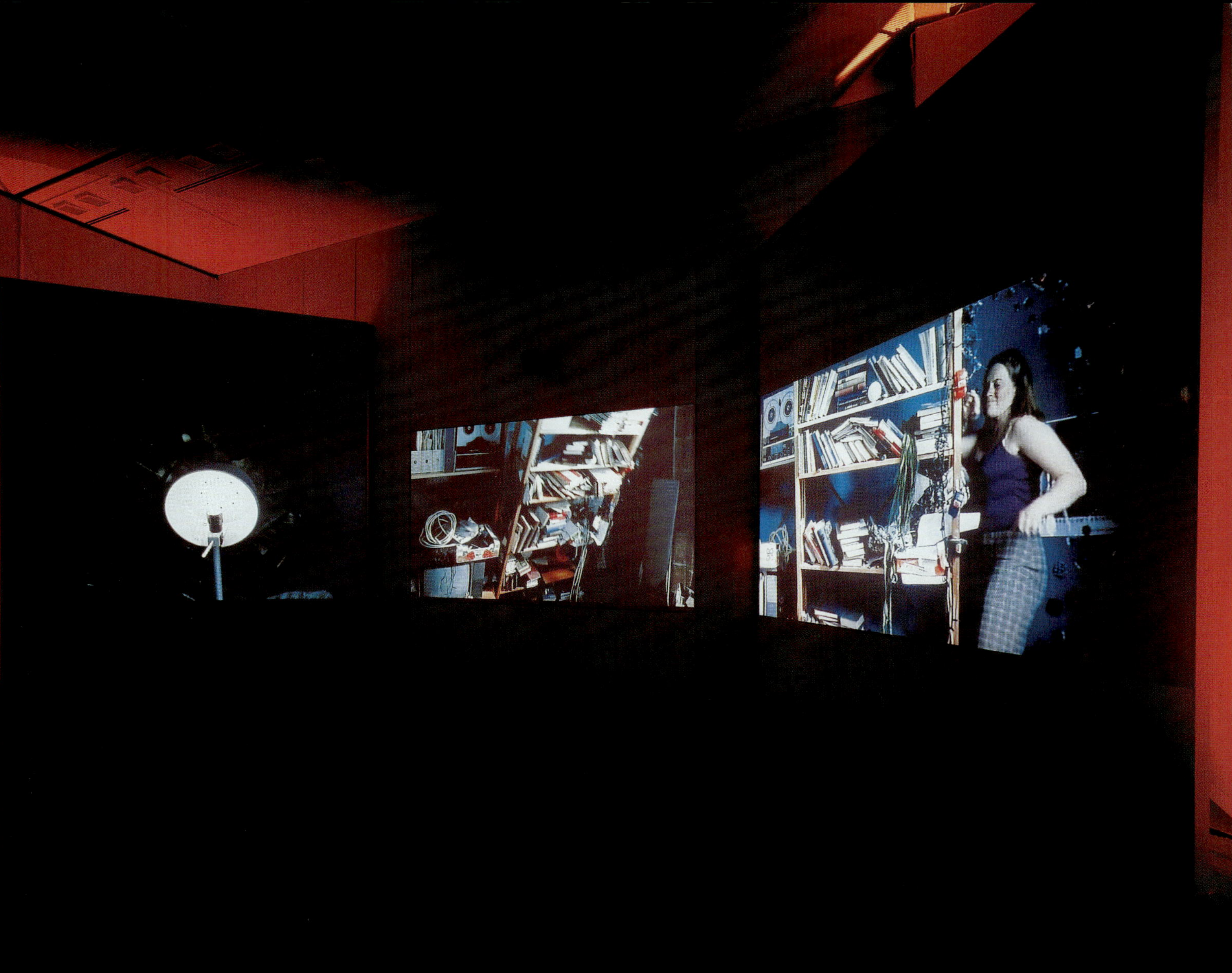

EIJA-LIISA AHTILA, THE WIND, 2002, 14 min. 20 sec. DVD installation for 3 projections with sound, Tokyo Opera City / DVD-Installation (14 Min. 20 Sek.) für 3 Projektionen mit Ton, Opera City Tokio.

Lefthand page / Linke Seite:
EIJA-LIISA AHTILA, THE WIND, 2002, DVD stills.

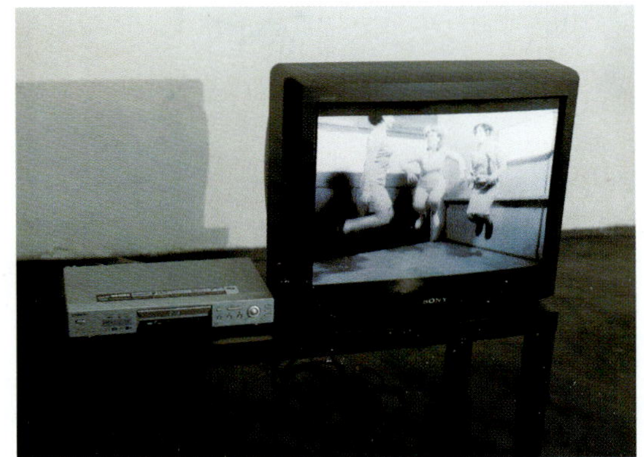

HOME MOVIES or The Hardship of Living in Houses

EIJA-LIISA AHTILA'S MOVING IMAGES OF LIFE AND DEATH

GERTRUD KOCH

How does one live in a house, how does one leave it, and how does one find accommodation?

Ahtila's moving pictures often revolve around the house: around the objects and people that enter it from the outside and close it off from the inside. Access roads, parking places, bridges along the way, doors that are opened into the house from outside by odd visitors, curtains that keep out the light, cars that traverse the walls of the rooms, beds under which one can hide, drafts that undo everything: the picture that Ahtila conjures of a house is a fragile affair, somewhere between dollhouse and house of cards, model and construction site. In one film, a house stands cut open in a courtyard like a giant dollhouse or like Jacques Tati's functional glass buildings in *Playtime*. In another, a woman is stuck to a spot on the wall, where ordinarily only elegant dancers in a musical, defying gravity, might tread. Some of her houses cannot be entered at all. Concrete steps look as if they were only propped up against the wall and instead of climbing them, it is preferable to lie down in a dirty puddle in front of the house that seems to be blocked by a mother standing at the top of the stairs.

GERTRUD KOCH is Professor for Cinema Studies at the Freie Universität in Berlin. Her most recent publication, *Kunst als Strafe* (Munich: Fink, 2003), contains collected essays on art as punishment.

EIJA-LIISA AHTILA, ME/WE; OKAY; GRAY, 1993, installation view, Kiasma, Finland. (PHOTO: MARJA-LEENA HUKKANEN)

In contrast to HAUS UR, which Gregor Schneider constructed inside the German pavilion at the Venice Biennale in 2001, Ahtila's houses are not so much architectural or sculptural structures as they are pictorial spaces, invested with the acrobatic flexibility that Schneider demanded of visitors to his HAUS UR. Ahtila shrinks and duplicates her houses both digitally and with the camera on location: the miniature replica of a hospital stands on the ground in front of its huge three-dimensional original—the lens and the movement of the crane make both versions appear real. Special effects transform the filmed or photographed world of three-dimensional objects into haunted houses as seen in horror films, where the "coziness" of the home, to use Sigmund Freud's terminology, is linked with the uncanniness of taboo zones. As we all know, Freud draws on the figure of the Sandman in E. T. A. Hoffmann's fantastic narrative to demonstrate the affinity between family home and house of horror. In Hoffmann's novella, the wondrous metamorphosis of the patriarchal home is first orchestrated with an array of optical utensils, upsetting the natural view of the world. "Opticus" Spalanzani sells a "perspective" (a small pocket telescope) to Nathaniel through which the sight of the doll Olympia is transformed into an affection-image (as discussed by Gilles Deleuze in his theory of film). In the close-up of the expanded telescope, the doll turns into the ideal image of woman: "Never in his life had he encountered a glass which brought objects before his eyes with such purity, sharpness, and clarity."[1] The optical transformation produces an obsessive picture: "For the first time he could see the wondrous beauty in the shape of her face; only her eyes seemed to him singularly still and dead. But as he looked more and more keenly through the glass, it seemed as if moist moonbeams were rising in Olympia's eyes. It was as if the power of seeing were being kindled for the first time; her glances flashed with steadily increasing life."[2] Hoffmann's narrative attracted the attention not only of Freud; film theory in particular has explored the optical premises underlying a new view of the world. However, in connection with Ahtila's uncanny houses, Spalanzani's displaced vision acquires an additional dimension. It is based on a premise in Hoffmann's tale that also prevails in Ahtila's fantastic grotesqueries: in the former, perception of the world goes awry through precise observation, while in Ahtila's work, descriptions of psychotic perception actually constitute the world. On the cover of the video LOVE IS A TREASURE (2002), we read that the film "consists of five episodes containing five different stories about women who have developed psychoses. Special cinematic techniques have been used to seamlessly situate impossibilities thrown up by the mind into realistic settings."[3] The substance of the film is derived from research and conversations with people who describe their psychotic disorders. Ahtila assembles the images, sounds, characters and texts of the interviews with poetic license, thereby lending them fictional status; she makes no attempt to provide documentary prose accounts of distorted perception. She focuses primarily on the transformational power of displacement itself as a processual means of re-constructing and -construing the visual world. Despite dramatic opening events, the films and videos take a cool, understated approach as if they were the "perspective" that empowers vision and not the enthused seer.

Compelling Obsession

In "Ground Control," an episode in LOVE IS A TREASURE, "a teenage girl becomes an assistant to the UFOs who control sounds on earth."[4] Transformations occur acoustically via sounds and optically via objects: an argument between the girl and her mother ends with the camera panning from the mother's nagging face to a close-up of a button on her blouse. A curiously shaped concrete water tower, topped with a kind of bowl, cuts to a detail of oval cladding that resembles the oval ornament of the button. Later, button-shaped digitized metallic spheres come barreling out of the night sky and race through the street, becoming ordinary buttons suspended on threads in mobiles hanging in the room. The UFO fantasies, though technically perfect, are made of everyday objects instead of being invested with high-tech allusions. In consequence, the digital image is almost ironically undermined. The blend of mental image and photographed or electronic image privileges a laconic approach. The artist has no interest in denouncing the illusionism of perception nor that of the imagination.

The logic of these pictures is inescapable: the compulsive act presupposes recognition of its self-evidence. If UFOs give the order, I obediently lie down again at night on the street, and so on. The self-evidence of my acts rests on my convictions, which give me no choice. If I believe in UFOs, I am obviously going to do what they say.

In the episode, "Underworld," a woman is curled up under the bed in a psychiatric ward. When the doctor, electronically miniaturized, marches toward her under the bed, the patient's fist swells and beats her back. These are not the spectacular special effects of science fiction and fantasy cinema. Their impact, in metaphorical terms, rests on a structure of repetition through which the sequence of pictures is thrust into a temporal axis where compulsive displacements acquire a self-evidence, making them part of the everyday world. The artist's bizarre imagery thereby strikes the viewer not only as grotesque but also as unexpectedly laconic. For Ahtila does not always place obsessive (dis-)orders centerstage; she also introduces visual metaphors, marvelous condensations of affect. In the episode, "The Wind," self-evidence becomes quintessentially natural when a woman's rage whips through the room and knocks everything down in its wake.

The interplay of things and their displacement constructs and demolishes orders, most of which are established as topographical orders, specifically the order of houses, streets, and bridges.

Room Projections

Although Ahtila's pictorial compositions tend to concentrate on the planar rather than on the sculptural effect of architecture, one cannot ignore the importance, in her works, of buildings, houses, rooms, streets, and bridges. On a plane, the house becomes a picture; in an installation, the picture becomes a wall and three pictures make a room. The room in which viewers find themselves has an order, a sequence in time based on repetition, i.e. a loop. In the final analysis, however, viewers have to orient themselves in space since they cannot take in the—usually—three screens at once. In contrast to films and videos projected on one screen, viewers find themselves thrown back from the flatness of the screen to a picture space with no fixed vantage point. The full impact of the images Ahtila projects emerges only in space. This is above all a consequence of proportion. The protagonists, most of them facing and speaking directly into the camera, confront the viewers at eye level. We see ourselves entering a room that shows a room in which someone seems to be addressing us. Only then does the effect of the many voices and sounds fully unfold.

The proportions in the installation are so conceived that they embed me in the space of the picture in a curious manner. As opposed to the small format of even the largest television screen and the optimal distance that we tend to occupy in front of a cinema screen in order to take in the entire picture, this installation keeps us at arm's length and at eye level. The space occupied by the pictures has the abstract shape of a room with walls. A performance of Ahtila's room drama generates the impression that we are in an inhabited room in which voices are addressing us or telling us plaintive episodes and stories of the kind we conceive of when happening to look into a ground floor apartment while crossing the street and unexpectedly discovering people watching television.

This mixture of the special effects of displacement, reminiscent of Valie Export's early work, and the evocation of a world at eye level is extremely disparate and explains the aesthetic appeal of Ahtila's works, the more so because a third aspect often joins the other two: a point of view, a little like a point-of-nowhere, neither narratively bound to the characters nor specifically reserved for mental projections but rather a kind of third gaze, brought into the world long ago by Opticus Spalanzani's venerable "perspective." The uncanniness is, of course, by nature precognitive in anticipation of mothers, UFOs, or accidents.

(Translation: Catherine Schelbert)

1) E.T. A. Hoffmann, *Der Sandmann* (1816) (Stuttgart: Reclam, 1969), p. 28.
2) Ibid., pp. 28–29.
3) LOVE IS A TREASURE (2002), (55 min.:1:1.85, DD5.1) Copyright: Crystal Eye, 2002.
4) Ibid.

EIJA-LIISA AHTILA, ME/WE; OKAY; GRAY, 1993, 3 x ca. 90 sec.
35-mm film and DVD installation for 3 monitors with sound, installation view, Kiasma, Finland /
3 x ca. 90 Sek. 35-mm-Film- und DVD-Installation für 3 Monitore mit Ton.
(PHOTO: MARJA-LEENA HUKKANEN)

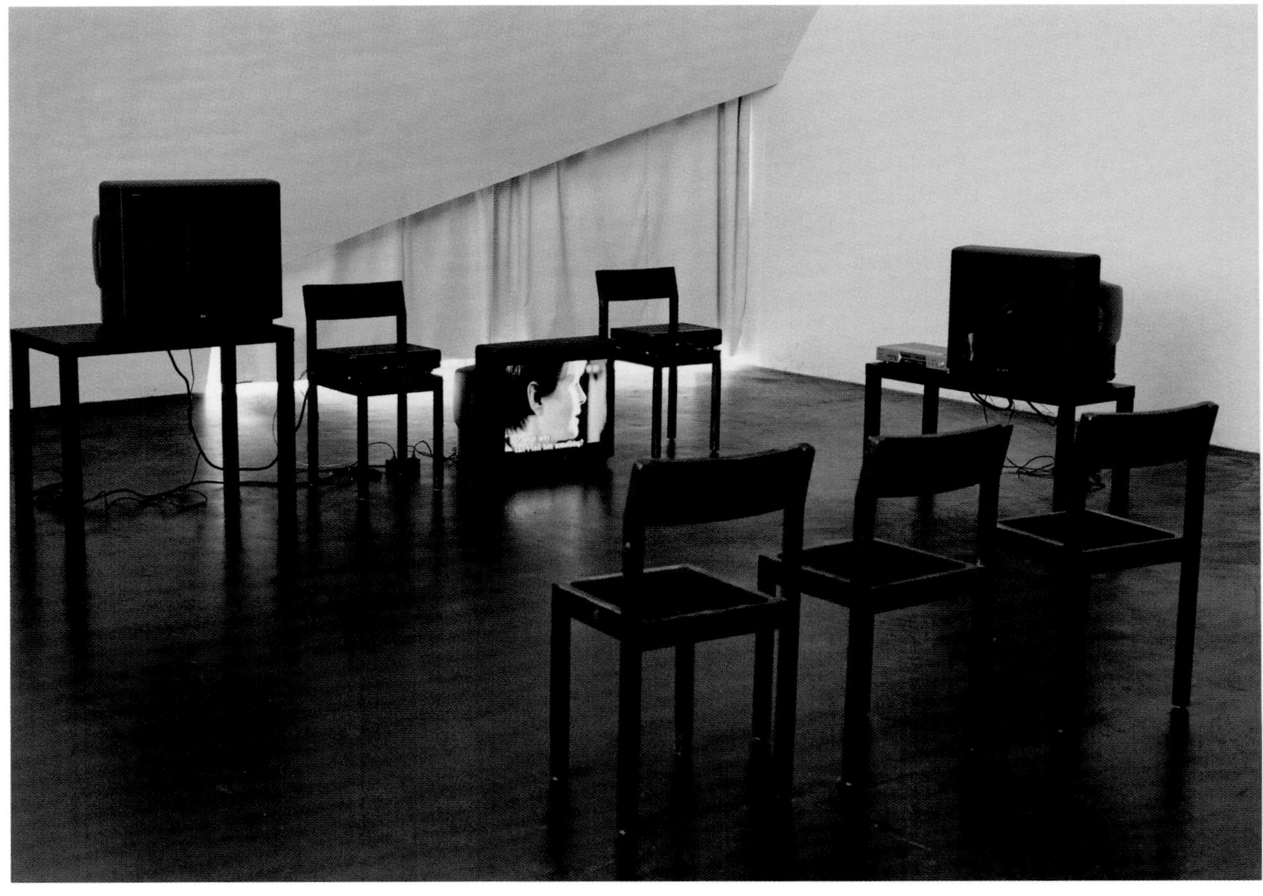

EDITION FOR PARKETT **EIJA-LIISA AHTILA**

VEIL OF IGNORANCE, 2003

Pure wool jacket with text printed on front (mirror-inverted) and back.

Handprinted silkscreen lettering by Atelier für Siebdruck Lorenz Boegli, Zurich.

Available in 5 sizes (see size table below).

Edition of 70, signed certificate.

Reines Wolljackett mit aufgedrucktem Text vorn und hinten (vorne spiegelverkehrt).

Handbedruckt bei Atelier für Siebdruck Lorenz Boegli, Zürich.

Erhältlich in 5 Grössen (siehe untenstehende Tabelle).

Auflage: 70, signiertes Zertifikat.

MEASUREMENTS IN CM / MASSE IN CM:

Men's Sizes / Herrengrössen:

Continental European	US/UK	shoulder width / Schulter-breite	back width / Rücken-breite	back length / Rücken-länge	sleeve length / Ärmel-länge	chest measurement / Brust-umfang
48	38	62	48	77	65	110
C 96	38 short	62	48	75	63	114
50	40	64	49	79	66	114.5
C 100	40 short	64	49	76	64	116.5
52	42	66	51	81	67	117

(PHOTO: MANCIA/BODMER, FBM STUDIO, ZÜRICH)

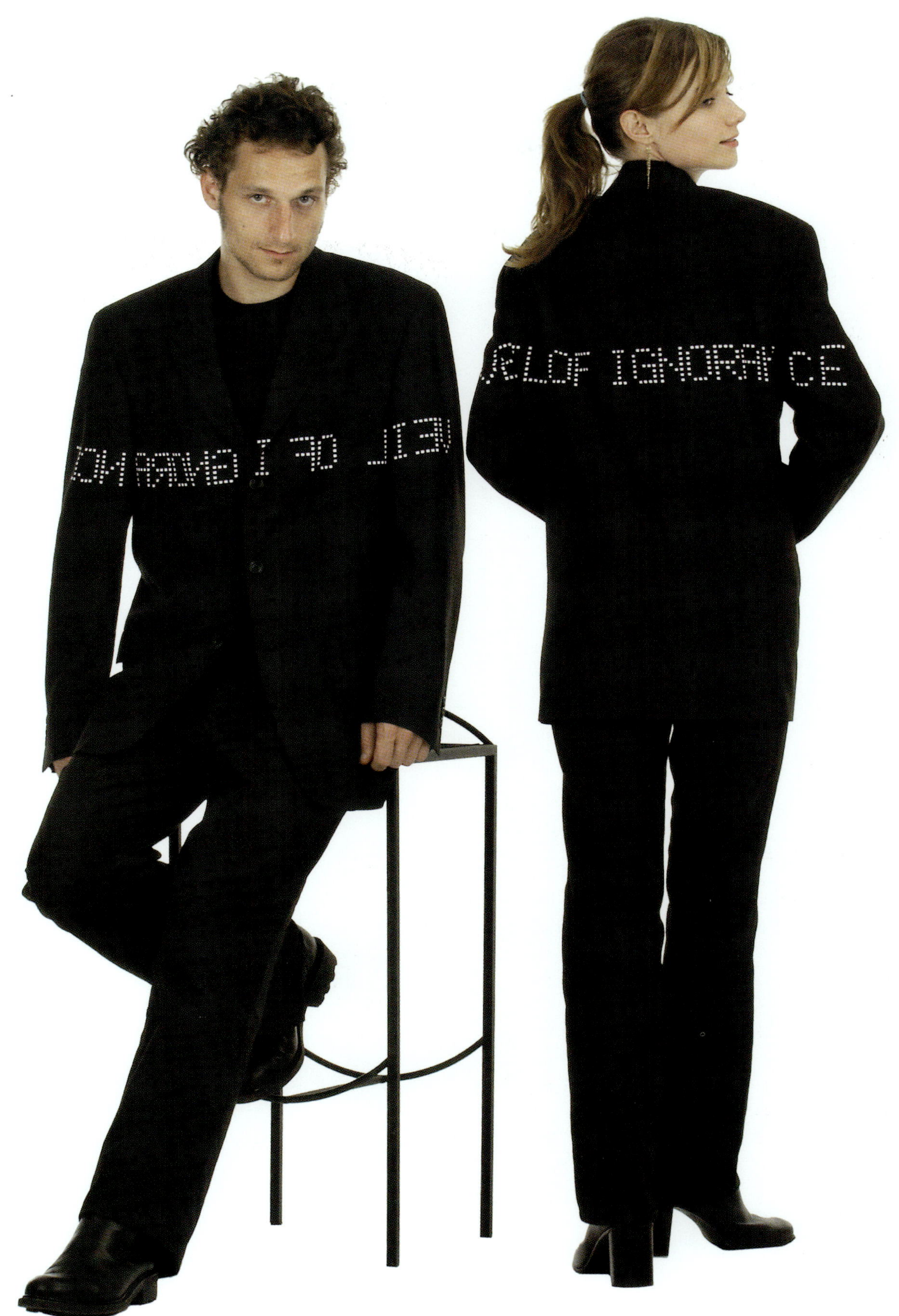

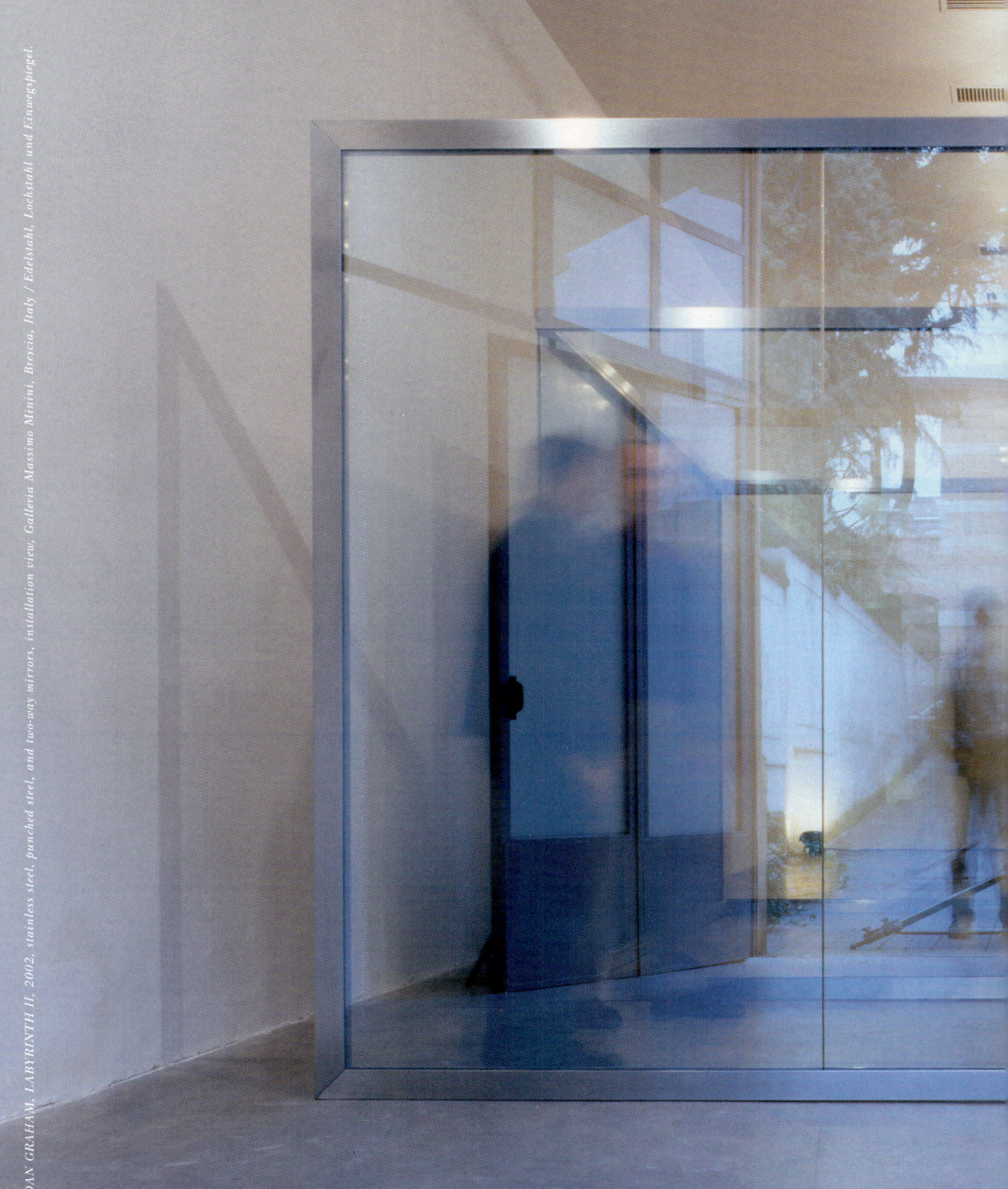

DAN GRAHAM, LABYRINTH II, 2002, stainless steel, punched steel, and two-way mirrors, installation view, Galleria Massimo Minini, Brescia, Italy / Edelstahl, Lochstahl und Einwegspiegel.

Dan Graham

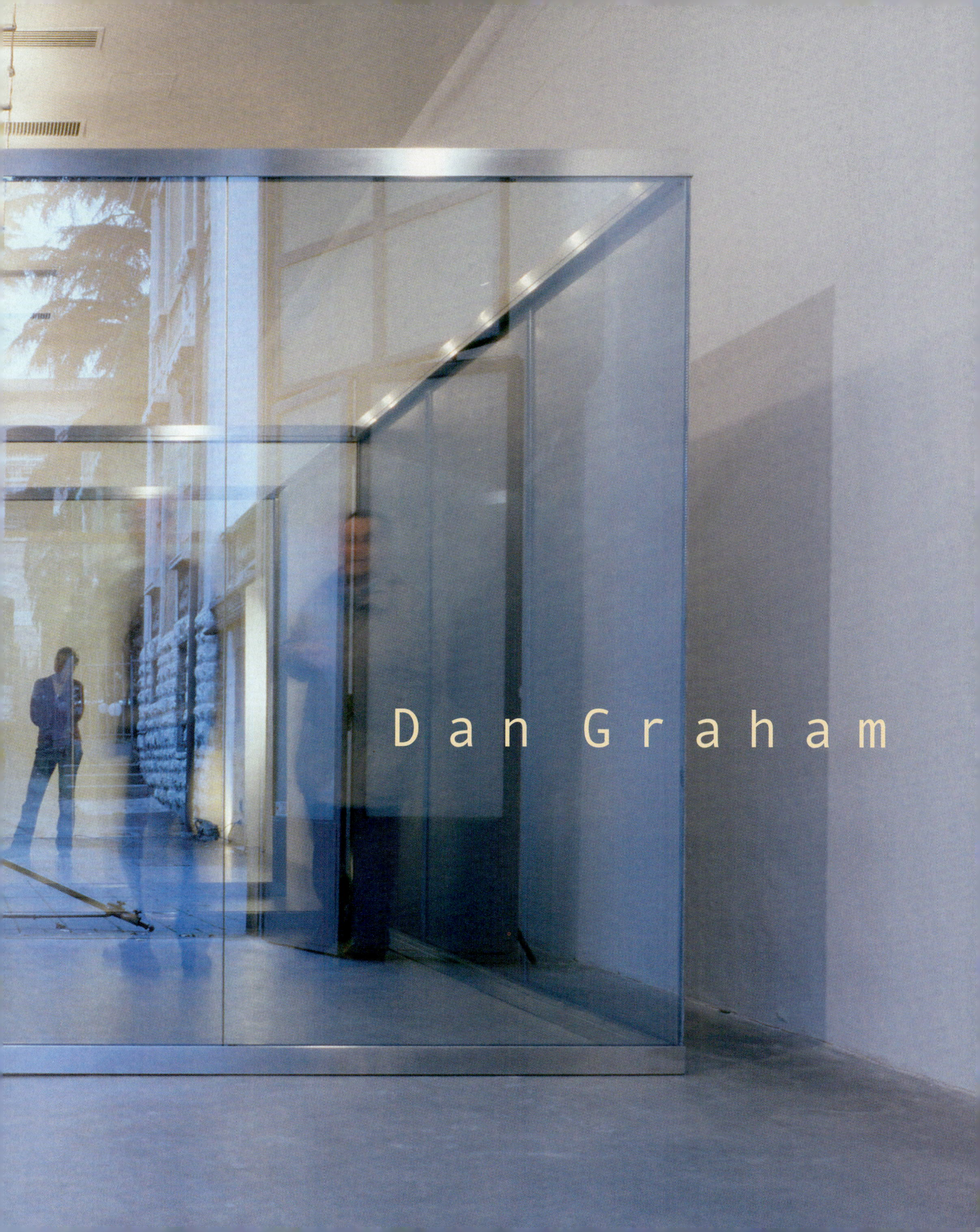

KARIN SCHNEIDER & NICOLAS GUAGNINI

Quasi Schizophrenia

Notes for a Liberated Condition

Temporality is evidently an organized structure. The three so-called "elements of time," past, present, and future, should not be considered as a collection of "givens" for us to sum up. (...) The only possible method by which to study temporality is to approach it as a totality which dominates its secondary structures and which confers on them their meaning.

–Jean-Paul Sartre [1]

Dan Graham first encountered this text at age sixteen.[2] Fourteen years later, in 1972, he would implement PAST FUTURE/SPLIT ATTENTION, performed without audience at Lisson Gallery in London and videotaped. Graham's premise for the piece is expressed in plain behaviorist terms: "Two people who know each other are in the same space. While one person predicts continuously the other person's behavior, the other person recounts (by memory) the other's past behavior."[3]

PAST FUTURE/SPLIT ATTENTION is one of Graham's first video works, preceded by a series of film pieces. In early video pieces from the same period by Bruce Nauman and Vito Acconci, one structure repeatedly appears: camera/body/monitor. Graham displaces this implied interrogation of the self—linked to the romantic notion of the artist's subjectivity expressed in the sanctioned physical space for artistic practice, the studio—and moves more towards playing with the audience and defining social spaces. Although very influenced by Nauman, who presented himself as or in place of the object, Graham subverted the subject-object relationship altogether by making the perceptual process of the spectator both the subject matter and the material of his work.

Graham discovered in the then new availability of video technology the possibility of using temporality as the preferred vehicle to rip apart the subject and consciousness. Temporality's functioning within the specificity of each media is clearly identified in the artist's notes for this work, written in the same year of 1972.[4] "As video tape [sic] is a continuum (unlike film, which is discontinuous/an analytic re-construction) with separate sound (verbal) and visual tracks, it is an ideal medium for presenting this sequence."[5]

In the first seconds of the video, two unmistakably seventies looking young men begin to come to terms with the mind-boggling proposal. While the outcome and their attitude is clearly non-theatrical and anti-narrative, the psychological and projective dimension of the premise comes forward immediately.[6] The opening statement of the "predictor" is "... you will see your mother this year more than once ... you will also see Rosalynd." The assumed objective "descriptor" of the predictor's pasts starts talking on top

KARIN SCHNEIDER & NICOLAS GUAGNINI are New York based artists and writers. They are also the co-founders of Union Gaucha Productions, a collaborative and independent film production company for artists.

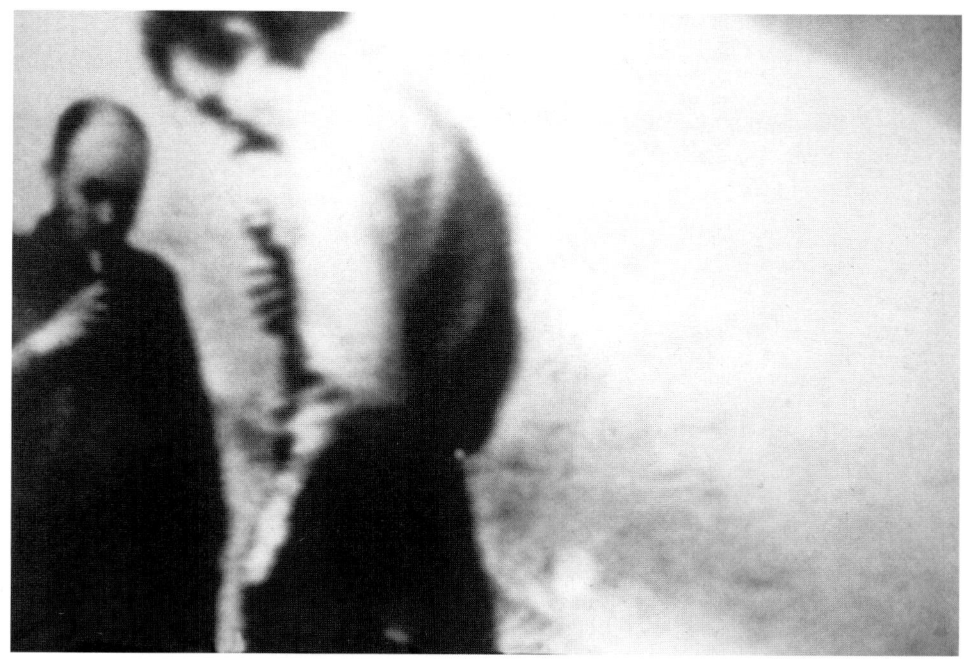

DAN GRAHAM, PAST FUTURE/SPLIT ATTENTION, 1972, performance video still / VERGANGENHEIT ZUKUNFT/ GETEILTE AUFMERKSAMKEIT.

of him. He cannot but answer aggressively: "... when you met your mother you were quite embarrassed to introduce your girlfriend."

As the performance progresses, both performers experience the happening of the just past and the very immediate predicted future. The present is never quite grasped, as it is permanently being projected forward and backwards. The tensions and accidents of their affection flow in spoken and bodily language while they struggle to keep within the given parameters. Their selves are irreversibly split: they perceive themselves as the other, continuously reflecting his perceptions in an endless feedback game.[7)] The linearity of their thinking process explodes in infinite yet not totally arbitrary reflections. Their behavior is not their own, as it is conditioned by the perception of each one by the other and the permanent attempt to reflect the other into himself. They are on different tracks, and at the same time they collapse in each other's observations. They become, for a brief moment, quasi schizophrenics.

The interpretative definition of schizophrenia favored by Graham comes from communication theory. Marshall McLuhan and Gregory Bateson were influential thinkers for the development of video art in the late sixties and early seventies.[8)] In Bateson's own words, "The theory of schizophrenia presented here is based on communication analysis, and specifically on the Theory of Logical Types. From this theory and from observations of schizophrenic patients is derived a description, and the necessary conditions for, a situation called the 'double bind'—a situation in which no matter what a person does, he 'can't win.' It is hypothesized that a person caught in the double bind may develop schizophrenic symptoms."[9)]

An atomization of the unified modern subject, a critique of Aristotelian time-space continuity, and a dismantling of Renaissance perspective and its organizing social presence are at the core of Graham's overall project from PAST FUTURE/SPLIT ATTENTION on, and in particular in the pavilion sculptures that he has developed since 1980 until today. This discrete series of constructions can also be seen as variations on the science fiction theme of the time machine.[10)] PAST FUTURE/SPLIT ATTENTION carries the model germ of the quasi-schizophrenic experience for the spectator that Graham has devised in different public pieces for the last twenty-five years of his work.

The creation of quasi-schizophrenic controlled situations through architectural, electronic and optical means gives the spectator-participant insight into the possibilities of the self, in a condition of joyful lucidity. Far from the anguish of being trapped in a pathological condition of self-alienation, the empowerment of inter subjective behavior and perception, enhanced through the use of two-way mirrors and simple geometrical forms in the situations generated by Graham's video installations and pavilions, reconciles being with becoming, constant change with identity.[11] Designed with extreme rationality and attention to the physical, urban and historical context, these works trigger irrationality inside the quotidian as they allow for an altered perception of familiar places. They free the spectator from established reality and awake the play impulse. In group situations people perceive each other perceiving each other, permitting alternative definitions of self and community. They are objects that activate the subject, and are activated by the spectator-participants. They dissolve the split between the reality principle and the pleasure principle, allowing us to be children again.

1) Jean-Paul Sartre, *Being and Nothingness*, transl. by Hazel E. Barnes (New York: Washington Square Press, 1966), p. 129.
2) Interview with Benjamin H.D. Buchloh in *Dan Graham, Works 1965–2000* (Düsseldorf: Richter Verlag, 2001), p. 169.
3) Graham, ibid., p. 139.
4) Sartre's existentialism is mostly pessimistic with regard to the possibilities of consciousness: "We can not perceive the world and at the same time apprehend a look fastened upon us; it must be either one or the other. This is because to perceive is to look at, and to apprehend a look is not to apprehend a look-as-object in the world (unless the look is not directed upon us); it is to be conscious of being looked at." Sartre, op. cit., p. 317.
Graham's video works were conceived and executed immediately after the hippie era with its explosion of psychedelic drugs and the release by Sony of the first portable video camera, the Portapak. It was a moment in time in which there was an intersection of a proliferation of available equipment and communities looking for an alternative lifestyle. The usage of all electronic equipment was briefly being utopically redefined. Thus the optimism towards the notion of an expanded consciousness is socio-historically specific.
5) Graham, op. cit., p. 139.
6) The distinction between real time and psychological time is rooted in the discussions around the late-nineteenth and early-twentieth century novel. Sartre wrote a five-volume, unfinished biography of Flaubert, *The Family Idiot: Gustave Flaubert, 1821–1857*, the pioneer and chief explorer of the psychological in the quotidian level. The other crucial development in the theorization of the opposition between real and psychological time (and the social consequences of the division of everyday life into work time and leisure time) comes from Herbert Marcuse and was pushed further politically in practice and theory by Guy Debord and the Situationists. The Brazilian artist Hélio Oiticica was working in New York in the early seventies in a series of works around a concept-proposition he developed, called "Creleisure." He wrote"(...) the discovery of Creleisure is essential to the conclusion of the participation-proposition: the catalysis of non-oppressive energies, and the proposition of the leisure connected to them (...) people + time + the possibility of expansion," August 1970. *Hélio Oiticica,* ex. cat. (Rotterdam: Witte de With Center for Contemporary Art, 1992), pp. 137–138.
7) Paul Ryan, a regular contributor to *Radical Software,* published his book *Cybernetics of the Sacred* in 1973. In this book Ryan discusses the use of videotape for communitarian and therapeutic uses and comes up with topological models using feedback loops. Topology had become a dominant mathematical metaphor around that time. Graham had encountered it much earlier at home, since his mother, an educational psychologist, had been a student of Kurt Lewin at the University of Iowa in the late thirties (Lewin had published in English his seminal *Principles of Topological Psychology* in 1936). Another artist who was attempting at the time a breakdown of the object-subject relationship using topology was the Brazilian Lygia Clark: "To capture a fragment of suspended time: If I use a Moebius strip for this experiment (CAMINHANDO/WALKING, 1964) it is because it breaks our spatial habits: Right-left, inside-outside, etc. It makes us experience limitless time and continuous space." Extract from "L'art c'est le corps," artist's text, 1973, in *Lygia Clark,* ex. cat. (Barcelona: Fundació Antoni Tápies, 1997), p. 187.
8) The magazine *Radical Software* was the arena to discuss video feedback and communication theory.
9) Gregory Bateson, *Steps to an Ecology of the Mind* (San Francisco: Chandler Publishing Company, 1972), p. 201. On temporality: "The ability to place an experience in time is one of the important cues [to diagnose schizophrenia]." p. 197.
10) Graham's favorite writer is Philip K. Dick, whose time paradoxes he read extensively. "In the living room of Ruth Rae's lavish, lovely, newly built apartment in the Fireflash District of Las Vegas, Jason Taverner said, 'I'm reasonably sure I can count on forty-eight hours on the outside and twenty-four on the inside. So I feel fairly certain that I don't have to get out of here immediately.' And if our revolutionary new principle is correct, he thought, then this assumption will modify the situation to my advantage. I will be safe. The theory changes the reality it describes." Philip K. Dick, *Flow My Tears, the Policeman Said,* (New York: Vintage Books, reissue edition 1993), p. 46.
11) Describing the use and meaning of a two-way mirror in his 1978–1982 TWO ADJACENT PAVILIONS, Graham writes: "These pavilions are used for people at restful play—a fun-house for children and a retreat for adults. They are both emblematic of the power of the corporate city and help to dissolve the city's alienation effects." *Two-Way Mirror Power: Selected Writings by Dan Graham on his Art* (Cambridge, MA: MIT Press, 1999), pp. 174–175.

KARIN SCHNEIDER & NICOLÁS GUAGNINI

Quasi schizophren

Notizen zu einem befreiten Zustand

Die Zeitlichkeit ist evidentermassen eine organisierte Struktur, und die drei sogenannten «Elemente» der Zeit: Vergangenheit, Gegenwart, Zukunft, dürfen nicht wie eine Kollektion von «Daten» betrachtet werden, aus denen die Summe zu ziehen ist (...) Die einzige mögliche Methode, die Zeitlichkeit zu untersuchen, ist, sie als eine Totalität anzugehen, die ihre sekundären Strukturen beherrscht und ihnen ihre Bedeutung verleiht.

– Jean-Paul Sartre [1]

Dan Graham ist mit sechzehn Jahren zum ersten Mal auf diesen Text gestossen.[2] Vierzehn Jahre später, 1972, entsteht PAST FUTURE / SPLIT ATTENTION (Vergangenheit Zukunft/geteilte Aufmerksamkeit), eine in der Lisson Gallery in London durchgeführte und auf Video aufgezeichnete Performance ohne Publikum. Grahams Ausgangspunkt für diese Arbeit wird mit knappen behavioristischen Begriffen umrissen: «Zwei Leute, die einander kennen, befinden sich im gleichen Raum. Während eine der beiden Personen fortwährend das Verhalten der anderen vorhersagt, rekapituliert die andere (aus der Erinnerung), wie sich die erste verhalten hat.»[3]

PAST FUTURE / SPLIT ATTENTION (1972) ist eine der ersten Videoarbeiten Grahams, der eine Reihe von Filmarbeiten vorausgegangen war. In frühen Videoarbeiten von Bruce Nauman und Vito Acconci aus derselben Zeit taucht eine bestimmte Struktur immer wieder auf: Kamera/Körper/Monitor. Graham ersetzt die darin implizierte Selbstbefragung – die mit einem romantischen Verständnis der künstlerischen Subjektivität zusammenhängt, welche sich in einem für die künstlerische Tätigkeit vorgesehenen realen Raum, dem Atelier, manifestiert – durch ein Spiel mit dem Publikum und ein Definieren sozialer Räume. Obwohl er sehr von Nauman beeinflusst war, der sich selbst als Objekt oder anstelle eines Objekts präsentierte, warf Graham die Beziehung von Subjekt und Objekt völlig über den Haufen, indem er den Wahrnehmungsprozess des Betrachters thematisierte, aber auch ganz konkret zum Gegenstand seines Werkes machte.

In der damals neu zur Verfügung stehenden Videotechnik erkannte Graham die Möglichkeit, unter Einsatz der dafür bestens geeigneten Dimension der Zeit, Subjekt und Bewusstsein auseinander zu dividieren. Die Funktion der Zeit in den jeweiligen Medien wird in den ebenfalls 1972 entstandenen Notizen des Künstlers zu dieser Arbeit deutlich angesprochen.[4] «Da Video (im Gegensatz zum Film, der eine analytische Re-Konstruktion ist) als kontinuierliche Aufzeichnung mit je separater (verbaler) Ton- und Bildspur entsteht, ist sie das ideale Medium zur Umsetzung dieser Sequenz.»[5]

In den ersten Sekunden des Videos versuchen zwei junge Männer – ganz unverkennbar aus den 70er Jahren – mit der verwirrenden Aufgabe zurechtzukommen. Obwohl das Resultat wie ihr Verhalten

KARIN SCHNEIDER & NICOLÁS GUAGNINI sind zwei Künstler und Kritiker aus New York. Sie sind Mitbegründer der Union Gaucha Productions, einer genossenschaftlichen, unabhängigen Filmproduktionsfirma für Künstlerinnen und Künstler.

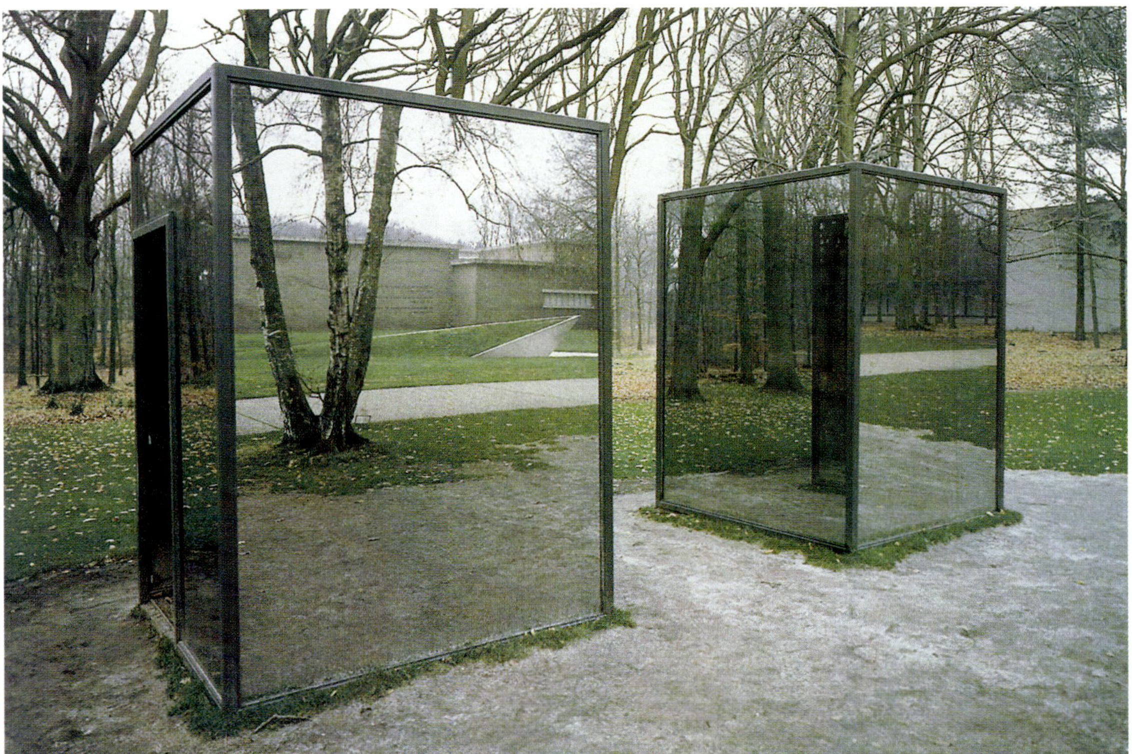

DAN GRAHAM, *TWO ADJACENT PAVILIONS, 1978–1982, two-way mirror, steel, 98¾ x 73⅕ x 73⅕", Kröller-Müller Museum, Otterlo, Holland* / ZWEI BENACHBARTE PAVILLONS, *Einwegspiegel, Stahl, 251 x 186 x 186 cm.*

absolut untheatralisch und nicht-narrativ ist, werden die psychologischen und projektiven Aspekte der Vorgaben sofort deutlich.[6] Die erste Aussage des «Prophezeienden» lautet: «... du wirst deine Mutter dieses Jahr mehr als einmal sehen... du wirst auch Rosalynd sehen.» Der so genannte objektive «Berichterstatter» über die Vergangenheit des Propheten beginnt ihm ins Wort zu fallen. Er kann gar nicht anders als aggressiv antworten: «... als du deine Mutter getroffen hast, war es dir ziemlich peinlich, ihr deine Freundin vorzustellen.»

Im Lauf der Performance erleben beide Beteiligten das eben Vergangene und die unmittelbar bevorstehende prophezeite Zukunft. Die Gegenwart wird nie ganz fassbar, weil sie andauernd nach vorn und rückwärts projiziert wird. Die Spannungen und Zufälle ihrer Gefühlsreaktionen fliessen in den verbalen Ausdruck und in ihre Körpersprache ein, während sie sich bemühen im Rahmen der verordneten Vorgaben zu bleiben. Ihr Selbst ist irreversibel gespalten: Sie nehmen sich selbst als anderen wahr und reflektieren in einem endlosen Spiel der Rückkopplung unablässig dessen Wahrnehmungen.[7] Die Linearität ihrer Denkvorgänge explodiert und geht in unendliche, aber nicht völlig willkürliche Reflexionen über. Ihr Verhalten ist nicht ihr eigenes, da es von der wechselseitigen Wahrnehmung des jeweils anderen und vom ständigen Versuch, den anderen in sich selbst zu reflektieren, bestimmt wird. Sie bewegen sich auf verschiedenen Schienen und gleichzeitig fallen sie in ihrer gegenseitigen Beobachtung zusammen. Für einen kurzen Moment werden sie quasi zu Schizophrenen.

Die Definition von Schizophrenie, die Graham bevorzugt, stammt aus der Kommunikationstheorie. Marshall McLuhan und Gregory Bateson waren die

Denker, die in den späten 60er und frühen 70er Jahren grossen Einfluss auf die Entwicklung der Videokunst ausübten.[8] Mit Batesons eigenen Worten: «Die hier vorgestellte Theorie der Schizophrenie beruht auf der Kommunikationsanalyse und insbesondere auf der Theorie der logischen Typen. Ausgehend von dieser Theorie und der Beobachtung schizophrener Patienten wird eine Beschreibung abgeleitet sowie die notwendigen Bedingungen für eine Situation, die *double bind* genannt wird – eine Situation, in der jemand, egal was er tut, ‹nicht gewinnen› kann. Die Hypothese lautet, dass ein Individuum, das in einem *double bind* gefangen ist, schizophrene Symptome entwickeln kann (...).»[9]

Die Atomisierung des einheitlichen modernen Subjekts, eine Kritik des aristotelischen Raum-Zeit-Kontinuums und die Demontage der Renaissance-Perspektive samt ihrer gesellschaftsordnenden Wirkung bilden den Kern von Grahams gesamter Arbeit seit PAST FUTURE/SPLIT ATTENTION; das gilt insbesondere auch für die Pavillon-Skulpturen, die er von 1980 bis heute entwickelt hat. Diese für sich stehende Serie von Konstruktionen kann auch als Variation auf das Sciencefictionthema der Zeitmaschine betrachtet werden.[10] PAST FUTURE/SPLIT ATTENTION bringt dem Betrachter den Urkern der quasi-schizophrenen Erfahrung nahe, die Graham in den vergangenen fünfundzwanzig Jahren in verschiedenen Arbeiten im öffentlichen Raum umsetzte.

Die Schaffung quasi-schizophrener, kontrollierter Situationen mit architektonischen, elektronischen und optischen Mitteln gewährt dem teilnehmenden Betrachter auf spielerisch einleuchtende Weise Einsicht in die Möglichkeiten des Ich. Fernab jeder Angst in einem pathologischen Zustand der Selbstentfremdung ertappt zu werden ermuntert uns zu intersubjektivem Verhalten und Wahrnehmen – in Grahams Videoinstallationen und Pavillonbauten besonders schön durch die Verwendung von Einwegspiegeln und einfachen geometrischen Formen – und versöhnt Sein und Werden, ständigen Wechsel und Identität.[11] Obwohl diese Arbeiten äusserst rational und unter sorgfältiger Beachtung des jeweiligen physikalischen, urbanen und historischen Kontexts geplant wurden, lassen sie das Irrationale im Alltäglichen aufblitzen, da sie eine ungewohnte Sicht auf Vertrautes zulassen. Sie befreien den Betrachter von der etablierten Realität und wecken den Spieltrieb. In Gruppensituationen nehmen die Leute einander beim gegenseitigen Wahrnehmen wahr, was ein neues Verständnis von Selbst und Gemeinschaft fördert. Es sind Objekte, die das Subjekt aktivieren, und gleichzeitig von den beteiligten Betrachtern zum Leben erweckt werden. Sie bringen die Kluft zwischen Realitäts- und Lustprinzip zum Verschwinden und erlauben uns wieder Kind zu sein.

(Übersetzung: Suzanne Schmidt)

1) Jean-Paul Sartre, *Das Sein und das Nichts*, übers. von T. König und H. Schöneberg, Rowohlt, Reinbek bei Hamburg 1994, S. 216.
2) Interview mit Benjamin H. D. Buchloh, in: *Dan Graham, Works 1965–2000*, Richter Verlag, Düsseldorf 2001, S. 169.
3) Graham, op. cit., S. 139.
4) Sartres Existenzialismus ist weitgehend pessimistisch, was die Möglichkeiten des Bewusstseins angeht. «Wir können nicht die Welt wahrnehmen und gleichzeitig einen auf uns fixierten Blick erfassen; es muss entweder das eine oder das andere sein. Wahrnehmen ist nämlich anblicken, und einen Blick erfassen ist nicht ein Blick-Objekt in der Welt erfassen (ausser, wenn dieser Blick nicht auf uns gerichtet ist), sondern Bewusstsein davon erlangen, angeblickt zu werden.» Sartre, op. cit., S. 467. Grahams Videoarbeiten entstanden unmittelbar im Anschluss an die Hippie-Ära und die explosionsartige Verbreitung psychedelischer Drogen und unmittelbar nachdem Sony die erste portable Videokamera auf den Markt brachte, die Portapak. Zu jenem Zeitpunkt wurden neue technische Geräte zugänglich, während gleichzeitig in Kommunen alternative Lebensstile erprobt wurden. Kurz, die Verwendung elektronischer Geräte wurde utopisch umdefiniert. Der Optimismus gegenüber der Idee des erweiterten Bewusstseins ist also in einem spezifischen soziologisch-historischen Umfeld zu verstehen.
5) Graham, op. cit., S. 139.
6) Die Unterscheidung zwischen Realzeit und psychologischer Zeit geht ursprünglich auf die Diskussion des Romans des späten neunzehnten und frühen zwanzigsten Jahrhunderts zurück. Sartre hat eine vierbändige, nicht vollendete Biographie Flauberts geschrieben *(Der Idiot der Familie: Gustave Flaubert, 1821–1857)*, des grossen Pioniers in Sachen Psychologie des Alltäglichen. Der andere entscheidende Entwicklungsschub für die Theorie des Gegensatzes zwischen realer und psychologischer Zeit (und seinen gesellschaftlichen Folgen der Aufteilung des Alltags in Arbeitszeit und Freizeit) stammt von Herbert Marcuse und wurde politisch in Theorie und Praxis von Guy Debord und den Situationisten weiterentwickelt. Der brasilianische Künstler Hélio Oiticica befasste sich in den frühen 70er Jahren in New York in einer Reihe von Arbeiten mit einem Begriffskonzept, das er «Creleisure» nannte (dt. etwa: Kreafreizeit). Im August 1970 schrieb er: «... die Entdeckung von Creleisure ist zentral für den Erfolg der Partizipationsidee: die Freisetzung nicht-

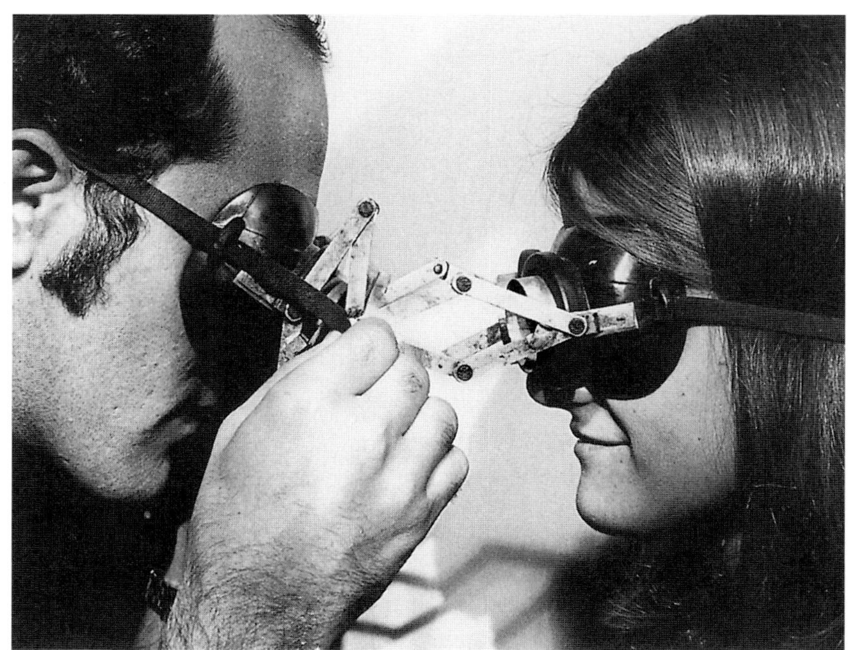

LYGIA CLARK, DIALOGUE: GOGGLES, 1968. Two participants, wearing specially equipped (diving) goggles, capture images of themselves and the surrounding space by means of mirrors. The rotating movement of the mirrors and their approaching and distancing from the eyes fragment the gaze of the participants who use this fragmentation in order to establish a dialogue. / DIALOG: SCHUTZBRILLEN. Zwei Leute mit speziell ausgerüsteten (Taucher-)Brillen sehen in kleinen Spiegeln Bilder von sich und ihrer Umgebung. Die Drehbewegung der Spiegel und ihre wechselnde Entfernung zum Auge zerstückeln das Sichtfeld der Beteiligten, welche diese Fragmentierung einsetzen, um miteinander zu kommunizieren.

oppressiver Energien und die Vorstellung von Musse, die damit verknüpft ist (...) Menschen + Zeit + Expansionsmöglichkeit.» *Hélio Oticica,* Ausstellungskatalog, Witte de With Center for Contemporary Art, Rotterdam 1992, S. 137–138.

7) Paul Ryan, der regelmässig für *Radical Software* schrieb, publizierte 1973 sein Buch, *Cybernetics of the Sacred.* Darin untersucht er den Einsatz von Videoaufzeichnungen für gemeinschaftliche und therapeutische Zwecke und erstellt mithilfe von Feedbackschleifen topologische Modelle. Die Topologie war in jener Zeit zu einer zentralen mathematischen Metapher geworden. Graham war sie im Elternhaus jedoch schon viel früher untergekommen, da seine Mutter als Schulpsychologin in den späten 30er Jahren an der Universität von Iowa bei Kurt Lewin studiert hatte. (Der deutsche Emigrant Lewin publizierte dort 1936 sein bahnbrechendes Werk *Principles of Topological Psychology.*) Einen weiteren Versuch, die herkömmliche Subjekt-Objekt-Beziehung mithilfe der Topologie zu durchbrechen, unternahm die brasilianische Künstlerin Lygia Clark: «Ein Fragment aufgehobener Zeit festhalten: Wenn ich für dieses Experiment – CAMINHANDO/WALKING (Spazieren, 1964) – eine Möbiusschleife verwende, so deshalb, weil sie die Gewohnheiten unserer Raumerfahrung aufbricht: rechts-links, innen-aussen usw. Sie macht eine grenzenlose Zeit und ein Raumkontinuum erfahrbar.» Aus «L'art c'est le corps» (1973), Text der Künstlerin, in: *Lygia Clark,* Ausstellungskatalog, Fundació Antoni Tápies, Barcelona 1977, S. 187.

8) Schauplatz der Diskussion von Video-Feedback und Kommunikationstheorie war damals die Zeitschrift *Radical Software.*

9) Gregory Bateson, *Steps to an Ecology of the Mind,* Chandler Publishing Company, San Francisco 1972, S. 201. Zum Thema Zeitlichkeit: «Die Fähigkeit eine Erfahrung zeitlich zu lokalisieren ist eines der wichtigen Schlüsselmomente [für die Diagnose von Schizophrenie], ebenda, S. 197. (Zitatübersetzung: Red.)

10) Grahams Lieblingsautor ist Philip K. Dick, dessen Zeitparadoxien er ausgiebig studiert hat. «Im Wohnzimmer von Ruth Raes luxuriösem, wunderschönem, Neubauappartment im Fireflash-Distrikt in Las Vegas sagte Jason Taverner: ‹Ich habe guten Grund zur Annahme, dass ich draussen mit 48 Stunden rechnen kann und drinnen mit 24. Deshalb bin ich mir ziemlich sicher, dass ich nicht sofort von hier verschwinden muss.› Und wenn unser revolutionäres neues Prinzip richtig ist, dachte er, dann wird diese Annahme die Situation zu meinem Vorteil verändern. Ich bin in Sicherheit. Die Theorie verändert die Realität, die sie beschreibt.» Philip K. Dick, *Flow My Tears, the Policeman Said,* Vintage Books, Neuauflage New York, 1993, S. 46. (Übersetzung: Red., die deutsche Ausgabe, *Eine andere Welt,* ist zurzeit vergriffen.)

11) In seinem Kommentar zu Gebrauch und Bedeutung eines Einwegspiegels in TWO ADJACENT PAVILIONS (Zwei benachbarte Pavillons, 1978–1982) schreibt Graham: «Diese Pavillons sind für das erholsame Spiel gedacht – ein Plauschhaus für Kinder und eine Rückzugsmöglichkeit für Erwachsene. Beide sind Sinnbilder für die Stadtgemeinschaft und tragen dazu bei, die Entfremdungseffekte der Stadt aufzuheben.» *Two-Way Mirror Power: Selected Writings by Dan Graham on his Art,* MIT Press, Cambridge, Mass. 1999, S. 174–175. (Übersetzung: Red.)

Glass *Perception*

MARIE-PAULE MACDONALD

In Manhattan, one readily accessible, poetically located sculptural work by Dan Graham is set in the roofscapes of Chelsea, at the Dia Center for the Arts. Assembled in 1991, it sits on top of a former light industrial building on West 23rd Street. The building shares the west end of the block traversed by the High Line, an abandoned elevated freight train track. The route to the Dia Center passes through the High Line's rows of rusted, paint-flaked steel columns and underneath its overgrown tracks. Getting up to the roof of the building involves ascending in the tiny elevator or narrow stairs with tall risers.

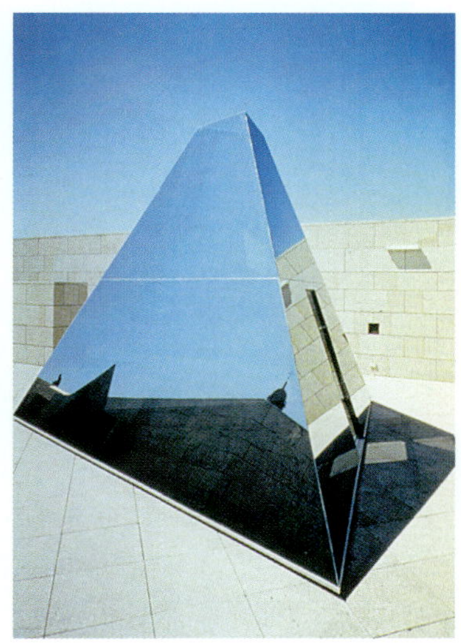

DAN GRAHAM, PYRAMID WITH TOP CUT OFF, 1989–1997, CGAC – Centro Galego de Arte Contemporánea, Santiago di Compostela / PYRAMIDE MIT ABGESCHNITTENER SPITZE.

The sculptural project on the roof, set on a raised wooden platform like an industrial version of a plinth, comprises a walk-in-size two-way mirror glass cylinder, scaled to the size of a water tower, set within a square glass frame, and an adjacent video café. The 360-degree vista from the Rooftop Park includes views of the High Line, Battery Park City, and New Jersey. Unused since 1981, the High Line can be "infiltrated"—one can sneak up and trespass, following a route through grass, native wild flowers, and trees, which have grown over the train track. A community group has tenaciously organized an attempt to transform the abandoned slice of rail infrastructure into an elevated public promenade. The initiative is inspired by the Viaduc des Arts in rue Daumesnil, Paris, a kilometer-long series of brick arches, renovated under the direction of architect Patrick Berger. Like the Parisian prototype, the Rooftop Park and the High Line offer a singular series of aerial vistas above the streets of a city whose density requires vertically stacked tiers of urban social life and architecture.

The adjacency and juxtaposition of these two quintessentially American works: the serial steel construction of the elevated rail infrastructure, and the two-way mirror glass and steel geometries of the rooftop pavilion, set up a contrapuntal urban resonance in the neighborhood. Dan Graham's interest developed into a desire to address, to express and confront issues of contemporary urbanism, landscape and public space. These concerns are apparent in a wide range of formal references, from the issues of scale, in the case of the water tower, to the choice of materials such as reflective glass and painted steel. For example, the rubber tile (flooring) on the Dia Center Rooftop Park is the same spongy material used to surface children's playgrounds, thickened at the base of playground slides.

MARIE-PAULE MACDONALD is an architect currently teaching in Montreal and the University of Waterloo, Canada.

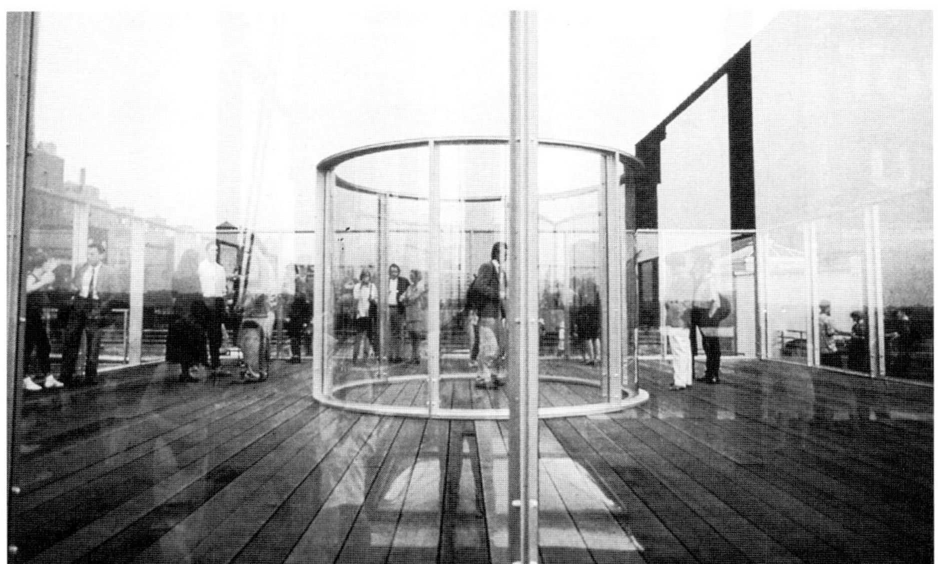

DAN GRAHAM, TWO-WAY MIRROR CYLINDER INSIDE CUBE AND VIDEO SALON, 1981/1988–1991, steel, two-way mirror, wood, aluminum, $8\frac{1}{2}$ x $36\frac{1}{8}$ x $36\frac{1}{8}$'; café: 12 x $36\frac{1}{8}$'; architects: Moji Baratloo, Clifton Balch / EINWEGSPIEGEL-ZYLINDER IN EINEM KUBUS UND VIDEOSALON, Stahl, Einwegspiegel, Holz, Aluminium, 260 x 1100 x 1100 cm, Café: 366 x 701 cm.

Citizens of the New York metropolis have been preoccupied with the problem of creating new public space as a result of the quest to redesign the Ground Zero site in Lower Manhattan. The design of urban public space has been a particular Achilles' heel of Modern Architecture and is often treated as mere public relations posturing in contemporary urban development. Modern architect and urbanist José Luis Sert acknowledged the issue in the fifties with a rudimentary statement of principle: "... places of public gatherings such as public squares, promenades, cafés, popular community clubs, etc., where people can meet freely, shake hands and choose the subject of their discussion are not things from the past, and, properly re-planned for the needs today, should have a place in our cities."[1] Manhattan's nineteenth- and twentieth-century responses to the need for urban public space introduced alternatives to the traditional public square or plaza of the European model, with extreme exaggerations: antimonies from the vast, metropolitan-scaled green common of Central Park, to the telescopically compressed diagonal views, created in the fortuitous intersection of streets and sidewalks, at Times Square.

What is public space, what should it be, and as Françoise Choay has publicly asked, where are the public spaces of our era?[2] Some answers from the nineties can be identified in the intimate spaces and speculative, self-conscious architectural programming of Graham's Rooftop Park, and in the paradoxical circumstances of public space in Manhattan, where the public realm is just as likely to be in the custody of private organizations and foundations. A *New Yorker* writer noted, "High is to New York what wet is to Venice."[3] In a vertical city, can civic public space be made democratically available six stories up in the air? Graham's work alludes to the scope of aerial urban places of leisure, from leafy penthouse terraces to the tar-papered tenement roof.

A public, theatrical quality emanates from Graham's exhaustive array of ambitions and aspirations for the Rooftop Park. He intended a gesture to the history of spontaneous performance traditions of previous twentieth century decades, when street, sidewalk, rented commercial or studio space, or community centers and alternative art spaces became temporary sites for street theater, dance, sound, events, etc. A specific reference is to the landfilled beach that preceded Battery Park City. Once the site of informal art collaborations, the site has since transformed into corporate headquarter lobbies and security stations. In response, Graham proposed programming the rooftop park for dance and performance. The video café complemented the reference as a place where recent video would be continuously available in relaxed circumstances.

The long, precise title of the sculpture of the rooftop park is TWO-WAY MIRROR CYLINDER INSIDE CUBE AND VIDEO SALON. The inner layer of the glass cylinder, centered inside the glass square posed on a wood deck set about three feet above the rubberized decking mat covering the roof, responds when visitors push on the pivot arc of the heavy door in the cylinder. The door's movement activates the sculpture as a perceptual device to mirror the skyline and set up a visual echo of the individual's place within it. The urban landscape reflects in the curved and planar glass: every visible element, from the water tower, adjacent billboards, to the cloud formations appear in superimposed strata. A cinematic tableau of subject and object, composed of the self, others, and of rooftop architecture, sky, and horizon is layered, stretched, curved, retransmitted, and bounced on the glass surfaces.

The "autoscopy" of seeing one's replicated self in the urban landscape is a usual feature of the ground level in the contemporary hyper-technological city. Around town—not just Manhattan, but in almost any post-industrial city—the ubiquity of the reflected image in glass store windows and mirrors has been augmented by the new ubiquity of the video image, delayed video image, or data-projected video image. It is a reminder of the prescience of Graham's video performance works of the seventies. Contemporary architecture and urbanism now almost automatically incorporate these technologies of a video-saturated urban existence. The narcissistic appeal of viewing one's self is a feature in suave contemporary renovations, projects such as Diller + Scofidio's fashionable restaurant interior, the Brasserie, in the Seagram building, where a delayed video image is relayed over the restaurant bar, recalling Graham's video installations from 1974 (PRESENT CONTINUOUS PAST[S]; TIME DELAY SERIES, etc.). The close-up viewing of one's body that was documented in Graham's live BODY PRESS spiral (1970) is "consumeristically" referenced in the intimate live video transmission found in underground dressing rooms in the cosmopolitan downtown store interior designed by Rem Koolhaas' office, OMA. The cylindrical glass elevator, also at Prada, could well be perceived as a form whose antecedents include Graham's reflective rooftop cylinder. City life is embellished, now perhaps cluttered with a high level of surveillance and self-viewing. What is compelling in Graham's open-air, atmospheric use of video, mirrors, and geometries of reflective glass is not only its focus on a refreshed perception of the self in the urban landscape, but also what Northrop Frye described, in his definition of "ethical criticism," as a "consciousness of the presence of society."[4] At a time that risks coming to be called a "posthuman" era, this informal, intuitive perception of the social seems crucial in the contemporary conception of public space.

1) *José Luis Sert, Arquitecto in Nueva York,* ex. cat., ed. by Xavier Costa, Guido Hartray (Barcelona: ACTAR & Museu d'Art Contemporani de Barcelona, 1997), p. 132.

2) Françoise Choay, "La Proximité comme problème anthropologique," notes for a public lecture at the Centre Georges Pompidou, circa 1996.

3) Adam Gopnik, "A Walk on the High Line," *The New Yorker,* May 21, 2001, p. 44.

4) "We may call this ethical criticism, interpreting ethics not as a rhetorical comparison of social facts to predetermined values, but as the consciousness of the presence of society." Northrop Frye, "Polemical Introduction" in *Anatomy of Criticism: Four Essays* (Princeton, NJ: Princeton University Press, 1957), p. 24.

Verspiegelte *Wahrnehmung*

MARIE-PAULE MACDONALD

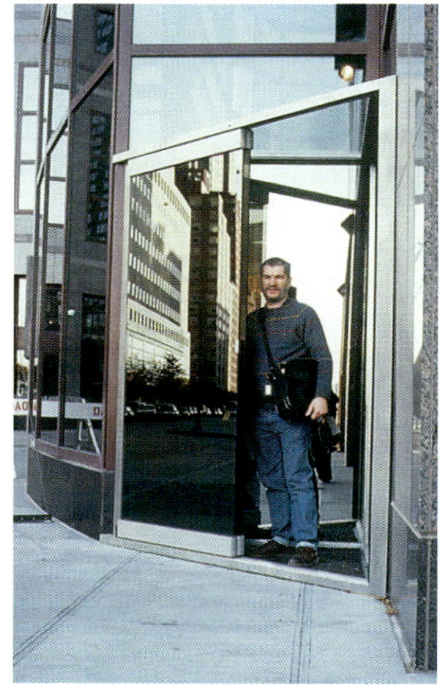

DAN GRAHAM, TRIANGULAR ENCLOSURE FOR NEW URBAN LANDSCAPE, 1988, New York City / DREIECKIGE KAMMER FÜR NEUE STADTLANDSCHAFT.

Eine leicht zugängliche Skulptur von Dan Graham befindet sich an poetischer Stelle in Manhattan, inmitten der Dachlandschaft von Chelsea auf dem Dia Center for the Arts. Sie wurde 1991 realisiert und sitzt nun auf dem Dach des ehemaligen Leichtindustrie-Gebäudes an der dreiundzwanzigsten Strasse West. Das Gebäude am Westende des Blocks stösst an das Gelände mit dem verlassenen Hochbahngeleise einer ehemaligen S-Bahn-Linie. Die Strasse zum Dia Center führt unter den rostenden Stahlträgern, von denen die Farbe abblättert, und den von Unkraut überwucherten Geleisen hindurch. Um aufs Dach des Gebäudes zu gelangen muss man den winzigen Lift benützen oder eine enge Treppe mit steilen Stufen erklimmen.

Die Dachskulptur steht auf einer erhöhten Holzplattform, die wie die industrielle Version eines Sockels anmutet, und besteht aus einem betretbaren Einwegspiegelglas-Zylinder von der Grösse eines Wasserturms, der in einem quadratischen Glasrahmen platziert ist, sowie einem Videocafé. Vom Dachgarten aus hat man eine 360-Grad-Rundsicht auf die Hochbahn, Battery Park City und New Jersey. Man kann die seit 1981 nicht mehr im Gebrauch befindlichen Geleise der Hochbahn betreten, das heisst sich unerlaubter Weise hinaufschleichen und dem von Gras, einheimischen Wildblumen und Bäumen überwachsenen Trassee folgen. Eine Bürgerinitiative hat sich hartnäckig dafür eingesetzt, aus dem verlassenen Eisenbahnteilstück eine öffentlich zugängliche Fussgängerpromenade zu machen. Die Initiative war vom Daumesnil-Viadukt in Paris inspiriert, jener kilometerlangen Aneinanderreihung von Backsteinbögen, die unter der Leitung des Architekten Patrick Berger renoviert wurde. Wie das Pariser Vorbild bieten auch der Dia-Dachgarten und die Hochbahnlinie eine Reihe einzigartiger Ausblicke über die Strassen einer Stadt, deren Dichte das urbane Leben und die urbane Architektur Schicht um Schicht in die Höhe zwingt.

Das kontrastreiche Nebeneinander dieser beiden zutiefst amerikanischen Bauwerke – der seriellen Stahlkonstruktion der Hochbahnbrücke und der Einwegspiegelglas- und Stahl-

---

MARIE-PAULE MACDONALD ist Architektin und lehrt zurzeit in Montreal und an der University of Waterloo, Kanada.

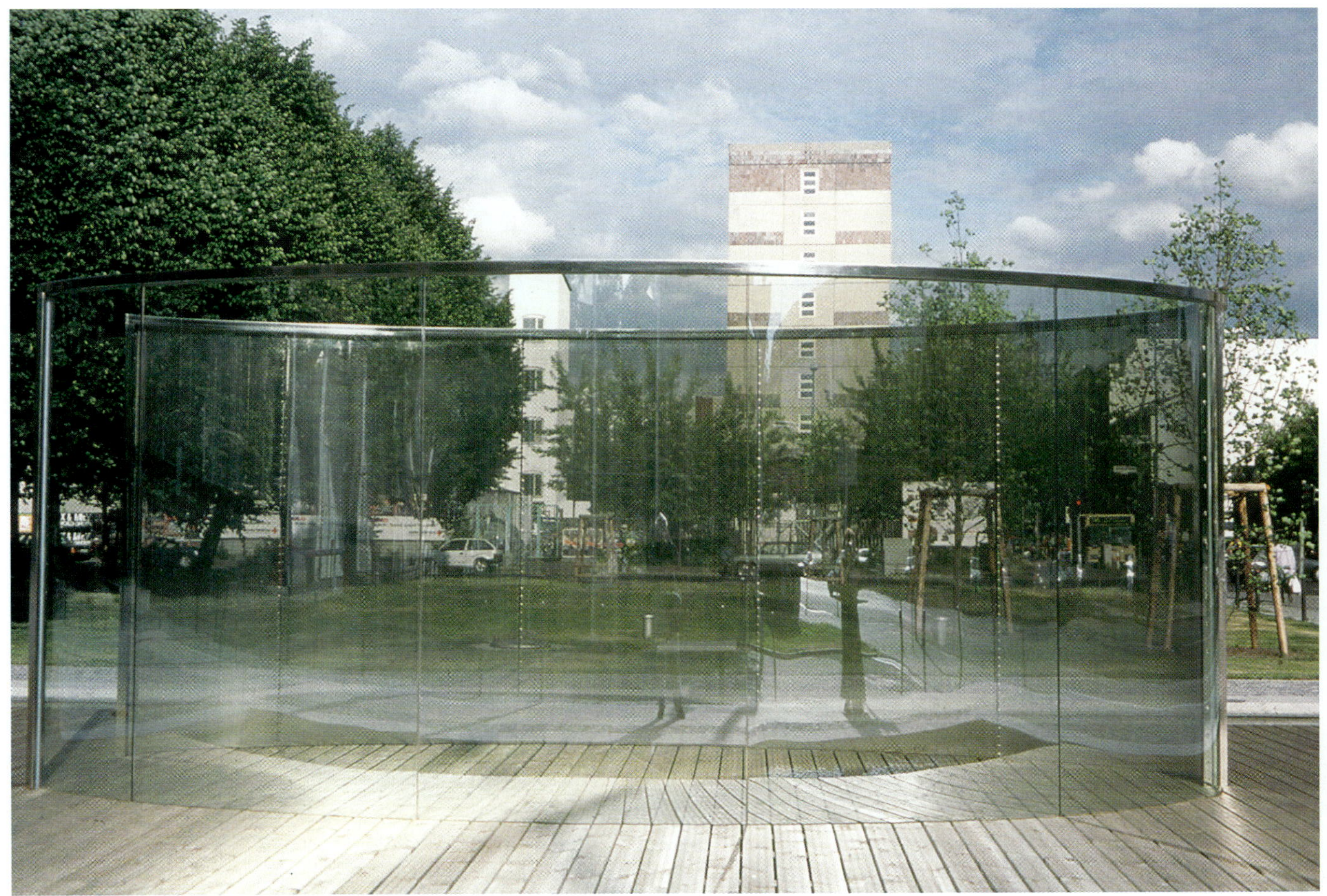

DAN GRAHAM, ELLIPTICAL PAVILION, 1996–1999, two-way mirror, aluminum, Bewag, Berlin, 94 1/2 x 197 x 71" / ELLIPTISCHER PAVILLON, Einwegspiegel, Aluminium, 240 x 500 x 180 cm.

geometrie des Dachpavillons – bildet einen urbanen Kontrapunkt zur unmittelbaren Umgebung. Dan Graham entwickelte zunehmend das Bedürfnis, Fragen zur zeitgenössischen Urbanität, zur Landschaft und zum öffentlichen Raum aufzuwerfen und sich damit auseinander zu setzen. Dieses Interesse ist an einer grossen Bandbreite formaler Referenzen ablesbar, von der Dimension, im Fall des Wasserturms, bis zur Wahl der Materialien, etwa des Spiegelglases und des bemalten Stahls. So ist etwa der Gummiplattenbelag auf dem Dach des Dia Centers aus demselben federnden Material, wie es auf Kinderspielplätzen Verwendung findet, unter Rutschbahnen in etwas dickerer Ausführung.

Die Einwohner der Metropole New York haben sich in jüngster Zeit mit der Frage der Schaffung neuer öffentlicher Räume im Zusammenhang mit der anstehenden Neugestaltung des *Ground Zero* an Manhattans Südspitze auseinander gesetzt. Die Gestaltung des öffentlichen urbanen Raums ist eine besondere Achillesferse der modernen Architektur und wird oft lediglich als PR-Pose zeitgenössischen Städtebaus missverstanden und praktiziert. Der moderne Architekt und Städteplaner José Luis Sert sprach dieses Thema in den 50er

Jahren in einer knappen, aber grundsätzlichen Formulierung an: «...Orte öffentlicher Begegnung, wie öffentliche Plätze, Promenaden, Cafés, gut besuchte Gemeinschaftszentren usw., wo Leute sich nach Belieben treffen, die Hand schütteln und frei unterhalten können, gehören nicht der Vergangenheit an und sollten, sorgfältig auf die Bedürfnisse von heute zugeschnitten, in unseren Städten Platz haben.»[1] Im neunzehnten und zwanzigsten Jahrhundert hat Manhattan als Antwort auf das Bedürfnis nach öffentlichen urbanen Räumen Alternativen zum traditionellen öffentlichen Platz oder Marktplatz europäischer Prägung entwickelt, und zwar durch eine extreme Steigerung: von der wahrhaft einer Metropole würdigen, riesigen Grünfläche des Central Park bis zu den teleskopisch verdichteten diagonalen Ausblicken, die dank der zufälligen Kreuzung der Strassen und Gehsteige am Times Square entstanden.

Was ist öffentlicher Raum, was sollte er sein, und, wie Françoise Choay in aller Öffentlichkeit fragte, wo sind die öffentlichen Räume unserer Zeit?[2] Einige Antworten aus den 90er Jahren lassen sich an den intimen Räumen und dem spekulativen, sich selbst reflektierenden architektonischen Programm von Grahams Dachgarten ablesen und auch an den paradoxen Bedingungen für den öffentlichen Raum in Manhattan, wo der öffentliche Grund oft in der Hand privater Organisationen und Stiftungen liegt. Ein Journalist des *New Yorker* meinte einmal: «Die Höhe ist für New York, was das Wasser für Venedig ist.»[3] Kann der öffentliche städtische Raum in einer vertikalen Stadt im sechsten Stockwerk allen gleichermassen demokratisch zugänglich gemacht werden? Grahams Arbeit ist eine Anspielung auf das Thema der luftigen urbanen Freizeiträume, von der begrünten Penthouseterrasse bis zum mit Teerpappe bedeckten Mietskasernendach.

Dan Grahams erschöpfende Aufstellung von Ambitionen und Zielen für den Dachgarten hat öffentlichen, performativen Charakter. Er beabsichtigte eine Reverenz an die Tradition der spontanen Performance vergangener Jahrzehnte, als die Strasse, der Gehsteig, der gemietete Laden oder Atelierraum oder auch Gemeinschaftszentren und alternative Kunsträume vorübergehend zu Aufführungsorten von Stassentheater, Tanz, Musik, Happenings usw. gemacht wurden. Eine Anspielung gilt insbesondere dem aufgeschütteten Uferstreifen, dort wo jetzt Battery Park City steht. Einst ein Ort informeller künstlerischer Gemeinschaftsprojekte ist er heute eine Ansammlung von Firmenhauptsitzen und Sicherheitsbüros. Grahams Vorschlag, den Dachgarten zu einem Ort für Tanz und Theater zu machen, ist eine Reaktion darauf. Ergänzt wird diese Bezugnahme durch das Videocafé, einen Ort, wo man sich jederzeit aktuelle Videos in entspannter Atmosphäre anschauen kann.

Der lange, präzise Titel der Dachgartenskulptur lautet TWO-WAY MIRROR CYLINDER INSIDE CUBE AND VIDEO SALON (Einwegspiegel-Zylinder in einem Kubus und Videosalon). Die Innenseite des Glaszylinders inmitten des gläsernen Quadrates auf dem Holzpodium, welches sich etwa 90 Zentimeter über den Gummibelag des Daches erhebt, entfaltet ihre Wirkung erst, wenn Besucher die Angel der schweren Zylindertür in Bewegung setzen. Die Bewegung der Tür macht die Skulptur zum Wahrnehmungswerkzeug, das den Horizont spiegelt und den Ort des Individuums darin wiedergibt. Die urbane Landschaft spiegelt sich im gekrümmten und planen Spiegelglas: Jedes sichtbare Element, vom Wasserturm, den benachbarten Plakatwänden, bis zu Wolkenformationen erscheinen in einander überlagernden Schichten. Ein kinematisches Tableau von Subjekt und Objekt, bestehend aus dem Selbst, den anderen, aus der Dacharchitektur, dem Himmel und dem Horizont wird geschichtet, gestreckt, gestaucht und noch einmal gespiegelt, so dass es buchstäblich auf den Spiegelglasflächen tanzt.

Diese «Selbstbeobachtung», das Erblicken des eigenen Spiegelbildes in der urbanen Landschaft, ist ein alltägliches Erlebnis im «Parterre» der zeitgenössischen hoch technologisierten Stadt. Überall in der Stadt – nicht nur in Manhattan, sondern in fast jedem postindustriellen Stadtzentrum – wird die Allgegenwart des Spiegelbildes in Schaufenstern und Spiegeln noch gesteigert durch die Allgegenwart des Videobildes, der zeitverschobenen Videoaufnahme oder des Videobildes als Datenprojektion. Das beweist nur die Weitsicht von Grahams Videoperformance-Arbeiten aus den 70er Jahren. Zeitgenössische Architektur und Stadtplanung beinhalten heute fast selbstredend diese Technologien einer videogesättigten urbanen Existenz. Der narzisstische Reiz des eigenen Bildes ist inzwischen integraler Bestandteil sanfter zeitgenössischer Renovationen, in Projekten wie Diller und Scofidios modischer Restaurantaufmachung oder der Brasserie im Seagram-Gebäude, wo ein zeitverschobenes Videobild über die Bar projiziert wird und an Dan Grahams Videoinstallationen von 1974 denken lässt (PRESENT CONTINUOUS PAST[S]; TIME DELAY SERIES und andere). An die Nahaufnahmen des eigenen Körpers, die Grahams BODY PRESS-Spirale (1970) live dokumentierte, erinnert die kommerzielle Variante der intimen Live-Videoübertragung in den Umkleidekabinen einer *Downtown*-Boutique im kosmopolitischen Design von Rem Koolhaas' Büro OMA. Den zylinderförmigen Glasfahrstuhl, auch bei Prada, könnte man ohne weiteres als eine Form betrachten, zu deren Vorgängern auch Grahams reflektierender Zylinder auf dem Dach gehört. Das Leben in der Stadt wird verschönert – mittlerweile vielleicht auch ein bisschen überladen – durch das hohe Mass an Überwachung und die Spiegelbilder unserer selbst. Was an Grahams atmosphärischem Open-Air-Einsatz von Video, Spiegeln und der Geometrie reflektierender Glasflächen überzeugt, ist jedoch nicht nur die Konzentration auf eine neue Sicht des Ich in der urbanen Landschaft, sondern auch, was Northrop Frye in seiner Definition einer «ethischen Kritik» als «Bewusstsein von der Gegenwärtigkeit der Gesellschaft» bezeichnete.[4)] In einer Zeit, die Gefahr läuft als «posthumane» Ära in die Geschichte einzugehen, ist diese informelle, intuitive Auffassung des Gesellschaftlichen wohl von entscheidender Bedeutung für das zeitgenössische Verständnis des öffentlichen Raumes.

(Übersetzung: Wilma Parker)

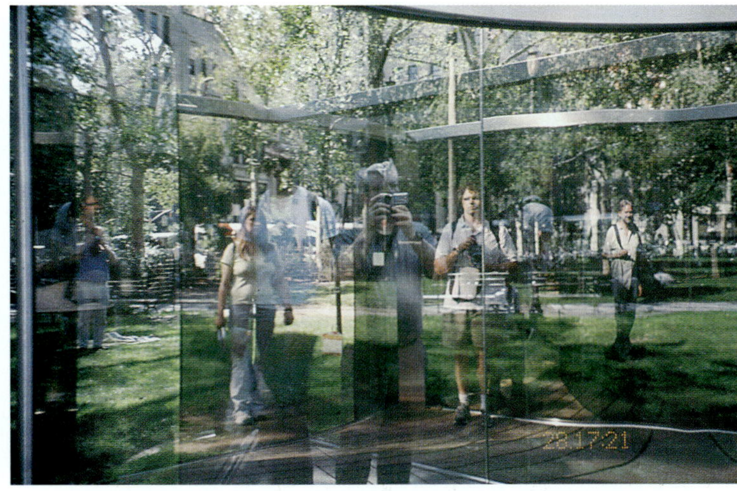

DAN GRAHAM, BISECTED TRIANGLE, INTERIOR CURVE, 2002, Madison Square Park, New York City, 20 x 24 x 24' / HALBIERTES DREIECK, INNERE KURVE, 600 x 730 x 730 cm.

1) *José Luis Sert: Arquitecto in Nueva York,* Ausstellungskatalog, hrsg. v. Xavier Costa und Guido Hartray, ACTAR & Museu d'Art Contemporani de Barcelona, 1997, S. 132.

2) Françoise Choay, «La Proximité comme problème anthropologique», Notizen zu einem öffentlichen Vortrag im Centre Georges Pompidou, ca. 1996.

3) Adam Gopnik, «A Walk on the High Line», *The New Yorker,* 21. Mai 2001, S. 44.

4) «Man könnte dies eine ethische Kritik nennen, wenn man Ethik nicht als rhetorischen Vergleich sozialer Gegebenheiten mit vorbestimmten Werten versteht, sondern als Bewusstsein von der Gegenwärtigkeit der Gesellschaft.» Northrop Frye, «Polemical Introduction», in: *Anatomy of Criticism: Four Essays,* Princeton University Press, Princeton 1957, S. 24.

Dan Graham

DAN GRAHAM, DOUBLE EXPOSURE: LANDSCAPE PHOTO PAVILION II, 1995, architectural model, two-way mirror, cibachrome transparency, 19¾ x 42 x 42". (PHOTO: PETER WHITE)

This pavilion is sited in a landscape with trees. The triangular pavilion, which is enterable through a sliding door, has two two-way mirror sides, while the third side is a huge cibachrome transparency. The transparency is of the landscape viewed from within the structure, 50 meters in front of the transparency side. The transparency is taken on a spring day, nearly at sunset. Spectators inside the structure can see the present landscape, slowly changing as to sunlight and time of the day, through the static image of the lightly exposed transparency of the past view. Each year, one year later, the photographed transparency is aligned, but slightly different from the original photographed view. This creates a time-delay with a still photo. Spectators inside the pavilion see a prismatically re-reflected, superimposed and continuously fluctuating (due to the change in outside lighting) image on the two-way mirror sides. There are continuous reflective and transparent views of the immediately surrounding landscape on both sides of the pavilion superimposed on images of gazing spectators inside and outside of the pavilion's sides, superimposed on the cibachrome distant landscape view through the actual distant landscape view.

Dan Graham, 1995–96

DOPPELBELICHTUNG. LANDSCHAFTSPHOTOPAVILLON II, Architekturmodell, Einwegspiegel, Cibachrome-Diapositiv, 50,2 x 106,7 x 106,7 cm.

Der Pavillon steht in einer Landschaft mit Bäumen. Der dreieckige Pavillon, in den man durch eine Schiebetür gelangt, hat zwei Einwegspiegelwände, die dritte Wand besteht aus einem riesigen Cibachrome-Diapositiv. Das Dia zeigt den Blick aus dem Innern des Pavillons auf die Landschaft 50 Meter vor der Diawand. Die Aufnahme entstand an einem Frühlingstag kurz vor Sonnenuntergang. Besucher innerhalb des Gebäudes sehen die reale, sich je nach Tageszeit und Sonneneinstrahlung langsam verändernde Landschaft durch das sich nicht verändernde transparente Diabild der früher aufgenommenen Landschaft hindurch. Nach einem Jahr wird das Dia jeweils neu angepasst, aber gegenüber der ursprünglichen Ansicht leicht verschoben. So wird mit einer Standaufnahme eine zeitliche Verschiebung erzeugt. Besucher im Pavillon sehen auf den Einwegspiegelwänden ein prismatisch zweimal gebrochenes, überlagertes Bild, das sich (dank des natürlichen Lichtwechsels) in ständigem Fluss befindet. Auf beiden Seiten des Pavillons sieht man mehrmals gespiegelte und transparente Bilder der unmittelbaren Umgebung, überlagert von Bildern der Betrachter hinter und vor den Pavillonwänden, welche wiederum die durch die aktuell gespiegelte Landschaft hindurch erkennbare Fernsicht auf dem Dia überlagern.

Dan Graham, 1995–96

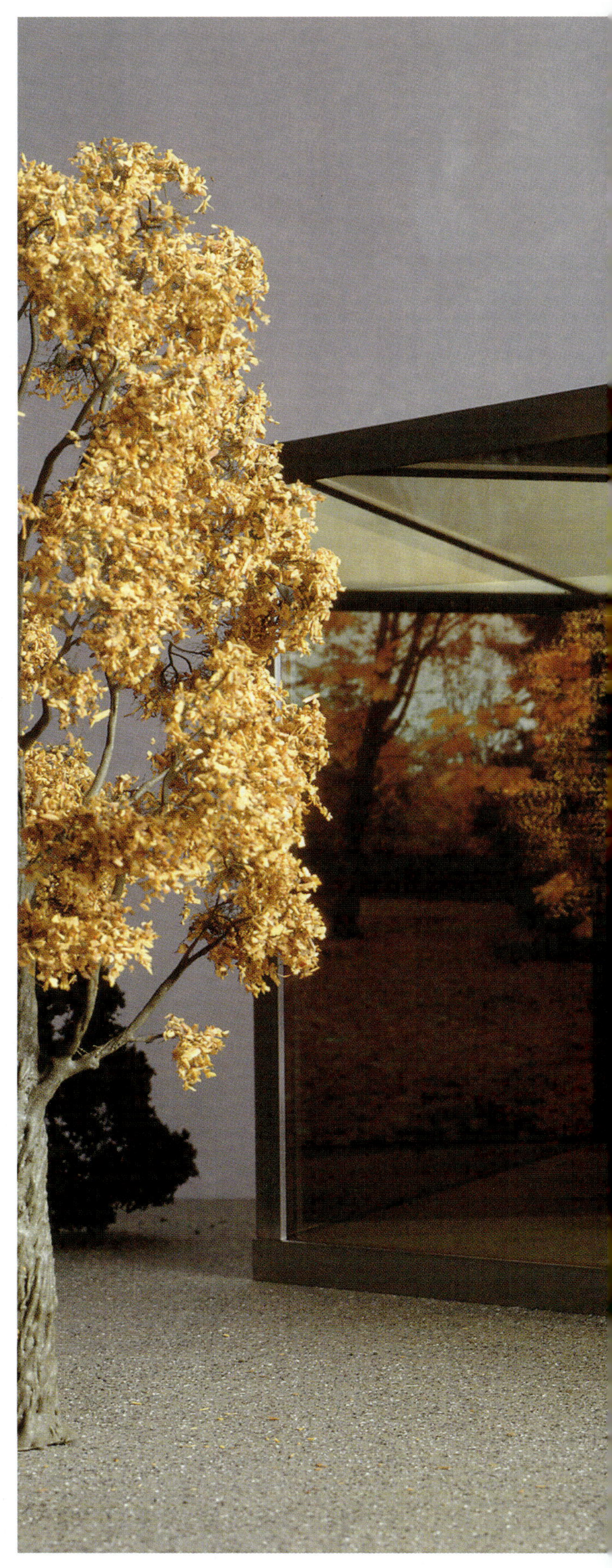

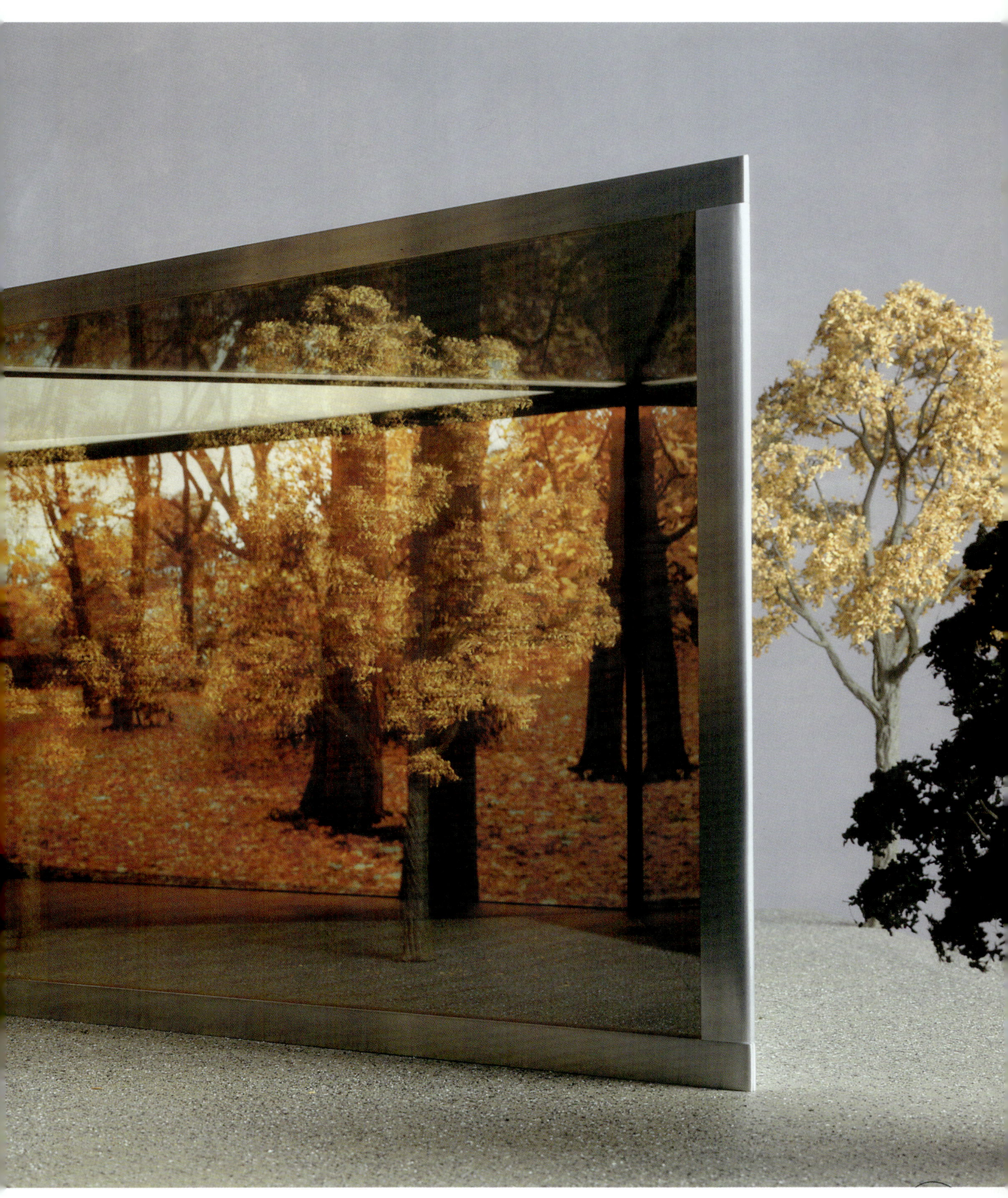

Dan Graham, ARTIST, Maybe ARCHITECT

MASSIMILIANO DI BARTOLOMEO

In 1976, during the "Ambiente/Arte" exhibition organized by Germano Celant at the Venice Biennale, Dan Graham showed a work titled PUBLIC SPACE/TWO AUDIENCES. A game of prestige, it took advantage of man's very ingenuous perception of space to double the reference coordinates of a place, using a "simple" mirror-wall and another in transparent glass that intersected a rectangular room. It was like looking through a bottomless mirror, with one's ego reflected in it; but it was also pervaded by a transparency. Meanwhile other wandering presences could be discerned, though it was impossible to ascertain their exact whereabouts. This work inaugurated a new approach by Graham to time delay: a dizzy perception postponed, an opportunity to observe a stranger, albeit only for an instant, before recognizing the stranger as oneself. The artificiality of the video and of the projectors, aided by mirrors and showcases, had enabled Dan Graham to explore perceptive dimensions that were in no way dependent on Renaissance perspective: an orderly and scientific rebellion that surveyed every spatial possibility. Again in 1976, the video TIME DELAY FOR TWO OPPOSING SHOP WINDOWS gave him an opportunity to explore this encroachment elsewhere. This time the observer's attention is focused on the object displayed, but distracted by his/her own reflection and by that of the passersby. Graham expands on that condition by installing two monitors, two television cameras and two mirrors, in two juxtaposed shop windows. This rigorous and exact, geometric and timely arrangement has the capacity, however, to set up infinite spatial combinations. These two experiences ferried Graham's work into an exploratory field far from the neutrality of an art specially prepared, but sharply conditioned by place.

Graham's "machines" have become instruments for surveying space, sectioning it according to sensorial sequences caused by incidents and fractures, screenings and television cameras that make the appreciation of a place ambiguous. The absolute and the relative interpenetrate alternatively, and the visitor can choose to observe one of the multiple realities, in the knowledge that no one possesses the dignity of the absolute except in the instant in which it is perceived. Place, on the other hand, is defined in its continuous denials, being projected and reflected according to contradictory coordinates. The concluded space of a room multiplies its dimensional planes by denying the truths of Cartesian geometry and releasing any subordination to a central and perspective representation: like optical benches on which to fix projections of reality while crossing the narrow border that separates the two worlds in which we are wrapped: the concrete one before our eyes, and the hazier one that resides in the tangle of our suggestions. If, therefore, in the closed spaces, Gra-

MASSIMILIANO DI BARTOLOMEO is an architect. He lectures on environmental architecture at Milan Polytechnic and writes regularly for *Domus*.

ham's pavilions represent the infinite as opposed to the finite, in the open spaces the reverse is true: the surfaces absorb the surrounding landscape, offering visitors the possibility of a synthesis, though this is never taken for granted. As, for example, in TWO CUBES/ONE ROTATED, which is a plain geometric interlocking of two glass and mirror cubes that can also be entered. This work, first shown at the ARC Musée d'Art Moderne de la ville de Paris, becomes naturally a frame for the space around it. Significantly, the dry and cold aluminum profiles hold back the portions of reality like pictures in a gallery of images rolled into themselves. In this case, the space is not subject to fractures recounting its complexity, as it is in the closed installations. Rather, it is simplified, harnessed to a geometrical pattern that seems to lend order to its comprehension. An exact reading is moreover denied by the fact that the simultaneity of information cannot be organized. And within this logic, the element of disturbance is necessary to our appreciation of Graham's work, while the reflections in the glass present a continual comparison between the observer and what is observed. In this way distraction can complete the observation. Speaking about his 1976 installation, Graham recalls that: "...If you entered and found yourself alone, it was like being inside minimalist art, but as soon as there was more than one person, you would get a double reflection, beside the feeling of bewilderment caused by the continuous reversal between the observer and the person observed." But it is still just as effective today, despite our having grown accustomed since then to an ever more technological and virtual existence. Indeed at the Italian Pavilion in this year's Venice Art Biennale, there were the same incredulous looks, nervous smiles and hands alternately raised, to get confirmation that the persons on the other side of the mirror were actually themselves. A feeling of dizziness may seize the viewer as he or she ingenuously observes a pavilion by Graham: a feeling that turns into contemplation or euphoria, a static or dynamic state. THE STAR OF DAVID PAVILION, from 1989, but finally realized in 1996, on the grounds of Buchberg Castle in Austria, is paradigmatic in this respect. Adults catch their breath as they grasp the intensity of images and sentiments crystallized in the transparent volume; the star shape is recognized in the intersection of the solid triangle, which can be entered, and another triangular water basin that seems to emerge from the two-dimensionality of the water. Its reflections thus also occupy an underground dimension, while the dizziness is in the eye, as it rapidly regains the tops of the star itself on the ground, later lost in its semi-extrusion. Children run towards the wall that isn't there, playing tag and going through a door almost concealed by the immateriality of glass. As the water on the interior of the solid two-way-mirror image position can be walked on by a metal grid, they gaze at their figures reflected in the water and superimposed on the sky, and point

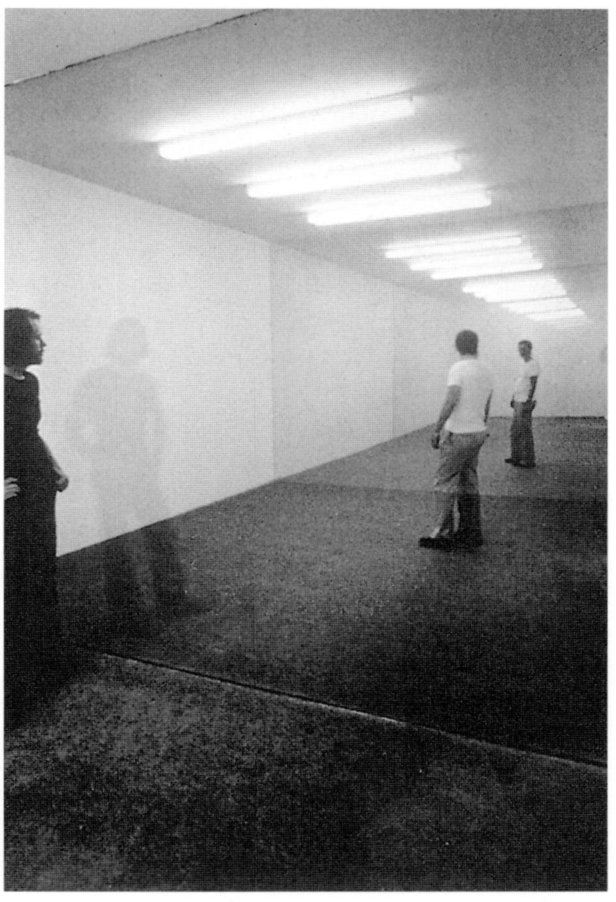

DAN GRAHAM, PUBLIC SPACE/TWO AUDIENCES, 1976, installation, "Ambiente/Arte," Venice Biennale / ÖFFENTLICHER RAUM/ZWEIFACHES PUBLIKUM.

at themselves through the two-way mirror planes. Dizziness becomes a game, and the dazed state is a venture beyond rationality. As Roger Caillois explains in his book *Man, Play, and Games* the coincidence that occurs between dizziness and the mask projects man's identity into a play-related and irrepressible dimension, until a state of stupefaction is reached. Certain propitiatory tribal dances, or more simply the children pirouetting in the courtyard in a hilarious crescendo until they lose their balance and feel sick as the ground starts to undulate, are actually a moment of exploration, an attempt to dig out the authenticity of a dimension that sometimes appears too static. Graham's pavilions convey this giddy sensation, setting off a continuous circular process, even in the visitor's absolutely static state while the space begins to rotate, absorbed or rejected by the screens with which the volume is constructed. In reality, the deception begins precisely with our attempt to grasp the complexity of the structure, the exact intersection of its planes and the geometry of its space. Seduced by the possibility of understanding, and trapped by our unconsciousness, we keep trying again, convinced that this time may be the lucky one, whilst in this reiterated deception the exploration continues.

At times, the distance between art and architecture is minimal; sometimes the two overlap and interpenetrate. This happens in the large suspended canvases by Anish Kapoor, in Richard Serra's magnetic spirals, in Kounellis's brutal labyrinths. The magazine *Domus* recently published a report on the excursion by the art world into the dynamics of architecture: and a recent article, titled "Art Eats Architecture," illustrated the sensational work installed by Kapoor at the Tate Modern in London. Kapoor himself has since been appointed to "design" a station on the Naples Underground. Dan Graham pushes beyond and succeeds in taming space, crystallizing it. However, he does not deprive it of possible changes. He transforms the viewer into an inhabitant, as his or her own privileged witness within the work. The drawing and the preparatory sketches, but also the models, reveal this designer's attitude: by means of axonometrics, perspectives, plans, and sections, where materials and finishes are indicated, but above all the visitor-inhabitant's entrances and routes, in a language detached from architecture. Functional diagrams anticipate the work's mechanism and the inhabitant's behavior, fostering a continual interaction between visitor and place. The CAFÉ BRAVO for the Berlin Biennale of 1998 therefore is a work of architecture, built with technical help from the architect Johanne Nalbach. It is composed of two cubes that intersect in the courtyard of an old factory converted into an exhibition space.

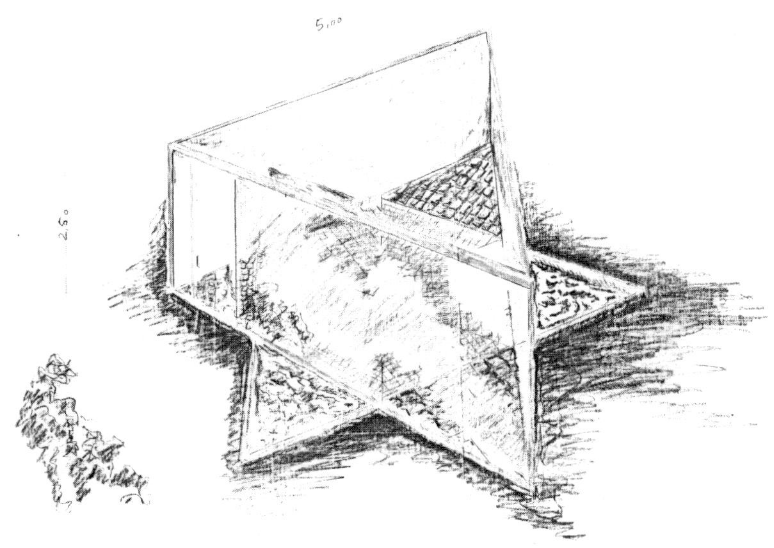

DAN GRAHAM, STAR OF DAVID PAVILION, 1989, drawing by the artist / DAVIDSTERN-PAVILLON, Skizze des Künstlers.

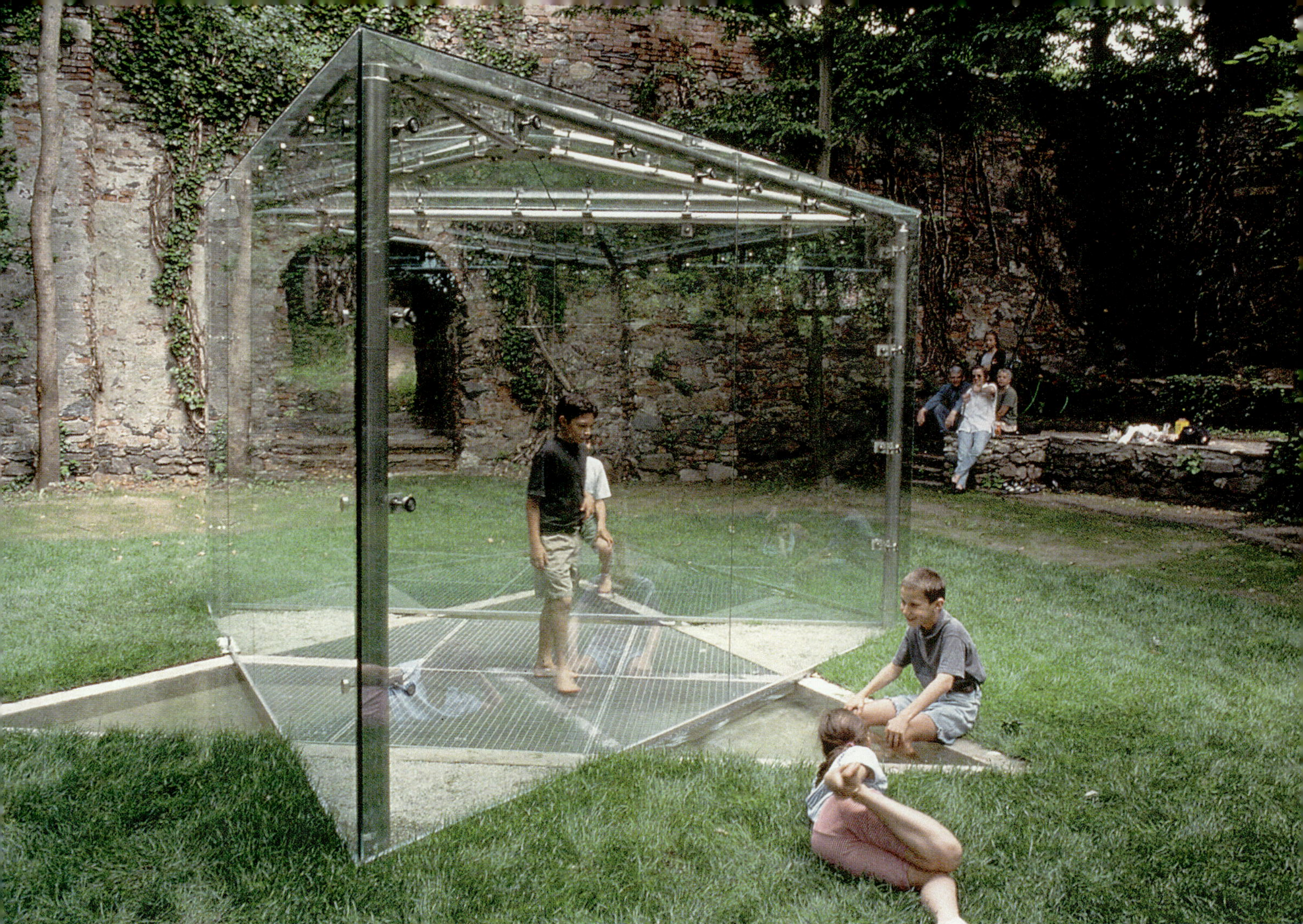

DAN GRAHAM, STAR OF DAVID PAVILION, 1989–1996, two-way mirror, aluminum, Plexiglas, Schloss Buchberg, Austria, 102 3/4 x 165 2/5 x 94" / DAVIDSTERN-PAVILLON, Einwegspiegel, Aluminium, Plexiglas, 261 x 420 x 238 cm.

Reflections in the two-way mirror glass and the mirrored profiles in chromed aluminum, distort the composition formed by the façades of surrounding buildings, while the two cubes seem to appropriate them for themselves. People in the café appear to be suspended in a bubble, yet they are reassured by its familiar furniture. They are distracted however, by the impossibility of defining the boundary between exterior and interior, public and private. Take M.C. Escher's ironic drawing PRINT GALLERY (1956), for example: is the visitor portrayed outside or inside the print?

And again, the fax used by Graham to technically illustrate his most recent work in Italy, at the Galleria Minini in Brescia: a sheet of paper on which four lines design the rectangle with the correct proportions to define the context of the exhibition space, and then, in a thicker line, the two "S" quoted and indicated in the materials. Live paths of glass, mirror and aluminum pursue one another to create an impossible labyrinth, where visitors enter and would like to get to the other side, through the sheet of stretched metal. In a moment of sensorial deprivation, we discover that we have once again been deceived, seduced and abandoned, left alone but infinitely greater.

(Translated from the Italian by Rodney Stringer)

Dan Graham, KÜNSTLER – oder ARCHITEKT?

MASSIMILIANO DI BARTOLOMEO

1976 zeigte Dan Graham an der von Germano Celant kuratierten Ausstellung «Ambiente» an der Biennale von Venedig eine Arbeit mit dem Titel PUBLIC SPACE/TWO AUDIENCES, ein Spiel mit Illusionen, das die naive räumliche Wahrnehmung des Menschen ausnützt, um die räumlichen Bezugskoordinaten mit einer «simplen» Spiegelwand und einer Wand aus transparentem Glas, die beide den rechteckigen Raum trennen, zu verdoppeln: Es ist, als blicke man in einen nach hinten offenen Spiegel; die eigene Gestalt wird gespiegelt, ist aber auch von Transparenz durchdrungen, während andere Gestalten sich durch den Raum bewegen, ohne dass sich ihre genaue Position ausmachen liesse. Mit diesem Werk machte Graham einen neuen Schritt in Richtung *time delay,* die Schwindel erregende zeitliche Verzögerung der Wahrnehmung: Sie erlaubt es, sich selbst einen Moment lang als Fremde(n) zu betrachten, ehe man sich erkennt. Das Künstliche von Bildschirmen und Projektoren, unterstützt von Spiegeln und Vitrinen, ermöglichte es Dan Graham, Wahrnehmungsdimensionen jenseits der Renaissanceperspektive zu erkunden: eine systematische, wissenschaftliche Rebellion, die alle Möglichkeiten des Raumes erforscht. Ebenfalls 1976 – im Video TIME DELAY FOR TWO OPPOSING SHOP WINDOWS – verwendete er Schaufenster, um dieses Vordringen in eine andere Dimension zu untersuchen: Die Aufmerksamkeit des Betrachters wird auf den ausgestellten Gegenstand gelenkt und zugleich durch die eigene Spiegelung und jene anderer Passanten abgelenkt. Graham erweitert diese Situation, indem er zwei Monitore, zwei Kameras und zwei Spiegel in zwei nebeneinander liegenden Schaufenstern installiert. Eine strenge und präzise, geometrisch exakte Anordnung, die aber unendliche Raumkombinationen hervorzubringen vermag. Mit diesen zwei Projekten stösst Grahams Arbeit in einen Untersuchungsbereich vor, der weit von der Neutralität einer «gemachten» Kunst entfernt und stark durch den Ort bestimmt ist. Grahams «Maschinen» werden zu Instrumenten, die den Raum erforschen und ihn durch sensorische Vektoren unterteilen, die sich durch Zwischenfälle und Brüche, Bildschirme und Kameras ergeben, und die Interpretation eines Ortes mehrdeutig werden lassen: Das Absolute und das Relative durchdringen

MASSIMILIANO DI BARTOLOMEO ist Architekt. Er lehrt umweltbezogene Architektur am Polytechnikum in Mailand und schreibt regelmässig für *Domus.*

einander, und der Betrachter kann wählen, welche der mannigfaltigen Realitäten er sich ansehen möchte, wohl wissend, dass sie alle einzig im Augenblick der Wahrnehmung die Würde des Absoluten besitzen, während der Ort durch seine fortwährenden Negationen definiert ist, da er anhand widersprüchlicher Koordinaten projiziert und gespiegelt wird. Der geschlossene Raum eines Zimmers vervielfacht seine Dimensionen, gerät in Widerspruch zur kartesianischen Geometrie und fügt sich nicht länger einer zentralperspektivischen Darstellungsweise: Die Wände werden zu optischen Schwellen, an denen man die Projektionen der Realität festmacht und dabei die feine Grenze zwischen den zwei Welten überschreitet, die uns umgeben – der konkreten Welt, die wir vor Augen haben, und der etwas verschwommeneren, die sich aus dem Wirrwarr unserer Eindrücke zusammensetzt.

Wenn Grahams Pavillons also in geschlossenen Räumen das Unendliche im Verhältnis zum Endlichen darstellen, so geschieht in offenen Räumen das Umgekehrte: Die Aussenflächen absorbieren die umliegende Landschaft und ermöglichen dem Betrachter eine Synthese, die jedoch nie vorausgesetzt werden darf. Ähnlich präsentiert sich TWO CUBES/ONE ROTATED, eine einfache geometrische Verschachtelung zweier Kuben aus Fenster- und Spiegelglas, die man auch betreten kann. Dieses Werk, das erstmals 1987 im ARC Musée d'Art Moderne de la Ville de Paris ausgestellt war, wird auf natürliche Weise zum Rahmen des umliegenden Raumes; nicht von ungefähr halten die hart und kalt wirkenden Aluminiumrahmen einzelne Stücke der Wirklichkeit fest wie Gemälde in einer Bildergalerie, die nur auf sich selbst verweisen. Hier ist der Raum keinerlei Brüchen unterworfen, die auf seine Komplexität hinweisen, wie das bei den Installationen in geschlossenen Räumen der Fall ist, sondern er erscheint eher vereinfacht, durch die geometrische Gliederung gebändigt, die ein deutliches Erkennen fördert: Die Eindeutigkeit der Interpretation wird dann aber gestört durch unsere Unfähigkeit, mit gleichzeitig auf uns einstürzenden Informationen umzugehen. Im Rahmen dieser Logik ist das störende Element notwendig, um Grahams Werk richtig zu würdigen. Denn die Spiegelungen im Glas lösen eine ständige

DAN GRAHAM, VIDEO PIECE FOR SHOP WINDOWS IN AN ARCADE, 1976, installation view, Corps de Garde, 1978, Groningen, Holland / VIDEOARBEIT FÜR SCHAUFENSTER IN EINER EINKAUFSPASSAGE.

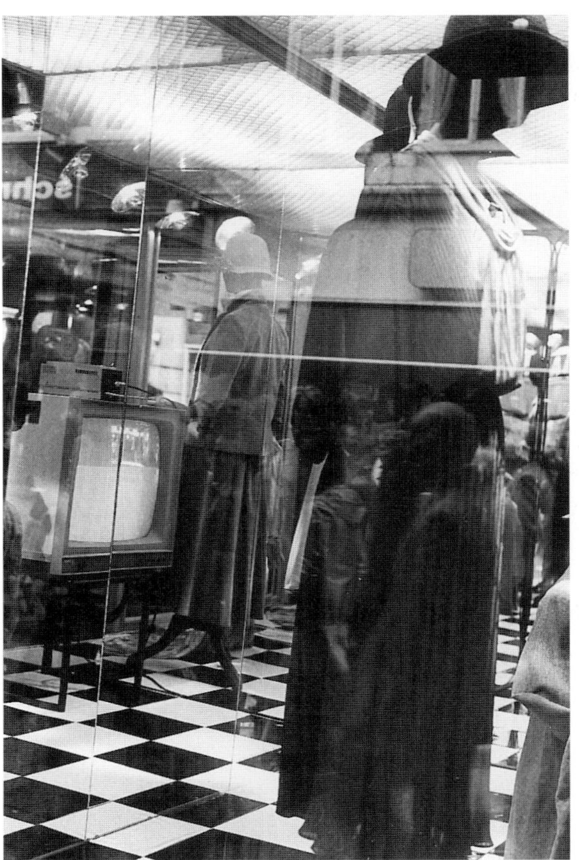

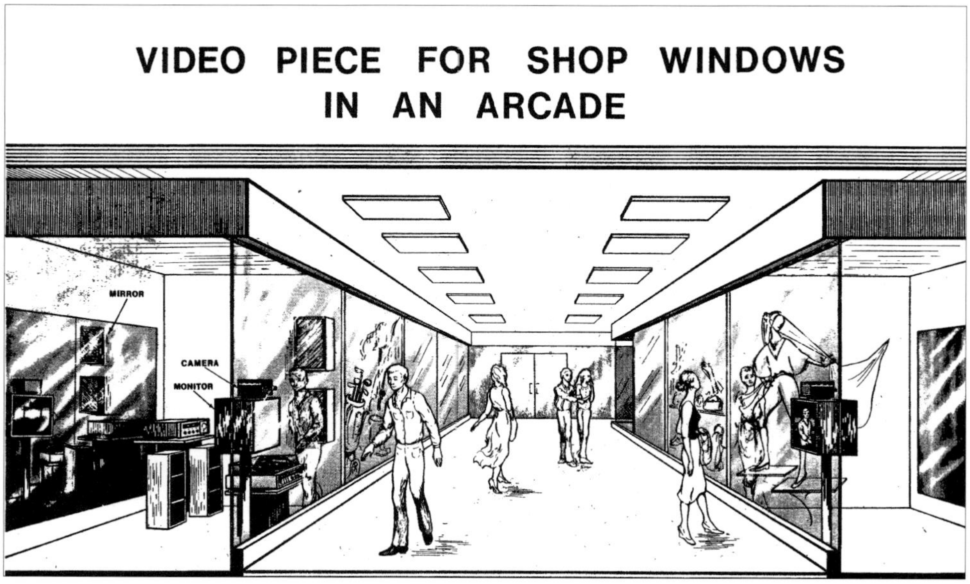

DAN GRAHAM, VIDEO PIECE FOR SHOP WINDOWS IN AN ARCADE, 1976, drawing / VIDEOARBEIT FÜR SCHAUFENSTER IN EINER EINKAUFSPASSAGE, Entwurf.

Auseinandersetzung zwischen Beobachter und Beobachtetem aus, welche auch die Ablenkung als Teil der Beobachtung zulässt: «...betrat man das Werk allein, hatte man das Gefühl, es mit Minimal Art zu tun zu haben, doch sobald mehr als eine Person anwesend war, [ergab sich] eine doppelte Spiegelung, zusätzlich zur Verwirrung, die durch die fortwährende Verkehrung der Rollen von Betrachter und Betrachtetem erzeugt wurde», erinnert sich Graham im Zusammenhang mit der Installation von 1976. Und obwohl wir mittlerweile an einen immer technoideren und virtuelleren Alltag gewöhnt sind, hat sich diese Wirkung – wie der italienische Pavillon der diesjährigen Biennale in Venedig beweist – bis heute unvermindert erhalten: ungläubige Blicke, verlegenes Lächeln und abwechselndes Heben der Hände, um die Bestätigung zu erhalten, dass wir es sind, die sich auf der anderen Seite des Spiegels bewegen.

Ein Betrachter, der arglos einen von Grahams Pavillons betrachtet, kann leicht von Schwindel erfasst werden: ein Gefühl, das sich alsbald in Kontemplation oder Euphorie, Statik oder Dynamik verwandelt. Der 1989 entworfene, aber erst 1996 im Park des österreichischen Schlosses Buchberg realisierte STAR OF DAVID PAVILION ist in dieser Hinsicht exemplarisch. Erwachsene halten den Atem an, wenn sie die Intensität der Bilder und Empfindungen spüren, die sich im transparenten Raum kristallisieren; die Sternform ergibt sich aus der Überschneidung eines betretbaren Elementes mit dreieckigem Grund und eines dreieckigen Wasserbassins, so dass der Stern gleichsam aus der Wasserfläche aufzutauchen scheint: Die Spiegelungen erhalten so auch eine unterirdische Dimension, während ein Schwindelgefühl den Blick erfasst, der blitzschnell die Zacken des Sterns am Boden erkennt, die sich zur Hälfte im Unsichtbaren verlieren. Kinder rennen gegen die nicht vorhandene Wand, spielen Fangen, treten durch die Tür, die in der Immaterialität des Glases nahezu unsichtbar ist, betrachten ihr Spiegelbild, das sich im Innern der Einwegspiegelkonstruktion auch im Wasser unter dem Bodengitter reflektiert und das Bild des Himmels überlagert, und sie zeigen durch die Einwegspiegelflächen hindurch mit dem Finger auf sich selbst: Das Schwindelgefühl wird zum Spiel und die Sprengung des Rationalen wirkt verblüffend. Wie Roger Caillois in seinem Buch *Les jeux et les hommes* erklärt, katapultiert das Zusammentreffen von Schwindel und Maske die menschliche

Identität in einen spielerischen, ungebändigten Zustand, der bis zur Benommenheit führen kann. Bestimmte Stammestänze oder ganz einfach Kinder, die sich im Hof immer ausgelassener um sich selber drehen, bis sie sich nicht mehr auf den Beinen halten können und das Übelkeit erregende Gefühl verspüren, dass die Erde schwankt: All dies ist nichts anderes als ein Moment der Erkundung, ein Versuch, die Wahrhaftigkeit einer Dimension zu überprüfen, die uns mitunter allzu statisch erscheint. Grahams Pavillons lösen genau diesen Schwindel aus und setzen einen kontinuierlichen, zirkulären Prozess in Gang, selbst wenn der Betrachter vollkommen reglos dasteht, während der Raum sich um ihn zu drehen beginnt, gleichzeitig absorbiert und zurückgewiesen von den Wänden, die sein Volumen begrenzen. In Wirklichkeit beginnt die Täuschung schon beim Versuch, die Komplexität der Struktur, die genaue Überschneidung der verschiedenen Flächen und die Raumgeometrie zu begreifen: verführt vom Glauben an die Möglichkeit zu verstehen und von unserem Unbewussten mit ständig neuen Versuchen überlistet, jedesmal überzeugt, dass es diesmal endlich gelingen werde, wobei sich gerade in dieser wiederholten Täuschung die Erkundung vollzieht.

Manchmal ist die Distanz zwischen Kunst und Architektur sehr gering; manchmal überlagern oder durchdringen sie einander – so im Fall von Anish Kapoors grossformatigen, im Raum aufgespannten Leinwänden, Richard Serras magnetischen Spiralen und Kounellis' brutalen Labyrinthen. Die Zeitschrift *Domus* thematisierte erst kürzlich, dass die Kunst zunehmend in den Bereich der Architektur vorstösst: Ein Artikel mit dem Titel «Kunst frisst Architektur» berichtete über Kapoors Aufsehen erregende Intervention in der Tate Modern in London, dank der Kapoor den Auftrag erhielt, eine U-Bahn-Station in Neapel zu gestalten. Aber Dan Graham geht noch weiter, er bringt es fertig, den Raum zu bändigen, indem er ihm feste Konturen verleiht, ohne ihn der Möglichkeit des Wandels zu berauben, und er macht den Betrachter zu einem Bewohner, der sich innerhalb des Werks selbst beobachtet. Die Zeichnungen, die vorbereitenden Skizzen, aber auch die Modelle zeugen von dieser Haltung: axonometrische und perspektivische Darstellungen, Grund- und Aufrisse, in denen in einer der Architektur entlehnten Sprache die Materialien und Details, vor allem aber die Eingänge und die Wege für die Betrachter-Bewohner angegeben sind. Zweckmässige Pläne, die den Mechanismus des Werks und das Verhalten potenzieller Bewohner vorwegnehmen und dabei der ständigen Interaktion zwischen Betrachter und Ort höchste Priorität einräumen. So ist auch das für die Biennale Berlin 1998 gestaltete CAFÉ BRAVO ein architektonisches Werk. Es entstand in Zusammenarbeit mit der Architektin Johanne Nalbach und besteht aus zwei in einem spitzen Winkel aneinander grenzenden Kuben im Innenhof einer ehemaligen Fabrik, die zum Ausstellungsraum geworden ist. Die Spiegelungen in den opaken und die Sicht durch die transparenten Glasflächen verdrehen – ebenso wie die Spiegelung der Konturen aus verchromtem Aluminium – die Fassadenstrukturen der umliegenden Gebäude, derer sich die Kuben zu bemächtigen scheinen. Der Cafébesucher erlebt das Ambiente, als schwebe er in einer Luftblase, wobei ihm die vertraute Ausstattung des kleinen Lokals Sicherheit vermittelt, während die Unmöglichkeit, die Grenze zwischen aussen und innen, zwischen Öffentlichkeit und Privatsphäre zu bestimmen, ziemlich verwirrend wirkt. Die Situation erinnert an M.C. Eschers ironische Zeichnung BILDERGALERIE (1956): Befindet sich der darauf abgebildete Galeriebesucher innerhalb oder ausserhalb des Bildes, das er betrachtet?

Und dann die Faxnachricht, in der Graham die technischen Illustrationen zu seiner neuesten Arbeit in Italien (in der Galerie Minini in Brescia) liefert: ein Blatt Papier, auf dem mit vier Linien im richtigen Verhältnis ein Rechteck gezeichnet ist, das den Ausstellungsraum darstellt, dann, mit dickerem Strich, die zwei S mit detaillierten Angaben zu den technischen Massen. *In natura* dann Gänge aus Glas, Spiegelglas und Aluminium, die aufeinander folgen und ein unmögliches Labyrinth bilden, das zu betreten bedeutet, sich auf die andere Seite der Streckmetallwand zu wünschen. Ein Augenblick, in dem man jeglicher Sinneseindrücke beraubt ist, um alsbald zu entdecken, dass man einmal mehr getäuscht, verführt und im Stich gelassen wurde, dass man allein ist, aber unendlich viel reicher als zuvor.

(Übersetzung aus dem Italienischen: Irene Aeberli)

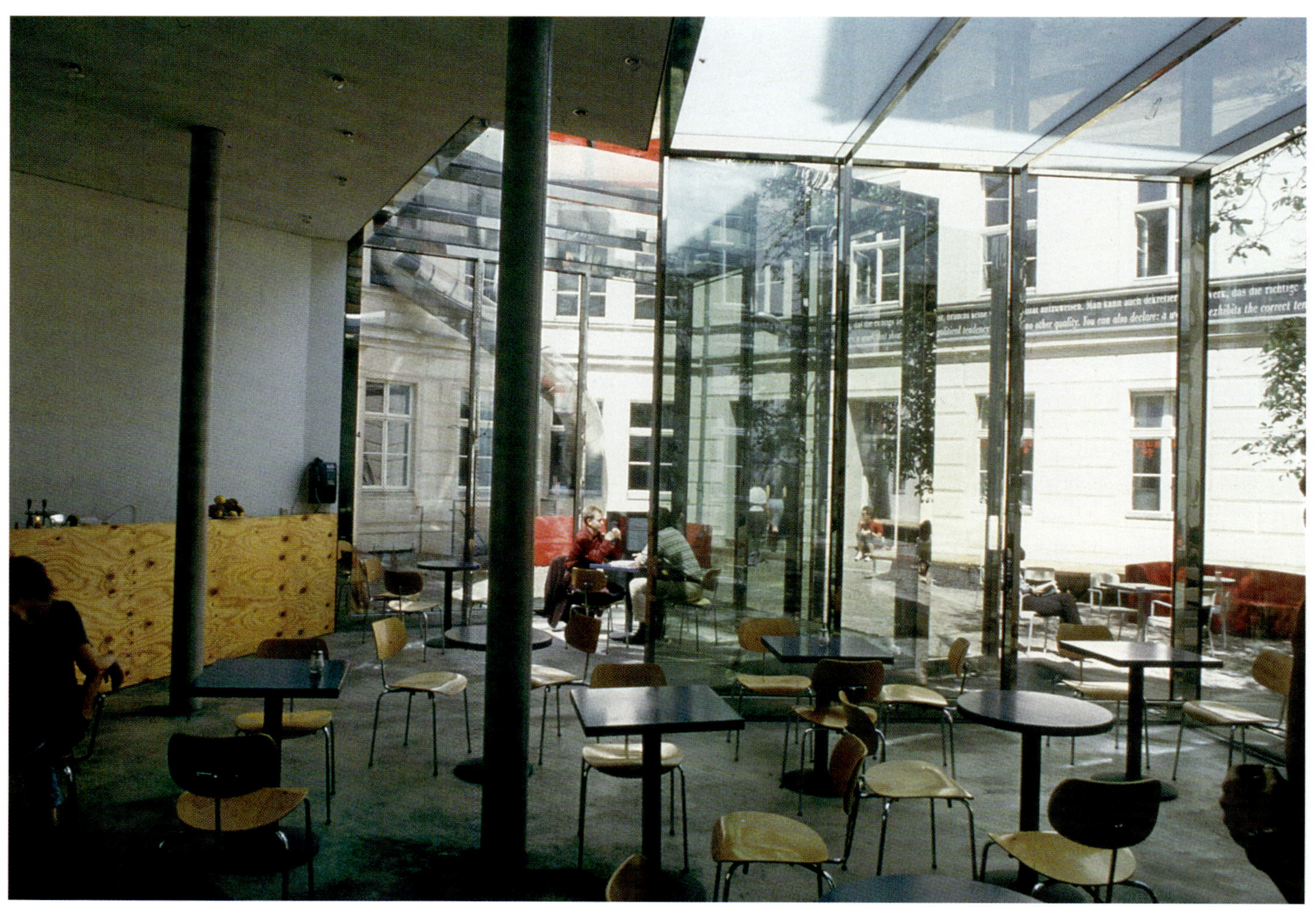

DAN GRAHAM, CAFÉ BRAVO, Kunst-Werke, Berlin, 1998, two-way mirror, opaque and transparent glass, polished steel frame, reflective aluminum walls, painted blue tables and wooden chairs, plywood counter, concrete floor; architect: Johanne Nalbach / Einwegspiegel, Milchglas und transparentes Glas, poliertes Stahlgerüst, reflektierende Aluminiumwände, blau bemalte Tische und Holzstühle, Theke aus Furnierholz, Asphaltboden.

QUESTIONNAIRE FOR MR. GRAHAM

CARMEN ROSENBERG MILLER

Carmen Rosenberg Miller: How did CAFÉ BRAVO (1998) get its name?

Dan Graham: The café is a functional café whose form is two adjacent two-way mirror cubes, which are placed at angles. It is named for the teenage German magazine, *Bravo*. I read it to learn about basic German and for the explicit content. I was never a real teenager when I grew up—so this is a vicarious pleasure for a semi-dirty old man. I like the name and want the magazine to be available for reading in the café.

CRM: What projects have you done for kids?

DG: My first work only for children was the 1986 CHILDREN'S PAVILION in Gent, which was part of the "Chambres d'amis" exhibition. As in my earlier OCTAGON PAVILION (1987) in Münster's second "Skulptur.Projekte Münster" exhibition, the interior uses a wooden pole for kids to try to climb or rotate around.

In 1989, when Jeff Wall, saw a videotape of this piece, he proposed we collaborate on a second CHILDREN'S PAVILION. Our proposal has not been realized. The idea is as follows. The CHILDREN'S PAVILION is built into, and enclosed by a landscaped hill. The structural shell of the hill-form is engineered in concrete. It is like the game "King of the Mountain" played by kids on a fake, grassy playground mountain. At the top is an oculus, which is a two-way mirror concave glass lens through which children can see an enlarged image of themselves as giants against the small image of adults and other children looking up from the inside superimposed on the changing skyscape and also superimposed on nine illuminated Cibachromes of children. Inside visitors can look up through the concave lens and see their own gazes against the sky superimposed on the gazes of the children outside. Nine illuminated Cibachromes by

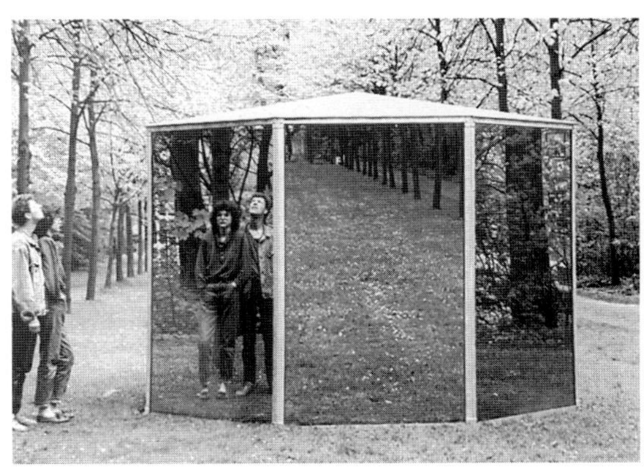

DAN GRAHAM, OCTAGON FOR MÜNSTER, 1987, 8 two-way mirror side panels, one of them a sliding door, wooden roof / 8 Einwegspiegel-Wandelemente, eines davon als Schiebetür, Holzdach.

CARMEN ROSENBERG MILLER lives in New York City and Berlin. She is a ninth-grade student at the Bronx High School of Science.

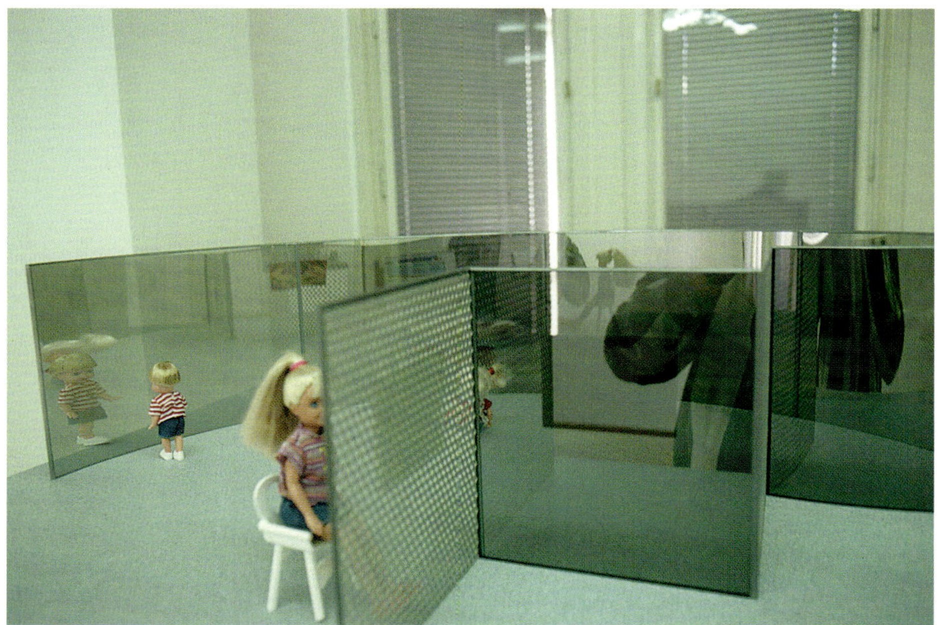

DAN GRAHAM, CHILDREN'S DAY CARE, CD-ROM, CARTOON AND COMPUTER SCREEN LIBRARY PROJECT, 1998–2000, architectural model, wood, glass, two-way mirror, punched aluminum, 12 x 36 x 42" / PROJEKT FÜR EINE KINDERTAGESSTÄTTE MIT CD-ROM-, CARTOON- UND COMPUTERBILDSCHIRM-BIBLIOTHEK, Architekturmodell, Holz, Glas, Einwegspiegel, Alu-Lochblech, 30,5 x 91,4 x 106,7 cm.

Jeff Wall are mounted on the interior wall of individual children of various nationalities set against different skies.

My 1989 project for a SKATEBOARD PAVILION, originally proposed for the Stuttgart "International Garden Year" of 1993, provided a special area for teenage visitors in the re-designed park. It allows itself to be "graffiti-ed" on its surface and creates a "sixties"-like psychedelic experience by using a truncated two-way mirror pyramidal canopy above the basin. This pyramid form parodies the eighties cliché of placing a glass pyramid on the roof of corporate buildings or shopping areas as in the I. M. Pei Louvre pyramid. The sun's light penetrates the form creating a psychedelic experience for skateboarders as they float weightlessly off the ramp. The two-way mirror glass shows both the skyscape and the skaters superimposed on the glass. The canopy is something akin to the nineteenth century gazebo roof.

The Dia Rooftop Pavilion from 1991 uses curved two-way mirror glass creating, for people inside the curved cylindrical form, an anamorphic enlargement of kids' (and adults') bodies like a funhouse mirror, while on the outside, reducing peoples' bodies as in a convex lens. On the roof outside the pavilion, I placed the rubber flooring used near the slides in a children's playground for people to lie on or for children to fall onto.

My FUNHOUSE FOR MÜNSTER (1997) was designed to relate to both a nearby children's playground and to CHILDREN'S DAY CARE, CD-ROM, CARTOON AND COMPUTER SCREEN LIBRARY PROJECT (1998–2000) conceived for the interior of the central city museum, but only realized later. The second project was designed for an educational function as well as for a children's playground. Both works used curved, anamorphic two-way mirror glass "mirroring" the city plan of Münster, which has a Roman circular plan with its main cathedral and museum at the center of a radiating series of circular streets. The FUNHOUSE was placed near a circular bicycle and footpath at the periphery of the city. I showed DAY CARE CENTER at the Marian Goodman Gallery.

GIRLS' MAKE-UP ROOM from 2000, consists of a 4½-feet high two-way mirror cylinder which is concave on the inside thus producing anamorphic reflections. The semi-circular form is bisected by two perforated stainless steel panels to allow entrance to the enclosure. When these panels slide open, the shifting imposition of the small "peep holes" on the glass creates a moving moiré pattern. Inside I supply a table with lipstick and small "normal" mirrors with fish-eye lenses attached to their centers. Manipulating the position of these mirrors creates an array of optical distortions.

CRM: What are your favorite bands?

DG: My favorite band of all time is *The Kinks.*

CRM: Do you like music more than art? Why?

DG: I used to love music more than art because it is more "play" than "business" ...because it is a form of communalism ...because it creates ecstatic pleasure and is closer to the body ...because it is "disposable" and about instant clichés of the moment like my first (conceptual) work for magazine pages ...because it is "pop" culture, which I can experience with normal people ... because it is kind of a hobby just as my first art was a hobby.

CRM: Are you still going through your second childhood?

DG: I think I am experiencing my second childhood through my two-way mirror work. I've never read Lacan, but I feel my work involves the Lacanian "mirror stage" of childhood, when the young child first experiences his/her sense or non-sense of an ego. I know that through my art I make new friends, which I barely had as a child. And through my "hobbies" of rock music, architectural tourism, and travel I stay young.

CRM: How did you know you were a child again?

DG: I know I am a child when I watch other Aries people (I am an Aries) behaving childishly, like me. It's difficult for me to directly answer your question, it's too perceptive for me—or maybe I am not that self-perceptive. But I thoroughly appreciate your question.

DAN GRAHAM, SKATEBOARD PAVILION, 1989, architectural model / SKATEBOARD-PAVILLON, Architekturmodell.

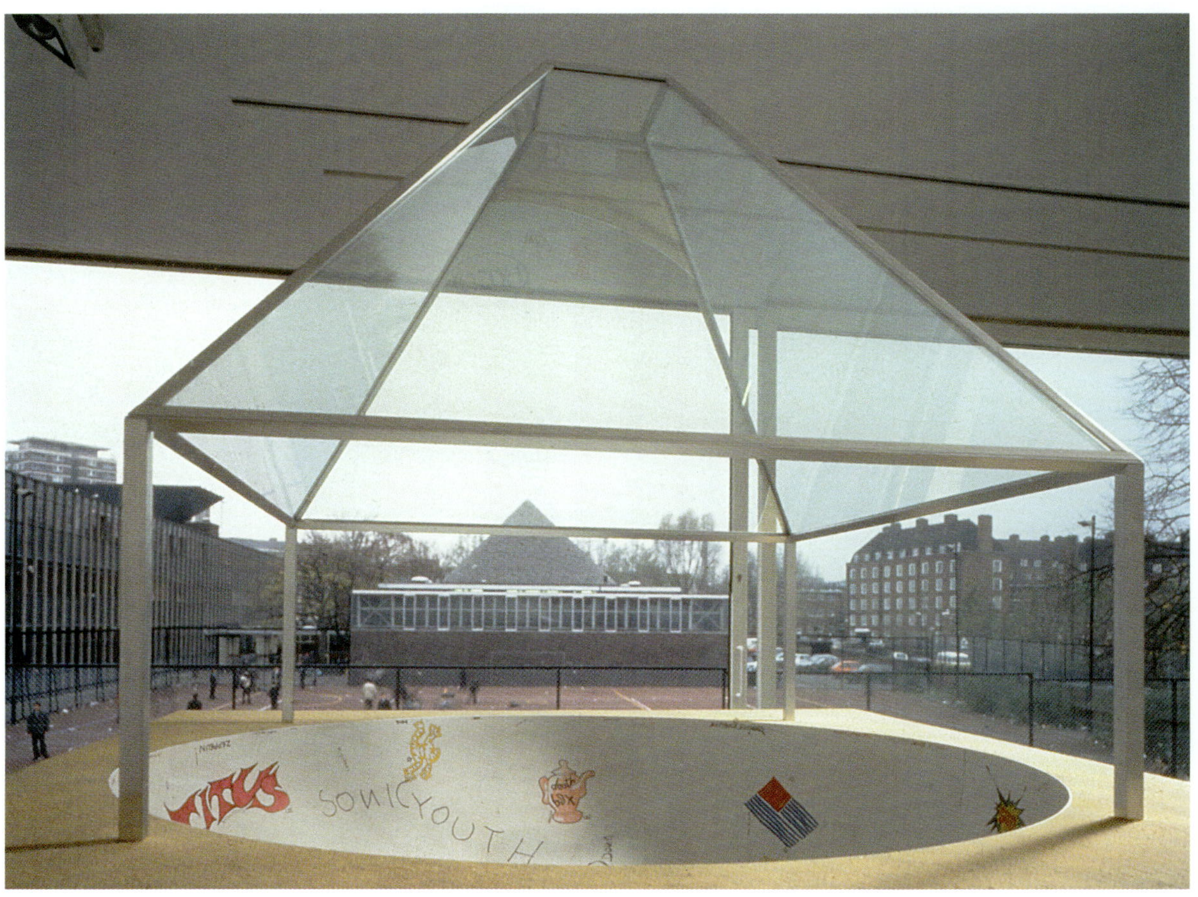

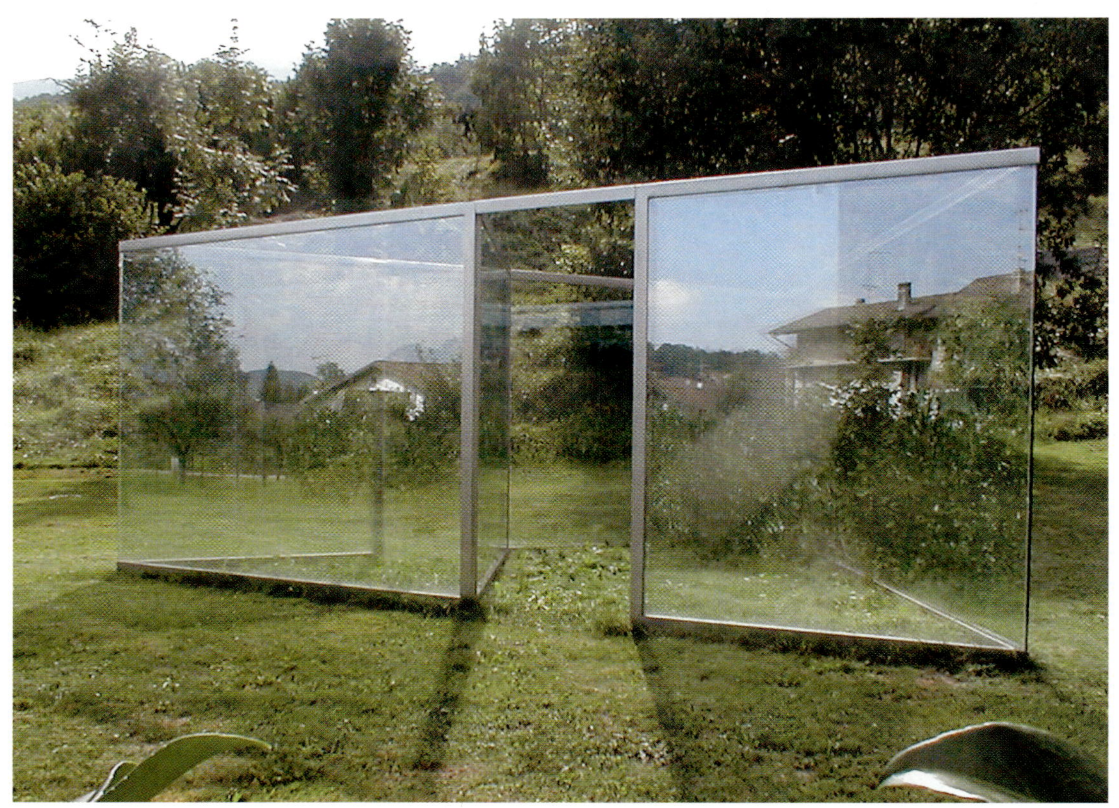

DAN GRAHAM, BISECTED TWO-WAY MIRROR TRIANGLE, 1998, stainless steel and two-way mirrors, $7^9/_{16}$ x $19^{11}/_{16}$ x $19^{11}/_{16}$' / ZWEIGETEILTES EINWEGSPIEGEL-DREIECK, Edelstahl und Einwegspiegel, 230 x 600 x 600 cm.

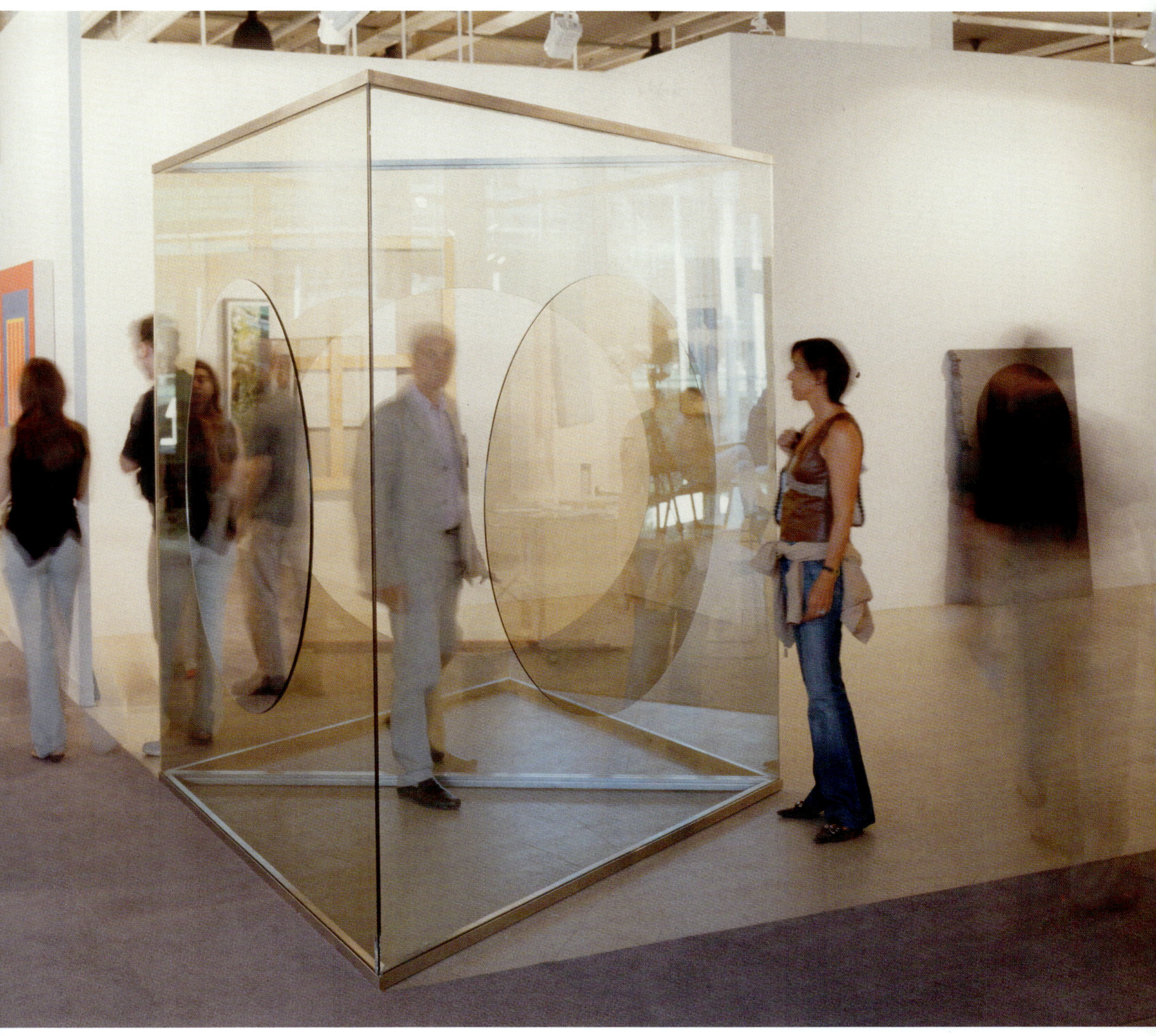

DAN GRAHAM, TRIANGULAR SOLID WITH CIRCULAR INSERTS, 1989–2003, stainless steel and two-way mirrors, exhibition view, Massimo Minini Gallery, Brescia, 7 9/16 x 7 9/16 x 7 9/16'/ DREIECKIGER KÖRPER MIT EINGESETZTEN KREISFORMEN, Edelstahl und Einwegspiegel, 230 x 230 x 230 cm.

FRAGEBOGEN FÜR MR. GRAHAM

CARMEN ROSENBERG MILLER

Carmen Rosenberg Miller: Wie ist das CAFÉ BRAVO (1998) zu seinem Namen gekommen?
Dan Graham: Das Café erfüllt eine bestimmte Funktion, es besteht aus zwei in einem schiefen Winkel aneinander grenzenden Kuben aus Einwegspiegelglas. Ich taufte es nach der deutschen Teenagerzeitschrift *Bravo,* die ich las, um mir ein paar Grundkenntnisse in Deutsch anzueignen, und weil es darin um Sex geht. Da ich als Junge nie ein richtiger Teenager war, ist das eine Art später Ersatzbefriedigung für den *dirty old man,* der ich mittlerweile vielleicht bin. Ausserdem gefällt mir der Name, und ich möchte, dass die Zeitschrift als Lesestoff im Café aufliegt.
CRM: Haben Sie auch Arbeiten für Kinder gemacht, und welche?
DG: Meine erste Arbeit nur für Kinder war der für die Ausstellung «Chambres d'amis» in Gent (1986) entworfene CHILDREN'S PAVILION (Kinderpavillon). Wie in meinem ersten OKTOGON FÜR MÜNSTER anlässlich der zweiten «Skulptur Projekte Münster» (1987) ist in seinem Innern eine Holzstange für Kinder angebracht, an der sie hochklettern oder sich herumschwingen können.

CARMEN ROSENBERG MILLER lebt in New York und Berlin. Sie besucht die neunte Klasse der Bronx High School of Science.

Als Jeff Wall 1989 eine Videoaufnahme dieser Arbeit sah, meinte er, wir sollten gemeinsam einen zweiten Kinderpavillon entwerfen. Der Entwurf wurde aber nie verwirklicht. CHILDREN'S PAVILION ist in einen künstlich angelegten Hügel hineingebaut. Die Stützstruktur der Hügelform ist in Beton gegossen. Das Ganze gleicht dem Spiel «Bergkönig», das Kinder auf einem künstlichen, mit Gras bewachsenen Spielplatzberg spielen. Oben befindet sich ein Rundfenster, eine konkave Linse aus Einwegspiegelglas, das die Kinder als wahre Riesen erscheinen lässt im Vergleich zum kleinen Bild der Erwachsenen und der anderen Kinder, die unten im Innern des Hügels stehen und nach oben schauen, ein Bild, das sich vor den ständig wechselnden Himmel und neun Cibachrom-Leuchtkästen schiebt. Von innen können die Besucher durch die konkave Linse hinausschauen und vor dem Hintergrund des Himmels ihre eigenen Blicke sehen, welche die Blicke der Kinder draussen überlagern. Jeff Wall hatte die Idee, neun Cibachrom-Leuchtkästen mit Bildern von einzelnen Kindern verschiedener Nationalität an der Innenwand aufzuhängen, die mit jeweils unterschiedlichem Himmel im Hintergrund aufgenommen wurden.

Mein Projekt SKATEBOARD PAVILION (1989), das ursprünglich für die Internationale Gartenschau in Stuttgart gedacht war, sah einen Bereich speziell für jugendliche Besucher innerhalb des umgestalteten

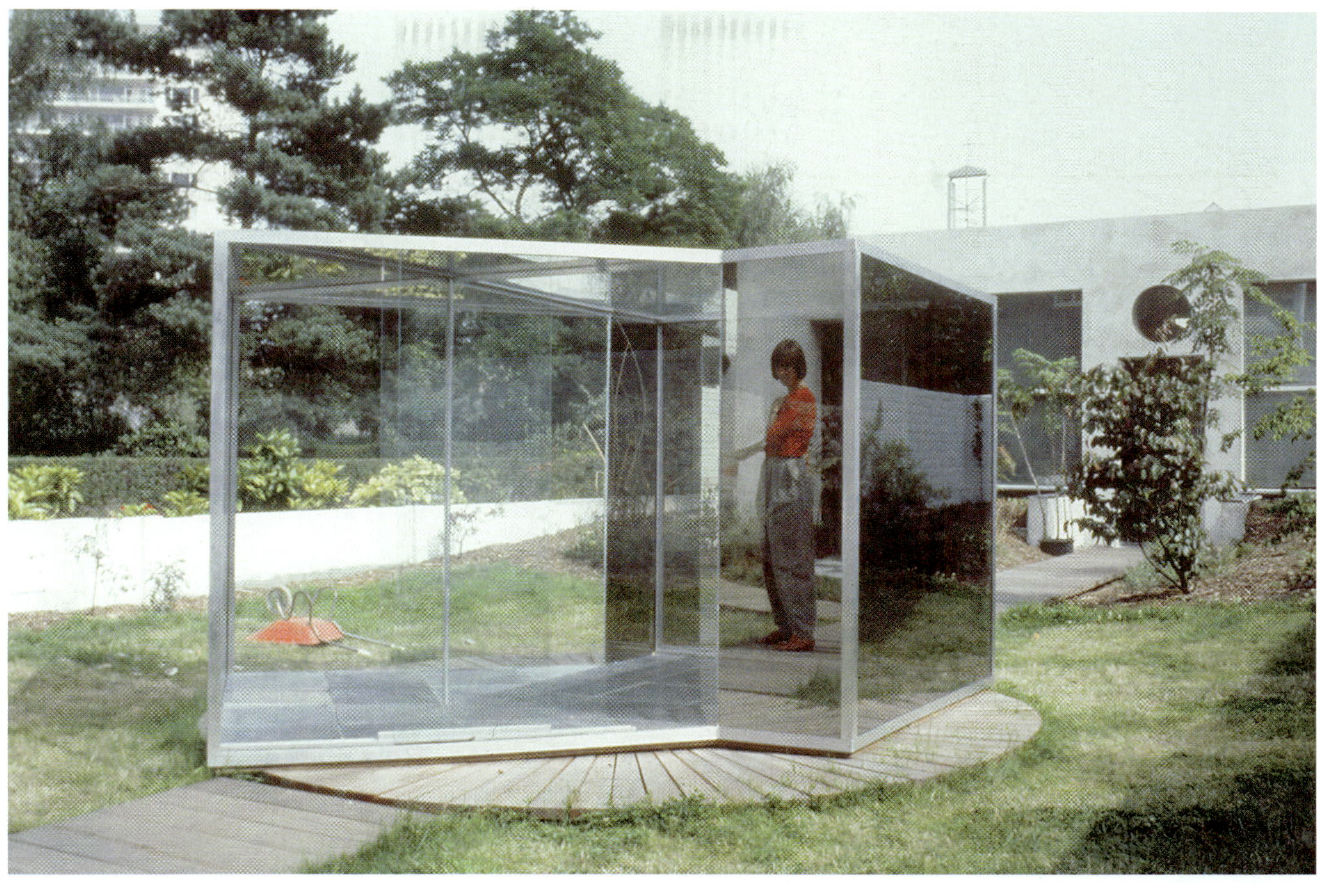

DAN GRAHAM, CHILDREN'S PAVILION, 1986, two-way mirror, glass, aluminum, installation "Chambre d'Amis," Gent, $64^1/_2$ x $123^1/_4$ x 91" / KINDERPAVILLON, Einwegspiegel, Glas, Aluminium, 164 x 313 x 231 cm.

Parks vor. Die Wände dürfen mit Graffiti besprüht werden, und eine stumpfe Pyramide aus Einwegspiegelglas, die sich über der Wanne erhebt, vermittelt eine Art psychedelische Erfahrung wie in den 60er Jahren. Die Pyramide parodiert auch ein Klischee der 80er Jahre, als man die Dächer grosser Firmengebäude oder Einkaufszentren mit Glaspyramiden im Stil von I. M. Peis Louvre-Pyramide krönte. Wenn die Skateboardfahrer schwerelos von der Oberkante der Wanne gleiten, vermittelt ihnen das einfallende Sonnenlicht ein rauschhaftes Gefühl. Auf dem Einwegspiegelglas sieht man sowohl den Himmel als auch die sich spiegelnden Skateboardfahrer. Die Überdachung erinnert an ein Gartenhaus aus dem neunzehnten Jahrhundert.

Der Pavillon auf dem Dach des Dia Centers in New York (1991) ist ein Zylinder aus Einwegspiegelglas, der bewirkt, dass die Leute im Innern die Körper von Kindern (und Erwachsenen) als riesige Verzerrungen sehen, fast wie in einem Spiegelkabinett, während sie von aussen wie durch eine konvexe Linse betrachtet zusammenschrumpfen. Für den Platz vor dem Dachpavillon benutzte ich einen gummiartigen Bodenbelag, wie man ihn neben Rutschbahnen auf Spielplätzen findet, damit sich die Leute darauf legen oder fallen lassen können.

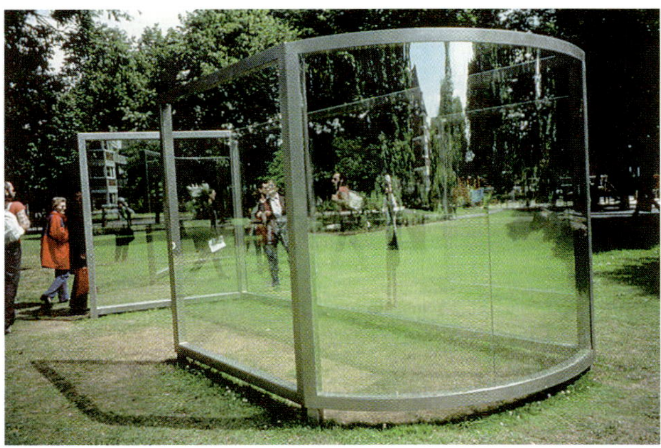

DAN GRAHAM, FUNHOUSE FOR MÜNSTER, 1997, two-way mirror, stainless steel, first installed for "Skulptur Projekte Münster," $90^{1}/_{2}$ x $216^{1}/_{2}$ x $78^{3}/_{4}$" / PLAUSCHHAUS FÜR MÜNSTER, Einwegspiegel, Edelstahl, 230 x 550 x 200 cm.

Mein FUNHOUSE FOR MÜNSTER (Plauschhaus für Münster, 1997) nahm sowohl auf einen nahe gelegenen Spielplatz Bezug als auch auf das CHILDREN'S DAY CARE, CD-ROM, CARTOON AND COMPUTER SCREEN LIBRARY PROJECT (1998–2000), das im Museum der Stadt aufgestellt werden sollte, aber erst später realisiert wurde. Das zweite Projekt sollte eine didaktische Funktion erfüllen und gleichzeitig auch ein Spielplatz sein. Für beide Arbeiten wurde rundes, die Formen verzerrendes Einwegspiegelglas verwendet, das gleichsam die Struktur der Innenstadt von Münster widerspiegeln sollte. Die Stadt ist nach römischem Muster kreisförmig angelegt, in der Mitte der in konzentrischen Kreisen verlaufenden Strassen befinden sich das Münster und das Museum. Das FUNHOUSE wurde am Stadtrand neben einem Rundweg für Fahrradfahrer und Fussgänger aufgestellt. DAY CARE CENTER war in der Marian Goodman Gallery ausgestellt.

GIRLS' MAKE-UP ROOM aus dem Jahr 2000 besteht aus einem 137 Zentimeter hohen Zylinder aus Einwegspiegelglas, der innen konkav ist und deshalb völlig verzerrte Spiegelbilder liefert. Das Halbrund wird durch zwei perforierte Platten aus Edelstahl unterteilt, so dass man den Zylinder betreten kann. Werden diese Platten auseinander geschoben, werfen die gleitenden Reflexionen der «Gucklöcher» ein fliessendes Wellenmuster (Moirée) auf das Glas. Im Innern stellte ich ein Tischchen mit Lippenstiften und normalen kleinen Spiegeln hin, in deren Mitte ein Fischauge angebracht war. Verändert man die Position dieser Spiegel, hat das eine ganze Reihe optischer Verzerrungen zur Folge.

CRM: Haben Sie eine Lieblingsband?

DG: Meine Lieblingsband sind seit eh und je *The Kinks.*

CRM: Mögen Sie lieber Musik oder Kunst, und warum?

DG: Früher war mir Musik lieber, weil sie mehr Spiel als Business ist, ...weil sie eine Art Gemeinschaftserlebnis bietet, ...weil sie wahnsinnig Spass machen kann und sinnlicher ist, ...weil sie verfügbar ist und im Augenblick gerade aktuelle Klischees aufgreift, wie meine ersten (konzeptuellen) Arbeiten für Zeitschriften, ...weil es eine populäre Form von Kultur ist, die ich zusammen mit ganz normalen Leuten erfahren kann, ...weil sie eine Art Hobby ist, so wie auch meine Kunst anfangs ein Hobby war.

CRM: Erleben Sie immer noch Ihre zweite Kindheit?

DG: Ich glaube, ich erfahre meine zweite Kindheit durch meine Einwegspiegelglas-Arbeiten. Ich habe nie Lacan gelesen, aber ich spüre, dass Lacans Spiegelstadien der Kindheit in diesem Zusammenhang sehr wichtig sind, wenn nämlich das Kind zum ersten Mal den Sinn oder Un-Sinn eines Ichs erfährt. Ich weiss, dass ich durch meine Kunst neue Freunde gewinne, Freunde, die ich als Kind kaum hatte. Und dank meiner Steckenpferde – der Rockmusik, den Ausflügen in die Architektur und dem Reisen – bleibe ich jung.

CRM: Und wie haben Sie gemerkt, dass Sie wieder ein Kind sind?

DG: Immer wenn ich sehe, wie kindisch sich andere im Sternzeichen des Widders geborene Leute benehmen (ich selbst bin auch Widder), weiss ich, dass ich ein Kind bin. Es fällt mir schwer, direkt auf deine Frage zu antworten, sie ist zu scharfsinnig für mich, vielleicht ist mein Blick auch nicht scharf genug, wenn es um mich selbst geht. Aber es ist eine gute Frage.

(Übersetzung: Uta Goridis)

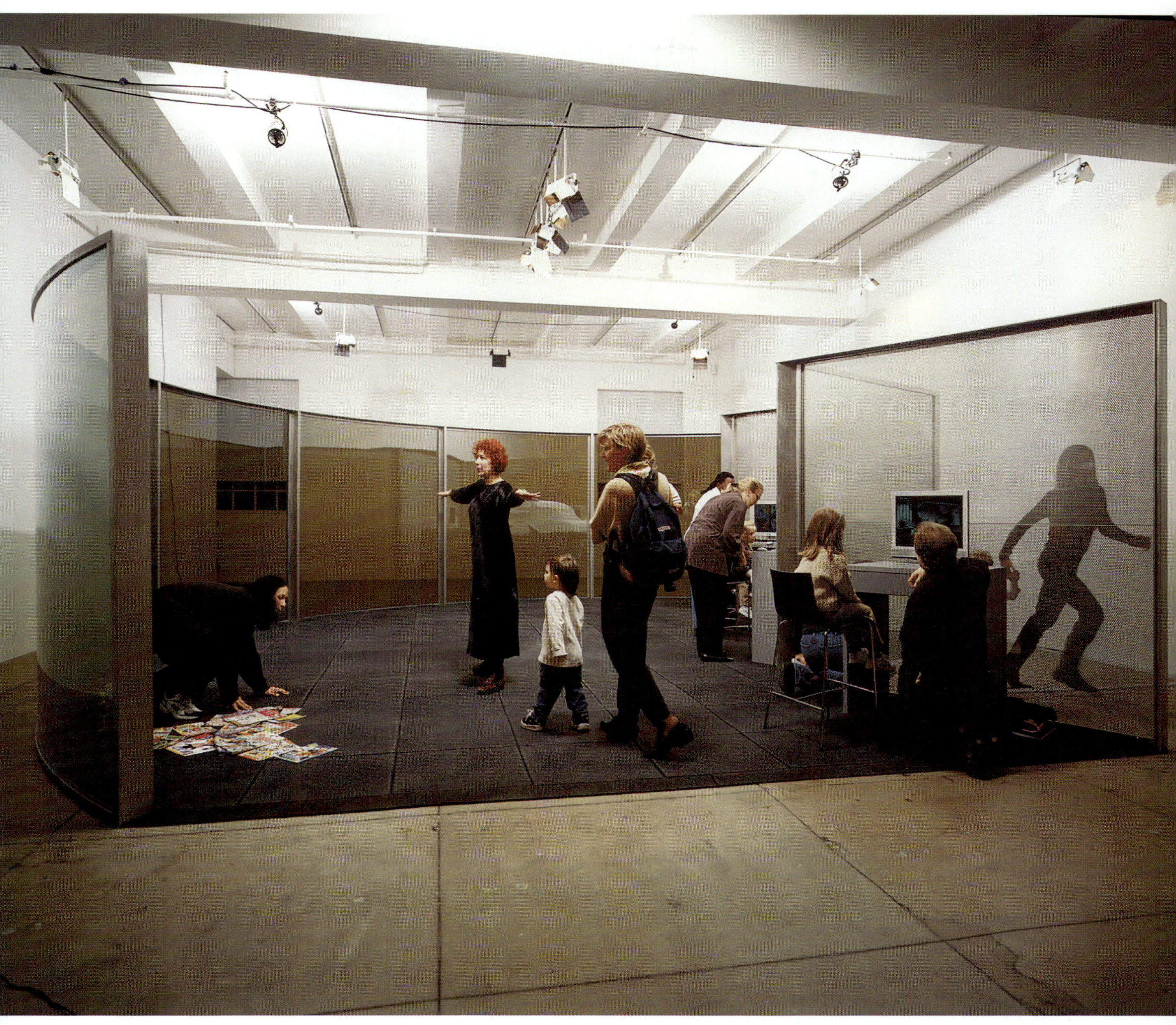

DAN GRAHAM, CHILDREN'S DAY CARE, CD-ROM, CARTOON AND COMPUTER SCREEN LIBRARY PROJECT, 1998–2000, two-way mirror, stainless steel, rubber, computer screens and computers, CD-ROM and cartoon library, desks and chairs, installation Marian Goodman Gallery, New York, April–May 2000, 90 x 296 x 273" / PROJEKT FÜR EINE KINDERTAGES-STÄTTE MIT CD-ROM-, CARTOON- UND COMPUTERBILDSCHIRM-BIBLIOTHEK, Einwegspiegel, Edelstahl, Gummi, Computer und Bildschirme, CD-ROM- und Cartoon-Bibliothek, Pulte, Stühle, 229 x 752 x 693 cm.

EDITION FOR PARKETT **DAN GRAHAM**

FUN FOR KIDS AT MY WORK IN A PARK IN MANHATTAN, 2003

Piezo Ultrachrome Pigment on Hahnemühle paper, 13 x 16 $^{1}/_{2}$".

Printed by Laumont Editions, New York.

Photograph by Rosalind Cutforth.

Edition of 60, signed and numbered on the reverse.

Piezo-Ultrachrome-Pigmentdruck auf Hahnemühle, 33 x 42 cm.

Gedruckt bei Laumont Editions, New York.

Photographie von Rosalind Cutforth.

Auflage: 60, auf der Rückseite signiert und nummeriert.

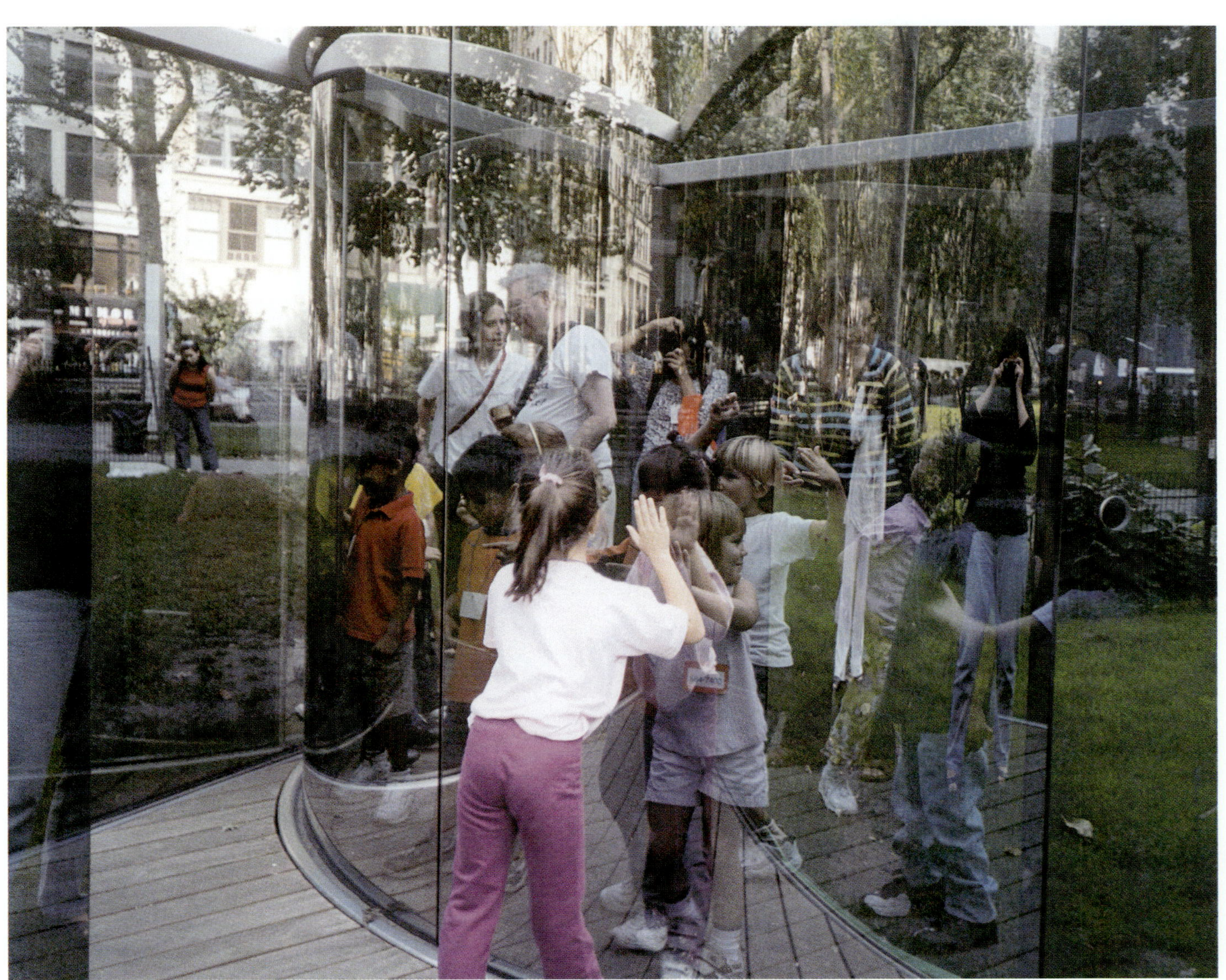

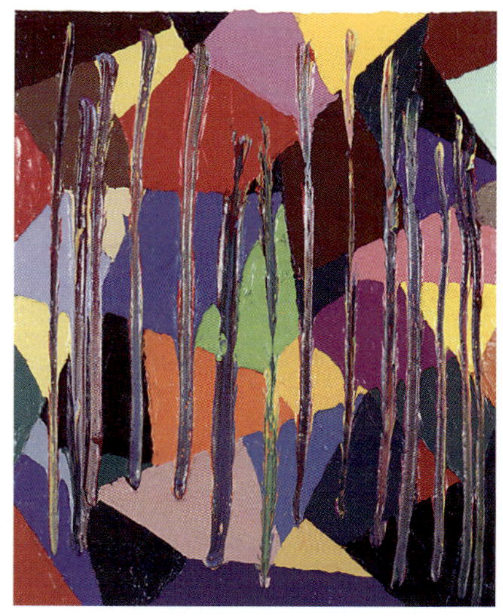

BERNARD FRIZE, *SIMPLETON*, 2002, acrylic and resin on canvas, $28\,^{3}/_{4}$ x $23\,^{5}/_{8}$"/ *SIMPEL*, Acryl und Kunstharz auf Leinwand, 73 x 60 cm.

The Taming of the Demiurge

A CONVERSATION WITH BERNARD FRIZE

HANS ULRICH OBRIST

Hans Ulrich Obrist: You mentioned, with regard to these paintings, the model of the urban network.
Bernard Frize: Yes, because the paradigm of the network is of course the city. The starting point of these paintings was a typology of city maps created by a couple of British architects whose name escapes me, and we used those patterns as grids for the surface. Take traffic, for example: cars move in all directions, but they stop at the same red lights and sometimes take the same thoroughfares; they pair up with other cars for some of the way, leave each other, then find each other again. Using these drawings as a support, the different people I work with make paintbrushes glide over the canvas and transport colors that corrupt each other on contact, as they criss-cross, meet or separate. All these traces merge together with no beginning or end, and thus the painting is completed.

Several things interest me here. First, there is a relationship to economy, to necessity and contingency in these paintings, but I also find it interesting to remain in touch with the idea of the image. It precludes any abstract formalism and engages the viewer's vision in an entirely different way.
HUO: This "many-hands-crafted" work, if you will, how did it begin?
BF: I started with simple images, like a shape similar to a fish bone. I thought I would be able to complete this series on my own, but I quickly realized that I didn't have enough "hands." *(Laughter.)* In this series, the brushes, each loaded with a different color, come from one side of the canvas, merge into a common trunk, and escape to the opposite side. There are three of us: one of us brings the brushes in, another one draws a more or less vertical line into which the brushes converge, and the third takes the brushes one after the other, carrying them out of the canvas. The colors are thoroughly mixed. I got help carrying these colors into and out of the canvas. The work manifests generation and corruption. It also shows how a mechanism is put into place. That's what I found interesting: setting up a movement and then arranging for this movement to occur on its own. I have always questioned this relationship to the painter's authority, to his demiurgic aspect. The assistants, the "machine," are strategies to find another role. For the

HANS ULRICH OBRIST is Curator at the Musée d'Art Moderne de la Ville de Paris.

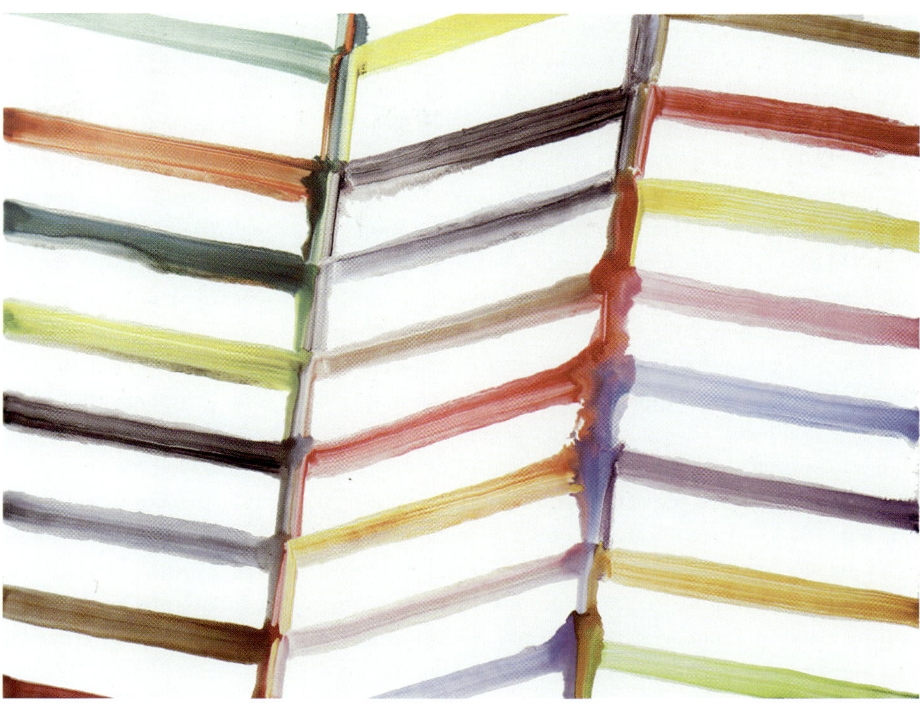

BERNARD FRIZE, ILLUSTRATION, 1998, acrylic and resin on canvas, 59 x 78¾" / Acryl und Kunstharz auf Leinwand, 150 x 200 cm.

last paintings, which look a little like curtains, I used a similar principle: as always, it is a question of mixing the colors on the canvas and here the result is a mottled color. I do not make a particular choice in the beginning: for example, these paintings were made with the same colors and the result is completely different. I am quite negligent with regard to the skill of painting in general. I use very ordinary procedures, without any savoir faire. As a matter of fact, the collaborators who help me are not painters at all.

HUO: They are not even artists?

BF: They are. But in general, they aren't painters, with the exception of Adam Adach, with whom I work less now, as he has started exhibiting more regularly... They work with video, installations. Marie Denis, for example, or Agnès Goffray, Gloria Saffont-Tria, etc.—these are artists who would never paint if I didn't ask them to.

HUO: In this studio, then, though it is more or less empty today, there are usually a lot of people.

BF: Before starting a painting, you have to prepare the canvas, stretch it, etc., and that is something I like to do myself. I do not use collaborators for the humble tasks. When I ask them to come over, I may have prepared a drawing for a certain number of people or I may feel like seeing some people who then invite a kind of drawing. It varies from two to four people. I have rarely used more people because that would imply a very different setting, which I haven't thought about yet. But I also make a lot of paintings on my own.

HUO: So what we're talking about is not, properly speaking, a "factory"?

BF: No. What would perhaps be comparable is the great quantity of paintings we produce, sometimes even in five minutes. But of course, a lot of them are failures. The same procedures, the same colors—because we prepare the colors once for the entire week, or for several meetings—offer a lot of variety and allow us to think about how both a failure and a success can result from the same combinations.

HUO: So you sort out the results after each method, you "edit" them?

BF: Exactly. I would like to show you a small painting. Last week, I met Katy Siegel and Paul Mattick and, to illustrate for them the banality of what I do, I told them that the procedures I use are as trivial as spreading butter on bread in the morning. Here it's the same thing. The finger traces mix all the colors together in this irritated gesture, and

produce a movement which generates the painting.
HUO: What is the date of this painting?
BF: 1989. It remained irrelevant for a very long time until the moment when I knew how to reintroduce it in my work.
HUO: Does it have a title?
BF: It is called SIMPLETON. Like a simple person, an idiot. The starting point of this painting came from a moment when I was watching my friend putting makeup on. Guerlain has this makeup powder made of many triangles of different colors: blue, bright pink, a few greens and browns. And when you mix the powders with a blush brush, it creates a nice flesh color. I liked the fact that such a simple gesture could produce something so unexpected. Another, earlier painting was made using the model of the *Mille-feuilles* pastry. Others borrowed from the decorations on clay pots. To use these day-to-day nothings gives me access to an activity in which I am not a different person once I step into the studio. As for the paintings themselves, they acquire a certain familiarity: their formal aspect is rejected and they become more accessible. Very simply put, my work oscillates between presentation and representation. Therefore, I have been looking for all those moments that become images. Each time my assistants and I meet, I try to suggest different ideas, so we have some fun. The methods are extremely reduced. In the end, it is always about registering the movement of a paintbrush from hand to hand without the brush leaving the surface of the canvas.
HUO: So there is a method, or some fixed rules of the game that you modulate with your assistants according to some practical ideas or new images?
BF: Usually there are three of us working on a painting. I have an assistant, who is very tall, and another one who is—unfortunately for the painting—short, and me, a little taller. *(Laughter.)* The reason I am saying this is because the canvas is very large—it's almost 9 feet—and since we work on a flat canvas on the floor, it is difficult to go all the way to the end of it. We paint with very large brushes (16 inches) and with five colors. We do a first run of these five colors on about 16 or 19 inches, then we move each color to the left, creating a staircase pattern. Once we have crossed the entire surface, we start again with the same brushes, without dipping them again in paint, moving each brush one step to the left. And over again, shifting rows each time. Black comes over yellow, yellow over green, etc. We start over until each color is no longer recognizable, the surface is mottled, and all the colors are combined. And that is the reason why two paintings made with exactly the same colors produce such different results. What I am looking for, through these permutations or these sequences, is a type of indifference to what happens, but not to the way it happened. In the case of these particular paintings, I felt there was something too rigid; it didn't really turn into an "image." In the beginning, we used to paint with brushes that weren't that large, and the paintings used to look like library shelves with multicolored book spines. I wanted to find yet another way to apprehend these movements, to be closer, in a sense, to discovering what happens when one passes several times over the same place.

This led me to the "curtains." We used the same principle, passing across the entire surface of the canvas and, in the last passage, evacuating all the brushes together on the side, or sometimes four, or two at a time, so the preceding moments are left uncovered. I don't know how long I will continue to find procedures that require several people. I think I will keep finding new ones as long as these exchanges produce images.
HUO: However, in parallel, you continue to work on your own?
BF: Yes. Let me show you another painting. I made it on my own. I made it with a brush that is, in a sense, too large for the painting. It is nearly 16 inches wide, which is almost half the size of the canvas. I am trying to fill in the surface with this brush, after having worked in about forty colors on the canvas. The brush drags the color with it, quite literally, and leaves a trace of its passage. Since the beginning of my work, I have been trying to avoid a demiurgic attitude, whose ambition would be to create a world in painting. On the contrary, I am trying to find the right attitude, and reducing the amount of decisions has seemed to me the most humble way of going about it. Hence my decision not to choose any color, or to choose too many of them so none of them stands out, or to let the trace of the brush be apparent so it is possible to reconstitute what happened, among other examples.
HUO: Is this painting one of its kind or is it part of a series?
BF: It is part of a series, because another aspect of this non-demiurgic attitude is the notion of labor. The work becomes visible if the paintings are related to each other. The idea of a series is also about emerging out of the series, i.e. exhausting it, carrying it out. I sometimes make a single painting and return to it later because I found where it fits

and where it concludes a series. In fact, there are a few reduced possibilities, a very small number of possibilities, and that's what I enjoy: to explore every possibility to the end. There are series that I started in 1986, and that I still haven't completed, in the sense that I haven't explored all their possibilities yet. I feel that the paintings work together like that, informing each other.

HUO: This non-demiurgic attitude was common in the sixties. It seems to me that you situate yourself in an in-between: one couldn't talk about your work in terms of a definition that is given and then consistently applied, but neither could one invoke a, let's say, "Picabian" attitude, with about-faces and changes of direction at every turn.

BF: What distinguishes my work from the artists who have used a systematic approach is that I rely a lot on chance. Hans Arp's chance cutouts have always been both a mystery and a spell for me. To invoke chance in one's work, and even to invoke it in a systematic way, is so paradoxical. That's what makes me different from Sol LeWitt or other artists who put a principle in place and stuck to it. Besides, I make my own paintings myself: to entirely delegate fabrication of the work doesn't seem to me to change anything other than the relationship of art to commerce. That is what allows me to constantly renew my painting strategies. I would add as well that I find ideas in industrial paint stores rather than within the field of art. This might be the only aspect that brings me closer to Picabia. As it happens, I am interested in mathematical reviews.

HUO: I didn't know that. Do you subscribe to any of them?

BF: No, but I often go to that excellent bookstore near the Pantheon.

HUO: And do you read René Thom's work, or are you interested in chaos theory?

BF: I'm interested above all in the idea of the game. There are very simple mathematical problems, such as: is it possible to cover every square of the chessboard with the knight? If so, what type of drawing does that produce? It is interesting because, in this case, I am delegating to a problem what I should be doing myself, i.e. creating the drawing.

Using these procedures structures the action and also allows me to distance myself. Similarly, each time I paint, I try to be further and further away from the painting. The same thing happens when I use collaborators: I remain at a distance, which reinforces the non-demiurgic aspect. The fact that my images and paintings are constantly changing is essentially a way of avoiding the trademark. An artist like Robert Ryman was very important for me when I started, but what I didn't like was that his idea of the ostensibly simple reduction to white became a trademark.

HUO: That's what Raymond Hains calls a "personified abstraction."

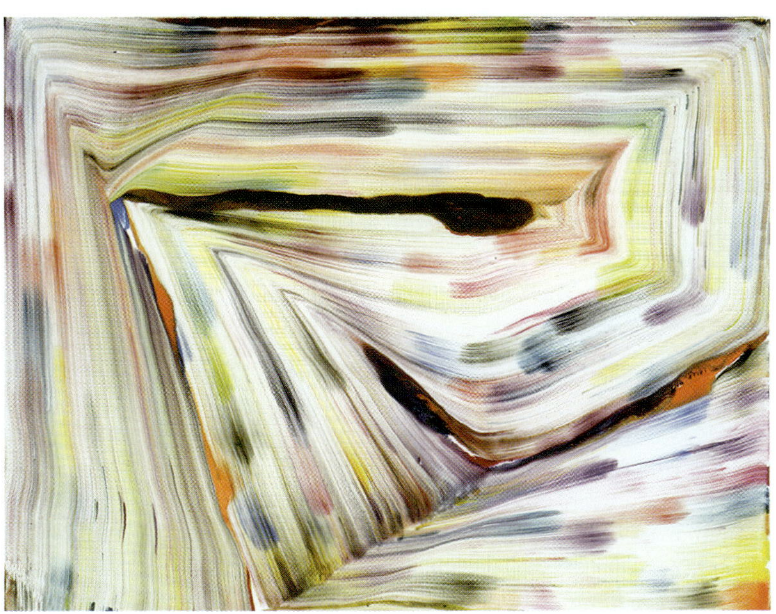

BERNARD FRIZE, CONDUCTEUR B, 2001, acrylic and resin on canvas, 35 x 45 1/2" / Acryl und Kunstharz auf Leinwand, 89 x 115,5 cm.

BF: Absolutely. So at the outset I told myself: "Let's use every color, every possibility, so no single one of them is recognizable. Obviously, as the work progresses, I will eventually feel like the traces of paint I am leaving are starting to look like trademarks, unless they reflect spent time. Then it is time to find other strategies to avoid becoming visible. It is a question of hiding behind procedures so as to prevent the "personification of abstraction." That's a very nice way of putting it.

The other thing I am interested in is the way a viewer activates a painting. There are some paintings you first look at from the side and then head on, there are others that are very different, once you get closer to them, from what they seemed viewed from a distance. Here too, I have used strategies, some of which, no doubt, have been used before. For example the idea of immersing a viewer in color, as with Barnett Newman, whose big paintings must be seen from up close, etc. This is why I want my traces to allow viewers to reconstitute what happened.

When I exhibit my works, I try to hang the paintings so their juxtaposition tells a story or a fiction that also invests a public space. A painting must address an audience, even though it is conceived in an individual world.

HUO: In this sense, is the exhibition a medium for you?

BF: Absolutely. And that's why I feel so frustrated with those museum exhibitions, where it's just a question of moving things I'm already familiar with from one place to another. Patricia (Falguières) recently told me a lot about Paolo Virno's book, *Grammaire de la multitude.* There are many similarities with what I think about production, about economy, about multitude and singularity.

HUO: Has the computer changed the way you work?

BF: Yes. It happened in two ways: when I started working with a computer, I first entered all my work with the images and their references. At the same time, I had started to catalogue the definitions and procedures I was using. Thanks to that list, which was not much longer than a page, I was able to create very different painting combinations.

HUO: How many paintings have you entered?

BF: More than 800.

HUO: A kind of imaginary museum?

BF: Or rather something a little "Warburgian." *(Laughter.)*

HUO: I also asked the question about your use of the computer because of the objects you showed at Micheline Szwajcer's gallery.

BF: There was one object I find absolutely fascinating; I

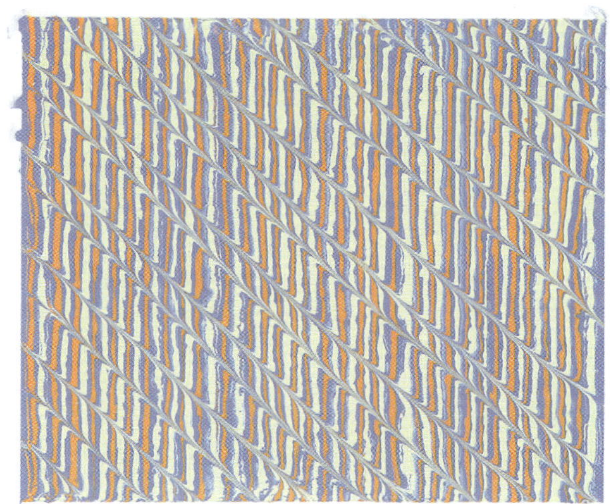

BERNARD FRIZE, XXX, 1995, acrylic and resin on canvas, $15^{3}/_{4}$ x $23^{5}/_{8}$" / Acryl und Kunstharz auf Leinwand, 40 x 60 cm.

first saw it when I was a kid at the *Palais de la Découverte.* It's a "map," painted over a volume, whose particularity is that each color shares a common border with all the others. There are eight colors and they are all connected to each other. About ten years ago, a mathematician named Szilassi found a simpler, much more geometric way to create this map. And whereas Heawood, in the nineteenth century, created his map empirically, Szilassi, in my opinion, probably used a computer. Look at this book, it is the *Récréations Mathématiques de la librairie technique Albert Blanchard.* There are several volumes, presenting different mathematical problems. For example, the problem of the bridges of Königsberg, where one must walk around the city without crossing the same bridge twice. Or the logic of family relationships. I use these things in my work all the time. I often make diagrams to make sure I don't use the same colors twice, or on the contrary to provoke repetitions of color. So I use a logical basis to find solutions.

HUO: Is logic to you a little like what Poincaré was for Duchamp?

BF: Yes, thanks. Most people approach my work from an

aestheticizing angle, but I am completely negligent with regard to the aesthetic result. I just try to make sure the blue is different from the green or the yellow, and that when I use two reds, it is clear that these two reds are very different. It is very important to me that procedures can be named and re-visited. The procedure isn't the object of the work, but it is its support, it informs it, just as the image is the shareable dimension of a sensorial experience.

HUO: Could you develop this readymade aspect a little?

BF: I think it is linked to the economy I put in place in my work: to avoid as much as possible working in a complicated or artistic manner, in a manner that requires a particular knowledge or skill. Another aspect is the use of chance. When I made these paintings I was preoccupied by the relationships between color and drawing. And in reality, I was looking for something entirely different; I only saw it because I was being negligent. One morning, I came to the studio and all the paint containers I had forgotten to seal the night before had dried up, so I cut them out. I had nowhere to put them so I put them on a canvas and all this was done without giving it much thought. The first time I showed it was in Lucien Durand's gallery—which no longer exists—and César's agent said something like: "What's the use of sticking plastic circles on a canvas?" I thought it was a mean but interesting comment, because the point was then to find a much better way to define these circles of color, to characterize their provenance, to try to show that paint drips and that these circles were not made of plastic. This happened at the beginning of my work and it really helped me later. Another aspect of the readymade is of course to distance and evacuate—ostensibly at least—the person from the act of making. But for a long time I didn't really like these paintings, because I thought they were too closely related to accumulation and the "New Realists." I preferred the Fluxus aspect. I always remember that image of Robert Filliou wiping up dust from a painting at the Louvre. That directness was interesting to me, that absence of mediation. At last, here was a possible relationship to language and memory, through images.

To return to the topic of chance, it's the idea of not choosing that pushed me to use these *Récréations Mathématiques.* And even with chance, the challenge is to find the freest, but at the same time of course the most determined manner of provoking chance. It is a question of eliminating all the parameters that could prevent a chance event from occurring. I spend all my time conceiving strategies that enable me to not intervene and to paint as lazily as possible.

HUO: There are many series you began and then put aside for a time, and to which you return sometimes years later. I was wondering if there were series you thought about but never realized?

BF: There are a lot of ideas for which I haven't found possibilities yet. But I might find them, most probably when a painting from the past resurfaces. This, by the way, is often the role of exhibitions: when two paintings are confronted, suddenly a third one becomes important, or possible. But it's not that I work on my own work either. An idea can come from a meeting with someone, from anything whatsoever. For example, I had the idea of making grids from noticing how you cross the edges of a cardboard box with tape or string to close it. And this "changing" moment, for example, is something I discovered in Italy, about mannerism, and about how the idea of representing a garment with a changing color was invented and then fought against during the Counter-Reformation because it was dangerous, inasmuch as it staked out the autonomy of painting. One is often confronted with ideas that are very simple on the level of fabrication, for example, but that are in fact of great relevance to an ideology or politics, as in this example of the Counter-Reformation.

HUO: So dialogues with art historians are crucial for understanding these matters?

BF: Yes. When I was at the *Ecole des Beaux Arts,* I read a lot of Russell, Wittgenstein, Austin, and later Quine, Cavell and other logicians or specialists in the philosophy of language. My understanding of them was above all a poetic one, they stimulated my imagination. We also encounter similar topics as we go about our daily business. For example, I was perplexed by the Mesdag Panorama in The Hague. It is fascinating on many levels, as a form of spectacle anticipating the cinema, but at the same time it remains an example of functional painting. In England there were a lot of moving paintings, painted on glass panels by well-known artists, that showed battle scenes, or you would move the panels to make a volcano erupt, for example. All these fields are still active today and seem to beg to be explored. Not to mention my interest in hearing these art historians discuss the art of today, because I do think, although one is not supposed to say it too loud, that art criticism here is rather impoverished. *(Laughter.)*

(Translated from the French by Anthony Allen)

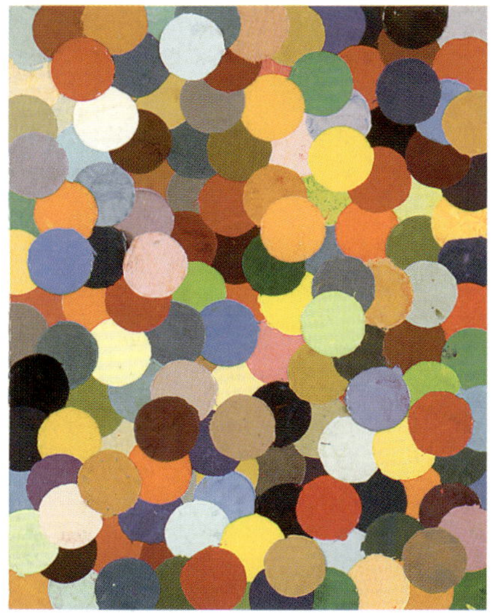

Die Zähmung des Demiurgen

EIN GESPRÄCH MIT BERNARD FRIZE

BERNARD FRIZE, SUITE SEGOND STRN30F100, 1980, alkyd urethane lacquer on canvas, 36 1/4 x 28 3/4" / Alkydurethan-Lack auf Leinwand, 92 x 73 cm.

HANS ULRICH OBRIST

Hans Ulrich Obrist: Im Zusammenhang mit diesen Bildern nanntest du als Vorbild das urbane Rasternetz.

Bernard Frize: Ja, weil die Stadt offensichtlich das Paradebeispiel eines Netzwerks ist. Der Ursprung dieser Bilder liegt in einer Typologie der Stadtpläne, die eine englische Architektengruppe erstellt hat, deren Name mir im Moment nicht einfallen will; wir haben diese Muster als Oberflächeneinteilung verwendet. Nehmen wir den Verkehr: Die Autos fahren in alle Richtungen, aber sie stoppen bei denselben Rotlichtern und verkehren manchmal auf derselben Achse; sie fahren ein Stück weit gemeinsam, trennen sich oder kommen wieder zusammen. Anhand dieser Muster lassen die Leute, mit denen ich zusammenarbeite, die Pinsel gleiten und transportieren Farben, die sich beim Zusammentreffen gegenseitig beeinflussen, sich kreuzen, wieder zusammenfinden oder sich trennen. Alle Spuren vermischen sich ohne Anfang und Ende, bis das Bild schliesslich vollendet ist. Mein Interesse geht dabei in verschiedene Richtungen: Einerseits haben diese Bilder eine Beziehung zu Ökonomie, Notwendigkeit und Zufall, aber ich finde es andrerseits auch interessant, die Idee des Bildes im Auge zu behalten. Das verhindert jeden abstrakten Formalismus und spricht das Auge des Betrachters auf ganz andere Weise an.

HUO: Wie hat diese Arbeit «zu mehreren Händen», wie du es nennst, begonnen?

BF: Ich habe mit einfachen Bildern angefangen, etwa einer Form, die man als Fischgräte verstehen konnte. Ich dachte zuerst, ich könnte diese Serie allein realisieren, merkte aber bald, dass ich nicht genug «Hände» dazu hatte. *(Gelächter.)* In dieser Serie kommen die Pinsel voll sauberer Farbe von der einen Seite der Leinwand, verschmelzen zu einem gemeinsamen «Rückgrat» und scheren dann auf die andere Seite aus. Wir sind zu dritt, einer führt die Pinsel, ein Zweiter zieht eine mehr oder weniger vertikale Linie, der diese Pinsel folgen, und der Letzte führt einen Pinsel nach dem anderen wieder aus der Leinwand hinaus; die Farben vermischen sich dabei völlig. Ich liess mir dabei helfen, die Farben auf die Leinwand zu bringen und wieder daraus zu entfernen. Diese Arbeit zeigt gleichzeitig einen Erzeugungs- und einen Zersetzungsprozess; sie zeigt

---

HANS ULRICH OBRIST ist Kurator am Musée d'Art Moderne de la Ville de Paris.

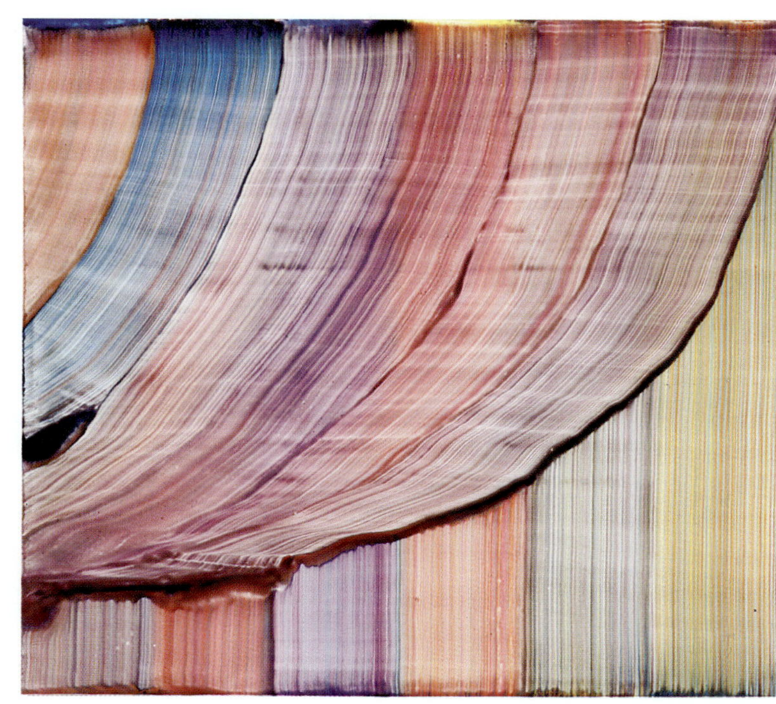

BERNARD FRIZE, MEROTOM, 2003, acrylic and resin on canvas, 63 x 70⅞" / Acryl und Kunstharz auf Leinwand, 160 x 180 cm.

auch, wie ein Mechanismus entsteht. Das habe ich interessant gefunden: eine Bewegung in Gang setzen und dafür sorgen, dass diese Bewegung dann von alleine weitergeht. Ich habe schon immer diese Beziehung zur Autorität des Malers, den demiurgischen Aspekt in Frage gestellt. Die Assistenten oder die «Maschine» sind Strategien, um einen anderen Standpunkt zu finden. Für die neusten Bilder, die ein bisschen Vorhängen gleichen, habe ich ein ähnliches Prinzip angewendet: die Farben immer auf der Leinwand mischen und dies zeigen. Dabei ist eine geflammte Farbe entstanden. Am Anfang steht nie eine bestimmte Entscheidung meinerseits; diese Leinwände hier sind mit denselben Farben gemalt, aber das Resultat ist ein völlig anderes. Ich bin sehr nachlässig, was das Metier des Malens im Allgemeinen angeht. Ich arbeite mit ganz banalen Mitteln ohne irgendein *savoir faire*. Im Übrigen sind auch meine Mitarbeiter keineswegs Maler.

HUO: Sind es auch keine Künstler?

BF: Doch. Aber im Allgemeinen sind es keine Maler, mit Ausnahme von Adam Adach, mit dem ich jetzt weniger zusammenarbeite, weil er selbst regelmässiger ausstellt… Sie machen Videos, Installationen. Da ist Marie Denis oder Agnès Geoffray, Gloria Saffont-Tria u.a., alles Künstlerinnen, die nie malen würden, wenn ich sie nicht darum bäte.

HUO: Also halten sich in diesem Atelier, das heute sozusagen leer ist, normalerweise viele Leute auf.

BF: Bevor man mit Malen beginnt, muss man erst einmal die Leinwände vorbereiten, sie auf Keilrahmen spannen usw.; das tue ich gern selbst. Ich brauche keine Mitarbeiter für Hilfsarbeiten. Wenn ich sie bitte zu kommen, ist der Entwurf entweder für die entsprechende Anzahl Personen vorbereitet oder, wenn ich einfach Lust habe mit ihnen zusammen zu sein, führt die Anzahl der Anwesenden zu einem bestimmten Entwurf. Das geht von zwei bis vier Personen. Mit mehr Leuten hab ich selten gearbeitet, denn da müsste man ganz anders vorgehen und darüber hab ich nie nachgedacht. Aber viele Bilder male ich auch allein.

HUO: Es handelt sich also nicht eigentlich um eine «Factory»?

BF: Nein, das Einzige, was dem vielleicht entspricht, ist die grosse Zahl von Bildern, die wir produzieren, manchmal innert nur fünf Minuten. Aber viele sind natürlich unbrauchbar. Dieselben Prozeduren, dieselben Farben – wir bereiten jeweils die Farben für eine ganze Woche oder mehrere Sitzungen vor – erlauben eine grosse Vielfalt und ein ebenso gründliches Abwägen, wie es mit denselben

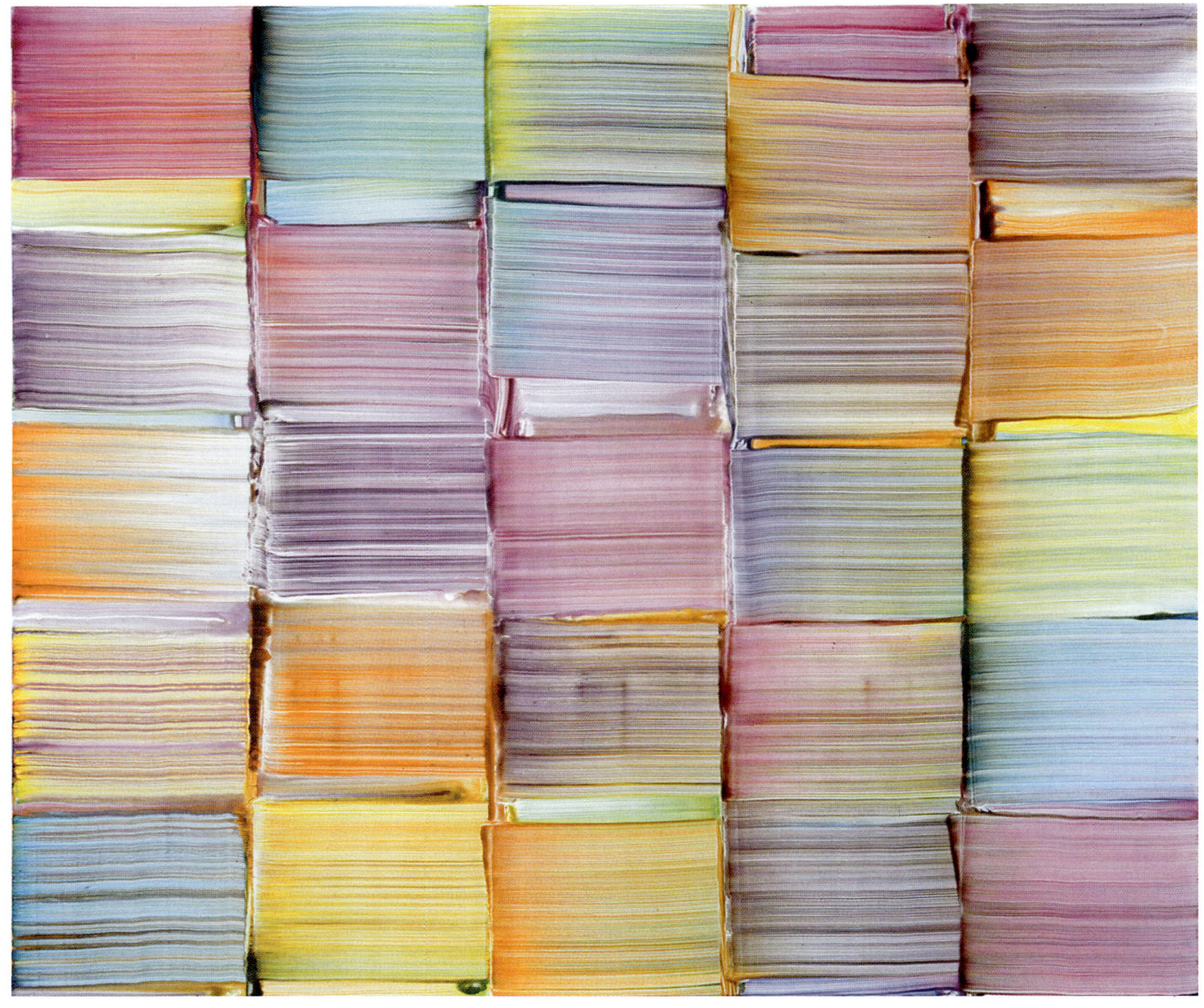

BERNARD FRIZE, AUNNO, 2003, acrylic and resin on canvas, 88 9/16 x 106 5/16" / Acryl und Kunstharz auf Leinwand, 225 x 270 cm.

Kombinationen zum Scheitern oder Gelingen kommt.
HUO: So sortiert ihr also aus, jede Methode wird einem «Redaktionsprozess» unterworfen...
BF: Genau: Ich möchte dir ein kleines Bild zeigen. Letzte Woche habe ich Kathy Siegel und Paul Mattick getroffen und um ihnen die Banalität dessen, was ich mache, vor Augen zu führen, sagte ich, dass die Methoden, die ich anwende so einfach seien wie die Butter am Morgen aufs Brot zu streichen. Hier ist es genauso: Die Fingerspuren vermischen mit dieser aufgeregten Geste alle Farben und erzeugen die Bewegung, die das Bild ausmacht.
HUO: Aus welchem Jahr ist das?
BF: 1989. Es blieb lange Zeit isoliert und folgenlos, bis ich es wieder in meine Arbeit einbringen konnte.
HUO: Hat es einen Titel?
BF: Es heisst SIMPLETON wie ein kleiner Simpel, ein Idiot.

Es ist aus einem Moment heraus entstanden, als ich meiner Freundin beim Schminken zuschaute. Bei Guerlain gibt es einen Wangenpuder, der aus mehrfarbigen Dreiecken besteht, Blau, Tiefrosa, Braun- und Grüntöne, und wenn man diesen Puder mit einem Rougepinsel mischt, entsteht ein schöner hautfarbener Ton. Mir gefiel, dass man mit einer einfachen Bewegung ein so unerwartetes Resultat erreichen kann. Ein anderes, etwas älteres Bild ist nach dem Vorbild der Blätterteigbäckerei entstanden. Für andere machte ich Anleihen bei Keramikdekors. Die Verwendung solch alltäglicher Kleinigkeiten erlaubt mir eine Tätigkeit, bei der ich kein anderer Mensch werde, wenn ich die Schwelle zum Atelier überschreite. Was die Malerei angeht, so bekommt sie lediglich einen vertrauten Zug, womit ihr formeller Aspekt beseitigt und der Zugang einfacher wird. Ich mache ganz einfach eine Arbeit, die zwischen Präsentation und Repräsentation oszilliert. Ich habe jeden Moment, der Bild wird, recherchiert. Wenn die Assistenten kommen, versuche ich jedesmal neue Ideen zu bringen, damit wir Spass haben. Die Methoden sind extrem reduziert, letztlich geht es immer darum, die Übergabe des Pinsels von Hand zu Hand zu schaffen, ohne den Kontakt mit der Leinwand zu verlieren.

HUO: Es gibt also eine feste Methode oder Spielregel, die du – entsprechend deinen praktischen Vorstellungen oder neuen Bildideen – mit deinen Assistenten durchspielst?

BF: Gewöhnlich arbeiten wir zu dritt an einem Bild. Ich habe eine Assistentin, die sehr gross ist, die andere ist – zum Unglück für das Bild – klein, und ich bin ein klein wenig grösser. *(Gelächter.)* Ich sage das, weil das Bild sehr gross ist, zwei Meter siebzig Spannweite, und da wir mit der Leinwand flach auf dem Boden arbeiten, ist es sehr schwer, überallhin zu gelangen. Wir malen mit sehr grossen Pinseln, vierzig Zentimeter lang, und mit fünf Farben. Wir machen einen ersten Durchgang mit diesen fünf Farben auf einer Breite von vierzig oder fünfzig Zentimetern, dann versetzen wir die Farben treppenartig abgestuft nach links. Wenn wir die ganze Fläche durchquert haben, beginnen wir mit denselben Pinseln wieder von vorn, jedoch ohne sie erneut mit Farbe zu tränken und um ein Feld versetzt. Und dann noch einmal mit einer weiteren Versetzung um jeweils ein Feld. Auf Gelb kommt Schwarz, auf Grün Gelb, usw. Wir überarbeiten alles so lange, bis die Spuren der einzelnen Farben nicht mehr erkennbar sind und eine mehrfarbige Fläche entsteht, auf der alles vermischt ist. Deshalb wirken zwei mit genau denselben Farben gemalte Bilder völlig verschieden. Was ich durch diese Verwandlungen, diese Sequenzen erreichen will, ist eine Art Gleichgültigkeit gegenüber dem, was geschieht, aber nicht gegenüber der Art und Weise, *wie* es geschehen ist. Bei diesen Bildern fand ich, sie hätten vielleicht etwas allzu Rigides; «es» gab als Bild nicht viel her. Zunächst hatten wir mit weniger grossen Pinseln gemalt, so dass die Bilder aussahen wie Ausschnitte von Bibliotheken, Büchertranchen in allen Farben. Ich wollte noch einen anderen Weg finden diese Bewegungen vorauszuahnen, um in gewisser Weise der Entdeckung näher zu kommen, was sich ereignet, wenn man mehrere Male am selben Ort vorbei kommt.

Das hat dann zu diesen «Vorhängen» geführt. Wir arbeiten nach demselben Prinzip, durchqueren die Leinwand ganz und beim letzten Durchgang nehmen wir alle Pinsel zugleich seitlich weg, oder manchmal in Vierergruppen, oder jeweils zwei und zwei zu den Seiten hin, damit die vorausgegangenen Momente sichtbar bleiben. Ich weiss nicht, wie lange es mir noch gelingt, Vorgehensweisen zu finden, die mehrere Leute erfordern. Ich glaube, ich werde sie so lange finden, wie aus dieser Zusammenarbeit Bilder entstehen.

HUO: Aber parallel dazu arbeitest du auch immer noch allein?

BF: Ja. Ich hole dir gleich ein anderes Bild. Das habe ich allein gemacht. Ich habe es mit einem Pinsel gemalt, der gewissermassen zu gross ist für das Bild, er ist vierzig Zentimeter breit, also fast die Hälfte des Bildes. Ich habe versucht die Bildfläche mit diesem Pinsel zu bedecken, indem ich etwa vierzig Farben durcheinander auf die Leinwand geschüttet habe. Der Pinsel zieht die Farbe mit, verpinselt sie buchstäblich und lässt eine Spur seines Weges zurück. Ich glaube, ich habe in meiner Arbeit von Anfang an versucht eine «demiurgische» Haltung zu vermeiden, eine Haltung, bei der ich den Ehrgeiz hätte, malerisch eine Welt zu erschaffen. Ich versuche lieber eine richtige Methode zu finden, und von Anfang an erschien mir die Reduktion der Entscheidungen als die demütigste Art, dies anzugehen. Also unter anderem: die Farben nicht auswählen oder wenigstens zu viele wählen, so dass keine dominiert, oder die Spuren der Pinsel sichtbar stehen lassen, so dass man rekonstruieren kann, was passiert ist.

HUO: Ist das ein Einzelbild oder ist es Teil einer Serie?

BF: Es gehört zu einer Serie, denn der andere Aspekt dieser nicht demiurgischen Haltung ist: eine *Arbeit* zu leisten. Diese Arbeit wird sichtbar, sobald Bilder aufeinander bezogen sind. Zur Idee der Serie gehört es gleichzeitig auch, aus der Serie hinauszutreten, das heisst sie zu erschöpfen, abzuschliessen. Es kommt manchmal vor, dass ich ein einzelnes Bild mache und es später wieder aufnehme, wenn ich einen Ort finde, wo ich es einbinden und ein Ensemble vervollständigen kann. Tatsächlich gibt es eine bestimmte Zahl beschränkter Möglichkeiten, also sehr wenige Möglichkeiten, und es macht mir Spass, alle Möglichkeiten bis zum Ende auszuschöpfen. Es gibt Serien, die ich 1986 begonnen und noch immer nicht abgeschlossen habe, in dem Sinn, dass ich noch nicht alle Möglichkeiten ausprobiert habe. Mir scheint, dass die Bilder miteinander Rücksprache halten.

HUO: Diese nicht-demiurgische Einstellung war in den 60er Jahren verbreitet. Mir scheint, dass du dich in einem Dazwischen befindest: Man kann bei deiner Arbeit nicht von einer einmal festgelegten und dann durchgängig angewandten Definition reden, aber genauso wenig könnte man behaupten, darin eine, sagen wir, «picabieske» Haltung zu erkennen, die sich mal da-, mal dorthin wendet und ständig die Richtung wechselt.

BF: Was meine Arbeit von jener von Leuten unterscheidet, die auf irgendeine Weise systematisch vorgehen, ist, dass ich viel mit dem Zufall arbeite. Die Zufalls-Scherenschnitte von Hans Arp hatten für mich immer zugleich etwas Rätsel- und Zauberhaftes. Sich in der Arbeit auf den Zufall zu berufen und sich gar noch systematisch darauf zu berufen ist absolut paradox. Das unterscheidet mich von Sol Lewitt und anderen Künstlern, die sich einem Prinzip verpflichten und ihm treu bleiben. Aber ich realisiere meine Bilder auch selbst; ich glaube nicht, dass das Delegieren der gesamten Fabrikation irgendetwas ändert ausser in Bezug auf den Kunsthandel. Deshalb kann ich meine Strategien immer wieder ändern und erneuern. Zudem finde ich meine Ideen eher in Zeitschriften über industrielle Maltechniken als im Bereich der Kunst. Das ist vielleicht das Einzige, was ich mit Picabia gemein habe. Im Übrigen interessiere ich mich für Mathematik-Zeitschriften.

HUO: Das wusste ich nicht. Bist du auf bestimmte Mathematik-Zeitschriften abonniert?

BF: Nein, aber ich gehe oft in diese tolle Buchhandlung beim Pantheon.

HUO: Liest du René Thom oder interessierst du dich für die Chaostheorien?

BF: Es hängt vor allem mit dem Spielgedanken zusammen. Es gibt ganz einfache mathematische Rätsel, wie: Kann man mit dem Springer alle Felder des Schachspiels benützen? Und wenn ja, was für eine Zeichnung entsteht dabei? Das ist interessant, weil ich auf der Stelle an dieses Rätsel delegiere, was ich eigentlich selbst machen sollte, nämlich, die Zeichnung erzeugen.

Die Anwendung solcher Prozeduren strukturiert mein Handeln und erlaubt mir auch Distanz zu nehmen. Genauso, wie ich beim Malen versuche mich jedesmal ein bisschen weiter von der Malerei zu entfernen. Dasselbe gilt für den Einsatz von Mitarbeitern: Ich gewinne Distanz und das stärkt die nicht-demiurgische Seite. Dass ich ständig die Bilder und Malweisen wechsle, soll eben das Entstehen von für mich typischen Bildern verhindern. Ein Künstler wie Robert Ryman war, als ich zu malen begann, sehr wichtig für mich, aber was mir weniger gefiel, war, dass seine scheinbar so simple Idee der Reduktion aufs Weisse einfach zu einem Markenzeichen wurde.

HUO: Also zu dem, was Raymond Hains eine «personifizierte Abstraktion» nennt.

BF: Genau. Deshalb hab ich mir im Voraus gesagt: «Verwenden wir alle Farben, alle Möglichkeiten, so dass man keine von ihnen wieder erkennt. Natürlich hätte ich bei der Arbeit mit der Zeit das Gefühl, dass die Spuren der Malerei, die ich hinterlasse, beginnen zu einem Markenzeichen zu werden, würden sie nicht auch Zeit transportieren. Und jetzt wird es Zeit, neue Strategien zu entwickeln, um nicht erwischt zu werden. Sonst wird es zum sich Verstecken hinter den Prozeduren, die dieser «Personifikation der Abstraktion» ausweichen; übrigens eine sehr schöne Formel. Das andere, was mich interessiert, ist, wie ein Betrachter ein Bild aktiviert. Es gibt diese Bilder, die man von der Seite und frontal betrachten kann, und es gibt andere, die aus der Nähe ganz anders aussehen als aus einer gewissen Entfernung. Auch da habe ich Strategien verwendet, die zum Teil natürlich schon früher untersucht wurden. Zum Beispiel, die Idee den Betrachter mit Farbe zu überschwemmen bei Barnett Newman, die grossen Bilder, die man aus der Nähe betrachten muss, usw. Deshalb möchte ich, dass die Spuren erkennen lassen, was geschehen ist.

In den Ausstellungen versuche ich zu erreichen, dass die Gegenüberstellung der Bilder eine Geschichte erzählt oder eine Fiktion erzeugt, die auch in den öffentlichen Raum mündet. Auch wenn es im individuellen Raum entsteht, muss ein Bild ein Publikum ansprechen.

HUO: In diesem Sinn ist die Ausstellung für dich also ein Medium?

BF: Absolut. Und deshalb bin ich auch immer so enttäuscht von diesen Museumsausstellungen, wo es nur darum geht, Dinge, die ich bereits kenne, von einem Ort zum andern zu transportieren. Patricia (Falguières) erzählt mir im Moment viel über das Buch von Paolo Virno, *Grammaire de la multitude*. Darin finden sich viele Ähnlichkeiten zu meinen Gedanken über die Produktion, die Ökonomie, die Menge und die Singularität.

HUO: Hat der Computer deine Arbeitsweise verändert?

BF: Ja, in zweierlei Hinsicht: Als ich mit dem Computer zu arbeiten begann, habe ich zunächst die ganze Arbeit mit den Bildern und all ihren Referenzen festgehalten und dann einen Katalog mit den Definitionen der diversen Vorgehensweisen angelegt. Diese Liste, die nicht länger als anderthalb Seiten war, ermöglichte ganz neue Bildkombinationen.

HUO: Wie viele Bilder hast du so erfasst?

BF: Mehr als 800.

HUO: Es ist also eine Art imaginäres Museum?

BF: Wohl eher etwas mit einem «warburgschen» Touch. *(Gelächter.)*

HUO: Ich habe dir diese Frage nach dem Einsatz des Computers auch im Hinblick auf die Objekte gestellt, die ich in der Ausstellung bei Micheline Szwajzer gesehen habe.

BF: Darunter war ein Objekt, das ich als kleiner Junge im *Palais de la Découverte* entdeckte und das mich total faszinierte: eine Landkarte, die auf einen dreidimensionalen Körper aufgemalt war, wobei das Besondere darin bestand, dass jede Farbe eine gemeinsame Grenze mit jeder anderen hatte. Es sind acht Farben und alle acht sind miteinander verbunden.

Vor rund zehn Jahren hat ein Mathematiker namens Szilassi eine einfachere, viel geometrischere Lösung für diese Karte gefunden. Und ich denke, während Heawood seine Karte gegen Ende des neunzehnten Jahrhunderts auf empirische Weise anfertigte, hat Szilassi natürlich den Computer verwendet. Schau dir dieses Buch an über die *Récréations Mathématiques de la librairie technique Albert Blanchard*. Es gibt mehrere Bände davon, die diverse mathematische Probleme behandeln. Zum Beispiel, das Problem der Königsberger Brücken, bei dem es darum geht, einen Weg durch die Stadt zu finden ohne zweimal dieselbe Brücke zu überqueren. Oder die Logik der Verwandtschaftsbeziehungen. Das sind Dinge, die ich immer wieder in meiner Arbeit verwende. Oft erstelle ich Diagramme, um nicht dieselben Farben zu verwenden oder aber die Wiederholung der Farben gerade zu provozieren. Solche Quellen aus dem Bereich der Logik hab ich angezapft um zu Lösungen zu kommen.

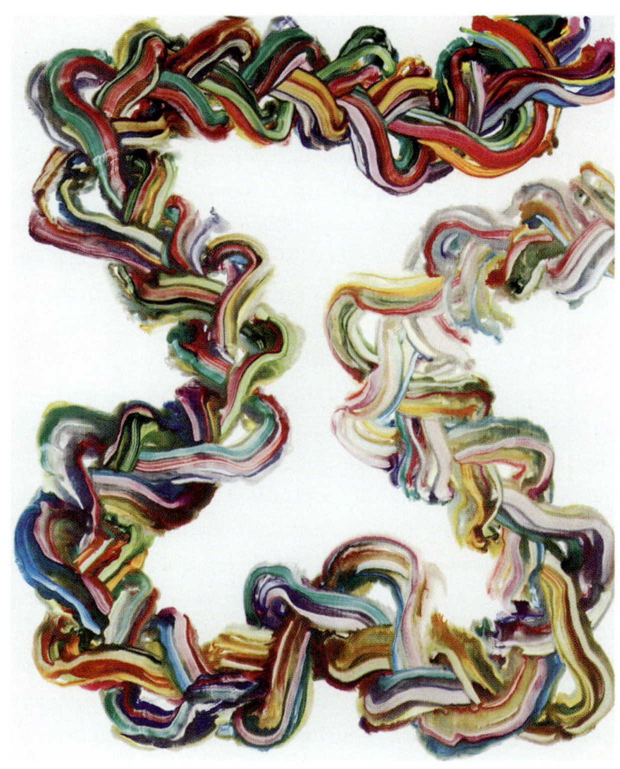

BERNARD FRIZE, PALACE, 2000, acrylic and resin on canvas, 86 5/8 x 70 7/8" / Acryl und Kunstharz auf Leinwand, 220 x 180 cm.

HUO: Das ist für dich also in etwa das, was Poincaré für Duchamp war?

BF: Ja, danke! Die meisten Leute betrachten meine Arbeit von einem ästhetischen Standpunkt, während ich selbst das ästhetische Resultat völlig vernachlässige. Mir geht es nur darum, dass das Blau sich vom Grün oder Gelb unterscheidet, und wenn ich zweimal Rot verwende, soll man sehen, dass es sich um zwei verschiedene Rot handelt. Es ist mir sehr wichtig, dass man die Dinge benennen und den Entstehungsprozess nachvollziehen kann. Die Vorgehensweise ist nicht Gegenstand der Arbeit, aber ihr Fundament. Sie verleiht ihr die Form, genauso wie das Bild eine Dimension sinnlicher Erfahrung eröffnet, an der man teilhaben kann.

HUO: Kannst du diesen *Readymade*-Aspekt etwas erläutern?

BF: Ich glaube, er hängt mit der Ökonomie zusammen,

die ich in meiner Arbeit anwende: so wenig wie möglich zu tun, aber auf eine komplizierte oder künstlerische Weise, die besonderes Wissen voraussetzt. Eine andere Sache ist das Arbeiten mit dem Zufall. Als ich diese Bilder machte, beschäftigte mich vor allem das Verhältnis zwischen den Farben und der Zeichnung. Aber eigentlich suchte ich etwas ganz anderes; ich bin nebenbei darauf gestossen. Eines Morgens kam ich ins Atelier und die Farbtöpfe, die ich am Vorabend zu verschliessen vergessen hatte, waren ausgetrocknet. Also habe ich den Inhalt in Scheiben geschnitten, und weil ich nicht wusste wohin damit, habe ich das Ganze ohne lange nachzudenken auf eine Leinwand gepappt. Als ich diese das erste Mal zeigte – es war in der Galerie Lucien Durand, eine Galerie, die nicht mehr existiert –, meinte der Agent von César mir gegenüber: «Wozu soll das gut sein, runde Plastikscheiben auf die Leinwand zu kleben?» Ich fand diesen Gedanken bösartig, aber doch auch interessant, denn es galt, diese Farbkreise irgendwie besser zu definieren, ihre Herkunft sichtbar zu machen, zu zeigen, dass die Farbe flüssig gewesen war und dass diese runden Formen nicht aus Plastik waren. Das war noch am Anfang meiner Arbeit und hat mir später sehr geholfen. Ein anderer Aspekt des *Readymade* ist offensichtlich das Distanznehmen und – wenigstens zum Schein – das Heraushalten der eigenen Person. Aber lange Zeit mochte ich diese Bilder nicht besonders, weil ich der Meinung war, dass sie eine zu enge Beziehung zum Akkumulativen und den «Neuen Realisten» hatten. Mir lag Fluxus näher. Ich habe immer dieses Bild im Kopf, wie Robert Filliou den Staub vom Rahmen eines Bildes im Louvre aufsammelt. Dieses Direkte, nicht lang Überlegte fand ich interessant. Endlich war eine Verbindung zu Sprache und Gedächtnis durch Bilder möglich.

Aber zurück zum Zufall: Es war die Idee des Keine-Wahl-Treffens, die mich dazu brachte, auf die *Récréations Mathématiques* zurückzugreifen. Selbst wenn es um den Zufall geht, muss man den freiest möglichen Weg finden, ihn herbeizuführen, aber gleichzeitig natürlich auch den sichersten. Man muss versuchen alle Parameter zu unterdrücken, die verhindern könnten, dass der Zufall spielt. Ich verbringe meine Zeit damit, Strategien zu entwickeln, die mir erlauben nicht einzugreifen und das Bild auf möglichst bequeme Weise zu produzieren.

HUO: Es gibt viele Serien, die du anfängst und dann vorläufig wieder aufgibst, um sie manchmal Jahre später wieder aufzugreifen. Ich frage mich, ob es auch Serien gibt, über die du nur nachgedacht hast, Projekte, die nicht realisiert wurden?

BF: Es gibt eine Menge Ideen, für die ich noch keine Möglichkeit zur Realisierung gefunden habe. Aber vielleicht werde ich sie finden; wahrscheinlich wenn eine Leinwand aus der Vergangenheit wieder auftaucht. Die Ausstellungen spielen übrigens ein bisschen diese Rolle: Wenn man zwei Bilder miteinander konfrontiert, gibt es oft plötzlich ein drittes Bild, das wichtig oder möglich wird. Aber ich arbeite nicht nur über meine eigene Arbeit. Das kann auch aus einer Begegnung entstehen, aus irgendwas. So ist etwa die Idee zu den Gittern entstanden, als ich gesehen habe, wie man die Kanten einer Schachtel kreuzt, wenn man sie zukleben oder -binden will. Und dieses «changierende» Moment ist etwas, was ich in Italien entdeckt habe, und zwar im Zusammenhang mit dem Manierismus und damit, dass die Idee ein Kleid zu malen, dessen Farbe oszilliert, während der Gegenreformation auftauchte und dann bekämpft wurde, weil sie insofern als gefährlich galt, als sie eine Autonomie der Malerei postulierte. Oft stösst man auf ganz einfache Ideen, etwa zu einer Frage der Fabrikation, die dann jedoch mit einer Ideologie oder Politik zusammenhängen wie in diesem Beispiel der Gegenreformation.

HUO: Dann ist der Dialog mit Kunsthistorikern also von zentraler Bedeutung, um diese Fragen zu verstehen?

BF: Ja. Als ich an der *Ecole des Beaux Arts* war, las ich viel; Russell, Wittgenstein, Austin, später Quine, Stanley Cavell und andere Logiker oder Philosophen, die sich mit Sprachphilosophie beschäftigten. Ich hatte vor allem ein poetisches Verständnis dieser Fragen, das meine Phantasie belebte. In der Ausübung unserer alltäglichen Tätigkeiten stösst man auf ähnliche Themen. So war ich zum Beispiel verwirrt von Mesdags Panorama in Den Haag. Als Schauspiel, das schon das Kino ankündigt, aber gleichzeitig noch ganz funktionelle Malerei ist, faszinierte es einen auf mehreren Ebenen. In England gab es viele bewegte Bilder, die von berühmten Künstlern auf Glasplatten gemalt wurden und Schlachten darstellten; oder man bewegte bemalte Glasscheiben, um einen Vulkanausbruch zu simulieren. All diese Bereiche bleiben noch zu erforschen und sind nach wie vor lebendig. Ganz zu schweigen davon, dass ich mich dafür interessiere, wie sie die heutige Kunst reflektieren, denn ich denke, aber das darf man nicht allzu laut sagen, dass die Kritik bei uns etwas armselig ist. *(Gelächter.)*

(Übersetzung aus dem Französischen: Suzanne Schmidt)

VERSICHERUNG DER *UNSICHERHEIT*

ZUM WERK VON DIRK SKREBER

GREGOR JANSEN

Da der Betrachter keine Bilder mehr erkannte, verurteilte er nur die fremden Genres. Eine Einigkeit, die der Bilderkriege bedurfte, verfehlte nach Ginsters Dafürhalten ihren Zweck.
– frei nach Siegfried Kracauer[1)]

Also gut, ich solle nicht wie üblich anfangen, bittet mich Dirk Skreber, es hänge ihm einfach zum Hals raus, immer auf ein Genre reduziert zu werden, und so beginne ich mit Ginster. Im gleichnamigen Roman von Siegfried Kracauer aus dem Jahre 1928 steht das Individuum als ich-lose Erscheinung in der Trostlosigkeit zwischen den Kriegen: Verhaltenslehren, Kältemetaphern, Wahrnehmungsverschiebungen zwischen unheilvoller Angst und verzehrender Sehnsucht bestimmen die 20er Jahre. Ginster im Krieg, das sei Chaplin im Warenhaus, schrieb Joseph Roth, und was hier interessant ist, Kracauer schrieb in einem Brief an Ernst Bloch, dass seine Romanfigur eine pflanzenhafte Erscheinung sei, die sich immer gewünscht hätte, an Bahndämmen zu leben.[2)]

An Bahndämmen leben. Das tat ich als Kind und eine der grössten Mutproben bestand darin, am Damm zu liegen und den vorbeidonnernden Zug, dieses gewaltige Ungeheuer aus Stahl, auszuhalten; wer weglief, verlor! Ginster, ein Anflug von Erhabenheit, von purer Existenz gegenüber der Herrschaft der Mechanisierung, der Macht der Maschine – Kindheitserinnerungen. Heute sind Züge weiter weg und

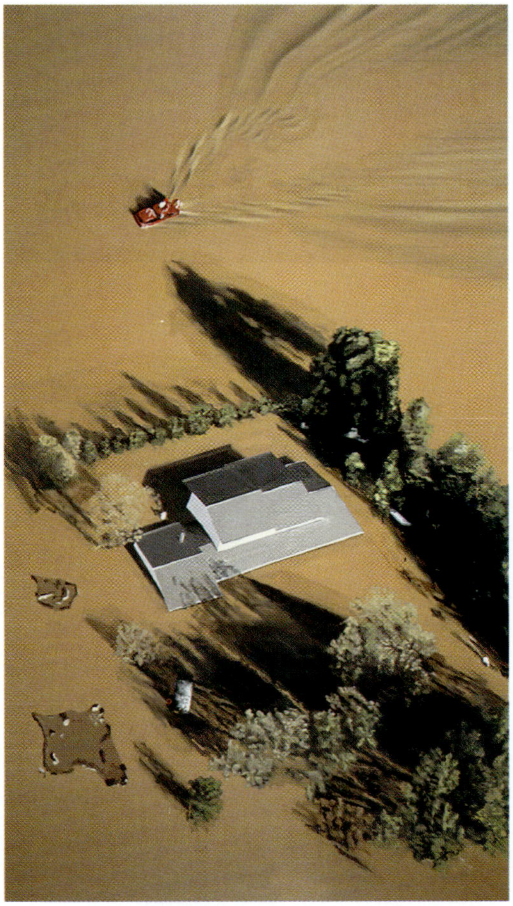

GREGOR JANSEN ist Dozent und Kunstwissenschaftler und lebt in Aachen.

DIRK SKREBER, OHNE TITEL, 2002,
Öl und Tape auf Leinwand, 290 x 170 cm /
oil and adhesive tape on canvas, 114 3/16 x 67".

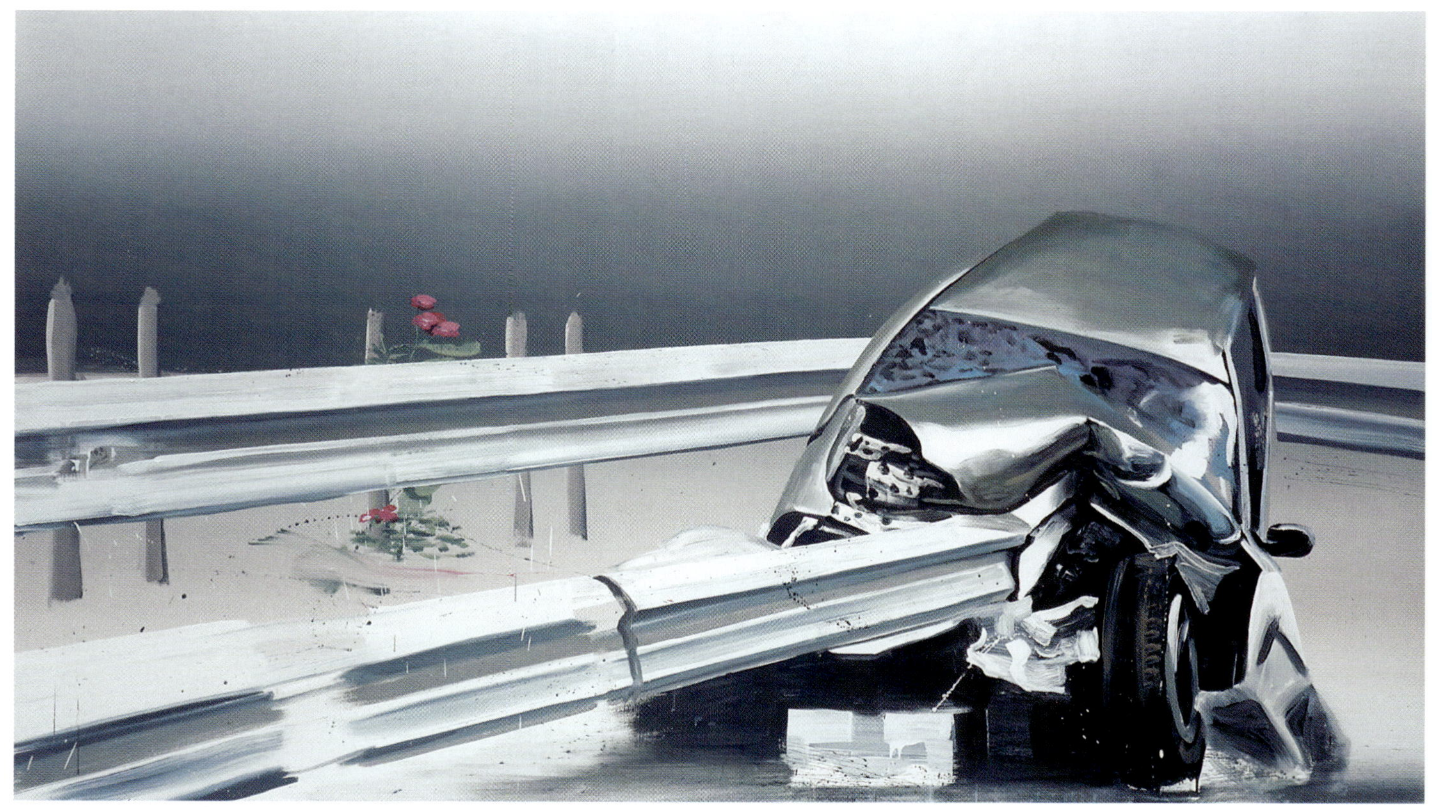

DIRK SKREBER, OHNE TITEL (IT ROCKS US SO HARD – HO HO HO 6.0), 2002,
Öl auf Leinwand, 160 x 280 cm / oil on canvas, 63 x 110¼".

schneller, viel schneller. Dennoch haben die Bilder der Lokomotiven und Sportstätten von Dirk Skreber eine ähnliche Faszination ausgeübt und Erinnerungsmomente ausgelöst, als ich sie erstmals sah. Markierungen, Rundungen, eine gewisse Leichtigkeit und Modellhaftigkeit des organisierten Sportwettstreits verklärten sich so von der banalen, flächigen Bodenhaftung zu einem an der Wand hängenden Bild, ähnlich Pollocks *drip paintings,* deren Wirklichkeit ebenfalls und eigentlich nur auf dem Boden denkbar ist.[3] All diese Bilder brannten sich ins Unterbewusstsein, wo sie auf alte Prägungen stiessen, auf sehr ähnliche Modelle, die bereits dort waren: menschenleer und doch immer durch den Menschen definiert. Wir waren wie Ginster und sahen ihn jetzt wieder, fühlten uns klein, mutig und irgendwie wohl, mit einem erhabenen Schauer, fragten nach dem Urheber dieser teilweise riesigen Bilder und sahen im gleichen Augenblick, wie klein die Welt und die Dinge in ihr geworden waren. Malerei ist oft Modellbau auf der Fläche, aber bei Dirk Skreber erscheint plastisch, was sonst nur im virtuellen Gefühl der Erhabenheit, des wohligen Schauers aufscheint. Hier stand gemalt die Modellpalette vor Augen und machte kein Hehl daraus, dass es sich um Malerei handeln sollte. Selbst das majestätische Matterhorn und seine umliegenden Wiesen konnten dem langen Krokodil nichts anhaben. Und meist sind die Hintergründe unendliche Landschaften ohne Halt, wie auf dem Meer, oder mitunter überwuchert alles eine undurchdringliche Wand aus Baumgrün, wie im Urwald. Dirk Skreber setzt unglaubliche Massstäbe.

Seine Bilder wirken häufig wie verhuschte, verlangsamte und gedehnte Abbilder: erstaunlich reine Flächen, analytisch und klar, sachlich, Möglichkeiten eines Traumes, der wie die Häuser in multiplen Ebenen oder transparent angelegt ist. Das Haus, Inbegriff städtischen Lebensgefühls und Wohlstandes, repräsentative Heimstätte mit Freifläche, zeigt im Allgemeinen den Besitzstand an. Nicht so bei Dirk Skreber, der in seiner Wahl des Bildmotivs früher mehr erfand, heute hingegen lieber auf photographische Vorlagen zurückgreift, dabei präzise selektiert, reinigt, plastisch denkt und flächig handelt. Das Haus an sich ist singulär, bei Skreber wird das deutlich, eine ebenfalls ich-lose Erscheinung mit fragwürdiger Identität, bis hin zu deutscher Spiessigkeit (aber ohne Mief!) und Harmlosigkeit; eine Verkörperung des schlechten Geschmacks, wobei die Menschen, die hier leben könnten, nicht sichtbar und kaum vorstellbar sind, obwohl es unsere Nachbarn sind. Ob noch im Rohbau mit offenem Dachstuhl oder als zerlegte, dekonstruierte Blockhütte, über der das abgehobene Dach schwebt: Skreber reduziert die Elemente und legt ein der Malerei inhärentes psychologisches Moment frei. Aus ihnen, hinter ihnen oder mit ihnen spritzt die Farbe wie nach einer Explosion heraus, eine machohafte Geste, als werde die Sachlichkeit selbst dem Maler zu viel. Jedoch stehen die eruptiven Schlieren und Farbsprenkel hinter den Häusern und bilden so eine abstrakte Grundierung der Bildfläche. Häufig auf dem Kopf gemalt, lösen sie eine Aggression aus, die als malerisches Bild wieder gezähmt wird und sich endlich als subtile Vorstellung von Energie und Horror zeigt. In den Gemälden lässt sich das ambivalente Spiel mit den Nuancen des abstrakten und gegenständlichen Motivwechsels als eigentlicher Farbwechsel nachvollziehen. Aber die Aggression steckt auch im Motiv, in der Auswahl der Themen und Bilder, deren Suggestivkraft auf das neutrale Bild eigentümlich ist. Teilweise geraten dann die faszinierenden Türme in den Wüsteneien aus Eis oder Sand (alle 1999) in bedrohliche Schieflage, und ein an John Martins Apokalypsen gemahnender Hintergrund belegt die Katastrophe, die durch die Namen der Hurrikane im Hilfstitel angezeigt ist, etwa im Fall von OHNE TITEL (MITCH) (1999). Diese Häuser sind die Katastrophe selbst, sind Teil eines Empfindens, in dem die Tragik des urbanen Alltags fein verwoben und gleichsam messerscharf seziert schlummert.

Ein Schlaf und mit ihm einhergehend ein Alptraum sind dann die um 2000 entstehenden Hochwasserbilder, in denen Skreber eine melancholische Ruhe dominieren lässt. Aus der Hubschrauber-Perspektive wird eine unbewohnbare weite Landschaft mit einsamen Häusern betrachtet, die voller Schönheit ist. Bei gleichzeitiger Trauer, bleibt zu fragen? Was ist faszinierend an der Katastrophe? Was kennzeichnet sie? «Das wunderbare an dieser Situation ist der ausgelöschte Alltag, die Abwesenheit von Alltäglichem», erläutert Skreber. «Menschen, die noch hier verweilen beziehungsweise wieder zurückkehren werden, sind all ihrer Alltäglichkeit beraubt und befinden sich in einem Zwischenraum, den sie von allein nicht hätten betreten können. Nur der Eingriff der Natur ermöglicht ihnen den Zutritt und die Kenntnis dieses Raumes. Es ist die Tragik des Verlorenen und die vielleicht verlorene Existenz, in der Verwandlung und Läuterung verborgen sind.»[4)] Die Gemälde bilden exakt jenen brutalen Zwischenraum als Gedankenraum ab. Fragen und antworten wir demnach so: Was macht uns lebendiger als das Sterben anderer?

Wirklich hinreissend nüchtern und kühl sind hier die Gemälde eines amerikanischen Schulgebäudes, OHNE TITEL (ULTRA VIOLENCE) (1999), und eines schmucken Vorort-Flachdachhauses mit Pool aus dem Jahr 2001, ebenfalls ohne Titel. Aus einem Hubschrauber geschossene Pressephotos sind die im kollektiven Bewusstsein verankerten Vorlagen. Frappierend gruselig und brutal schlagen die grossformatigen Leinwände mit dem Hintergrund und Kontext von Luftaufnahmen um: im ersten Fall der brutale Amoklauf eines Schülers, im zweiten der tragische Selbstmord Hannelore Kohls. Schlagartig verschwindet die objektive Nüchternheit der radikalen Vogelperspektive im Taumel der (medialen) Ereignisse. Die Bildatmosphären stimmen dem zu: klares Sonnenlicht und grauer Schulalltag. Die Wirklichkeit ist eine Illusion, gemalte Realität.

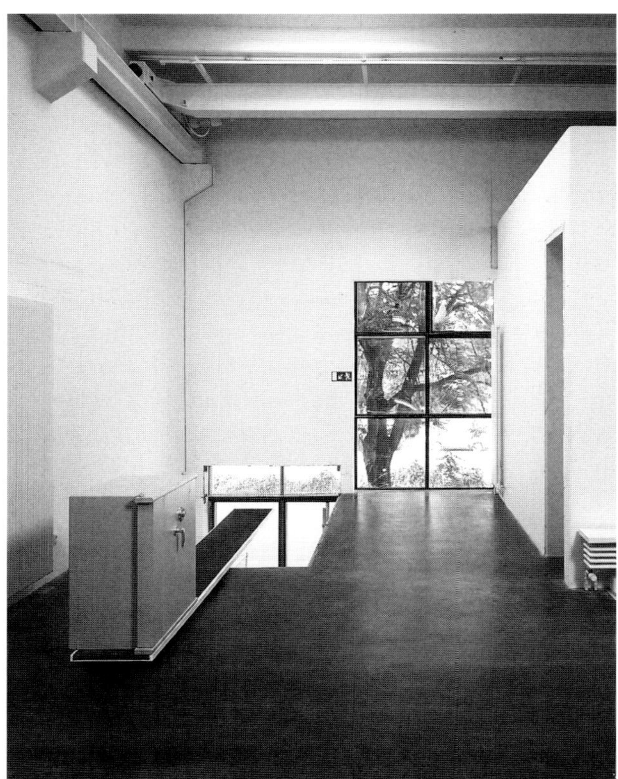

DIRK SKREBER, OHNE TITEL (THE INNER TYSON / HOLY DIRTBAG), 2002, Safe, Sprungbrett, Galerie Luis Campaña, Köln / safe, diving board, installation at Luis Campaña Gallery, Cologne.

Dirk Skreber benutzt häufig Klebeband, um einen gleichzeitig homogenen und strukturierten Hintergrund als Malfläche zu erhalten. Das Material ist absolut neutral und schichtet den Bildaufbau nicht mehr wie ein illusionistischer Tiefenraum, sondern zeigt die Fläche als horizontal, bisweilen auch vertikal aufgebautes strukturiertes Zeilenbild. Allen medialen Bezügen zum Trotz entsteht so eine stärkere Bindung an das Motiv und seine Relevanz, die vor dem Hintergrund der Klebefolie unwirklich deutlich ist. Eine weitere Folie, ebenfalls horizontal geschichtet und an den Rändern sauber beschnitten, besteht aus gedruckten Texten. In diesen äussert sich der Künstler selbst, vor allem als Interviewpartner Charles Kabold oder als Sammler tritt er in einen monologischen Dialog, der als Form zwar ein *fake* ist, als Inhalt jedoch mehr als die gewünschte Aussage ergibt, da er zumeist von Raumproblemen handelt. Deutlich wird hier wie dort die erstaunlich souveräne Behandlung der Themenbereiche «Natur/Romantik» oder «Aggression/Skeptizismus». Der einzige Mensch, der die Welt ironisch von hoher Warte mit ideologischem Blick sieht, ist der Maler mit seinem Blick auf Dinge, die das Chaos überstanden haben und in geläuterter Weise ihre klare Präsenz behaupten. Und danach steht der folienähnliche Malprozess zur Diskussion, macht sich daran, unsere lieb gewonnene Idylle einfach so in einer abstrakten Verflüssigung und irreversibel entropischen, nicht mehr sichtbaren Wirklichkeit *ad absurdum* zu führen.

Nicht zu vergessen sind die zahlreichen abstrakten, ebenfalls meist horizontal geschichteten Farbbahnen, die immer wieder zwischendurch entstehen. Ihre Anwesenheit ist wie die Sportstätten, Häuser oder Katastrophenbilder schlicht und einfach Präsenz. Und selbst wenn sie an Twombly und Ryman, Newman oder Richter und die pure Farbe als Oberfläche denken lassen, verkörpern diese Bilder einen Blick hinter die Dinge. Eine radikale Wirklichkeit, die immer abstrakt geordnet ist und danach in den figürlichen Arbeiten bewusster aufscheint.

Parallel hierzu stehen die Raum-Modelle. Modulen gleich – wie er sie im Jahr 2000 souverän für den Preis der Freunde der Berliner Nationalgalerie als Baustellensituation im Hamburger Bahnhof entwickelte – stehen Gänge als Zu-, Über- und Abgänge meist in räumlicher Abfolge mit irritierend tiefen oder engen Passagen und Einblicken. In der Kölner Galerie Luis Campaña liess er die Besucher auf ein Sprungbrett über dem Abgrund treten. Wandelgänge zwischen den Welten des geistigen Traums und der körperlichen Anwesenheit, zwischen Ruhe und Bewegung, zwischen idyllischer Stille und schrillem Horror. Manchmal wird ihm das Malen einfach auch ein wenig zu viel.

Seine neuesten Werke beruhen ebenfalls auf horizontalen Streifen. Gemeinste Op-Art aus Schaumstoffklebeband auf dunkel lackierten Hölzern – irgendwo im Niemandsland gegenständlicher Malerei.

DIRK SKREBER, OHNE TITEL (RADIOLOGICAL CLEANUP CONTAINMENT STRUCTURE), 2002, Öl auf Leinwand, 300 x 170 cm / oil on canvas, 118 1/8 x 67".

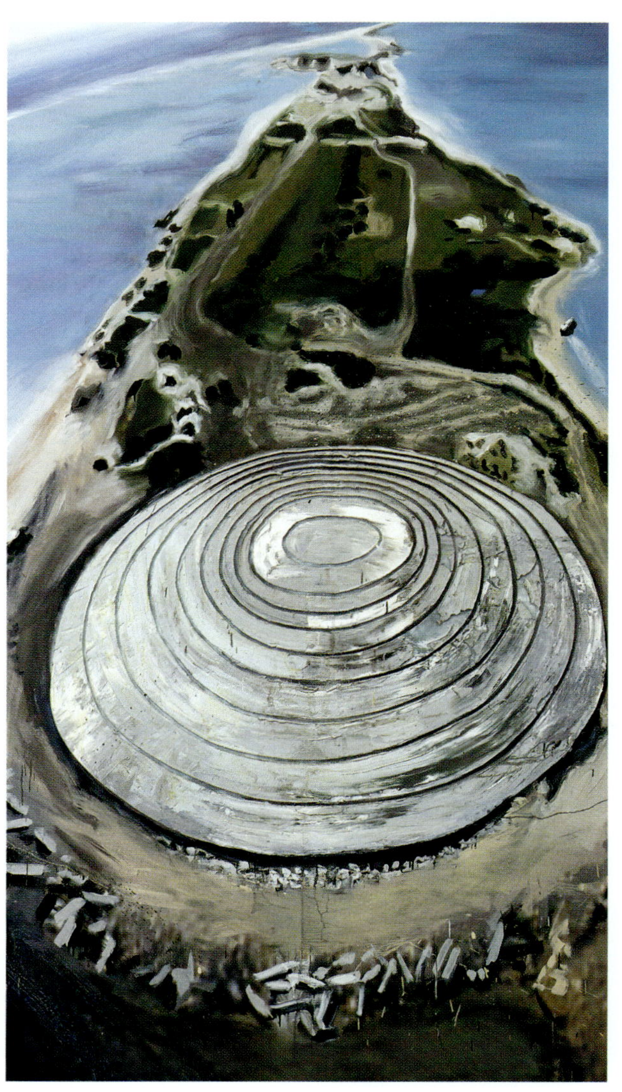

Akkurat in einem regelmässigen Abstand entsteht so eine vibrierende, reliefartige Grundstruktur, die den Augen wenige Anhaltspunkte liefert und nur durch die dem Material inhärente Farbschwankung des Gelbs eine zarte Modulation erzielt. Aus diesen erhabenen Bändern pult Skreber Teile heraus, so dass in den Vertiefungen die Farbe des Untergrundes deutlicher hervorscheint. Er entwirft so, gleichsam aus dem Zeilenraster, heroische Figuren aus dem Bilderkosmos der Comics der 50er und 60er Jahre. Die flimmernde Erscheinung und Formwerdung von *Wonderwoman*, *Modesty Blaise* oder des *Silver Surfer* lassen die Augen schmerzen. Zum ersten Mal arbeitet er an Personen, auch wenn diese sehr artifiziell und distanziert bleiben. Dennoch bleibt sein Standort gewagt – sowohl was die Betrachtung als auch was die Machart dieser profanen Wirkungsästhetik angeht –, und deshalb ist es eine Freude zu sehen, besser: zu fühlen, wohin die Reise geht. Die ich-lose Sachlichkeit ist das Ziel dieser Objektivität, eine aufrichtige, ehrliche, aber nicht aufklärende Malerei in deren Widerhall dennoch der postmoderne Geist unruhig flimmert. Lassen wir Frau van C. (aus Kracauers *Ginster*) diesen Text über Dirk Skreber – den visuelle Ruhe und Bewegung, Konzentration und Provokation kombinierenden Maler – wie den Anfangsdialog einer guten Beziehung beschliessen: «Sie sind ein merkwürdiger Mensch», sagt sie, «man ist gezwungen, aufrichtig Ihnen gegenüber zu sein.»[5]

1) Siegfried Kracauer, *Ginster* (1928), in: ders., *Schriften*, Bd. 7, Suhrkamp Verlag, Frankfurt/Main 1973, S. 39: «Da der Kaiser keine Parteien mehr kannte, verurteilte er nur die fremden Nationen. Eine Einigkeit, die der Kriege bedurfte, verfehlte nach Ginsters Dafürhalten ihren Zweck.» – Auch Robert Musil hätte hier seine Berechtigung gehabt, musste aber der pflanzenhaften Erscheinung Ginsters weichen.
2) Freundlicher Hinweis von Carola Dahmen, Aachen, auf den Brief von Siegfried Kracauer an Ernst Bloch vom 17. Januar 1928, in: Ernst Bloch, *Briefe 1903–1975*, Bd. 1, hrsg. v. Karola Bloch u.a., Suhrkamp, Frankfurt am Main 1975, S. 293.
3) Ebenfalls erstaunlich ist der von Rita Kersting beschriebene Vergleich der Sportfelder Skrebers mit einer Kritik von Michael Fried an Barnett Newman, 1962, laut der er Newmans Bilder als misslungen empfand, weil sie das Gefühl der langweiligen Leere eines Handballfeldes vermittelten. Vgl. den Ausstellungskatalog *Rotation*, mit einer Einleitung von Rita Kersting & Martijn van Nieuwenhuyzen, Köln u.a. 1999–2000, S. 9.
4) Dirk Skreber in einer E-Mail an den Autor vom 12. Juli 2003.
5) Kracauer, op cit., S. 125.

SECURING *INSECURITY*

ON THE WORK OF DIRK SKREBER

GREGOR JANSEN

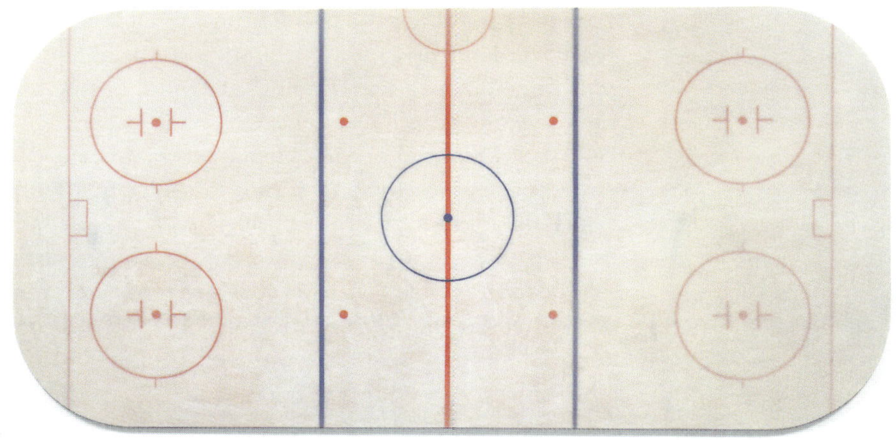

DIRK SKREBER, OHNE TITEL (EISHOCKEY), 1993, Acryl und Epoxitharz auf Holz, 170 x 340 cm / acrylic and epoxy resin on wood, 67 x 133 7/8".

Since the viewer no longer recognized any pictures, he only condemned foreign genres. A unity that required iconoclasm would miss the mark, as Ginster saw it.

– after Siegfried Kracauer[1)]

Please don't start as usual, Dirk Skreber tells me. He is sick and tired of being reduced to one genre. And so I start with Ginster. In Siegfried Kracauer's novel of the same name written in 1928, the individual appears without a self, a self-less being in the desolation between the wars: principles of behavior, metaphors of coldness, and perception shifting between anxiety and all-consuming longing characterized the twenties. According to Joseph Roth, Ginster in wartime is tantamount to Chaplin in the department store and, as Kracauer wrote in a letter to Ernst Bloch, the interesting thing is that his protagonist is a plant-like character who always wanted to live on railroad embankments.[2)]

Living on railroad embankments. I did, as a child, when the greatest test of courage consisted of lying on the embankment and staying put, waiting for the train, the mighty steel monster, to thunder past. The first to get up and run for his life was the loser! Ginster: a flight of superiority, of pure being in the face of tyrannical mechanization, the power of the machine—childhood memories. Trains are farther away

GREGOR JANSEN is a lecturer and art theoretician, living in Aachen.

today and faster, much faster. Even so, the first time I saw Dirk Skreber's pictures of locomotives and sporting facilities, they exerted a similar fascination and triggered distant memories. Convexities, a certain lightness and modeled examples of organized athletic competitions were rarefied from banal, planar ground adhesion to a picture hanging on the wall, similar to Pollock's drip paintings, whose reality essentially is also conceivable only on the ground.[3)]

All of these images were branded into the subconscious, there bumping into old, ingrained imprints, into similar, long-established models: deserted and yet still defined by people. We were like Ginster and we saw him again, felt small, brave, and good somehow, asking about the maker of these at times gigantic pictures, with a sublime shudder, and immediately realizing how small the world and the things in it had become. Painting is often a matter of building models on a plane but in Dirk Skreber's work, things become sculptural that usually emerge only in the virtual feeling of a third dimension, a pleasurable shudder. The model palette stood painted before us and made no bones about being painting. Even the majestic Matterhorn and its surrounding meadows are no match for the long crocodile. And the backgrounds are usually endless landscapes with nothing to hold on to, like the ocean, or occasionally impenetrable walls of forest green running rampant, like the jungle. Dirk Skreber sets incredible standards.

DIRK SKREBER, OHNE TITEL (MODESTY BLAISE), 2002, Tesamoll auf Holz, 250 x 150 cm / adhesive foam tape on wood, 98 7/16 x 59".

His paintings often look like distracted, decelerated, and stretched mimetic depictions: surprisingly pure surfaces, analytical and clear, matter-of-fact, the possibilities of a dream laid out in multiple layers, like the buildings, or transparent. The building, quintessential feeling of urban life and prosperity, is a residential status symbol with empty spaces generally indicative of ownership. Not so in Skreber's case. His choice of motif, once a product of invention, now relies more frequently on photographic source material, precisely selected, purified, sculpturally reflected, and two-dimensionally implemented. The building as such is singular; Skreber makes that clear, it is another self-less item with a questionable identity to the point of harmlessness and German philistinism (but without being musty!): an embodiment of bad taste, whereby the potential tenants are not visible and can, in fact, barely be envisioned although they are our neighbors. Whether a roofless shell still under construction or a dismantled, deconstructed log cabin above which the roof hangs suspended: Skreber reduces the elements and brings to the fore a psychological aspect intrinsic to painting. The paint splatters out of the paintings or behind them or within them, like the aftermath of an explosion, a macho-like gesture as if objectivity were too much even for the painter. Nonetheless, the streaks and sprinkles of paint have erupted behind the buildings and form an abstract ground on the picture plane. Often painted upside-down, they provoke an aggres-

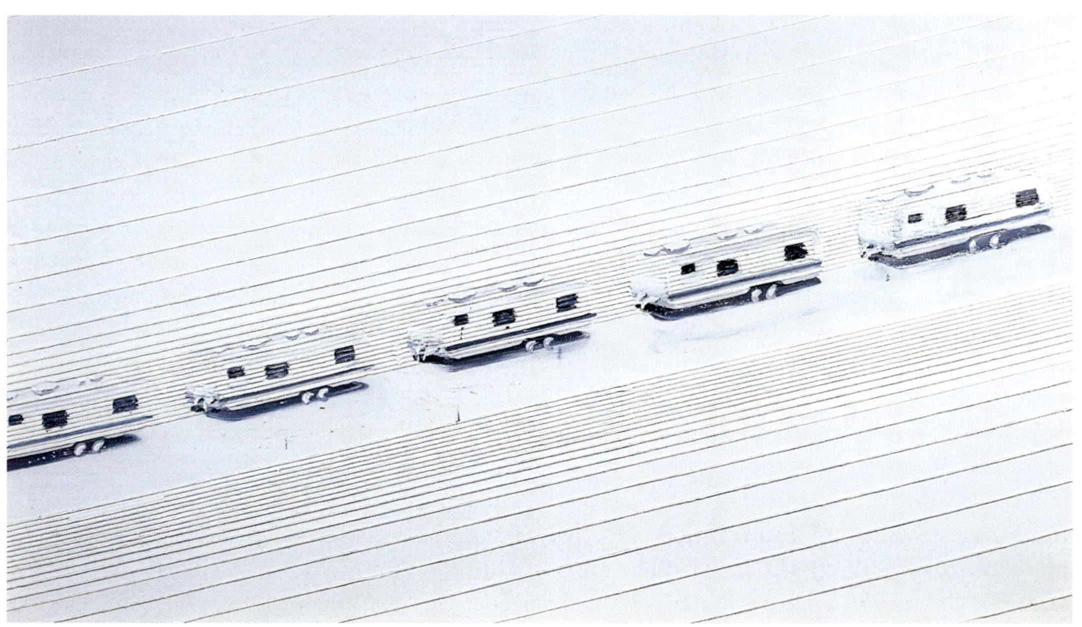

DIRK SKREBER, OHNE TITEL (TRAILER BOMBS), 2003, Öl auf Leinwand, 220 x 380 cm / oil on canvas, $86\,^{5}/_{8}$ x $149\,^{5}/_{8}$".

sion that is tamed in the painterly image, ultimately yielding a subtle vision of energy and horror. The ambivalent, nuanced play of abstract and figurative motifs is expressed in the paintings through variations in color. But the aggression also springs from the motif itself, from the choice of scenes and images whose suggestive implications have a curious impact on the neutral image. The fascinating towers in wastelands of ice or sand (all 1999) may show a menacingly precarious tilt, and a background reminiscent of John Martin's visions of the apocalypse testifies to the catastrophe conjured by names of hurricanes, as in UNTITLED (MITCH), 1999. These buildings are the catastrophe itself, they belong to sensations in which the dormant tragedy of everyday urban life is subtly interwoven but also remorselessly dissected.

Sleep and its attendant nightmares constitute the floods painted around the year 2000, in which Dirk Skreber allows a melancholy tranquility to dominate. A vast, uninhabitable landscape with isolated buildings is seen from a helicopter view; it is full of beauty. Coexistent with mourning, one asks? What makes the catastrophe fascinating? What distinguishes it? "The wonderful thing about the situation is the obliteration of the everyday, the absence of ordinariness," Skreber explains. "The people who are still there or who have come back have all been robbed of their daily lives and find themselves in a limbo, a state of suspension they would never have encountered by themselves. Only the intervention of nature allows them to enter and become cognizant of this space. It is the tragedy of loss and possibly lost existence, which is embodied in transformation and purification."[4] This limbo, this brutally suspended space is exactly what the paintings depict as a mental space. We therefore ask and answer as follows: does anything make us more alive than the death of others?

Remarkably captivating matter-of-factness and understatement characterize the paintings of an American school, UNTITLED (ULTRA VIOLENCE) (1999), and a lovely suburban flat-roof home with a pool, also untitled (2001). They are painted after press photographs shot from a helicopter, pictures anchored in the collective consciousness. The large-format canvases with the framework and context of aerial photography suddenly become stunningly horrific and brutal: in the first case, the atrocious gunning rampage of a student, in the second the tragic suicide of Hannelore Kohl. The objective reportage of the radical bird's-eye view instantly vanishes in the turbulence of the (media) events, underscored by the atmosphere in which the pictures are immersed: limited sunlight and gray school days. Reality is an illusion; it is a painted reality.

Dirk Skreber often uses adhesive tape to produce a homogeneous and yet structured background on which to paint. The material is absolutely neutral and does not layer the composition any more than does illusionist depth; instead it presents the surface as a horizontal or, at times, vertical structure of lines. Thus, despite potential reference to media events, there is a stronger link to the motif and its relevance, which acquires an unreal lucidity against the taped background. Another layer, also horizontal and cleanly cut at the edges, is formed by printed text. Texts in which Dirk Skreber himself speaks, above all as the interview partner, Charles Kabold, or as a collector: he launches into a monologistic dialogue, whose form is obviously fake but whose content yields more than the desired statement since it generally deals with problems of space. Unmistakably manifest in both cases is the astonishingly masterful treatment of such concerns as "nature/romanticism" or "aggression/skepticism." The only person who takes an ironic view of the world from lofty ideological heights is the painter with his rendition of things that have survived chaos and his purified assertion of their clear presence. The follow-up: a discussion of the foil-like process of painting, in which our cherished idyll is pursued *ad absurdum* in an abstract liquefaction and an irreversibly entropic, no longer visible reality.

Not to forget the countless abstract and also, for the most part, horizontal bands of color that crop up in between. Their presence is as plain and simple as the athletic facilities, buildings, or pictures of catastrophe. And even though they evoke Twombly and Ryman, Newman or Richter and pure color as surface, these paintings still embody a view behind things. A radical reality that is always abstract in arrangement and therefore makes an even more conscious appearance in the figurative works.

The paintings are complemented by the artist's three-dimensional models. They are like modules, as in the construction-site situation at the Hamburg railroad station, created in the year 2000 for the prize of the Friends of the National Gallery in Berlin. Corridors provide access, transit and egress, generally as sequences in space with disturbingly deep or narrow passageways and views. At the Luis Campaña Gallery in Cologne, Skreber had visitors walk out over the abyss on a diving board. Ambulatories between the worlds of mental dreams and physical presence, between stasis and movement, between idyllic serenity and shrill horror. Sometimes painting is simply too much for him as well.

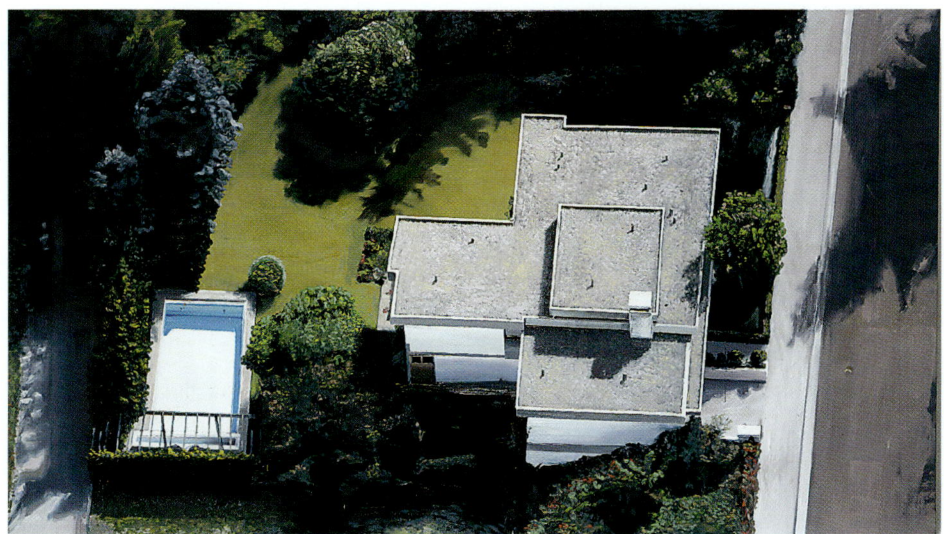

DIRK SKREBER, OHNE TITEL (THE HOUSE), 2001, Öl auf Leinwand, 160 x 280 cm / oil on canvas, 63 x 110 1/4".

*DIRK SKREBER, OHNE TITEL (AUGENAIDS), 2001,
Öl und Tape auf Leinwand, 160 x 280 cm /
oil and adhesive tape on canvas, 63 x 110 1/4".*

Skreber's most recent works are also based on horizontal strips. Perfectly ordinary Op Art out of adhesive foam tape on dark varnished wood—figurative paintings somewhere in a no man's land. At precise, regular intervals a vibrant, relief-like underlying structure emerges that gives the eye little to focus on, a delicate modulation generated only by variations in the yellow of the material itself. Dirk Skreber plucks bits and pieces out of these raised bands, so that the color of the background comes forth more clearly in the recesses. In this way, out of the linear grid as it were, he designs heroic figures drawn from the picture universe of comics in the fifties and sixties. The shimmering appearance of *Wonderwoman, Modesty Blaise* or the *Silver Surfer* makes one's eyes hurt. It is the first time that he works on people, though they do remain artificial and detached. Even so, his vantage point is daring both with respect to the choice of approach and to the making of this profane aesthetic. Which is why it is a joy to see or rather to feel where the journey is taking us. Self-less matter-of-factness is the goal of this objectivity: painting that is straightforward and honest, but not enlightening, in whose reverberations the spirit of postmodernism still restlessly shimmers. Like the opening lines of a good relationship, we shall permit Frau van C. (from Kracauer's *Ginster*) to conclude this text about Dirk Skreber, the painter who combines visual stillness and movement, concentration and provocation: "You are a curious person," she says, "you force people to be honest with you."[5)]

(Translation: Catherine Schelbert)

1) Siegfried Kracauer, *Ginster* (1928) in: Kracauer, *Schriften,* vol. 7 (Frankfurt/Main: Suhrkamp Verlag, 1973), p. 39: "Since the emperor no longer recognized any parties, he only condemned foreign nations. A unity that required wars would miss the mark, as Ginster saw it."—Robert Musil would have served the purpose equally well but had to yield to Ginster's vegetal appearance. (*Ginster* is also the German botanical name for "gorse.")
2) My thanks to Carola Dahmen, Aachen, for drawing my attention to Siegfried Kracauer's letter to Ernst Bloch of January 17, 1928 in: Ernst Bloch, *Briefe 1903–1975,* vol. 1, ed. by Karola Bloch, et. al. (Frankfurt am Main: Suhrkamp, 1975), p. 293.
3) Equally astonishing is Rita Kersting's link between Skrebner's sports fields and Michael Fried's 1962 critique of Barnett Newman. Fried questioned the success of Newman's pictures, likening them to the boring emptiness of a handball court. See *Rotation,* ex. cat., with an introduction by Rita Kersting & Martijn van Nieuwenhuyzen, Cologne, 1999–2000, p. 9.
4) Dirk Skreber in an e-mail message to the writer, July 12, 2003.
5) Kracauer, op cit., p. 125.

TITEL BILD · Untertitel und Graphik GmbH

http://www.titelbild.de

TITEL BILD · Joachim-Friedrich-Strasse 37 · D-10711 Berlin

e-mail: info@titelbild.de

Tel.: + 49.30.890 923 39

Fax: + 49.30.892 96 51

TITEL ▼ BILD

Englischer Ausgangstext

Robert Barry

Telepathic Piece 1969

[During the exhibition I will try to communicate telepathically a work of art, the nature of which is a series of thoughts that are not applicable to language or image]

Französische Übersetzung

Robert Barry

Telepathic Piece 1969

[Dans cette exposition, je tente de transmettre par télépathie une œuvre d'art constituée d'une série de pensées qui ne peuvent être illustrées ni par le langage ni par l'image.]

Geschäftsführer:
Mary Carroll
Volker Hagemeier
Handelsregister:
Amtsgericht
Berlin-Charlottenburg
HRB 39 431
USt-IdNr. DE 136 59 4822
Bankverbindung:
Commerzbank AG
Potsdam
BLZ 160 400 00
Konto 13 13 733

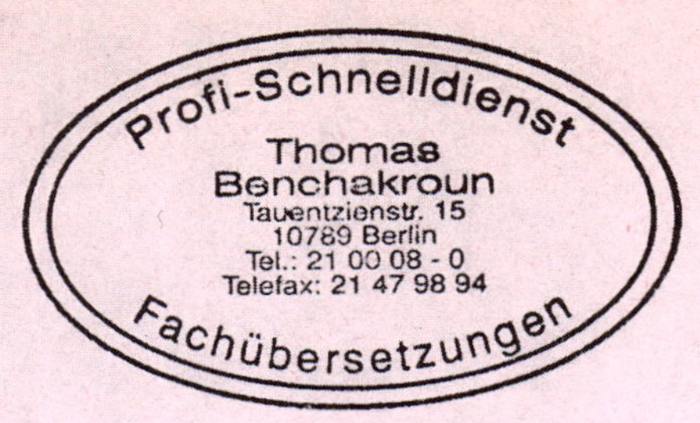

Robert Barry

Telepathic Piece 1969

Dans cette exposition, je tente de transmettre par télépathie une œuvre d´art constituèe d´une série de pensées qui ne peuvent être illustrées ni par le langage ni par l`image.

Robert Barry

Telepathic Piece 1969 (telepathisch stuk)

In deze voorstelling probeer ik door middel van telepathie een kunstwerk
door te geven dat bestaat uit een reeks gedachten die noch met woorden noch
met afbeeldingen geïllustreerd kunnen worden!

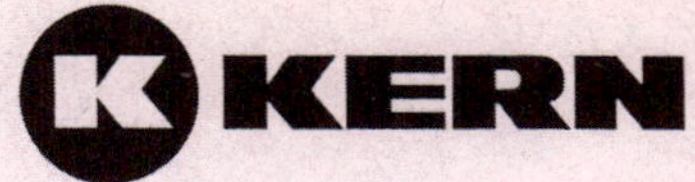

KERN AG, Panoramastraße 1, 10178 Berlin

✉	**KERN AG** **Panoramastraße 1** **10178 Berlin**
Telefon:	**(030) 24 72 12 50**
Telefax:	(030) 24 72 12 75
e-mail:	KERN.Berlin@e-kern.com
Bankkonten:	Dresdner Bank AG, Frankfurt 4 901 046 (BLZ 500 800 00) Deutsche Bank AG, Frankfurt 2 472 942 (BLZ 500 700 10) Postbank Frankfurt 5602-601 (BLZ 500 100 60)
Internet:	**www.e-kern.com**

Ihre Zeichen Your reference Votre référence	Ihre Nachricht vom Your letter of Votre lettre du	Unsere Zeichen Our reference Notre référence	**Geschäftsbereich** **Division** **Domaine d'activité**	Datum Date Date

Robert Barry

Telepathic Piece 1969 (telepathisch stuk)
In deze voorstelling probeer ik door middel van telepathie een kunstwerk door te geven dat bestaat uit een reeks gedachten die noch met woorden noch met afbeeldingen geillustreerd kunnen worden!

Robert Barry

Telepathic Piece (telepathisches Stück)
In dieser Vorstellung versuche ich, durch Telepathie ein Kunstwerk herüberzubringen, das aus einer Reihe von Gedanken besteht, die weder mit Worten noch mit Abbildungen illustriert werden können!

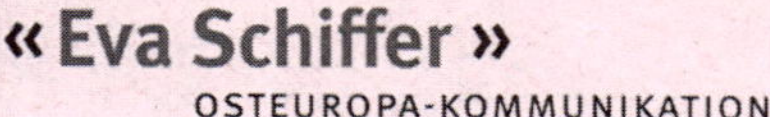

»

Robert Barry

Telepathic Piece (telepathisches Stück)
In dieser Vorstellung versuche ich, durch Telepathie ein Kunstwerk herüberzubringen, das aus einer Reihe von Gedanken besteht, die weder mit Worten noch mit Abbildungen illustriert werden können!

Robert Barry

Telepathic Piece (Telepatický kousek)
V této ukázce se prostřednictvím telepatie pokouším přiblížit umělecké dílo, skládající se z řady myšlenek, jež slovně ani obrazně nelze vyjádřit!

Dolmetscher- u. ÜbersetzerDienst (DÜD) – A Translation

Dolmetscher- u. Übersetzerbüro für alle Sprachen u. Fachgebiete

Dipl.-Ing. Gautam Bhattacharja (BDÜ) & Kollegen
Postanschrift: DÜD, PF: 47 02 05, 12311 Berlin
Zentrale: Wesenberger Ring 6 B; 12359 Berlin
Telefon: (030) 602 12 04 oder 666 22 188
Funk: 0171 - 681 33 60 Fax: (030) 666 22 189
Email: dued@epost.de

Übersetzungsnummer: 03022501Ü Datum: 25.02.2003

Übersetzung: Tschechisch-Polnisch

Tschechisch

Robert Barry

Telepathic Piece (Telepatický kousek)

V této ukázce se prostřednictvím telepatie pokouším přiblížit umělecké dílo, skládající se z řady myšlenek, jež slovně ani obrazně nelze vyjádřit!

Polnisch

Robert Barry

Telepathic Piece (Wyciąg telepatyczny)

W tym wzorcu spróbuję drogą telepatyczną zbliżyć dzieło artystyczne, składające się z toku myśli, które nie mogące być wyrażone ani słowami, ani obrazami.

Für die Richtigkeit und Vollständigkeit der Übersetzungen:

A + TRANSLATION
-Alle Sprachen u. Fachgebiete-
Dipl.-Ing. Gautam Bhattacharja & Kollegen
Postanschrift: DÜD, PF: 47 02 05, 12311 Berlin
Tel: (030) 666 22 188 Fax: (030) 666 22 189

ABC-GLOBAL

Dolmetscher- und Übersetzerbüro GmbH

Geschäftsführerin : Andrea Rickelt

ABC-GLOBAL ®
über 140 Sprachen

Hauptbüro: Kurfürstendamm 235, 10719 Berlin Tel : (030) 88 47 29 18 o. 29 00 56 35 Handy : 0172 59 62 69 1
(Vis-à-vis Kaiser-Wilhelm-Gedächtniskirche) Fax : (030) 88 47 29 20 E-mail : ari@abcglobal.de

Übersetzung vom Polnischen ins Ukrainische:

Polnisch:

Robert Barry

"Telepathic Piece (Wyciag telepaticzny)
W tym wzórcu sprobuję drogą telepaticzną zbliżyć dzielo artystyczne, skladające się z toku myśli, które nie mogące być wyraźone ani slowami, ani obrazami".

Ukrainisch:

Роберт Баррі

Телепатична фігура (Текст, отриманий за допомогою телепатії)

В тому візерунку (образі) телепатичний шлях спробує зблизити артистичну справу, вона складається з потоку думок, який неможливо виразити ні словами ні образами.

Küster – **Übersetzungsservice**
Nürnberger Str. 27
10789 Berlin
T: 030-21969480, 2362 0770 Fax 2196 9489
Tel: +49-171-74 28 143

alle Sprachen
alle Fachgebiete
Eilaufträge
Stadtführungen, alle Sprachen
e-mail: kuester-translation@t-online.de

Übersetzung aus dem Ukrainischen ins Russische:

Перевод с украинского языка на русский:

Ukrainisch – украинский язык	Russisch – Русский язык
Роберт Баррі Телепатична фігура (Текст, отриманий за допомогою телепатії) В тому візерунку (образі) телепатичний шлях спробує зблизити артистичну справу, вона складається з потоку думок, який неможливо виразити ні словами ні образами.	Роберт Барри Телепатическая фигура (Текст, полученный с помощью телепатии) В том рисунке (образе) телепатический путь попытается сблизить артистическое дело, оно складывается из потока мыслей, который невозможно выразить ни словами ни образами.

ABC-GLOBAL

Dolmetscher- und Übersetzerbüro GmbH

Geschäftsführerin : Andrea Rickelt

ABC-GLOBAL ® über 140 Sprachen

Hauptbüro: Kurfürstendamm 235, 10719 Berlin (Vis-à-vis Kaiser-Wilhelm-Gedächtniskirche) Tel : (030) 88 47 29 18 o. 29 00 56 35 Fax : (030) 88 47 29 20 Handy : 0172 59 62 69 1 E-mail : ari@abcglobal.de

Übersetzung vom Russischen ins Kasachische:

Russisch:

Роберт Барри

Телепатическая фигура (текст полученный с помощью телепатии)

В том рисунке (образе) телепатический путь попытается сблизить артистическое дело, оно складывается из потока мыслей, который невозможно выразить ни словами ни образами.

Kasachisch:

Роберт Баррі

Телепатия турі
(телепатия арқылы алынған текст)

Сол суретте (турде) телепатия жолы артистік істі уқсатуға тырмысады, ол ой ағымынан қурылады, оны сөзбен де білдіруге турменде көрсетуге мумкін емес.

ABC-GLOBAL

Dolmetscher- und Übersetzerbüro GmbH

Geschäftsführerin : Andrea Rickelt

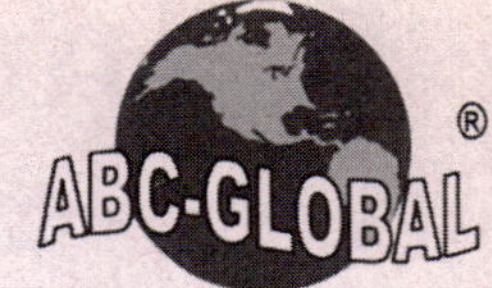

Hauptbüro: Kurfürstendamm 235, 10719 Berlin
(Vis-à-vis Kaiser-Wilhelm-Gedächtniskirche)
Tel : (030) 88 47 29 18 o. 29 00 56 35 Handy : 0172 59 62 69 1
Fax : (030) 88 47 29 20 E-mail : ari@abcglobal.de

Übersetzung vom Kasachischen ins Mongolische:

Kasachisch (kyrill.Schrift):

Телепатия турі
(телепатия арқылы алынған текст)

Сол суретте (турде) телепатия жолы артистік істі уқсатуға тырмысады, ол ой ағымынан қурылады, оны сөзбен де білдіруге турменде көрсетуге мумкін емес.

Mongolisch:

Зайнаас мэдрэх хэлбэр
(зайнаас медрэх чадварын тусламжтай бий болсон бичиг)

Үгээр ч, дүрээр ч илэрхийлэх боломжгүй бодол сэтгэлгээний урсгалаас
бүрддэг жүжиглэх урлагийг энэ зурагт (хэлбэрт) зайнаас медрэх арга ойртуулахыг оролдож байна.

ABC-GLOBAL

Dolmetscher- und Übersetzerbüro GmbH

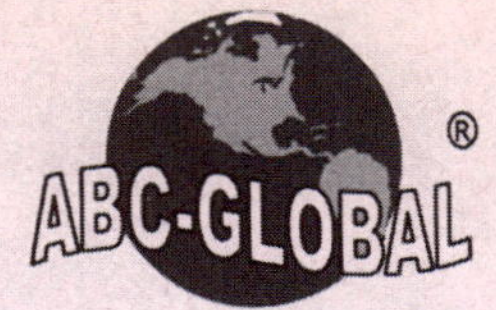

Geschäftsführerin : Andrea Rickelt

Hauptbüro: Kurfürstendamm 235, 10719 Berlin (Vis-à-vis Kaiser-Wilhelm-Gedächtniskirche) Tel : (030) 88 47 29 18 o. 29 00 56 35 Fax : (030) 88 47 29 20 Handy : 0172 59 62 69 1 E-mail : ari@abcglobal.de

Übersetzung vom Mongolischen ins Chinesische:

Mongolisch:

Роберт Барри

Зөн совингийн мэдрэмжээс бүтсэн дүрс бүтээл (зөн совингийн мэдрэмжийн замаар бичигдсэн бичиг)

Үгээр болон дүрсээр дүрслэгдэшгүй бодол мөрөөдлийн урсгалаар бүрдсэн уран бүтээлийг танд энэ зураг (дүрслэл)-ээр, зөн совингийн мэдрэмжийн замаар хүргүүлэхийг оролдов.

Chinesisch:

罗伯特　巴瑞 (Robert Barri)

心灵感应图(通过心灵感应得到的信息)

在这个图象中心灵感应的表述方式尝试着更加接近于由思维意识流组成的艺术作品，而她们既不能通过文字也不可以具体形象地表达出来。

ABC-GLOBAL

Dolmetscher- und Übersetzerbüro GmbH

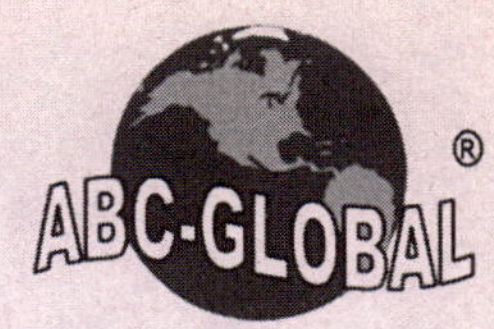

über 140 Sprachen

Geschäftsführerin : Andrea Rickelt

Hauptbüro: Kurfürstendamm 235, 10719 Berlin (Vis-à-vis Kaiser-Wilhelm-Gedächtniskirche)
Tel : (030) 88 47 29 18 o. 29 00 56 35 Handy : 0172 59 62 69 1
Fax : (030) 88 47 29 20 E-mail : ari@abcglobal.de

Übersetzung vom Chinesischen ins Englische:

Chinesisch:

罗伯特　巴瑞

心灵感应图(通过心灵感应得到的信息)

在这个图象中心灵感应的表述方式尝试着更加接近于由思维意识流组成的艺术作品，

而她们既不能通过文字也不可以具体形象地表达出来。

Englisch:

Robert Barri

Image of the reaction of the soul (information obtained through reactions of the soul)

In this image the way of expression of reactions of the soul attempts to come close to a work of art that is composed

of the course of thinking and consciousness, being elements that cannot be expressed either in writing or through

concrete forms.

INSERT
JONATHAN
MONK

INSERT FOR PARKETT 68, 2003:
JONATHAN MONK, TRANSLATION PIECE, 2002 .

"YANOMAMI, SPIRIT OF THE FOREST" & THE SIGNS OF THE TIMES

JAY MURPHY

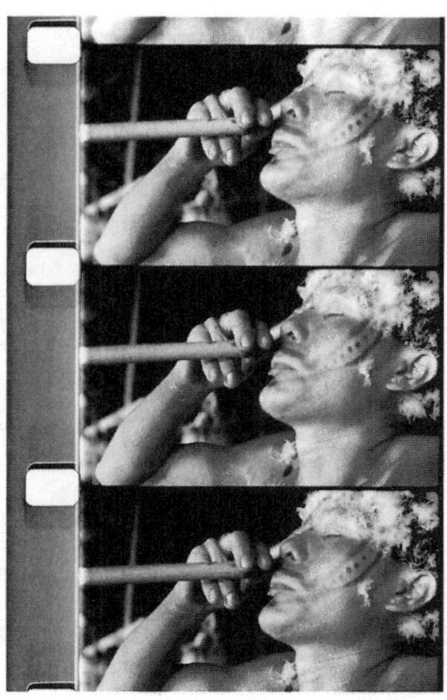

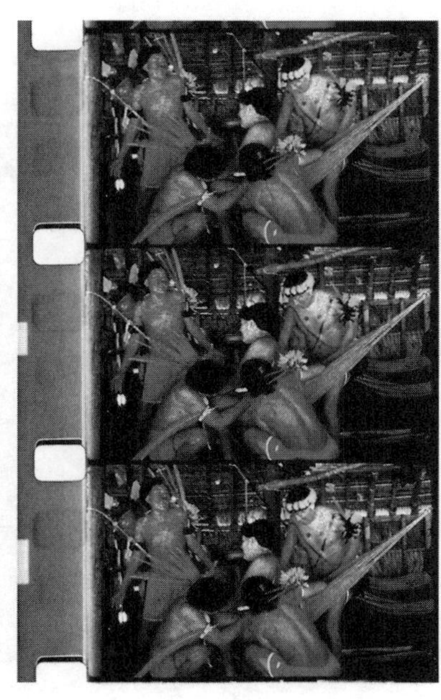

RAYMOND DEPARDON, CHASSEURS ET CHAMANS, 2002, film transferred to DVD, stills.

The artists in "Yanomami, Spirit of the Forest,"[1] have all, to a greater or lesser extent, opted for what Flemish critic and art historian Jeroen Boomgaard has called "exchanging the cynicism of the code for the optimism of the contact."[2] Until what was to be a devastating encounter with the *chercheurs d'or* and other typical representatives of the "outside" world (missionaries, military, and development planners) beginning in the eighties, the Yanomami Indians along the Brazilian-Venezuelan border in the northern Amazon region were the most populous, still intact indigenous people in South America who had retained their customary way of life. That included sorcery, a ritualized existence based on interpretation of the myriad malefic and benign gods and spirits teeming in their midst, as well as consumption of the pulverized bones of their dead ancestors, contributing to the Yanomami's reputation as cannibals. The exhibition was organized by the Cartier Foundation with anthropol-

---

JAY MURPHY is a writer and critic living in New York City. He is writing *The Art of Disorder: A Life of Emile de Antonio*; a new version of his 1993 anthology *For Palestine* is also forthcoming; his collaborative Internet project *privilege* was shown in the 2002 Sundance Online Film Festival.

ogist Bruce Albert, who speaks one of the four Yanomami languages and has spent several months with them each year since his first visit in 1973, along with Survival International (where Albert is vice president) and the Brazilian NGO *Comissão Pró-Yanomami.* The exhibition was conceived in cooperation with the Yanomami shamans themselves, especially Davi Kopenawa, a prominent national and international spokesperson for the Indians and his village Watoriki. Their purpose was to provoke a "confrontation" and comparison between their cosmology and visionary experience, and the "savage mind" at the heart of our own artistic enterprise. Five of the artists traveled to the Amazon to develop their works *in situ* with the Yanomami, three worked from materials provided by the Indians whether texts, drawings, or video, and three others had already spent considerable time with the Indians making works that predated the exhibition in some instances by more than twenty years.

To its credit, much of the catalogue details the cosmologies and facets of life of the Yanomami, their shamans' séances and relation to animal and ancestor spirits, their relationship to their rich ecological habitat, and traumatic meeting with the "whites" which included a massacre of 16 Yanomami in 1993 in Haxima. Having shamans from the village work with each artist, the exhibition disavows presentation as another "Amerindian" art or humanitarian/documentary exhibit, rather it banks on the interchange of "free associations" between the shamanic visions and the image-making of contemporary artists from the "developed world." The great virtue of "Yanomami, Spirit of the Forest" is the immersion of experience afforded many of the artists, and the variety of their sensibility and means of interpretation—ranging from Claudia Andujar's extremely sensitive and dignified photographs of the Yanomami (her later works through multiple exposures highlight the metamorphoses and absorption of shamanic trances) that draw on the humanist, documentary tradition to the more high-tech artistry of Gary Hill, Tony Oursler and the celebratory, dynamic video installation made largely from Yanomami drawings of Issey Miyake protégé Naoki Takizawa.

At their best, the ensemble of works in this exhibition illustrate the polyvalent, multi-leveled "feedback" loops that constitute our wider ecological relations, here enacted by artists of the "First World" with those of the "Fourth

WOLFGANG STAEHLE, PAREAKIKI (AYNO HARANI), 2003 / MOUNTAIN SEEN FROM THE HOUSE-VILLAGE, 24-hour color film / BERG VOM HAUSDORF AUS GESEHEN, 24 Std. Film.

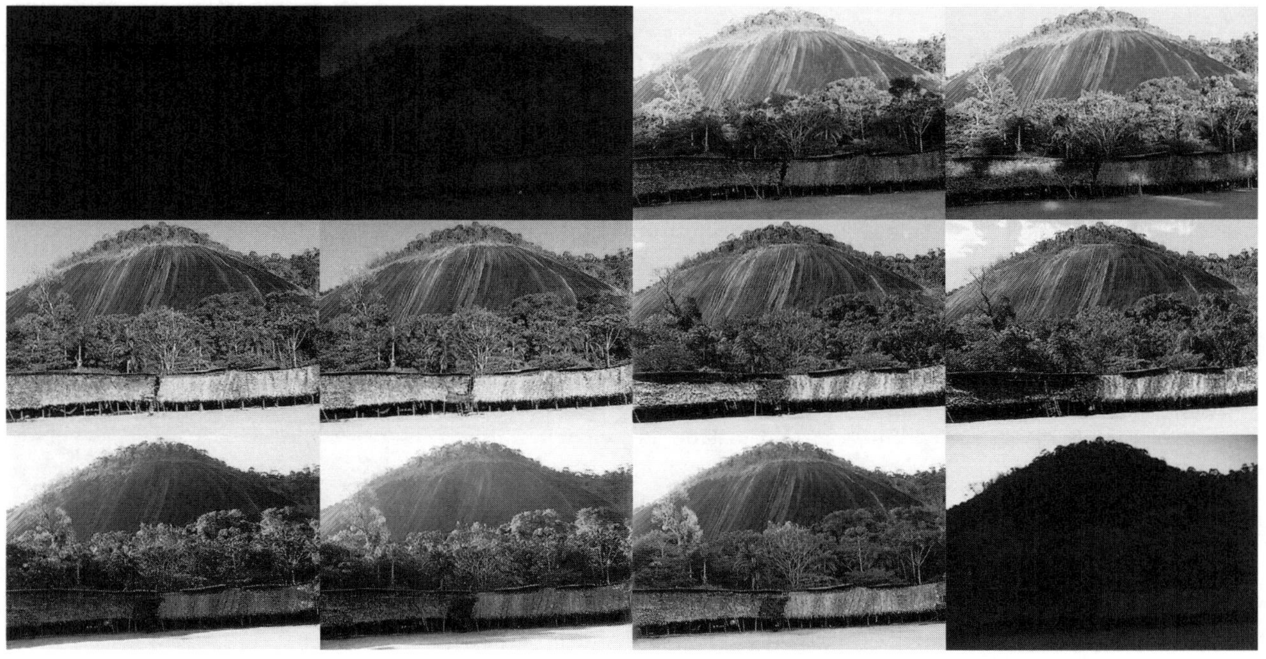

World," not just of the "natural" world or social-economic groups, but of image-blocks, states of feeling, and perceptions, keeping in mind Félix Guattari's notion that "an ecology of the virtual is just as pressing as ecologies of the visible world."[3] The exhibition is filled with abstracted or virtual analogues of Yanomami experience. In a Warholian representation, Wolfgang Staehle provided dual 24-hour video-cams broadcasting complementary views of Watoriki village seen from its mythical *La montagne du vent*, and the mountain seen from the village. Tony Oursler, long preoccupied with fraught, disembodied psyches and mental disturbances translated through projective technology, uses a bestiary from Watoriki children's drawings and art of shamanic ceremonies, which overlay his signature eyes in his video

JOSECA YANOMAMI, OKARIMARI, 2002, THE SPIRIT OF THE ANACONDA AND ITS SONS-IN-LAW, drawing / DER GEIST DER ANAKONDA UND SEINE SCHWIEGERSÖHNE, Zeichnung.

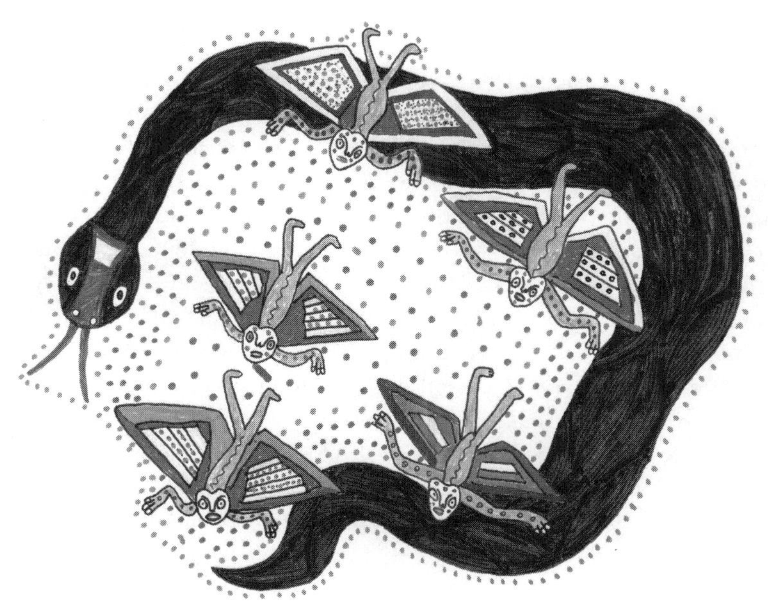

AYNO A (PAREAKIKI HARANI), 2003 / HOUSE-VILLAGE SEEN FROM THE MOUNTAIN, 24-hour color film / HAUSDORF VOM BERG AUS GESEHEN, 24 Std. Farbfilm.

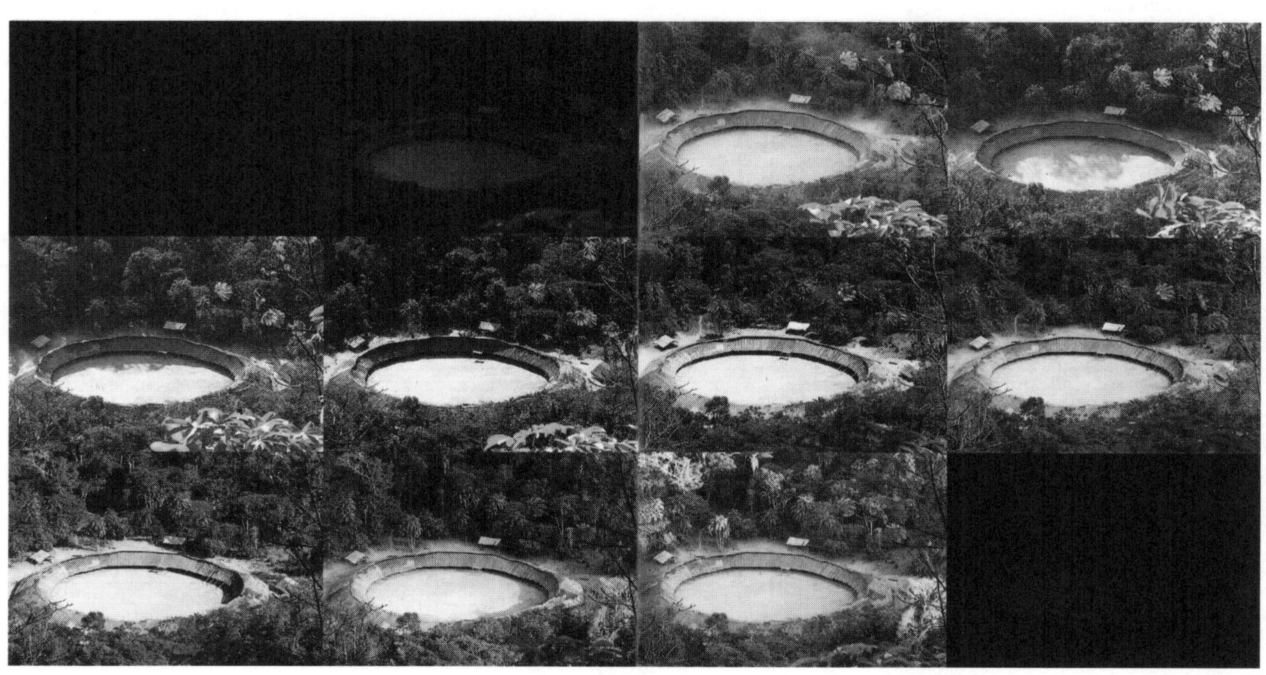

projection MIRROR MAZE (DEAD EYES LIVE) (2003). Gary Hill brought his concern with testing the limits of the body and of language through an ongoing catastrophe theory using video and other technologies, attempting to represent in IMPRESSIONS D'AFRIQUE (2003) his drug experience with the Yanomami elders. Others, who had extended experience working with the Yanomami, sought to present their history to the world, as with Volkmar Ziegler's feature-length film *La Maison et la Forêt* (1994). While Adriana Varejão's oil and mixed media paintings seemed to truly partake of a similar itinerary to Yanomami shamanism in her Baroque, hybrid exploration of out-of-body experience, bodily dismemberment, cannibalism, and shamanic initiation, cut in with a history of the Americas. Vincent Beaurin's sculptures pointed out the more dubious and superficial aspects of contrasting the semiotics of contemporary art with the Yanomami or aboriginal "dreamtime."

This enterprise of comparing the artistic visions of avant-garde/modernism or now post-avant-garde/postmodernism with the works of non-Western cultures of course has a long and problematic history. As old as Toulouse-Lautrec's fondness for Japanese woodcuts or Paul Gauguin's move to Tahiti, this always-controversial tendency has recently been expanded exponentially by processes of the international art market's "globalization." In describing the "return to the real" in the nineties, critic Hal Foster characterized the decade as that "of the itinerant curator who gathers nomadic artists at different sites."[4] This trend that critic Peter Schjeldahl dubbed "festivalism" was often explicitly a part of the new economic order's global trouncing of frontiers and breaking of barriers, putting into exchange all that had remained foreign, and it accompanied the opening of art biennials celebrated in such previously inaccessible spots as Kwangju, Johannesburg, Istanbul, Lima, and Abu Dhabi. A key statement of this was the 5th Lyon biennial of contemporary art in 2000, where the curators Thierry Prat and Thierry Raspail announced their theme of "Sharing Exoticisms" (*Partage d'Exotismes*), explaining that the term "art" played the same role in regard to individual works as the term "globalization" did in respect to economics.[5] They claimed the success of this "expansionist principle"—"the victory of modernity"—leaves no room for further expansion but is rather a "sharing of exoticisms." To this end, they brought in as guest curator Jean-Hubert Martin, who takes this thinking to its logical end by proclaiming the end of art in a globalized *la ronde* of anthropology—"the prepossessing dominance of strictly artistic categories has faded out in favor of more general values deriving from the human sciences and anthropology."[6]

Martin had ushered in much of this art world "globalization" in a big way with his 1989 exhibition "Magiciens de la terre" at the Centre Georges Pompidou and Grande Halle de La Villette. There, in the interests of world dialogue and reciprocity, *objets d'art* collected from around the globe, were juxtaposed on the basis of visual criteria, excitement, and novelty, and united by a common spiritual search, as Martin adumbrated in interviews. "Magiciens de la terre" claimed a true universality, gathering so many works from formerly "marginal contexts." In shades of the Yanomami exhibit, Lawrence Weiner was sent to Papua New Guinea. The show opened with Zulu dancers. In the catalog for the exhibit, it was left to two critics, Guy Brett and Jean Fisher, to point out that the "marginal contexts" were often due not to what Martin termed "Western contamination" or spiritual pollution, but to land struggles and brutal economic exploitation, a crucial subtext missing from the exhibit. The show's slighting of the extremely heterogeneous modernisms alive in say India, or Brazil, led artist and critic Rasheed Araeen to ask, "If all things were equal and the same, why was nobody sent to the villages of Europe? If the purpose of the exhibition was to question distinctions between modern works of art and folk or traditional art, why was this not done also within or in relation to Western culture?"[7] For Araeen the show merely duplicated the reigning view of the "West" as dynamic/modern and the "Other" as static/traditional. Araeen's criticism pointed to some of the rocky terrain of these projects that slip from artistic into socio-anthropological or ethnographic realms. They must of necessity interrogate themselves, circling back into questions of museology and the circumstances of the West's dominance. Otherwise, they risk becoming what analyst Slavoj Zizek denounced as yet another form of racism—"it 'respects' the Other's identity, conceiving the Other as a self-enclosed 'authentic' community towards which he, the multiculturalist, maintains a distance rendered possible by his privileged universal position."[8]

Another representation of these quandaries is exemplified by French author Michel Leiris, an early pioneer of the tendency that put so much into question, which James Clifford dubbed "ethnographic surrealism." Clifford notes the obsessive character of Leiris' remarkable journal of his African expedition *L'Afrique fantôme,* its "dada ideas of data," its disenchantment, as well as its "strange childlike innocence emerging somehow, each time, a f t e r experience ... No moment of truth: *Afrique fantôme* is only a pen starting up every day." Clifford leaves us this intriguing image of the "surrealist-ethnographer": after a long, intense period studying *zâr* possession in Ethiopia, a sacrifice is made especially for Leiris. He tastes the animal's blood but does not perform the *gourri,* the dance of the possessed. Seated with the *zâr* adepts in a room thick with incense, sweat, blood, and perfume, Leiris' head is covered in butter, and "the dead animal's entrails are coiled around his brow. He does not, however, interrupt his note taking."[9)]

One of the morals Clifford draws from this is that "Perhaps there's no return for anyone to a native land—only field notes for its reinvention."[10)] That, strangely enough, also seemed to be one of the meanings from another visitor to the Yanomami, Juan Downey, in his 1978 video *Laughing Alligator.* At one point in the video, Downey's guides turn on him with their bows and arrows, as if to ask who is "shooting" whom? Perhaps "Yanomami, Spirit of the Forest" also asks if, despite looming conditions of ecocide and the vast increases in destitution since Downey's video, at last we can approach more of a semblance of mutual cooperation and negotiation.

1) "Yanomami, l'esprit de la fôret," May 14–October 12, 2003, Fondation Cartier pour l'art contemporain, Paris.
2) Jeroen Boomgaard, "Theory Today" in *Conventions in Contemporary Art. Lectures and Debates Witte de With, 2001,* ed. by Valentijn Byvanck (Rotterdam: Witte de With Center for Contemporary Art, 2002), p. 65.
3) See Félix Guattari, *Chaosmosis,* transl. by Paul Bains and Julian Pefanis (Bloomington & Indianapolis: Indiana University Press, 1995); *The Three Ecologies,* transl. by Ian Pindar and Paul Sutton (London/New Brunswick, NJ: Athlone Press, 2000).
4) Hal Foster, "The Artist as Ethnographer" in *The Return to the Real* (Cambridge: MIT Press, 1996), note 44, p. 282.
5) Thierry Prat and Thierry Raspail, *Partage d'Exotismes,* vol. 1 (Lyon: Réunion des Musées Nationaux, 2000), p. 20. The artists Chris Ofili and Hassan Musa refused to share their exoticism, the latter writing to the curators that "African art" was only a European category that hindered appreciation of his work.
6) Jean-Hubert Martin, ibid, p. 46.
7) Rasheed Araeen, "Our Bauhaus Others' Mudhouse," *Third Text* 6 (Spring 1989): 3–14, p. 11.
8) Slavoj Zizek, "Multiculturalism, or the Cultural Logic of Multinational Capitalism," *New Left Review* 225 (1997): 28–51, p. 44.
9) James Clifford, *The Predicament of Culture* (Cambridge: Harvard University Press, 1988), pp. 172, 168.
10) Ibid, p. 173.

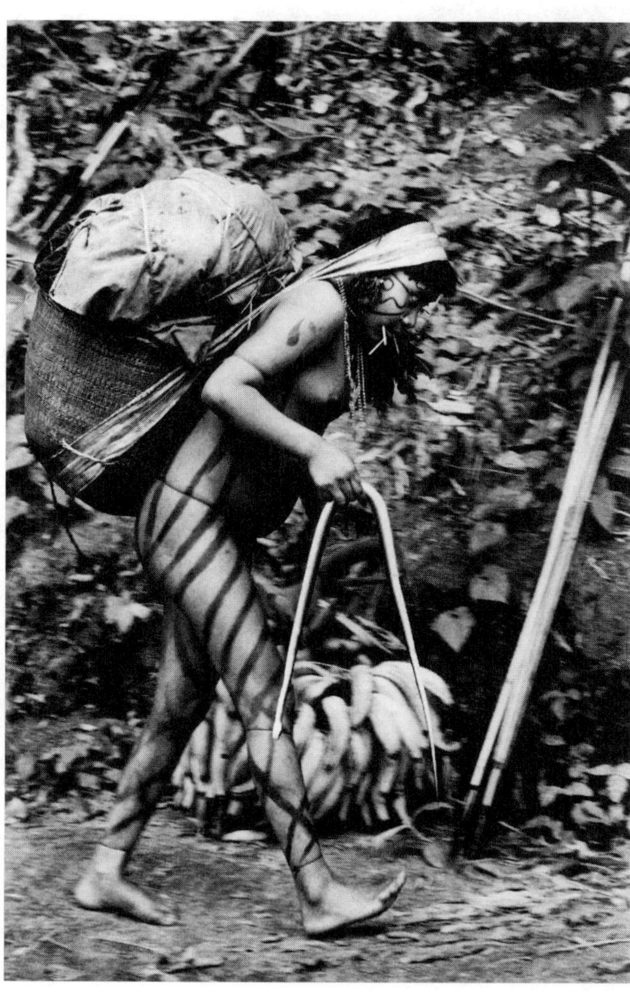

LOTHAR BAUMGARTEN, RIVER-CROSSING, KASHORAWËTHERI, 1978, from a series of 6 gelatin silver prints, 14 x 11" / FLUSSÜBERQUERUNG, aus einer Serie von 6 Gelatinsilber-Abzügen, 35,5 x 28 cm.

(ALL IMAGES FROM THE CATALOGUE "YANOMAMI, L'ESPRIT DE LA FORÊT," FONDATION CARTIER, PARIS.)

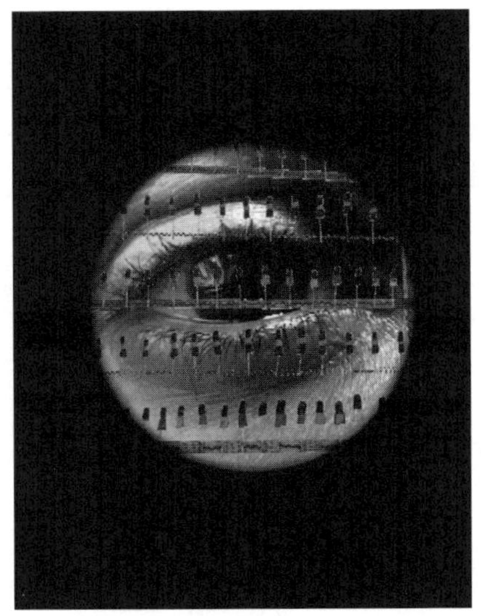

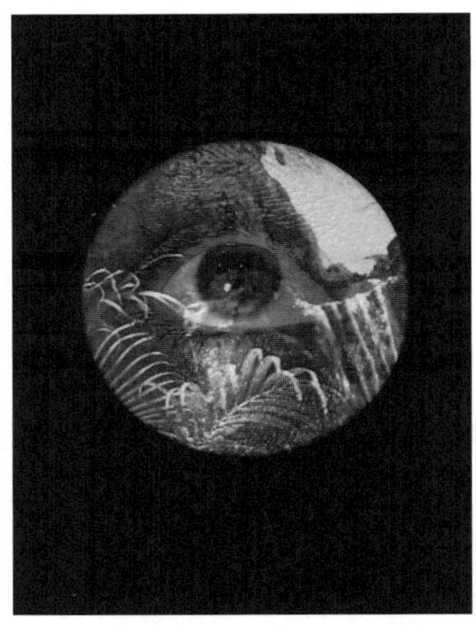

TONY OURSLER, MIRROR MAZE (DEAD EYES LIVE), 2003, details from video projection with sound on 10 resin spheres of 70 7/8" diameter / SPIEGEL-LABYRINTH (TOTE AUGEN LEBEN) Videoprojektion mit Ton auf 10 Kunstharzkugeln von 180 cm Durchmesser.

«YANOMAMI, L'ESPRIT DE LA FORÊT» UND DIE ZEICHEN DER ZEIT

JAY MURPHY

Alle an der Pariser Ausstellung «Yanomami, l'esprit de la forêt»[1] beteiligten Künstler votierten mehr oder weniger entschieden dafür, «den Zynismus der Chiffre durch den Optimismus des Kontakts zu ersetzen», wie der flämische Kritiker und Kunsthistoriker Jeroen Boomgaard es einmal formulierte.[2] Bis zu ihrer unheilvollen Begegnung mit Goldsuchern und anderen typischen Vertretern der «Aussenwelt» waren die Yanomami-Indianer entlang der Grenze zwischen Brasilien und Venezuela im nördlichen Amazonas das grösste noch intakte Urvolk Südamerikas, das seine traditionelle Lebensweise zu bewahren vermochte. Zu dieser Tradition gehört auch die Zauberei, eine ritualisierte Existenzweise, die auf der Interpretation von Myriaden bös- und gutartiger, in ihrer Mitte lebender Götter und Geister beruht, aber auch auf dem Konsum der zu Staub zerriebenen Gebeine ihrer Vorfahren, was mit zu ihrem Ruf als Kannibalen beitrug. Die Ausstellung wurde von der Fondation Cartier organisiert, und zwar durch den Anthropologen Bruce Albert, der eines der vier Yanomami-Idiome spricht und seit seinem ersten Besuch 1973 – zusammen mit *Survival International* (dessen Vizepräsident er ist) und der brasilianischen NGO *Comissão Pró-Yanomami* – jedes Jahr mehrere Monate bei den Yanomami verbrachte. Die Ausstellung wurde in Zusammenarbeit mit den Yanomami-Schamanen

JAY MURPHY, Schriftsteller und Kritiker, lebt in New York City. Zurzeit schreibt er *The Art of Disorder: A Life of Emile de Antonio*; eine überarbeitete Neuauflage seiner Anthologie *For Palestine* (1993) steht kurz bevor, und am Sundance-Online-Filmfestival 2002 wurde sein Gemeinschafts-Internetprojekt *privilege* vorgestellt.

konzipiert, insbesondere mit Davi Kopenawa, einem wichtigen nationalen und internationalen Vertreter indianischer Interessen, und seinem Heimatdorf Watoriki. Den Yanomami ging es darum, eine «Konfrontation» und einen Vergleich zwischen ihrer Kosmologie und visionären Erfahrung und dem «wilden Geist», der unserem eigenen künstlerischen Tun zugrunde lag, zu erreichen. Fünf der Künstler reisten ins Amazonasgebiet um ihre Werke vor Ort mit den Yanomami zu entwickeln, drei arbeiteten mit von den Indianern vorgegebenen Materialien wie Texten, Zeichnungen oder Videos, und drei weitere hatten bereits vorher beträchtliche Zeit mit den Indianern verbracht und trugen Werke bei, die teilweise mehr als zwanzig Jahre vor dieser Ausstellung entstanden waren.

Man muss dem Katalog zugute halten, dass er die Kosmologien und Lebensumstände der Yanomami detailliert darstellt: ihre schamanistischen Séancen und ihre Beziehung zu den Geistern von Tieren und Vorfahren, ihr Verhältnis zu ihrem reichen ökologischen Habitat und ihre verhängnisvolle Begegnung mit den «Weissen», einschliesslich des Massakers an 16 Yanomami-Indianern 1993 in Haxima. In der Zusammenarbeit von Dorfschamanen und Künstlern wendet sich die Ausstellung gegen eine Präsentation in Form einer weiteren amerikanisch-indianischen Kunst- oder humanitären Dokumentations-Ausstellung und setzt stattdessen auf den Austausch «freier Assoziationen» zwischen schamanistischen Visionen und der Bildproduktion zeitgenössischer Künstler der «entwickelten Welt». Die Stärke dieser Ausstellung liegt im Eintauchen in Erfahrungen, das viele Künstler auf sich nahmen (nehmen durften), sowie in der Vielfalt ihrer Sensibilitäten und Interpretationsweisen – von Claudia Andujars äusserst feinfühligen und würdevollen Photographien (ihre späteren Arbeiten veranschaulichen dank Mehrfachbelichtungen die Metamorphosen und die tiefe Versunkenheit schamanistischer Trancezustände), die in einer humanistischen, dokumentarischen Tradition stehen, über die sich eher durch High-Tech auszeichnenden Kunstwerke eines Gary Hill oder Tony Oursler, bis zu der feierlich dynamischen, weitgehend auf Yanomami-Zeichnungen gestützten Videoinstallation des Issey-Miyake-Schützlings Naoki Takizawa.

Im glücklichsten Fall sind die Werke in dieser Ausstellung eine Illustration der polyvalenten vielschichtigen Rückkopplungsvorgänge, die unsere ökologischen Beziehungen im weiteren Sinn ausmachen und hier für ein-

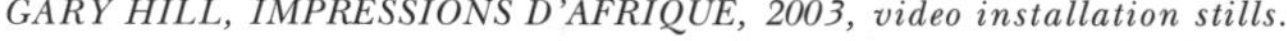

GARY HILL, IMPRESSIONS D'AFRIQUE, 2003, video installation stills.

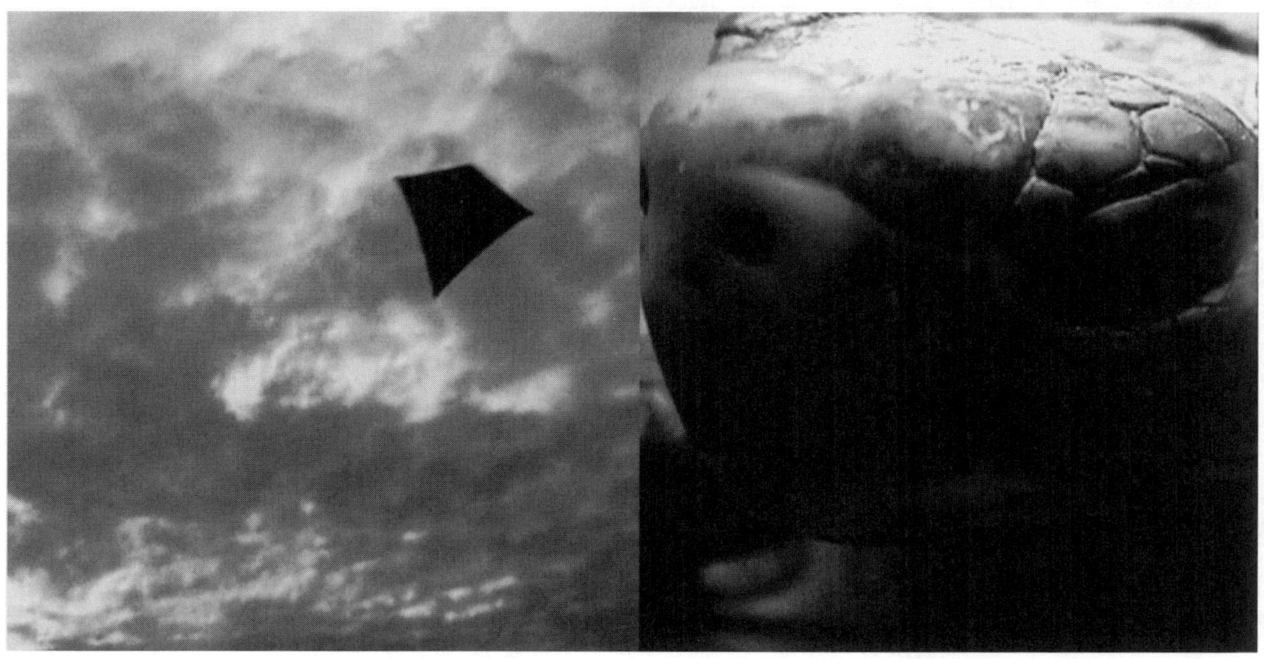

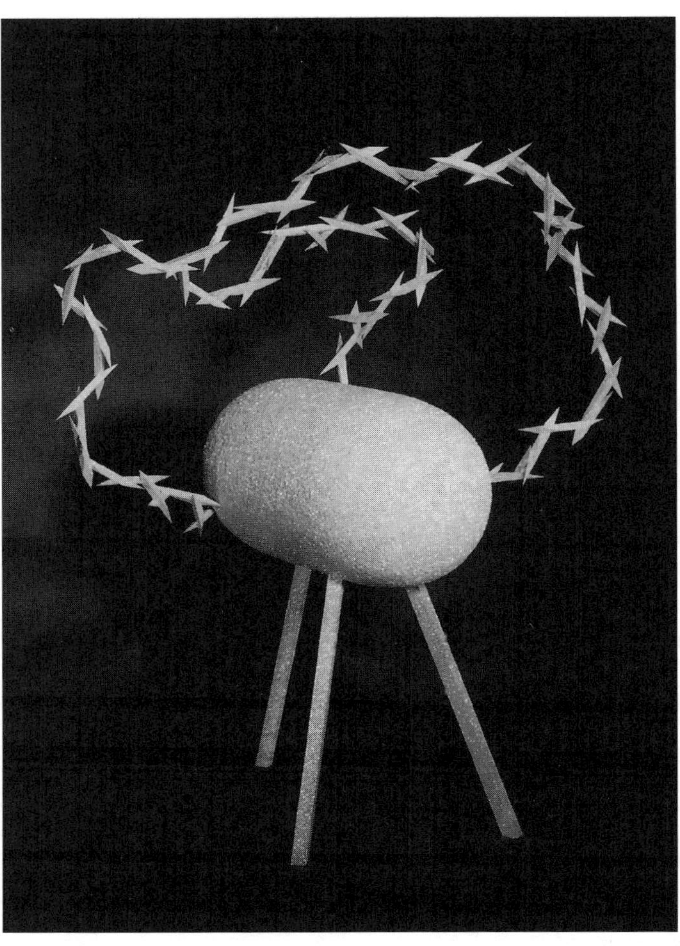

VINCENT BEAURIN, DESIGNATION: ENSEIGNE ANIMAL JAUNE, 2003 / DESIGNATION: YELLOW ANIMAL SIGN, 38 1/5 x 33 1/2 x 23 5/8" / BESTIMMUNG: GELBES-TIER-ZEICHEN , 97 x 85 x 60 cm.

mal von Künstlern der «Ersten Welt» zusammen mit denen der «Vierten Welt» dargestellt werden, also nicht nur durch die «natürliche» Welt oder sozioökonomische Gruppen, sondern durch Bildblöcke, Gefühlszustände und Wahrnehmungen, getreu Félix Guattaris Idee, dass eine Ökologie des Virtuellen genauso dringend nötig sei wie die Ökologien der sichtbaren Welt.[3)] Die Ausstellung ist voller abstrahierter oder virtueller Analogien zum Leben der Yanomami. In einer warholschen Re-Präsentation schuf Wolfgang Staehle eine 24-stündige Videoschau, die jeweils komplementär eine Aufnahme des Dorfs Watoriki vom mythischen «Berg des Windes» aus zeigt und eine Ansicht des Berges vom Dorf aus. Tony Oursler, der sich lange mit der Darstellung von Gefährdungen, körperlosen Seelen und psychischen Störungen durch Videoprojektionen auseinander gesetzt hat, verwendet in seiner Videoprojektion MIRROR MAZE (DEAD EYES LIVE) – Spiegellabyrinth (tote Augen leben) – Tierdarstellungen aus Zeichnungen der Kinder von Watoriki und Kunstobjekte aus schamanistischen Zeremonien und kombiniert sie mit seinen typischen Augenbildern. Gary Hill wiederum brachte seine Untersuchung körperlicher und sprachlicher Grenzsituationen im Rahmen einer Katastrophentheorie mittels Video und anderen Technologien mit ein und versuchte in IMPRESSIONS D'AFRIQUE (Eindrücke aus Afrika, 2003) seine Drogenerfahrung mit den Yanomami-Ältesten darzustellen. Andere, die bereits längere Zeit mit den Yanomami zusammengearbeitet hatten, suchten deren Geschichte zu vermitteln, so auch Volkmar Ziegler in seinem Film *La Maison et la Forêt* (1994), der die Länge eines Spielfilms hat. Während Adriana Varejãos Öl- und Mischtechnik-Bilder einen ähnlichen Weg zum Schamanismus der Yanomami einzuschlagen schienen mit ihrer barocken, hybriden Untersuchung von ausserkörperlicher Erfahrung, körperlicher Verstümmelung, Kannibalismus und schamanistischer Initiation, gewürzt mit einem Schuss Geschichte der amerikanischen Kontinente, verwiesen Vincent Beaurins Skulpturen auf einen etwas dubioseren und oberflächlicheren Zug dieser Gegenüberstellung von Semiotik zeitgenössischer Kunst und «Traumzeit» der Yanomami oder Aborigines.

Dieser Vergleich von künstlerischen Visionen der Avantgarde/Moderne beziehungsweise Post-Anvantgarde/Postmoderne mit Werken nichtwestlicher Kulturen hat natürlich eine lange und problembeladene Vorgeschichte. So alt wie Toulouse-Lautrecs Vorliebe für japanische Holzschnitte oder Paul Gauguins Reisen nach Tahiti hat diese schon immer umstrittene Tendenz in jüngster Zeit durch die Globalisationsprozesse des internationalen Kunstmarktes massiv an Bedeutung gewonnen. In seiner Beschreibung der «Rückkehr zur Wirklichkeit» charakterisierte der Kritiker Hal Foster die 90er

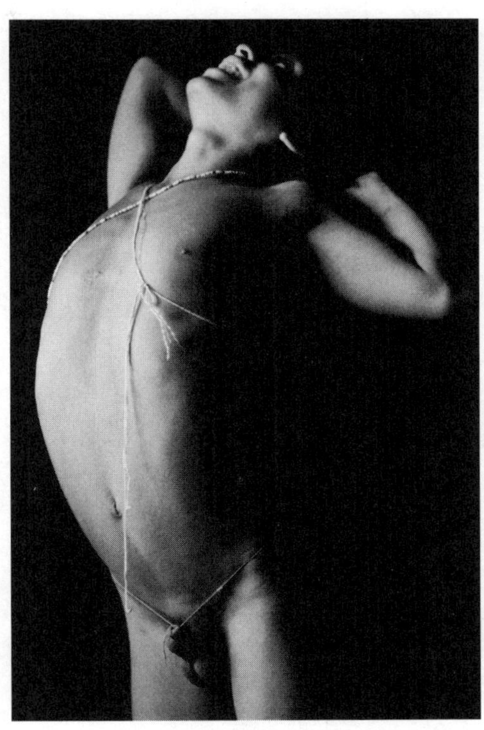

CLAUDIA ANDUJAR, IDENTITE, WAKATHA U, 1977, from a series of 11 b/w prints, 39 x 34¼" / aus einer Serie von 11 Schwarzweissabzügen, 99 x 87 cm.

Jahre als Jahrzehnt des «wandernden Kurators, der an verschiedenen Orten nomadische Künstler um sich schart».[4] Diese Entwicklung, von Peter Schjeldahl als «Festivalismus» gebrandmarkt, war oft ganz explizit Teil des Grenzen sprengenden und Schranken niederreissenden Vormarschs der neuen globalen Wirtschaftsordnung, die alles, was noch fremd geblieben war, in den allgemeinen Austausch mit einzubeziehen suchte, und führte zur Eröffnung von Kunstbiennalen an bis dahin so entlegenen Orten wie Kwangju, Johannesburg, Istanbul, Lima und Abu Dhabi. Ein Schlüsselereignis dieser Art war die fünfte Biennale zeitgenössischer Kunst in Lyon, 2000, zu deren Thema die Kuratoren Thierry Prat und Thierry Raspail das «Teilen von Exotismen» (*Partage d'Exotismes*) erhoben, wobei sie erklärten, dass der Begriff «Kunst» für das Werk des Individuums dieselbe Rolle spiele wie der Begriff «Globalisierung» für die Wirtschaft.[5] Sie behaupteten, dass der Erfolg dieses Expansionsprinzips – der Sieg der Moderne – keinen Raum mehr liesse für weiteres Expandieren, sondern lediglich noch für ein «Teilen der Exotismen». Zu diesem Zweck luden sie als Gastkurator Jean-Hubert Martin ein, der dieses Denken zu seinem logischen Ende führte, indem er in einem anthropologischen Ringelreihen das Ende der Kunst verkündete: «Die überwältigende Dominanz streng künstlerischer Kategorien hat an Bedeutung verloren gegenüber allgemeineren Werten, die aus den Humanwissenschaften und der Anthropologie stammen.»[6]

Martin hatte diese Globalisierung der Kunstszene bereits 1989 in seiner Ausstellung «Magiciens de la terre» im Centre Georges Pompidou und in der Grande Halle de La Villette im grossen Stil angekündigt. Dort waren im Namen des weltumspannenden Dialogs und der Reziprozität Kunstobjekte aus aller Welt versammelt und nach visuellen, spannungs- und neuheitsbedingten Kriterien einander gegenübergestellt worden; gemeinsamer Nenner war, wie Martin in diversen Interviews andeutete, eine spirituelle Suche. «Magiciens de la terre» behauptete wahrhaft universell zu sein, weil so viele Werke aus bisher «marginalen Kontexten» gezeigt wurden. Zur Kontrastierung des Ausstellungsgutes der Yanomami wurde Lawrence Weiner nach Papua Neuguinea geschickt. Zulu-Tänzer eröffneten die Ausstellung. Im Katalog blieb es den beiden Kritikern Guy Brett und Jean Fisher überlassen, darauf hinzuweisen, dass die so genannten «marginalen Kontexte» weniger mit «westlicher Kontamination» oder spiritueller Verunreinigung zu tun hatten, wie Martin es nannte, sondern vielmehr mit Landstreitigkeiten und brutaler wirtschaftlicher Ausbeutung; ein entscheidender Subtext, der in der Ausstellung selbst völlig unterging. Die Vernachlässigung bestehender, äusserst heterogener Modernismen in Indien oder Brasilien

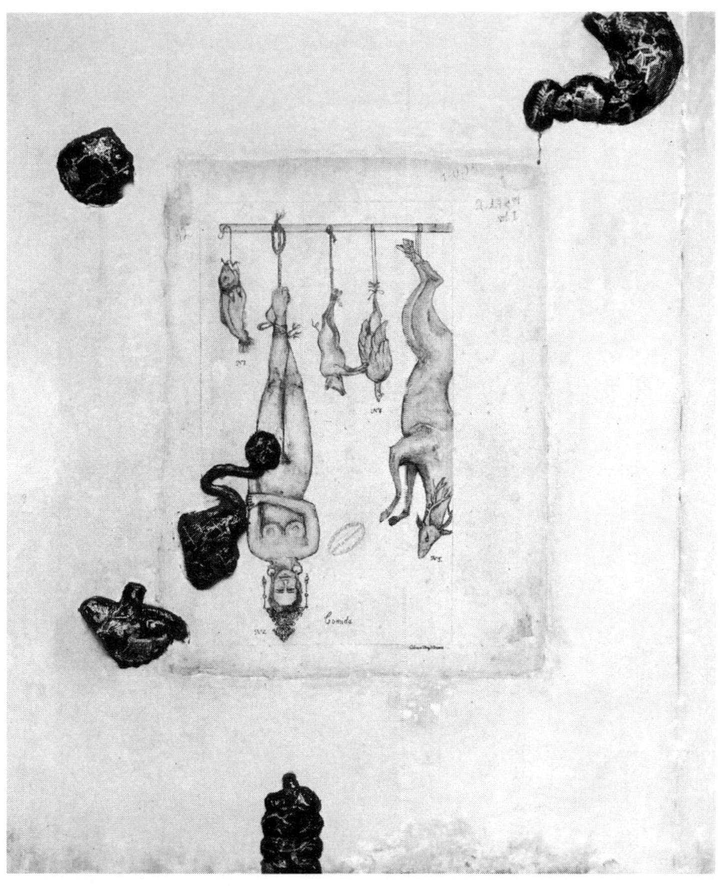

ADRIANA VAREJAO, COMIDA (FOOD), 1992, oil on canvas, $47^1/_4$ x $39^3/_8$" / NAHRUNG, Öl auf Leinwand, 120 x 100 cm.

veranlasste den Kritiker Rasheed Araeen zur Frage: «Wenn doch alles gleich und gleichwertig ist, weshalb wurde dann niemand in die europäischen Dörfer entsandt? Und wenn der Zweck der Ausstellung die Hinterfragung der Unterscheidung zwischen modernen Kunstwerken und Volkskunst oder traditionellen Kunstformen war, warum hat man das nicht auch innerhalb der westlichen Kultur getan?»[7] Laut Araeen wiederholte die Ausstellung lediglich das bestehende Vorurteil des dynamisch-modernen Westens gegenüber dem statisch-traditionellen «Anderen». Araeens Kritik machte das steinige Terrain sichtbar, auf dem sich Projekte bewegen, die vom Künstlerischen ins Sozialanthropologische oder Ethnologische ableiten. Diese müssten sich unbedingt selbst reflektieren und sich auf Fragen der Museologie und die Umstände westlicher Dominanz zurückbesinnen. Andernfalls laufen sie Gefahr zu dem zu werden, was der analytische Denker Slavoj Zizek als eine andere Form von Rassismus bezeichnet: «Er respektiert die Identität des Anderen, während er dieses doch nur als eine in sich geschlossene ‹authentische› Gemeinschaft versteht, der gegenüber er als multikultureller Mensch eine Distanz aufrechterhält, die nur dank seiner privilegierten universalen Stellung möglich ist.»[8]

Eine weitere Darstellung dieses Dilemmas liefert der französische Autor Michel Leiris in seiner frühen und gründlichen Auseinandersetzung mit dem, was James Clifford «ethnologischen Surrealismus» nennt. Clifford hebt den obsessiven Charakter von Leiris' bemerkenswertem Tagebuch seiner Afrikaexpedition hervor, seine dadaistische Behandlung von Daten, seine Ernüchterung, aber auch die «seltsam kindliche Unschuld, die sich jeweils nach einem Erlebnis einstellt... Kein Moment der Wahrheit: *L'afrique fantôme* ist nur eine Feder, die jeden Tag von neuem zu schreiben beginnt.» Clifford lässt uns mit diesem beunruhigenden Bild eines «surrealistischen Ethnologen» zurück: Nachdem er lange und intensiv die *Zâr*-Besessenheit in Äthiopien studiert hat, wird speziell für Leiris ein Tier geopfert. Leiris kostet vom Blut des Tieres, aber er tanzt nicht den *gourri,* den Tanz der Besessenen. Er sitzt mit den *Zâr*-Jüngern in einem von Weihrauch, Schweiss, Blut und Düften geschwängerten Raum, den Kopf mit Butter beschmiert und «die Eingeweide des Tiers um die Stirn gewunden. Aber er hört nicht auf, Notizen zu machen.»[9]

Eine der Lehren, die Clifford daraus zieht, ist, dass es «vielleicht für niemanden eine Rückkehr ins gelobte Land gibt, sondern lediglich Feldforschungen zwecks seiner Neuerfindung».[10] Und seltsamerweise scheint das Video *Laughing Alligator* (1978) eines anderen Besuchers der Yanomami, Juan Downey, auf dasselbe hinauszulaufen. An einer Stelle dieses Videos wenden sich Downeys Führer samt ihren Pfeilen und Bögen zu ihm um, als wollten sie fragen: «Wer jagt hier wen?» Vielleicht stellt uns «Yanomami, l'esprit de la forêt» ja auch die Frage, ob wir jetzt, trotz drohendem Umweltkollaps und dem fortschreitenden Niedergang seit der Entstehung von Downeys Video, endlich zu echter Zusammenarbeit und gegenseitiger Verständigung in der Lage seien.

(Übersetzung: Wilma Parker)

1) «Yanomami, l'esprit de la forêt», 14. Mai–12. Oktober 2003, Fondation Cartier pour l'art contemporain, Paris.
2) Jeroen Boomgaard, «Theory today», in: *Conventions in Contemporary Art: Lectures and Debates, Witte de With 2001,* hrsg. v. Valentijn Byvanck, Witte de With Center for Contemporary Art, Rotterdam 2002, S. 65.
3) Vgl. Félix Guattari, *Chaosmose,* Galilée, Paris 1992; *Die drei Ökologien,* hrsg. v. Peter Engelmann, übers. v. Alec A. Schaerer, Passagen-Verlag, Wien 1994.
4) Hal Foster, «The Artist as Ethnographer», in: *The Return to the Real,* MIT Press, Cambridge, MA, 1996, Anm. 44, S. 282.
5) Thierry Prat und Thierry Raspail, *Partage d'Exotismes,* Bd. 1, Réunion des Musées Nationaux, Lyon 2000, S. 20. Die Künstler Chris Ofili und Hassan Musa weigerten sich, «ihren exotischen Standpunkt mit anderen zu teilen»; Letzterer schrieb den Kuratoren, dass «Afrikanische Kunst» lediglich eine europäische Kategorie sei, welche die Anerkennung seiner Arbeit verhindere.
6) Jean-Hubert Martin, ebenda, S. 46.
7) Rasheed Araeen, «Our Bauhaus Others' Mudhouse», *Third Text* Nr. 6 (Frühjahr 1989), S. 11.
8) Slavoj Zizek, «Multiculturalism, or the Cultural Logic of Multinational Capitalism», *New Left Review* Nr. 225 (1997), S. 44.
9) James Clifford, *The Predicament of Culture,* Harvard University Press, Cambridge, MA 1988, S. 172, 168.
10) Ebenda, S. 173.

NAOKI TAKIZAWA, MIREKOPE (SHAMANIC MIRRORS), 2003, mirrors, aluminum, steel, DVD projection; DVD still / SCHAMANENSPIEGEL, Installation mit Spiegeln, Aluminium, Stahl, DVD-Projektion; Standaufnahme.

(ALLE BILDER AUS DEM KATALOG «YANOMAMI, L'ESPRIT DE LA FORÊT», FONDATION CARTIER, PARIS.)

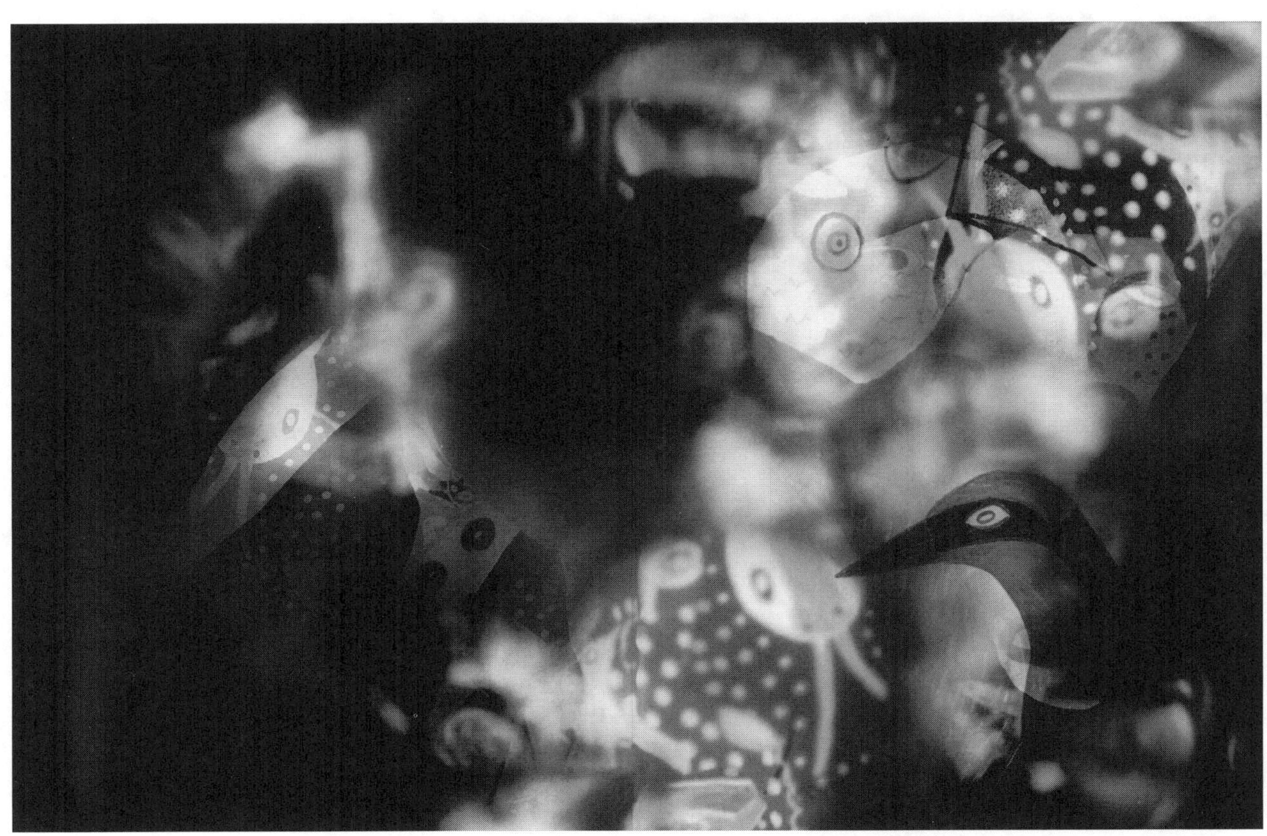

CUMULUS

From America

IN EVERY EDITION OF PARKETT, TWO CUMULUS CLOUDS, ONE FROM AMERICA, THE OTHER FROM EUROPE, FLOAT OUT TO AN INTERESTED PUBLIC. THEY CONVEY INDIVIDUAL OPINIONS, ASSESSMENTS, AND MEMORABLE ENCOUNTERS—AS ENTIRELY PERSONAL PRESENTATIONS OF PROFESSIONAL ISSUES.

OUR CONTRIBUTORS TO THIS ISSUE ARE CAY SOPHIE RABINOWITZ, SENIOR U.S. EDITOR FOR "PARKETT" IN NEW YORK, AND BERLIN BASED CURATOR AND WRITER JENS HOFFMANN.

Seeing Being Seen

CAY SOPHIE RABINOWITZ

Mary Jane Jacobs' 1993 exhibition "Culture in Action" introduced a series of artist and community projects in Chicago that began to shift the ideological position of art from a self-referential practice confined within museum interiors to a social and public activity. While "Culture in Action" may have been inspired by international precedents and has engendered numerous valiant attempts to democratize visual culture since, few exhibition projects have managed to do much more than either perpetuate a "top down" dispensation of cultural values or force a grass roots leveling of the criteria for what kind of work belongs in the museum.

My thoughts on the subject of exhibitions and the public sphere were provoked recently when invited to visit Panama City, Panama, for "Multiple City," curated by Gerardo Mosquera and Adrienne Samos. "Multiple City" was not localized in any institution; no venue was its host or its parasite. Instead twelve international and local artists were invited to install, perform, and enact works on, in, and for Panama City, a uniquely hybrid urban center on a narrow strip of land connecting the Americas. Thus, the city became a platform and each work part of a narrative not bound by the wide space or the white cube.

While several works in "Multiple City" measured the torn social fabric of this formerly occupied canal city with its diverse and competing ethnic and cultural traditions, its commercial banks and crowded barrios, the most accomplished participating artists addressed the public and exposed local histories without pretense. No reform strategies were assessed, no charity cases were named, no special privileges were offered. International artists created new works for specific sites, Panamanians participated fully, and visitors like myself learned more than can be gleaned from the annals and books published. Several artists created works in an atyp-

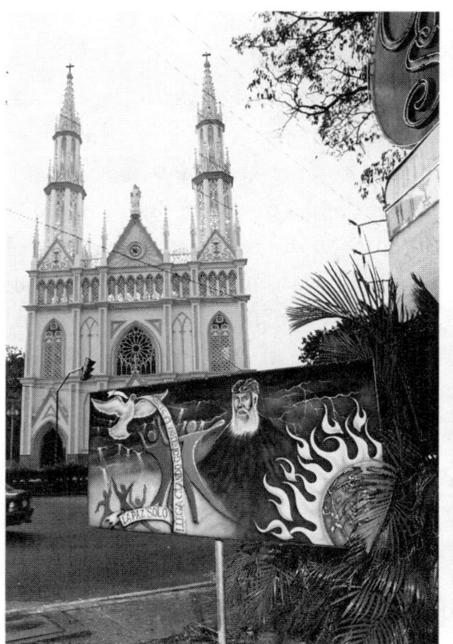

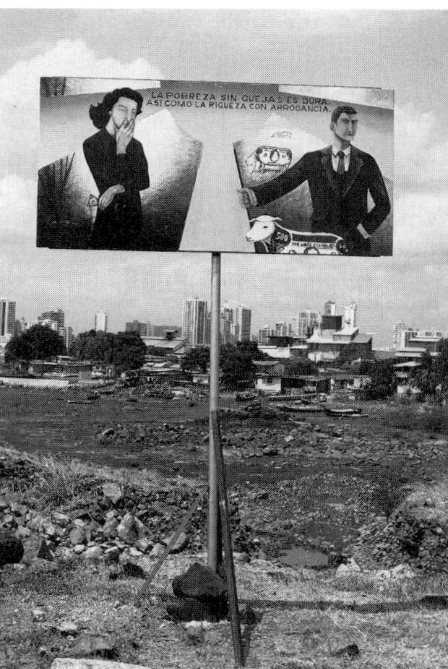

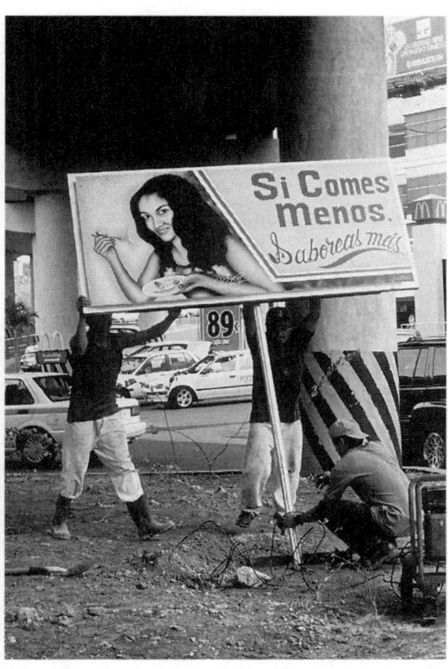

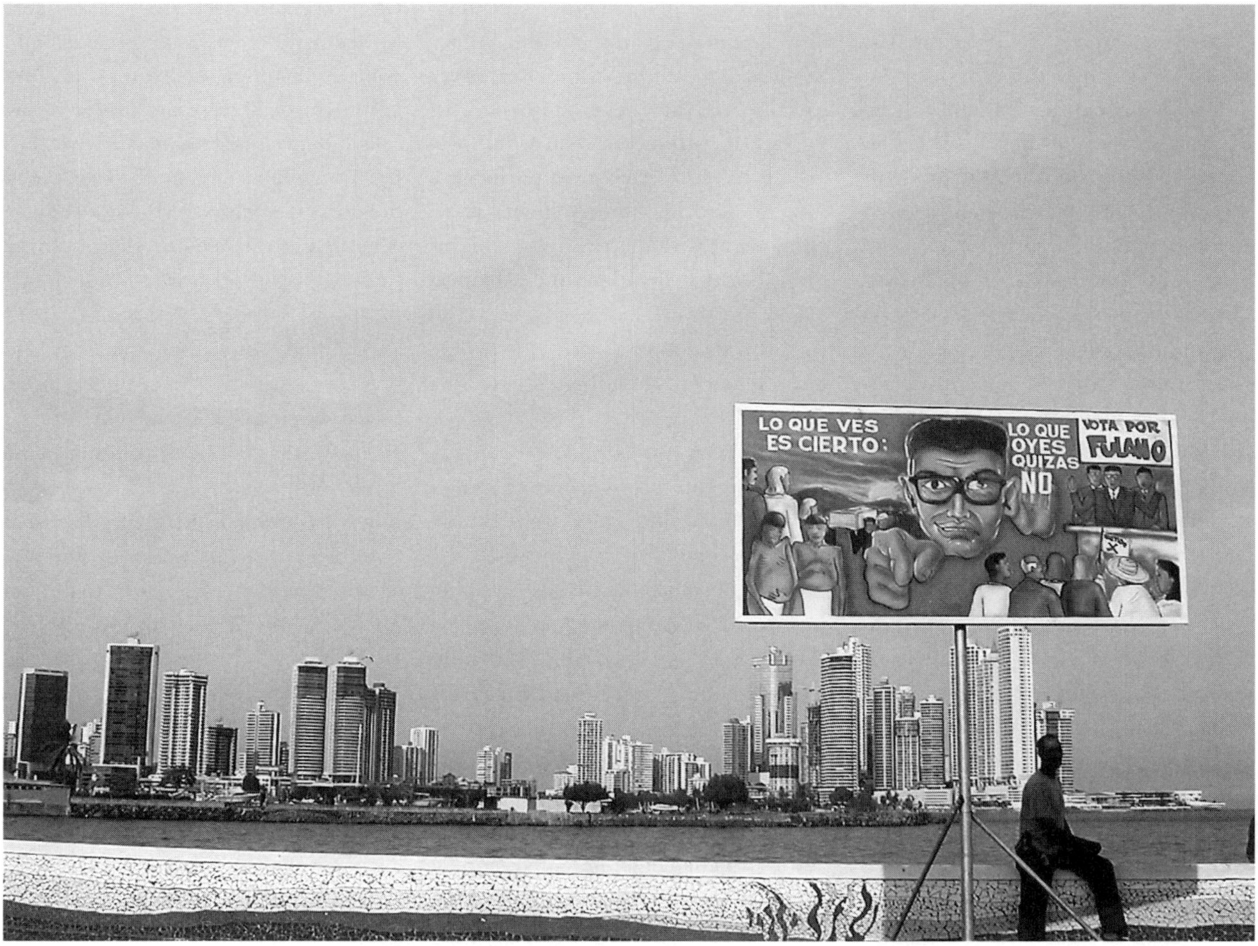

GHADA AMER, CHINESE PROVERBS, 2003, paintings on wood / CHINESISCHE SPRICHWÖRTER, Malerei auf Holz. (PHOTOS: FUNDACION ARPA)

ical medium or style from that common to their oeuvre. For example, Ghada Amer strayed from her signature machine stitched canvases of cavorting nudes to produce billboards incorporating Chinese proverbs and graffiti art, both common cultural elements in Panama. Through such works, I gained access to the city, its range of inhabitants, their wildly diverse standards of living, and the way history remains as a crumbling façade on building structures and social infrastructures alike. Because "Multiple City" expressed no didactic goal, I returned to my editorial office and began to reflect on how or why this exhibition was able to teach me so much about Panama.

My first afternoon in Panama City was spent touring exhibition locations with assistant curator Ramon Zafrani, whose discussion of the works' materials, composition, and content gradually gave way to the extensive site analysis and local cultural history that led to my patchwork understanding of Panama City. He recalled incidents of the works' reception (or more likely rejection) by conservative Panamanians (often former Noriega sympathizers). We trailed city busses called "red devils," explosively painted by the graffitists who produced Amer's proverbial billboards, and we traversed a ghetto striving for gentrification where the presidential offices are protected by two species of guards: peacocks and paramilitary. In this neighborhood, called San Filipe, Cuban artist Yoan Capote's work ANALYSIS OF BEAUTY (2003) revealed the urban district's complex character. Capote adorned ten trash dumpsters, each upholstered in decoratively patterned material and trim. I spotted one next to the French embassy and noticed that the dumpster's white lace fabric seemed to match the building's ornate wooden lattice-trimmed colonial architecture. I walked further into the neighborhood and identified a lightless open doorway flanked on one side by a thin man dressed in a loose fitting T-shirt and on the other by a decorated dumpster. I soon learned from local newspaper reports that residents, most of them third-generation squatters, had been moving the artist's containers to their homes, and were using the dumpsters as always to discard trash but with care so as to preserve the fine detail of the artist's hand.

Brook Alfaro's NINE (2003) was a hugely successful experience, which revealed much about the city's community, commerce, and culture. Alfaro worked for months with rival street gangs from a slum neighborhood called Barraza to produce a dual video projection in which each gang performs a song by "Roockie," one of the most celebrated local rappers. For two nights only, local Panamanians and members of the press were bussed to Barraza to view the videos projected side-by-side onto tenement buildings where the gangs live.

In NINE, as the two groups of gangsters dressed in baggy jeans and sleeveless T's, exposing knife wounds and tattoos, gradually move forward, the camera becomes active by panning around each group and creating the appearance of a face-off. Tensions mount as they seem to confront each other and a long pause is shattered by neighborhood children who cheer when one leader passes a soccer ball to his rival opponent. Understood to be a gesture of challenge, not an attempt at conciliation, this moment communicates the likely futility of most cultural projects designed to produce social reform. In the end, the art public enters a neighborhood thought to be off limits and dangerous and two rival gangs appear to cooperate and perform together but continue shooting each other when the rehearsals are done.

While most approached the neighborhood expecting Alfaro's piece to resolve some of the obvious problems localized in this urban district, no semblance of social or economic resolution is offered. Rather a relentless dramatic tension is conveyed through the artist's uniquely constructed choreography with the actors and his camera. Alfaro often collaborates with marginal persons and his work generally challenges the relation between artist, subject, and viewer in a controversial and complex manner. Alfaro does not disguise the social disparity between himself and his subjects, making obvious the potentially exploitative treatment of outcasts as actors. As the closeness of Alfaro's surveillance nears invasiveness, that extensively explored post-colonial problem of occident and orient, viewer and viewed, or desiring spectator and object of desire, becomes a more complex configuration. In the end, Alfaro's video works put into question the artist's own activity. Thus, this director-filmmaker-artist of the ghetto becomes the object of his own critique and this viewer-spectator-critic starts to reflect on and reconsider her own role.

With each passing day, each work, and each person encountered, Panama City's complex identity began to reveal itself while my manner of approaching an exhibition changed accordingly. My method began to resemble that of an ethnographer, a participant-observer, doing fieldwork to experience and record local activity. The most radical change in my professional protocol was provoked and initiated by Humberto Velez and his work BANDA DE MI HOGAR (2003). Velez collaborated with a brass and percussion marching band made up of mostly black musicians and majorettes, of all ages, who are affiliated with the Sanchez family-operated vocational school. Though widely popular and even played on the radio, the Banda del Hogar is only invited to parade publicly once a year on Independence Day. Breaking Panama's rigid social traditions, Velez and the band marched numerous times on non-holidays, modeling their homemade uniforms and banners in public squares and on busy streets and performing their Samba based rhythms, which are so different from the American military style marching bands that are most common in Panama.

After I had viewed video documentation of BANDA DE MI HOGAR and engaging in a lengthy discussion with the artist, Velez decided to ask Señora Sanchez if I might audition to be a majorette. As I was curious and never expected to keep up with these very young marching musical talents, I showed up outside Sanchez's beauty salon to learn a few routines. Expecting my young instructor and Señora Sanchez to laugh at my novice North-of-the-border-moves, I was astonished when they asked me to attend another rehearsal to prepare me to be "Major Majorette" in Valez's BANDA DE MI HOGAR's final performance on the last day of "Multiple City." After several nights of restless sleep, I awoke early Sunday, took a taxi to the salon to have beauty school students do my make-up and hair and let the six teenage majorettes help me into a costume that was several sizes too small. We boarded a "red devil" bus crowded with musicians and headed for the "Canal Zone." After the bus and band were spuriously denied access to the scheduled parade site, Velez and the exhibition organizers decided to move to the central square in San Filipe. Back in the area that I had visited on my first day in Panama City, surrounded by the run-down ornate design of the former bank buildings and hotels, alongside Yoan Capote's trash dumpsters, I concentrated on twirling my large tasseled baton in time with the majorette's hips and the band master's horn directing cymbals, tubas, clarinets, and drummers to play their version of "Gonna Fly Now," also known as "The *Rocky* Theme."

I tried to avoid conscious contact with colleagues, new acquaintances, and strangers in the crowd, but suddenly the raised eyes of "Multiple City" curator Gerardo Mosquera caught me by surprise. He seemed consumed with a mixture of disbelief and pure satisfaction. For a brief moment I believe we enjoyed a collaborative sense of accomplishment, one best conveyed in person, or, when not possible, in the first person. Thus my once planned objective reading of this exhibition or of this place had become instead something which to some might read like a new script for *National Lampoon's Panama Vacation.*

When my embarrassment subsides, I have to think seriously about my encounter in Panama City. Admittedly, participation might have corrupted my ability to evaluate the exhibition's shortcomings or its placement within a chronology of contemporary art exhibitions. I still return to that exchange of glances. I went from viewing and reporting on an exhibition of contemporary art (as I have done for more than a decade) to participating and even becoming part of the work exhibited. I came to see what the curators had done and ended up letting them see me or, rather, see me being seen.

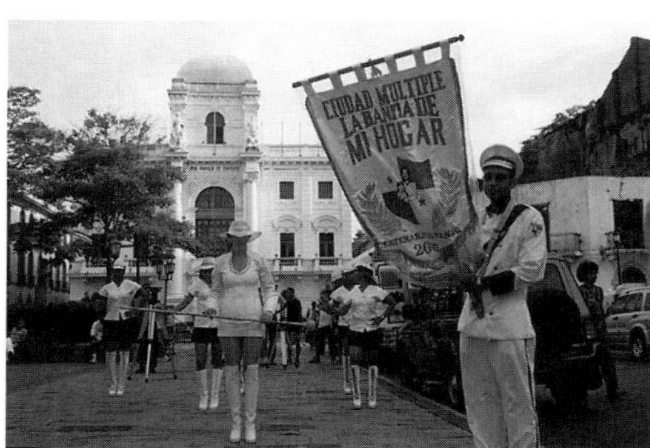

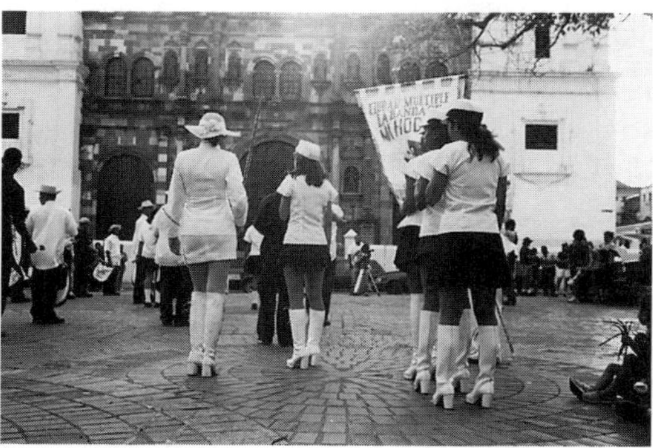

HUMBERTO VELEZ, LA BANDA DE MI HOGAR, 2003, final performance on the last day of "Multiple City" / Parade am letzten Ausstellungstag. (PHOTOS: GUSTAVO ARAUJO)

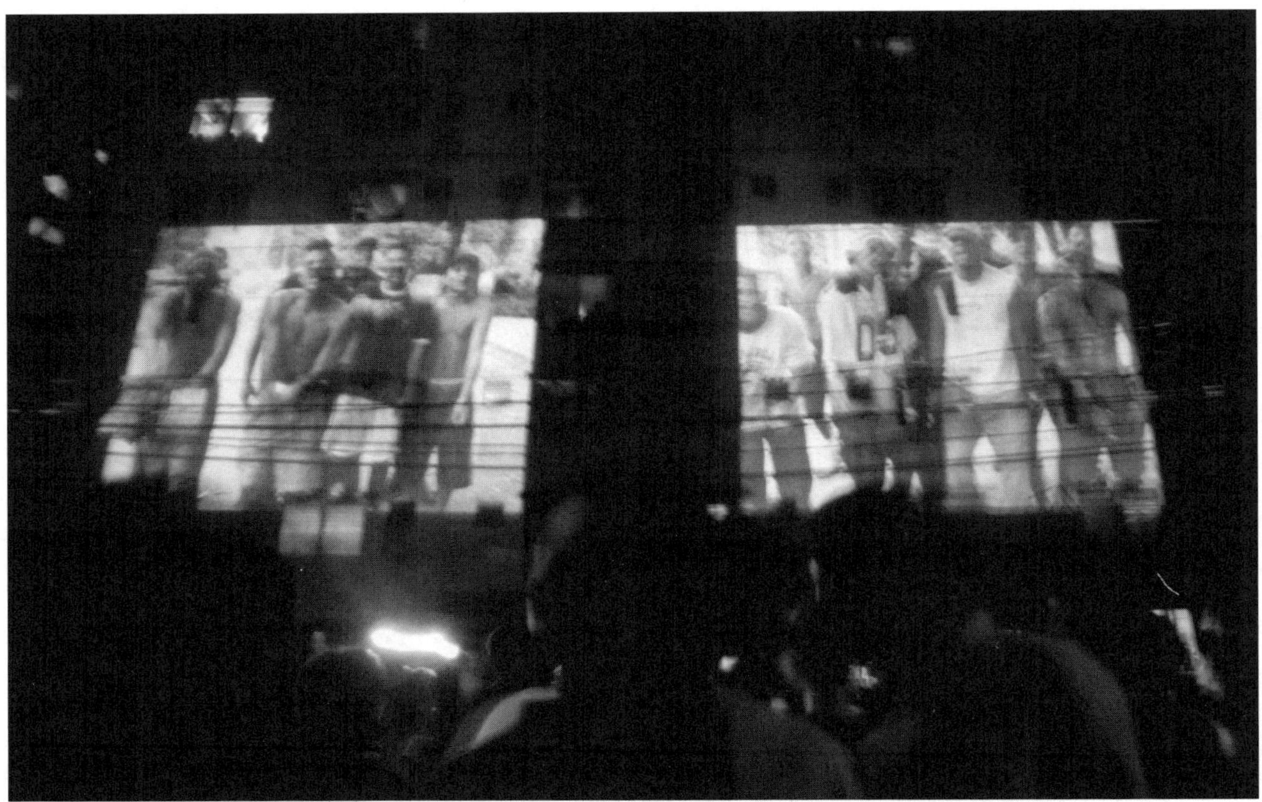

Beim Sehen gesehen

CAY SOPHIE RABINOWITZ

Die Ausstellung «Culture in Action», die Mary Jane Jacobs 1993 in Chicago organisierte, präsentierte eine Serie von Künstler- und Nachbarschaftsprojekten, die die Kunst zunehmend aus der selbstreferenziellen Ideologie der Museen herauslöste und als soziale und öffentliche Praxis präsentierte. Auch wenn «Culture in Action» von Vorgängerausstellungen inspiriert gewesen sein mag, und trotz der zahlreichen ehrgeizigen Versuche der letzten Dekade, visuelle Kultur zu demokratisieren, haben es wenige Ausstellungen geschafft, mehr als nur eine «von oben verordnete» Verbreitung kultureller Werte oder eine Einebnung der Kriterien für Museumskunst auf unterstem Niveau zu erreichen. Dieser Zustand wurde zudem von Politikern verschärft, die zusammenhanglose Sammelausstellungen mit Kunst aus ihren Wahlkreisen eröffneten oder Werke von Hobbykünstlern und Kindern in die Museen brachten unter dem Vorwand im Sinne der Kunst zu handeln.

Vor kurzem erhielten meine Gedanken zum Thema Ausstellungen im öffentlichen Raum neue Anregung durch die Einladung, nach Panama City zu reisen und die von Adrienne Samos und Gerardo Mosquera organisierte Ausstellung «Multiple City» zu besuchen. «Multiple City» fand in keiner Institution statt und kein Museum fungierte als Wirt oder Schmarotzer. Die Ausstellung lud vielmehr zwölf internationale und lokale Künstler ein, Arbeiten in, über und für Panama City

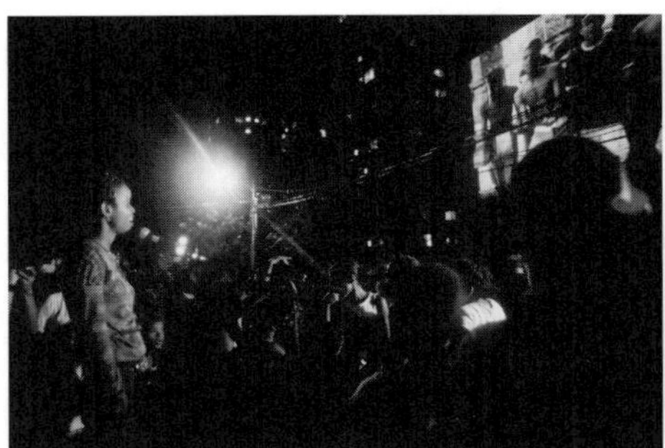

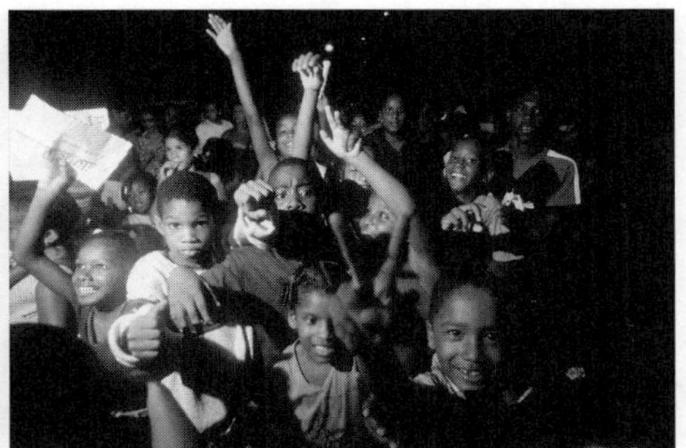

BROOKE ALFARO, NINE, 2003, the dual video projection and its public, during the exhibition "Multiple City" in Panama City / die Videodoppelprojektion und ihr Publikum. (PHOTOS: FUNDACION ARPA)

zu entwickeln, in diesem einzigartig hybriden, urbanen Zentrum jener schmalen Landmasse, welche die beiden amerikanischen Kontinente verbindet. So wurde die Stadt zur Plattform und die einzelnen Arbeiten zu Teilen einer Erzählung, die weder von der Weite der Landschaft noch vom White Cube bestimmt war.

Viele Arbeiten versuchten das rissige soziale Gewebe dieser ehemals besetzten Kanalstadt mit ihren diversen und konfliktreichen ethnischen und kulturellen Traditionen, ihren kommerziellen Banken und übervölkerten Vorstädten auszuloten, und die erfolgreichsten schafften es, das Publikum einzubeziehen und lokale Geschichte(n) aufzudecken ohne auf vorgefasste Meinungen zurückzugreifen. Sie verzichteten darauf, Reformstrategien zu entwickeln, Mitleid zu erregen oder besondere Privilegien anzubieten. Stattdessen produzierten die Künstler neue Arbeiten für spezifische Orte und ermöglichten den Bewohnern Panama Citys die Teilnahme und Besuchern wie mir die Möglichkeit, mehr zu lernen als das, was in Büchern und Lexika steht. Einige Künstler arbeiteten in Medien oder Formaten, die für ihr übriges Werk untypisch sind. Ghada Amer, zum Beispiel, zeigte nicht die mit der Nähmaschine produzierten Bilder nackter Frauen in eindeutigen Posen, für die sie bekannt ist, sondern schuf Plakatwände, auf denen chinesische Sprichwörter im Comicstil dargestellt sind, und nahm so auf zwei in Panama geläufige kulturelle Elemente Bezug. Durch diese Arbeiten fand ich Zugang zur Stadt und ihrem bunten Bevölkerungsgemisch, den drastisch divergierenden Lebensstandards, aber auch zu den Spuren ihrer Geschichte, die an verwitterten Hausfassaden und sozialen Infrastrukturen ablesbar sind. Und da «Multiple City» ohne didaktisches Ziel angetreten war, kehrte ich in meine Redaktion zurück mit der Frage, wie und warum es dieser Ausstellung gelungen war, mir so viel über Panama beizubringen.

An meinem ersten Nachmittag in Panama City besuchte ich die Orte, an denen Arbeiten installiert waren, geführt von Assistenzkurator Ramon Zafrani, dessen Beschreibung der Materialien, Kompositionen und Inhalte der einzelnen Werke in eine ausführliche Ortsbeschreibung und lokale Kulturgeschichte mündete, die mir schliesslich zu meinem patchworkartig zusammengetragenen Verständnis Panama Citys verhalf. Zafrani berichtete von den unterschiedlichen (meist ablehnenden) Reaktionen konservativer panamaischer Würdenträger (oft ehemalige Noriega-Sympatisanten) auf die Arbeiten, während wir in überbordend bunten, so genannten «Rote Teufel»-Bussen fuhren, die von den gleichen Graffitikünstlern bemalt worden waren, die auch Ghada Amers Plakatwände ausgeführt hatten. Wir durchquerten ein in wirtschaftlich-gesellschaftlichem Aufschwung begriffenes Ghetto, wo der Präsidentenpalast von zweierlei Wachpersonal beschützt wird: Pfauen und Paramilitär. Die Arbeit ANALYSIS OF BEAUTY (Analyse der Schönheit, 2003) des kubanischen Künstlers Yoan Capote unterstrich den komplexen Charakter dieses Stadtbezirks, San Felipe: Capote verzierte zehn Mülltonnen mit dekorativ gemusterten Stoffbezügen und -bändern. Eine solche Mülltonne stand neben der französischen Botschaft und mir fiel auf, wie der weisse Spitzenstoff der Tonne mit dem prunkvollen Zierrat der kolonialen Architektur harmonierte. Ein paar Strassenecken weiter bemerkte ich einen dunklen offenen Hauseingang, der auf der einen Seite von einem dünnen Mann in einem viel zu grossen T-Shirt und auf der anderen von einer dekorierten Mülltonne flankiert war. Zafrani erklärte, dass die Anwohner begonnen hätten, die Mülltonnen zu ihren Häusern zu rollen. Und wenig später erfuhr ich aus der Zeitung, dass

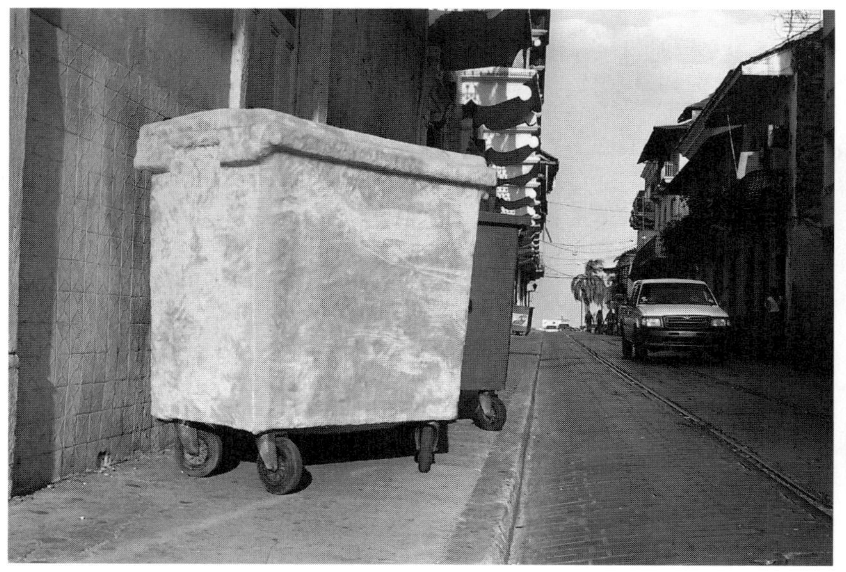

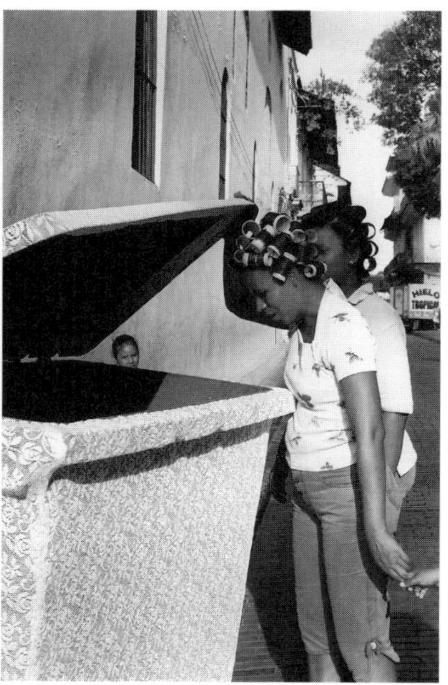

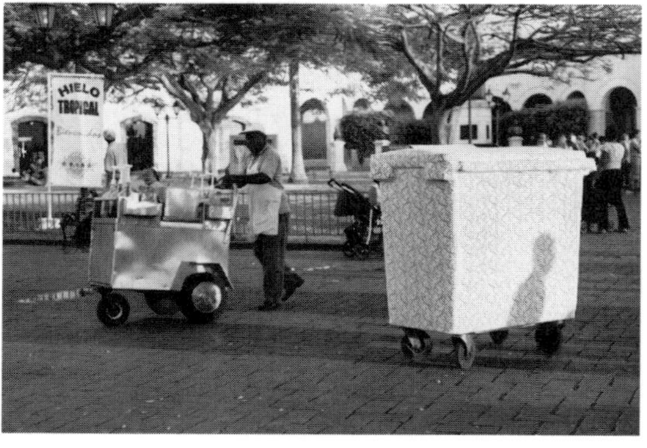

YOAN CAPOTE, ANALYSIS OF BEAUTY, 2003, *mixed media sculpture* / ANALYSE DER SCHÖNHEIT. (PHOTOS: FUNDACION ARPA)

die Anwohner, meist Hausbesetzer der dritten Generation, die Mülltonnen zu ihren Häusern geschafft hätten, wo sie diese ganz normal für ihre Abfälle benützten, sie jedoch mit besonderer Vorsicht behandelten um die feinen Details der künstlerischen Arbeit zu bewahren.

Brooke Alfaros Arbeit NINE (Neun, 2003) war ein durchschlagender Erfolg und verriet viel über die Sozialstrukturen, den Kommerz und die Kultur der Stadt. Alfaro arbeitete monatelang mit zwei rivalisierenden Strassenbanden aus der Slumgegend Barraza und produzierte eine Doppelbild-Videoprojektion, die je eine Gang zeigt, wie sie ein Lied von Roockie, einem der bekanntesten lokalen Rapper, singt. An zwei Abenden hatten Gäste und Stadtbewohner die Möglichkeit, per Bus nach Barraza zu fahren, wo die Videos nebeneinander auf die Hauswand eines Sozialwohnungsblocks projiziert wurden.

Als sich die beiden Gangs mit ihren übergrossen Jeans, ärmellosen T-Shirts, Messerwunden und Tätowierungen langsam in Bewegung setzen, schwenkt die Kamera allmählich aus der Frontalansicht der beiden Gruppen zur Profilansicht, so dass sich beide Gruppen gegenüberstehen. Die Anspannung dieser Konfrontation steigert sich über einen längeren Zeitraum hinweg und wird erst vom Geschrei der Kinder aus dem Quartier durchbrochen, als einer der Anführer seinem Gegenüber einen Fussball zuschiesst. Dieser Moment, der klar als Herausforderung und nicht etwa als Geste der Versöhnung zu verstehen ist, verdeutlicht die Vergeblichkeit der zahllosen sozialen Reformprojekte. Die Kunst mag in einen Bezirk eingedrungen sein, der als gefährlich und unzugänglich galt, und die beiden rivalisierenden Banden mögen sich zur Kooperation bereit erklärt haben, aber sobald die Proben vorbei sind, werden sie wieder aufeinander schiessen.

Auch wenn die meisten Besucher in diese Gegend gekommen waren, weil sie sich von Alfaros Arbeit einen Lösungsversuch für einige der augenfälligsten Probleme des Bezirks erhofft hatten, blieb jegliche Form von Konfliktlösung aus. Stattdessen erzeugte die sorgfältige Choreographierung von Darstellern und Kamera eine erbarmungslose Spannung. Alfaro arbeitet oft mit sozial Randständigen und seine Werke hinterfragen fast immer auf kontroverse und komplexe Weise das Verhältnis zwischen Künstler, Darsteller und Betrachter. Der Künstler verbirgt die soziale Ungleichheit zwischen sich und seinen Darstellern nie und macht die potenzielle Ausbeutung der Unterprivilegierten als Darsteller deutlich. Obwohl die Genauigkeit von Alfaros Beobachtung schon fast persönlichkeitsverletzend ist, zeigt sich die ausführlich untersuchte postkolonialistische Problematik um Orient und Okzident, Beobachter und Beobachtetes, begehrenden Betrachter und Objekt der Begierde in ihrer ganzen Komplexität. Am Ende stellen Alfaros Videoarbeiten das Tun des Künstlers selbst zur Debatte: Der im Ghetto arbeitende Regisseur/Filmemacher/Künstler wird zum Objekt seiner eigenen Kritik und die Besucherin/Betrachterin/Kritikerin beginnt, ihre eigene Rolle zu überdenken.

Mit jedem Tag, jeder Arbeit und jeder neuen Begegnung verstand ich Panama Citys komplexe Identität besser und gleichzeitig veränderte sich auch mein Zugang zur Ausstellung. Ich wurde mehr und mehr zur Ethnologin, einer teilnehmenden Betrachterin, die Feldversuche durchführt und die eigenen Erfahrungen und lokalen Gebräuche aufzeichnet. Die radikalste Veränderung meiner professionellen Berichterstattung bewirkte jedoch Humberto Velez und seine Arbeit BANDA DE MI HOGAR (2003). Velez arbeitete mit einer Bläser-und-Schlagzeug-Marschkapelle zusammen, die aus vornehmlich

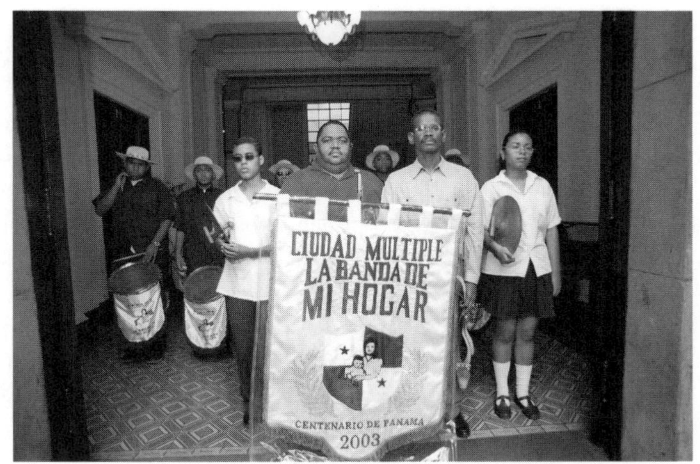

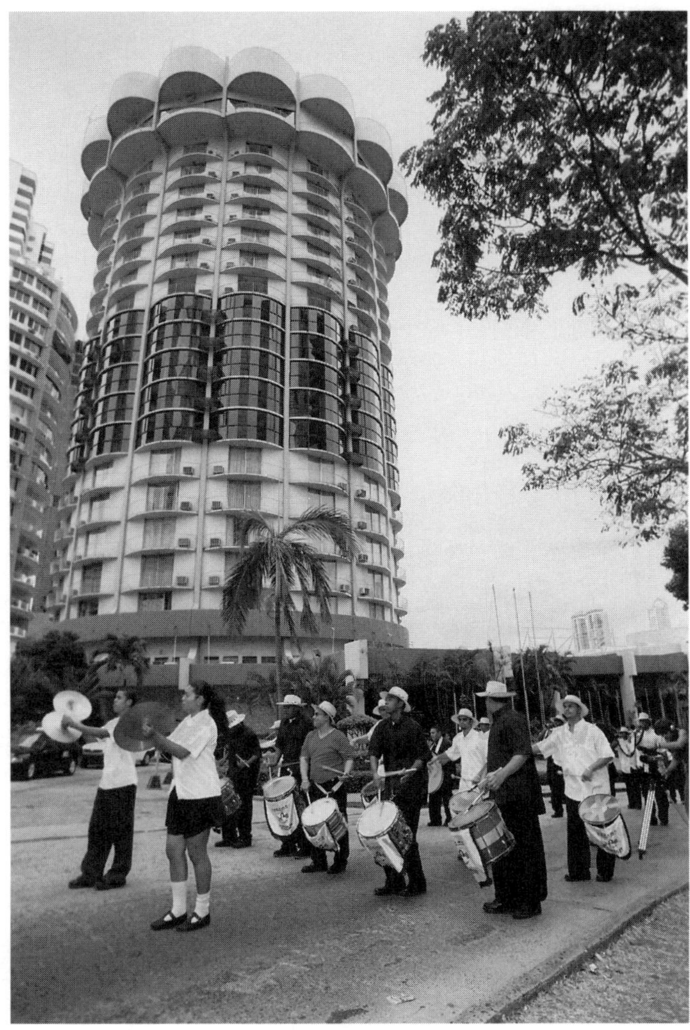

HUMBERTO VELEZ, LA BANDA DE MI HOGAR, 2003. (PHOTOS: FUNDACION ARPA)

schwarzen Musikern und Majoretten jeden Alters besteht und zu einer von der Sanchez-Familie geleiteten Berufsschule gehört. Obwohl die Kapelle Banda del Hogar sehr populär ist und sogar im Radio zu hören ist, wird sie jeweils nur einmal im Jahr, am Unabhängigkeitstag, zur offiziellen Parade geladen. Velez und die Kapelle brachen mit dieser strikten Tradition und paradierten mehrmals an ganz gewöhnlichen Tagen. Sie zeigten ihre selbst gemachten Uniformen und Standarten auf öffentlichen Plätzen und belebten Strassen und spielten ihre Sambarhythmen, die ganz anders klingen als die Musik der anderen Kapellen in Panama, welche eher dem Vorbild amerikanischer Militärkapellen nacheifern.

Nachdem ich die Videodokumentation der Arbeit BANDA DE MI HOGAR gesehen und mich in eine lange Diskussion mit dem Künstler verstrickt hatte, fragte Velez Señora Sanchez, ob ich für eine Rolle als Majorette vorsprechen könne. Neugierig, aber überzeugt, dass ich sowieso nicht mit den anderen jungen Majoretten und ihrem musikalischen Talent würde mithalten können, ging ich zu Frau Sanchez' Schönheitssalon um ein paar Grundschritte zu lernen. Ich erwartete, dass meine junge Ausbildnerin und Señora Sanchez herzlich über die ungelenken Bewegungen dieses nordamerikanischen Greenhorns lachen würden, umso grösser der Schock, als ich zu einer weiteren Probe gebeten wurde, die mich auf die Rolle als Haupt-Majorette in der letzten öffentlichen Performance von Velez' BANDA DE MI HOGAR am letzten Ausstellungstag vorbereiten sollte. Nach einigen schlaflosen Nächten fuhr ich am Sonntag früh per Taxi zum Schönheitssalon, wo Kosmetikschülerinnen mir Make-up und Frisur richteten, und liess mir von sechs Teenagern, ebenfalls Majoretten, in ein um etliche Nummern zu knappes Kostüm helfen. Wir bestiegen einen «Roten Teufel», der bereits mit Musikern voll gepackt war, und fuhren Richtung Kanalzone. Nachdem sowohl Bus als auch Kapelle der Zugang zur Kanalzone verweigert wurde, entschieden Velez und die Ausstellungsorganisatoren, die Veranstaltung auf den zentralen Platz in San Felipe zu verlegen. Just an dem Ort, den ich an meinem ersten Tag in Panama City besucht hatte, umgeben von den ehemals prunkvollen Banken und Hotels und von Yoan Capotes' dekorierten Mülltonnen, konzentrierte ich mich darauf, einen grossen mit Fransen verzierten Stab im Takt des Hüftschwungs der jungen Majoretten und der Trompeten, Zimbeln, Tuben, Klarinetten und Trommeln zu bewegen, die eine eigene Version von «Gonna Fly Now» spielten, besser bekannt als «The *Rocky* Theme».

Ich vermied den direkten Blickkontakt mit meinen Kollegen, neuen Bekannten und sogar den fremden Betrachtern in der Menge, wurde jedoch plötzlich von den grossen Augen des Kurators der Ausstellung, Gerardo Mosquera, überrascht. Er schien ungläubig und zugleich von grösster Genugtuung erfüllt. Für einen kurzen Moment war es, als ob wir ein gemeinsames Gefühl des Gelingens teilten, das sich am ehesten im unmittelbaren Erlebnis, oder, wenn dies nicht möglich ist, in der ersten Person Singular vermitteln lässt. So wurde mein geplanter objektiver Besuch der Ausstellung und des Landes zu etwas, was auf den ersten Blick wie eine Drehbuchfolge für *Versteckte Kamera in Panama* klingen mochte.

Doch je mehr das Gefühl peinlicher Verlegenheit wich, desto intensiver musste ich über meine Begegnungen in Panama City nachdenken. Möglicherweise hat die aktive Teilnahme mein Urteilsvermögen in Bezug auf die Versäumnisse der Ausstellung oder ihren Stellenwert vor dem Hintergrund anderer zeitgenössischer Kunstausstellungen beeinträchtigt. Immer wieder muss ich an jenen Blickwechsel denken. Statt eine Ausstellung zeitgenössischer Kunst lediglich anzuschauen und von ihr zu berichten (was ich seit über zehn Jahren betreibe), wirkte ich an einer der gezeigten Arbeiten mit und wurde schliesslich zu einem Teil von ihr. Ich war gekommen um zu sehen, was die Kuratoren geleistet hatten, und nun liess ich zu, dass sie mich sahen beziehungsweise mir beim Sehen zusahen.

(Übersetzung: Christian Rattemeyer)

GHADA AMER, CHINESE PROVERBS, 2003, paintings on wood / CHINESISCHE SPRICHWÖRTER, Malerei auf Holz. (PHOTOS: FUNDACION ARPA)

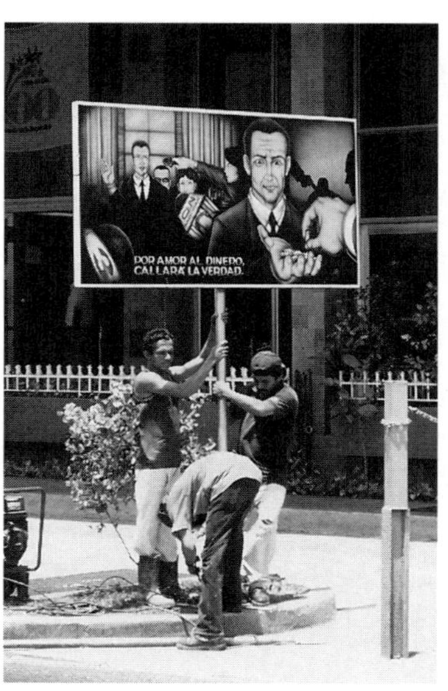

CUMULUS

Aus Europa

IN JEDER AUSGABE VON PARKETT PEILT EINE CUMULUS-WOLKE AUS AMERIKA UND EINE AUS EUROPA DIE INTERESSIERTEN KUNSTFREUNDE AN. SIE TRÄGT PERSÖNLICHE RÜCKBLICKE, BEURTEILUNGEN UND DENKWÜRDIGE BEGEGNUNGEN MIT SICH – ALS JEWEILS GANZ EIGENE DARSTELLUNG EINER BERUFLICHEN AUSEINANDERSETZUNG.

IN DIESEM BAND ÄUSSERN SICH JENS HOFFMANN, FREISCHAFFENDER KRITIKER UND KURATOR IN BERLIN, SOWIE CAY SOPHIE RABINOWITZ, PARKETT-REDAKTORIN IN NEW YORK.

THIS IS TINO SEHGAL

JENS HOFFMANN

Tino Sehgal möchte nichts produzieren. Zumindest nichts, was als herkömmliches, physisch vorhandenes Kunstwerk betrachtet werden könnte. Er möchte keine greifbaren Dinge schaffen; es liegt ihm nichts daran, eine sichtbare Spur zu hinterlassen. Sein Medium ist das Immaterielle und er benutzt es, um äusserst flüchtige Werke hervorzubringen, die den traditionellen Museumskontext herausfordern.

Auch wenn Sehgals Werk auf den ersten Blick recht zugänglich erscheinen mag, ist es doch ausserordentlich komplex und oszilliert zwischen verschiedenen künstlerischen und intellektuellen Spannungsfeldern, um Grundlagen der heutigen Gesellschaft in Frage zu stellen. Sehgal ist als Künstler erst vor kurzem in Erscheinung getreten, hat aber – unter Künstlern, Kuratoren und Kritikern gleichermassen – bereits eine bemerkenswerte Reputation erlangt. Diese gründet vor allem in der Charakteristik seiner Arbeiten, die dem Besucher oft buchstäblich ins Gesicht springen. Der Schlüssel zu einem Verständnis von Sehgals künstlerischem Anliegen liegt einerseits in seiner Beschäftigung mit Choreographie und andererseits in seinem Studium der politischen Ökonomie: Beides ist zentral im Hinblick auf seine Positionierung in der bildenden Kunst. Die Konzeptkunst und insbesondere Werke von Künstlern wie Michael Asher, Marcel Broodthaers, Daniel Buren oder James Coleman sind signifikante Vorläufer. Auch wenn Sehgal einen direkten Einfluss dieser Künstler nicht hervorheben würde, besetzt sein Werk letztlich dennoch vergleichbares Terrain, da es das filigrane Fundament der Kunst und ihre Konventionen, ihre ungeschriebenen Gesetze und Machtstrukturen hinterfragt, indem es die Beziehung zwischen Mensch und Objekt einer genauen Prüfung unterzieht.

Sehgal sieht den untrennbaren Zusammenhang zwischen Kunst und Gesellschaft aus der Perspektive ihrer

Note: Le Plein 2003

~~Connemara Landscape~~, ~~1980~~, is to be experienced as an exhibition ~~projected image~~. The artist kindly requests that the piece ~~image~~ is not photographed or visually recorded.

♡ Tino Sehgal

~~© James Coleman~~

identischen ökonomischen Prämissen: der Produktion und des Austauschs von Gütern und Waren. Seine Werke fordern diese Prämissen heraus, indem sie Bedeutung durch die Transformation von Handlungen in einer transitorischen Situation hervorbringen, und nicht durch die Transformation physischer Materialien. Sein Werk ist hoch politisch, weil es ein System in Frage stellt, das auf einer kulturellen Hierarchie fusst, die Gegenständliches und Stofflichkeit glorifiziert. Sehgal schafft flüchtige Gesten, die auf der Bewegung oder dem gesprochenen Wort basieren (Tanz oder Gesang). Er inszeniert diese auf höchst artifizielle Weise und es ist äusserst interessant zu beobachten, was passiert, wenn sie in dem musealen Raum stattfinden, der gewöhnlich für die Ewigkeit geschaffene Objekte beherbergt.

Seine bisher vielleicht bekannteste Arbeit ist OHNE TITEL (2001), die im Moderna Museet in Stockholm uraufgeführt wurde. Das Werk hat eigentlich mehrere Titel, doch der Künstler zieht es vor, diese jeweils erst bei der Aufführung mündlich zu verkünden. Auf Deutsch heisst es ...DAS XX. JAHRHUNDERT; auf Französisch MUSÉE D'ART MODERNE, SECTION XXIÈME SIÈCLE, DÉPARTEMENT, und auf Englisch 20 MINUTES FOR THE 20TH CENTURY. Sehgal wollte ein Stück machen, dessen Bedeutung nicht im Inhalt oder in der Form liegt, sondern das vielmehr den spezifischen Produktionsmodus ausstellt, der dem Medium Tanz inhärent ist. Er führt OHNE TITEL selbst auf und stellt offensichtlich eine Verbindung her zwischen dem institutionellen Kontext des Museums beziehungsweise dessen archivarischer Funktion und dem Kontext des Tanzes. Was Sehgal macht, ist zwar simpel, aber in seiner konzeptuellen Komplexität schlicht brillant. Er wird selbst zum Museum, einem Museum des Tanzes. Für die Dauer von 55 Minuten sehen wir ihn alles tanzen, was die Ästhetik des Tanzes im zwanzigsten Jahrhundert ausmacht. Von Isadora Duncan bis Merce Cunningham und jüngeren Protagonisten der internationalen Tanzszene wie Xavier Le Roy zeigt Sehgal einen Abriss der Geschichte des Tanzes. Angesichts der Tatsache, dass Sehgal völlig neue Elemente in den Museumskontext einführt, ist es letztlich aber gar nicht so wichtig, welche Choreographen er in seinem Stück Revue passieren lässt. In der Tat wird an keiner Stelle ein choreographisches Werk rekonstruiert, vielmehr eignet er sich die verschiedenen Formen des Tanzes an und kreiert daraus eigene Bewegungsabläufe, so dass das Publikum konsequent mit einer Historisierungspraxis konfrontiert wird, die der des Museums entgegenläuft. Noch erstaunlicher ist, dass Sehgal den spezifischen Produktionsmodus des Tanzes nicht nur intellektuell, sondern auch physisch zu erfahren sucht, indem er sämtliche Tanzstile durchexerziert und sich selbst in ein lebendes Archiv der Choreographie verwandelt. OHNE TITEL ist eine frühe Arbeit, die eine klare Gratwanderung zwischen Tanz und bildender Kunst darstellt. Sie ist nicht für den Ausstellungsraum, sondern für die Bühne eines Museumsauditoriums gedacht. Und es ist genau diese Veränderung des Dispositivs, die im Zentrum von Sehgals Arbeit steht. Es werden nicht länger immobile, starre Gegenstände von angeblich ewiger Gültigkeit gezeigt, sondern Bewegung, Transformation und Vergänglichkeit sind jetzt die leitenden Prinzipien.

Sehgal interessiert die Idee des Œuvre und deshalb ist er bei der Platzierung seiner Arbeiten in Ausstellungen und Institutionen äusserst sorgfältig. Man merkt, dass ihn der Kontext, den er abzulehnen scheint, gleichzeitig anzieht. Gute Beispiele dafür liefern eine Reihe von Arbeiten, in denen er Museumswärter einsetzt, wie etwa in THIS IS GOOD (2001), einer Arbeit, die 2002 im Rahmen der Gruppenausstellung «I promise it's political» im Kölner Museum Ludwig gezeigt wurde. Beim Betreten des entsprechenden Ausstellungsraums erblickte das Publikum einen Wärter, der ohne ersichtlichen Grund plötzlich von einem Bein aufs andere hüpfte, dabei ein paar Sekunden lang die Arme vor dem Körper kreisen liess und schliesslich sagte: «TINO SEHGAL, THIS IS GOOD, 2001. Im Besitz des Künstlers.» Jedes Mal, wenn ein Besucher den Raum betrat, wiederholte die Aufsicht diese Bewegungen und denselben Satz, und zwar während der gesamten Dauer der Ausstellung. THIS IS GOOD ist mit Sicherheit mehr als die blosse Verwandlung eines Museumswärters in ein Kunstwerk. Mit Hilfe der Choreographie wirft Sehgal ein neues Licht auf das Verhältnis zwischen Kunst und Kunstgegenstand, Objekt und Subjekt, Museum und Gesellschaft. Wenn Sehgal gerade jene Personen, die physisch unsere Traditionen und unser kulturelles Erbe schützen, als Medium seiner Arbeit einsetzt und sie darüber hinaus zum mündlichen Übermittler der Werkbezeichnung macht, rüttelt er fraglos an den Grundfesten der herkömmlichen Kunstpraxis. In THIS IS PROPAGANDA (2002), einem Werk, das unter anderem an der Biennale in Venedig 2003 Bestandteil der «Utopia Station» war, wird nicht Tanz, sondern Gesang als transitorischer Akt eingesetzt. Der Künstler engagierte für die Ausstellung eine Gruppe von Sängerinnen als Aufseherinnen und bat sie, jedes Mal, wenn ein neuer Besucher auftauchte, «This is propaganda, you know, you know» zu singen und dann den Satz zu sprechen: «TINO SEHGAL, THIS IS PROPAGANDA, 2002, im Besitz des Künstlers». Während THIS IS GOOD mit der Ambivalenz der Titelaussage spielt – worauf bezieht sich THIS IS GOOD, auf seine Arbeit, auf die Ausstellung oder das Museum? –, ist THIS IS PROPAGANDA weit weniger kryptisch und bezieht sich offensichtlich auf das, was wir im Ausstellungsraum sehen und hören: auf Sehgals eigene Arbeit und auf die anderen Werke in der Ausstellung. Diese Arbeiten propagieren zwei völlig verschiedene Produktionsweisen; die eine stützt sich auf die Transformation von Materie, die andere auf jene flüchtiger Handlungen.

Man könnte annehmen, Sehgal verurteile den Kunstmarkt und seine Ökonomie, tatsächlich betrachtet er ihn jedoch als integralen Bestandteil des Kunstbetriebs, der ihm erlaubt, seinen eigenen Ansatz weiterzuentwickeln. Eine interessante Wendung brachte seine erste Ausstellung im kommerziellen Rahmen, als er die Arbeit LE PLEIN in der Galerie Jan Mot in Brüssel zeigte (20. Februar – 5. April 2003). Das vom Galeristen und seiner Assistentin ausgeführte Werk bestand aus allen Arbeiten, die der Künstler bis dato geschaffen hatte, einschliesslich einiger noch nicht realisierter Projekte. LE PLEIN begann mit einem leeren Galerieraum. Jedes Mal, wenn ein Besucher eintrat, traten der Galerist oder seine Assistentin rückwärts aus ihrem Büro in die Galerie und sagten: «Ceci n'est pas un vide» (Dies ist keine Leere). Dann begannen sie Sehgals gesamtes Repertoire vorzuführen und boten die Arbeiten zum Verkauf an.

Der Verkauf eines Werks von Sehgal ist an sich beinah schon ein Kunstwerk und ist offenkundig völlig unkonventionell: Es wird ein Termin mit einem Notar vereinbart, bei welchem sich der Künstler und ein potenzieller Käufer treffen. Sehgal stellt dann mündlich einen Vertrag auf, den der Notar als Zeuge beglaubigt, worauf die Transaktion rechtsgültig wird: Der Künstler bekommt das Geld bar auf die Hand und die Arbeit geht in den Besitz des

Note:

~~Connemara Landscape~~ this is propaganda, ~~1980~~ 2002, is to be experienced as ~~a projected image~~ sung. The artist kindly requests that the ~~image~~ piece is not photographed or visually recorded.

♡ Tino Sehgal ~~© James Coleman~~

Sammlers über. Es gibt kein Zertifikat, keine schriftliche Vereinbarung, keine Quittung und auch sonst keine sichtbare Spur des getätigten Verkaufs. Sehgal realisiert also endlich die seit langem proklamierte Entmaterialisierung des Kunstobjekts.

Auch wenn Sehgals Werk eine noch so kritische Position gegenüber dem Kunstbetrieb und seinen Mechanismen einnimmt, so ist es doch unübersehbar, dass es diesen Rahmen auch immer wieder affirmiert und ihn braucht, um selbst existieren zu können; in diesem Sinn enthält es – wie der Künstler bestätigt – durchaus ein konservatives Element. Sehgal besteht darauf, dass seine Arbeiten bildende Kunst sind, denn nur so sind sie in der Position, die der Ausstellungspraxis zugrunde liegenden Überzeugungen in Frage zu stellen. Vielleicht braucht die Kunst hin und wieder einen Künstler wie Sehgal, der ihren Codes und Konventionen gründlich misstraut. Beschäftigt man sich jedoch eingehender mit seinem Werk, wird deutlich, dass er dies nur kann, weil er absolut Teil dessen ist, was er dekonstruiert. Sehgal will das Kunstsystem nicht auflösen, er will es meistern.

(Übersetzung: Uta Goridis unter Mitwirkung des Autors)

THIS IS TINO SEHGAL

JENS HOFFMANN

Tino Sehgal does not want to produce anything. Or at least anything that could be perceived as a conventional, physically existing work of art. He does not want to create tangible objects, nor is he interested in leaving any visible trace. His medium is immateriality, and he uses it to generate highly provisional pieces of art that challenge the traditional museological context.

Even though at first glance Sehgal's work seems rather accessible, it is enormously complex, oscillating between various artistic and intellectual fields to radically question the groundwork of contemporary society. Sehgal has only been making art for a short while, but he has already gained a considerable reputation among artists, curators, and critics alike. This stems particularly from the distinctiveness of his works, which often literally jump right into the audience's face. The keys to an understanding of Sehgal's artistic concerns are his background in choreography and his education in political economy, since both play a fundamental role in the way he situates himself in the sphere of art. Conceptual art, especially the work of artists such as Michael Asher, Marcel Broodthaers, Daniel Buren, and James Coleman, is a significant precedent. Sehgal would refuse to acknowledge being directly influenced by such artists, yet his work ultimately occupies similar territory by questioning the delicate substructure of art and its conventions, unwritten rules, and power by looking closely at the relationship between humans and objects.

Sehgal views the art world as being completely interrelated with the rest of society and functioning along identical economic conditions, namely the production and exchange of goods and commodities. He is interested in challenging these conditions by creating works that appear as the transformation of acts and the production of meaning through a transitory situation, rather than as a transformation of solid materials. His work is intensely political, as it questions a system that is built on a cultural hierarchy that glorifies objects and materiality. Sehgal creates fleeting gestures, based on movement or spoken word (dancing or singing). He stages them in a highly artificial manner, and it is extremely interesting to see what happens when he places them in museological spaces that are mostly used to house objects created for eternity.

Perhaps his best-known work to date is UNTITLED (2001), which was first presented in 2001 at the Moderna Museet in Stockholm. The piece in fact has titles, but the artist decided to only announce them orally when he is presenting the work. In German it is called ...DAS XX. JAHRHUNDERT, in French MUSÉE D'ART MODERNE, SECTION XXÈME SIÈCLE, DÉPARTEMENT, and in English 20 MINUTES FOR THE 20TH CENTURY. Sehgal wanted to make a piece that would have no meaning in terms of its content or form but would focus primarily on exposing the specific form of production inherent to the medium of dance. In UNTITLED he performs the piece himself and clearly connects the institutional context of the museum and its role as an archive of art to the context of dance. What Sehgal does is rather simple, but brilliant in its conceptual complexity. He turns himself into a museum, a museum of dance. For the duration of 55 minutes, we see him dancing the most significant dance aesthetics of the twentieth century. Sehgal displays a survey of the history of modern dance from Isadora Duncan to Merce Cunningham, up to younger protagonists of the international dance scene, such as Xavier Le Roy. Ultimately, it is less significant which choreographers are reviewed in his piece, when you consider the fact that Sehgal introduces a completely different set of elements into the context of museums. Although he never actually reenacts a classic choreographic style but rather appropriates the different dance forms and creates individual moves, he confronts the audience with a consequential disarrangement of common museological practices. What is even more astonishing is that Sehgal has attempted not only to intellectually comprehend the specific mode of dance production, but also to physically experience it while dancing in all the various styles, turning himself into a living archive of choreography. UNTITLED is an early piece that clearly navigates between the practice of dance and the practice of visual art. It is not supposed to take place in an exhibition space but rather on a stage in a museum auditorium, a theatrical setting, and it is exactly this change of dispositive that is at the core of Sehgal's work. No longer are motionless, inflexible, and supposedly eternal objects displayed, but rather the guiding principles are now movement, transformation, and ephemerality.

Sehgal is keen on building an oeuvre and is very careful about how he places his pieces into exhibitions and institutions. One realizes that he is actually extremely attracted to the context that he seemingly despises. A good example is a series of works employing museum guards, including the piece THIS IS GOOD (2001), which was presented in a group show at the Museum Ludwig in Cologne, 2002, entitled "I promise it's political." Upon entering one of the exhibition spaces, the audience saw a guard who, for no apparent reason, suddenly began to jump from one leg to the other while rotating his arms in front of his body for a couple of seconds before saying: "Tino Sehgal, THIS IS GOOD, 2001. Courtesy the artist." Every time a visitor entered the room, the guard repeated the sequence of movements and the sentence. The guard executed the piece every day for the duration of the

Note: this is propaganda
~~Connemara Landscape~~, ~~1980~~ [2002], is to be experienced as ~~a projected image~~ [sung]. The artist kindly requests that the ~~image~~ [piece] is not photographed or visually recorded.

♡ Tino Sehgal ~~© James Coleman~~

exhibition. THIS IS GOOD is certainly more than the simple act of turning a museum guard into a work of art. By way of choreography, Sehgal offers a different perspective on issues surrounding the relationship between art and art object, object and subject, museum and society. When Sehgal uses the persons who are in fact physically guarding our traditions and our cultural heritage to express such a conception, while also turning them into the label of his piece, he clearly cracks the foundation of common art practice. THIS IS PROPAGANDA (2002), which was included in "Utopia Station" at the 50th Venice Biennale in 2003, does not employ dancing, but instead singing as a momentary act. The artist hired a group of female singers to work as guards during the exhibition and asked them to sing, every time a new visitor entered the space: "This is Propaganda, you know, you know." Then they would say: "Tino Sehgal, THIS IS PROPAGANDA, 2002. Courtesy the artist." While THIS IS GOOD introduces an ambiguous play on titles (What is the artist actually referring to with THIS IS GOOD? His work, the exhibition, or the museum?). THIS IS PROPAGANDA is less cryptic and clearly relates to what we see and hear in the exhibition space, Sehgal's own piece and the other artworks in the exhibition. These works propagate very different modes of production, one based on the transformation of material, and the other based on the transformation of transitional acts.

One would think that Sehgal condemns the art market and its economy, but in fact he sees it as an integral part of the art system that allows him to develop his particular approach even further. An interesting turn occurred when he presented the work LE PLEIN, his first exhibition in a commercial setting, at the Jan Mot Gallery in Brussels in 2003. Executed by the gallery owner and his assistant, the work consists of all of the pieces the artist has created to date, including several unrealized projects. LE PLEIN began with an empty gallery space, and every time a visitor entered, the owner or his assistant walked backward into the gallery from the office and said: "Ceci n'est pas un vide." Then they began to perform all of the works in Sehgal's repertoire and offered them for sale.

The actual act of selling a Sehgal piece is almost an artwork in its own right and is obviously completely unconventional. An appointment is arranged with a notary, during which the artist and the potential buyer meet. Thereafter Sehgal states an oral contract that is carefully witnessed by the notary who legally approves the whole transaction. The artist is immediately paid in cash and the piece becomes the possession of the collector. There is no certificate, no written agreement, no receipt, or any other trace of the sale. Thus, Sehgal finally realizes the fulfillment of the long-proclaimed dematerialization of the art object.

As much as Sehgal's work seems to maintain an unconditionally critical stance toward the context of art and its mechanisms, one also realizes that his work constantly affirms this framework and needs it to exist. Thus, as the artist readily acknowledges, his work is also somewhat conservative. He insists that his pieces are visual artworks, since that is the only way they have the power to question inherent beliefs about exhibition practices. It might be that the visual arts periodically need an artist like Sehgal to fundamentally mistrust their codes and conventions. Yet, when one carefully observes his work, it becomes apparent that he can only do so because he is also absolutely fascinated by the very thing that he tries to take apart. Sehgal does not want to dissolve the art system; he wants to master it.

Note:
this is exchange 2003
~~Connemara Landscape~~, ~~1980~~, is to be experienced as a
situation
~~projected image~~. The artist kindly requests that the Piece **~~image~~ is not photographed or visually recorded.**

Tino Sehgal
~~© James Coleman~~

BALKON

«Partnerbilder»
Thomas Struths neue Videoarbeit: READ THIS LIKE SEEING IT FOR THE FIRST TIME...

HANS RUDOLF REUST

Dabei hat der Film so etwas Interessantes an sich, was sich sonst nirgendwo anders wiederfinden lässt: er erlaubt einem nämlich, nicht zu wissen/savoir, aber zu sehen/voir, um dann im Nachhinein vielleicht zu wissen.
– Jean-Luc Godard [1)]

I. Mit einer erfolgreichen Tournee durch verschiedene Museen der USA – Dallas, Los Angeles, New York und Chicago – hat das photographische Werk von Thomas Struth weitere Anerkennung und breiteres Verständnis erfahren. Der Katalog, aber auch verschiedene Formen der Hängung haben viele bekannte Aufnahmen in anderen Konstellationen gezeigt und Vergleiche über die einzelnen Werkgruppen hinaus ermöglicht. Städtebilder, Museumsphotos, Einzel- und Familienporträts, die Blumen- und Dschungelbilder lassen – gemischt in einem Raum oder bei Durchblicken zwischen den Sälen – in je unerwarteten Nachbarschaften eine übergreifende künstlerische Haltung erkennen: Struths direkte, nie zudringliche Interpretation.

Weniger bekannt ist die Projektion, sind seine Videoarbeiten. Durch eine Auswahl von Video-Einzelporträts in der Eingangshalle des Metropolitan Museum wurde an prominenter Stelle auf diesen Aspekt seines Werkes hingewiesen. Nach Eröffnung der Ausstellung in New York hat Thomas Struth seine Arbeit in diesem Medium wieder aufgenommen: mit einem Gruppenporträt.

II. «Es hat eigentlich schon immer eine Sehnsucht gegeben oder eine Phantasie, einen Film zu machen. Aber mehr in der Hinsicht, dass ich dachte,

HANS RUDOLF REUST ist Kunstkritiker und Dozent an der Hochschule der Künste Bern.

ich möchte nicht einen kleinen Experimentalfilm machen, sondern ich müsste dann gleich eine Familiensaga drehen. Also Familienporträts, komplizierte Lebensumstände. Das hängt auch mit meiner eigenen komplexen und ungewöhnlichen Familiensituation zusammen. Es faszinieren immer die Themen, die man am eigenen Leib erfährt.»[2] Thomas Struth hatte seine Sehnsucht zum Film schon 1998 in einem Interview mit Ulrich Loock formuliert. Ein äusserer Anlass bot nun Gelegenheit, dieser Phantasie erstmals nachzugehen: Anfang September 2003 entstand aus dem Zusammenschluss der Hochschule für Musik und Theater und der Hochschule für Gestaltung, Kunst und Konservierung in Bern die erste Hochschule der Künste der Schweiz. Die Biennale Bern (4.–14. September 2003) sollte daher über ein reiches Musikprogramm hinaus auch künstlerische Beiträge umfassen. Thomas Struth nahm die Einladung der neuen Hochschule an, während vier Tagen zur Eröffnung in der grossen Halle eine Videoprojektion einzurichten. Ein Film, eine Familiensaga, konnte in der gegebenen Frist nicht entstehen. Dennoch erwuchs aus der kleinen Anfrage und einem kleinen Team eine grössere Produktion. Zunächst war da nur der Gedanke, nach den Einzelporträts ein Video-Gruppenporträt zu versuchen. Anders als bei der Konfrontation einer Person mit einer Kamera während einer Stunde, beginnt mit der Interaktion unter mehreren Menschen in der Aufzeichnung zwingend eine filmische Erzählung. Wie würde sich ein überzeugender Rahmen finden lassen, in dem die Handlung nicht erfunden, ihre Dauer nicht künstlich begrenzt werden musste?

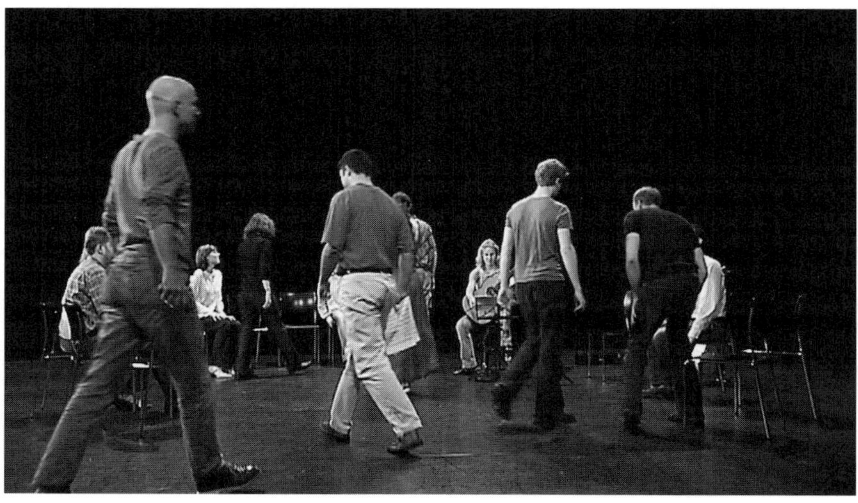

THOMAS STRUTH, READ THIS LIKE SEEING IT FOR THE FIRST TIME (FRANK BUNGARTEN UND SEINE KLASSE FÜR GITARRE AN DER MUSIK-HOCHSCHULE LUZERN), 2003, Videostills aus der 270-Min.-Videodoppelprojektion / stills from 270 min. dual video projection. (© THOMAS STRUTH & HOCHSCHULE DER KÜNSTE BERN)

Auch in seinen photographischen Porträts zeigt Struth immer wieder Menschen, mit denen ihn eine besondere persönliche Beziehung verbindet. Aus der langjährigen Freundschaft zum Gitarristen Frank Bungarten ergab sich schliesslich die Idee, eine Reihe von Gruppenlektionen aufzunehmen, wie Bungarten sie an den Musikhochschulen in Luzern und Hannover hält. Die Handlung besteht aus dem, was sich zwischen Dozent und Studierenden sowie unter den zuhörenden Mitstudentinnen und -studenten ereignet. Die Dauer der Lektion bestimmt auch jene der Aufnahme. Nie sollte dabei ein Musikvideo entstehen, wie man es kennt, mit dramatischer Lichtführung und Close-Up-Aufnahmen von virtuosen Fingern und glitzernden Instrumenten, vom magischen Ort der Klangerzeugung oder von einer zerfurchten Stirn, dem Brennpunkt von Konzentration und Verinnerlichung. Die Kamera durfte nichts inszenieren, sondern sollte möglichst ohne Zudringlichkeit und Effekte die persönliche Auseinandersetzung unter Menschen wahrnehmen; sie musste ihrerseits zum Instrument werden, um genauer sehen zu lassen, was sich zeigt.

Entstanden ist eine fünfteilige Sequenz aus vier Einzel-Lektionen und einer Lektion mit einem Quartett in einer Runde von zwölf Studierenden, aufgenommen von zwei Kameras, deren unterschiedliche Blickwinkel im Format 16:9 und 4:3 auf zwei einander in einem leichten Winkel zugewandten Grossleinwänden ungeschnitten und in Realzeit wiedergegeben werden. Der beiden Projektionen gemeinsame Ton stammt aus drei Klangquellen, welche auf beiden Seiten und in der Mitte zwischen den Leinwänden stehen. Gefilmt wurde vor einem schwarzen Vorhang auf einer Bühne, die keine Kulisse bot, sondern vor neutralem Hintergrund lediglich die dreizehn Individuen hervortreten liess. Über Funkkontakt zu den Kameraleuten konnte Thomas Struth die beiden Bilder, die er live an zwei Monitoren verfolgte, gleichzeitig aufeinander abgestimmt entwerfen. In wenigen Bewegungen führte er die Kameras zu ruhigen, klaren Einstellungen, kadriert mit photographischer Genauigkeit, behutsam wechselnd zwischen Totale und Detail dem Geschehen folgend.

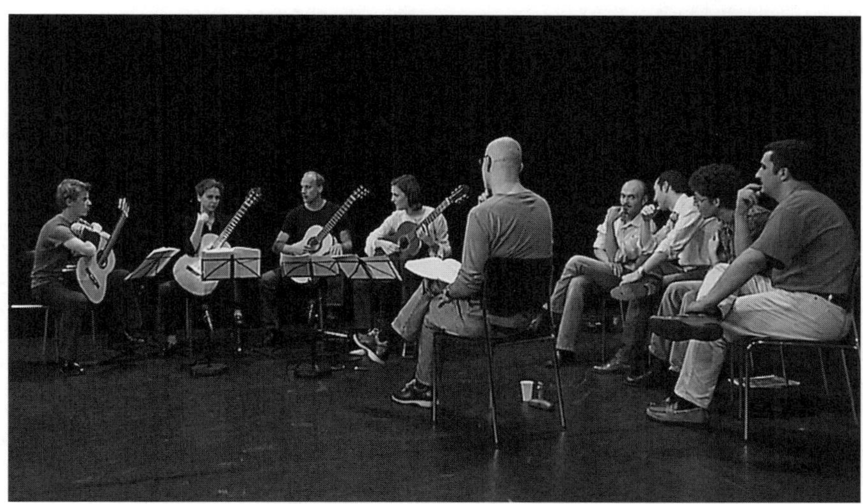

III. Die Lektionen beginnen mit einer Passage des Vorspielens. Dann aber wird der musikalische Vortrag durch verbale Einschübe, Wechselrede und Wiederholungen in der Übung aufgebrochen. Mit jeder Stunde entsteht eine unwiederbringlich besondere Atmosphäre unter Menschen, welche durch das Musikstück eingeführt wird, um im Dialog zwischen Frank Bungarten und der Persönlichkeit der jeweiligen Studierenden erweitert und vertieft zu werden. Von der Präsenz genau dieser Menschen rührt auch hier die Faszination des Porträts.

Unterricht mischt sich als ein Drittes die Wortsprache ein und unterbricht den stummen Austausch über Klang. Erst in der Aufzeichnung der Musikstunden verbinden sich schliesslich Klang, Bild und Sprache wieder zu einer neuen Einheit. Eine Aufzeichnung von Gesprächen über Kunstwerke wäre gelähmt durch die Konkurrenz zweier Bildmedien. Allein der Gattungswechsel zur Musik erlaubt dem Video diese Freiheit in der Reflexion über künstlerische Haltungen. Bungarten: «Musik Spielen ist ständiges Beginnen. Insofern wird die Auseinandersetzung um Musik zum Medium des Nachdenkens über Kunst. «Read this like seeing it for the first time... (Lesen Sie das, als sähen Sie's zum ersten Mal...)», rät Bungarten. Immer wieder geht es um die Öffnung für den Moment der Interpretation, um das Verlassen vorgefasster Konzepte und eingeschliffener Wahrnehmungsweisen und um die Arbeit an der eigenen Persönlichkeit, die bei aller Übung letztlich den Umgang mit dem Instrument bestimmt. Beim ist vergänglich.» Und darin, so Struth, treffen sich die Momenthaftigkeit der Photographie und der Musik. Auch der Photograph ist letztlich ein Interpret: Interpret einer Situation, die er zum Ort – zum unbewussten Ort[3] – werden lässt.

Thomas Struth hat eine sehr enge Beziehung zur Musik und zum Unterrichten, immerhin war er zuzeiten Professor an der Hochschule für Gestaltung in Karlsruhe. Auch ihm war damals das Gruppengespräch besonders wichtig, weil die kleine Öffentlichkeit

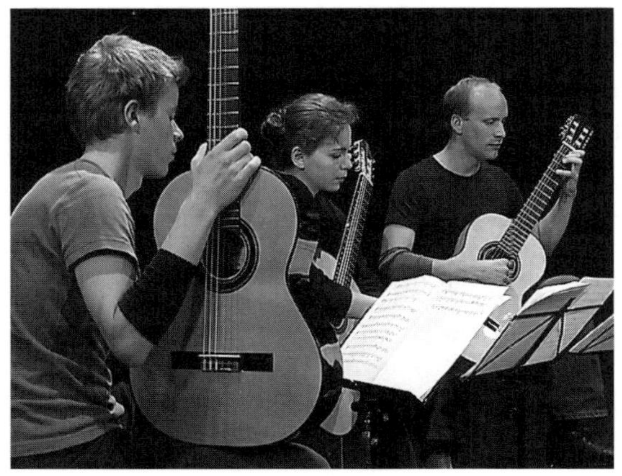

THOMAS STRUTH, READ THIS LIKE SEEING IT FOR THE FIRST TIME (FRANK BUNGARTEN UND SEINE KLASSE FÜR GITARRE AN DER MUSIKHOCHSCHULE LUZERN), 2003, Videostills aus der 270-Min.-Videodoppelprojektion, / stills from 270 min. dual video projection. (© THOMAS STRUTH & HOCHSCHULE DER KÜNSTE BERN)

von allen Beteiligten verbindlichere Aussagen fordert als ein Gespräch unter vier Augen. In einem unserer vielen Gespräche führte er auf einmal das Wort «Partnerbilder» ein: Bilder von Partnern in der Auseinandersetzung um Kunst, aber auch Bilder als Partner: paarweise einander zugeordnet oder Bilder als Partner der Betrachtenden. Sein Konzept voneinander abweichender, gleichwertiger Ansichten führt zu einer ungewohnten Konstellation von zwei unabhängigen, durch die Realzeit jedoch streng aufeinander bezogenen Bildern. Aus angemessener Distanz betrachtet liegen beide Projektionen zugleich im Blick. Wir können uns fortwährend entscheiden, wohin wir unsere Aufmerksamkeit lenken wollen, wohin wir uns ziehen lassen. Zwar dominiert auf der breiteren Leinwand öfters die Totale. Es besteht jedoch nie eine starre Aufteilung der Rollen zwischen Totale und Referenzbild. Die Sichtweisen wechseln, durch die hohe Präsenz des verbindenden Tons jedoch bleiben wir stets dem Geschehen verhaftet.

Die Gleichzeitigkeit zweier Ansichten mag an die kubistisch vielperspektivische Brechung des Raumes in die Fläche erinnern. Schon Manet hat das Kontinuum der Malerei wieder aufgebrochen, wie Michel Foucault zu dessen bekanntem Bild UN BAR AUX FOLIES-BERGÈRE (1881) ausführt: «... nicht wissen, wo der Maler stehen müsste, um dieses Gemälde so zu malen, wie er es gemalt hat, und wo wir stehen müssten, um die Szene zu sehen. Mit dieser Technik hat Manet die Eigenschaft des Gemäldes ins Spiel gebracht, kein normativer Raum zu sein, dessen Darstellung den Betrachter auf einen einzigen Punkt festlegt, von dem aus er betrachtet, sondern ein Raum, dem gegenüber man verschiedene Positionen einnehmen kann...» [4] Entscheidend bleibt die Freiheit der Betrachterinnen und Betrachter. Die Beiordnung zweier Bilder aus unterschiedlichen Blickwinkeln ist das alte Verfahren der Stereoskopie, das erst durch Synthese im Hirn ein einheitlich plastisches Bild entstehen lässt. Zugleich ist sie ein Prinzip des Films: «Film heisst nicht: ein Bild nach dem anderen, sondern ein Bild plus ein Bild, woraus ein drittes Bild entsteht. Dieses Bild wird übrigens vom Zuschauer in dem Augenblick gebildet, wo er den Film sieht...» [5] Zwei gleichzeitig sich durch den Raum bewegende Kameras spalten den Blick und verbinden ihn zugleich wieder: Sie lassen uns die Menschengruppe durch zwei Bewegungen in einem einzigen Augenblick wie eine Skulptur in der Zeit er-fahren.

IV. Die neue Videoarbeit vereinigt in sich Momente aus den vorangehenden Sonderprojekten und aus dem photographischen Werk: Die Hingabe an eine Dauer in Realzeit, die Konzentration auf Weniges und Momente der unausweichlichen Konfrontation waren schon in EINE STUNDE, der Reihe von Video-Einzelporträts, zentral. Obwohl es in den Lektionen bewusst keine Binnenschnitte gibt und Thomas Struth, bis auf die Übergänge zwischen den einzelnen Stunden, bewusst auf eine filmische Montage verzichtet hat, gibt es durch die Doppelvision ein ständiges Wieder-Sehen, eine augenblicklich wiederholte Lektüre. Über die fünf Stunden hin stellt sich damit eine Verlangsamung der Wahrnehmung ein, die sich der fortwährenden Beschleunigung unserer Kultur widersetzt. Insofern nimmt die neuste Arbeit auch ein Element aus den Dschungelphotographien von NEW PICTURES FROM PARADISE auf: Versenkung und das Leeren des Blicks durch die Membran des dichten Blattwerks hindurch.

Bei den Skulptur-Projekten in Münster 1987 hat Thomas Struth eine Reihe von acht Stadtansichten nachts auf ausgewählte Fassaden der Altstadt projiziert. Die begrenzte Dauer des Sehens und die Spezifik des Ortes bestimmen nun auch die Aufführung der neusten Arbeit während den vier Tagen im Rahmen der Biennale. Durch die Möglichkeit zur Konsumation, zum Kommen und Gehen, ergibt sich keine Konzertsituation, wohl aber eine Anwesenheit im Bewusstsein begrenzter Dauer. Eine Choreographie filmischer Sequenzen – verteilt auf vier Leinwände – war schliesslich schon bei der Projektion des BERLIN-PROJEKTS mit Klaus vom Bruch in der Galerie Max Hetzler in Berlin und im Kunstmuseum Luzern 1998 zu sehen. Erstmals hat Thomas Struth nun aber Regie geführt bei einer Aufnahme mit einem Team und mehreren Akteuren. Dies ist der Anfang für das Einlösen einer Sehnsucht. Noch steht die Familiensaga aus.

1) Jean-Luc Godard, «Wie kann man sexuelle Beziehungen filmen – Ein Interview mit *Libération*», dt. in: Jean-Luc Godard, *Liebe, Arbeit, Kino: Rette sich wer kann (Das Leben)*, aus dem Franz. übers. v. Lothar Kurzawa, Merve Verlag, Berlin 1981, S. 75.
2) Thomas Struth im Gespräch mit Ulrich Loock, 13. März 1998, Nîmes, in: *Thomas Struth / Klaus vom Bruch, Berlin-Projekt*, Ausstellungskatalog, hrsg. v. Ulrich Loock, Kunstmuseum Luzern, 1998, S. 11.
3) Thomas Struths Ausstellung von Städtebildern in der Kunsthalle Bern 1987 trug den Titel «Unbewusste Orte».
4) Michel Foucault, *Die Malerei von Manet*, aus dem Franz. übers. v. Peter Geble, Merve Verlag, Berlin 1999, S. 46. (Transkript eines Vortrags vom 20. Mai 1971 im Club Tahar Haddad in Tunesien, zuerst erschienen in einer Foucault gewidmeten Sondernummer der *Cahiers de Tunisie*, Tunis 1989.)
5) Jean-Luc Godard, «Reden mit Unterbrechungen», Auszüge aus einer Pressekonferenz anlässlich der Erstaufführung von *Rette sich wer kann (Das Leben)* im Juli 1980 in Avignon, dt. in: Jean-Luc Godard, *Liebe, Arbeit, Kino: Rette sich wer kann (Das Leben)*, op. cit., S. 43f.

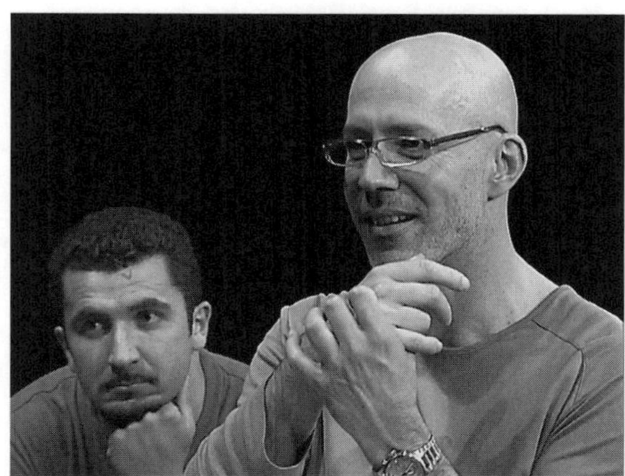

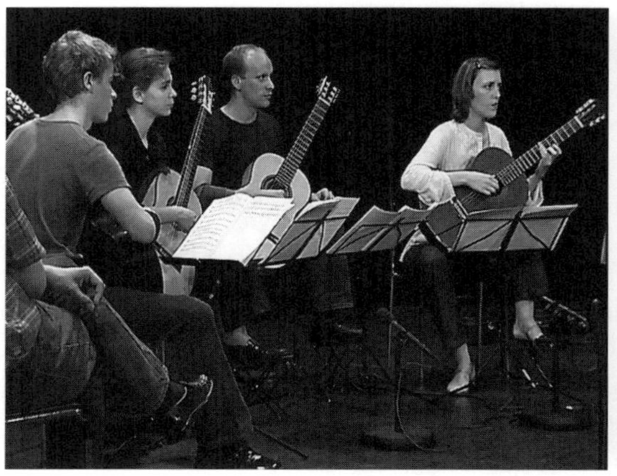

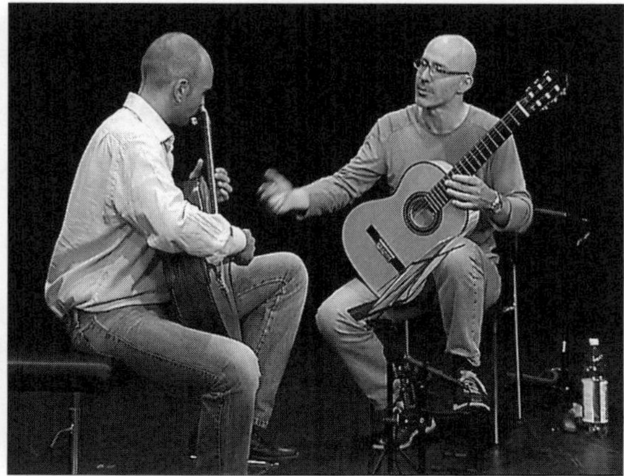

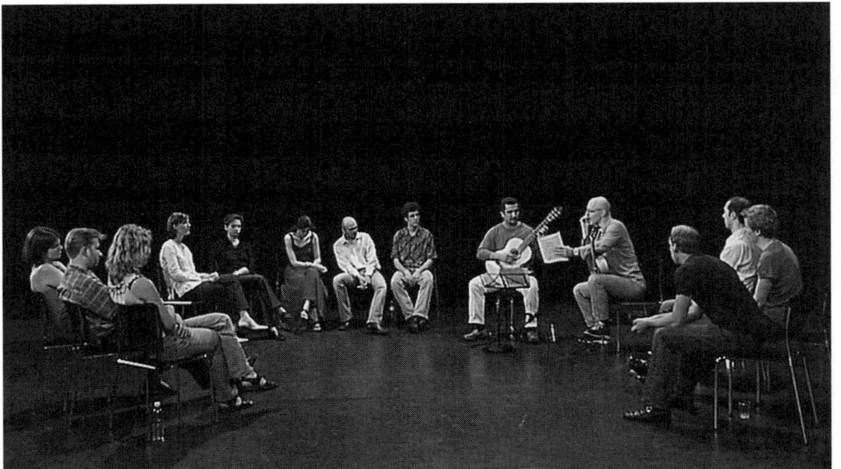

THOMAS STRUTH, READ THIS LIKE SEEING IT FOR THE FIRST TIME, 2003, Videostills aus der 270-Min.-Videodoppelprojektion / stills from 270 min. dual video projection. (© THOMAS STRUTH & HOCHSCHULE DER KÜNSTE BERN)

"Partner Pictures"

On Thomas Struth's New Video: READ THIS LIKE SEEING IT FOR THE FIRST TIME...

HANS RUDOLF REUST

And there's an interesting thing about filming that you don't find anywhere else: it allows you not to know/savoir, but to see/voir, so that you might know in retrospect.

–Jean-Luc Godard[1)]

I. In a successful exhibition that toured several museums in the United States—in Dallas, Los Angeles, New York, and Chicago—Thomas Struth's photography enjoyed widespread appreciation and understanding. Both in the catalogue and in the hanging of the works, new combinations cast a different light on a number of familiar prints and allowed comparison within a larger context. Cityscapes, museum photographs, individual and family portraits, the flowers and the jungle shots, juxtaposed in a single gallery or viewed from one room to the next, offered unexpected affinities within the cogent, compact artistic approach of Struth's direct, but never intrusive interpretation.

Less well-known are his projected works, his videos. A selection of video portraits, prominently displayed in the lobby of the Metropolitan Museum,

HANS RUDOLF REUST is an art critic and lecturer at the University of Arts Berne, Switzerland.

drew attention to this aspect of his oeuvre. After the exhibition opened in New York, Thomas Struth started working in the medium of moving pictures again and made a group portrait.

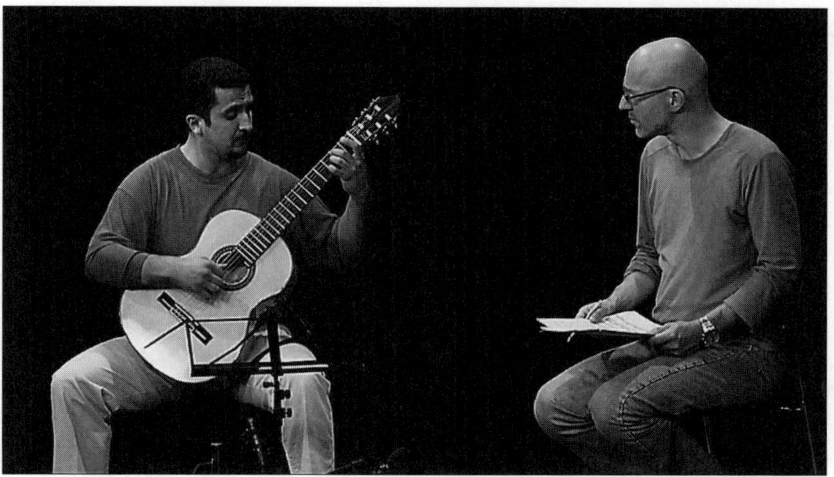

II. "There was always this desire or fantasy of making a film. But more in the sense that I didn't want to make a small experimental film but thought I had to start right away with a family saga. That is, family portraits, complicated circumstances. That's also related to my own complex and unusual family situation. You're always fascinated with things you've experienced yourself."[2] Thomas Struth expressed this desire to make films back in 1998 in an interview with Ulrich Loock. External circumstances finally provided an opportunity to put it into action: the fusion, at the beginning of September 2003, of the University of Music and Drama and the University of Applied Arts in Berne into a single institution, now known as the University of Arts Berne.

For the Biennale Berne from September 4–14, therefore, a diverse program of music was to be accompanied by artistic contributions. Thomas Struth accepted the new University's invitation to present a film for four days in the main auditorium during the opening ceremonies. The production of a film, a family saga, was out of the question in such a short period of time. Nonetheless, the modest commission with a small team evolved into a relatively elaborate production. Initially, Struth planned to follow up the individual portraits with a video group portrait. The interaction of several people in the course of an hour inevitably generates a cinematic narrative, as opposed to confronting a single person with a camera for the duration of an hour. How, then, could a compelling framework be found in which the plot is not invented and its duration not artificially limited?

As in his photographed portraits, Thomas Struth always selects people with whom he has a special relationship. His long-standing friendship with the guitarist Frank Bungarten finally led to the idea of filming a series of group lessons conducted by Bungarten at the Universities in Lucerne and Hanover. The plot consists of the interaction between teacher and students and their listening peers. One lesson defines the length of the film. The final product had no intention of featuring the techniques that generally characterize music videos: dramatic lighting in conjunction with close-ups of virtuoso fingering, of glistening instruments as the magical place where sounds are generated, or of furrowed brows as signs of concentration and focused interpretation. Nothing would be staged; the camera would interfere as little as possible in its perception of the personal interaction among the "actors"; it would itself turn into an instrument capable of seeing what it is looking at with greater precision.

Struth ended up with a five-part sequence of four private lessons and one lesson with a quartet. Two cameras filmed a group of twelve students, playing or listening, from two different angles in a format of 16:9 and 4:3. The films are presented uncut in real-time on two large screens facing each other at a slight angle. The sound shared by both projections comes from three sources placed between and on either side of the two screens. The cameras filmed the 13 individuals on a stage against the neutral backdrop of a black curtain. The artist watched the images live on two monitors and composed them via radio contact with the camera people. With a sparing use of movement, he directed the cameras to shoot clear and calm takes, framed with photographic precision, and thoughtfully alternating between long shot and close-up in following the course of action.

III. At the beginning of a lesson, the student plays a passage. The musical interpretation is then broken up by spoken intervention, exchanges between teacher and student, and the repetition of the passage. In each lesson an irrevocable, special atmosphere emerges among a group of people, which is engendered by the music and grows in intensity and depth in the dialogue between Frank Bungarten and his students. The fascination of the portrait rests on the presence of precisely those people.

Playing means beginning over and over again. In that respect the use of music as subject matter becomes a medium for reflection on art. "Read this like seeing it for the first time...," Bungarten advises. Everything is geared towards being open to moments of interpretation, suspending judgment, becoming conscious of ingrained patterns of perception, and acquiring insight into one's own personality, which ultimately—no matter how much the musician practices—determines the handling of his/her instrument. A third factor when teaching is the language of words which breaks up the nonlinguistic exchange through sound. The act of recording the music lessons creates a new unity of sound, image, and language. In contrast, the attempt to record a conversation about works of art would be obstructed by the competition between two visual media. It is the change of genre, from vision to sound, that gives the video the freedom to reflect on artistic attitudes. Bungarten: "Music is ephemeral." In that respect, according to Struth, photography and music meet; they are both of the moment. The photographer is ultimately also an interpreter: the interpreter of a situation, which turns it into a place—an unconscious place.[3]

Thomas Struth is a stranger neither to music, nor to education. When he was teaching at the University of Design in Karlsruhe, he placed particular emphasis on group instruction because, unlike a conversation in private between teacher and student, the slightly more public atmosphere fosters a more committed exchange. In one of our many conversations Struth once introduced the idea of "partner pictures": pictures of partners in the exploration of art, but also pictures as partners, arranged in pairs, and pictures as partners for viewers. His concept of deviating but equivalent viewpoints has led to an unusual combination of two independent pictures, which are, however, compellingly related to each other by the factor of real time. At a certain distance, both of the projections are within our range of vision. We can decide to which of the two we wish to direct our attention; we can allow ourselves to be drawn to the one or the other. Often the long shot dominates the wider screen, but there is never a rigid assignment of roles between long shot and close-up; they are interchangeable. Although the viewpoints vary, we remain glued to the scene through the strong presence of the unifying sound.

The simultaneity of two angles of vision may recall cubism's multi-perspectival dissection of space on the two-dimensional plane. Manet had already undermined the continuum of painting, as Michel Foucault observes in discussing the well-known UN BAR AUX FOLIES-BERGÈRE (1881): "...not knowing where the painter would have to stand in order to paint the painting as he has done, and where we would have to stand in order to see the scene. With this technique, Manet has brought into play the property of painting as a space that is not normative, whose representation does not restrict the viewer to a single standpoint from which to view the picture, but rather as a space that allows us to take up various positions..."[4] Crucial in this respect is the freedom of the viewer. The partnership of two pictures taken from different vantagepoints underlies the venerable technique of stereoscopy, which is based on the brain's capacity to synthesize two images into a single 3D picture. Cinema also exploits this technique. In the words of Jean-Luc Godard, "Film does not mean one picture after another, but one picture plus another picture out of which a third picture emerges. This picture, by the way, is formed by the viewer the moment he sees the film..."[5] Two cameras moving through the room at the same time split the view and immediately reassemble it. We experience the group of people as two moving pictures of one single moment, like a sculpture in time.

IV. Struth's new video unites aspects of his photography as well as the special projects that preceded it. A commitment to duration in real time, concentration on a restricted scope, and moments of inescapable confrontation already characterized his series of single portraits, EINE STUNDE (ONE HOUR). Although there are no cuts within the single lessons and no montage, except for the transition between them, the dual projection produces a constant re-visiting of instantly repeated readings. Perception therefore slows down in the course of the five lessons, defying the relentless acceleration of contemporary civilization. This most recent work by Struth therefore also incorporates an element of the jungle photographs, the NEW PICTURES FROM PARADISE: the immersion and the emptying of the gaze in and through the membrane of dense foliage.

For his sculpture project in Münster in 1987, Thomas Struth projected a series of eight cityscapes on selected façades in the Old Town. The restricted length of viewing and the specific nature of the place also determined the presentation of his most recent work on view for four days at the Biennale Berne. The presentation did not resemble a concert: visitors could have a bite to eat, could come and go, but they did sense a presence generated by the awareness of restricted duration. On another occasion, Struth choreographed film sequences on four different screens—in his BERLIN PROJECT with Klaus vom Bruch at Galerie Max Hetzler in Berlin and at the Kunstmuseum Luzern in 1998—but this is the first time that he has functioned as a director in collaboration with a team and a cast of several "actors." This is the beginning of gratifying a long-cherished desire. The family saga is yet to come.

(Translation: Catherine Schelbert)

1) Jean-Luc Godard, "Wie kann man sexuelle Beziehungen filmen – Ein Interview mit *Libération*" in Jean-Luc Godard, *Liebe, Arbeit, Kino: Rette sich wer kann (Das Leben)* (Berlin: Merve Verlag, 1981), p. 75. (Quotation translated from the German.)
2) Thomas Struth in conversation with Ulrich Loock in Nîmes, March 13, 1998, in *Thomas Struth / Klaus vom Bruch, Berlin-Projekt,* ex. cat., ed. by Ulrich Loock, Kunstmuseum Luzern, 1998, p. 11.
3) Thomas Struth's exhibition of cityscapes at the Kunsthalle Bern in 1987 was titled "Unbewusste Orte / Unconscious Places."
4) Michel Foucault, "La peinture de Manet" in *Les cahiers de Tunisie,* special issue: *Foucault en Tunisie,* Tunis, 1989.
5) Jean-Luc Godard, excerpts from a press conference held at the premiere of *Sauve qui peut (la vie) / Every man for himself* in Avignon in July 1980. See Jean-Luc Godard, *Liebe, Arbeit, Kino: Rette sich wer kann (Das Leben),* op. cit., pp. 43f. (Quotation translated from the German.)

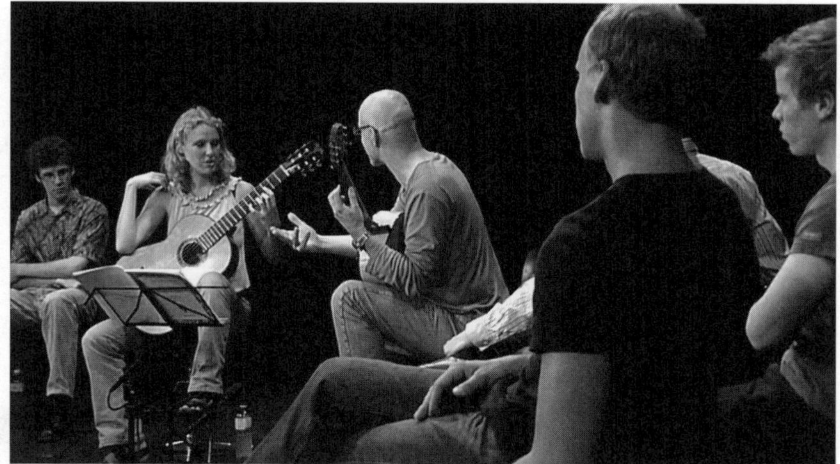

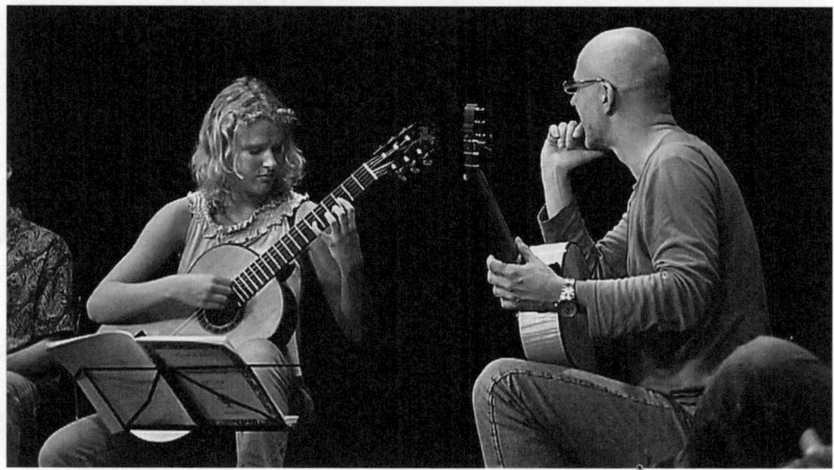

THOMAS STRUTH, READ THIS LIKE SEEING IT FOR THE FIRST TIME, 2003, Videostills aus der 270-Min.-Videodoppelprojektion / stills from 270 min. dual video projection.
(© THOMAS STRUTH & HOCHSCHULE DER KÜNSTE BERN)

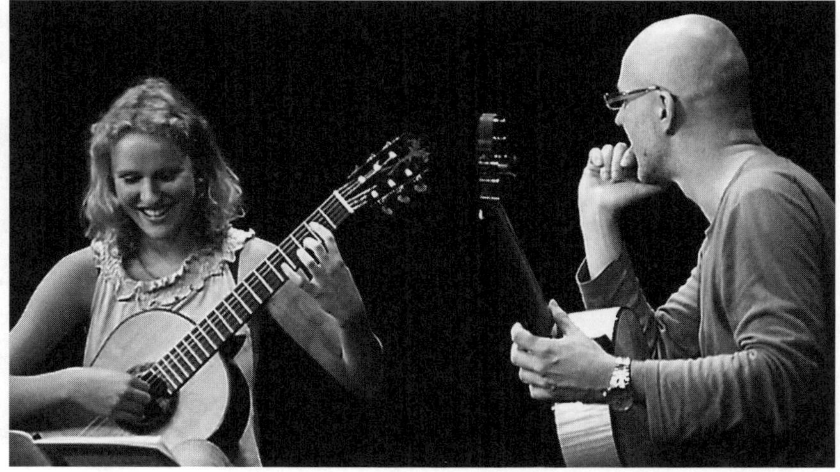

COMPLETE YOUR PARKETT LIBRARY
VERVOLLSTÄNDIGEN SIE IHRE PARKETT-BIBLIOTHEK

OUT OF PRINT / VERGRIFFEN: **NO. 1** ENZO CUCCHI, **2** SIGMAR POLKE, **3** MARTIN DISLER, **4** MERET OPPENHEIM, **5** ERIC FISCHL, **6** JANNIS KOUNELLIS, **7** BRICE MARDEN, **8** MARKUS RAETZ, **9** FRANCESCO CLEMENTE, **10** BRUCE NAUMAN, **12** ANDY WARHOL, **13** REBECCA HORN, **16** ROBERT WILSON, **17** FISCHLI/WEISS, **19** JEFF KOONS, MARTIN KIPPENBERGER, **20** TIM ROLLINS&K.O.S., **22** CHRISTIAN BOLTANSKI, JEFF WALL, **25** KATHARINA FRITSCH, **26** GÜNTHER FÖRG, PHILIP TAAFFE, JAMES TURRELL, **27** LOUISE BOURGEOIS, ROBERT GOBER, **29** CINDY SHERMAN, JOHN BALDESSARI, **30** SIGMAR POLKE, **31** DAVID HAMMONS, MIKE KELLEY, **35** GERHARD RICHTER, **38** ROSS BLECKNER, MARLENE DUMAS, **45** MATTHEW BARNEY, SARAH LUCAS, ROMAN SIGNER

For out-of-print issues you can register your name and address with Parkett and you will be notified, if your issue(s) become(s) available on the secondary market / Für vergriffene Bände nimmt der Verlag gerne Ihren Suchauftrag entgegen und macht Ihnen bei allfälliger Verfügbarkeit im Handel ein Angebot.

COLLABORATIONS

FRANZ ACKERMANN
EIJA-LIISA AHTILA
DAN GRAHAM
FOGLE, DECTER, STANGE; ILES, ELFVING, KOCH; GUAGNINI/SCHNEIDER, MACDONALD, DI BARTOLOMEO, ROSENBERG MILLER
INSERT: **JONATHAN MONK**
DANIEL KURJAKOVIC: **BOJAN SARCEVIC**
HANS ULRICH OBRIST: **BERNARD FRIZE**
GREGOR JANSEN: **DIRK SKREBER**
LES INFOS: JAY MURPHY
CUMULUS: C.S. RABINOWITZ, J. HOFFMANN
BALKON: HANS RUDOLF REUST

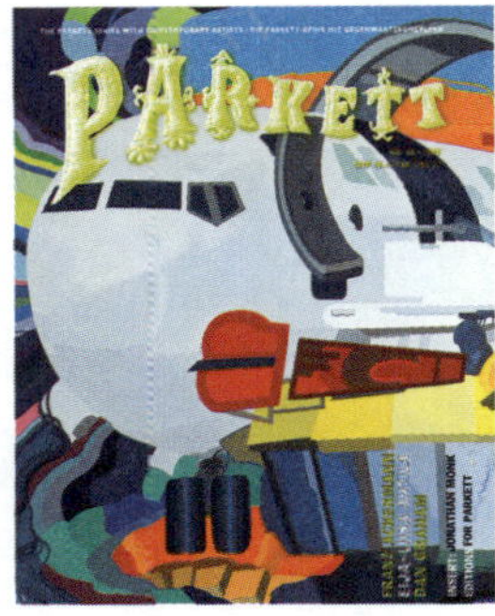

No. 68 - ISBN 3-907582-18-7

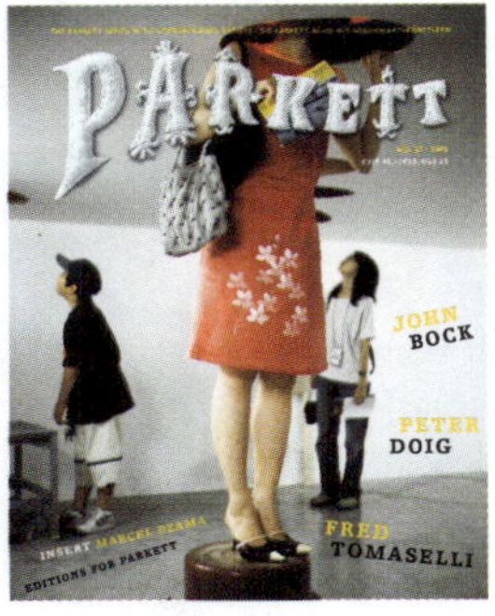

No. 67 - ISBN 3-907582-17-9

JOHN BOCK
PETER DOIG
FRED TOMASELLI
HOFFMANN, BIRNBAUM, AVGIKOS BONAVENTURA, FUCHS, RUF CAMERON, RONDEAU, PINCHBECK
INSERT: **MARCEL DZAMA**
T. SELVARATNAM: **SIMON STARLING**
S. OMLIN: **HANNE DARBOVEN**
T. VISCHER/J. HERZOG: SCHAULAGER BASEL
LES INFOS: H. BÖHME ON **WANG FU**
CUMULUS: L. FIRSTENBERG, R. KERSTING
BALKON: DANIELE MUSCIONICO

ANGELA BULLOCH
DANIEL BUREN
PIERRE HUYGHE
REBENTISCH, WILSON, PRINZHORN RORIMER, GINGERAS, BUREN/HUYGHE MILLAR, OBRIST, HOBBS
T. NICHOLS GOODEVE/GIULIANA BRUNO
EDWARD DIMENDBERG: **ALLAN SEKULA**
LES INFOS: ROBERTO OHRT ON **MONICA BONVICINI**
CUMULUS AMERICA: NATO THOMPSON
CUMULUS EUROPA: GREG HILTY

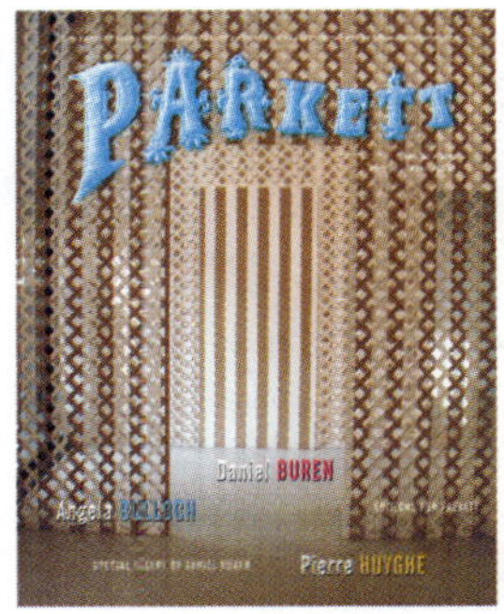

No. 66 - ISBN 3-907582-16-0

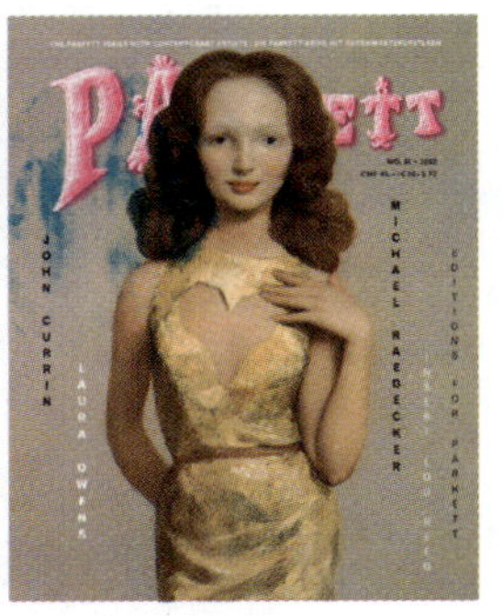

No. 65 - ISBN 3-907582-15-2

JOHN CURRIN
LAURA OWENS
MICHAEL RAEDECKER
SEWARD, VAN DE WALLE, BERG, FERGUSON, THOMSON, WEISSMAN, VERSCHAFFEL, MYERS, EGGERS
INSERT: **LOU REED**
KURT W. FORSTER: **JEFF WALL**
STORR: **DIETER ROTH & DOROTHY IANNONE**
KONRAD BITTERLI: **HUBBARD/BIRCHLER**
LES INFOS: CHRISTINA VÉGH
CUMULUS: OLAV WESTPHALEN, THOMAS HAH
BALKON: SHEENA WAGSTAFF

OLAFUR ELIASSON
TOM FRIEDMAN
RODNEY GRAHAM
BLOM, MORGAN, CAMERON, MATSUI, WATERS/FRIEDMAN, COOKE, HALE
INSERT: **AMY SILLMAN**
VÉRONIQUE D'AUZAC: **XAVIER VEILHAN**
A.M. HOMES: **CHRIS VERENE** (INTERVIEW)
HAKAN NILSSON: **ANNIKA LARSSON**
INQUIRY/UMFRAGE: LEARNING FROM "DOCUMENTA"

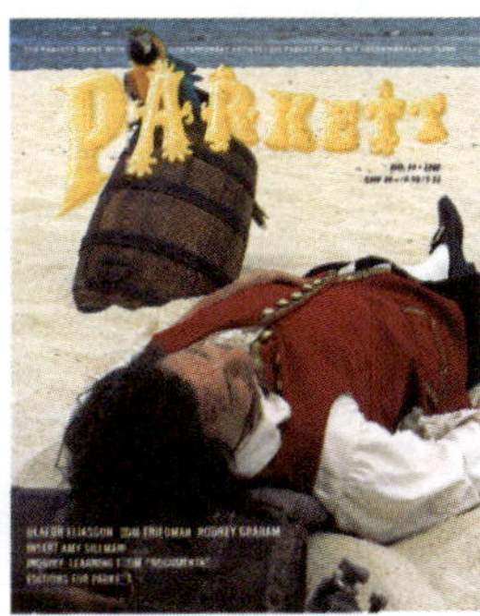

No. 64 - ISBN 3-907582-14-4

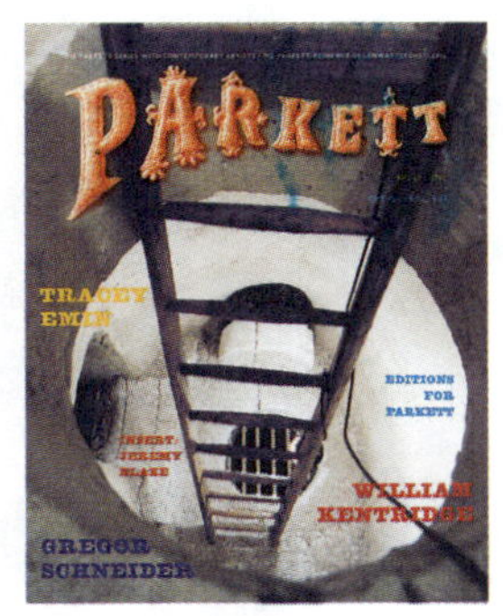

No. 63 - ISBN 3-907582-13-6

TRACEY EMIN
WILLIAM KENTRIDGE
GREGOR SCHNEIDER
BARBER, MUIR, PREECE, GUNNING, STEWART, GOLDBERG, PUVOGEL, LOOCK
INSERT: **JEREMY BLAKE**
CLAUDIA SPINELLI: **FABRICE GYGI**
RAINER FUCHS: **KATHARINA GROSSE**
ADRIAN DANNATT: **THE THREE**
CUMULUS: CH. RATTEMEYER, D. BIRNBAUM
BALKON: MICHAEL OPPITZ

JOHN WESLEY
TACITA DEAN
THOMAS DEMAND
MILLAR, CARABELL, SCHWARZ
NORDEN, KÖNIG/STOCKEBRAND
HAINLEY, SEARLE, RUBY, HEISER
INSERT: **G. STEINER & J. LENZLINGER**
PHILIP URSPRUNG: **ALLAN KAPROW**
RUSSELL FERGUSON: **GLEN WILSON**
EDWARD A. SCHEER: **MIKE PARR**
LES INFOS: DAVID GREENBERG
CUMULUS: G. CARMINE, S. DIETZ

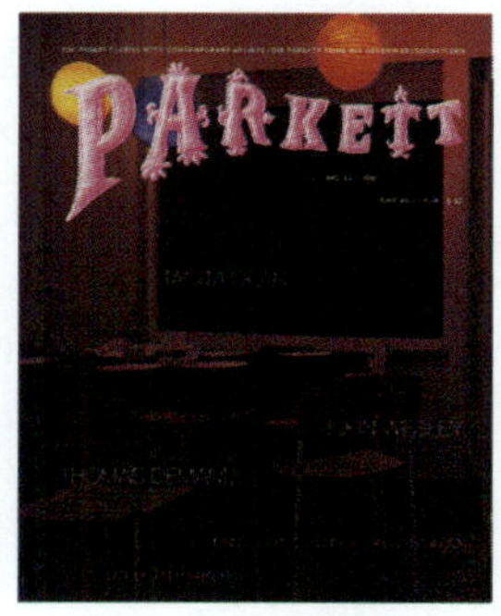

No. 62 - **ISBN 3-907582-12-8**

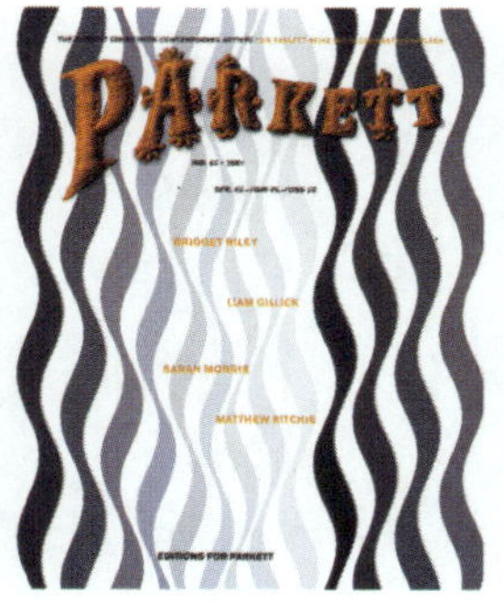

No. 61 - **ISBN 3-907582-11-X**

BRIDGET RILEY
LIAM GILLICK
SARAH MORRIS
MATTHEW RITCHIE
KUDIELKA, HICKEY
GILLICK, STEMMRICH, WOLLEN
NICHOLS GOODEVE, KLEIN, PRINZHORN
RABINOWITZ, GALISON/JONES, MARCUS
ELISABETH KLEY: **PAUL LINCOLN**
CUMULUS: O. ENWEZOR, M. WARNER
BALKON: STELLA ROLLIG

CHUCK CLOSE
DIANA THATER
LUC TUYMANS
PROSE, CLOSE/PEYTON, SHIFF,
CLOSE/CURIGER
ARRHENIUS, HASLINGER, GILBERT-ROLFE
HOPTMAN, MOSQUERA, REUST
INSERT: **SHIRANA SHAHBAZI**
GREG HILTY: **JEREMY DELLER**
HOWARD SINGERMAN: **DAVID BUNN**
LES INFOS: THIERRY DE DUVE—INTERVIEW
CUMULUS: FRAZER WARD, HANS ULRICH RECK

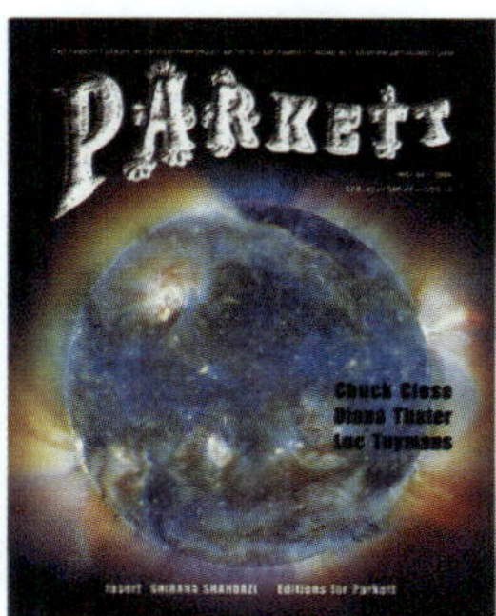

No. 60 - **ISBN 3-907582-10-1**

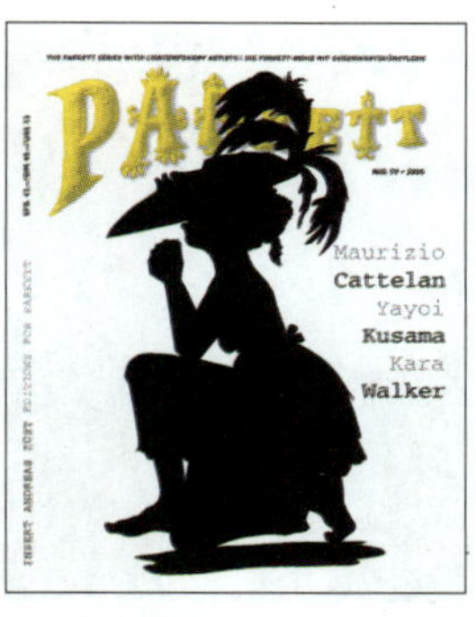

No. 59 - **ISBN 3-907582-09-8**

MAURIZIO CATTELAN
YAYOI KUSAMA
KARA WALKER
BOURRIAUD, GINGERAS, BONAMI
PANHANS-BÜHLER, MATSUI, POLLOCK
DUBOIS SHAW, JANUS, WALKER
INSERT: **ANDREAS ZÜST**
VINCENT KATZ,
ELISABETH BRONFEN: **ANNETTE MESSAGER**
JAN AVGIKOS: **ANNA GASKELL**
LES INFOS: ALI SUBOTNICK
CUMULUS: M. ROWELL, L. FÖLDENYI
BALKON: MICHELLE NICOL

JAMES ROSENQUIST
SYLVIE FLEURY
JASON RHOADES
USSELL, KOONS/ROSENQUIST, HULTEN, FELIX
GLENN, LOBEL, DANNATT, RUF, KOETHER
FERGUSON, ORTH, SCHEIDEMANN/HERMANN
INSERT: **HENRY BOND**
GILDA WILLIAMS: **JANE & LOUISE WILSON**
SLAVOJ ZIZEK, PAUL D. MILLER & CHRIS OFILI
LES INFOS: ANNA HELWING
CUMULUS: DAVID ROBBINS, HILDE TEERLINCK
BALKON: KNUT EBELING

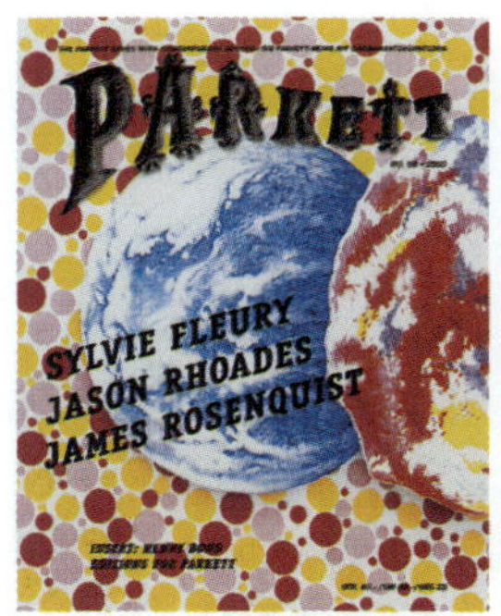

No. 58 - **ISBN 3-907582-08-X**

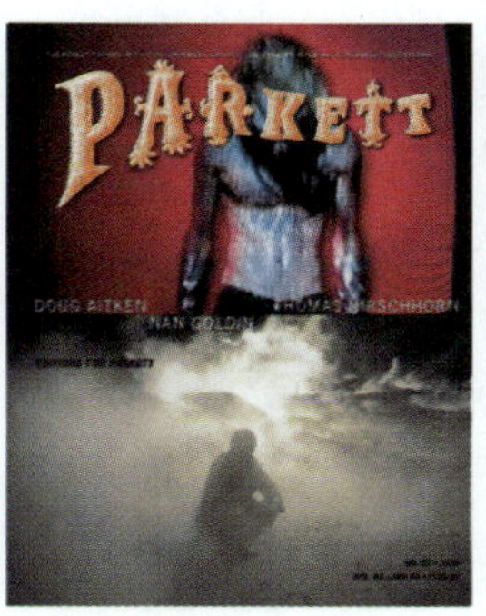

No. 57 - **ISBN 3-907582-07-1**

DOUG AITKEN
NAN GOLDIN
THOMAS HIRSCHHORN
ROBERTS, BONAMI, VAN ASSCHE, LEBOVICI
DANTO, LIEBMANN, FRIIS-HANSEN, HAKERT,
EISENBERG, FLECK, GINGERAS, VERGNE, STEINWEG
DAVID GREENBERG: **DONALD BAECHLER**
ANDREA KROKSNES: **LOUISE LAWLER**
LIONEL BOVIER: **JOHN MILLER**
LES INFOS: RUDOLF SCHMITZ
CUMULUS: H.U. OBRIST, CONNIE BUTLER
BALKON: JURI STEINER & ANNELISE COSTE

ELLSWORTH KELLY
VANESSA BEECROFT
JORGE PARDO
KELLEIN, FER, MAURER, RIMANELLI
BRYSON, TAZZI, SEWARD, AVGIKOS
FERGUSON, VÉGH, VAN WINKEL
FRANGENBERG, BUSH
GREG HILTY: **CERITH WYN EVANS**
THOMAS Y. LEVIN: **CHRISTIAN MARCLAY**
LYNNE COOKE: **DIANA THATER**
LES INFOS: DIANE LEWIS
CUMULUS: ADRIAN DANNATT, PETR NEDOMA

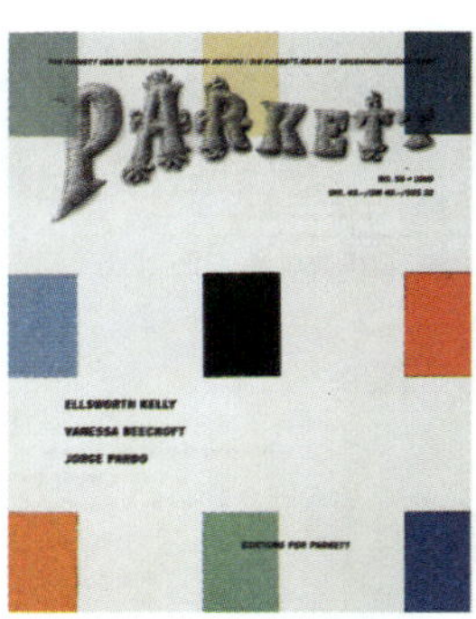

No. 56 - **ISBN 3-907582-06-3**

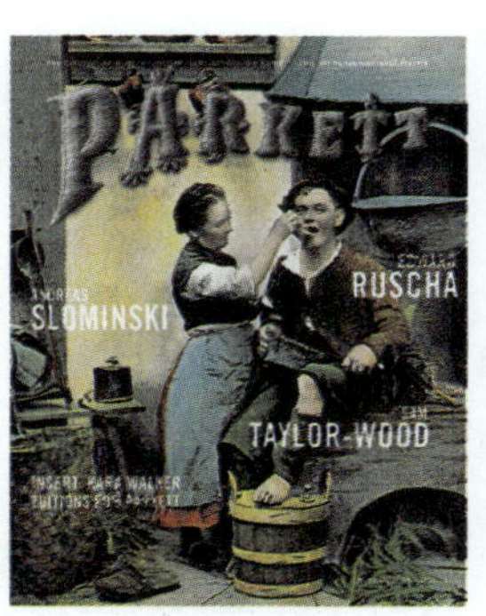

No. 55 - **ISBN 3-907582-05-5**

EDWARD RUSCHA
ANDREAS SLOMINSKI
SAM TAYLOR-WOOD
PERRONE, HIGGIE, SINGERMAN, SCHENKER
SCANLAN, SPECTOR, FREY, HEYNEN
GROYS/FUNCKE/HOFFMANN, BRONFEN
BONAMI, LAJER-BURCHARTH
INSERT: **KARA WALKER**
BORIS GROYS: **PAVEL PEPPERSTEIN**
RUDOLF SCHMITZ: **ALEXANDER KLUGE**
BEATRIX RUF: **EIJA-LIISA AHTILA**
CUMULUS: MICHELLE NICOL, SUELY ROLNIK

RONI HORN
MARIKO MORI
BEAT STREULI
SCHORR, GUNNARSSON, GOROVOY, LEWIS
SPECTOR, BRYSON, NAKAZAWA, NICHOLS
GOODEVE, STALS, DANTO, AMANO, SMITH
INSERT: **MATTHEW RITCHIE**
VINCENT KATZ: **ALEX KATZ**
HORST BREDEKAMP: **STEPHAN VON HUENE**
PAUL D. MILLER: **SHIRIN NESHAT**
LES INFOS:
OKWUI ENWEZOR & WILLIAM KENTRIDGE
CUMULUS: VALÉRIA PICCOLI, MARIA LIND

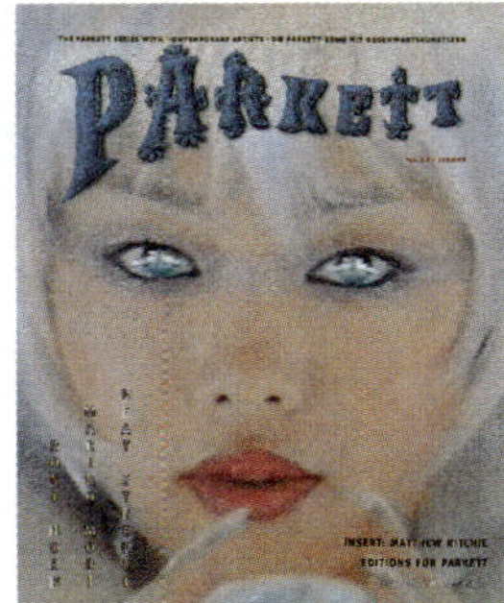

No. 54 - **ISBN 3-907582-04-7**

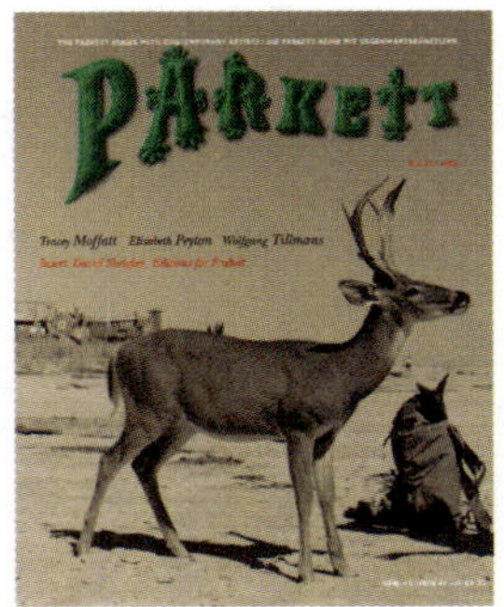

No. 53 - **ISBN 3-907582-03-9**

TRACEY MOFFATT
ELIZABETH PEYTON
WOLFGANG TILLMANS
MARTIN, LAJER-BURCHARTH, RIMANELLI
PILGRIM, URSPRUNG, LIEBMANN, MATSUI
WAKEFIELD, BUDNEY, NESBITT, ZIEGLER
INSERT: **DAVID SHRIGLEY**
CATHERINE BERNARD: **JOHAN GRIMONPREZ**
BERNARD MARCADÉ: **ROBERT GOBER**
LES INFOS DE L'ENFER: VALERIA LIEBERMANN
CUMULUS: BLESSING, AUPETITALLOT
BALKON: STEINER/MAGNAGUAGNO

KAREN KILIMNIK
MALCOLM MORLEY
UGO RONDINONE
SCHORR, BÜRGI, JUNCOSA, MORLEY,
LEBENSZTEJN, BONAMI, VERWOERT, HOPTMAN,
INSERT: **THOMAS BAYRLE**
ED WHITE: **JEAN MICHEL OTHONIEL**
NEVILLE WAKEFIELD: **RICHARD SERRA**
GILDA WILLIAMS: **GILLIAN WEARING**
ROBERT GRESKOVIC: **MERCE CUNNINGHAM**
CUMULUS: WALKER, KURZMEYER
BALKON: CECILIA VICUÑA

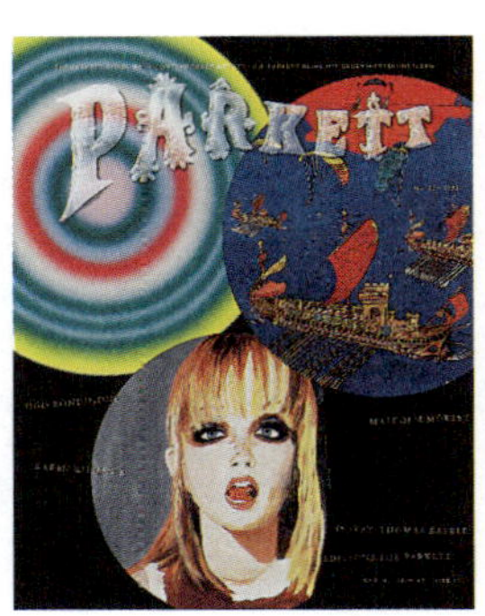

No. 52 - **ISBN 3-907582-02-0**

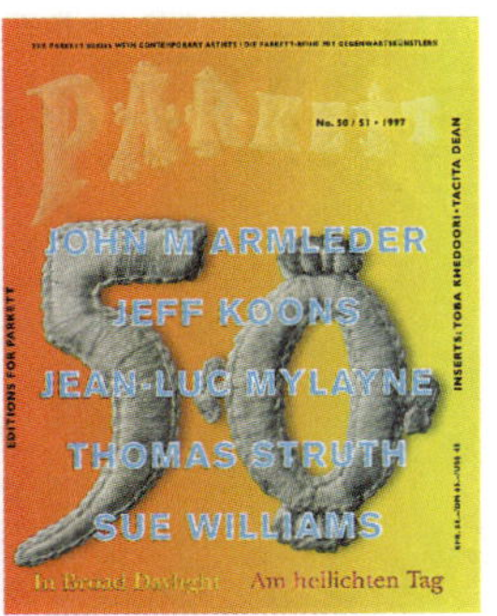

50/51 - **ISBN 3-907582-00-4**

JOHN M ARMLEDER, JEFF KOONS
JEAN-LUC MYLAYNE
THOMAS STRUTH, SUE WILLIAMS
DI PIETRANTONIO, BOVIER, MUNIZ,
SEWARD, LOERS, NICHOLS GOODEVE,
COOKE, DION, ARNAUDET, MYLAYNE,
CURIGER, LINGWOOD, OKUTSU, BRYSON,
SCHJELDAHL, NESBIT, DANNATT, CAMHI
INSERTS: **TOBA KHEDOORI, TACITA DEAN**
ONFRAY: **HYACINTHE RIGAUD,** NICOL: **SAM SAMO**
MURPHY, VAN DER WALLE, STEINER,
KURT W. FORSTER: **FRANK GEHRY**
CUMULUS: COLEMAN, BIRNBAUM

LAURIE ANDERSON
DOUGLAS GORDON
JEFF WALL
FLOOD, BEZZOLA, FERGUSON
GILLICK/GORDON, BRYSON, PONTBRIAND
SCHORR, ANDERSON, BURCKHARDT, BUDNEY
INSERT: **SILVIA BÄCHLI**
COLIN DE LAND: **JOHN WATERS**
ROBERT STORR: **SEYDOU KEITA**
DANIELA SALVIONI: **CLEGG & GUTTMANN**
CUMULUS: KITTELMANN, MEYER

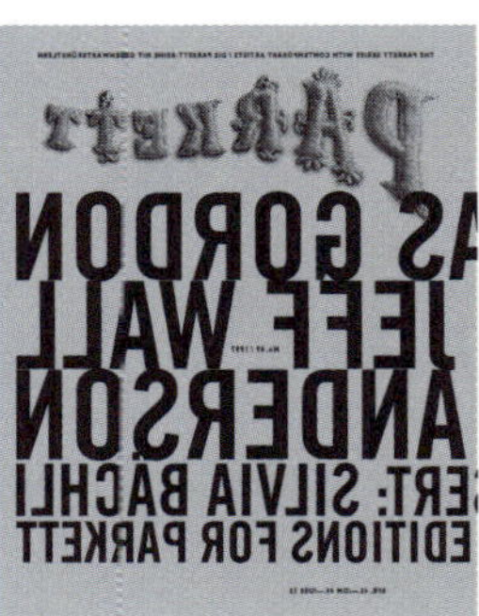

No. 49 - **ISBN 3-907509-99-4**

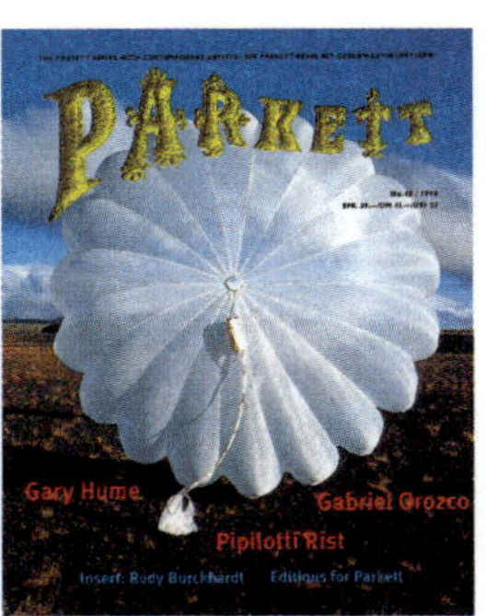

No. 48 - **ISBN 3-907509-98-6**

GARY HUME
GABRIEL OROZCO
PIPILOTTI RIST
BOVIER, MUIR, FOGLE, BONAMI
DE ZEGHER, SPECTOR, URSPRUNG
BABIAS, COLOMBO, ANDERSON
INSERT: **RUDY BURCKHARDT**
VINCENT KATZ: **RUDY BURCKHARDT**
VAN DER WALLE: **CHARLES LONG**
& STEREOLAB
FAYE HIRSCH: **BRUCE CONNER**
CHRISTOPH DOSWALD: **IAN ANÜLL**
CUMULUS: LEGGAT, SCHNEIDER

TONY OURSLER
RAYMOND PETTIBON
THOMAS SCHÜTTE
COOKE, RICHARD, NERI,
LEWIS, GROYS, ALS, RUGOFF,
GOODEVE, SEARLE, MARI, REUST,
WAKEFIELD, LOOCK, JANUS
INSERT: **ZOE LEONARD & CHERYL DUNYE**
JURI STEINER: **EMMA KUNZ**
MAX WECHSLER: **CHRISTOPH RÜTIMANN**
SUSAN MORGAN: **DIANE ARBUS**
CUMULUS: PRINCENTHAL, BOVIER/CHERIX

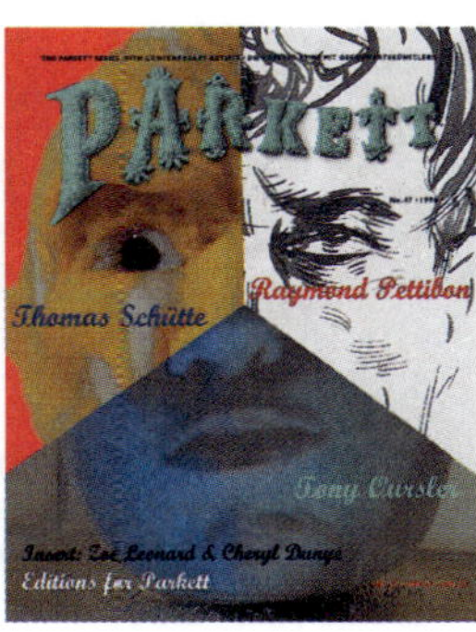

No. 47 - **ISBN 3-907509-97-8**

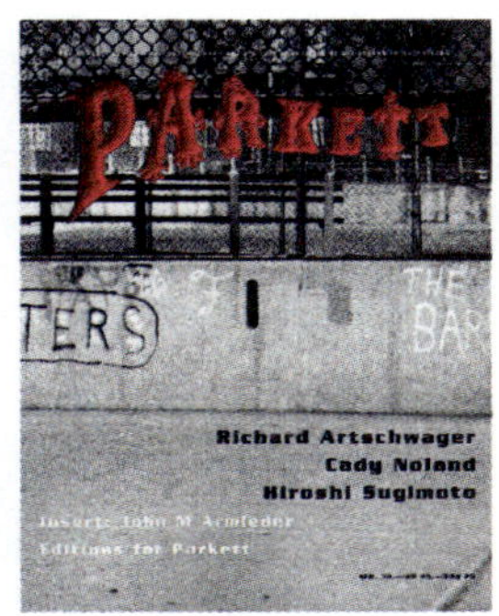

No. 46 - **ISBN 3-907509-96-X**

RICHARD ARTSCHWAGER
CADY NOLAND
HIROSHI SUGIMOTO
DEITCHER, SCHAFFNER, FORSTER, MUNIZ
ARMSTRONG, RELYEA, BOGDAN, GOODEVE
NICKAS, BRYSON, RUGOFF, DENSON
INSERT: **JOHN M ARMLEDER**
ROLAND WÄSPE: **ERWIN WURM**
DANIEL BIRNBAUM: **ÖYVIND FAHLSTRÖM**
LES INFOS DU PARADIS: ROBERT FLECK
CUMULUS: MILLER, VETTESE
BALKON: MARTIN HELLER

VIJA CELMINS
ANDREAS GURSKY
RIRKRIT TIRAVANIJA
PRINCENTHAL, LEWIS, SILVERTHORNE
SHIFF, CRIQUI, BURCKHARDT, WAKEFIELD
SCHORR, MELO, GILLICK, FLOOD, STEINER
INSERT: **HANS DANUSER**
LES INFOS: LIAM GILLICK & DOUGLAS GORDON
LYNNE COOKE, DAVID DEITCHER
DANIEL KURJAKOVIC: **MARIE JOSÉ BURKI**
NAN GOLDIN: **PETER HUJAR**
NOEMI SMOLIK: **ANDREAS SLOMINSKI**
JASON SIMON: **MARK DION**
LUK LAMBRECHT: **MARK LUYTEN**

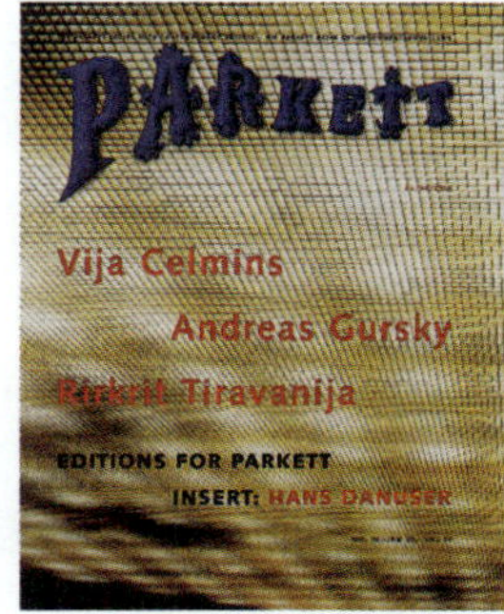

No. 44 - ISBN 3-907509-94-3

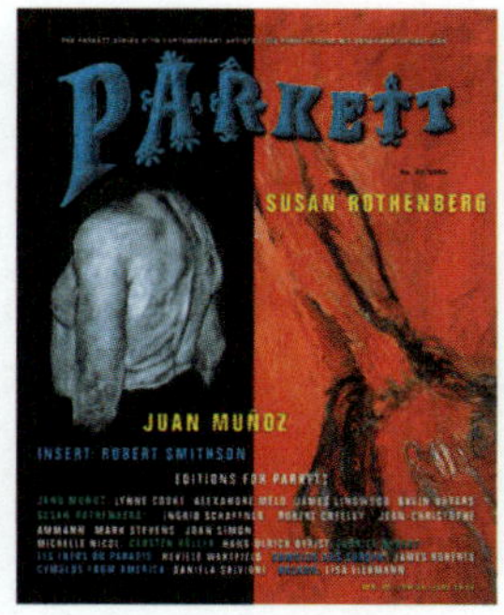

No. 43 - ISBN 3-907509-93-5

JUAN MUÑOZ
SUSAN ROTHENBERG
LYNNE COOKE, ALEXANDRE MELO
JAMES LINGWOOD, GAVIN BRYARS
ROBERT CREELEY, INGRID SCHAFFNER
JEAN-CHRISTOPHE AMMANN
MARK STEVENS, JOAN SIMON
INSERT: **ROBERT SMITHSON**
NEVILLE WAKEFIELD
MICHELLE NICOL: **CARSTEN HÖLLER**
HANS-ULRICH OBRIST: **FABRICE HYBERT**

LAWRENCE WEINER
RACHEL WHITEREAD
BROOKS ADAMS, FRANCES RICHARD
DIETER SCHWARZ, DANIELA SALVIONI
ED LEFFINGWELL, LANE RELYEA
NEVILLE WAKEFIELD, RUDOLF SCHMITZ
TREVOR FAIRBROTHER, SIMON WATNEY
INSERT: **NAN GOLDIN**
VINCE LEO: **ROBERT FRANK**
CLAUDE RITSCHARD: **MARKUS RAETZ**

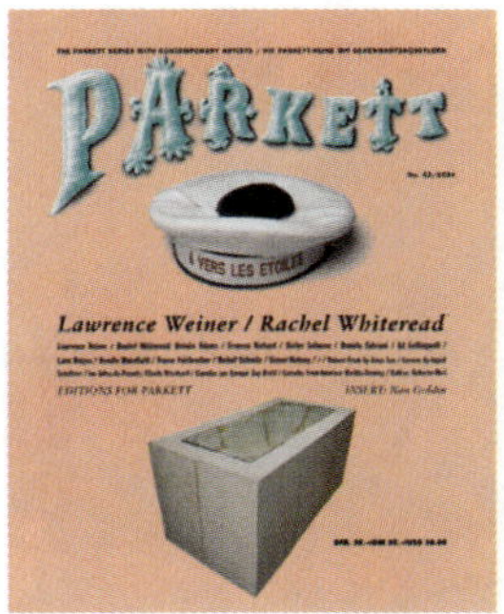

No. 42 - ISBN 3-907509-92-7

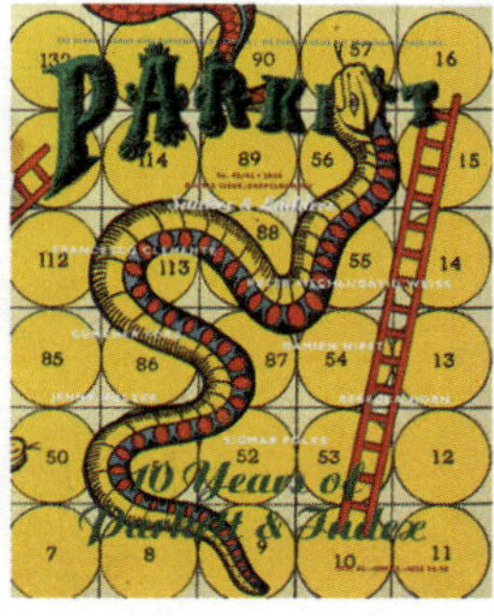

40/41 - ISBN 3-907509-90-0

FRANCESCO CLEMENTE
GÜNTHER FÖRG
PETER FISCHLI/DAVID WEISS
DAMIEN HIRST
JENNY HOLZER
REBECCA HORN
SIGMAR POLKE
HOLLAND COTTER, BORIS GROYS
MAX WECHSLER, DAVID RIMANELLI
JOAN SIMON, GORDON BURN
GILBERT LASCAULT, WERNER SPIES
BICE CURIGER, JEFF PERRONE
G. ROGER DENSON, VIK MUNIZ
DAVE HICKEY

FELIX GONZALEZ-TORRES
WOLFGANG LAIB
NANCY SPECTOR, SIMON WATNEY,
SUSAN TALLMAN, DIDIER SEMIN,
CLARE FARROW, JEAN-MARC AVRILLA,
THOMAS McEVILLEY
CLAUDE GINTZ: **GABRIEL OROZCO**
WALTER GRASSKAMP: **AXEL KASSEBÖHMER**
NEVILLE WAKEFIELD: **MATTHEW BARNEY**
INSERT: **RONI HORN**
LES INFOS DU PARADIS: **BURT BARR**
CUMULUS: **MEYER VAISMAN**

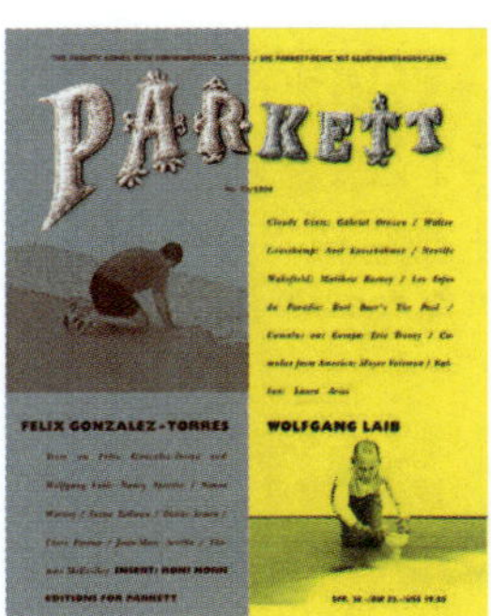

No. 39 - ISBN 3-907509-89-7

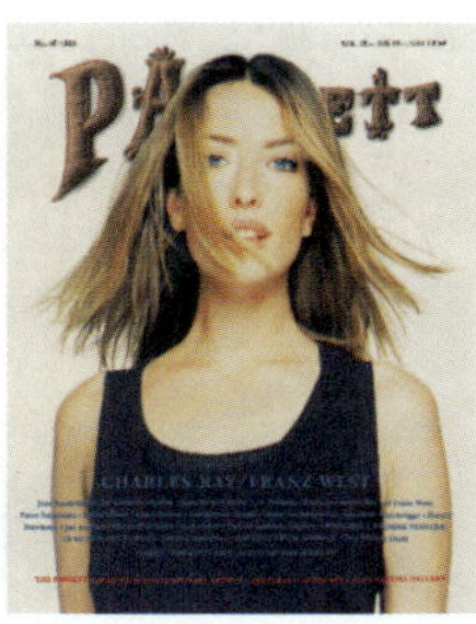

No. 37 - ISBN 3-907509-87-0

CHARLES RAY
FRANZ WEST
KLAUS KERTESS, CHRISTOPHER KNIGHT
PETER SCHJELDAHL, ROBERT STORR
JAN AVGIKOS, AXEL HUBER
MARTIN PRINZHORN, ELISABETH
SCHLEBRÜGGE, HARALD SZEEMANN,
DENYS ZACHAROPOULOS
INSERT: **PIPILOTTI RIST**
JEAN BAUDRILLARD
HANS RUDOLF REUST: **LUC TUYMANS**
PARKETT INQUIRY:
CHERCHEZ LA FEMME PEINTRE!

ILYA KABAKOV
RICHARD PRINCE
BORIS GROYS, ROBERT STORR
JAN THORN-PRIKKER
CLAUDIA JOLLES, EDMUND WHITE
SUSAN TALLMAN, DANIELA
SALVIONI, KATHY ACKER
INSERT: **TATSUO MIYAJIMA**
GUDRUN INBODEN: **ASTA GRÖTING**
LYNNE COOKE: **GARY HILL**
PATRICK McGRATH: **STEPHEN ELLIS**

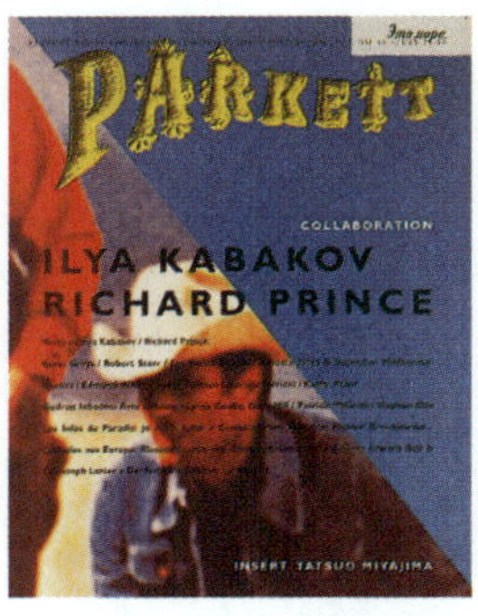

No. 34 - ISBN 3-907509-84-6

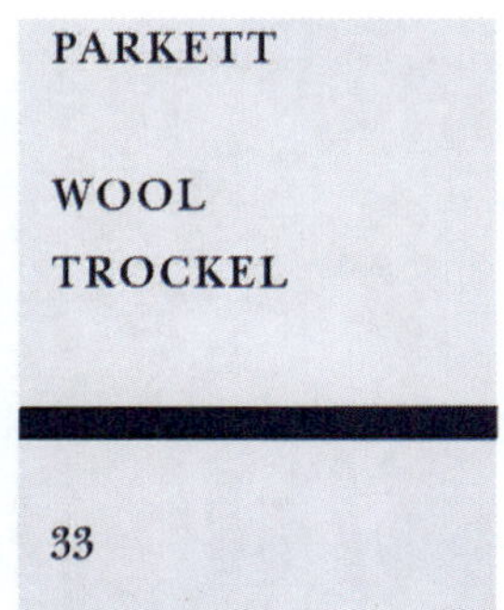

No. 33 - ISBN 3-907509-83-3

ROSEMARIE TROCKEL
CHRISTOPHER WOOL
VERONIQUE BACCHETTA,
BARRETT WATTEN,
ANNE WAGNER, JIM LEWIS,
GREIL MARCUS, JEFF PERRONE,
DIEDRICH DIEDERICHSEN
INSERT: **ADRIAN SCHIESS**
MARINA WARNER: **PENIS PLENTY**
G. ROGER DENSON:
DENNIS OPPENHEIM
CAMIEL VAN WINKEL

IMI KNOEBEL
SHERRIE LEVINE
RUDOLF BUMILLER
RAINER CRONE/DAVID MOOS
LISA LIEBMANN, DANIELA SALVIONI
ERICH FRANZ, HOWARD SINGERMANN
INSERT: **DAMIEN HIRST**
SHEENA WAGSTAFF: **VIJA CELMINS**
JIM LEWIS: **LARRY CLARK**
LIAM GILLICK: **BETHAN HUWS**
THOMAS KELLEIN: **WALTER DE MARIA**

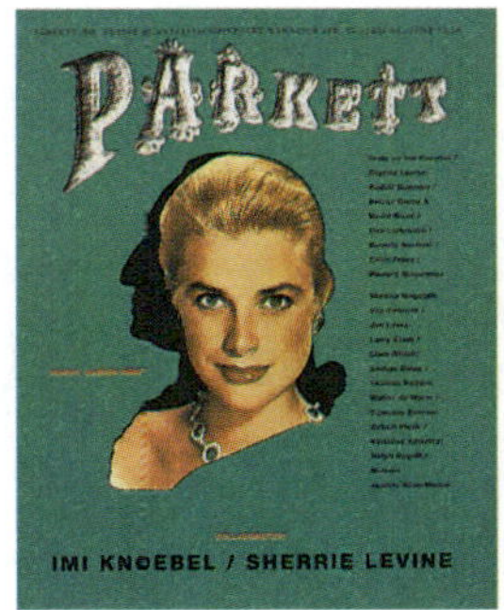

No. 32 - ISBN 3-907509-82-X

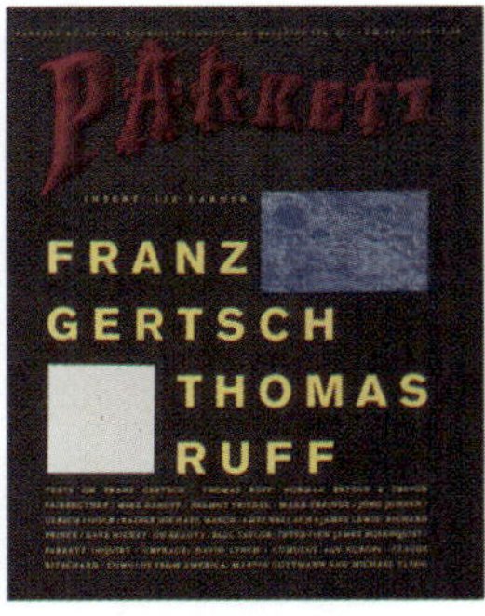

No. 28 - ISBN 3-907509-78-1

FRANZ GERTSCH
THOMAS RUFF
HELMUT FRIEDEL, ULRICH LOOCK
I. MICHAEL DANOFF, AMEI WALLACH
RAINER MICHAEL MASON
MARC FREIDUS, JÖRG JOHNEN
TREVOR FAIRBROTHER/NORMAN BRYSON
INSERT: **LIZ LARNER**
JAMES LEWIS: **RICHARD PRINCE**
DAVID HICKEY:
THE INVISIBLE DRAGON/
DER UNSICHTBARE DRACHEN
PAUL TAYLOR: **JAMES ROSENQUIST**

ALIGHIERO E BOETTI
JEAN-CHRISTOPHE AMMANN
GIOVAN BATTISTA SALERNO
RAINER CRONE & DAVID MOOS
FRIEDEMANN MALSCH
JEAN-PIERRE BORDAZ
ALAIN CUEFF
INSERT: **CINDY SHERMAN**
SHEENA WAGSTAFF:
SOPHIE CALLE
HERBERT LACHMEYER/
BRIGITTE FELDERER: **FRANZ WEST**
JUTTA KOETHER: **MIKE KELLEY**

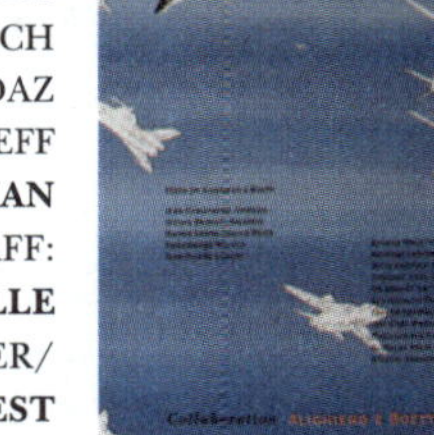

No. 24 - ISBN 3-907509-74-9

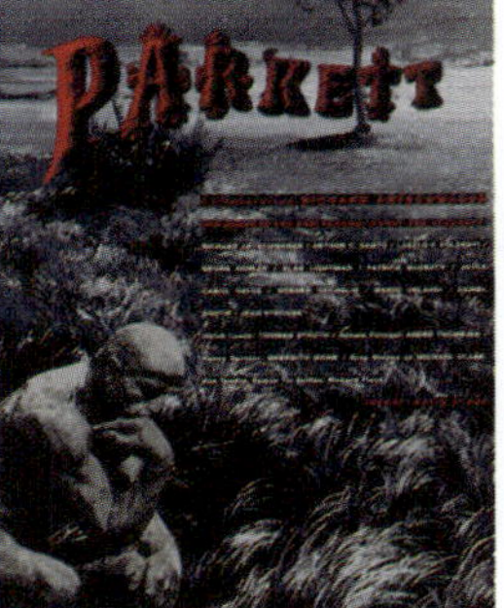

No. 23 - ISBN 3-907509-73-0

RICHARD ARTSCHWAGER
ARTHUR C. DANTO, GEORG KOHLER,
MARIO A. ORLANDO, JOYCE
CAROL OATES, WERNER OECHSLIN,
ALAN LIGHTMAN, PATRICK
McGRATH, DANIEL SOUTIF,
LASZLO F. FÖLDENYI, JEAN STROUSE
INSERT: **DAVID BYRNE**
RENATE PUVOGEL: **ANDRÉ THOMKINS**
ULRICH LOOCK: **THOMAS STRUTH**
NANCY SPECTOR: **MEREDITH MONK**

ALEX KATZ
JOHN RUSSELL, BROOKS ADAMS,
DAVID RIMANELLI, FRANCESCO
CLEMENTE, MICHAEL KRÜGER,
RICHARD FLOOD, PATRICK FREY,
CARL STIGLIANO, BICE CURIGER,
GLENN O'BRIEN
INSERT: **WILLIAM WEGMAN**
LISA LIEBMAN: **ROBERT GOBER**
JACQUELINE BURCKHARDT:
GIULIO ROMANO

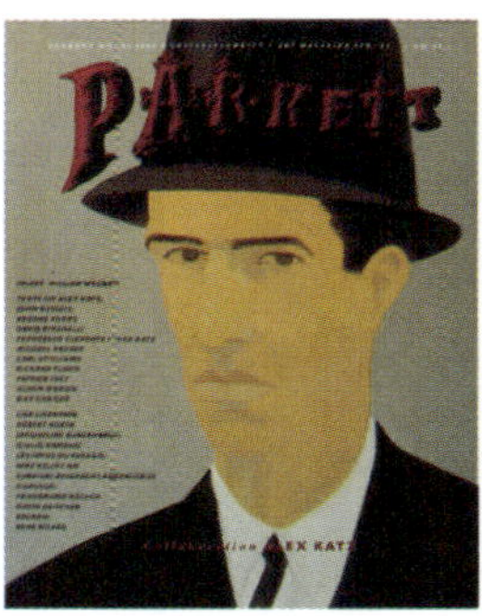

No. 21 - ISBN 3-907509-71-4

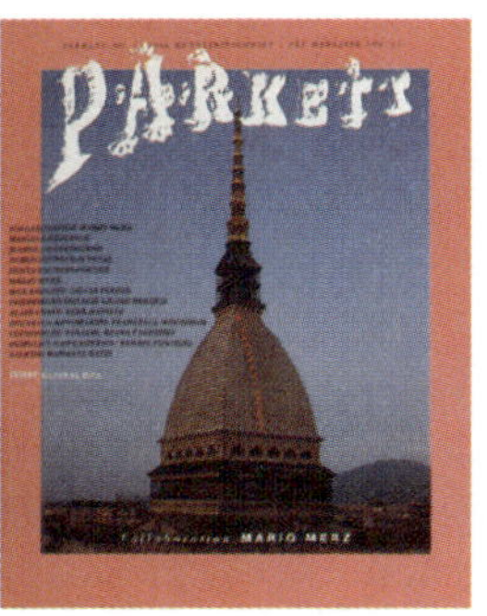

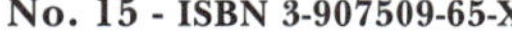

No. 15 - ISBN 3-907509-65-X

MARIO MERZ
MARLIS GRÜTERICH, JEANNE
SILVERTHORNE, DEMOSTHENES
DAVVETAS, HARALD SZEEMANN,
DENYS ZACHAROPOULOS
INSERT: **GENERAL IDEA**
MAX KOZLOFF: **GILLES PERESS**
FRIEDEMANN MALSCH:
GEORG HEROLD
BRUNELLA ANTOMARINI:
FRANCESCA WOODMAN

GILBERT & GEORGE
DUNCAN FALLOWELL, MARIO
CODOGNATO, JEREMY COOPER,
DEMOSTHENES DAVVETAS,
WOLF JAHN
INSERT: **ROSEMARIE TROCKEL**
ROBERT STORR: **NANCY SPERO**
HAIM STEINBACH: **MANIFESTO**
JÖRG ZUTTER: **THOMAS HUBER**

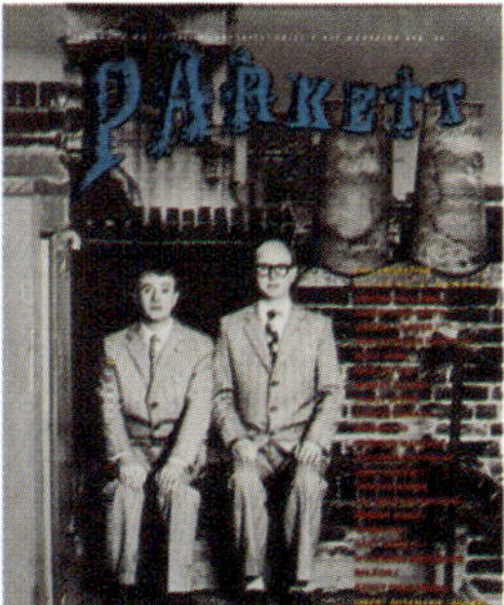

No. 14 - ISBN 3-907509-64-1

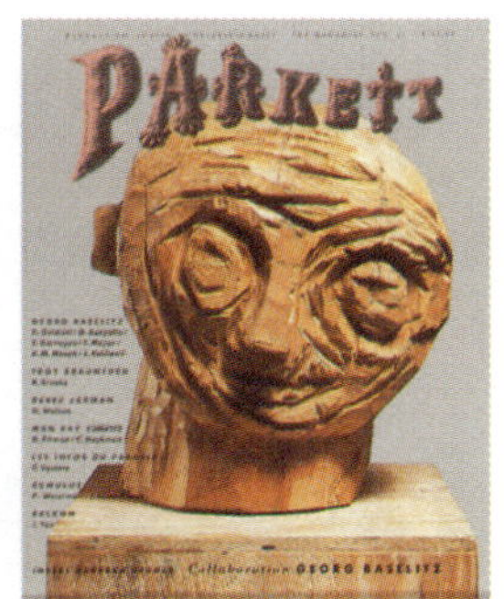

No. 11 - ISBN 3-907509-61-7

GEORG BASELITZ
REMO GUIDIERI, DIETER
KOEPPLIN, ERIC DARRAGON,
RAINER MICHAEL MASON, FRANZ
MEYER, JOHN CALDWELL
INSERT: **BARBARA KRUGER**
GRAY WATSON: **DEREK JARMAN**
CAROL SQUIERS:
PHOTO OPPORTUNITY
ROSETTA BROOKS:
TROY BRAUNTUCH

Each volume of PARKETT is created in collaboration with artists, who contribute an original work specially made for the readers of PARKETT. The works are available in a signed and numbered Special Edition. Prices are subject to change. Postage is not included.

EDITIONS FOR PARKETT

Jeder PARKETT-Band entsteht in Collaboration mit Künstlern, die eigens für die Leser von PARKETT Originalbeiträge gestalten. Diese Vorzugsausgaben sind als nummerierte und signierte Editionen erhältlich. Preisänderungen vorbehalten. Versandkosten und MwSt. (Schweiz) nicht inbegriffen.

SAISONALE GRAVITATION:
INDIVIDUELLE SPUREN UND
KRISTALLISATIONSPUNKTE
IM SOG DER MASSENNESTER
DES GEKRÜMMTEN RAUMS.

SEASONAL GRAVITATION:
INDIVIDUAL TRACES AND POINTS
OF CRYSTALLIZATION IN THE
MAELSTROM OF MASS NESTING
FROM PLACE TO PLACE.

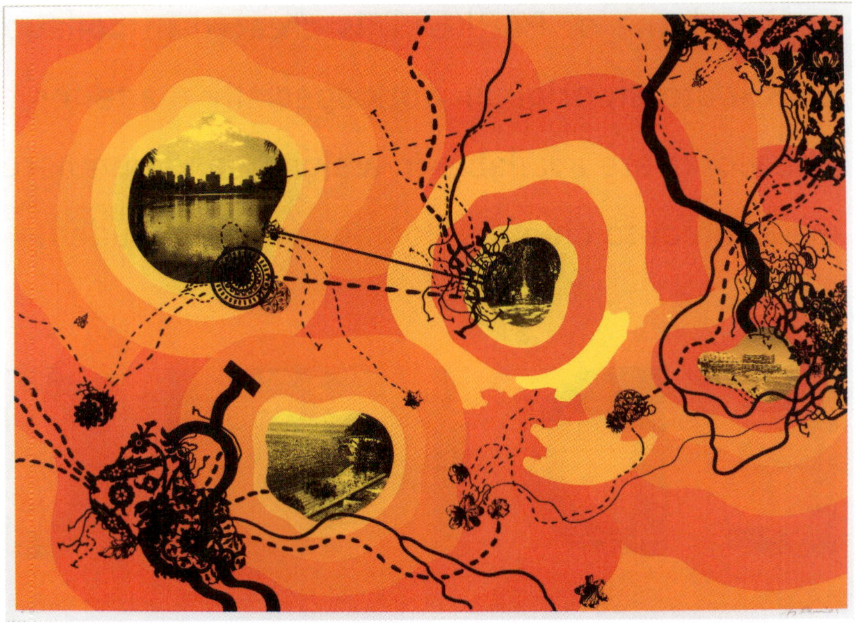

PARKETT 68

FRANZ ACKERMANN

PEAK SEASON, 2003

Siebdruck (10 Farben) auf Somerset 300g/m2;
Blattformat 50 x 70 cm, Bildformat 48 x 68 cm.
Druck: Werkstatt für Kunstsiebdruck München.
Auflage: 70, signiert und nummeriert.
CHF 1700 / € 1100

10-color silkscreen print on Somerset 300 g/m2;
paper size 19 11/16 x 27 9/16", image size 18 7/8 x 26 3/4".
Printed by Werkstatt für Kunstsiebdruck Munich.
Edition of 70, signed and numbered.
$ 1400 / € 1100

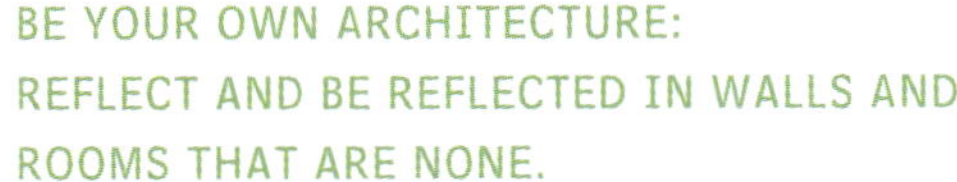

BE YOUR OWN ARCHITECTURE:
REFLECT AND BE REFLECTED IN WALLS AND
ROOMS THAT ARE NONE.

ADDITION, SUBTRAKTION, MULTIPLIKATION,
DIVISION: DAS VERSPIE(GEL)LTE EINMALEINS
EINER MEHRDIMENSIONALEN ARCHITEKTUR.

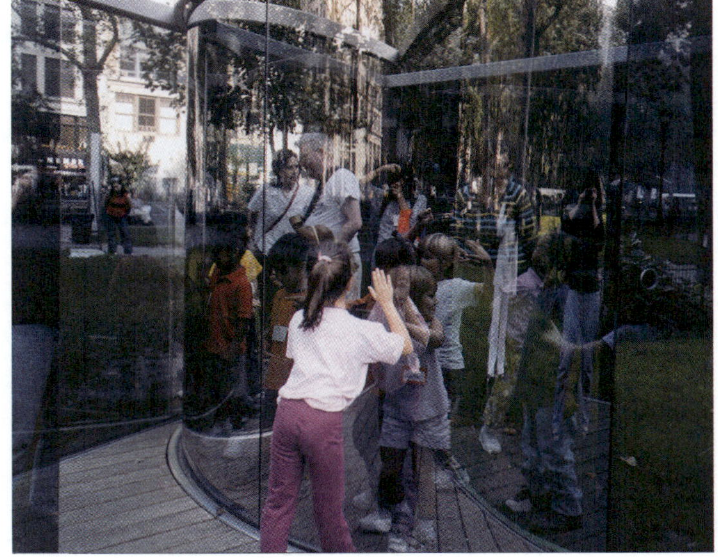

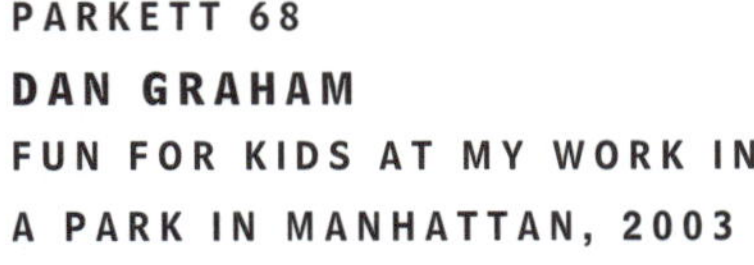

PARKETT 68

DAN GRAHAM

FUN FOR KIDS AT MY WORK IN
A PARK IN MANHATTAN, 2003

Piezo Ultrachrome Pigment on Hahnemühle paper, 13 x 16 1/2".
Printed by Laumont Editions, New York.
Photograph by Rosalind Cutforth.
Edition of 60, signed and numbered on the reverse.
$ 1400 / € 1200

Piezo-Ultrachrome-Pigmentdruck auf Hahnemühle, 33 x 42 cm.
Gedruckt bei Laumont Editions, New York.
Photographie von Rosalind Cutforth.
Auflage: 60, auf der Rückseite signiert und nummeriert.
CHF 1800 / € 1200

IGNORANCE IS THE MIRROR OF KNOWLEDGE

KNOWLEDGE IS THE MIRROR OF IGNORANCE

UNWISSEN IST DER SPIEGEL DES WISSENS

WISSEN IST DER SPIEGEL DES UNWISSENS

PARKETT 68

EIJA-LIISA AHTILA,

VEIL OF IGNORANCE, 2003

Pure wool jacket with text printed on front (mirror-inverted) and back. Handprinted silkscreen lettering by Atelier für Siebdruck Lorenz Boegli, Zurich. Available in 5 sizes (see size table below). Edition of 70, signed certificate.

$ 1400 / € 1200

Reines Wolljackett mit aufgedrucktem Text vorn und hinten (vorne spiegelverkehrt). Handbedruckt bei Atelier für Siebdruck Lorenz Boegli, Zürich. Erhältlich in 5 Grössen (siehe untenstehende Tabelle). Auflage: 70, signiertes Zertifikat. **CHF 1800 / € 1200**

Measurements in cm / Masse in cm:

Men's Sizes / Herrengrössen: Continental European	US/UK	shoulder width / Schulter-breite	back width/ Rücken-breite	back length Rücken-länge	sleeve length / Ärmel-länge	chest measurement Brust-umfang /
48	38	62	48	77	65	110
C 96	38 short	62	48	75	63	114
50	40	64	49	79	66	114.5
C 100	40 short	64	49	76	64	116.5
52	42	66	51	81	67	117

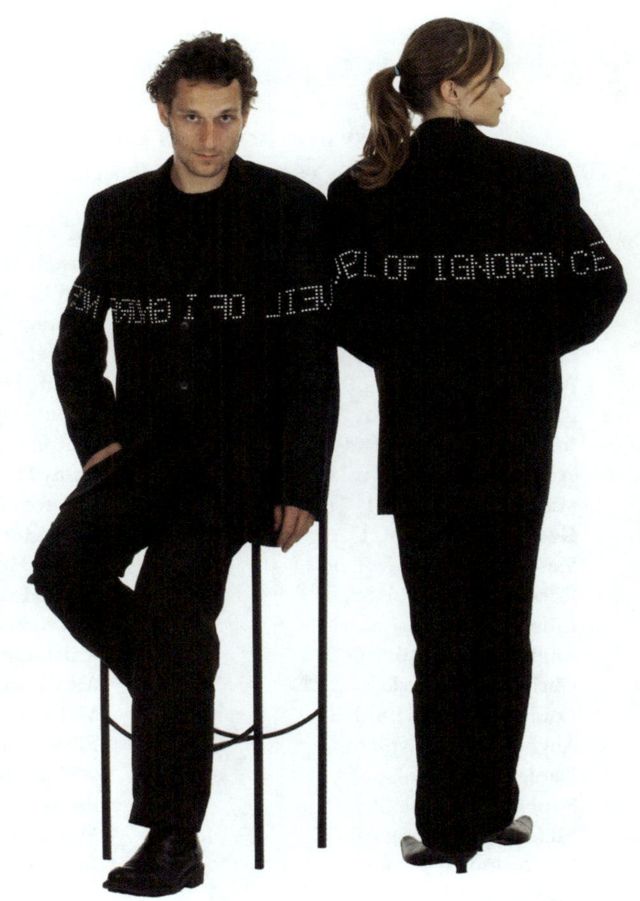

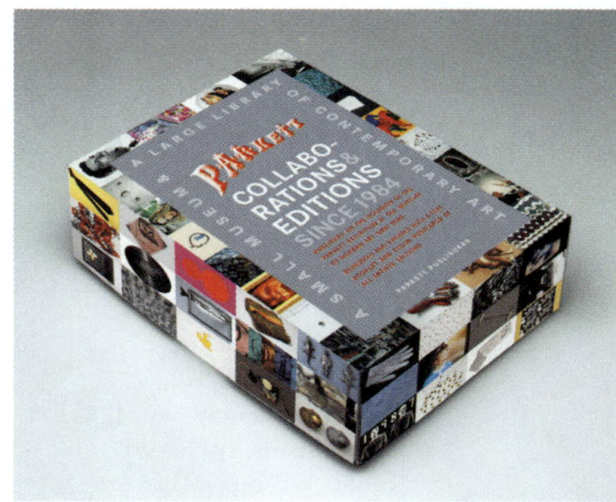

CHF 45 / $ 29 / € 30

ISBN 3-907582-23-3

PARKETT POSTCARD SET WITH TEXT BOOKLET ON MOMA SHOW

Featuring the artists' editions made for PARKETT since 1984 and a booklet with essays by Deborah Wye (Chief Curator Illustrated Books and Prints at MoMA) and Susan Tallman. 128 color postcards, booklet with 2 texts, color reproductions of 64 PARKETT covers. 64 p., packed in a white box, $6\frac{1}{4}$ x $4\frac{3}{4}$ x $2\frac{3}{8}$".

PARKETT-POSTKARTEN-SET MIT TEXTBÜCHLEIN ZUR MOMA-AUSSTELLUNG

Mit Postkarten der seit 1984 von Künstlern für PARKETT geschaffenen Editionen. Das Textbüchlein enthält 2 Essays zur Ausstellung im MoMA, New York, von Deborah Wye (Chefkuratorin für illustrierte Bücher und Grafik am MoMA) und Susan Tallman. 128 Farbpostkarten, Büchlein mit zwei Texten, Farbabb. von 64 PARKETT-Titelblättern u.a.m. 64 S., in weisser Schachtel, 16 x 12 x 6 cm.

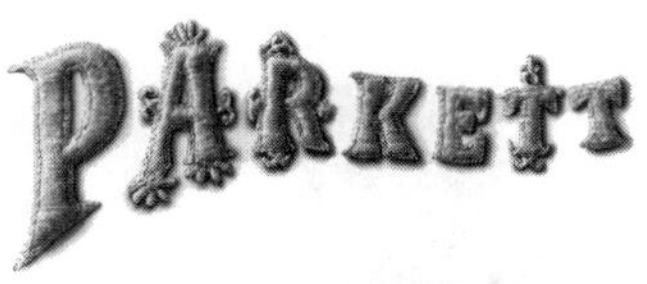

ARTISTS' MONOGRAPHS & EDITIONS / KÜNSTLERMONOGRAPHIEN & EDITIONEN

FOR AVAILABILITY SEE NEXT PAGE / LIEFERBARKEIT SIEHE FOLGENDE SEITE

Franz Ackermann, vol. 68
Eija-Liisa Ahtila, vol. 68
Doug Aitken, vol. 57
Francis Alÿs, vol. 69
Laurie Anderson, vol. 49
John Armleder, vol. 50/51
Richard Artschwager, vol. 23, vol. 46
John Baldessari, vol. 29
Stephan Balkenhol, vol. 36
Matthew Barney, vol. 45
Georg Baselitz, vol. 11
Vanessa Beecroft, vol. 56
Ross Bleckner, vol. 38
John Bock, vol. 67
Alighiero e Boetti, vol. 24
Christian Boltanski, vol. 22
Louise Bourgeois, vol. 27
Angela Bulloch, vol. 66
Daniel Buren, vol. 66
Sophie Calle, vol. 36
Maurizio Cattelan, vol. 59
Vija Celmins, vol. 44
Francesco Clemente, vol. 9 & 40/41
Chuck Close, vol. 60
Enzo Cucchi, vol. 1
John Currin, vol. 65
Tacita Dean, vol. 62
Thomas Demand, vol. 62
Martin Disler, vol. 3
Peter Doig, vol. 67
Marlene Dumas, vol. 38
Olafur Eliasson, vol. 64
Tracey Emin, vol. 63
Eric Fischl, vol. 5
Peter Fischli/David Weiss, vol.17, 40/41
Sylvie Fleury, vol. 58
Günther Förg, vol. 26 & 40/41
Tom Friedman, vol. 64
Katharina Fritsch, vol. 25
Liam Gillick, vol. 61
Isa Genzken, vol. 69
Franz Gertsch, vol. 28
Gilbert & George, vol. 14
Robert Gober, vol. 27
Nan Goldin, vol. 57
Felix Gonzalez-Torres, vol. 39
Douglas Gordon, vol. 49
Dan Graham, vol. 68
Rodney Graham, vol. 64
Andreas Gursky, vol. 44
David Hammons, vol. 31
Thomas Hirschhorn, vol. 57
Damien Hirst, vol. 40/41
Jenny Holzer, vol. 40/41
Rebecca Horn, vol. 13 & 40/41
Roni Horn, vol. 54
Pierre Huyghe, vol. 66
Gary Hume, vol. 48
Ilya Kabakov, vol. 34
Anish Kapoor, vol. 69
Alex Katz, vol. 21
Mike Kelley, vol. 31
Ellsworth Kelly, vol. 56
William Kentridge, vol. 63
Karen Kilimnik, vol. 52
Martin Kippenberger, vol. 19
Imi Knoebel, vol. 32
Jeff Koons, vol. 19, 50/51
Jannis Kounellis, vol. 6
Yayoi Kusama, vol. 59
Wolfgang Laib, vol. 39
Sherrie Levine, vol. 32
Sarah Lucas, vol. 45
Brice Marden, vol. 7
Mario Merz, vol. 15
Tracey Moffatt, vol. 53
Mariko Mori, vol. 54
Malcolm Morley, vol. 52
Sarah Morris, vol. 61
Juan Muñoz, vol. 43
Jean-Luc Mylayne, vol. 50/51
Bruce Nauman, vol. 10
Cady Noland, vol. 46
Meret Oppenheim, vol. 4
Gabriel Orozco, vol. 48
Tony Oursler, vol. 47
Laura Owens, vol. 65
Jorge Pardo, vol. 56
Raymond Pettibon, vol. 47
Elizabeth Peyton, vol. 53
Sigmar Polke, vol. 2, 30 & 40/41
Richard Prince, vol. 34
Michael Raedecker, vol. 65
Markus Raetz, vol. 8
Charles Ray, vol. 37
Jason Rhoades, vol. 58
Gerhard Richter, vol. 35
Bridget Riley, vol. 61
Pipilotti Rist, vol. 48
Matthew Ritchie, vol. 61
Tim Rollins & K.O.S., vol. 20
Ugo Rondinone, vol. 52
James Rosenquist, vol. 58
Susan Rothenberg, vol. 43
Thomas Ruff, vol. 28
Edward Ruscha, vol. 18 & 55
Gregor Schneider, vol. 63
Thomas Schütte, vol. 47
Cindy Sherman, vol. 29
Roman Signer, vol. 45
Andreas Slominski, vol. 55
Beat Streuli, vol. 54
Thomas Struth, vol. 50/51
Hiroshi Sugimoto, vol. 46
Philip Taaffe, vol. 26
Sam Taylor-Wood, vol. 55
Diana Thater, vol. 60
Wolfgang Tillmans, vol. 53
Rirkrit Tiravanija, vol. 44
Fred Tomaselli, vol. 67
Rosemarie Trockel, vol. 33
James Turrell, vol. 25
Luc Tuymans, vol. 60
Kara Walker, vol. 59
Jeff Wall, vol. 22 & 49
Andy Warhol, vol. 12
Lawrence Weiner, vol. 42
John Wesley, vol. 62
Franz West, vol. 37
Rachel Whiteread, vol. 42
Sue Williams, vol 50/51
Robert Wilson, vol. 16
Christopher Wool, vol. 33

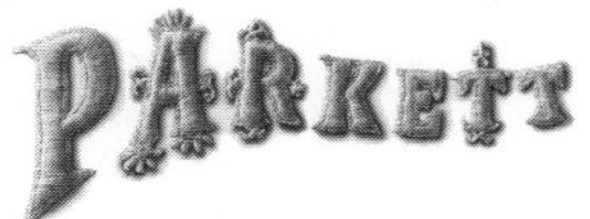

ARTISTS' EDITIONS FOR PARKETT SUBSCRIBERS
WWW.PARKETTART.COM

The PARKETT Series is created in collaboration with artists, who contribute an original work available exclusively to the subscribers in the form of a signed limited SPECIAL EDITION. The available works are also reproduced in each PARKETT issue.

Each SPECIAL EDITION is available by order from any one of our offices in New York or Zurich. Just fill in the details below and send this card to the office nearest you. Once your order has been processed, you will be issued with an invoice and your personal edition number. Upon receipt of payment, you will receive the SPECIAL EDITION. (Please note that supply is subject to availability. PARKETT does not assume responsibility for any delays in production of SPECIAL EDITIONS. Postage is not included.)

☐ As a subscriber to PARKETT, I would like to order the following Special Edition(s), signed and numbered by the artist.

PARKETT No. ARTIST ______ NAME: ______

PARKETT No. ARTIST ______ ADDRESS: ______

PARKETT No. ARTIST ______ CITY: ______

PARKETT No. ARTIST ______ STATE/ZIP: ______

PARKETT No. ARTIST ______ COUNTRY: ______

PARKETT No. ARTIST ______ PHONE: ______

☐ I have indicated my way of payment on the reverse side of this form.

Send this form to the PARKETT office nearest you:

PARKETT PUBLISHERS 155 AV. OF THE AMERICAS NEW YORK, NY 10013 PHONE (212) 673-2660 FAX (212) 271-0704

PARKETT VERLAG QUELLENSTRASSE 27 CH-8031 ZÜRICH TELEFON +41-1-271 81 40 FAX +41-1-272 43 01

Visit our website: www.parkettart.com

PARKETT

KÜNSTLEREDITIONEN FÜR PARKETT-ABONNENTEN
WWW.PARKETTART.COM

68

Die PARKETT-Buchreihe entsteht in Zusammenarbeit mit Künstlern, die eigens für die Abonnenten einen Originalbeitrag in Form einer limitierten und signierten EDITION gestalten. Diese Editionen sind auch in der Zeitschrift abgebildet und können mit dieser Bestellkarte in jedem unserer Büros in Zürich, Frankfurt oder New York bestellt werden. Sie erhalten dann Ihre persönliche Editionsnummer und eine Rechnung. Sobald wir Ihre Zahlung erhalten haben, schicken wir Ihnen Ihre Edition(en). Lieferung solange Vorrat. PARKETT übernimmt keine Verantwortung für allfällige Verzögerungen bei der Herstellung der Vorzugsausgaben. Versandkosten und MwSt (Schweiz) nicht inbegriffen.

☐ Ich bin PARKETT-Abonnent(in) und bestelle folgende EDITION(EN), nummeriert und vom Künstler signiert:

PARKETT Nr. KÜNSTLER/IN ______ NAME: ______

PARKETT Nr. KÜNSTLER/IN ______ STRASSE: ______

PARKETT Nr. KÜNSTLER/IN ______ PLZ/STADT: ______

PARKETT Nr. KÜNSTLER/IN ______ LAND: ______

PARKETT Nr. KÜNSTLER/IN ______ TEL.: ______

☐ Meine Zahlungsweise habe ich auf der Rückseite angegeben.

Senden Sie die Bestellkarte an das PARKETT-Büro in Ihrer Nähe:

PARKETT VERLAG QUELLENSTRASSE 27 CH-8031 ZÜRICH TELEFON +41-1-271 81 40 FAX +41-1-272 43 01

PARKETT PUBLISHERS 155 AV. OF THE AMERICAS NEW YORK, NY 10013 PHONE (212) 673-2660 FAX (212) 271-0704

Besuchen Sie unsere Website: www.parkettart.com

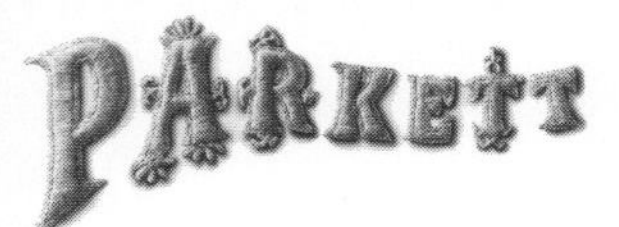

SUBSCRIBE, COMPLETE OR SEND A GIFT SUBSCRIPTION TO THE BEST BOOK SERIES ON CONTEMPORARY ARTISTS – WWW.PARKETTART.COM

68

☐ I wish to subscribe to the PARKETT Series, starting with issue no. _____

☐ I wish to send a gift subscription, starting with issue no. _____ (a gift card in my name will be sent to the recipient):

- ☐ for 1 year (3 issues) at US $ 80 (USA/Canada), € 82 (Europe), € 98 (Rest of the World)
- ☐ for 2 years (6 issues) at US $ 145 (USA/Canada), € 150 (Europe), € 188 (Rest of the World)
- ☐ for 3 years (9 issues) at US $ 205 (USA/Canada), € 212 (Europe), € 278 (Rest of the World)
- ☐ for 1 year (3 issues) at the special student discount (US $ 65 for USA/Canada, € 67 for Europe). A copy of my student ID is enclosed.

Postage included. All prices subject to change.

☐ I wish to complete my PARKETT library and order the following issue(s):

No. ______________________

at € 30 each (up to no. 43: € 20; no. 44–48: € 28), postage not included. Within the USA & Canada $ 32 (up to no. 43: $ 22.50; no. 44–48: $ 29), add postage: $ 5 (USA), $ 10 (Canada). (Sold out: No. 1–10, 12, 13, 16, 17, 19, 22, 25, 26, 27, 29–31, 35, 36, 38, 45).

☐ I wish to order _____ copies of the PARKETT Postcard Set with Text Booklet on MoMA Show. Featuring all artists' editions made for PARKETT since 1984 and a booklet with essays by Deborah Wye (Chief Curator Illustrated Books and Prints at MoMA) and Susan Tallman. 128 color postcards, booklet with 2 texts, color reproductions of all 64 PARKETT covers. 64 p., packed in a box, 6¼ x 4¾ x 2⅜", € 30 (USA $ 27) per set, plus postage.

NAME: ______________________

ADDRESS: ______________________

CITY: ______________________

STATE/ZIP/COUNTRY: ______________________

TEL.: ______________ FAX: ______________

E-MAIL: ______________________

GIFT RECIPIENT: ______________________

ADDRESS: ______________________

CITY: ______________________

STATE/ZIP: ______________________

COUNTRY: ______________________

☐ Charge my Visa Card ☐ Mastercard ☐ AMEX

Card No. | | | | | | | | | | | | | | | | | Expiration date _______

☐ Payment enclosed (US check or money order) ☐ Bill me

DATE ______________________

SIGNATURE ______________________

Send this form to the PARKETT office nearest you:

PARKETT PUBLISHERS 155 AV. OF THE AMERICAS NEW YORK, NY 10013 PHONE (212) 673-2660 FAX (212) 271-0704

PARKETT VERLAG QUELLENSTRASSE 27 CH-8031 ZÜRICH TELEFON +41-1-271 81 40 FAX +41-1-272 43 01

Visit our website: www.parkettart.com

ABONNIEREN, VERVOLLSTÄNDIGEN ODER VERSCHENKEN SIE DIE UMFASSENDSTE BUCHREIHE ÜBER GEGENWARTSKÜNSTLER – WWW.PARKETTART.COM

68

☐ Ich abonniere die PARKETT-Reihe ab Nr. _____

☐ Ich verschenke ein PARKETT-Abonnement ab Nr. _____ (Der/die Beschenkte erhält eine Geschenkkarte in meinem Namen)

- ☐ für 1 Jahr (3 Bände) zu: € 78 (Deutschland), CHF 116.– (Schweiz), € 82 (übriges Europa)
- ☐ für 2 Jahre (6 Bände) zu: € 140 (Deutschland), CHF 216.– (Schweiz), € 150 (übriges Europa)
- ☐ für 3 Jahre (9 Bände) zu: € 200 (Deutschland), CHF 312.– (Schweiz), € 212 (übriges Europa)
- ☐ für 1 Jahr (3 Bände) zum Studenten-Sonderpreis (Deutschland: € 65 /Schweiz: CHF 96.– / übriges Europa: € 67). Eine Kopie meines gültigen Studentenausweises lege ich bei.

Preise einschliesslich Versandkosten. Preisänderungen vorbehalten.

☐ Ich möchte meine PARKETT-Bibliothek vervollständigen und bestelle die folgenden noch erhältliche(n) Ausgabe(n):

Nr. ______________________

zu je € 30 / CHF 45.– (bis Nr. 43: € 20 / CHF 30.–; Nr. 44–48: € 28 / CHF 39.–), zzgl. Versandkosten (vergriffen: Nr. 1–10, 12, 13, 16, 17, 19, 22, 25, 26, 27, 29–31, 35, 36, 38, 45).

☐ Ich bestelle _____ Ex. des PARKETT-Postkarten-Sets mit Textbüchlein zur MoMA-Ausstellung. Mit Postkarten der seit 1984 von Künstlern für PARKETT geschaffenen Editionen. Das Textbüchlein enthält 2 Essays zur Ausstellung im MoMA, New York, von Deborah Wye (Chefkuratorin für illustrierte Bücher und Grafik am MoMA) und Susan Tallman. 128 Farbpostkarten, Büchlein mit zwei Texten, Farbabb. aller 64 PARKETT-Titelblätter u.a.m. 64 S., in bunter Schachtel, 16 x 12 x 6 cm. € 30 / CHF 45.– pro Set, zzgl. Versandkosten.

NAME: ______________________

STRASSE: ______________________

PLZ/STADT: ______________________

LAND: ______________________

TEL.: ______________ FAX: ______________

E-MAIL: ______________________

BESCHENKTE(R): ______________________

STRASSE: ______________________

PLZ/STADT: ______________________

LAND: ______________________

☐ Ich zahle mit Visa ☐ Eurocard/Mastercard ☐ AMEX

Karten Nr. | | | | | | | | | | | | | | | | | Gültig bis _______

☐ Mein Scheck über CHF/€ ______________ liegt bei.

☐ Bitte senden Sie mir eine Rechnung.

DATUM ______________________

UNTERSCHRIFT ______________________

Senden Sie die Bestellkarte an das PARKETT-Büro in Ihrer Nähe:

PARKETT VERLAG QUELLENSTRASSE 27 CH-8031 ZÜRICH TELEFON +41-1-271 81 40 FAX +41-1-272 43 01

PARKETT PUBLISHERS 155 AV. OF THE AMERICAS NEW YORK, NY 10013 PHONE (212) 673-2660 FAX (212) 271-0704

Besuchen Sie unsere Website: www.parkettart.com

vol.	Collaboration		
69	Francis Alÿs	m	e
	Isa Gentzken	m	e
	Anish Kapoor	m	e
68	Franz Ackermann	m	e
	Eija-Liisa Ahtila	m	e
	Dan Graham	m	e
67	John Bock	m	e
	Peter Doig	m	e
	Fred Tomaselli	m	e
66	Angela Bulloch	m	e
	Daniel Buren	m	e
	Pierre Huyghe	m	e
65	John Currin	m	
	Laura Owens	m	e
	Michael Raedecker	m	e
64	Olafur Eliasson	m	
	Tom Friedman	m	
	Rodney Graham	m	
63	Tracey Emin	m	e
	William Kentridge	m	e
	Gregor Schneider	m	
62	Tacita Dean	m	e
	Thomas Demand	m	
	John Wesley	m	e
61	Liam Gillick	m	
	Sarah Morris	m	e
	Bridget Riley	m	e
	Matthew Ritchie	m	e
60	Chuck Close	m	
	Diana Thater	m	e
	Luc Tuymans	m	e
59	Maurizio Cattelan	m	
	Yayoi Kusama	m	e
	Kara Walker	m	
58	Sylvie Fleury	m	
	Jason Rhoades	m	e
	James Rosenquist	m	e
57	Doug Aitken	m	e
	Nan Goldin	m	
	Thomas Hirschhorn	m	
56	Vanessa Beecroft	m	
	Ellsworth Kelly	m	
	Jorge Pardo	m	e
55	Edward Ruscha	m	
	Andreas Slominski	m	
	Sam Taylor-Wood	m	
54	Roni Horn	m	e
	Mariko Mori	m	
54	Beat Streuli	m	
53	Tracey Moffatt	m	
	Elizabeth Peyton	m	
	Wolfgang Tillmans	m	
52	Karen Kilimnik	m	e
	Malcolm Morley	m	e
	Ugo Rondinone	m	e
50/51	John Armleder	m	
	Jeff Koons	m	e
	Jean-Luc Mylayne	m	
	Thomas Struth	m	
	Sue Williams	m	
49	Laurie Anderson	m	e
	Douglas Gordon	m	
	Jeff Wall	m	
48	Gary Hume	m	
	Gabriel Orozco	m	
	Pipilotti Rist	m	
47	Tony Oursler	m	
	Raymond Pettibon	m	
	Thomas Schütte	m	e
46	Richard Artschwager	m	
	Cady Noland	m	
	Hiroshi Sugimoto	m	
45	Matthew Barney		
	Sarah Lucas		
	Roman Signer		e
44	Vija Celmins	m	
	Andreas Gursky	m	
	Rirkrit Tiravanija	m	e
43	Juan Muñoz	m	
	Susan Rothenberg	m	
42	Lawrence Weiner	m	e
	Rachel Whiteread	m	
40/41	Francesco Clemente	m	
	Fischli/Weiss	m	
	Günther Förg	m	
	Damien Hirst	m	
	Jenny Holzer	m	
	Rebecca Horn	m	
	Sigmar Polke	m	
39	Felix Gonzalez-Torres	m	
	Wolfgang Laib	m	
38	Ross Bleckner		
	Marlene Dumas		
37	Charles Ray	m	
	Franz West	m	e
36	Stephan Balkenhol		
36	Sophie Calle		
35	Gerhard Richter		
34	Ilya Kabakov	m	
	Richard Prince	m	
33	Rosemarie Trockel	m	
	Christopher Wool	m	
32	Imi Knoebel	m	
	Sherrie Levine	m	
31	David Hammons		
31	Mike Kelley		
30	Sigmar Polke		
29	John Baldessari		
29	Cindy Sherman		
28	Franz Gertsch	m	
	Thomas Ruff	m	
27	Louise Bourgeois		
	Robert Gober		
26	Günther Förg		
	Philip Taaffe		
25	Katharina Fritsch		e
	James Turrell		e
24	Alighiero e Boetti	m	e
23	Richard Artschwager	m	
22	Christian Boltanski		
	Jeff Wall		
21	Alex Katz	m	
20	Tim Rollins + K.O.S.	m	
19	Martin Kippenberger		
	Jeff Koons		
18	Ed Ruscha	m	
17	Fischli/Weiss		
16	Robert Wilson		
15	Mario Merz	m	
14	Gilbert & George	m	
13	Rebecca Horn		
12	Andy Warhol		
11	Georg Baselitz	m	
10	Bruce Nauman		
9	Francesco Clemente		
8	Markus Raetz		
7	Brice Marden		
6	Jannis Kounellis		
5	Eric Fischl		
4	Meret Oppenheim		
3	Martin Disler		
2	Sigmar Polke		
1	Enzo Cucchi		

m = available monograph / erhältliche Monographie, e = available edition / erhältliche Edition
Delivery subject to availability at time of order / Lieferung solange Vorrat

PARKETT IN BOOKSHOPS (Selection)

PARKETT IS AVAILABLE IN 500 LEADING ART BOOKSHOPS AROUND THE WORLD. FOR FURTHER INFORMATION CONTACT:

PARKETT GIBT ES IN 500 FÜHRENDEN KUNSTBUCHHANDLUNGEN AUF DER GANZEN WELT. FÜR WEITERE INFORMATIONEN WENDEN SIE SICH BITTE AN:

PARKETT VERLAG, QUELLENSTRASSE 27, CH-8031 ZÜRICH, TEL. +41-1 271 81 40, FAX 272 43 01, WWW.PARKETTART.COM;

PARKETT*, 155, AVENUE OF THE AMERICAS, 2ND FLOOR, NEW YORK, N.Y. 10013, PHONE +1 (212) 673-2660, FAX 271-0704, WWW.PARKETTART.COM*

NORTH & SOUTH AMERICA, ASIA, AUSTRALIA

DISTRIBUTOR / VERTRIEB
D.A.P. (DISTRIBUTED ART PUBLISHERS)
155 AVENUE OF THE AMERICAS, 2ND FLOOR,
NEW YORK, NY 10013

USA

AUSTIN, TX
BOOK PEOPLE
603 N. LAMAR

BERKELEY, CA
BERKELEY ART MUSEUM
2625 DURANT AVENUE
CODY'S BOOKS
2454 TELEGRAPHE AVENUE

BEVERLY HILLS, CA
RIZZOLI
9501 WILSHIRE BOULEVARD

BOSTON, MA
INSTITUTE OF CONTEMPORARY ART
955 BOYLSTON STREET
TRIDENT BOOKSELLERS
338 NEWBURY STREET

BUFFALO, NY
TALKING LEAVES
3158 MAIN STREET

CAMBRIDGE, MA
MIT PRESS BOOKSTORE
292 MAIN STREET

CHICAGO, IL
ART INSTITUTE OF CHICAGO
104 S. MICHIGAN
MUSEUM OF CONTEMPORARY ART
220 EAST CHICAGO AVENUE
QUIMBY'S
1854 W. NORTH AVENUE
SMART MUSEUM OF ART
5550 S. GREENWOOD AVENUE

CINCINNATI, OH
CONTEMPORARY ARTS CENTER
115 E. 5TH STREET

COLUMBUS, OH
COLUMBUS MUSEUM OF ART
372 COMMONS MALL
WEXNER CENTER BOOKSTORE
30 W. 15TH STREET

CORAL GABLES, FL
BOOKS & BOOKS
296 ARAGON ROAD

HOUSTON, TX
BRAZOS BOOKSTORE
2421 BISSONNET
CONTEMPORARY ARTS MUSEUM
5216 MONTROSE BOULEVARD
MENIL COLLECTION
1520 SUL ROSS

HUNTINGTON, WV
HUNTINGTON MUSEUM OF ART
2033 MCCOY ROAD

LOS ANGELES, CA
BOOKSOUP
8818 SUNSET BOULEVARD
MUSEUM OF CONTEMPORARY ART
250, S. GRAND
UCLA / ARMAND HAMMER MUSEUM OF ART
10899 WILSHIRE BOULEVARD

MIAMI, FL
BOOKS & BOOKS
296 ARAGON AVENUE, CORAL GABLES
MUSEUM OF CONTEMPORARY ART
770 N.E. 125TH STREET NORTH MIAMI

MINNEAPOLIS, MN
THE WALKER ART CENTER BOOKSTORE
VINELAND PLACE

NEW YORK, NY
GUGGENHEIM DOWNTOWN MUSEUM
575 BROADWAY
MUSEUM OF MODERN ART
11 W. 53RD STREET
NEW MUSEUM OF CONTEMPORARY ART
583 BROADWAY
RIZZOLI
454 WEST BROADWAY
SAINT MARK'S BOOKSTORE
31 3RD AVENUE

OAKLAND, CA
DIESEL, A BOOKSTORE
5433 COLLEGE AVENUE

OAK PARK, MI
BOOK BEAT LTD.
26010 GREENFIELD

OMAHA, NE
JOSLYN ART MUSEUM
2200 DODGE STREET

PHILADELPHIA, PA
AVRIL 50
3406 SANSOM STREET
WATERSTONE BOOKSELLERS
2191 HORNIG ROAD

PITTSBURGH, PA
CARNEGIE INSTITUTE
4400 FORBES AVENUE

PORTLAND, OR
POWELL'S BOOKS
7 NW 9TH STREET

PROVIDENCE, NY
ACCIDENT OR DESIGN
128 N. MAIN STREET
RHODE ISLAND SCHOOL OF DESIGN
2 COLLEGE STREET, 1765

SAN ANTONIO, TX
SLOAN / HALL SAN ANTONIO
5930 BROADWAY

SAN FRANCISCO, CA
A CLEAN WELL LIGHTED PLACE
601 VAN NESS AVENUE
CITY LIGHTS BOOKSHOP
261 COLUMBUS AVENUE
SAN FRANCISCO MUSEUM OF MODERN ART,
MUSEUMBOOKS
151 3RD STREET, 1ST FLOOR

ST. LOUIS, MO
LEFT BANK BOOKS
399 NORTH EUCLID

SANTA MONICA, CA
ARCANA
1229 3RD STREET PROMENADE
HENNESSEY & INGALLS BOOKS
1254 3RD STREET PROMENADE

ST. PAUL, MN
HUNGRY MIND BOOKSTORE
1648 GRAND AVENUE

SEATTLE, WA
UNIVERSITY BOOKSTORE
4326 UNIVERSITY WAY

WASHINGTON D.C.
NATIONAL GALLERY OF ART
6TH STREET & CONSTITUTION AVENUE, NW

CANADA / KANADA

CALGARY
TREPANIER BAER GALLERY
105 999 8TH STREET SW

MONTREAL
ARTEXTE
3575 STREET LAURENT
OLIVIERI LIBRAIRIE BOOKSTORE
185 STREET CATHERINE WEST

TORONTO
ART GALLERY OF ONTARIO
317 DUNDAS STREET WEST
ART METROPOLE
788 KING STREET WEST
DAVID MIRVISH BOOKS ON ART
596 MARKHAM STREET

VANCOUVER
VANCOUVER ART GALLERY
750 HORNBY STREET

AUSTRALIA / AUSTRALIEN

DARLINGHURST
EAST SYDNEY BOOKSTORE
THE DOME, THE ELAN BUILDING
1 KINGS CROSS ROAD

SYDNEY
MUSEUM OF CONTEMPORARY ART
140 GEORGE STREET, CIRCULAR QUAY NORTH
GLEE BOOKS
191 GLEBE POINT ROAD, GLEBE

NEW ZEALAND / NEUSEELAND

AUCKLAND
PROPAGANDA
2 CARR ROAD, MT ROSKILL

ASIA / ASIEN

JAPAN

TOKYO
AOYAMA BOOK CENTRE, SHIBUYA-KU
COSMOS AOYAMA GARDEN FLOOR B2F
5-53-97, JINGUMAE
ART & BOOKS
2-1-13-307
TAKANAWA, MINATO-KU
WATARI MUSEUM OF CONTEMPORARY ART,
ON SUNDAYS BOOKSHOP
376 JINGUMAE SHIBUYA-KU

SINGAPORE / SINGAPUR

PAGE ONE BOOKSTORE
20 KAKI BUKIT VIEW TECHPARK

GREAT BRITAIN / GROSSBRITANNIEN

DISTRIBUTOR / VERTRIEB
CENTRAL BOOKS
99, WALLIS ROAD
LONDON E9 5LN

BRISTOL
ARNOLFINI BOOKSHOP
16 NARROW QUAY

LONDON
BORDERS BOOKSHOP
120 CHARING CROSS ROAD

BORDERS BOOKSHOP
203–207 OXFORD STREET
CAMDEN ARTS CENTRE
ARKWRIGHT ROAD
HAYWARD GALLERY
SOUTH BANK
IAN SHIPLEY BOOKSHOP
70 CHARING CROSS ROAD
INSTITUTE OF CONTEMPORARY ARTS
12 CARLTON HOUSE TERRACE
THE MALL
SERPENTINE GALLERY
KENSINGTON GARDENS
TATE MODERN
BANKSIDE
ZWEMMER LTD. ART BOOKS
24 LITCHFIELD STREET

IRELAND / IRLAND
DUBLIN
DOUGLAS HYDE GALLERY
TRINITY COLLEGE

GERMANY / DEUTSCHLAND
DISTRIBUTOR / VERTRIEB
GVA VERLAGSSERVICE GÖTTINGEN
PF 2021
D-37010 GÖTTINGEN
BERLIN
BÜCHERBOGEN AM SAVIGNYPLATZ
STADTBAHNBOGEN 593
GALERIE 2000 KUNSTBUCHHANDLUNG
KNESEBECKSTRASSE 56/58
WALTHER KÖNIG BUCHHANDLUNG, MUSEUM FÜR GEGENWARTSKUNST
IM HAMBURGER BAHNHOF INVALIDENSTRASSE 50–51
WIENS LADEN & VERLAG
LINIENSTRASSE 158 (HOF)
WASMUTH GMBH & CO.
PFALZBURGERSTRASSE 43–44
BREMEN
BEIM STEINERNEN KREUZ GMBH
BEIM STEINERNEN KREUZ 1
DÜSSELDORF
LITERATUR BEI RUDOLF MÜLLER
NEUSTRASSE 38
WALTHER KÖNIG BUCHHANDLUNG
HEINRICH-HEINE-ALLEE 15
FRANKFURT
KUNST-BUCH, KUNSTHALLE SCHIRN
RÖMERBERG 7
WALTHER KÖNIG BUCHHANDLUNG
DOMSTRASSE 6
HAMBURG
HELMUT VON DER HÖH BUCHHANDLUNG
GROSSE BLEICHEN 21
SAUTTER + LACKMANN BUCHHANDLUNG
ADMIRALITÄTSTRASSE 71/72
HANNOVER
MERZ KUNSTBUCHHANDLUNG
KURT-SCHWITTERS-PLATZ
KARLSRUHE
HANS MENDE BUCHHANDLUNG
KARLSTRASSE 76
KÖLN
SCHADEN.COM BUCHHANDEL
BURGMAUER 10
WALTHER KÖNIG BUCHHANDLUNG
EHRENSTRASSE 4
KIOSK-BUCH-EVENT GMBH
IM MEDIAPARK 7
MÜNCHEN
HANS GOLTZ BUCHHANDLUNG FÜR BILDENDE KUNST
TÜRKENSTRASSE 54
ILKA KÖNIG BUCHHANDLUNG
MAXIMILIANSTRASSE 35

L. WERNER BUCHHANDLUNG
RESIDENZSTRASSE 18
NÜRNBERG
WALTHER KÖNIG BUCHHANDLUNG
LUITPOLDSTRASSE 5
STUTTGART
LIMACHER BUCHHANDLUNG
KÖNIGSTRASSE 28 / KÖNIGSBAU

SPAIN / SPANIEN
BARCELONA
LAIE – CAIXAFÒRUM
MARQUES DE COMILLAS 6–8
LAIE – CCCB (CENTRE DE CULTURA CONTEMPORÀNIA DE BARCELONA)
MONTALEGRE 5
MADRID
MUSEO NACIONAL REINA SOFIA
C/ SANTA ISABEL, 52

FRANCE / FRANKREICH
PARIS
CENTRE POMPIDOU, FLAMMARION 4
26, RUE JACOB
GALERIE NATIONALE DU JEU DE PAUME
1, PLACE DE LA CONCORDE
LIBRAIRIE DU MUSÉE D'ART MODERNE
9, RUE GASTON DE SAINT-PAUL
CHRISTOPH DAVIET-THERY, LIVRES & EDITIONS D'ARTISTES
10, RUE DUCHEFDELAVILLE
COLETTE
213, RUE SAINT-HONORÉ

ITALY / ITALIEN
MILANO
A&M BOOKSTORE
30, VIA TADINO
ROMA
GALLERIA NAZIONALE D'ARTE MODERNA
131, VIA DELLE BELLE ARTI
GALLERIA PRIMO PIANO
203, VIA PANISPERNA

NORWAY / NORWEGEN
OSLO
THE NATIONAL MUSEUM OF CONTEMPORARY ART
BANKPLASSEN 4 / SKATTEFOG

PORTUGAL
LISBOA
MODULO CENTRO DIFUSOR DE ARTE
CALÇADA DOS MESTRES 34 A–B
PORTO
MODULO CENTRO DIFUSOR DE ARTE
AV. BOAVISTA 854

SWEDEN / SCHWEDEN
STOCKHOLM
KULTURHUSET KONSTIG
MEDIA & KONSTBOKHANDEL
SERGELS TORG 3
MODERNA MUSEET
SKEPPSHOLMEN
GÖTEBORG
GÖTEBORGS KONSTMUSEUM
GÖTAPLATSEN / AVENYN

TURKEY / TÜRKEI
ISTANBUL
ROBINSON CRUSOE BOOKS PUSULA PRODUCTIONS
389 ISTIKAL CADDESI BEYOGLU

NETHERLANDS, BELGIUM AND LUXEMBURG
DISTRIBUTOR / VERTRIEB
IDEA BOOKS
NIEUWE HERENGRACHT 11
NL-1011 RK AMSTERDAM

NETHERLANDS / NIEDERLANDE
AMSTERDAM
ART BOOK
VAN BAERLESTRAAT 126
ATHENAEUM NIEUWSCENTRUM
SPUI 14–16
ROBERT PREMSELA BOOKSHOP
VAN BAERLESTRAAT 78
GRONINGEN
SCHOLTENS / WRISTERS BOOKSHOP
FULDENSTRAAT 20
ROTTERDAM
DONNER BOOKSHOP
LIJNBAAN 150

BELGIUM / BELGIEN
ANTWERPEN
F.N.A.C.
GROENPLAATS
BRUXELLES
TROPISMES LIBRAIRIES
GALERIE DES PRINCES 11
GENT
COPYRIGHT BOOKSHOP
JACOBIJNENSTRAAT 8

LUXEMBOURG / LUXEMBURG
LUXEMBOURG
CASINO LUXEMBOURG
41, RUE NOTRE-DAME

SWITZERLAND / SCHWEIZ
DISTRIBUTOR / VERTRIEB
SCHEIDEGGER & CO. C/O AVA
CENTRALWEG 16
CH-8910 AFFOLTERN A. A.
BASEL
FONDATION BEYELER
BASELSTRASSE 77, RIEHEN
GALERIE STAMPA
SPALENBERG 2
JÄGGI BUCHHANDLUNG
FREIE STRASSE 32
KUNSTHALLE BASEL
KLOSTERGASSE 5
BERN
STAUFFACHER BUCHHANDLUNG
IM KUNSTMUSEUM
HODLERSTR. 12
LUZERN
RÄBER BÜCHER AG
FRANKENSTRASSE 7-9
GENÈVE
LIBRAIRIE PAYOT
5, RUE DE CHANTEPOULET
MENDRISIO
GABRIELE CAPELLI LIBRERIA ARCHITETTURA
4, VIA NOBILI BOSIA
ST. GALLEN
RÖSSLITOR BÜCHER
WEBERGASSE 5
ZÜRICH
CALLIGRAMME BUCHHANDLUNG
HÄRINGSTRASSE 4
HOWEG BUCHHANDLUNG
WAFFENPLATZ 1
KUNSTGRIFF BUCHHANDLUNG
LIMMATSTRASSE 270
KUNSTHAUS ZÜRICH
HEIMPLATZ 1
KUNSTKIOSK
LIMMATQUAI 31
ORELL FÜSSLI KRAUTHAMMER
MARKTGASSE 12
ORELL FÜSSLI BUCHHANDLUNG
FÜSSLISTRASSE 4
SCALO BOOKS & LOOKS
WEINBERGSTRASSE 22 A
SEC 52 BUCHHANDLUNG
JOSEFSTRASSE 52

E X H I B I T I O N S

ZÜRICH

Gallery	Address	Exhibition	Dates
ARS FUTURA GALERIE AG	Bleicherweg 45 8002 Zürich Tel. 01 201 88 10 www.arsfutura.com info@arsfutura.com	ELKE KRYSTUFEK	**21.8.–11.10.2003**
		GIANNI MOTTI	**24.10.–24.12.2003**
		Artissima, Turin	**6.11.–9.11.2003**
FIRST ART TRADE	Stauffacherstrasse 153 8004 Zürich Tel. 043 317 95 11 Tel. 0848 200 777 www.first-art-trade.ch office@first-art-trade.ch	KAREN LA KAR – Körper Felder	**30.10.–12.12.2003**
		G. MICHAEL SCHLEENHAIN – Zeichnungen	**18.12.–5.2.2004**
ELISABETH KAUFMANN	Müllerstrasse 57 8004 Zürich Tel./Fax 043 322 01 15 elkauf@yahoo.com	ERAN SCHAERF "Index of Distances"	**21.8.–18.10.2003**
		Art Cologne + Förderprogramm: SHAHRYAR NASHAT, JAN FABRE	**22.11.–10.1.2004**
GALERIE LEHMANN LESKIW + SCHEDLER	Josefstrasse 53 8005 Zürich Tel. 01 440 61 20 www.schedler.ch zurich@schedler.ch	Art Cologne 2003	
		JAMES SHEEHAN	
GALERIE LELONG	Utoquai 31 8008 Zürich Tel. 01 251 11 20 galerie.lelong@dplanet.ch	KIKI SMITH Near	**20.9.–8.11.2003**
MAI 36 GALERIE	Rämistrasse 37 8001 Zürich Tel. 01 261 68 80 www.artgalleries.ch/mai36 mai36@artgalleries.ch	THOMAS RUFF	**3.10.–15.11.2003**
		Frieze Art Fair London	**17.10.–20.10.2003**
		PIA FRIES	**21.11.–10.1.2004**
		ART Basel Miami Beach	**4.12.–7.12.2003**
MARK MÜLLER	Gessnerallee 36 8001 Zürich Tel. 01 211 81 55 www.markmueller.ch mark.mueller@dplanet.ch	Katharina Grosse "Punkbreite bewegt" KARIM NOURELDIN "131 X 207,5 CM"	**21.8.–11.10.2003**
		ART Forum Berlin Freestyle mit KNUT ECKSTEIN + ULRICH KOCHINKE	**1.10.–5.10.2003**
		CHRISTINE STREULI "longing belonging" DENNIS HOLLINGSWORTH "Malerei"	**18.10.–20.12.2003**
		ART Cologne – KünstlerInnen der Galerie	**28.10.–2.11.2003**
GALERIE SEMINA RERUM IRÈNE PREISWERK	Cäcilienstrasse 3 8032 Zürich Tel. 01 251 26 39 www.seminarerum.ch ipreiswerk@bluewin.ch	ROMEO VENDRAME	**bis 11.10.2003**
		NIVES WIDAUER	**18.10.–29.11.2003**
		SIMONE KAPPELER	**6.12.–31.1.2004**

E X H I B I T I O N S

BOB VAN ORSOUW	Limmatstrasse 270 8005 Zürich Tel. 01 273 11 00 mail@bobvanorsouw.ch	JULIAN OPIE new films and paintings	**23.8.–11.10.2003**
		Paint: DAVID CHIEPPO, ANNELISE COSTE, LUTZ / GUGGISBERG, HANSPETER HOFMANN, MARKUS WEISS u.a.	**25.10.–20.12.2003**
ANNEMARIE VERNA	Neptunstrasse 45 8032 Zürich Tel. 01 262 38 20 www.annemarie-verna.ch office@annemarie-verna.ch	ANTONIO CALDERARA (1903–1978) zum 100. Geburtstag	**3.10.–15.11.2003**
		FRED SANDBACK (1943–2003) In Memory	**22.11.–24.1.2004**
GALERIE JAMILEH WEBER	Waldmannstrasse 6 8001 Zürich Tel. 01 252 10 66 www.jamilehweber.com info@jamilehweber.com	SILVIA GERTSCH, XERXES ACH from dusk till dawn – new works	**21.8.–4.10.2003**
		SEAN SCULLY – photographs	**10.10.–22.11.2003**
BRIGITTE WEISS	Müllerstrasse 67 8004 Zürich Tel. 01 241 83 35 www.likeyou.com/brigitteweiss brigitteweiss@bluewin.ch	GRAEME TODD	**bis 11.10.2003**
		CHARLES BOETSCHI	**Nov. / Dez. 2003**

BASEL

NICOLAS KRUPP	Erlenstrasse 15 4058 Basel Tel. 061 683 32 65 www.nicolaskrupp.com nic@nicolaskrupp.com	REMO HOBI & MARKUS MÜLLER	**31.7.–20.9.2003**
		HEIMO ZOBERNIG	**25.9.–15.11.2003**
		THOMAS BAUMANN	**20.11.–31.12.2003**
		ART Basel Miami Beach	**4.12.–7.12.2003**

ST. GALLEN

WILMA LOCK	Schmiedgasse 15 9000 St. Gallen Tel. 071 222 62 52 wilmalock@freesurf.ch	MARK FRANCIS Painting BERNARD FRIZE Peinture KELLY WOOD Photos ERWIN WURM Photos	
SUSANNA KULLI	Davidstrasse 40 9000 St. Gallen Tel. 071 223 59 58 www.susannakulli.ch info@susannakulli.ch ab Februar 2004: Dienerstrasse 21, CH-8004 Zürich	JOHN M ARMLEDER GERWALD ROCKENSCHAUB ADRIAN SCHIESS works on paper	**5.9.–31.10.2003**

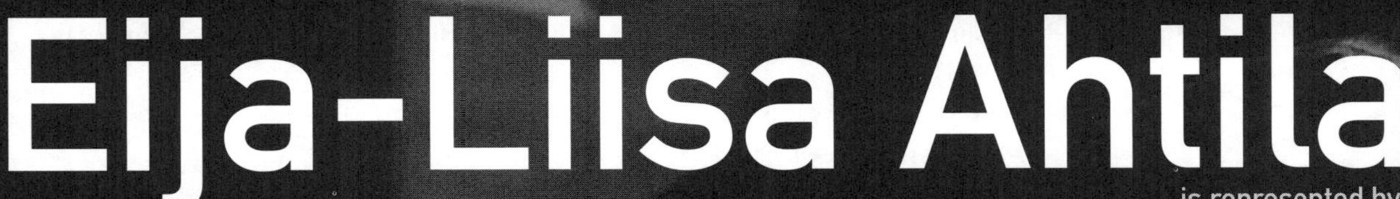

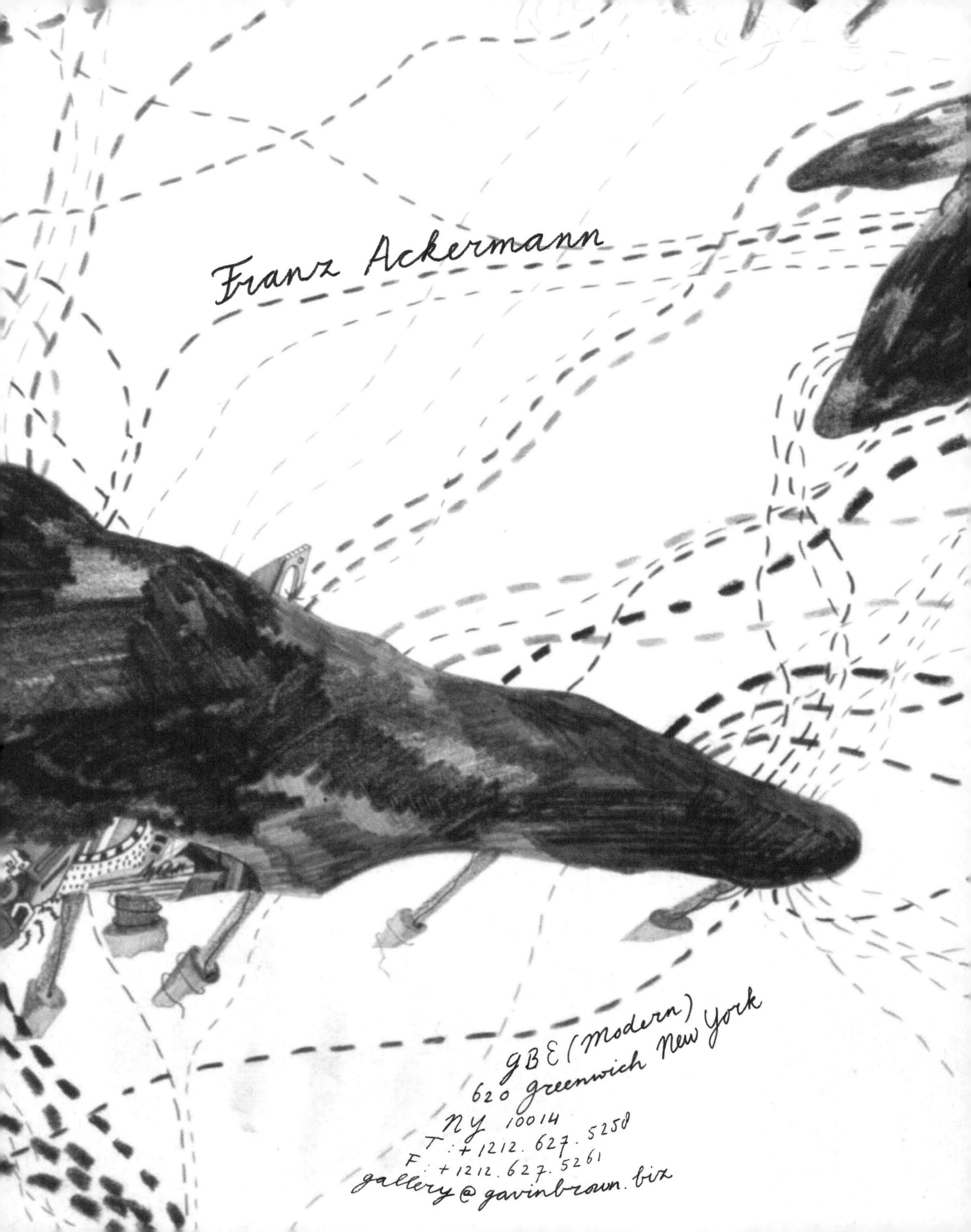

Franz Ackermann

GBE (Modern)
620 Greenwich New York
NY 10014
T: +1212. 627. 5258
F: +1212. 627. 5261
gallery@gavinbrown.biz

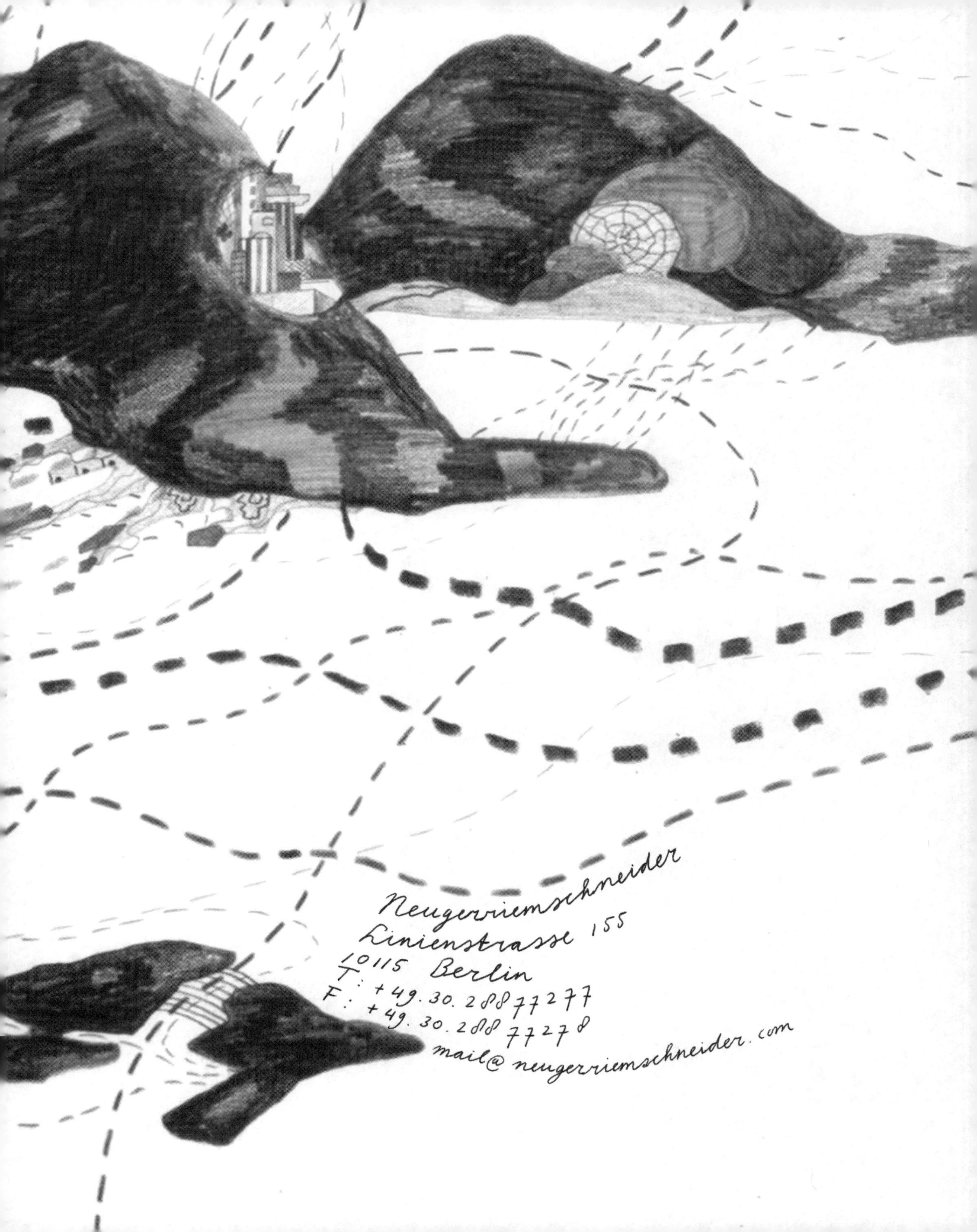

Neugerriemschneider
Linienstrasse 155
10115 Berlin
T: +49.30.288 77277
F: +49.30.288 77278
mail@neugerriemschneider.com

JONATHAN MONK

CASEY KAPLAN YVON LAMBERT LISSON GALLERY LONDON Meyer Riegger Galerie GALLERI NICOLAI WALLNER

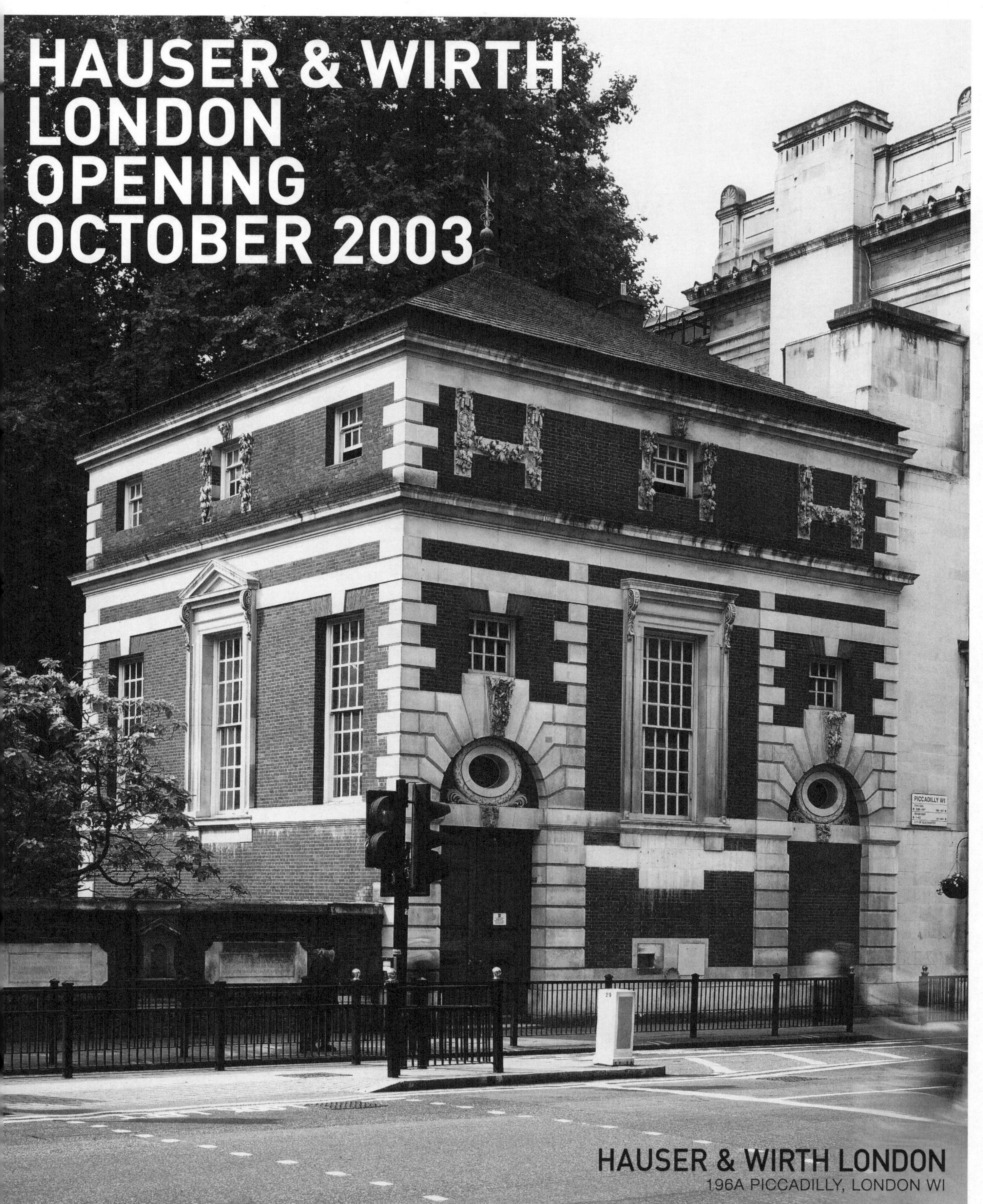
HAUSER & WIRTH
LONDON
OPENING
OCTOBER 2003
PICCADILLY W1
HAUSER & WIRTH LONDON
196A PICCADILLY, LONDON WI

11 SEPTEMBER - 26 OCTOBER 2003

William Eggleston

From the Seventies

11 SEPTEMBER - 26 OCTOBER 2003

Phillip Allen

8 - 13 OCTOBER 2003

FIAC Paris

13 NOVEMBER 2003 - 11 JANUARY 2004

Peter Rogiers

13 NOVEMBER 2003 - 11 JANUARY 2004

Stephen Wilks

4 - 7 DECEMBER 2003

Art Basel Miami Beach

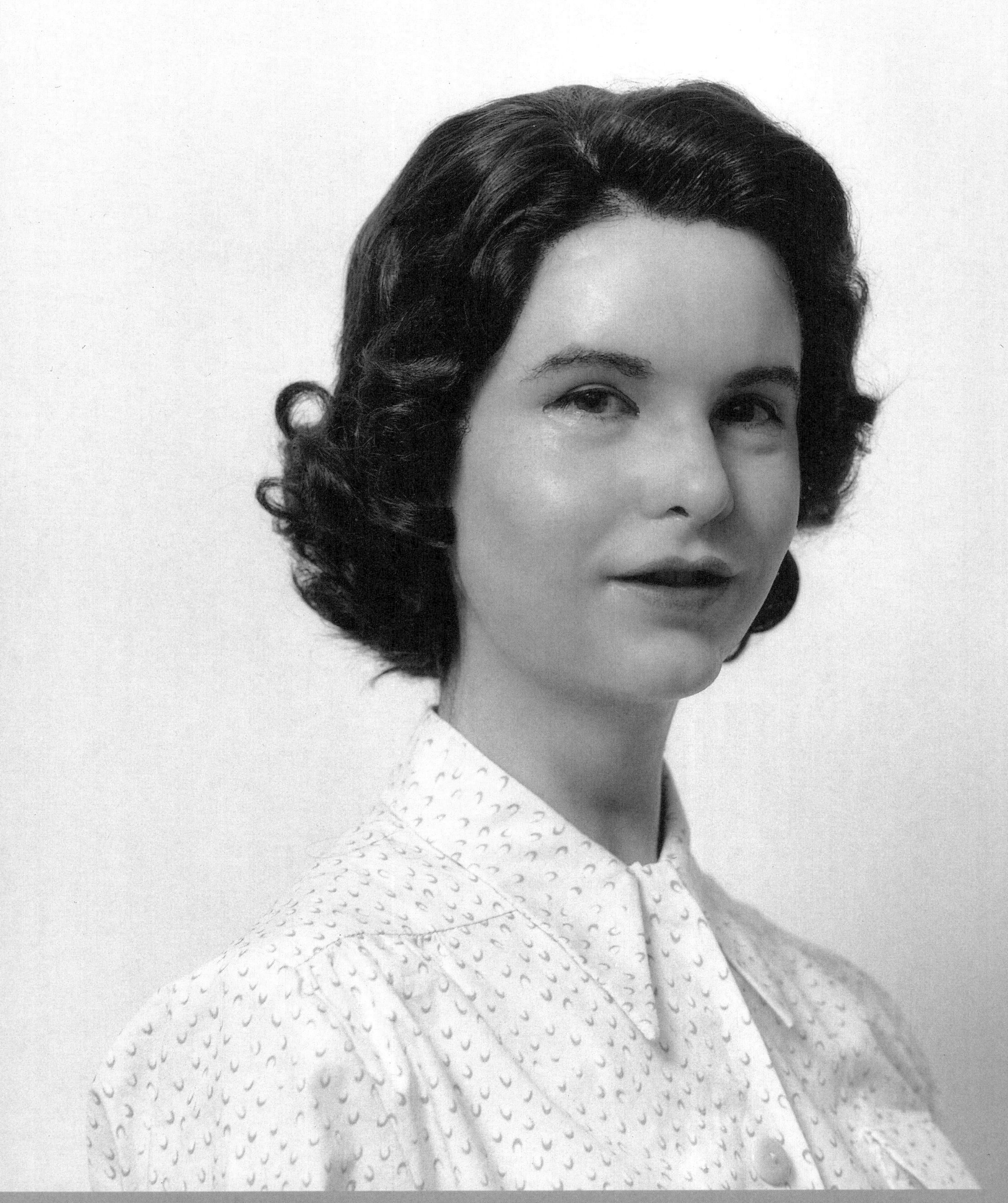

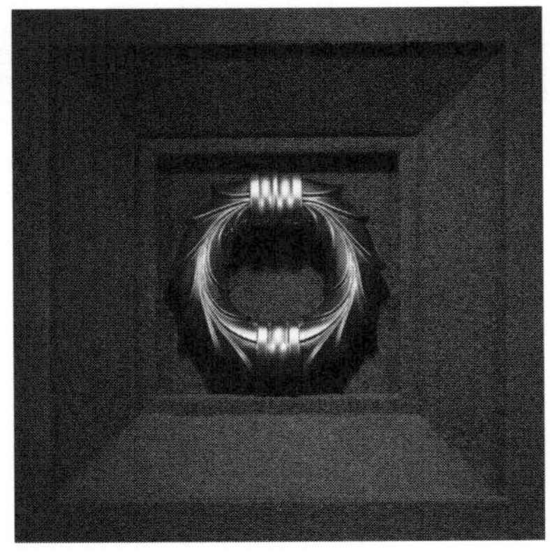

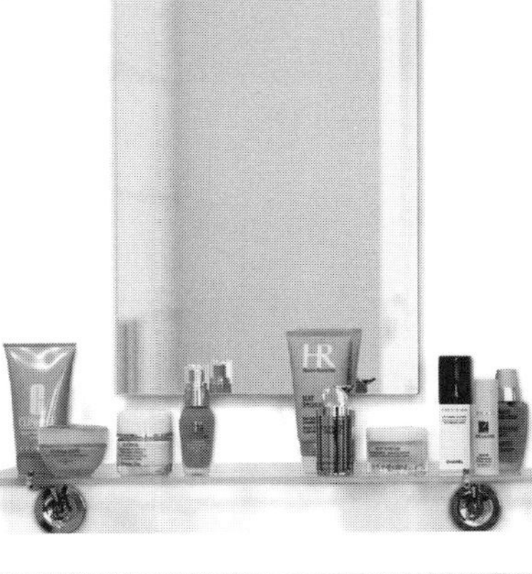

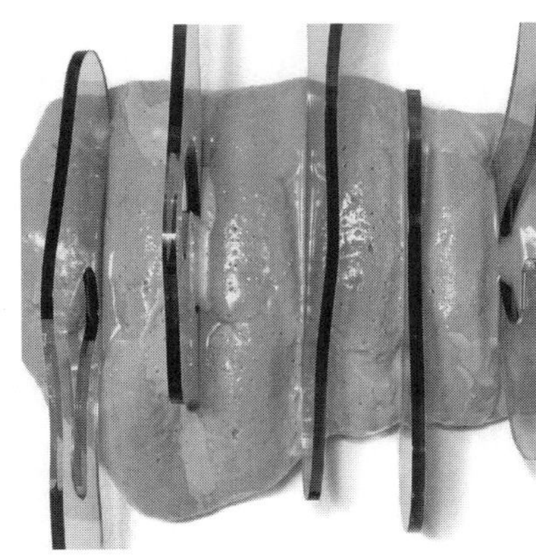

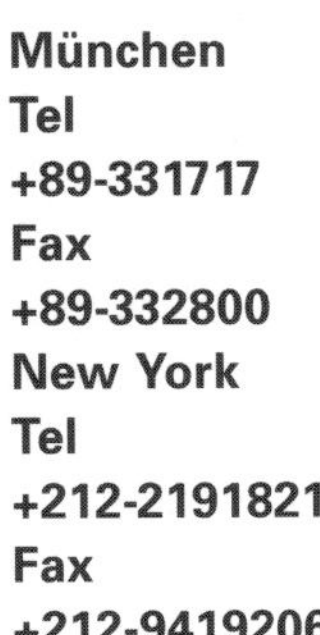

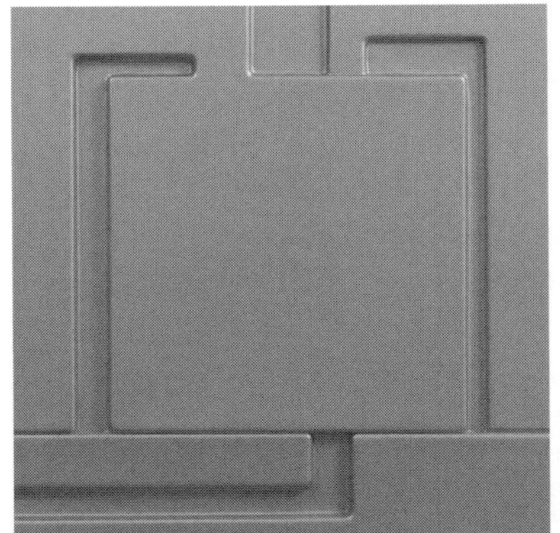

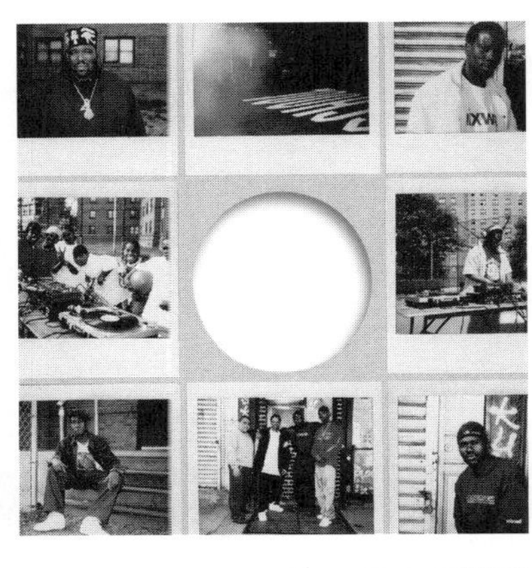

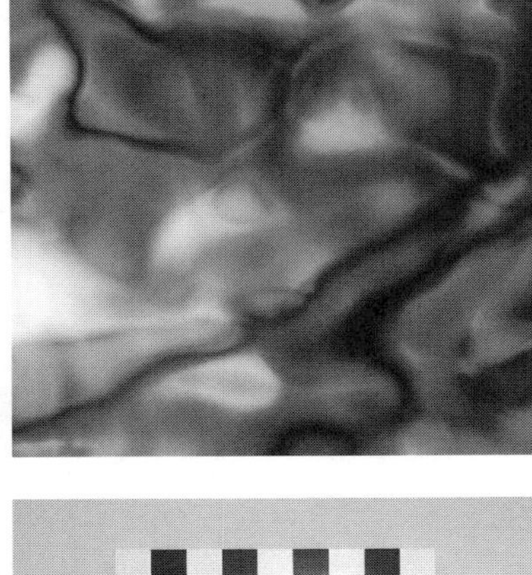

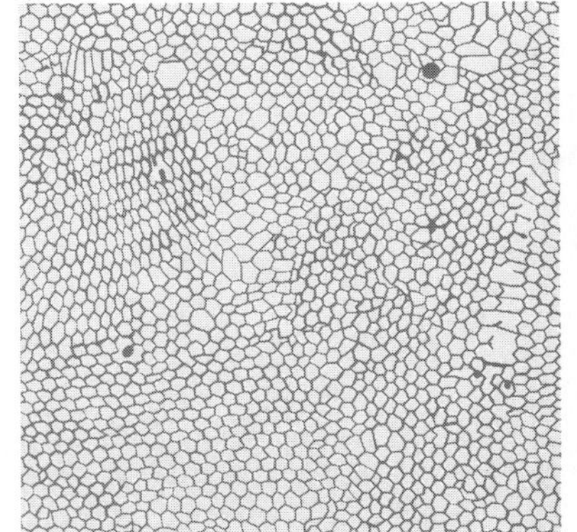

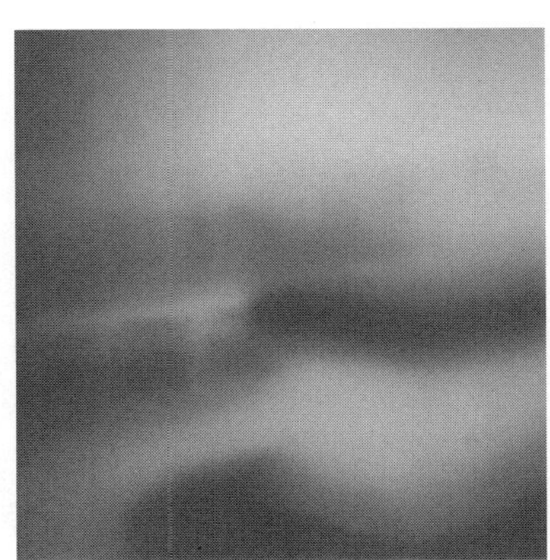

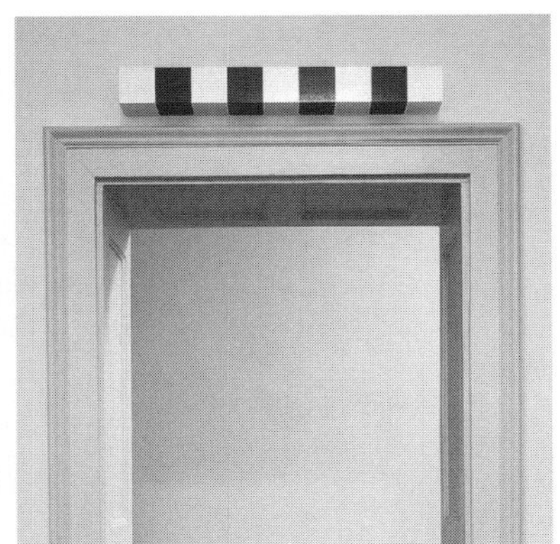

GEORGE CONDO

SCULPTURE

SEPTEMBER – NOVEMBER 2003

WOLFGANG LAIB

NOVEMBER 2003 – FEBRUARY 2004

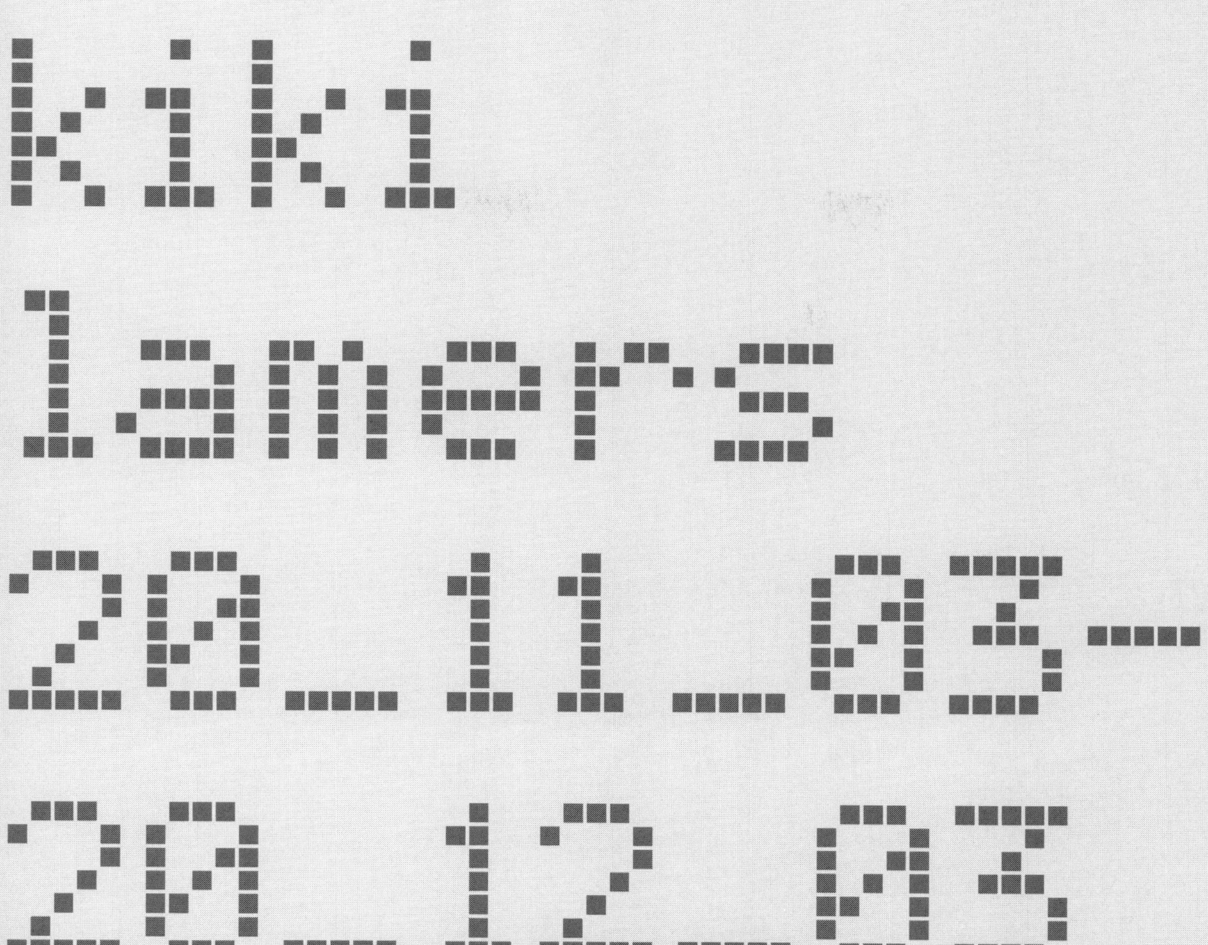

5 rue de la muse

'Works from 1996 to 2003'

Exhibition in collaboration with Annet Gelink Gallery, Amsterdam

■ BFAS
Blondeau Fine Art Services

5 rue de la Muse
1205 Geneva _ Switzerland
T +41 (0)22 544 95 95
F +41 (0)22 544 95 99

■ contact _ Philippe Davet
philippe@bfasblondeau.com

■ exhibition
TUE-FRI 14h-18h30
SAT 11h-17h
■ office
MON-FRI 9h-12h30 / 14h-18h30

20.21

Galerie Edition Kunsthandel GmbH
Meisenburgstraße 169–173
45133 Essen
Tel. **+49 201 87100-0**
Fax **+49 201 87100-10**
info@2021art.com
www.2021art.com

Di–Fr 10–18 · Sa 11–16
und nach Vereinbarung

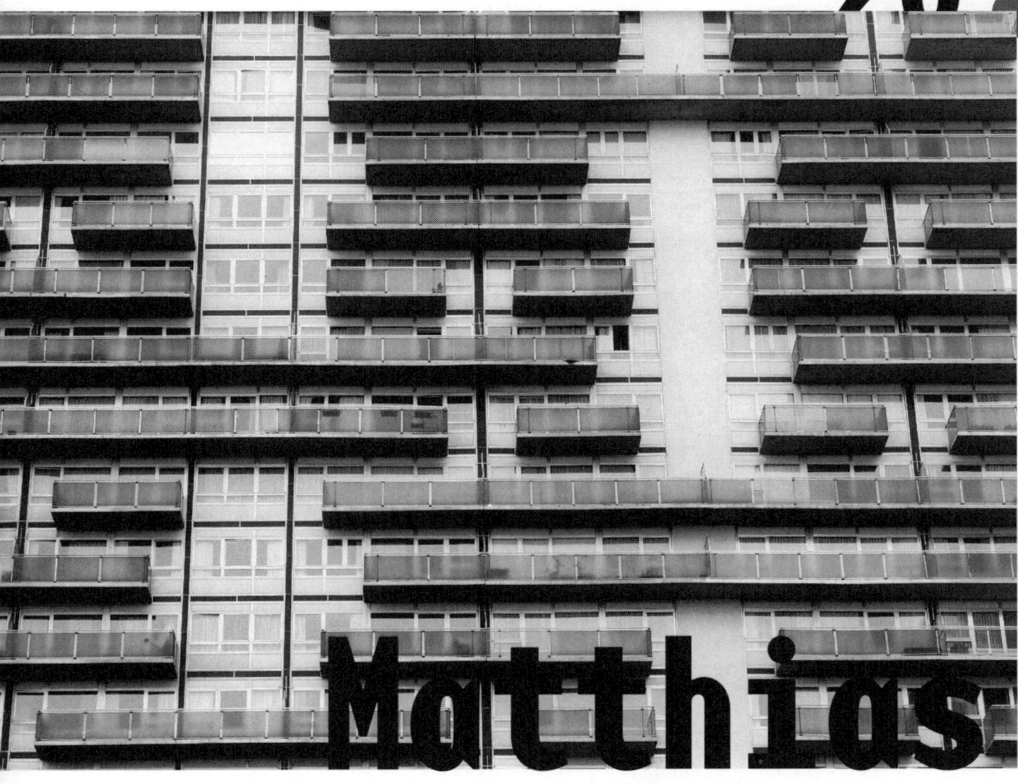

Matthias Hoch

20|9–14|11|2003

Bogomir Ecker

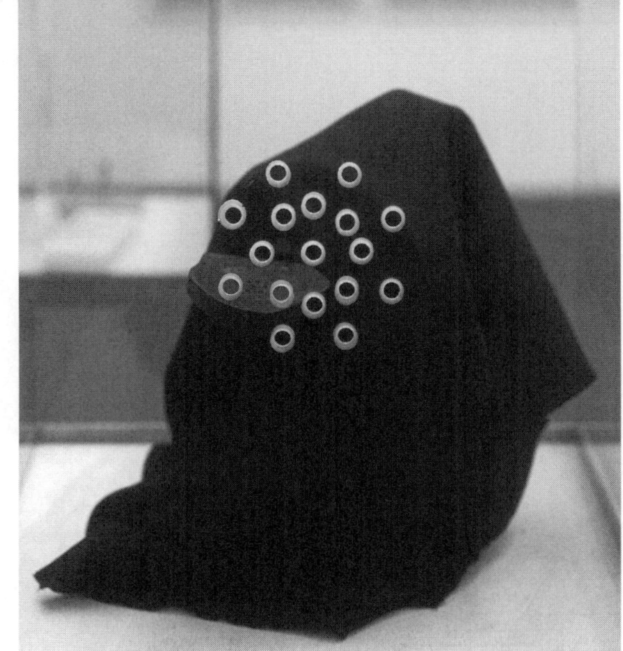

Dezember: Martin Parr

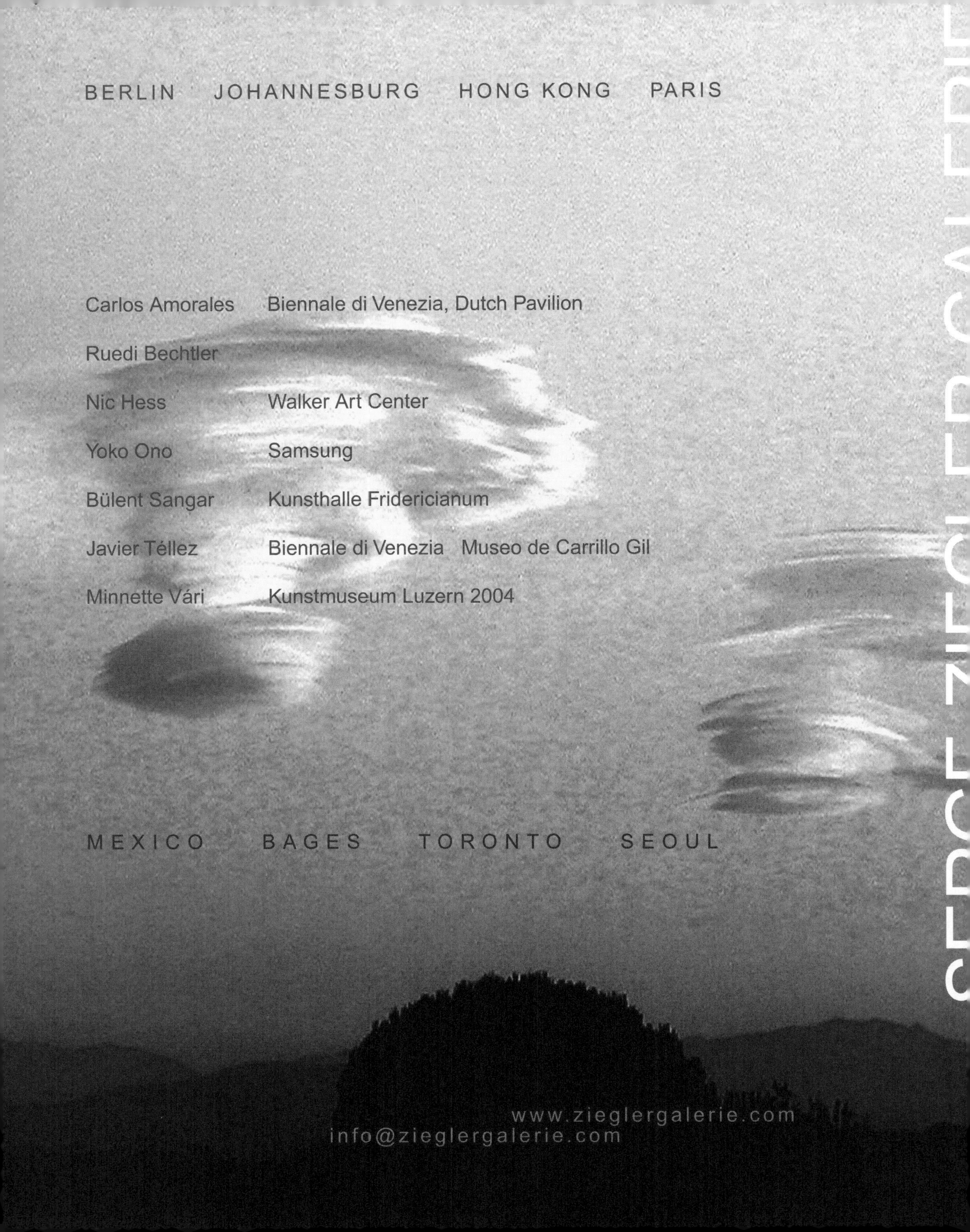
BERLIN JOHANNESBURG HONG KONG PARIS
Carlos Amorales Biennale di Venezia, Dutch Pavilion
Ruedi Bechtler
Nic Hess Walker Art Center
Yoko Ono Samsung
Bülent Sangar Kunsthalle Fridericianum
Javier Téllez Biennale di Venezia Museo de Carrillo Gil
Minnette Vári Kunstmuseum Luzern 2004
MEXICO BAGES TORONTO SEOUL
www.zieglergalerie.com
info@zieglergalerie.com

gallery bob van orsouw limmatstrasse 270 8005 zurich
phone +41-01 273 11 00 fax +41-01 273 11 02 mail@bobvanorsouw.ch

august 23
until
october 11, 2003
julian opie new films and paintings

october 25
until
december 20, 2003
paint david chieppo, annelise coste, lutz/guggisberg, hanspeter hofmann, markus weiss u.a.

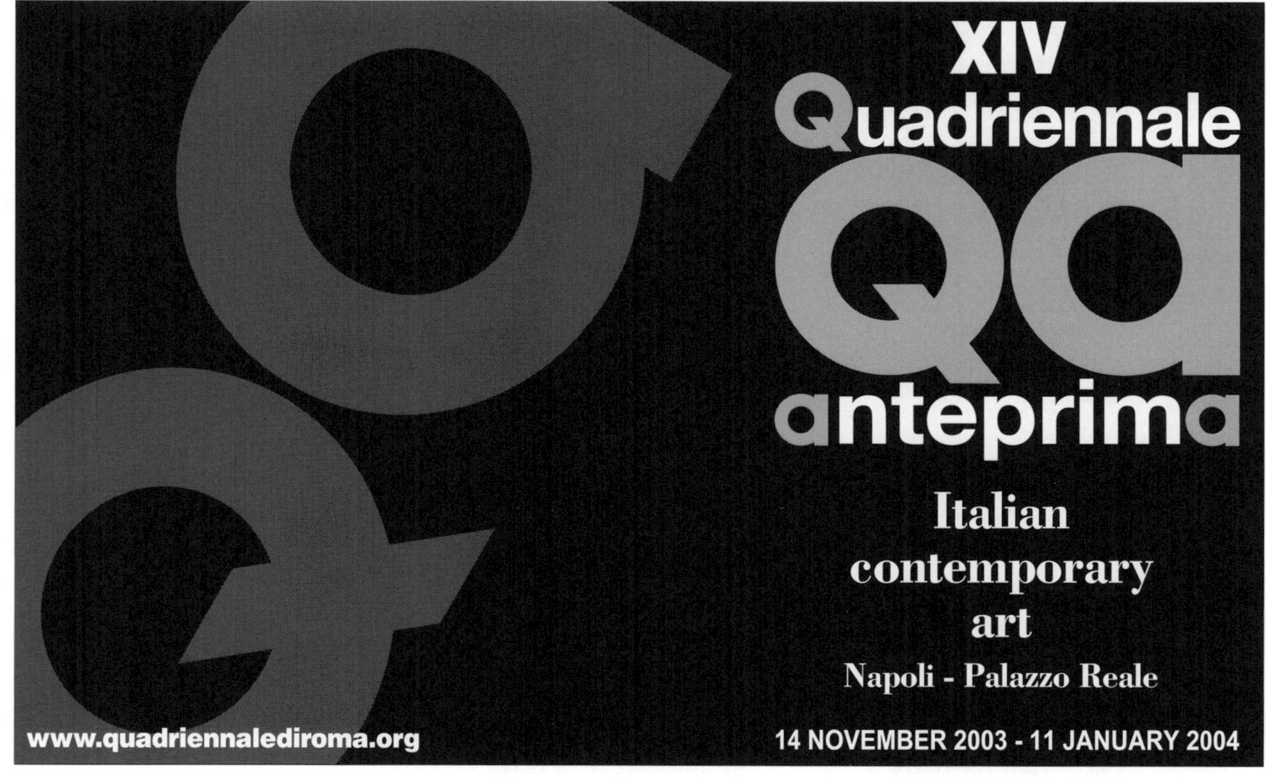

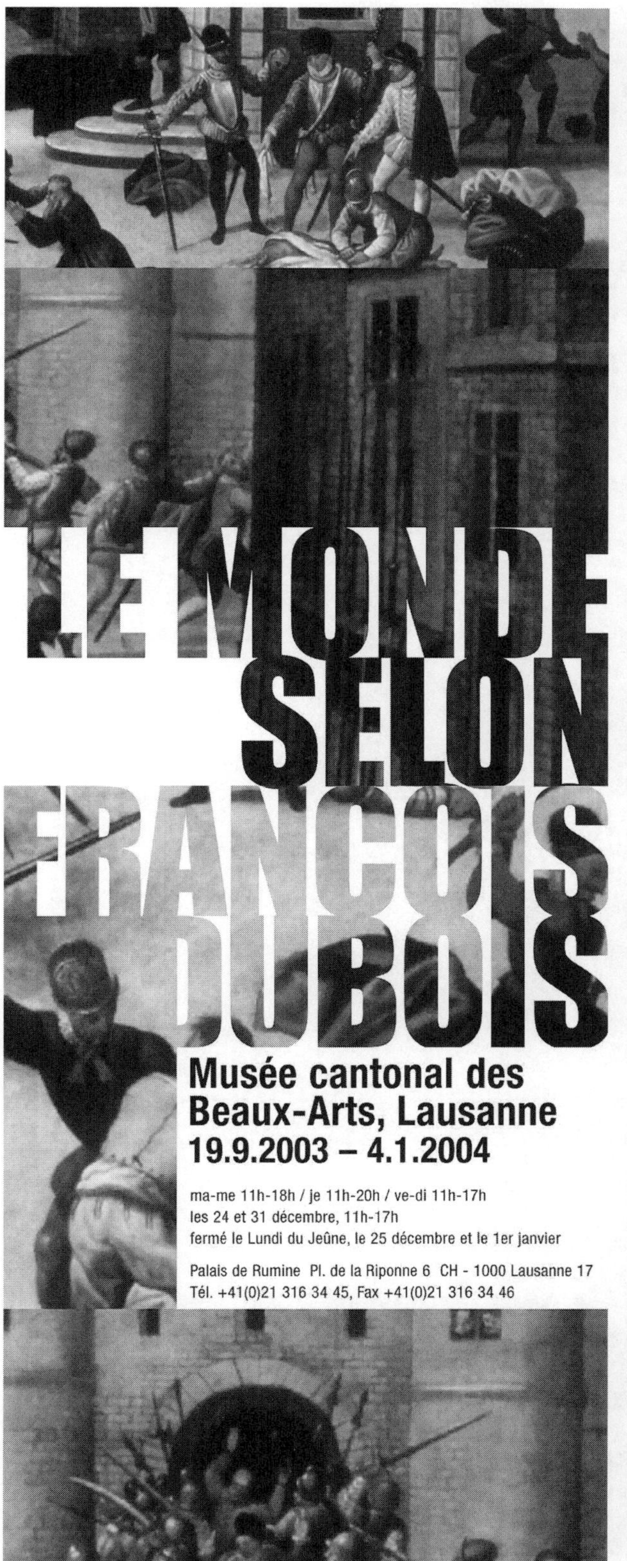
LE MONDE
SELON
FRANÇOIS
DUBOIS
Musée cantonal des
Beaux-Arts, Lausanne
19.9.2003 – 4.1.2004
ma-me 11h-18h / je 11h-20h / ve-di 11h-17h
les 24 et 31 décembre, 11h-17h
fermé le Lundi du Jeûne, le 25 décembre et le 1er janvier
Palais de Rumine Pl. de la Riponne 6 CH - 1000 Lausanne 17
Tél. +41(0)21 316 34 45, Fax +41(0)21 316 34 46

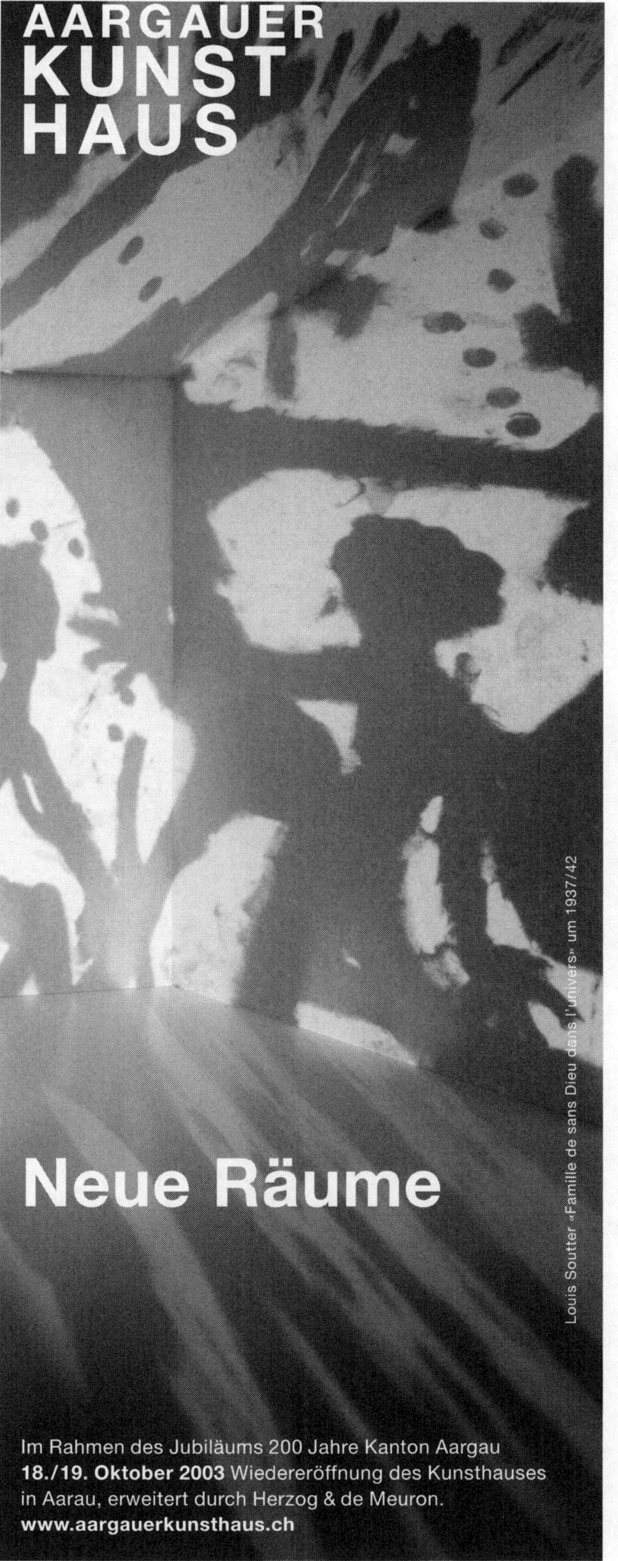
AARGAUER
KUNST
HAUS
Neue Räume
Louis Soutter «Famille de sans Dieu dans l'univers» um 1937/42
Im Rahmen des Jubiläums 200 Jahre Kanton Aargau
18./19. Oktober 2003 Wiedereröffnung des Kunsthauses
in Aarau, erweitert durch Herzog & de Meuron.
www.aargauerkunsthaus.ch

A R C O

Arco 04 international contemporary art fair

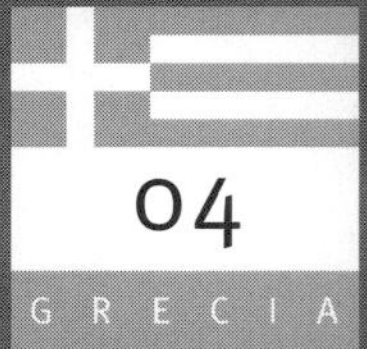

23rd Edition
Parque Ferial Juan Carlos I, Madrid
Halls 7 and 9
www.arcospain.org

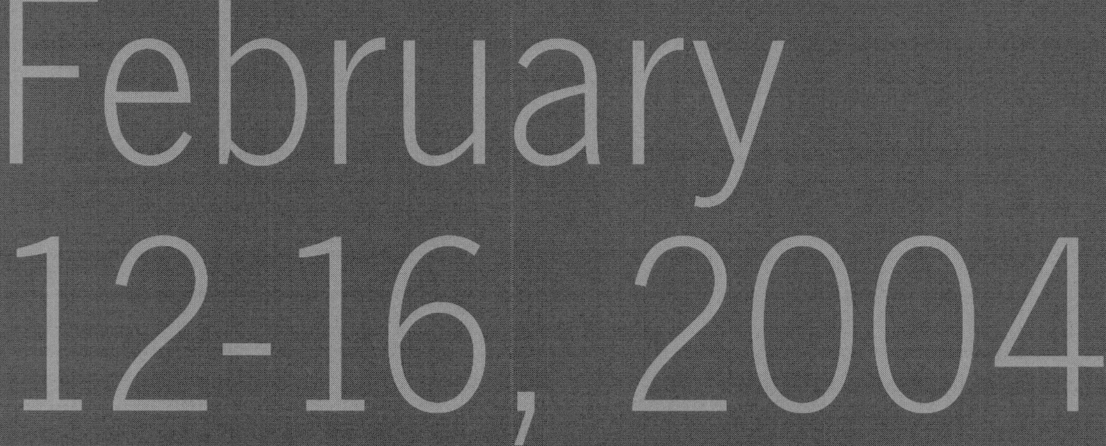

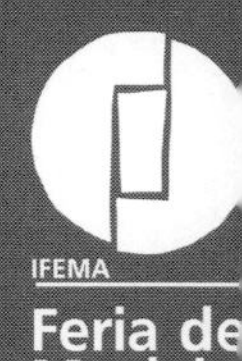

Feria de Madrid

Official opening:
(by invitation): Wednesday 11th February: 7 p.m.

Professional visit:
(by invitation): Wednesday 11th February: from 4 p.m. Thursday 12th February: from 11 a.m.

Open to the general public:
Thursday 12th February: 2 p.m. to 9 p.m. Friday 13th, Saturday 14th, Sunday 15th and Monday 16th: Noon to 9 p.m.

IBERIA
Official Carrier

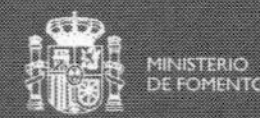

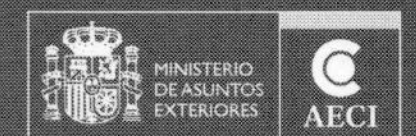

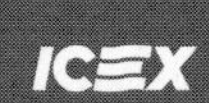

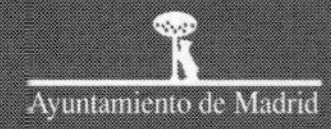

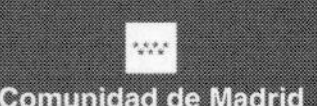

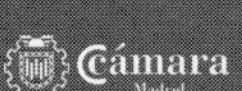

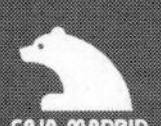

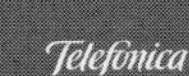

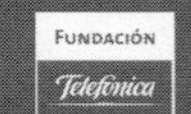

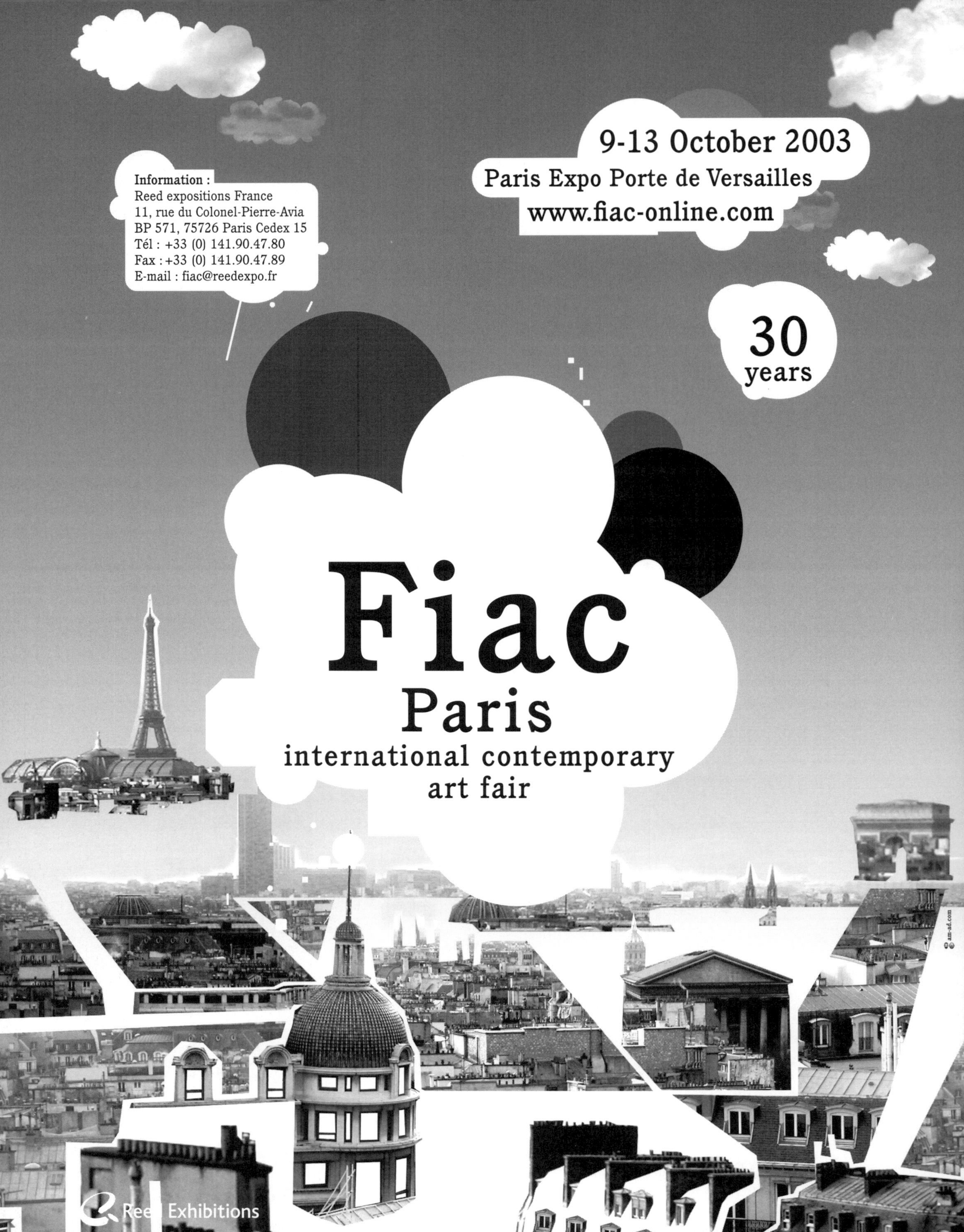
9-13 October 2003
Paris Expo Porte de Versailles
www.fiac-online.com
Information :
Reed expositions France
11, rue du Colonel-Pierre-Avia
BP 571, 75726 Paris Cedex 15
Tél : +33 (0) 141.90.47.80
Fax : +33 (0) 141.90.47.89
E-mail : fiac@reedexpo.fr
30
years
Fiac
Paris
international contemporary
art fair
Reed Exhibitions

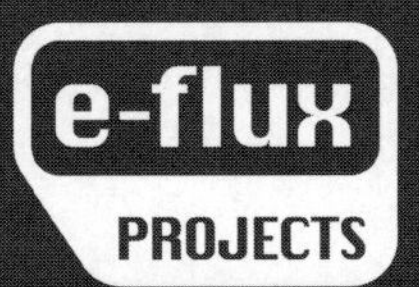

In 2001 we initiated an ongoing program of special projects curated and produced for our site. The focus of this program is to present individual works and exhibitions that explicitly engage participation of our audience.

JULY 2003

The Next Documenta Should Be Curated by an Artist

curated by **Jens Hoffmann**

What happens if artists take over and occupy territory usually reserved for curators? What happens if artists are asked to propose a concept for a large-scale group exhibition and to take control over a prestigious show such as Documenta? These are some of the questions that The Next Documenta Should Be Curated By An Artist is trying to investigate. With: **John Baldessari / Ricardo Basbaum / Laura Belém / Daniel Buren / AA Bronson / Michael Elmgreen & Ingar Dragset / Morgan Fisher / Liam Gillick / Carsten Höller / Cildo Mereiles / John Miller / Jonathan Monk / Lawrence Weiner and many others...**

MAY 2003

Utopia Station Poster Project

Posters by more than 150 artists.
View them online, download and print them out!

A 2003 Venice Biennial project, curated by **Molly Nesbit, Hans Ulrich Obrist and Rirkrit Tiravanija**, including works by **Matthew Barney, Rodney Graham, Thomas Hirschhorn, Ilya and Emilia Kabakov, Steve Mc Queen, Elizabeth Peyton, Ed Ruscha, Lawrence Weiner, Franz West, Yoko Ono, Leon Golub, Nancy Spero, Patti Smith and many many others.**

MAY 2002

DOiT

curated by **Hans Ulrich Obrist**

DOiT is an autonomous show that exists in a form of artist's instructions to be actualized by the audience. Should you decide to participate, segments of the show can materialize in your home, office or any other place you may find appropriate. DOiT is also an online compendium of artists' writings; a 'webzine' containing fascinating essays on the peculiar subject of artworks in the form of instructions and experimental exhibitions, as well as an informal community of people interested in such subjects.

JANUARY 2001

101 Art Ideas You Can Do Yourself

by **Rob Pruitt**

Think you can't be an artist? Think Again. In 101 Art Ideas You Can Do Yourself, a new York based artist Rob Pruitt supplies the instructions and leaves the art making to the viewer.

Creative Partner
FDTdesign
communication architects
www.fdtdesign.com

www.e-flux.com
For further information please contact
projects@e-flux.com

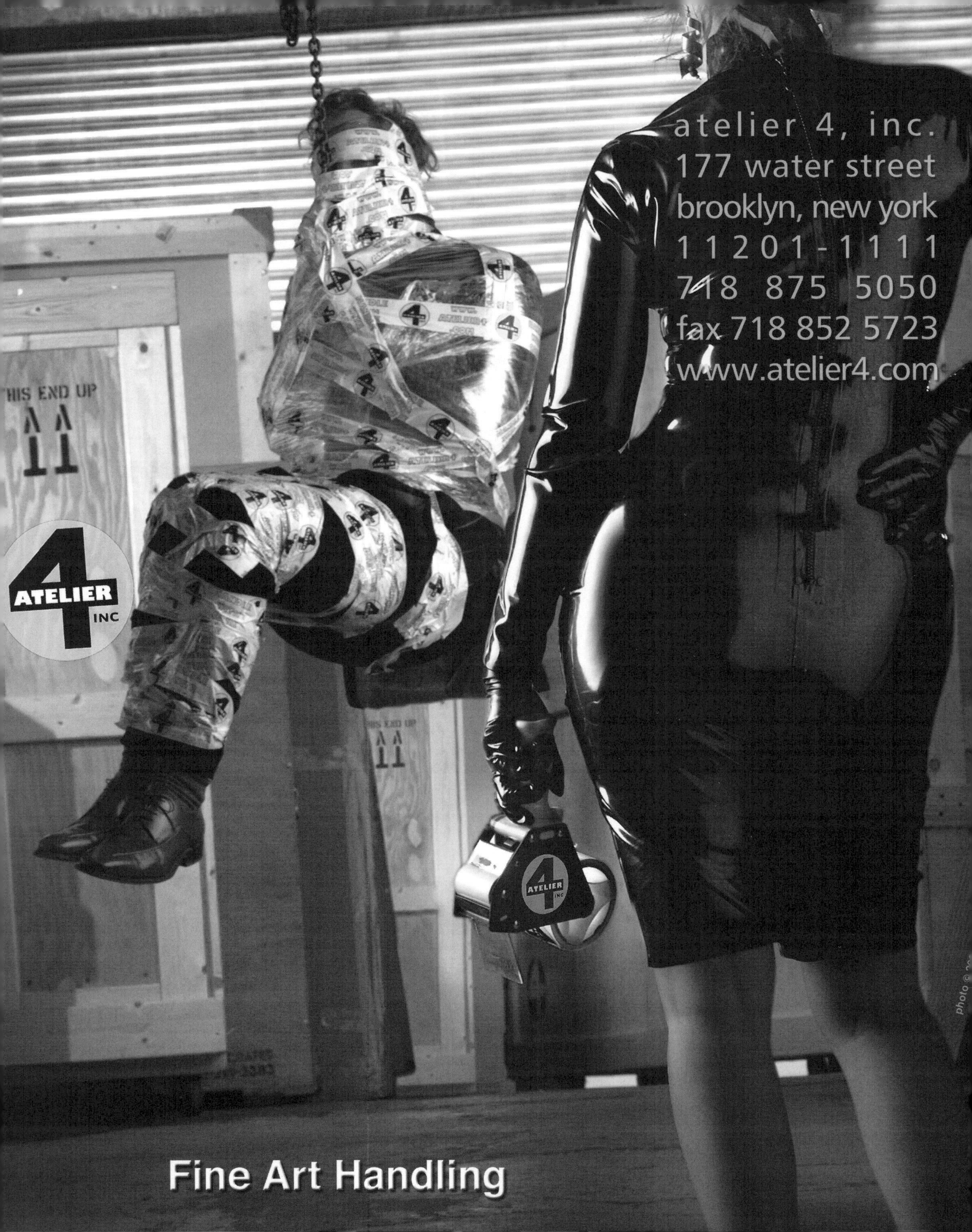
atelier 4, inc.
177 water street
brooklyn, new york
11201-1111
718 875 5050
fax 718 852 5723
www.atelier4.com
THIS END UP
ATELIER
INC
Fine Art Handling

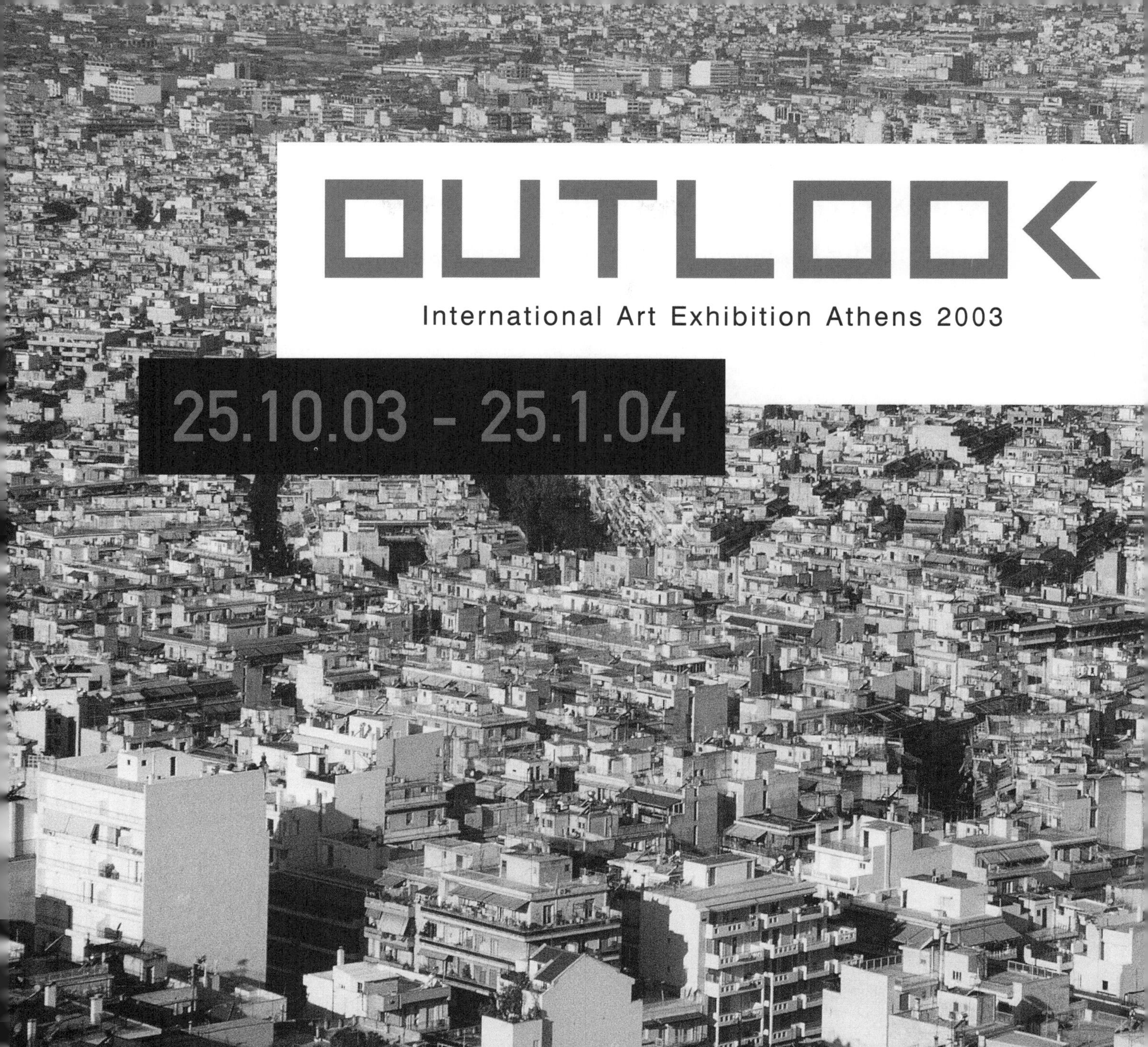

GALLERIAGOTTARDO
dal 17.9 al 22.11.2003
THE SPIRI TUAL LAND SCAPE
Gleizes Kandinsky Marc Mondrian Münter Nolde
dalle collezioni del Solomon R. Guggenheim Museum di New York
Galleria Gottardo
una fondazione per la cultura
della Banca del Gottardo
Martedì
14.00 - 17.00
Mercoledì
- sabato
11.00 - 17.00
Domenica
11.00 - 16.00
Entrata libera
Galleria Gottardo
Viale Franscini 12
CH 6900 Lugano
Telefono 091 808 1988
Fax 091 808 2447
E-mail galleria@gottardo.com

SI-FALL + WINTER PROGRAM + EVENTS:

FRANCIS BAUDEVIN, NIC HESS AND MATHIEU MERCIER, SEPT 9 – OCT 25 2003

NEW SI-PROJECTS BY ALEKSANDRA MIR, JONATHAN MONK, MOMOYO TORIMITSU AND OTHERS,

AS WELL AS SI-LECTURE SERIES WITH CURATORS AND ARTISTS, HALLOWEEN PARTY, AND MORE.

SAVE THE DATE: OCT 30TH SI-BENEFIT AUCTION AND DINNER

HOW MANY EXTRA LAYERS CAN WE GRAFT ONTO REALITY BEFORE IT COLLAPSES?

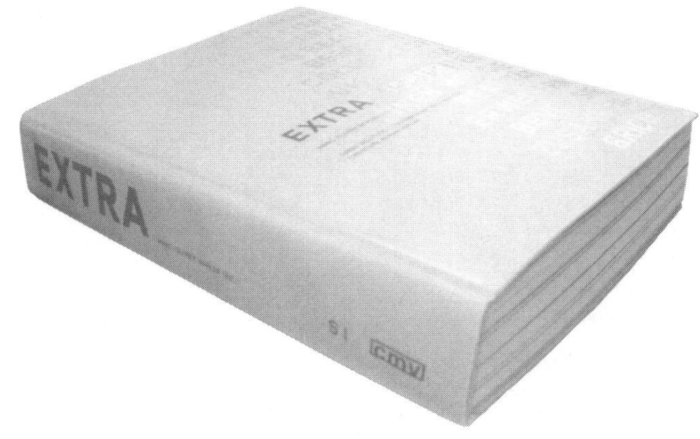

EXTRA / THE BOOK

WITH EXTRA, 28 ARTISTS HAVE COME TOGETHER, JOINED BY CRITICS, CURATORS AND PHYSICISTS, TO EXPOSE THE DEPTH AND COMPLEXITY OF REALITY IN A GRAND COLLABORATION.

EACH ARTIST HAS CONTRIBUTED AN ORIGINAL VISUAL ESSAY IN FULL COLOR. THEIR IMAGES ARE COMPLIMENTED BY SEVERAL FASCINATING TEXTS. DAVID DEUTSCH AND SETH LLOYD, QUANTUM PHYSICISTS, DELIVER A PASSIONATE ROUND OF "BRAIN TENNIS" IN THEIR CORRESPONDENCE DISCUSSING THE CONCEPT OF MULTIPLE UNIVERSES. MARC-OLIVIER WAHLER'S TEXT ABOUT GLIDING THROUGH THE FOLDS OF REALITY IS AN INTRICATE COMPANION TO HIS EXHIBITION. THE TEXTS OF ART CRITIC BOB NICKAS AND SEVERAL ARTISTS (JOHN GIORNO, JUTTA KOETHER, OLIVIER MOSSET AND STEVEN PARRINO) SERVE TO ROUND OUT AND COMPLETE THIS MULTILAYERED COLLABORATION.

EXTRA ORIGINAL VISUAL ESSAYS BY:
VIRGINIE BARRÉ, OLIVIER BLANCKART, OLAF BREUNING, STÉPHANE DAFFLON, WIM DELVOYE, DANIEL FIRMAN, URS FISCHER, PETER FISCHLI / DAVID WEISS, SYLVIE FLEURY, GELATIN, JOHN GIORNO, JANINE GORDON, FABRICE GYGI, LORI HERSBERGER, CHRISTIAN JANKOWSKI, OLIVIER MOSSET, GIANNI MOTTI, ERIK PARKER, STEVEN PARRINO, JUTTA KOETHER, BRUNO PEINADO, UGO RONDINONE, JEAN-CLAUDE RUGGIRELLO, STÉPHANE SAUTOUR, JIM SHAW, ROMAN SIGNER, OLAV WESTPHALEN AND ERWIN WURM.

EXTRA, 440 PAGES, FULL COLOR
EDITED BY MARC-OLIVIER WAHLER
PUBLISHED BY THE SWISS INSTITUTE - CONTEMPORARY ART AND CHRISTOPH MERIAN VERLAG
DISTRIBUTED IN NORTH-AMERICA BY D.A.P.
TO ORDER NOW VISIT WWW.SWISSINSTITUTE.NET

S I

SWISS INSTITUTE - CONTEMPORARY ART,
495 BROADWAY 3RD FLOOR / NEW YORK NY 10012
TUESDAY – SATURDAY 11 A.M. – 6 P.M. / p 212 925 2035 / f 212 925 2040
www.swissinstitute.net / info@swissinstitute.net

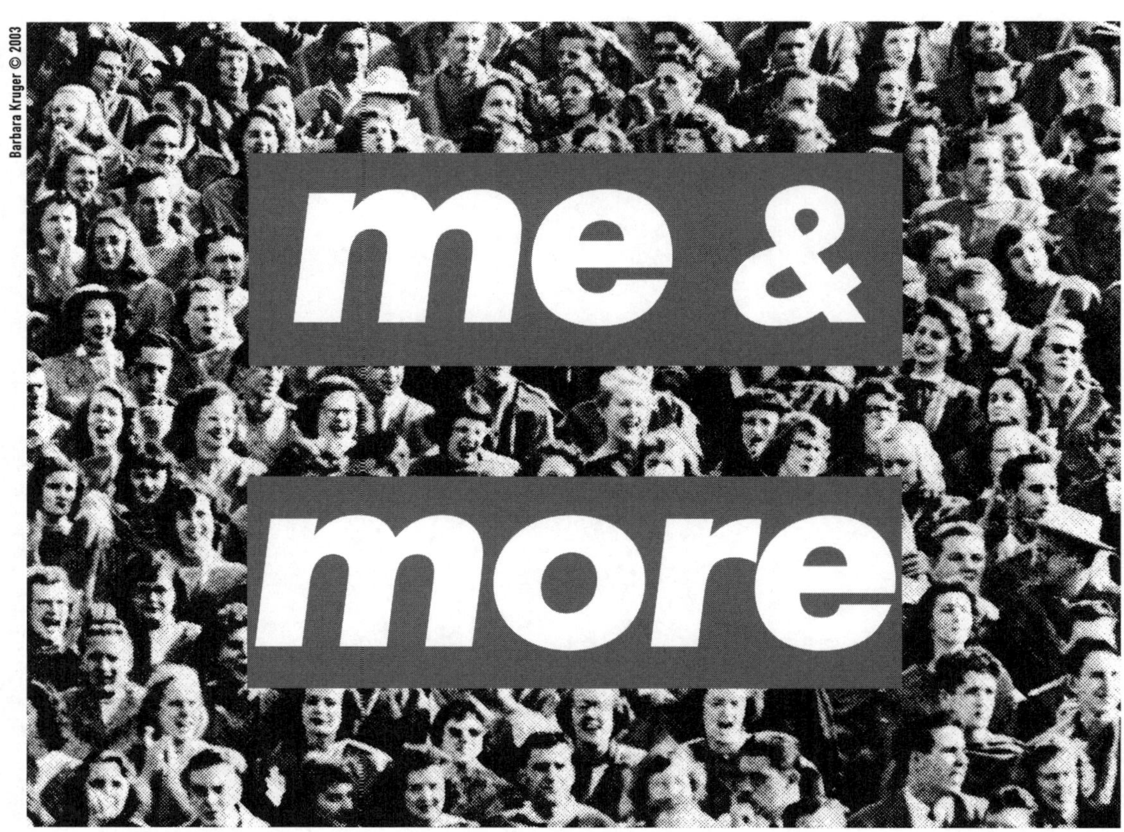

me & more with Magdalena Abakanowicz, Laylah Ali, Ross Bleckner, Antony Gormley, Yishai Jusidman, Barbara Kruger, Elke Krystufek, Urs Lüthi, Tatjana Marusic, Miao Xiaochun, Ernesto Neto, Chloe Piene, Kiki Smith, Zhang Huan

August 9 - November 23

Kunstmuseum Luzern Museum of Art Lucerne

Europaplatz 1 (KKL Level K) CH-6002 Luzern Tel. +41 (0)41 226 78 00
Infotel. +41 (0)41 226 78 78 www. kunstmuseumluzern.ch

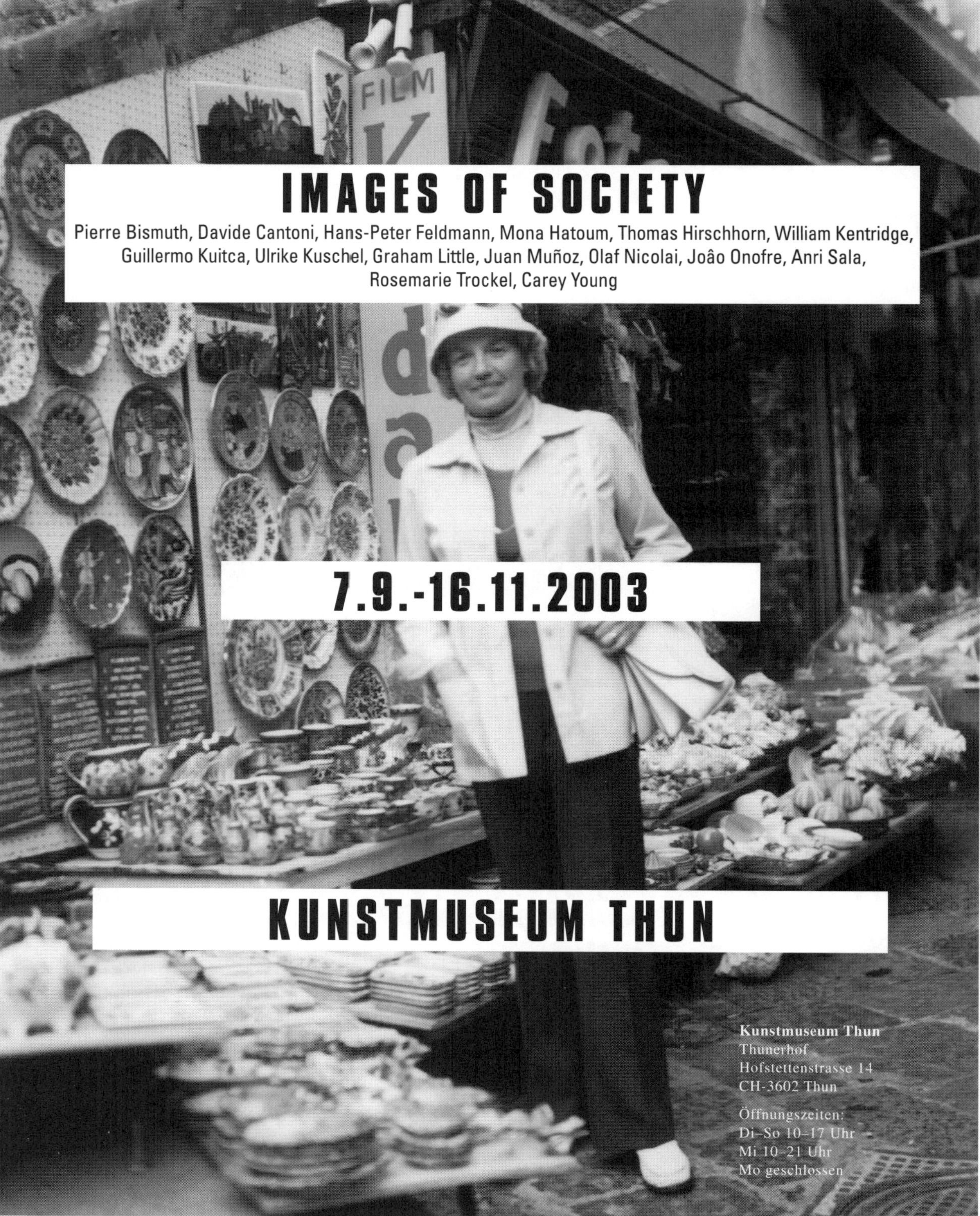
FILM
IMAGES OF SOCIETY
Pierre Bismuth, Davide Cantoni, Hans-Peter Feldmann, Mona Hatoum, Thomas Hirschhorn, William Kentridge,
Guillermo Kuitca, Ulrike Kuschel, Graham Little, Juan Muñoz, Olaf Nicolai, Joâo Onofre, Anri Sala,
Rosemarie Trockel, Carey Young
7.9.-16.11.2003
KUNSTMUSEUM THUN
Kunstmuseum Thun
Thunerhof
Hofstettenstrasse 14
CH-3602 Thun
Öffnungszeiten:
Di–So 10–17 Uhr
Mi 10–21 Uhr
Mo geschlossen

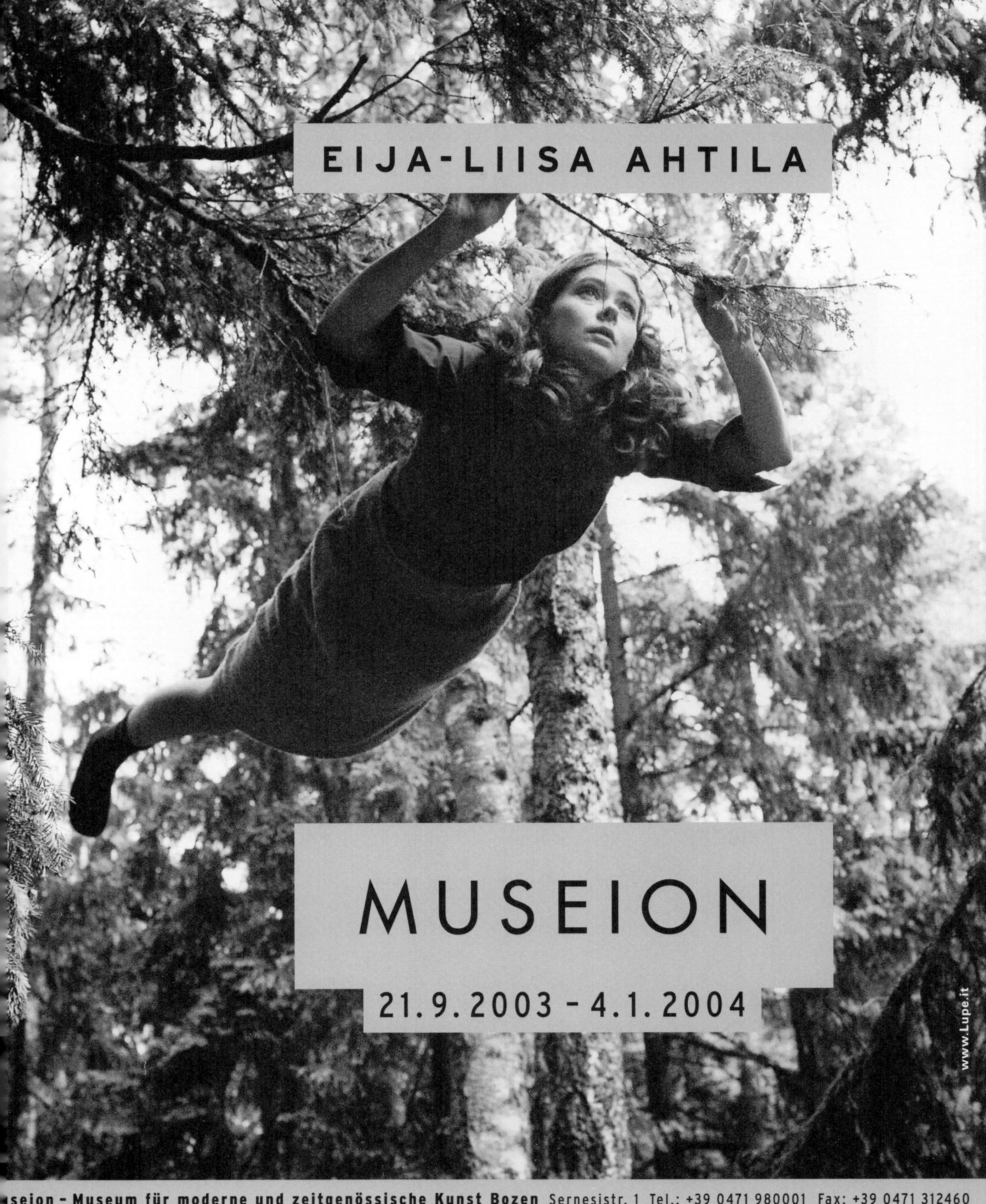
EIJA-LIISA AHTILA
MUSEION
21.9.2003 – 4.1.2004
www.Lupe.it

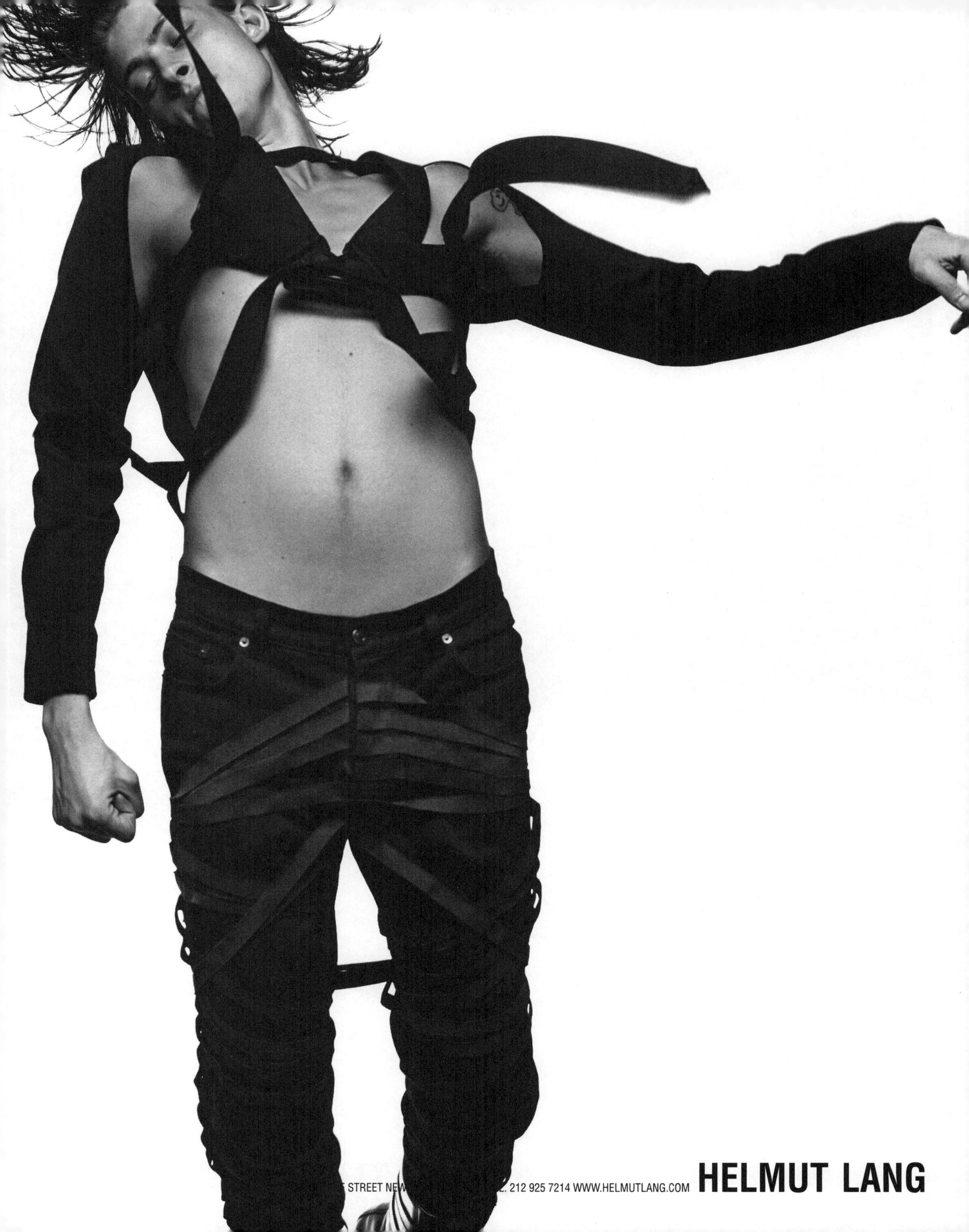
STREET NEW
212 925 7214 WWW.HELMUTLANG.COM
HELMUT LANG

JEAN-MARC **BUSTAMANTE**

RECENT WORKS

SEPTEMBER 27 - NOVEMBER 8, 2003

GALERIE THADDAEUS ROPAC

MIRABELLPLATZ 2, 5020 SALZBURG TEL: 43 662 881 393 FAX: 43 662 881 3939 www.ropac.net

silvia gertsch
xerxes ach

from dusk till dawn – new works

august 21 – october 4, 2003

sean scully

photographs

october 10 – november 22, 2003

galerie jamileh weber

waldmannstrasse 6
ch–8001 zurich
telefon +41 1 252 10 66
telefax +41 1 252 11 32
www.jamilehweber.com
info@jamilehweber.com
tu-fr 11–18h, sa 10–16h